ADOBE® PHOTOSHOP®

LIGHTROOM®
CLASSIC CC

THE MISSING FAQ

VERSION 7 / 2018 RELEASE

D1364818

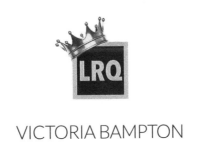

VICTORIA BAMPTON

Adobe Photoshop Lightroom Classic CC—The Missing FAQ (Version 7)

Publication Date 26 January 2018

TABLE OF CONTENTS

BONUS CHAPTERS IN THE EBOOK APPENDIX

FAST TRACK INDEX

ACKNOWLEDGMENTS

A lot of people have contributed to this project, and although I'd love to thank everyone personally, the acknowledgments would fill up the entire book. There are some people who deserve a special mention though.

I couldn't go without thanking the whole Lightroom team at Adobe, especially Tom Hogarty, Sharad Mangalick, Priya Alexandre, Ben Warde, Josh Haftel, Jeff Tranberry, Julieanne Kost, Thomas Knoll, Eric Chan, Max Wendt, Josh Bury, Simon Chen, Matt Johnson, Julie Kmoch, Kelly Castro, Becky Sowada, Paul Kleczka, Sreenivas Ramaswamy and Sunil Bhakskaran who have willingly answered my endless questions.

My heartfelt thanks go to Paul McFarlane, who yet again did a great job of editing and proof-reading, and who kept me going through the chaos of attempting to write two books at once.

Thanks are also due to the team of Lightroom Gurus, who are always happy to discuss, debate and share their experience, especially Rikk Flohr, Jim Wilde, Sean McCormack, Laura Shoe, Jeff Schewe, Martin Evening, Andrew Rodney, Peter Krogh, Ian Lyons, John Beardsworth, George Jardine, Rob Sylvan, Jeffrey Friedl, Linwood Ferguson, Johan Elzenga and the rest of the crew!

I'm also grateful to the members of the various Lightroom forums and my social media followers, who constantly challenge me with questions, problems to solve, and give me ideas for this book.

And finally I have to thank you, the Reader. Yet again, many of the changes in the book are based on the suggestions and questions that you've sent in. It's your book. The lovely emails I've received, and the reviews you post online, make all the late nights and early mornings worthwhile—so thank you.

Victoria Bampton—Southampton, UK, January 2018

INTRODUCTION

1

Adobe® Photoshop® Lightroom™ 1.0 was released on February 19th 2007, after a long public beta period, and it rapidly became a hit. Thousands of users flooded the forums looking for answers to their questions. In the years that have followed, Lightroom has continued to gain popularity, becoming the program of choice for amateur and professional photographers alike.

In October 2017, Adobe announced that Lightroom was dividing in two different directions, so that each program can focus on its strengths. Lightroom Classic CC continues the desktop folder-based workflow we've used for the last 10 years, whereas the Lightroom CC ecosystem is cloud-native, so all of your photos are stored in the cloud and accessible from any device.

Lightroom Classic CC and Lightroom CC are like distant cousins, so their communication is limited. We'll discuss their interactions in the Cloud Sync chapter starting on page 483, but the rest of the book will focus on the desktop workflow that is Lightroom Classic's primary focus. To save writing it's full name—*Adobe Photoshop Lightroom Classic CC*—over and over again, we'll refer to it as Lightroom in this book.

Google now turns up around 48,500,000 web pages when you search for the word Lightroom. So when you have a question or you get stuck with one of Lightroom's less intuitive features, where do you look?

Do you trawl through thousands of web pages looking for the information you need? Perhaps post on a forum, wait hours for anyone to reply, and hope they give you the right information? From now on, you look right here! *Adobe Photoshop Lightroom Classic CC - The Missing FAQ* is a compilation of the questions most frequently asked—and many not so frequently asked—by real users on forums all over the world.

Unlike many 'how-to' books, this isn't just the theory of how Lightroom is supposed to work, but also the workarounds and solutions for the times when it doesn't behave in the way you'd expect. We're going to concentrate on real-world use, and the information you actually need to know.

I know you're intelligent (after all, you chose to buy this book!), and I'll assume you already have some understanding of computers and digital photography. Unlike the other books, I'm not going to tell you what you 'must' do. I'm going to give you the information you need to make an informed decision about your own workflow so you can get the best out of Lightroom.

Two of my favorite comments about this series of books are "it's like a conversation with a trusted friend" and "it's like having Victoria sit next to you helping." That's my aim - I'm here to help.

THE BOOK FORMAT

Let's just do a quick guided tour so you can get the best out of the book...

The Fast Track for New Lightroom Users

Lightroom's a big program these days, and when you're just getting started, it can be overwhelming. Have you heard of the Pareto principle or 80/20 rule? In short, the idea is that 20% of the effort creates 80% of the results. But when you're just starting out, it's hard to know which information you need to understand, so I've done the work for you.

Starting on page 5, the Fast Track weaves its way through the book, giving you the essential information you need to get started. At the end of each Fast Track section is another red arrow, along with a page reference and clickable link which takes you to the next Fast Track section.

The aim of the Fast Track is to make the information accessible to less experienced users, while retaining all of the advanced geeky detail, so the book's useful to you throughout your whole Lightroom journey.

You can either read the book cover to cover, or you can follow the Fast Track to understand the basics, and then dive into the rest of the book to round out your knowledge, or use it as a reference when you have a question.

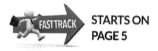

STARTS ON PAGE 5

Workflow Order

If you read the book from front to back, I'll lead you through a typical workflow. It begins with getting your photos and videos

into Lightroom, then viewing them, selecting the best photos, grouping them, adding metadata and filtering the photos. Next, we move on to editing your photos, both in the Develop module and external editors, and then outputting the photos as individual images, emails and publishing them on social media websites. Finally, we discuss how to access your photos on multiple computers or mobile devices.

Index

If you're using the book as a reference, you can find the information you need using the index starting on page 495. In the eBook formats, you can also use the search facility or bookmarks to find the specific words, and you can add your own bookmarks and notes too.

Appendices

In the complimentary eBook formats, there are additional appendices covering the less frequently used Book (page A-1), Slideshow (page B-1), Print (page C-1) and Web (page D-1) modules, but you'll also find introductory tutorials for these modules in the Output Modules chapter in the main book (page 381).

In The Geeky Bits appendix starting on page E-1 (only available in the eBook formats), we explore the pros and cons of the DNG format and other geeky topics such as how to use the DNG Profile Editor, how to hack the TranslatedStrings file and how to import from other software.

Keyboard Shortcuts

Many controls can be accessed in multiple different ways—buttons in the user interface, menu commands, context-sensitive menus and keyboard shortcuts. If I listed every single one, you'd be bored stiff, so I've noted the most frequently used (and most easily remembered) commands and shortcuts. They're also listed at the end of each related chapter, and you can download the complete printable keyboard shortcuts list from https://www.Lrq.me/keyboard-shortcuts/

On both platforms, in addition to keyboard shortcuts, the standard modifier keys are used in combination with mouse clicks to perform various tasks.

Ctrl (Windows) / Cmd (Mac) selects or deselects multiple items that are not necessarily consecutive. For example, hold down Ctrl (Windows) / Cmd (Mac) to select multiple photos, select multiple folders, select multiple keywords, etc.

Shift selects or deselects multiple consecutive items. For example, hold down Shift while clicking to select multiple photos, select multiple folders, select multiple keywords etc.

Alt (Windows) / Opt (Mac)—Changes the use of many controls. For example, in Quick Develop, it swaps the 'Clarity' and 'Vibrance' buttons for 'Sharpening' and 'Saturation.' In Develop panels, it changes the panel label to a panel 'Reset' button, and holding it down while moving some sliders shows masks or clipping warnings.

Links

The links in the eBooks are all clickable. In order to keep the website links current, and make them easy for you to access, I've used my own short-url domain https://www.Lrq.me (that's LRQ.ME) to handle the redirections.

Multiple Formats

You can choose how to you wish to read the book - PDF, ePub, Kindle, Paperback, or all 4! You might want the PDF version on your computer for searching while you work with Lightroom, the Kindle version for reading cover-to-cover while relaxing in the garden, and the paperback for scribbling extra notes. It's up to you. I would suggest:

PDF - used on computer or large tablets.

ePub - used on smaller mobile devices and most eReaders.

Kindle - used on Kindle eReaders.

Windows or Mac?

It doesn't matter whether you're using the Windows or Mac platform, or even both. Lightroom is cross-platform, and therefore this book will follow the same pattern. The screenshots are mainly of the Mac version because I'm writing on a Mac, but the Windows version is almost identical in functionality, and any significant differences will be explained and illustrated.

Where keyboard shortcuts or other commands differ by platform, both are included. The exception is the shortcut to view a context-sensitive menu, which is right-click on Windows or Ctrl-click on Mac. I'll keep that simple and just refer to right-clicking. If you use a trackpad on a Mac, right-click is a two-finger tap and dragging two fingers up or down the trackpad is the same as scrolling.

TALK TO ME!

This book is based entirely around user feedback, so I'd love to hear the things you like about this book, and anything you feel could be improved. I'm always looking for ways to make this book even better, so if you come across a question that I've missed, something that's not clear, or you just want to tell me how much you love the book, you can send me your feedback using the Contact form on the website at https://www.lightroomqueen.com/contact I promise to read every email, even if I can't reply to them all personally.

I've also included a year's Premium Email Support with your purchase, via the form in the Premium Members Area, in case you get stuck while you're reading (see page 494).

If you enjoy the book, posting a review on Amazon or your favorite online bookstore would make my day, and would help other Lightroom users find it too. Thank you!

Now, where shall we start...?

BEFORE YOU START

2

If you're anything like me, the first thing you want to do with a new program is dive right in. Who wants to read an instruction manual when you can experiment? If you're nodding in agreement, that's fine, but do yourself a favor and just skim through the Fast Track before you jump in head first.

Lightroom's designed around a database, so it doesn't work in the same way as most other image editing software. You'll save yourself a lot of headaches by understanding the basics!

WHAT IS A LIGHTROOM CATALOG?

There are basically two different types of image management software – databases (catalogs) and file browsers. So what's the difference? Let's compare to a physical library of books to illustrate. **(Figure 2.1)**

A file browser looks at the files directly on the hard drive and organizes photos by folder. This is like walking straight into the library and looking round the shelves of books. If someone's borrowed a book, you won't even know it exists.

A database is a series of text records. This is like the library's catalog of books. In the old days, it was made up of drawers full of cards, but these days it's all computerized. Each card – or computerized record – contains information about the book, who wrote it, a description, its ISBN number, perhaps a picture of the cover, and most importantly, which shelf the book is stored on. **(Figure 2.2)**

The books themselves are still on the shelves. They're not IN the catalog. If someone's borrowed a book so it's no longer on the shelf, you can still see the information describing the book, but you can't read the book until it's returned to its shelf. If

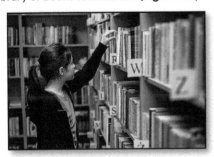

Figure 2.1 *The Lightroom catalog is like a library of books.*

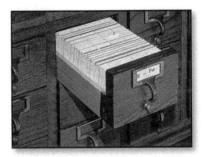

Figure 2.2 *There's a text record describing each photo.*

someone moves the book to a new shelf, the information on the card is incorrect and you'll be looking in the wrong place until the record is updated.

Lightroom uses a database rather than acting as a file browser. Photos are never IN the catalog. The Lightroom catalog contains text records of information describing the photos, with small previews stored nearby, and most importantly, a note of where each photo is stored on the hard drive. If the hard drive is disconnected or a photo is moved to a new location, you can still see the information describing the photo and a small preview in the catalog, but you can't work with the photo until the original file is found.

Why does understanding the catalog matter?

We're very familiar with working in file browsers. Windows Explorer and Mac Finder are used on every single Windows and Mac computer, so handling files in a browser comes naturally to most computer users.

Catalogs are different. If you move, rename or delete a file outside of Lightroom, the records in the catalog won't get updated to match. Lightroom will still be looking in the old location on the hard drive for the file, and won't be able to find it. When this happens, you may not be able to edit or export the photos (just like you can't read a library book until you find the book itself).

As well as the information about the original image files, the catalog contains a record of all of the work you've done to the photos. This includes flags, stars, keywords, captions, collection membership, and more. Even your Develop edits are stored as a series of text instructions in the catalog itself. While it's possible to store some of

this metadata with the files (in a format called XMP), by default it's only stored in the catalog. If you remove the photos from the catalog, all of your Lightroom edits will be gone. Even if you reimport the photos later, you won't get this information back.

What do I need to remember?

• Always rename photos within Lightroom, using the *Library menu > Rename Photos* command. If you don't, you have to fix the links one at a time. BIG job! (See page 116 for more detail.)

• Move photos within Lightroom by dragging and dropping them on another folder – or if you move them using Explorer/ Finder/other software, update Lightroom's records immediately, before you forget where you put them. (See page 118 for more detail.)

• Don't remove photos from the catalog unless you're also intentionally deleting the original photos (e.g. the fuzzy ones). (See page 115 for more detail.)

• Back up your catalog regularly. It contains a lot of essential information! (See page 53 for more detail.)

DESIGNING YOUR WORKFLOW

Finally, before we start using the software itself, let's talk briefly about workflow. It's one of the most popular topics among photographers, but why? What does it actually mean?

The term workflow simply describes a series of steps undertaken in the same order each time. For photographers, this workflow runs from the time of shooting (or even before), through transferring the photos to

...continues on page 9

Basic Lightroom Workflow

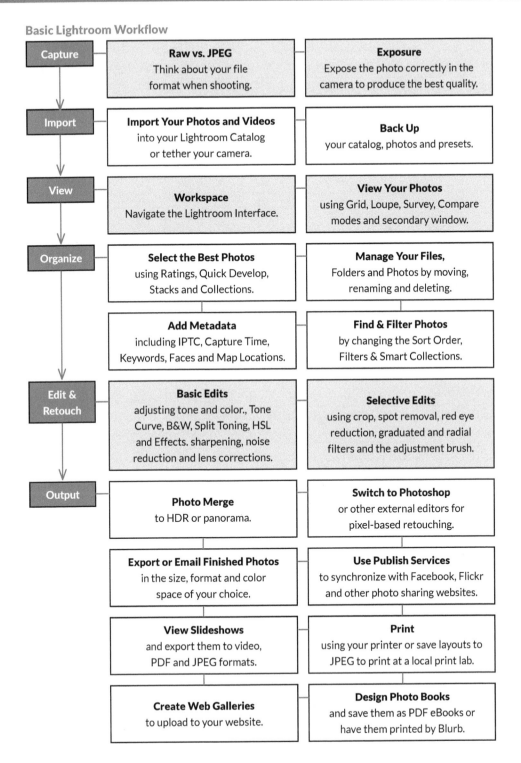

Capture

Raw vs. JPEG	Exposure
Think about your file format when shooting.	Expose the photo correctly in the camera to produce the best quality.

Import

Import Your Photos and Videos	Back Up
into your Lightroom Catalog or tether your camera.	your catalog, photos and presets.

View

Workspace	View Your Photos
Navigate the Lightroom Interface.	using Grid, Loupe, Survey, Compare modes and secondary window.

Organize

Select the Best Photos	Manage Your Files,
using Ratings, Quick Develop, Stacks and Collections.	Folders and Photos by moving, renaming and deleting.

Add Metadata	Find & Filter Photos
including IPTC, Capture Time, Keywords, Faces and Map Locations.	by changing the Sort Order, Filters & Smart Collections.

Edit & Retouch

Basic Edits	Selective Edits
adjusting tone and color., Tone Curve, B&W, Split Toning, HSL and Effects. sharpening, noise reduction and lens corrections.	using crop, spot removal, red eye reduction, graduated and radial filters and the adjustment brush.

Output

Photo Merge	Switch to Photoshop
to HDR or panorama.	or other external editors for pixel-based retouching.

Export or Email Finished Photos	Use Publish Services
in the size, format and color space of your choice.	to synchronize with Facebook, Flickr and other photo sharing websites.

View Slideshows	Print
and export them to video, PDF and JPEG formats.	using your printer or save layouts to JPEG to print at a local print lab.

Create Web Galleries	Design Photo Books
to upload to your website.	and save them as PDF eBooks or have them printed by Blurb.

Figure 2.3 *Each photographer's Lightroom workflow is different, but there are similar themes.*

My Personal Workflow

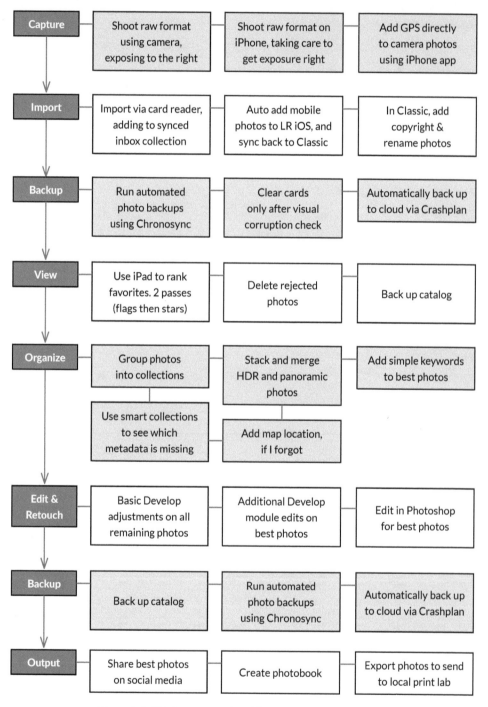

Figure 2.4   *This is my personal workflow. Your workflow won't look exactly the same, but it'll share the same principles.*

your computer, sorting and selecting your favorites, editing and retouching them, and then outputting to various formats, whether on screen or in print.

The initial aim for your workflow is consistency. If you do the same thing in the same order every time, you reduce the risk of mistakes. Files won't get lost or accidentally deleted, metadata won't get missed, and you won't end up redoing work that you've already completed **(Figure 2.3)**

There is no perfect workflow for everyone, as everyone's needs are different. The Fast Track sections of this book guide you through a simple workflow, but outside of the Fast Track, we'll also consider other workflow variations and the thought processes behind them, so you can start to build your own ideal workflow. I've also included a diagram of my personal workflow to help get you started. **(Figure 2.4)**

Once you've settled on a good workflow, that isn't the end of the story. You'll likely find that you continue to tweak it, finding slightly more efficient ways of doing things. It'll continue to build with time and experience, as well as with the introduction of new technology. The principles, however, remain the same.

INSTALLING LIGHTROOM

Just in case you haven't installed Lightroom Classic yet, we'll briefly run through the installation and upgrade processes. If you're already up and running, you can move on to the next chapter starting on page 15.

Minimum System Requirements

The minimum system requirements for installing Lightroom Classic are found at https://www.Lrq.me/classic-sysreq

These are the absolute minimum required in order to actually install Lightroom, but it is likely to 'walk' rather than run on these specs! Lightroom does benefit from higher specification hardware.

Installing Lightroom

To install Lightroom, click on the Creative Cloud icon in the System Tray (Windows) / Menubar (Mac) and select the *Apps* tab. Scroll down to *Lightroom Classic CC* and press *Install*. **(Figure 2.5)**

If you don't have the Creative Cloud desktop app installed, log in to your account at https://www.adobe.com and select the Desktop Apps from the menu. Find Lightroom Classic CC and click the Download button. It prompts you to install the Creative Cloud desktop app, and then you can follow the previous instructions.

Opening Lightroom

To open Lightroom again in future, go to *Start > Adobe Lightroom Classic CC* (Windows) / *Applications > Adobe Lightroom Classic CC > Adobe Lightroom Classic CC.app* (Mac).

While Lightroom's open, you can set up a shortcut for easier access. On Windows, right-click on the icon in the Taskbar and select *Pin to Taskbar*. On macOS, right-click on the icon in the Dock and select *Options > Keep in Dock*.

As Lightroom loads, it display a splash screen. **(Figure 2.6)** but if you'd prefer to display your own photo, create a folder called Splash Screen in the following locations, and put the photo inside:

Windows—C: \ Users \ [your username] \ AppData \ Roaming \ Adobe \ Lightroom \ Splash Screen

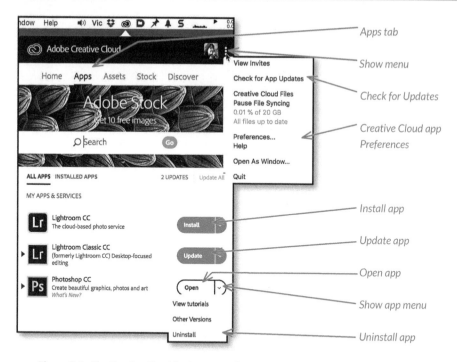

Figure 2.5 *The Creative Cloud Desktop app allows you to easily install and update Adobe software.*

Mac—Macintosh HD / Users / [your username] / Library / Application Support / Adobe / Lightroom / Splash Screen

If you add multiple photos to this folder, Lightroom cycles through them.

To turn it off completely, uncheck **Show splash screen during startup** in Lightroom's Preferences dialog.

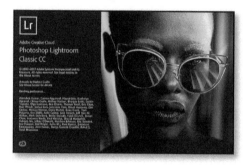

Figure 2.6 *The splash screen displays when you start Lightroom.*

Setting the Language

Lightroom's not just limited to English—it's also available in Chinese Simplified, Chinese Traditional, Dutch, French, German, Italian, Japanese, Korean, Portuguese, Spanish, or Swedish.

By default, it uses the same language as the operating system. To switch to another language, go to *Edit menu* (Windows) / *Lightroom menu* (Mac) > *Preferences > General tab*, select the language you want to use and then restart Lightroom.

Some keyboard shortcuts don't work on international keyboards. In Appendix E on page E-17, you'll find instructions for editing the keyboard shortcuts.

Activation

Lightroom Classic requires online activation, and it allows activation on two machines at any time (although you can have it installed on additional computers). The activation process runs automatically while installing Lightroom, and all you need to do is remained signed in with your Adobe ID.

You don't need to remain connected to the internet after activation, so even traveling to remote areas isn't a problem. Lightroom just needs to be able to 'phone home' at least every 99 days. If you're going to be away from internet, make sure your laptop battery doesn't die, as this can reset the activation.

If you need to switch computers, you can go to *Help menu > Sign Out* to deactivate a computer, but if you forget, don't worry. When you try to activate on a third computer, Lightroom warns that you're already activated on two machines and offers to deactivate them remotely.

Desktop App Usage Information

When you start Lightroom for the first time, it warns you that it'll send some usage information back to Adobe, to help them improve the program. This includes information about your Lightroom usage, but not your photos or other personal information.

If you don't want to share this information with Adobe, go to *Help menu > Manage My Account*, log in, and select *Desktop App Usage Information* under *Security & Privacy*, then uncheck the checkbox.

Creating Your First Catalog

Once Lightroom's installed, there are very few differences between the Windows and Mac versions, apart from the slightly different appearance. We'll carry on using the Mac version for screenshots, but where there are notable differences, we'll show both. Let's get started...

(If you're upgrading from a previous Lightroom version, skip to page 12.)

If you haven't used Lightroom before, it asks where to store the catalog and how to name it. **(Figure 2.7)** This is important, because the catalog contains your Lightroom edits. By default, the catalog is called Lightroom Catalog.lrcat and it's stored in a Lightroom folder in your main Pictures folder.

Next to the catalog, Lightroom creates a Previews folder (Windows) / file (Mac) called Lightroom Catalog Previews.lrdata. The previews folder/file contains a small JPEG preview of all the photos you import so it can grow very large.

If you have plenty of space on your boot drive (usually C:\ on Windows or Macintosh HD on Mac), click *Continue* to select the default location.

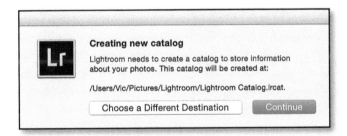

Figure 2.7 *Lightroom asks where to store your new Lightroom catalog.*

If your boot drive's low on space or you'd prefer an alternative location for your catalog, click *Choose a Different Destination* and select your chosen folder and catalog name. (The catalog must be stored on an internal or external hard drive, not network storage.)

Either way, make a note of the catalog name and location you choose, as you'll need to ensure these files are backed up.

Lightroom may ask whether you want to sync your photos, so you can access them in Lightroom CC on your mobile phone, tablet or another computer. We'll come back to these options in more detail in the Cloud Sync chapter starting on page 483. If in doubt, turn it off for now.

Lightroom's main interface opens with some initial tips in the center of the screen. **(Figure 2.8)** These tips give you a quick guided tour of Lightroom. Press *Next* to view the tips or click anywhere else on the screen to hide them.

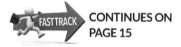

CONTINUES ON PAGE 15

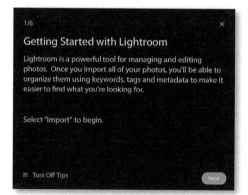

Figure 2.8 *Tips appear in the center of the screen.*

MULTIPLE COMPUTERS

Lightroom's license agreement is cross-platform (both Windows and Mac) and it allows the main user to use Lightroom on two computers, for example, a desktop and a laptop.

Lightroom isn't designed to be used over a network. The Lightroom catalog needs to be stored on a locally attached drive (internal or external), and can only be used by one person at a time. The photos, however, can be stored on a network drive or NAS unit.

There are options for using your catalog on multiple machines, such as between your desktop and laptop. We'll explore the options in the Multiple Computers chapter starting on page 404.

UPGRADING FROM EARLIER VERSIONS

If you're upgrading from a previous version (Lightroom CC 2015, Lightroom 6 or earlier), you'll need to upgrade your catalogs in addition to upgrading the program. The good news is that's an easy process and any release version catalogs (Lightroom 1-6, CC 2015) can be upgraded to the Lightroom Classic version 7 catalog format.

How do I install the Lightroom upgrade?

To install Lightroom Classic, open the Creative Cloud app and click *Install* next to *Lightroom Classic CC*. It doesn't happen automatically.

Installing the upgrade doesn't update your shortcuts/dock icons, but it does upgrade the catalog.

How do I upgrade my catalog for use in Lightroom Classic?

Before you install a major upgrade (usually October each year), make sure you have a current catalog backup, just in case something goes wrong. Proper measures have been put in place to avoid disasters, but you can never be too careful.

When you open Lightroom Classic, it automatically finds your last-used Lightroom catalog and asks for permission to upgrade it. **(Figure 2.9)** This creates a copy of your Lightroom catalog, adds -2 to the end of the catalog name, borrows the previews files from the earlier version, and upgrades the catalog format.

Your original catalog remains untouched, so you may want to move it to your backups folder once the upgrade is complete.

If Lightroom doesn't automatically find your catalog, or you want to upgrade a different one, go to *File menu > Open Catalog.*

Once I've upgraded the catalog, can I go back to an earlier Lightroom version?

Once you've upgraded your catalog, you won't be able to open the upgraded catalog in an earlier version. You'll still have your earlier catalog untouched, however if you work on the upgraded copy in Lightroom Classic, for example, using a trial version, and then decide to go back to Lightroom 6 or earlier, the changes you've made to your photos in Lightroom Classic will not show up in your earlier catalog.

DOT RELEASES

Lightroom's usually updated with new camera and lens support on a 3-4 monthly basis. The updates also include bug fixes, particularly in the early dot releases such as 7.1, so it's worth staying current with these updates.

How do I check which version I'm currently running?

To check which version you're running, go to the *Help menu > System Info* and the first line

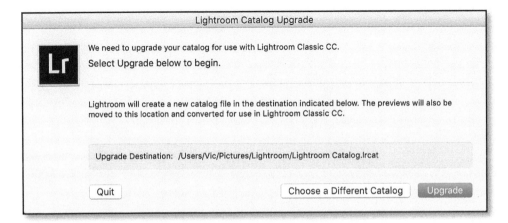

Figure 2.9 *When you try to open an older Lightroom catalog, Lightroom asks for permission to upgrade it to the current format.*

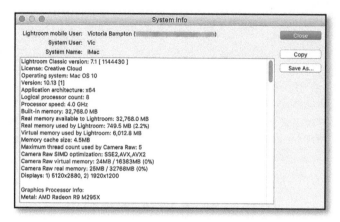

Figure 2.10 *The first line of the System Info dialog shows your current build number.*

confirms the version and build number. **(Figure 2.10)**

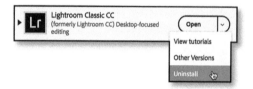

Figure 2.11 *To uninstall, click the cog icon in the Creative Cloud app.*

How do I update to a newer Lightroom dot release?

If you have a Creative Cloud subscription, the updates appear automatically in the Creative Cloud system tray/menubar app. Click the Update button to install the update. Lightroom displays a simple What's New dialog, but you'll find more extensive release notes on my blog at https://www.Lrq.me/whatsnew/classic/

How do I uninstall Lightroom?

If you have the Creative Cloud app, the easiest option is to click the arrow to the right of the *Lightroom Classic CC Open* button and select *Uninstall.* **(Figure 2.11)**

What happens to Lightroom if my subscription expires?

If you cancel your subscription, most of Lightroom carries on working, so you don't lose access to your photos or the work you've done to them. You can still view and export your photos, and even add new ones, but the Develop module, Map module and Sync all stop working.

HELP SHORTCUTS

		Windows	Mac
Help	Lightroom Help	F1	F1
	Current Module Help	Ctrl Alt /	Cmd Opt /
	Current Module Shortcuts	Ctrl /	Cmd /

IMPORTING PHOTOS & VIDEOS

3

As Lightroom is built around a database, the first thing you need to do is add the information about your photos and videos to this database. This process is called Importing, but don't let that confuse you. Although it's called Importing, the photos don't go 'into' Lightroom. A better word to describe the process might be reference, link, or register.

Importing the photos simply means that the information describing the photos and videos is added to the database as text records, along with a link to that file on the hard drive and a small JPEG preview. Remember, it's like an index of the books in a library. The library catalog tells you a little about the book and which shelf it's stored on, and maybe even gives you a preview of the cover, but it doesn't contain the book itself. **(Figure 3.1)**

Where are my photos?

Before you can start adding your photos to Lightroom, you need to know where they're currently stored. I can't answer that question for you, but there are a few common places to look:

- Your phone or tablet.

- Your camera's memory card.

- The Pictures or Photos folder on your computer.

- Other internal or external hard drives.

- Cloud services, such as Google Photos and Dropbox.

- If you've been using Photoshop Elements to organize your photos, there's an Import tool to transfer your existing photos into Lightroom. See Appendix E (page E-28) for more detail.

- On macOS, iPhoto, Photos and Aperture default to storing photos in a special kind of folder called a package file, which is not accessible using other software. To access the photos, you can use that software to export them to a folder as normal photos. Select the "Original" format option where possible, to avoid degrading the quality.

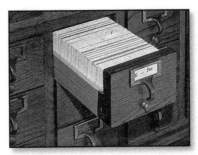

Figure 3.1 *Like a manual library card catalog, Lightroom keeps track of where your photos and videos are stored, and information about them, but it doesn't contain the photos/videos themselves.*

There's more information on transferring photos from these apps in Appendix E (starting on page E-23).

Once you've found your photos, you then need to decide where you'll store them in future.

Where should I store my photos?

Lightroom doesn't hide your photos away from you. They're kept as normal image files in folders on your hard drive.

The benefit? You have complete control over where your photos are stored, you're not locked in to using Lightroom forever, and you can access the photos using other software.

The downside? That makes you responsible. You need to know where they're stored, how to back them up, and you need to understand how what you do in Lightroom affects these files on the hard drive. Don't worry, we'll learn all the basics you need to know in the Fast Track sections of this book.

When you import your photos, YOU make the decision on where to store the photos (even if that decision is to accept Lightroom's defaults). It's possibly the most important decision you'll make in Lightroom, so it's worth taking the time to pay attention to the choice you make.

At the top of the Import dialog, you're given three main choices: will you copy the photos to a new location, move them to a new location or just add links to the catalog, leaving the image files where they are. **(Figure 3.2)**

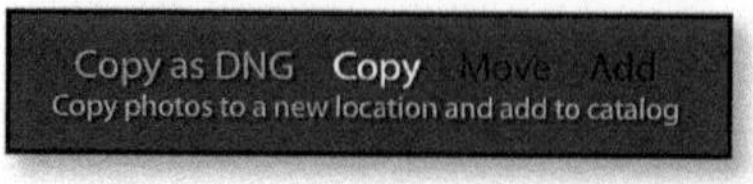

Stop and think about these options for a moment. Your choice will depend on whether you're copying new photos from a camera/memory card or adding existing

Figure 3.2 *Select Copy at the top of the dialog to copy the photos to your hard drive, or Add to leave them in their current location.*

photos.

If your photos are currently on a memory card, and you tell Lightroom to "add" them at their existing location, Lightroom will record their location as being on the memory card. What will happen when you eject the card? Lightroom will look for the photos on the memory card but won't be able to find them any more, so you won't be able to edit and export them. And when you format the memory card? Gone forever! There won't be a copy on your computer's hard drive, because you didn't tell Lightroom to copy them. So when you're importing photos from a memory card, it's ESSENTIAL that you select *Copy* at the top of the Import dialog.

But what if you're adding photos that are already on your hard drive? Your choice will depend on how organized your photos are:

If your photos are beautifully organized into an existing folder structure, you'll want to select Add. This simply adds the information describing the photos to Lightroom's catalog, but the photos remain in their current location. Remember, if you then rename, move or delete the photos outside of Lightroom, Lightroom will no longer be able to find them.

If your photos aren't quite so organized – or if they're spread haphazardly across your computer's hard drives—then you might want to consolidate them in a single location. While importing, Lightroom can copy them to a new location, leaving the originals scattered across your computer (and therefore taking up twice the hard drive space), or it can move them to a new location.

If you're copying or moving photos, you pick the location in the Import dialog's Destination panel. You have to make a one-time decision... where will you store your photos?

The default location is the Pictures folder in your user account. This is a perfectly good location, as long as you don't have too many photos and you have a big hard drive. But what if your hard drive is too small?

Lightroom doesn't mind where you choose to store the photos. They can be on an internal drive, an external drive, a network drive, or even a mix of different drives. The important detail is that YOU know where they are so you can back them up.

You can make life easier for yourself by keeping your folders of photos under a single parent folder (or one for each drive), rather than scattering them in random locations. Why?

• If the folders of photos are grouped in a folder called "Lightroom Photos" or another easily identifiable name, it reminds you not to rename, move or delete these photos.

• If you need to move them to another drive or another computer, it's far easier to copy/move a single folder with its subfolders than it is to hunt around 300 different folders on your computer.

• It's easier to back them up when they're all stored under a single parent folder.

As your collection of photos grows, you may need to expand onto additional hard drives, which isn't a problem for Lightroom.

So where will you store your photos? Made your decision? Then let's start importing your photos...

How do I import my photos?

When you initially open the Import dialog **(Figure 3.3)**, it may look a little overwhelming, but don't worry, it's simpler than it looks. There are three main decisions to make: where to find the photos (the source), how to handle the photos (copy/move/add) and if you're copying or moving the photos, where to put them (destination). The rest of the options are, well, optional!

First, we'll step through the basics of getting your photos into Lightroom, and then we'll go back through the individual elements of the Import dialog in more detail. Although we'll mainly refer to importing photos throughout the chapter, the instructions apply to videos too. Let's get started...

1. If you're importing from a memory card, insert your memory card into the card reader or attach the camera to the computer. Card readers usually work more reliably with Lightroom than USB camera connections.

2. If the Import dialog doesn't open automatically, go to *File menu > Import Photos and Videos* or by pressing the **Import** button in the lower left corner of the Library module.

3. On the left of the Import dialog is the Source panel, with memory cards at the top and hard drives listed below.

4. If you're importing from a memory card, click on its name. If you only have a single device (i.e. card reader, camera or phone) attached, it's selected automatically.

5. If you're importing existing photos,

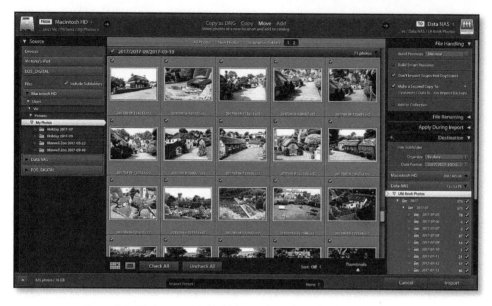

Figure 3.3 *Photos are added to Lightroom's catalog using the Import dialog.*

navigate to the location of your photos in the lower *Files* section of the Source panel.

6. If the photos are stored under a single folder, such as the My Photos folder in

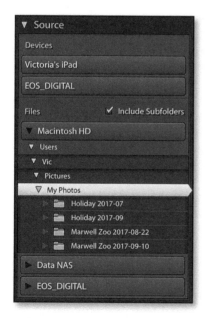

Figure 3.4 *Select the memory card or folder of photos in the Source panel.*

Figure 3.4, select that folder and check the *Include Subfolders* checkbox.

7. If your photos are spread across multiple folders, hold down Ctrl (Windows) / Cmd (Mac) while clicking on each folder, or hold down Shift while clicking on the first and last folder in a series of consecutive folders.

8. Thumbnails start to appear in the central preview area. They make take a while to appear if you have thousands of photos, but you don't need to wait for them to finish appearing before continuing. It's possible to view and check/uncheck photos in the Import dialog, but it's easier to sort through them in the Library module after import.

9. At the top of the Import dialog **(Figure 3.5)**, decide how to handle the files you're importing.

If you're importing from a memory card, select Copy, to copy the photos to your computer's hard drive.

If you're importing from a hard drive, you

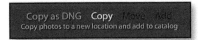

Figure 3.5 *Select Copy at the top of the dialog to copy the photos to your hard drive, or Add to leave them in their current location.*

have a choice: do you want to leave the photos where they are, or copy/move them to a new location? Select...

Add—To reference the photos at their current location, select *Add*. This is a good choice if your photos are already arranged in a tidy folder structure that you'd like to keep.

Move—To let Lightroom move the photos to a new location and automatically reorganize them, select *Move*. This is most useful if your photos are spread across your hard drives in a slightly disorganized fashion.

Copy—To leave the original photos alone and create a copy in the location you choose in the Destination panel, select *Copy*. You'll need twice as much hard drive space if you choose this option, as you'll be duplicating all of your photos, but it leaves your current system intact.

10. On the right-hand side of the Import dialog are a variety of different settings you can apply while importing the photos. We'll use some default settings to get started, and explore the options in more detail later in the chapter.

11. In the File Handling panel **(Figure 3.6)**, set the following:

Build Previews—*Standard*.

Build Smart Previews—checked.

Don't Import Suspected Duplicates—checked.

Make a Second Copy—If you're importing existing photos, leave it unchecked. If you're importing from a memory card, check it then click on the file path and choose a location on another hard drive as a temporary backup.

Add to Collection—unchecked.

12. In the File Renaming panel **(Figure 3.7)**, if it's available, leave *Rename Files* unchecked or turn to the File Renaming panel section starting on page 30 to learn more.

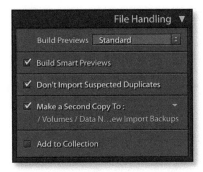

Figure 3.6 *In the File Handling panel, choose your preview size and temporary backup location.*

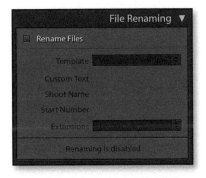

Figure 3.7 *In the File Renaming panel, set a new file naming template, or leave it unchecked to retain the camera filename.*

13. In the Apply During Import panel (**Figure 3.8**), set the following:

Develop Settings—*None.*

Metadata—*None* or turn to page 35 to learn how to create your copyright metadata preset.

Keywords—*leave it blank.*

14. If you've set the import type to *Add*, your work is done—press *Import* and allow Lightroom to register all the selected photos in the catalog.

15. If you've chosen *Move* or *Copy*, you need to choose where to put the photos. By default, Lightroom copies your photos into the Pictures folder in your user account, but you can choose another location. In the Destination panel, you'll see a volume bar for each drive that's attached to your computer. When you click on the bar, the drive opens to show the enclosed folders. To see hidden subfolders, click the small triangles.

To select a folder, click on it so it's highlighted in white, like the Lightroom Photos folder shown in **Figure 3.9**. Double check this destination every time you export photos.

16. Then you need to decide how you're going to organize the photos. The options at the top of the Destination panel allow you to set the folder structure. As you try different settings, the folders in the lower half of the Destination panel update, so you can test different options to see what will happen. The folders in italic will be created by your import settings.

We'll go into more detail on the pros and cons of different systems starting on page 36. If you're not sure what to choose, I'd recommend a simple dated folder structure, with one folder per month, grouped by year, but here's a few different options:

To copy/move the photos **directly into the folder** you've selected, select *Into One Folder* in the ***Organize*** pop-up.

To **create a named subfolder** for the photos, check *Into Subfolder*, enter the name of the new subfolder, and select *Into One Folder* in the *Organize* pop-up. (**Figure 3.10**) This is useful when copying photos from a memory card into a manually-created folder structure.

To **create a date-based folder structure** automatically, select *By Date* from the *Organize* pop-up and a folder structure from the *Date Format* pop-up. If you're not sure

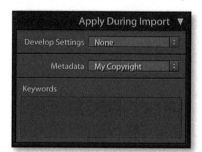

Figure 3.8 *In the Apply During Import panel, add your copyright metadata.*

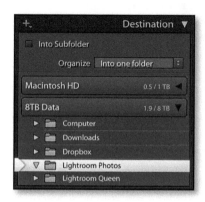

Figure 3.9 *Select the Destination folder, highlighted in white.*

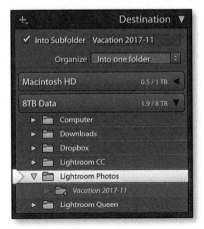

Figure 3.10 *You can place the photos into a named subfolder.*

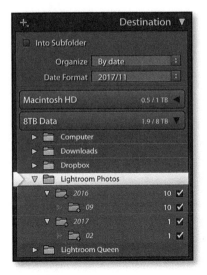

Figure 3.11 *Alternatively, you can automatically create a dated folder structure based on the metadata of the selected photos.*

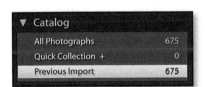

Figure 3.12 *The recenly imported photos are grouped in the Current Import / Previous Import collection.*

which to select, the YYYY/MM option is a good default. **(Figure 3.11)** We'll go into more detail in the Destination panel section starting on page 36.

17. Before you start the import, double check the folders in italic, to make sure the folder structure looks correct. The wrong parent folder being selected can cause confusion (see page 40 for more detail), so it's worth checking this italic preview every single time you import new photos.

18. Finally, press *Import*.

19. The Import dialog closes and the new photos start to appear in the Library module. The photos are grouped in a special collection in the Catalog panel called *Current Import* (which then changes to *Previous Import*) **(Figure 3.12)**, and their folders also appear in the Folders panel.

Congratulations, your photos are now cataloged by Lightroom! If you're itching to start using Lightroom, you can now skip on to backing up your photos (page 53) and then viewing them in Lightroom (page 75), and come back to the rest of this chapter later. If you're still with me, let's go back and explore the individual elements of the Import dialog in more detail.

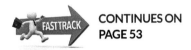

CONTINUES ON PAGE 53

IMPORT IN DETAIL

In Lightroom, there are usually multiple ways to accomplish the same task. For example, to open the Import dialog you can go to *File menu > Import Photos*, press the *Import* button at the bottom of the left panel group in the Library module, or use the keyboard shortcut Ctrl-Shift-I (Windows) / Cmd-Shift-I (Mac).

How do I automatically open the Import dialog?

Lightroom can also open the Import dialog automatically when you insert a memory card. There are two different behaviors involved in the Import dialog opening automatically: whether Lightroom opens the Import dialog when the program is already open, and whether the program launches by itself even though it was closed.

To change this auto-open behavior, go to Lightroom's *Preferences dialog > General tab* and check or uncheck **Show Import dialog when a memory card is detected**. (Figure 3.13)

On Windows, this checkbox controls whether the Import dialog opens automatically when a card is detected, and also whether the program launches from closed (using Windows Auto Play).

On a Mac, the checkbox only controls whether Lightroom opens the Import dialog when the program is already open. To set Lightroom to launch from closed, insert the memory card or plug in the device. Go to the Applications folder, open the Image Capture app, and select the memory card or device on the left-hand side. In the lower left corner, click the arrow, and select Lightroom as the program to automatically open when

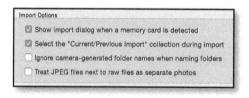

Figure 3.13 *The Show import dialog when a memory card is detected checkbox in the Preferences dialog > General tab controls whether the Import dialog automatically opens when a device is connected. On Windows it also launches Lightroom if it's closed.*

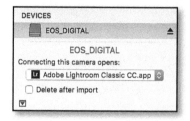

Figure 3.14 *On macOS, Image Capture controls whether Lightroom opens.*

that device is detected. (**Figure 3.14**)

The same logic applies, not just to card readers and cameras, but also to mobile phones and tablets, USB keys, printers with card readers, and various other devices.

SOURCE PANEL

When importing photos into Lightroom, you first need to select the source of the photos using the Source panel. (**Figure 3.15**) Remember, at the top of the panel are your devices—cameras, card readers, mobile devices, and so forth—and below that are the hard drives attached to your computer, as well as any mounted network drives. To select a source, simply click on the folder or device of your choice.

Why do the folders keep jumping around when I click on them?

When you click on different folders in the Source panel (and later in the Destination panel too), Lightroom can appear to have a mind of its own, with different behavior depending on whether you single-click or double-click, but it's actually a useful feature.

If you navigate around by single-clicking on the folder arrows or folder names, the navigation behaves normally. If you double-click, or if you right-click and choose **Dock**

Folder from the context-sensitive menu, you can collapse the folder hierarchy to hide unnecessary folders. **(Figure 3.16)** It makes it easier to navigate through a complex folder hierarchy, especially if it's many levels deep and the panel is too narrow to read the folder names. If you collapse it down too far,

just double-click on the parent folder to show the full hierarchy again. **(Figure 3.17)**

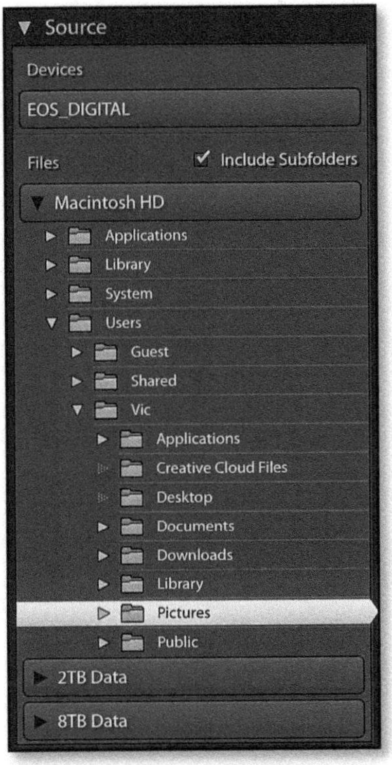

How do I import from multiple folders or memory cards in one go?

If all the photos you want to import are in subfolders under a single parent folder, for example, within a Photos folder, then you can select that parent folder and check the *Include Subfolders* checkbox. All the photos from the subfolders display in the preview area, ready to be imported.

If your photos are spread around multiple folders, hold down Ctrl (Windows) / Cmd (Mac) while clicking on each folder. **(Figure 3.18)** The multiple folders don't even have to be on the same drive as long as they appear in the *Files* section of the Source panel. If the folders are consecutive, hold down Shift while clicking on the first and last folder in a series to select them without having to click on each one.

Figure 3.15 *The Source panel on the left of the Import dialog allows you to select the folder or device to import.*

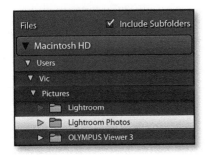

Figure 3.16 *With the My Photos folder docked, some non-essential folders are hidden.*

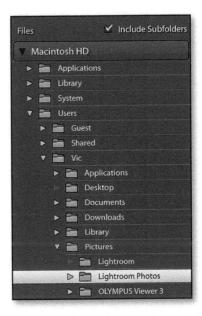

Figure 3.17 *When the folders list is undocked, the folder list can become very long.*

Multiple selections are limited to folders shown in the *Files* section. You can't import from two separate devices in one go, for instance, two card readers. However if the operating system sees the memory cards as two drives in the lower *Files* part of the Source panel, you can Ctrl-click (Windows) / Cmd-click (Mac) on the folders to import both at once.

Can I use the operating system dialog to navigate to a folder instead of using Lightroom's Source panel?

If you're more comfortable using the operating system dialog to select a folder, click on the large button in the top left corner of the Import dialog. **(Figure 3.19)** (Yes, those corners are large buttons, even though they don't look like it!) The *Other Source* option in that menu displays the operating system dialog. It also lists shortcuts to popular folders such as *Desktop* and *Pictures*, as well as recent sources. When

you select a folder using any of these options, the Source panel automatically updates to display that folder.

The top right corner behaves the same way, except it updates the Destination panel.

PREVIEWING AND SELECTING INDIVIDUAL PHOTOS

Having selected the source of the photos, the photo thumbnails start to populate the central preview area. In this grid, you can view the photos and select the ones you want to import.

A photo count displays in the bottom left corner of the dialog, showing how many photos are checked and how much hard drive space they fill. **(Figure 3.20)**

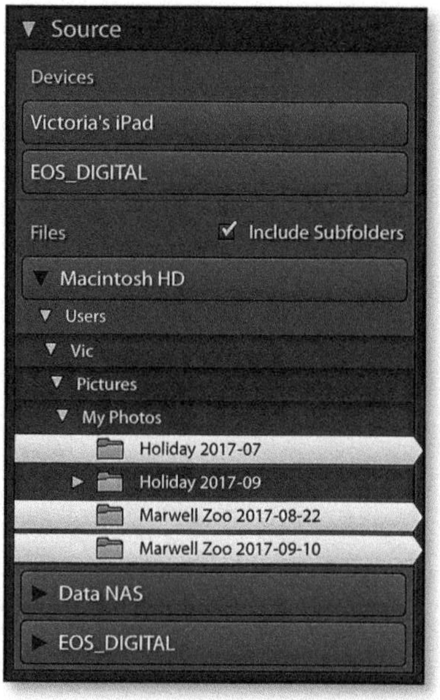

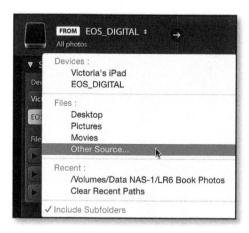

Figure 3.19 *Click on the top corners of the Import dialog to view a menu of recent sources and to access the operating system dialog.*

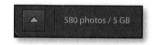

Figure 3.20 *A photo count displays in the bottom left corner.*

Figure 3.18 *You can select multiple folders for import.*

How do I select only certain photos to import?

The checkbox in the corner of the thumbnail controls whether the photo is included in the import. They're all checked by default. The **Check All** and **Uncheck All** buttons below the grid check/uncheck all the photos in one go, or you can click the individual checkboxes to select or deselect specific photos.

To check or uncheck a series of photos, hold down Ctrl (Windows) / Cmd (Mac) while clicking on photos to select non-consecutive photos, or Shift-click on the first and last photo to select a group of consecutive photos. Once you have the photos selected, shown by a lighter gray surround, check or uncheck the checkbox on a single photo to apply that same checkmark setting to all of the selected photos.

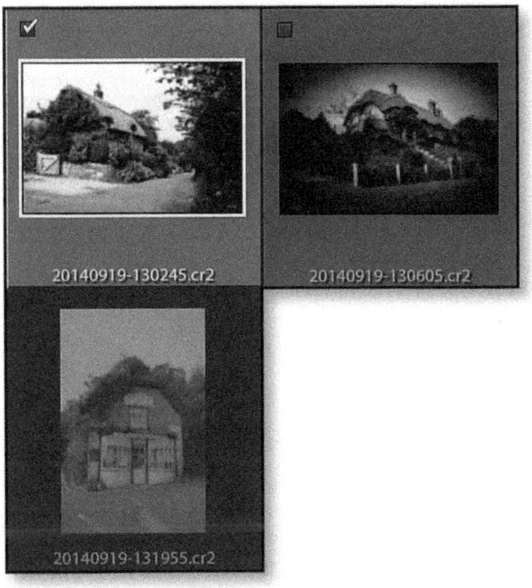

Figure 3.21 *Dimmed thumbnails without a checkbox (bottom) aren't available for import. Thumbnails with a vignette are unchecked and can be imported by checking the box (top right).*

Why are some photos unavailable or dimmed in the Import dialog?

You might notice that some of the photos appear dimmed in the Grid. Photos shown with a vignette are unchecked photos, but they can be selected for import by toggling the checkbox. **(Figure 3.21)**

Dimmed photos that don't have a checkbox are unavailable for import, either because they're already in your current Lightroom catalog at that location, or they're already in your catalog at a different location and you have *Don't Import Suspected Duplicates* checked in the File Handling panel.

How do I change the preview size?

On the Toolbar below the grid, to the right, the **Thumbnails** slider adjusts the size of the thumbnails. The thumbnails embedded in the files are usually small and low quality, but there's also a larger JPEG preview embedded in most photos. These larger previews aren't used for the Grid view as they're slower to load, but the Loupe view allows you to take advantage of the larger preview.

Can I change the sort order?

Also on the Toolbar is the **Sort** pop-up **(Figure 3.22)**, which allows you to sort the thumbnails in the Grid.

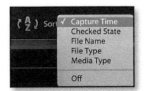

Figure 3.22 *At the bottom of the Import dialog grid, you'll find the sort order pop-up and thumbnail size slider.*

The options are:

Capture Time sorts the photos based on their capture time.

Checked State displays the checked photos first, followed by the unchecked photos.

Filename sorts the photos in alpha-numeric filename order.

File Type displays the photos grouped by file type, for example, all of the CR2 files, then the JPEGs, then the TIFFs.

Media Type displays the videos first, followed by the photos.

Off disables sorting.

Can I filter the photos?

As well as changing the sort order, you can filter the photos shown in the Grid using the Filter bar above the thumbnails. **(Figure 3.23)**

All Photos—displays all the photos in the selected source.

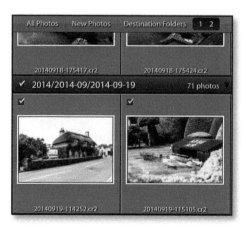

Figure 3.23 *Along the top of the Import dialog grid is a Filter bar. Clicking on Destination Folders divides the thumbnails into groups.*

New Photos—hides any photos that have already been imported and are recognized as duplicates.

Destination Folders—breaks up the grid into sections based on the folder structure you set in the Destination panel, for example, by date. These grid sections can be collapsed by clicking on the triangle on the left, and whole groups of photos can be checked or unchecked using the checkbox on the dividing row.

How do I select specific file types?

Select the *File Type* sort order in the *Sort* pop-up in the toolbar. This groups the photos by their file type. Click *Uncheck All*, then hold down Shift, click on the first photo of your selected file type, then click on the last photo of the same type. Finally, check one of the selected photos to check all of them.

Can I see a larger preview before importing?

To show a larger Loupe view of a photo, select any thumbnail and press the Loupe button on the Toolbar **(Figures 3.24 & 3.25)** or double-click on the thumbnail. (If it doesn't work, the file may not include a larger preview, or Lightroom may be having trouble reading it, so go ahead and import the photos and view them in the Library module instead).

Below that Loupe preview is the checkbox to include or exclude the photo from the Import. Be careful marking photos in the Import dialog, because if you accidentally close the Import dialog before importing, you can lose all the work you've done selecting files, whereas marking photos in the Library module saves as you go along.

Press the Grid button on the Toolbar or

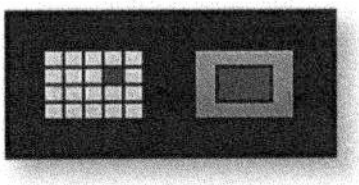

Figure 3.24 *Below the thumbnails or preview are Grid and Loupe buttons for switching between these views.*

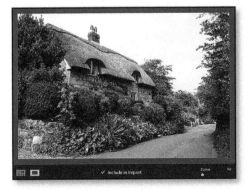

Figure 3.25 *The Loupe view allows you to see a larger preview of the photo before importing.*

double-click on the photo to return to Grid view again.

IMPORT METHOD

Having selected the photos, you need to decide how to handle them. While importing, you can copy them, move them, or leave them where they are. **(Figure 3.26)** These options are found at the top of the Import dialog.

Copy as DNG copies the photos to a folder of your choice, and converts the copies of any raw files to DNG format, leaving the originals untouched. DNG, or Digital Negative, is an openly documented raw file format. Some cameras create DNG files

natively, and other raw files can also be converted to the DNG format. It's worth understanding the pros and cons so you can make an informed decision. In the Geeky Bits Appendix starting on page E-1, we explore all the benefits and disadvantages, as well as how DNG can be integrated into your workflow.

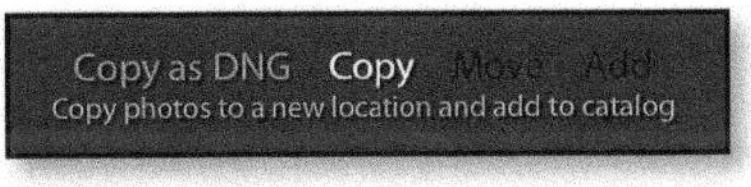

Copy also copies the photos to a folder structure of your choice but it doesn't convert them to DNG format. As it's duplicating the photos, it takes up additional hard drive space, so it's primarily used when copying photos from a memory card or other device, rather than importing existing photos from the hard drive.

Move copies the photos to the folder structure of your choice but it also removes the files from their original location. The *Move* option is particularly useful if you want Lightroom to reorganize your existing photos while importing, as it doesn't take up additional hard drive space.

Add leaves the files in their current folder structure with their existing filenames, and references them, or links to them, in that original location. This is a great option for importing existing photos if you already have an organized filing system. You'll note that the File Renaming and Destination panels on the right are missing, since they don't apply when adding photos without moving them.

Why can't I select *Move* or *Add*?

When you're importing from a device such as a camera or card reader, Lightroom disables the *Move* and *Add* options to protect you from accidental loss. Most file corruption happens during file transfer, and if you moved the files instead of copying them, you would no longer have an uncorrupted copy on the card. Also, if you use *Add* to reference

Copy as DNG   **Copy**   Move   Add
Copy photos to a new location and add to catalog

Figure 3.26 *At the top of the Import dialog, choose how to handle the files.*

the photos directly on the card, you could format the card believing that the files are safely imported into Lightroom, only to discover that Lightroom can no longer find the files.

For that same reason, there's no *delete photos from memory card once uploaded* option, because it's good practice to verify that the data is safe before you delete the files. Formatting the cards in your camera, rather than the computer, also minimizes the risk of corruption.

FILE HANDLING PANEL

Further file handling options appear in the File Handling panel on the right. **(Figure 3.27)** Using this panel, you choose the size of the previews to be created after

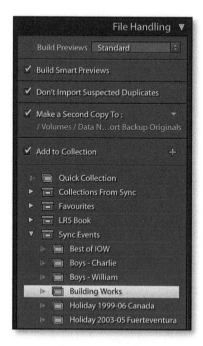

Figure 3.27 *The File Handling panel on the right of the Import dialog allows you to set initial preview size, duplicate handling, temporary backups and collection membership.*

importing, how to handle duplicate photos, and whether to copy the photos to a temporary backup location.

Why do I have to create previews? Why can't I just look at the photos?

The first option in the File Handling panel is **Build Previews**. All raw processors create their own previews because raw data has to be converted in order to be viewed as an image. Lightroom creates previews of all file types, so that non-destructive edits can be previewed without damaging the original image data. These previews also allow you to view the photos when the original files are offline, for example, when your external drive is disconnected.

What size previews should I build?

There are four preview size options:

Minimal—extracts the thumbnail preview embedded in the file. It's a quick option initially, but it's a very small low quality preview, usually with a black edging and about 160px along the long edge, so you then have to wait to for previews to build as you browse. They're useful if you're in a hurry to import, but don't need to look at the photos until later. Minimal previews aren't color managed.

Embedded & Sidecar—extracts the JPEG preview embedded in a raw file or the sidecar JPEG for viewing in the Library module. This is quicker than building standard or 1:1 previews, so they're useful for initially viewing the photos and selecting your favorites. They don't have any Lightroom adjustments applied, so they look like the camera JPEGs. We'll discuss embedded previews in more detail on page 83.

Standard—builds Lightroom's own previews

Import Preview Decision Tree

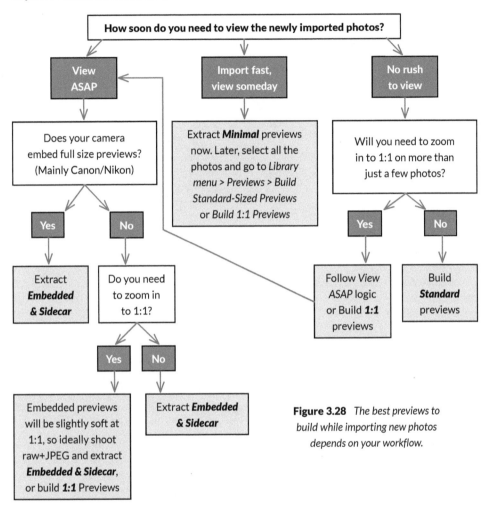

Figure 3.28 *The best previews to build while importing new photos depends on your workflow.*

immediately after import, so the photos look the same as they do in the Develop module. Lightroom will have to build standard previews at some point, so if you're not in a hurry to start viewing the photos, this is a good choice.

1:1—builds full size versions of standard previews. They're slower to build, and take up more space on the hard drive, but if you need to zoom in when viewing the photos, and your camera doesn't embed a full size embedded preview, they're a good choice.

Still confused? Try following the decision tree. **(Figure 3.28)**

There's also a **Build Smart Previews** checkbox. Smart Previews are proxy files that can be used in place of the original files when the original files are offline. They're partially processed raw data (lower resolution Lossy DNG), so they behave like the original raw files when editing in the Develop module. They also help to speed up indexing the image content and mobile sync. We'll come back to Smart Previews in more detail in the Multiple Computers chapter on page 420 and in the Performance chapter on page 465 and page 468.

What does Don't Import Suspected Duplicates do?

Next in that panel is **Don't Import Suspected Duplicates**. If it's checked, Lightroom matches the photos that you're importing against those that are already in the catalog, to see whether you're trying to import duplicates.

For example, if you forget to reformat the card in the camera before shooting more photos, it recognizes the photos that are already in the catalog and skips them rather than duplicating the files. It's worth leaving checked unless you're intentionally importing duplicate photos.

To be classed as a suspected duplicate, the files must match on the original filename (as it was when imported into Lightroom), the EXIF capture date and time, and the file length (size).

If it doesn't recognize the duplicates, make sure you've inserted the card before opening the Import dialog, as it can be more temperamental if you open the Import dialog first. It also only works if the photos are still in the catalog, so if you've deleted some, they will be reimported from the card. It also won't recognize photos that you've re-saved as an alternative format—only exact duplicates.

What does the Make a Second Copy option do?

When using one of the Copy or Move options, the **Make a Second Copy To** checkbox becomes available in the File Handling panel. This backs up your original files to the location of your choice, in a dated folder

called "Imported on [date]". If you choose to rename your files while importing, these backups are renamed to match, but they always remain in their original file format, even if you're converting the working files to DNG while importing.

The Second Copy option is useful as a temporary backup, while the photos make their way into your primary backup system, but it's not a replacement for good primary backups as it doesn't replicate your working folder structure. We'll consider backup systems in the next chapter starting on page 53.

How do I add imported photos to a collection while importing?

While you're importing the photos, you can also add them to a collection. This is particularly useful if you use sync photos to the cloud to access on your mobile devices, your workflow is designed around collections, or you're importing photos from an event that spans multiple days, such as a vacation.

Enable the **Add to Collection** checkbox to display and select your existing collections and collection sets, or click on the + button to create a new collection. You can only add the photos to a single collection while importing, although you can add them to additional collections once the import completes.

FILE RENAMING PANEL

Most cameras use fairly non-descriptive file names such as IMG_5968. The problem with these names is, over the course of time, you'll end up with multiple photos with the same name.

Using the options in the File Renaming panel

(**Figure 3.29**), you can rename your photos while you're importing them. (If your Import dialog is set to *Add*, you won't be able to rename while importing. Either change to one of the *Copy* or *Move* options, or wait until the photos are imported and rename in the Library module.)

How will you name your photos?

The main thing to consider when naming your files is how you'll make the names unique. If a file doesn't have a unique name, and it's accidentally moved to another folder, other photos could be overwritten.

The date and time works well as a unique file name, for example, YYYYMMDD-HHMMSS (year month day—hour minute second). If you regularly shoot in sub-second bursts or you prefer to keep to the camera file name, YYYYMMDD-original file number (and a camera code if you're shooting with more than one camera) can work well with a low risk of duplication.

Others prefer a sequence number combined with some custom text, for example, *Vacation2017_003.jpg*. Don't add the words *Vacation2017* into the template itself, otherwise you'll have to go back to the

Filename Template Editor each time you need to change it. Instead, use the *Custom Text* and *SequenceNumber(001)* tokens, so you can enter *Vacation2017* directly in the Import dialog.

You can rename the files at any time, as long as you do it within Lightroom, but doing so while importing means your initial backups will have the same names as the working files. This can be invaluable if you have to restore from import backups.

Which characters can I use in my filenames?

It's sensible to only use standard characters, such as plain letters and numbers, and use underscores (_) or hyphens (-) instead of spaces when you're setting up your filenames, so your filenames will be fully compatible with web browsers and other operating systems without having to be renamed again. Some characters, such as / \ : ! @ # $ % < > , [ ] { } & * ( ) + = may have specific uses in the operating system or Lightroom's database, causing all sorts of trouble, so those are best avoided.

For more information on recommended filename limitations, check https://www.Lrq.me/cv-filenames

How do I rename the files while importing?

To rename the files, check the **Rename Files** checkbox and select a template from the pop-up to the right. There's a selection of templates built in to Lightroom, but if you select *Edit* in the **Template** pop-up, you can create your own template using tokens in the Filename Template Editor. (**Figures 3.30, 3.31 & 3.32**)

How do I build a filename template?

1. In the Filename Template Editor, click

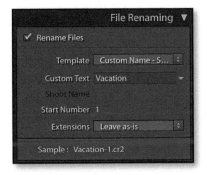

Figure 3.29 *The File Renaming panel allows you to rename the photos at the time of import, which means that all versions and backups of the photos will have the same name.*

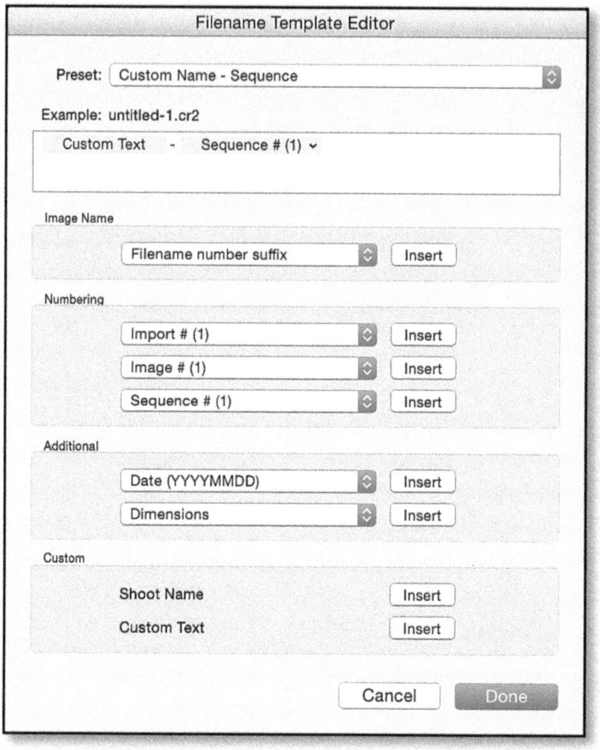

Filename Template Editor

Preset: Custom Name - Sequence

Example: untitled-1.cr2

Custom Text - Sequence # (1) ⌄

Image Name

Filename number suffix   Insert

Numbering

Import # (1)   Insert

Image # (1)   Insert

Sequence # (1)   Insert

Additional

Date (YYYYMMDD)   Insert

Dimensions   Insert

Custom

Shoot Name   Insert

Custom Text   Insert

Cancel   Done

Figure 3.30 *Use the Filename Template Editor to build a filename structure of your choice.*

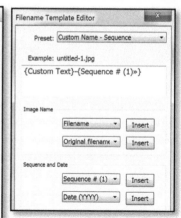

Figure 3.31 *The Windows version displays the tokens as curly brackets rather than blue lozenges.*

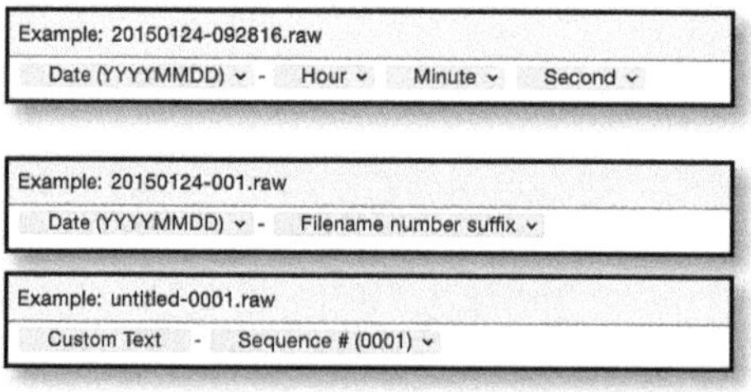

Example: 20150124-092816.raw

Date (YYYYMMDD) ⌄ -   Hour ⌄   Minute ⌄   Second ⌄

Example: 20150124-001.raw

Date (YYYYMMDD) ⌄ -   Filename number suffix ⌄

Example: untitled-0001.raw

Custom Text - Sequence # (0001) ⌄

Figure 3.32 *These are a few example filename templates:*
The first one becomes 20150124-092816.jpg.
The second one becomes 20150124-001.jpg.
The last one becomes London2015-0001.jpg.

in the white field and delete the existing tokens. The tokens appear as text in curly brackets on Windows, or blue lozenges on Mac.

2. Below the white field is a selection of pop-ups, each containing different types of tokens. There's a huge selection to choose from! The tokens are grouped into pop-ups. The first contains filename tokens (i.e. current filename), then there are 3 pop-ups for numbering tokens (i.e. sequence numbers) with 1 to 5 digits, then date-based tokens (i.e. YYYYMMDD, and metadata-based tokens (i.e. camera model, star ratings, etc.). Finally there are *Insert* buttons for two custom text fields—*Shoot Name* and *Custom Text*.

3. To add a token, click the Insert button next to one of the pop-ups or select a different option from a pop-up.

4. Repeat to add additional tokens.

5. You can type directly into the white field to add punctuation such as hyphens and underscores between tokens. You can also add text such as your initials. Add a custom text field for text that changes regularly, such as the name of the shoot or other descriptive text.

6. Finally, save it as a preset by selecting the Preset pop-up at the top of the dialog and choosing *Save Current Settings as New Preset* and giving it a name.

7. Press *Done* to close the dialog, and check that your new preset is selected in the File Renaming panel.

How do I add additional padding zeros to sequence numbers?

In the *Numbering* pop-ups, such as Sequence #, you'll note that there are options from (1) to (00001). Some programs can have problems sorting in intelligent numerical order, so they sort files as 1, 10, 11... 19, 2, 20, 21. The solution is to add extra padding zeros to set the filenames to 001, 002, and so forth.

To use a padded 3-digit sequence number, select *Sequence # (001)* instead of *Sequence # (1)* from the pop-up menu. **(Figure 3.33)**

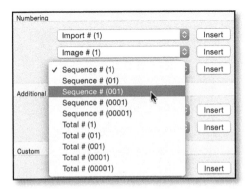

Figure 3.33 *Lightroom offers a range of numbering systems, including a standard Sequence number which you set in the Import dialog.*

What's the difference between Import#, Image#, Sequence# and Total#?

While you're looking at the *Numbering* pop-ups, you'll notice that there are a number of different types of sequence number available.

Sequence # is the most useful, and the most familiar type of numbering. It's an automatically-increasing number which starts at the number you set in the File Naming panel in the Import dialog or in the Rename Photos dialog in the Library module.

Import # increases with each batch of photos you import. The first time you use the token during import, it's set to 1, then the next time it's 2, etc. It's only available while importing photos.

Image # increases with each individual photo you import. The first photo is set to 0, then the next is 1, etc.

Both *Import #* and *Image #* have starting numbers set in *Catalog Settings > File Handling tab*, with **Import Number** used for *Import #* and **Photos Imported** used for *Image #*. **(Figure 3.34)** If you don't use these tokens, the count doesn't increase. Later, when renaming in the Library module, Image # always starts at 1 regardless of the Catalog Settings.

Total # refers to the number of photos it's renaming in one go, so if you're renaming 8

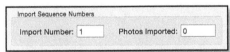

Figure 3.34 *In Catalog Settings > File Handling tab, you can set the Import Sequence Numbers which are used for the Import # and Image # tokens.*

photos, the *Total #* token is replaced with 8. It's only available in Library module Rename Photos dialog.

Lightroom can't automatically restart the numbering for each day (i.e. day3-001.jpg) or remember the last number used in a folder (i.e. start at London-253.jpg). To use that type of numbering system, rename the photos in chunks in the Library module, using the *Sequence #* token and setting a start number manually for each batch.

Where do I enter custom text and start numbers?

After creating your filename template, the availability of the additional fields in the File Renaming panel **(Figure 3.35)** depends on which tokens are used in the selected template.

There are two custom text fields—**Custom Text** and **Shoot Name**—which allow you to add custom text into your filename without returning to the Filename Template Editor each time you want to change the text. The arrow to the right of each field displays recent entries.

Start Number is used with the *Sequence #* token, allowing you to set a starting number

of your choice. For example, you may want your numbering to start at 1, or you may want to carry on from a specific number such as 253.

The **Extensions** pop-up sets the case of the file extension (i.e. .jpg, .JPG, etc.). The default is *Leave as-is*, but you can change it to *uppercase* or *lowercase* if you prefer. That choice is personal preference.

At the bottom of the File Renaming panel is the **Sample** filename, which allows you to double check you have the correct template selected.

APPLY DURING IMPORT PANEL

Next in line is the Apply During Import panel **(Figure 3.36)**. These options allow you to apply settings to the photos as they're imported—Develop Settings, Metadata or Keywords. The settings apply to all the photos in the current import.

You can't apply different settings to different photos in the same import. You could start the first import with selected photos, however doing so runs the risk of missing a photo or two. It's easier to import

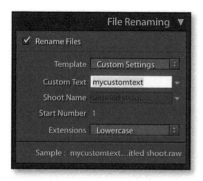

Figure 3.35 *If a template includes Custom Text or Shoot Name tokens, they can be updated in the File Renaming panel.*

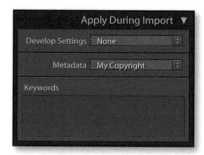

Figure 3.36 *The Apply During Import panel allows you to apply initial Develop settings to your photos at import, as well as adding any Metadata or Keywords that will apply to all of the selected photos.*

all the photos in a single process and then add the different settings, or move photos into different folders in the Library module once they've all finished importing. All the settings that are available in the Import dialog, such as Metadata and Develop presets, can also be applied in the Library module.

What Develop settings should I apply in the Import dialog?

The **Develop Settings** pop-up allows you to apply a Develop preset to the photos while importing, for example, you may always apply a specific preset to all studio portraits as a starting point. *None* just applies the default settings to new photos but preserves any existing Develop settings stored with the files, so it's the option to choose if you're ever uncertain. Be careful not to confuse *None* with *Lightroom General Presets > Zeroed* which sets every slider back to zero even if there were existing settings.

How do I add copyright metadata to my photos?

Import is the ideal time to apply copyright metadata to ensure that all of your photos include this vital information. To create a metadata preset:

1. Select *New* in the **Metadata** pop-up and the New Metadata Preset dialog appears. **(Figure 3.37)** At the top, enter a name for the preset such as "Copyright Preset".

2. Enter your copyright information below. Only checked fields are saved in the preset.

3. In many countries, the copyright notice requires the copyright symbol ©, the year of first publication and then the name of the copyright owner, for example, © 2017 Victoria Bampton. Copyright laws vary by country, so please check your local laws for exact specifications. You may also want to include personal details such as your name, address, website and other contact details.

4. To add a © symbol in the Copyright field, hold down Alt while typing 0 1 6 9 on the numberpad (Windows) or type Ctrl-Alt-C (Windows) / Opt-G (Mac).

5. Press the *Create* button to return to the Import dialog, where your new preset is automatically selected.

Should I apply keywords in the Import dialog?

Keywords can also be applied while importing the photos by typing them in

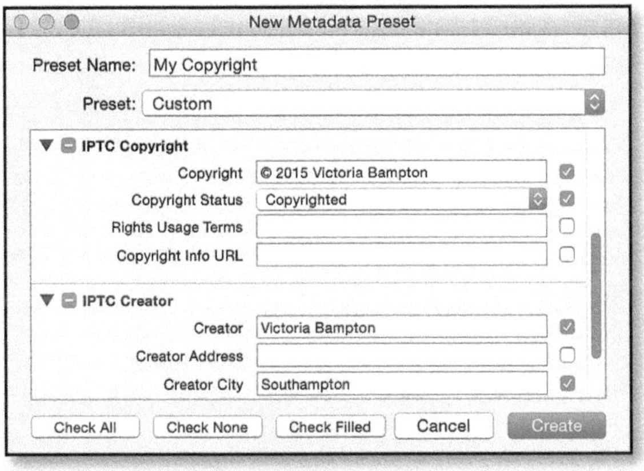

Figure 3.37 *Create a Metadata preset to automatically embed your copyright data in every photo.*

the **Keywords** field, however remember that they're applied to all the photos in the current import, so it's only useful for keywords that apply to everything. Specific keywords are better applied individually in the Library module.

Can I remove existing metadata?

To remove metadata while importing the photos, perhaps because you've entered metadata in other software and want a fresh start, check the applicable fields in a Metadata preset but leave the fields blank. This prevents the metadata being added to Lightroom's catalog. Simply leaving the Apply During Import panel *Keywords* field blank without checking the tick box retains any existing keywords.

DESTINATION PANEL

Finally, you need to decide where to put the photos (unless you're using *Add* to leave them in their current location) and that's where the Destination panel comes into play. It's worth taking the time to get this right before you start importing, as moving the photos after import is a manual process. We decided where to store the photos in the Fast Track at the beginning of the chapter (starting on page 17), but now let's look at how you'll organize them into folders.

What's the best way to organize my photos into folders?

Once you've decided where to store the photos on the hard drive, you then need to decide how to organize them. There's no right or wrong way of organizing photos on your hard drive, but there are some basic principles that can help you avoid problems. It's worth spending the time to set up a logical folder structure before you start importing photos into Lightroom.

As far as Lightroom's concerned, your choice of folder structure doesn't make a lot of difference. Folders are just a place to store the photos, and you can use metadata and keywords to organize them. You could just dump them all into a single folder, but that would become unwieldy in time, so some kind of organization helps. You may also want to find the photos outside of Lightroom, which may influence your choice of folder structure.

We'll come back to some sample folder structures in a moment, but first, let's consider the basic principles behind the widely accepted best practices of digital asset management:

Scalable—You may only have a few thousand photos at the moment, but your filing system needs to be capable of growing with you, without having to go back and change it. Can you go back and add new photos to your system without disturbing existing folders, especially if some of the folders are archived offline?.

Easy Backup & Restore—Your folder structure needs to be easy to back up, otherwise you may miss some photos, and it needs to be easy to restore if you ever have a disaster. This is particularly important as your library grows and becomes split over multiple hard drives.

Storing photos in a single parent folder (per drive), rather than scattering photos around your hard drives, makes it much easier to back up the photos, or move them onto another drive when you outgrow your current drive.

No Duplication—Each photo should be stored in a single location (in addition to your backups).

Besides taking up additional hard drive

space, having the same photo in multiple folders can create chaos when you start trying to add metadata or edit them.

Standard Characters—When naming your folders, stick to standard characters—A-Z, 0-9, hyphens (-) and underscores (_)—to prevent problems in the future.

Consistent—You should always know where a photo should go without having to think about it. If you have to debate each time, there's a higher chance of making a mistake.

We could write a whole book on Digital Asset Management, and the pros and cons of various systems, but fortunately, the world-renowned DAM expert Peter Krogh has already done so. If it's a subject that you would like to learn more about, I recommend The DAM Book https://www.Lrq.me/dambook

Why not organize the photos by topic?

Before you used photo management software, such as Lightroom, you may have organized your photos by subject, so why not carry on doing that? The main reason... a file can only be in one folder at a time, so if you divide your photos up by topic, how do you decide where a photo should go?

For example, if you have a photo of John and Susan, should it go in the John folder or the Susan folder? Perhaps you duplicate in both folders, but then, what happens when you have a larger group of people? Do you duplicate the photo in all of their folders too, rapidly filling your hard drive and making it difficult to track? And if you duplicate the photo in multiple folders, when you come to edit that photo, do you have to update all of the copies too?

Folders work best as storage buckets rather than organizing tools. If you keep

a single copy of each photo (plus backups elsewhere, of course!) in a folder, you can then use keywords, collections and other metadata to group and find photos easily. Using metadata as your organizational tool, the photo of John and Susan may be stored in a single 2017/12 folder, but it would show up when you searched for photos of John, Susan, or even photos shot at a wedding.

Why use a date-based folder structure?

The simplest option for most people is to use a date-based folder structure. It ticks all of the boxes, and more:

• It's scalable, because you just keep adding new dates to the end.

• It's easy to back up the original photos, even to write-once media like DVD/Blu-ray, because you're adding new photos to the latest folders. (Note that if you save derivative files with the original files, such as those edited in other software, you might still be adding photos to older folders too.)

• It's easy to restore from a good backup. In the event of a disaster, it's even possible to rebuild from files rescued by recovery software, because the capture dates are stored in the file metadata.

• It uses standard characters which are accepted by all operating systems.

• The folders can be nested with days inside of months inside of years, so you don't have a long unwieldy list of folders.

• Lightroom can create the folder structure for you automatically on import, so you don't even have to organize it manually. Photos synced from the Lightroom CC family of apps can also drop photos into the same folder structure.

- It's easy to go back and move older photos into the same folder structure, especially if you're only using one folder per month.

Can I adapt a dated folder structure to suit me?

That's not to say you shouldn't adapt the folder structure to suit your needs.

As long as you follow the basic principles above, you can adapt the folder structure to suit your needs without causing unnecessary headaches. It just requires a little more thought initially. Here are a few examples to consider, and I'm sure you can think of a few more:

- Unless you're shooting thousands of photos a day, you probably don't need a full folder hierarchy with one folder per day. A folder for each month, nested inside a folder for each year is a very popular choice, and it's the system I use personally.

- If you want to be able to find photos outside of Lightroom, you might want to use a named folder per shoot, nested inside a year folder. The "random" photos that don't fit inside a full shoot folder can go directly into the year parent folder, and it still follows the basic principles.

- If you're grouping photos by day, you may want to add a descriptive word to the folder name to describe the overall subject, for example, 2017-04-21 Zoo. This makes it possible to find the photos in a file browser, however the folder list can get quite long, so it's worth nesting them in month folders and showing the folder hierarchy so you can collapse them down.

- An event photographer may prefer to use a folder for each event within a parent year folder, sorted by name rather than date, for example, 2017/

John_Kate_wedding_20170421.

- If you shoot for work as well as pleasure, you may want to have separate dated folder structures for Work vs. Personal. But if you decide to split your system, make sure there are no overlaps where a photo may fit into more than one category.

Alternative filing systems aren't 'wrong' but you'll save yourself a lot of headaches if you follow the basic principles. If you're not using a basic dated structure, make sure you think it through properly, and perhaps discuss it with other experienced digital photographers, in case they can see a pitfall that you've missed.

Also, consider how you're going to manage derivatives—retouched masters, and copies exported for other purposes. Are you going to manage these alongside your originals, and if so, how are they going to be backed up and archived?

How do I select a Destination folder?

The Destination panel works just like the Source panel (page 22), including single-clicking for standard navigation, double-clicking to dock folders, and the large button in the top right corner which shows recent destination folders and the operating system dialog.

Select your Destination folder by clicking to highlight it. Any folders that Lightroom creates are placed inside your selected folder. (Figure 3.38)

If the Destination panel is empty, click on the + button and select View : All Folders. The other option—Affected folders only—only displays folders that are receiving new photos, so they only appear when you have photos selected for import.

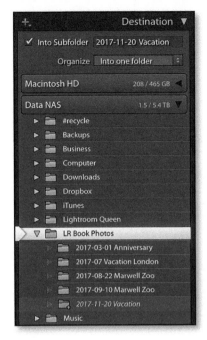

Figure 3.38 *Select the Destination folder and preview the results before starting the import.*

pop-up selection. You have three choices:

By date gives you a choice of date-based folder structures. It automatically organizes your photos into a tidy folder structure.

Into one folder places the photos in the single folder that you select. It allows you to create your own folder structure manually. For example, a portrait photographer may create a folder for each shoot, or you may choose to create a folder for each family event you attend.

By original folders imports in the same nested hierarchy as their existing structure, but at a new location. This is useful if you're importing existing folders of photos and you wish to keep the existing organization.

Any of these folder structures can also be placed into an existing folder on your hard drive or a new folder.

How do I create a new folder?

There are two main ways of creating a new folder. If you click the + button on the Destination panel header, you can use the operating system dialog to create a new folder in the location of your choice.

Alternatively, select a folder in the Destination panel and check the **Into Subfolder** checkbox at the top of the Destination panel. Enter the name of your new subfolder in the field to the right. The new subfolder appears in italic below your selected folder, showing that it will be created by the import process.

I've chosen Copy or Move—how do I organize the photos into a folder structure that suits me?

How the photos are organized within your selected folder depends on your **Organize**

How do I pick a date structure?

If you select *By date*, the **Date Format** pop-up appears, giving you a choice of difference dated folder structures, based on the capture date stored in each file. **(Figure 3.39)**

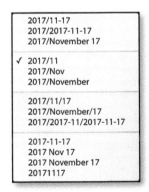

Figure 3.39 *A selection of dated folder structures are available in the Date Format pop-up menu.*

The slash (/) creates nested folders so 2014/10/07 creates a folder 07 inside of a folder 10 inside of a folder 2014, not a single folder called 2014/10/07.

If you want a single folder, you need to use a format with hyphens (-) or underscores (_), such as the 2014-10-07 format.

For most amateur photographers, the best of these options is YYYY/MM, which creates month folders inside year folders.

I'd suggest ignoring the ones with the month spelled alphabetically, as the Folders panel sorts in alpha-numeric order and isn't quite smart enough to know that May should come before August. **(Figure 3.40)**

Why are some of the Destination folders in italic?

As you test the different *Organize* and *Date Format* options, watch the folder hierarchy below. The folders shown in italic are folders that don't currently exist, but will be created by the import. It's an easy way to check that the folder organization setting that you've chosen is the one that you want.

To the right of the folder names are numbers and checkmarks. The numbers show how many photos in the current import will be placed in that folder. Two numbers divided by a slash are checked (left) and unchecked (right) photos.

The checkmarks next to the italicized folders select and deselect photos from those folders. They're particularly useful when you're using a dated folder structure, allowing you to select or deselect a whole day or month's photos in one go.

How do I avoid incorrectly nesting dated folders?

There's one particular thing to look out for when selecting the folder... nested year folders. For example, notice in **Figure 3.41**,

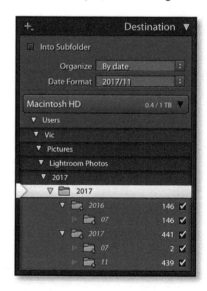

Figure 3.41 *In this case, we've selected the wrong folder, resulting in nested 2017 folders. We should have selected the Lightroom Photos folder.*

Figure 3.40 *The Folders panel sorts in alpha-numeric order and isn't quite smart enough to know that May should come before August.*

there's a new italic 2017 folder being created inside the existing 2017 folder, which is inside yet another 2017 folder. This happens when you select an existing year folder, and tell Lightroom to create dated folders inside it. But look how easy it is to spot in the Destination preview!

To fix it, if you click on the parent folder – Lightroom Photos, in this case – the dated folders slip back into the correct place in the hierarchy, shown in **Figure 3.42**.

Something as simple as double-checking the preview in the Destination panel each time you import new photos can save hours of work tidying up later. You just need to know where to look.

How do I create a manual shoot-based folder structure?

If you need to find photos outside of Lightroom, you may want to store your photos in a year/shoot-named hierarchy instead of purely date-based folder structure.

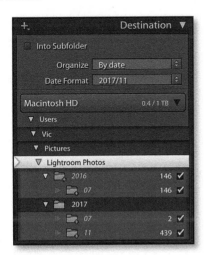

Figure 3.42 *Your selected folder structure is previewed in italic. Make sure you check the folder structure is correct before importing the photos.*

First, in the Destination panel, look for the parent folder that contains all of your photos. Earlier in the chapter, we suggested calling it something like *Lightroom Photos* (page 16).

Inside that *Lightroom Photos* folder, I'd recommend you have a folder per year. This makes it easy to split your photo archive over multiple drives, or archive some photos offline, as you outgrow your hard drives. For most of the year, this folder will already exist, but if it's January and you don't have a 2018 folder yet, right-click on your *Lightroom Photos* folder and select *Create New Folder* (or create it in Windows Explorer/Finder and then select it in the Destination panel, if that's more comfortable for you).

Select this year's folder so that it's highlighted in white. In the *Organize* pop-up at the top of the Destination panel, select Into one folder. This places the photos into the selected/highlighted year folder. This is a great choice for random photos that don't need their own shoot subfolder.

But let's go one stage further. Let's create a new subfolder to hold the photos you're importing, because they're from a specific shoot. At the top of the Destination panel, check the *Into Subfolder* checkbox, and then enter a name for the shoot. In this example, we'll call it *Marwell Zoo*, but you can add the date if you prefer. **(Figure 3.43)**

Before you click Import, remember to double check that the photos are landing in the right place. Remember we said that Lightroom previews any new folders in italic? This is a useful double check to ensure that you have the right folder selected.

Can Lightroom manage my photos, like iTunes moves my music files?

Lightroom doesn't automatically manage

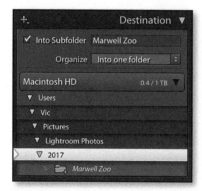

Figure 3.43 Your selected folder structure is previewed in italic. Make sure you check the folder structure is correct before importing the photos.

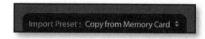

Figure 3.44 Import Presets save the combinations of settings you use regularly.

importing existing photos. You can save these sets of settings as Import presets.

How do I create Import presets, and what do they include?

The **Import Preset** pop-up is tucked away at the bottom of the Import dialog in both the compact and expanded Import dialog views. **(Figure 3.44)** Select your import settings and then choose *Save Current Setting as New Preset* from the pop-up menu and give it a name.

All of the settings in the right-hand panels are included in the presets, along with the *Copy as DNG/Copy/Move/Add* choice. Source panel selections and checked/unchecked thumbnails aren't included in the preset, as these change each time you import.

To use these settings again later, simply select the preset from the *Import Presets* pop-up. You can also update or delete existing presets by selecting the preset, editing it and then selecting *Update* (or *Delete*) from the same pop-up.

THE COMPACT IMPORT DIALOG

If you click the arrow in the lower left corner of the Import dialog, it toggles between compact and expanded dialog views. The compact Import dialog allows you to change a few of the settings, such as the Source or Destination folders, and add basic metadata. **(Figure 3.45)** It doesn't read thumbnails of the photos so it's usually quicker, especially on a slow machine or when importing large numbers of photos. The compact Import

or rearrange your photos once they've been imported. You can move the photos manually by dragging and dropping them into other folders within the Library module, but that could be a big job, so it's better to decide on a sensible filing system at the outset.

Once you've imported the photos, don't tidy up or rename them using Explorer (Windows) / Finder (Mac) or other software, because Lightroom would no longer know where to find them, leaving you the labor-intensive job of relinking the files individually. We'll investigate how do to that in the Missing Files section starting on page 435, but it's easier to prevent than to fix.

SAVING & REUSING IMPORT SETTINGS

Don't worry, having made all these decisions the first time, you can save them to reuse again later. Lightroom remembers your last used settings, but you might need different settings for different uses. For example, you may use different settings when copying from a memory card than you do when

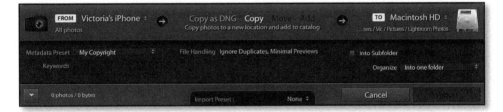

Figure 3.45 *The compact Import dialog only offers a summary of settings. Click the triangle in the lower left corner to switch to the expanded Import dialog*

dialog also displays a quick summary of your other settings, but if you want to change these settings, you need to switch to the expanded Import dialog.

AFTER PRESSING IMPORT

Having set up your import preferences, click the *Import* button in the lower right corner of the dialog to start the import. The *Cancel* button closes the dialog without importing any photos.

The import runs as a background task, allowing you to start (or continue) working in Lightroom while it adds the new photos to the catalog. The progress bar displays in the Activity Center in the top left corner of the screen.

Lightroom selects the *Current Import* collection in the Library module's Catalog panel while importing the photos. If you switch to another folder or collection, it then flips back to the same collection (now called *Previous Import*) automatically when the import completes. This can be frustrating if you're trying to work on other photos while the import runs in the background, so there's a **Select the 'Current/ Previous Import' collection during import** checkbox in the *Preferences dialog > General* tab. **(Figure 3.46)** It's checked by default, but unchecking it prevents Lightroom from automatically switching view.

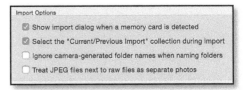

Figure 3.46 *Unchecking the Select 'Current/ Previous Import' collection during import checkbox stops Lightroom automatically switching views when an import completes.*

Once the import completes and you've built standard-sized or 1:1 previews, visually check the files to ensure that they're not corrupted and your backups are safe before wiping your memory cards.

Some photographers like to delete the files from the memory card using Explorer (Windows) / Finder (Mac), as a reminder that the card's ok to reuse, but it's worth then reformatting the card in the camera. This reduces the risk of corruption.

TROUBLESHOOTING IMPORT

We've covered all the controls you need to know about, but there are a few issues that could prevent you importing your photos. To avoid you tripping at the first hurdle, we'll run through the most frequent of these problems and error messages now, and translate them into more helpful terms.

FILE FORMATS

Lightroom can import photos and videos in the following formats:

• Camera raw file formats for supported cameras. You can check whether your camera is supported by the latest version of Lightroom by visiting Adobe's website: https://www.Lrq.me/camerasupport
• Digital Negative (DNG) format
• PSD files set to Maximize Compatibility (8-bit & 16-bit only)
• TIFF (8-bit, 16-bit & 32-bit)
• JPEG
• PNG files
• Some video formats from digital still cameras—AVI, MOV, MP4 and the video files from within AVCHD folders. There's a full list at https://www.Lrq.me/video-support

There are a few limitations to be aware of:

• Photos can be no larger than 65,000 pixels along the longest edge, and no more than 512 megapixels (not megabytes)—whichever is smaller. A photo that is 60,000 x 60,000 is under the 65,000 pixel limit, but it still won't import as it's over the 512 megapixel limit. As most cameras range between 8-36 megapixels, that's only likely to become an issue for huge panoramic or poster shots created in Photoshop.

• CMYK, Lab and Grayscale photos can be imported and managed, but editing and exporting them converts them to RGB. This could result in unexpected shifts in files with other color modes, so you may prefer to control the conversion to RGB yourself using Photoshop, and then import the RGB file into Lightroom for further editing.

• PNG files can be imported and managed, but editing in Photoshop or exporting requires conversion to another format (i.e. TIFF/PSD). Transparency shows as white in Lightroom.

• 32-bit HDR files can only be DNG or TIFF format.

• AVCHD format has limited support—Lightroom imports the MTS video clips but not the whole AVCHD folder structure. You'll need to manually copy the AVCHD folder structure from the memory card to your hard drive if you want to retain the additional metadata.

• Sound files (i.e., WAV and MP3) with the same names as imported photos are copied and marked as sidecar files. This means that they're listed in the Metadata panel, and if you move or rename the original file, the sidecar is also updated.

• Files that aren't created by digital cameras, for example, text files that you may have placed alongside the photos, are not copied to the new location, so always check before formatting the card or drive if you've added extra files.

How do I stop the Import dialog hanging?

If the Import dialog simply hangs before displaying any or all of the thumbnails, it's usually caused by having a mobile phone or tablet attached to the computer. It can also be caused by a drive that's slow to respond (perhaps a network drive), or cloud drives that appear as network drives (e.g. JungleDrive). Try detaching all peripherals from your computer and ejecting network drives before attempting to open the Import dialog again, to narrow down the cause of the problem.

Why can't I see my photos in the Import dialog?

Assuming you've correctly selected a source, there are a few reasons why the thumbnails of the photos might not be visible.

If the photo cells are visible, but the thumbnails are gray and say *Preview unavailable for this file* (**Figure 3.47**), there are a few likely reasons:

• The raw file format isn't supported by your Lightroom version.

• The file is corrupt or has the wrong file extension.

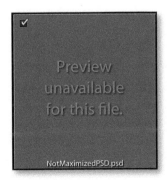

Figure 3.47 *If a preview is unavailable, Lightroom displays a gray thumbnail in the Import dialog.*

• The file doesn't have an embedded preview.

• Lightroom is unable to get the previews from the images. If your camera's connected directly to the computer, a lack of previews can be a result of problems with the camera driver at the operating system level. You may consider purchasing a card reader, as they're usually quicker, reduce the wear and tear on your camera, and can show previews more reliably.

• Lightroom simply hasn't finished retrieving all the embedded previews yet.

Regardless of the cause, you can go ahead and press *Import* as normal. Lightroom displays a more descriptive error message if it can't import the photos. We'll discuss some of these errors shortly.

If the photos are completely missing from the Import dialog, there are three main possibilities:

• The photos are in a subfolder inside the selected source, but you've forgotten to check the *Include Subfolders* checkbox.

• The file type isn't supported, for example, Lightroom won't display Word documents. See the File Formats sidebar (page 44) for a list of supported file types.

• In Lightroom's *Preferences > General tab* is an option to *Treat JPEG files next to raw files as separate photos*. With this option checked, Lightroom displays the JPEG files alongside the raw files, ready for import. If the checkbox is unchecked, the JPEGs are added as sidecars when you import the matching raw file but they're not visible in the Import dialog. (**Figure 3.48**)

How does Lightroom handle Raw+JPEG pairs?

If you shoot raw+JPEG, there's a couple of ways to handle them, controlled by the *Preferences > General tab > **Treat JPEG files next to raw files as separate photos*** checkbox.

To keep them both visible in Lightroom as separate photos, tick the checkbox. They'll be treated as entirely different photos.

To keep them as a pair, with only the raw file visible in Lightroom, uncheck the checkbox. The JPEGs are handled as sidecar files. Sidecar files aren't treated like photos, so you can't view them separately. If you move or rename the visible file, the sidecar file is moved or renamed too.

(Other file types can also be sidecar files, for example, XMP files or audio annotations. They're listed in the Metadata panel.)

If you've imported the raw files already, and you now want to import the JPEGs as separate photos, you can turn off the checkbox and re-import that folder—the raw files are skipped as they already exist in the catalog, and the JPEGs are imported as separate photos. The raw files remain marked as Raw+JPEG, and there isn't an easy way of changing that. Removing them from the catalog and reimporting them resets that label, but if you've made any changes since import, these changes may be lost, so the best solution currently is to close your eyes and ignore them.

What does this error message mean?

If Lightroom can't import the selected files, it displays an error message **(Figure 3.49)** starting with ***Some import operations were not performed*** followed by the reason:

"Could not copy a file to the requested

Figure 3.48   In Preferences dialog > General tab, the Treat JPEG files next to raw files as separate photos checkbox controls the handling of Raw+JPEG pairs.

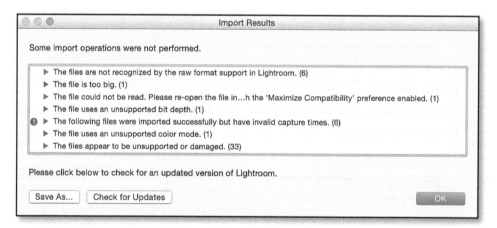

Figure 3.49   If Lightroom can't import your photos, it lists the photos in the Import Results dialog, along with an error message explaining the reason for the failure. Many of these issues can easily be overcome.

location."

If Lightroom can't copy or move the photos to their new location, it's usually because the Destination folder is read-only. Try another location with standard folder permissions, such as the desktop, to confirm that permissions are the problem. If it works correctly on the desktop, use the operating system to correct the permissions for that folder. If the permissions appear to be correct already, it may be a parent folder that has the incorrect permissions. (You'll need to Google for instructions on correcting file/folder permissions, as it's an operating system function rather than Lightroom.)

Other possibilities include the drive being nearly full or the drive being formatted using an incompatible format, such as a Mac computer trying to write to an NTFS formatted drive.

"The files could not be read."

When Lightroom says *"The files could not be read,"* it more frequently means that they couldn't be written. Yes, I know that's not very helpful! As with the *"Could not copy a file to the requested location"* error, check the folder permissions for the Destination folder and its parent folders.

Lightroom also shows *"The files could not be read"* error if the memory card or camera is removed while the photos are still copying, or if the photos are deleted from the source folder before the import completes.

"The files already exist in the catalog."

If you're importing a large number of photos and you press the Import button before Lightroom's finished checking the new photos against the catalog, it may get to the end of the import and say *"The*

files already exist in the catalog." It simply means that Lightroom didn't need to import them as they're already registered in your catalog at that location. If you search the *All Photographs* collection or look in the folder in the Folders panel, you'll be able to find them.

"The file is from a camera which isn't recognized by the raw format support in Lightroom."

Each time a new camera is released, Adobe has to update Lightroom (and ACR plug-in for Photoshop) to be able to read and convert the raw files. The list of supported cameras can be found at: https://www.Lrq.me/camerasupport

The Lightroom updates are released at 2-4 monthly intervals. Go to *Help menu > Check for Updates* to make sure you're running the latest version. If your brand new camera doesn't appear on the list yet, you can also check to see if Adobe has released an Release Candidate of the next update.

There's one other possibility if Lightroom says *"The file is from a camera which isn't recognized by the raw format support in Lightroom."* If a raw file is corrupted, it may show this error instead of the *"unsupported or damaged"* error.

"The file uses an unsupported color mode."

Lightroom supports RGB, CMYK, Lab and Grayscale color modes. If you try to import a photo in another color mode, for example, Duotone, Lightroom shows the *"unsupported color mode"* error. In this case, you'll need to convert the photo to a supported color mode, or import an RGB copy as a placeholder instead.

"The file is too big."

Lightroom has a file size limit of 65,000 pixels along the longest edge, and up to 512 megapixels, whichever is the smaller. If it tells you that the file is too big, then you're trying to import a photo that's larger than that—perhaps a panoramic photo. If you have any such files that you can't import, create a small version of the photo (i.e. using Photoshop) to import into Lightroom to act as a placeholder.

"The files could not be read. Please reopen the file and save with 'Maximize Compatibility' preference enabled."

Lightroom doesn't understand layers, so if there isn't a composite preview embedded in a layered PSD file, it can't import it and Lightroom displays an error asking you to save the file with *Maximize Compatibility* enabled.

To do so, you'll need to open the PSD files in Photoshop and re-save them. You'll find Photoshop's Preferences dialog under the *Edit menu* (Windows) / *Photoshop menu* (Mac), and in the *File Handling > File Compatibility section*, there's an option to *Maximize Compatibility* with other programs by embedding a composite preview in the file. **(Figure 3.50)** The preference only applies to PSD and PSB format files, as other formats (such as TIFF) embed the composite by default.

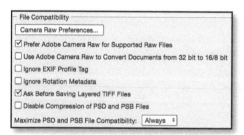

Figure 3.50 *Maximize Compatibility in Photoshop saves a composite layer.*

Maximize Compatibility does increase file size, but it ensures that other programs—not just Lightroom—can read the embedded preview even if they can't read the layers. It's safest to set your Photoshop Preferences to *Always*, or simply use TIFF format, which is generally a better choice now anyway.

"The file appears to be unsupported or damaged."

Files that have the wrong file extension, or 32-bit PSD files, can trigger the *"unsupported or damaged"* error message. 32-bit HDR floating point TIFF or DNG files are supported, but not 32-bit PSD's. Most unsupported file formats aren't even shown in the Import dialog, but those are the exceptions.

More frequently, severe file corruption triggers the *"unsupported or damaged"* error message, although files with less significant corruption may import without warning.

If you don't have an uncorrupted version, Instant JPEG from RAW may be able to extract a readable embedded JPEG preview from a corrupt raw file. You can learn more at https://www.Lrq.me/instantjpegfromraw

TETHERED SHOOTING & WATCHED FOLDERS

Before we move on to backing up your photos, we should mention one final way of getting photos into Lightroom. Tethered shooting involves connecting your camera directly to the computer. As you shoot, the photos appear on the computer's monitor, rather than having to download them later. Lightroom offers two different options, depending on your requirements.

If you're using one of the supported cameras, you can use the Tethered Capture tool, which allows you to connect your camera to the computer, view your camera settings and trigger the shutter using Lightroom's interface.

If you're shooting wirelessly, for example, using an Eye-Fi card, or other remote capture software, you can use Auto Import to monitor a watched folder instead. Auto Import collects photos from a folder of your choice as they appear and automatically imports them into Lightroom, moving them to a new location in the process.

Which cameras are supported by the built-in Tethered Capture?

The current list of cameras supported for tethering can be found on Adobe's website at: https://www.Lrq.me/tethersupport

Lightroom uses the manufacturer's own SDKs to control the camera, which results in some slight differences between manufacturers. For example, if there's a memory card in the camera, Canon cameras can write to the memory card in addition to the computer hard drive, whereas Nikon cameras only write to the computer hard drive. Waiting for the manufacturer to release an updated SDK can also lead to delays in tethering support for new cameras. Nikon cameras are limited to the list linked above, but due a difference in the SDK's, some unlisted Canon cameras may work.

How do I set Lightroom up to use Tethered Capture?

To set Lightroom up for tethering:

1. Connect your camera to the computer using your USB or Firewire cable. A few cameras need to be in PC Connection mode, but most need to be in PTP Mode.

2. Go to *File menu > Tethered Capture > Start*

Tethered Capture and choose your settings in that dialog: **(Figure 3.51)**

Enter a name into the *Session Name* field. This becomes the folder name for the photos.

(Optional) Check the *Segment Photos by Shot* checkbox. This subdivides the photos into further subfolders, inside the *Session Name* subfolder. The *Shot Name* can be changed from the main Tethered Capture window while you're shooting.

Select a file naming template. The default *Session Name—Sequence* template uses the *Session Name* you've entered at the top of the dialog, followed by a 3 digit sequence number.

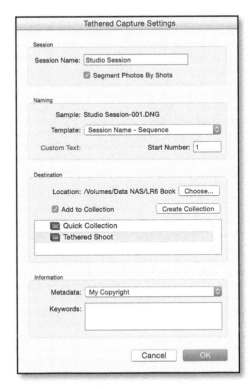

Figure 3.51 *The Tethered Capture Settings dialog sets initial import settings including the Destination folder, file renaming and metadata.*

3. Select a *Destination* folder. The *Session Name/Shot Name* folder hierarchy is placed inside your selected folder.

4. For performance reasons, Tethered Shooting doesn't offer the option to convert to DNG while importing. If you prefer the DNG format, once you've completed the shoot, select the files and go to *Library menu > Convert Photos to DNG* to automatically convert the files.

5. (Optional) Select your *Metadata Preset* and any keywords to apply to the photos as they're imported.

6. Press OK to display the Tethered Capture window. **(Figure 3.52)** The Tethered Capture window displays the current camera settings, but doesn't allow you to change the settings remotely. You can drag the dialog to another location if it's getting in your way. It floats over the top of Lightroom's standard window so you can carry on working without closing the Tethered Capture window.

(Optional) If *Segment Photos by Shot* is enabled, enter a shot name in the Shot Name dialog. To update it for future shots, click on the *Shot Name* field in the Tethered Capture window (just below the camera name) to show the dialog again.

(Optional) Select a Develop preset to apply to each photo on import. Certain settings, such as Crop, can't be included in Develop presets, however that doesn't prevent you from applying them automatically. Simply shoot the first photo, apply your crop along with any other Develop settings, and then select the *Same as Previous* option in the Develop presets pop-up menu. Any further tethered shots automatically have those previous settings applied, including the crop.

7. Press the shutter button on the camera or the silver button on the dialog to trigger the shutter.

8. When you're finished, close the Tethered Capture window by clicking the X in the top right corner.

How do I set Lightroom up to use a watched folder?

If Lightroom's tethering doesn't support your camera, you need to change the camera settings remotely, or you're shooting wirelessly, you can use other tethering tools such as EOS Utility, Camera Control Pro or Eyefi to capture the photos and drop them into Lightroom's watched folder. Lightroom then collects the files from that watched folder, and moves them to another folder of your choice, importing them into your Lightroom catalog, renaming if you wish, and applying other settings automatically.

To set it up:

1. Go to *File menu > Auto Import Settings*.

2. In the *Watched Folder* section, select an empty folder, perhaps on your desktop. **(Figure 3.53)**

3. Select a destination folder and subfolder to store the photos.

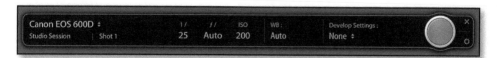

Figure 3.52 *The Tethered Capture window shows the current camera settings and triggers the capture.*

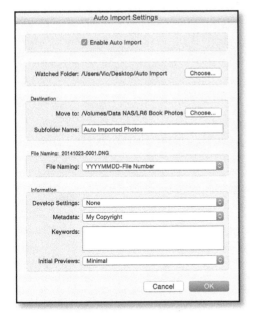

Figure 3.53 *You can use alternative tethered capture software to capture your photos, and automatically import the photos into Lightroom using Auto Import.*

works, then you've set up Lightroom properly.

8. Switch to your camera's remote capture software and set it to drop the photos into that folder. Make sure the remote capture software doesn't create a dated subfolder as Lightroom won't look in any subfolders in the watched folder.

9. Finally, connect the camera to the capture software, and ensure it's saving to the right folder. Release the shutter. The file appears in the watched folder, and then Lightroom moves to your destination folder and imports it into your catalog.

4. Select your filename template in the *File Naming* pop-up.

5. Choose any other import options in Auto Import Settings dialog—*Develop Settings, Metadata Preset, Keywords* and *Preview Size.* These are the same as the choices in the main Import dialog.

6. Enable the *Auto Import* checkbox at the top of the dialog or go to *File menu > Auto Import > Enable Auto Import.* The watched folder needs to be empty when you enable Auto Import, and Lightroom needs to remain open.

7. To check you've set it up correctly, copy a file from your hard drive into the watched folder. As soon as the file lands in the folder, it should start the import, and you should see the file vanish from the watched folder. It should then appear in the destination folder and in Lightroom's catalog. If that

IMPORT SHORTCUTS

		Windows	Mac
Import Dialog	Open Import Dialog	Ctrl Shift I	Cmd Shift I
	Grid View	G	G
	Loupe View	E	E
	Move between photos	Left/Right Arrows	Left/Right Arrows
	Zoom	Spacebar	Spacebar
	Check Selected Photos	P	P
	Uncheck Selected Photos	X	X
	Toggle Checkbox	`	`
	Auto Advance	Caps Lock	Caps Lock
	Add Copyright Symbol	Ctrl Alt C	Opt G
	Begin Import	Enter	Enter
	Cancel / Close Import Dialog	Escape	Escape
Tethered Capture	Hide Tethered Capture Window	Ctrl T	Cmd T
	Shrink Tethered Capture Window	Alt-click on close button	Opt-click on close button
	New Shot	Ctrl Shift T	Cmd Shift T
	Trigger Capture	F12	F12

BACKUP

4

Before we move on to viewing your photos, it's essential to know how to back up your work. This is 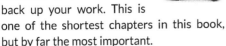 one of the shortest chapters in this book, but by far the most important.

There are three main categories of files that you'll want to include in your backups:

- The catalog(s)

- The photos

- The extras, such as presets and templates

We'll work through each in turn. If you already have a reliable backup system, you can skip to the checklist on page 61.

BACK UP YOUR CATALOG

All the work you do in Lightroom is stored as text metadata in your Lightroom catalog. There are four main things that could go wrong with the catalog:

User error—you may accidentally remove photos from the catalog or unintentionally change settings.

Hard drive failure—if your hard drive dies, you'll need to restore your catalog from a backup on another drive.

Catalog corruption—although rare, the database can become corrupted, usually due to hardware errors.

Software bugs—all software has bugs even though it's tested carefully. It's best to err on the safe side!

Most backup software just backs up the latest version, overwriting the previous backup. That's fine if your hard drive dies, but what if you make a mistake and don't spot it for a few days? That's where versioned backups come into their own.

Versioned backups keep multiple copies of a file so you can 'step back in time' to an earlier version. Lightroom's catalog backup tool does this automatically by zipping up a copy of the catalog and using the current date/time as the folder name so you can identify it later.

How do I back up Lightroom's catalog?

By default, Lightroom prompts you to back up the catalog weekly when you quit Lightroom, and it's as simple as pressing the *Back Up* button in this dialog.

Let's dive a little deeper into the settings, however, to make sure your catalog backups are safe.

PHOTOS NOT INCLUDED

Lightroom's catalog backup doesn't include your original image files. It only backs up the catalog containing metadata about the photos. I regularly hear from people who have deleted their original photos, thinking that Lightroom has them backed up, and I don't want to hear that you've fallen into the same trap. We'll investigate photo backup in the next section starting on page 56.

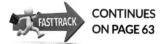

CONTINUES
ON PAGE 63

Where are the backups stored?

Unless you change the location, Lightroom saves the catalog backups in a *Backups* subfolder next to the original catalog. This is a fairly logical place, as long as these folders are also backed up to another drive by your primary backup system. However, it won't help if they're your only catalog backups and your hard drive dies.

To change the backup folder:

1. Go to *Edit menu > Catalog Settings* (Windows) / *Lightroom menu > Catalog Settings* (Mac) and select the *General tab*.

2. In the *Back up catalog* pop-up, change the backup frequency to *When Lightroom next exits*.

3. Quit Lightroom so that the Back Up Catalog dialog appears **(Figure 4.1)**

4. Press *Choose* and navigate to the folder of your choice.

5. Press *Backup* to confirm your choice and run your first backup at the new location.

The backup catalog is compressed into a zip file and placed in a dated subfolder at your chosen location.

Should I turn on Test integrity and Optimize catalog each time I back up?

Also in the Back Up Catalog dialog, there are two important checkboxes which are worth leaving permanently checked.

Test integrity before backing up checks that the catalog hasn't become corrupted and attempts to repair any problems.

Optimize catalog after backing up tidies up and helps to keep your catalog running smoothly and quickly.

```
                        Back Up Catalog

          Note: This only backs up the catalog file, not your photos.

   Back up catalog:  Once a day, when exiting Lightroom          ◊

   Backup Folder:  /Users/Vic/Pictures/Lightroom/LR Book Catalog/Backups   Choose...

          Also:  ☑ Test integrity before backing up
                 ☑ Optimize catalog after backing up

    Skip until tomorrow                    Skip this time    Back up
```

Figure 4.1 *When the backup runs, you can change the backup location or frequency.*

How often should I back up the catalog?

We said that Lightroom prompts you to back up weekly, however if you're working on a large number of photos every day, a week's worth of work is a lot to potentially lose. You can change the backup frequency to prompt you daily, weekly, monthly, or every time Lightroom exits.

To change the backup frequency:

1. Go to *Edit menu > Catalog Settings* (Windows) / *Lightroom menu > Catalog Settings* (Mac) and select the *General tab*. **(Figure 4.2)**

2. Using the *Back up catalog* pop-up, select the frequency of your choice.

You can also change the frequency in the Backup dialog itself, when a backup runs.

How much work can you afford to lose if the worst happened?

I haven't got time to back up now—can I postpone the backup?

If, on occasion, you don't have time to wait for the backup to run, you can skip the backup. There are two buttons in the Back Up Catalog dialog. *Skip this time* postpones the backup until the next time you close the catalog. *Skip until tomorrow/next week/next month* offers a longer postponement, depending on your selected backup frequency. Don't be tempted to skip it too often, or you could find yourself without a recent backup.

How do I run an extra backup on demand?

If you've done a large amount of work (or moved/renamed files) and your backup isn't scheduled to run for a few days, or you hit skip because you were in a hurry last time you closed Lightroom, you can run an unscheduled backup. Go to *Catalog Settings > General tab* and change the backup frequency to When Lightroom next exits and then quit Lightroom so that the backup can run. When you reopen that catalog, it automatically reverts to your normal backup schedule.

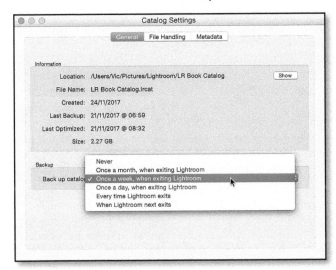

Figure 4.2 *Set your backup frequency in the Catalog Settings dialog.*

Can I delete the oldest backups?

Lightroom compresses the backups using ZIP compression so they don't take up too much space on your hard drive, but if you're backing up every day, they can start to add up. The backups aren't automatically deleted, but you can go to the Backups folder using Explorer (Windows) / Finder (Mac) and delete older backups yourself.

I'd recommend keeping a couple of older backups in addition to the current ones, for example, 1 year old, 6 months old, 3 months old, 1 month old, plus the most recent 4 or 5 backups. You never know when you might discover a mistake you made a few months ago, and want to retrieve settings for some photos from a much older backup.

Why does Lightroom say it's unable to backup?

If Lightroom says it can't back up your catalog, there are a few possibilities to check:

• Check the backup location—is the drive accessible and does the folder still exist?

• Check the folder permissions for the backup location—do you have read/write permissions?

• Is there enough space on the drive?

If everything looks correct, try changing the backup location to a different folder. If this works, try changing it back to your normal backup location.

Should I also write the metadata to the files as an extra backup?

As long as you're sensible about backups, then you have nothing to fear from keeping your data in a single catalog. However if you

like a belt-and-braces approach to backup, you can also save the metadata to the files in a format called XMP which is stored in the header of JPEG/TIFF/PSD/DNG files and in sidecar files for proprietary raw files. XMP doesn't hold all the information that's stored in the catalog, but as the XMP is stored with the image files, it has been known to save the day on occasion. We'll come back to XMP in the starting on page 345.

BACK UP YOUR PHOTOS

Lightroom's Catalog Backup is just that—a backup of your catalog. Your photos are not stored 'in' Lightroom and Lightroom's Catalog Backup doesn't back up the photos, so we need to consider how you're going to protect your photos from disaster.

There are a few questions to ask yourself when planning your photo backup system:

1. How many backups do I need?

Backups can fail. For important files such as your original photos, consider keeping 3 copies (1 working plus 2 backups) on 2 different kinds of media (e.g. hard drive and online), with at least 1 copy at a different location.

When considering your backup system, don't limit the backups to internal/external hard drives or network attached storage (NAS), because viruses, theft, computer malfunctions, lightning strikes, floods, and other similar disasters could wipe out all of your backups along with the working files.

Online backups, such as Crashplan (Small Business Edition), Backblaze or Carbonite, are an excellent choice if you have a fast internet connection, or there's always the lower-tech solution of leaving an external hard drive with a friend or family member.

It's possible to back up to Adobe's cloud , but not through Lightroom Classic (see page 486).

2. Are my backups reliable?

Is the backup media (e.g. external hard drive) free from errors? Avoid using old hard drives for your primary backups.

Are they easily checked to make sure they don't develop errors over time? If your backup system is a mountain of DVD's, checking whether they still read correctly is a long job!

Think about what could go wrong and whether your backups would be protected. This includes hardware errors, software bugs, transfer errors, viruses, hacking, theft, fire, water damage, lightning strike and human error.

Is the file transfer validated? Byte-for-byte verification ensures that the files are copied to the backups without introducing corruption.

3. Are the backups protected from user error?

If you accidentally delete a file, could you easily recover it from your backups? For example, RAID1 is not a sufficient backup system as the file is immediately deleted from both drives.

Is the backup system automated, or does it rely on you remembering which files you've already copied?

4. Could I easily restore the photos to their working folder structure with the correct filenames?

If the backups are stored in a different folder structure, or you've renamed the

working photos after backing up, you'll have a nightmare trying to restore them.

How will you keep your primary backups updated with any changes?

5. Will my derivative files (e.g. photos edited in Photoshop) be included?

If you back up to write-once media such as DVD or Blu-Ray, how will you back up the files you've edited in other software or added to the photo folders?

How do I back up my photos?

Every computer system is different, so I can't give you step-by-step instructions on how to back up your photos. Your choices will depend on your workflow, where your photos are stored, how they're organized, and the available backup media, among other things.

If you're not currently backing up your photos, anything is better than nothing. The simplest way to back up your photos is to include them in your main system backups. Windows comes with its own Backup and Restore tool, and macOS includes Time Machine, both of which can back up your computer files to an external drive. For a little more control, you can run dedicated backup software. Ensure that all of your photos are included in the backups, especially if you store them on external drives, as these may be excluded from the default backup settings.

If you're looking for a slightly more flexible option, file synchronization software makes it very easy to keep a mirrored backup on another drive without wrapping your photos up in a proprietary backup format. These can also verify your data during the transfer, as most file corruption happens while copying or moving files between hard drives. Vice Versa and Chronosync are my personal favorites.

FreeFileSync (Windows/Mac)—
https://www.Lrq.me/freefilesync

Vice Versa (Windows)—
https://www.Lrq.me/viceversa

Chronosync (Mac)—
https://www.Lrq.me/chronosync

I back up photos using the Import dialog—isn't that enough?

We mentioned in the Import chapter (page 30) that the *Second Copy* backup in the Import dialog isn't a replacement for a backup system. It simply copies the imported photos into folders called 'Imported on [date]' so it's great as a temporary backup while you ensure the photos have been safely added to your main backups, or even as a write-once backup stored on DVD/Blu-ray. It won't, however, replicate your working folder structure, back up any additional photos such as those edited in Photoshop, update photos you've moved or renamed, or remove any photos you've deleted.

Should you ever have to try to restore from these backups, you'd have a very time-consuming job reorganizing all the photos.

BACK UP THE EXTRAS

Over the course of time, you'll also gather presets and templates that you've created or downloaded from other websites, so you'll want to back these up too. You can manually copy them from their various locations listed in the checklist on page 61, or set file synchronization software to do it for you.

RESTORING FROM BACKUPS

Now you can relax in the knowledge that your data is protected, but while we're on the subject of backups, let's talk about restoring them. After all, what good is a backup if you don't know how to recover from a disaster?

We'll step through restoring individual backups in this chapter, and restoring everything (after an OS reinstall or moving to a new computer) in the Multiple Computers chapter starting on page 399.

How do I restore a backup of my catalog?

If you're restoring your whole catalog, for example, due to corruption, find your current catalog (*.lrcat file) and rename it, move it or zip it up temporarily. To restore your backup catalog:

1. Find your most recent backup in your Backups folder. The backups are stored in dated subfolders, with the zip file named to match your catalog name, to make them easy to identify.

2. Double-click on the zip file to open the backup. The *.lrcat file displays next to the zip file.

3. If you're on a Mac and your catalog is large, double-click might not correctly unzip the file. In this case, download StuffIt Expander from the App Store (it's free). Open the app and drag the backup zip file onto the icon to unzip it.

4. Move the backup *.lrcat file to your normal catalog location, replacing (or alongside) the existing damaged catalog. Don't be tempted to work on your backup catalog without moving it first. It gets confusing when you're working in a backup folder!

5. Double-click on the *.lrcat file to open it.

6. If everything's now working correctly, you can delete the previous (corrupted) catalog and you should be ready to continue working. If the catalog opens but is behaving strangely, for example, showing the wrong previews or running slowly, you may also need to rebuild the preview cache. We'll discuss this in the Troubleshooting chapter starting on page 448.

How do I restore part of my backup catalog?

But what if you only want to restore part of the backup catalog? Perhaps you accidentally synchronized Develop settings across a folder of photos, or you accidentally removed specific photos from your catalog. If you've worked on other photos since the backup was created, you probably won't want to restore the entire backup catalog, as you'd lose the other work you've done. Instead, you can restore just the settings for specific photos. There are a few additional steps:

1. Find your most recent backup in your Backups folder that includes the missing photos. The backups are stored in dated subfolders, with the zip file named to match your catalog name, to make them easy to identify.

2. Double-click on the zip file to open the backup. The *.lrcat file displays next to the zip file.

3. If you're on a Mac and your catalog is large, double-click might not correctly unzip the file. In this case, download StuffIt Expander from the App Store (it's free). Open the app and drag the backup zip file onto the icon to unzip it.

4. Move the backup *.lrcat file to a

temporary location, such as the desktop.

5. Double-click on the *.lrcat file to open it into Lightroom.

6. Find the photos you'd like to transfer to the working catalog.

7. Select the photos and go to *File menu > Export as Catalog*. Select a temporary location, such as the desktop, and give the exported catalog a name such as "Transfer. lrcat". Check *Export Selected Photos only* and leave the other checkboxes unchecked.

8. Go to *File menu > Open Recent* and open your normal working catalog.

9. In your main working catalog, go to *File menu > Import from Another Catalog* and direct it to the temporary *Transfer.lrcat* you created in step 6.

10. At the top of the Import from Catalog dialog, check the *All Folders* checkbox. **(Figure 4.3)**

11. The availability of the options below depends on your reason for restoring the data from the backup catalog. We'll discuss

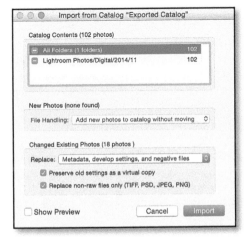

Figure 4.3 *Use Import from Catalog to recover part of a backup catalog.*

the options in more detail in the Multi-Computer chapter starting on page 423, but these are the most likely options:

If you're restoring photos you accidentally removed from the catalog, select *Add new photos to catalog without moving* in the *New Photos* section.

If you're restoring metadata for photos that still exist in the catalog, select *Metadata and develop settings only* from the *Replace* pop-up in the *Changed Existing Photos* section. (To keep the current settings as a virtual copy, check the checkbox below too.)

12. Press *Import* to transfer the metadata into your working catalog.

13. Once you've confirmed everything's working well, delete the temporary catalog from the desktop.

There is one limitation worth mentioning. When importing from other catalogs, Lightroom imports all of the data about your chosen photo. For example, you can't import just the Develop settings for a photo without also importing its keywords. There is, however, a workaround. If you check the *Preserve old settings as a virtual copy* checkbox, your current settings are retained as a virtual copy. You can then use John Beardsworth's Syncomatic plug-in to sync specific metadata (e.g. keywords) from the virtual copies to the updated masters. https://www.Lrq.me/beardsworth-syncomatic

How do I restore a backup of photos?

If you have good backups, restoring photos is as simple as copying the backup photos to their correct locations.

1. Open your photo backups in an Explorer (Windows) / Finder (Mac) window.

2. Open another Explorer (Windows) / Finder (Mac) window and navigate to your normal working folder structure.

3. Copy the photo backups (whether specific photos or whole folders) back to their correct location in your working folders.

4. Open Lightroom and check that none of the photos are marked as missing. To double-check, go to *Library menu > Find All Missing Photos*. If any photos are missing, copy them from the backups.

That's the simple option, but let's consider a couple of variations that might arise:

What happens if I'm restoring to a new hard drive.

1. Open your photo backups in an Explorer (Windows) / Finder (Mac) window.

2. Open another Explorer (Windows) / Finder (Mac) window and navigate to your new drive.

3. Copy the photo backups to the new drive, being careful to retain the same folder structure.

4. Open Lightroom. The folders and photos are marked as missing unless you've given the new drive the same drive letter (Windows) / drive name (Mac) as the old one.

5. Turn to the Missing Files instructions starting on page 435 to reconnect Lightroom's records to the new location.

Test it!

The true test of a backup system is how easily you can restore from these backups and continue working in the event of a disaster. If you're reading this before your hard drive dies, prevention is better than cure, so now is an excellent time to make sure you know how to restore your backups in the event of a disaster.

BACKUP CHECKLIST

Ideally you'll be running a full system backup, but as far as Lightroom is concerned, there are a few essentials to ensure you've included. I've listed the default locations, but you may have chosen alternative locations for some items such as the catalog.

☐ **The catalog(s)**—holds all the information about your photos, including all the work you've done on the photos within Lightroom.
   o Windows Default—C: \ Users \ [your username] \ My Pictures \ Lightroom \ Lightroom Catalog. lrcat
   o Mac Default—Macintosh HD / Users / [your username] / Pictures / Lightroom / Lightroom Catalog.lrcat
Go to *Edit menu* (Windows) / *Lightroom menu* (Mac) > *Catalog Settings* to confirm the location of your catalog. Your catalog may have a different name, but they all have *.lrcat as the extension. You may have created more than one catalog.

☐ **The catalog backups**—just in case your working catalog gets corrupted.
   o By default, they're stored in a Backups folder next to the catalog.

☐ **The previews**—standard and smart previews.
These would be rebuilt on demand as long as you have the original photos. If you have available backup space, backing them up would save time rebuilding them, and if you deleted your original photos accidentally, they may be the only copy left.
If you run a versioned backup system, which keeps additional copies each time a file changes, you may want to exclude the previews as they change constantly and will rapidly fill your backup hard drives.
Previews are stored next to the catalog as folders (Windows) or files (Mac) with a *.lrdata extension.

☐ **The photos**—in their current folder structure, in case you ever have to restore a backup. You'll want to include your edited files too.
These are stored in the location of your choice. To locate a specific folder, go to the Folders panel, right-click and select *Show in Explorer* (Windows) / *Show in Finder* (Mac).

☐ **Mobile uploads**—photos uploaded from your mobile phone or tablet using the Lightroom mobile app.

  ○ Windows—C: \ Users \ [your username] \ My Pictures \ Lightroom \ Mobile Downloads.lrdata
  ○ Mac—Macintosh HD / Users / [your username] / Pictures / Lightroom / Mobile Downloads. lrdata

The Mobile Downloads.lrdata file is always stored in your Pictures folder, regardless of where your catalog and other photos are stored, but you can select an alternative location for downloaded photos in *Preferences > Lightroom mobile*.

☐ **Presets**—includes Develop presets, Slideshow, Print and Web templates, Metadata presets, Export presets, etc.

  ○ Windows—C: \ Users \ [your username] \ AppData \ Roaming \ Adobe \ Lightroom \
  ○ Mac—Macintosh HD / Users / [your username] / Library / Application Support / Adobe / Lightroom /

If *Preferences > Presets tab > Store presets with this catalog* is checked, most presets and templates are stored in a Lightroom Settings folder next to your catalog.

☐ **Default settings and custom camera/lens profiles**—includes Develop default settings and Lens Profile defaults, which are shared with ACR.

  ○ Windows—C: \ Users \ [your username] \ AppData \ Roaming \ Adobe \ CameraRaw \
  ○ Mac—Macintosh HD / Users / [your username] / Library / Application Support / Adobe / CameraRaw /

☐ **Plug-ins**—includes export plug-ins, web galleries and any other extensions that you may have downloaded for Lightroom. Don't forget to keep their serial numbers safe too. These are stored in your choice of location. Check File menu > Plug-in Manager for the location of each plug-in.

☐ **Preferences**—includes last used settings, view options, FTP settings for uploading web galleries, some plug-in settings, etc. The preferences could be rebuilt if necessary, but you may save yourself a little time by backing them up and restoring them.

  ○ Windows—C: \ Users \ [your username] \ AppData \ Roaming \ Adobe \ Lightroom \ Preferences \ Lightroom Classic CC 7 Preferences.agprefs
  ○ Mac—Macintosh HD / Users / [your username] / Library / Preferences / com.adobe. LightroomClassicCC7.plist

☐ **Startup Preferences**—includes the last used catalog path, the recent catalog list, which catalog to load on startup and the catalog upgrade history. The preferences could be rebuilt if necessary, but you may save yourself a little time by backing them up and restoring them.

  ○ Windows—C: \ Users \ [your username] \ AppData \ Roaming \ Adobe \ Lightroom \ Preferences \ Lightroom Classic CC 7 Startup Preferences.agprefs
  ○ Mac—Macintosh HD / Users / [your username] / Library / Application Support / Adobe / Lightroom / Preferences / Lightroom Classic CC 7 Startup Preferences.agprefs

THE LIGHTROOM WORKSPACE

5

It's worth becoming familiar with the whole Lightroom interface as you'll be using different areas in all future tasks, so on the following double page spread, there's a quick guided tour. Flip over to get an overview **(Figure 5.2 overleaf)**, and then we'll do a deeper dive into the Lightroom workspace, and then come back here to continue...

The highlights are shown on the diagram overleaf are for quick reference, but if they're too small (e.g., on your eReader or tablet), don't worry, as we'll discuss them in detail in the text too.

THE TOP BAR

Let's work our way round the different elements of the screen in more detail, starting at the top.

Module Picker

Lightroom is divided up into modules. Library is where you manage your photos, Develop is where you edit them, Map allows you to add location metadata, and then Book, Slideshow, Print and Web are for displaying your photos in different formats.

In the top-right corner of the Lightroom workspace is the Module Picker where you click to switch modules. **(Figure 5.1)** When

you open Lightroom for the first time, the Library module is selected and its name is highlighted in the Module Picker. To switch to a different module, click on its name.

As you'll likely spend most of your time switching between the Library and Develop modules, it's worth learning those keyboard shortcuts—G for Grid view, E for Loupe view, and D to switch to the Develop module. We'll come back to the Library view modes a little later in the Viewing Your Photos chapter starting on page 75.

If the Module Picker won't fit because you're working on too small a screen, an arrow appears on the right, allowing access to the other modules. If you don't use a specific module often, for example, you don't print from your netbook, you can right-click on the module name and uncheck to hide it. The hidden module is still accessible from the *Window menu*, and you can show it again at any time by right-clicking on the Module Picker and reselecting the module name in the context-sensitive menu.

...continues on page 66

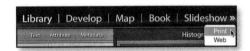

Figure 5.1 *If modules become hidden, right-click on one of the other module names or click on the double arrows at the right hand end of the Module Picker.*

The Lightroom Interface Overview

Title Bar

The Title Bar shows the name of the current catalog, along with the standard window buttons. If it goes missing, along with the minimize/maximize/close buttons, press Shift-F once or twice to cancel the Full Screen modes. If the whole interface goes missing, leaving just the photo on screen, press Escape.

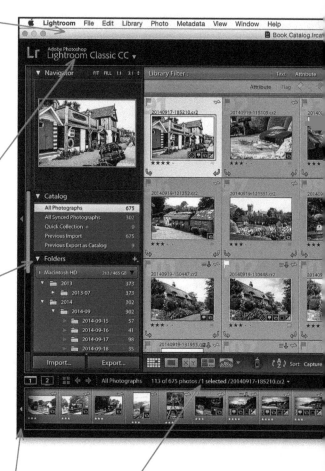

Identity Plate & Activity Center

The Identity Plate allows you to add your own branding to your catalogs. When a background task is active, such as building previews, it's replaced by the Activity Center status bars.

Panels

Panels can be opened and closed by clicking on the panel header. If you right-click on the panel header, you can show/hide specific panels.
In that right-click menu, you'll also find Solo Mode, which automatically closes a panel when you open another panel in the same panel group. It's particularly useful when working on a small screen.

Show/Hide Panel Groups

The left and right-hand sides are called panel groups. If you click on the black bars along the outer edges of the screen, you can show/hide the left/right panel groups, as well as the Module Picker and the Filmstrip. Right-clicking on the black bars gives additional options.

Breadcrumb Bar

The breadcrumb bar at the top of the Filmstrip has controls for the secondary window, as well as information about the selected source folder or collection, the number of photos in the current view and the number of selected photos. If you click on it, there's a list of recent sources for easy access.

Figure 5.2 *The sections of the workspace for quick reference.*

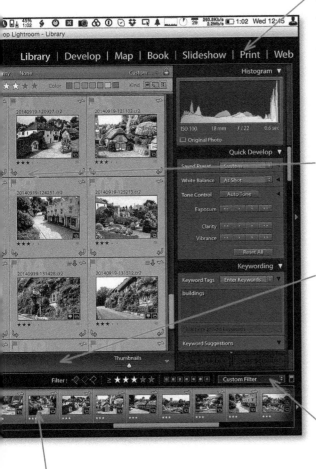

Module Picker

The Module Picker gives you access to the Library, Develop, Map, Book, Slideshow, Print and Web modules. The selected module is highlighted, and you can click on another module name to switch modules. If you right-click on a module name, you can hide modules from view.

Preview Area

The central area of the screen is the Preview Area or main work area.

Toolbar

The Toolbar gives easy access to often used tools. Press T on your keyboard if it goes missing, and click on the arrow at the right-hand end to choose which tools show in the Toolbar.

Filter Bar

When viewing Grid view, the Filter Bar appears above the thumbnails. It allows you to filter the current view to only show photos meeting your chosen criteria. If it goes missing, press the \ key on your keyboard. You can also access frequently used filters by clicking the word Filter on the Filmstrip.

Filmstrip

The Filmstrip is available in all modules and shows the set of photos you're currently viewing. When you select a different photo in the Filmstrip, the main Preview Area is updated too.

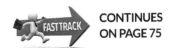

CONTINUES ON PAGE 75

If you select a custom Identity Plate, you can also change the font used for the Module Picker to a smaller size or narrower font, allowing them to fit on small screens without hiding any modules.

Identity Plate

To the left of the Module Picker is the Identity Plate, which allows you to add your own branding to your catalogs. **(Figure 5.3)**

To change the Identity Plate, go to *Edit menu* (Windows) / *Lightroom menu* (Mac) > *Identity Plate Setup.* **(Figure 5.4)** In the **Identity Plate** pop-up, there are three options:

Lightroom Mobile displays your name when you're signed into an Adobe ID, or reminds you to sign in.

Lightroom simply says "Adobe Lightroom Classic CC".

Personalized allows you to create your own

To add your logo, select *Use a graphical identity plate.* Use the *Locate File* button to navigate to your logo, or drag it from Explorer (Windows) / Finder (Mac) into the preview field below. PNG format is a good choice, as it retains any transparency.

To create a text Identity Plate, perhaps using the catalog name, select *Use a styled text identity plate* and type the text of your choice. Select the text and change the font, size and color using the pop-ups below. Different sections of text can have different styling.

These Identity Plates can also later be used in the Slideshow, Print and Web modules, so you may keep a selection of Identity Plate presets for different uses. To save your settings as a preset, select *Save As* in the second pop-up menu at the top of the dialog and give your Identity Plate a name. The Identity Plates settings are stored in the catalog, so if you have multiple catalogs, you'll need to set them up in each catalog.

Activity Center

When there's an active process running in the background, for example, a large import or previews building, the Identity Plate is temporarily replaced by the Activity Center.

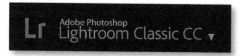

Figure 5.3   *The Identity Plate is to the left of the Module Picker.*

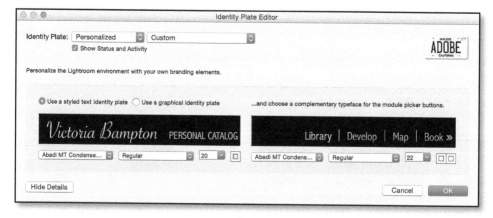

Figure 5.4   *You can design your own Identity Plate to brand your catalog.*

(Figure 5.5) It shows the progress of any current tasks, and clicking on the X at the end of any of the progress bars cancels the task. Lightroom is multi-threaded, which means it can do lots of tasks at once, so you don't need to wait for it to finish before doing something else. When there are too many tasks to show in one view, for example, more than three exports, it displays a combined progress bar. Clicking the arrow at the end of the combined progress bar displays each of the individual active tasks in turn.

If you click on the Activity Center, it expands to show more detail on the current tasks, including the name of the file that Lightroom's working on, and in some cases, how many photos are left to complete. (Figure 5.6) Clicking the X on the right cancels the selected task.

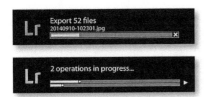

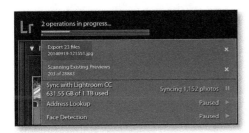

Figure 5.5 *The Activity Center shows the progress of current tasks. When more than one task is running, they show as separate lines. The arrow at the end shows more detail for each line.*

Figure 5.6 *Click on the Identity Plate to show the expanded Activity Center which includes additional information and background processes.*

In the Activity Center you can also control the ongoing tasks that run silently in the background: **Sync with Lightroom CC, Address Lookup** and **Face Detection**. If these tasks are running in the background and slowing down the computer, you can temporarily pause them using the toggle play/pause button to the right, enabling them again at a time when you don't need to use the computer.

If you right-click on the Identity Plate, you can show these background tasks above the main Identity Plate when they're running. (Figure 5.7) By default, *Sync with Lightroom mobile* is enabled but the others are disabled.

Title Bar & Full Screen Modes

Above the Identity Plate and Module Picker is the standard window title bar and menu. (Figure 5.8) If you find these distracting when working with Lightroom, they can be hidden using Lightroom's Full Screen modes. They're all listed under *Window menu > Screen Mode.*

Normal window mode allows you to resize or move the window. The title bar along the top of the window shows the name of the current catalog, along with the standard minimize/maximize/close window buttons.

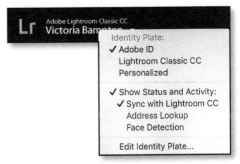

Figure 5.7 *Right-click on the Identity Plate to always show background activity for selected tasks.*

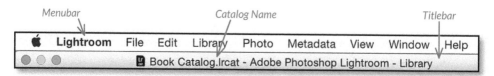

Figure 5.8 *The Menu bar, Title bar and catalog name.*

Full Screen with Menu Bar fills the screen but leaves the menu bar showing.

Full Screen hides the menu bar, as well as filling the screen. Floating the mouse right to the top of the screen briefly displays the menu bar.

Full Screen Preview mode hides everything except the photo, allowing you to view it without any distractions. Even the cursor hides if the mouse is stationary. Press the F key to switch to and from the Full Screen Preview mode.

PANELS & PANEL GROUPS

Down the left and right-hand sides of the screen are panel groups, each holding individual panels. The panel group on the left always holds the Navigator or Preview panel and other sources of information— folders, collections, templates, presets, etc. The panels on the right allow you to work with the photos themselves, adding metadata, changing Develop settings, and adjusting settings for books, slideshows,

prints and web galleries.

The black bar along the outer edges of the panels controls whether that panel group is showing or hidden. Click on that bar to open or close the panel group. There are matching black bars at the top and bottom of the screen to hide the Module Picker and Filmstrip too. (**Figure 5.9**)

The panel groups are set to **Auto Hide & Auto Show** by default, which means that if you click on the black bar to hide the panel, every time you float the mouse close to the edge, the panels will pop into view. If you right-click on the black bars, you can change the behavior for each panel group, setting it to **Auto Hide** or **Manual. Sync with Opposite Panel** opens or closes the panel group at the same time as the panel group on the opposite side. (**Figure 5.10**)

Within the panel groups are individual panels, and they can be opened and closed by clicking on the panel header. If there's a panel you never use, right-click on the panel header and uncheck the panel name in the context-sensitive menu. To bring it back, just check it again or select the panel name

Figure 5.9 *A solid arrow indicates that the panel is locked into position, and an opaque arrow indicates that the panel group is set to automatically show or hide when you float the mouse over that black bar.*

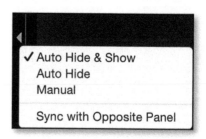

Figure 5.10 *Change the panel show and hide settings by right-clicking on the black bars.*

under *Window menu > Panels.*

Solo Mode

In that right-click menu, you'll also find *Solo Mode*, which automatically closes a panel when you open another panel in the same panel group, so you just have one panel open at a time. It's especially useful when working on a small screen, to save scrolling up and down. To open another panel without closing the first one, hold down the Shift key while clicking on the panel header.

Panel Preferences

As well as showing/hiding panels, you can adjust the way they're displayed. Dragging the inner edge of the panel groups (or top edge of the Filmstrip), you can make them wider or narrower. This also changes the width of the sliders, making them easier to adjust. (On Mac, hold down the Opt key while dragging the inner edge to stretch beyond their normal limits.) **(Figure 5.11)**

There are additional controls in the *Preferences dialog > Interface tab*, where you can adjust the **Font Size** slightly and add panel **End Marks** to the bottom of each panel group. **(Figure 5.12)** You can create your own panel end marks, for example, you can

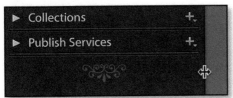

Figure 5.11 *Panel groups can be resized by dragging the inner edge. The Panel End Marks show below the panels.*

display your logo or notes such as the meanings of your star ratings and color labels.

To create your own panel end mark, you'll need a pixel editor such as Photoshop or Photoshop Elements. Create a transparent file of up to 250px wide (140px wide generally looks good), type your chosen text or add your logo, and save it as PNG, TIF, PSD or GIF. If you're creating a Panel End Mark for a retina display, make it double the size and end the name in @2x (e.g. mypanelendmark@2x.png).

In the *Preferences dialog > End Marks* pop-up, select *Go to Panel End Marks Folder* and copy your file to that folder. Finally, select your panel end mark name from the pop-up and close the dialog.

THE FILMSTRIP

The bottom panel is called the Filmstrip. It displays thumbnails of the photos in your current view, making them accessible in the other modules. When you select a different photo in the Filmstrip, the main Preview Area is updated too.

To change the size of the thumbnails, drag the top of the Filmstrip to enlarge it or right-click on that edge to view a menu of preset thumbnail sizes.

If you find that the Filmstrip thumbnails become too cluttered with icons, or you like them there for information but don't want them to do anything if you accidentally click, you can select which ones to view using the *Preferences dialog > Interface tab*

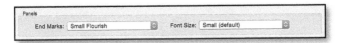

Figure 5.12 *Change the Panel End Marks in the Interface tab of the Preferences dialog.*

in the *Filmstrip* section, or by right-clicking and selecting *View Options*. The square badges automatically disappear when the thumbnails become too small.

Breadcrumb Bar

Along the top of the Filmstrip are other useful tools, including breadcrumb navigation that allows you to retrace your steps. **(Figure 5.13)**

From left to right, they are:

Secondary Display controls allow you to display a second Lightroom window.

Grid button gives you quick access to the Grid view from any module.

Forward and Back buttons step backwards and forwards through recent sources, like your web browser buttons. For example, it remembers each time you switch between different folders.

The Breadcrumb shows additional information about your current view. It shows whether you're viewing a folder or a collection, the folder or collection name, the number of photos that are currently visible and aren't hidden by a filter or

collapsed stack, the total number of photos in that folder/collection, the number of photos selected, and finally the name of the currently selected photo.

Even wondered why it's called a breadcrumb bar? It comes from the story of Hansel & Gretel, where they left a trail of breadcrumbs to retrace their steps. When you click on Lightroom's breadcrumb bar, it shows all of your recent sources.

Recent & Favorite Folders are displayed when you click on the breadcrumb, so you can easily skip back to a recent view. It also allows you to add favorite folders/collections that you visit regularly, using the *Add to Favorites* option at the bottom of the menu.

Quick Filters display on the right hand side. They give easy access to basic filtering without having to switch back to Grid view. We'll come back to filtering in the Finding & Filtering chapter starting on page 167, but to toggle between the compact and expanded views, click the word Filter, and to disable the filters temporarily, toggle the switch on the right. **(Figure 5.14)**

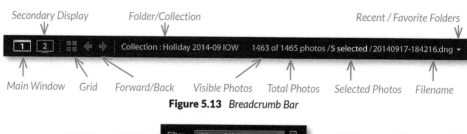

Figure 5.13 *Breadcrumb Bar*

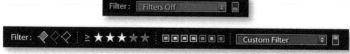

Figure 5.14 *The Quick Filters are displayed on the Filmstrip, and if you click the word Filter (above), it opens up to show additional filter options (below).*

Preview Area

In the center of the window is the preview area, or main work area, which shows the photo(s) that you're currently working on. In the Library module, this can be Grid, Compare, Survey or People view with multiple photos, or a large Loupe view of the whole photo. We'll come back to these view options in the next chapter starting on page 75. In the Develop module it displays a high quality preview of your photo, and in the other modules the main preview area displays the output layout you're working on, such as book pages, slides, print packages or web gallery previews.

By default, the background surrounding the photo is mid-gray, however you can change it to white, black, or other shades of gray. To change it, go to Lightroom's *Preferences dialog > Interface tab*, or right-click on that gray surround and select an alternative shade from the context-sensitive menu.

Filter Bar

When viewing Grid view, the Filter Bar appears above the thumbnails. It allows you to filter the current view to show only photos meeting your chosen criteria. We'll come back to the different filter options and their icons in the Finding & Filtering chapter starting on page 167. If it goes missing, press the \ key on your keyboard. You can also access frequently used filters by clicking the word **Filter** on the Filmstrip.

Toolbar

Beneath the preview area you'll see the Toolbar. If it goes missing, press the T key on your keyboard or select *View menu > Show Toolbar*. **(Figure 5.15)** The options that are available on this Toolbar change depending on your current module or view, and if you click the arrow at the right-hand end, you can choose to show different tools.

Now let's move on to the fun part... viewing your photos!

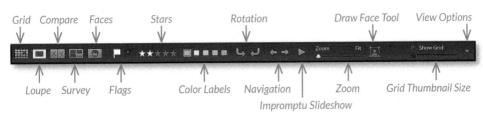

Grid   Compare   Faces   Stars   Rotation   Draw Face Tool   View Options

Loupe   Survey   Flags   Color Labels   Navigation   Zoom   Grid Thumbnail Size

Impromptu Slideshow

Figure 5.15 *The Toolbar appears below the grid or preview area, and gives you easy access to frequently used tools. This is the Loupe view toolbar.*

WORKSPACE SHORTCUTS

		Windows	Mac
Moving between Modules	Library Module	G/E/C/N or Ctrl Alt 1	G/E/C/N or Cmd Opt 1
	Library Module - Grid view	G	G
	Library Module - Loupe view	E	E
	Library Module - Compare view	C	C
	Library Module - Survey View	N	N
	Library Module - Faces View	O	O
	Develop Module	D or Ctrl Alt 2	D or Cmd Opt 2
	Map Module	Ctrl Alt 3	Cmd Opt 3
	Book Module	Ctrl Alt 4	Cmd Opt 4
	Slideshow Module	Ctrl Alt 5	Cmd Opt 5
	Print Module	Ctrl Alt 6	Cmd Opt 6
	Web Module	Ctrl Alt 7	Cmd Opt 7
	Go Back to Previous Module	Ctrl Alt up arrow	Cmd Opt up arrow
	Go Back	Ctrl Alt left arrow	Cmd Opt left arrow
	Go Forward	Ctrl Alt right arrow	Cmd Opt right arrow
Panels	Show / Hide Side Panels	Tab	Tab
	Show / Hide All Panels	Shift Tab	Shift Tab
	Show / Hide Module Picker	F5	F5
	Show / Hide Filmstrip	F6	F6
	Show / Hide Toolbar	T	T
	Show / Hide Filter Bar in Grid view	\	\
	Show Left Panels	F7	F7
	Show Right Panels	F8	F8

		Windows	Mac
	Expand / Collapse Left Panels	Ctrl Shift 0 - 9 panel number	Cmd Ctrl 0 - 9 panel number
	Expand / Collapse Right Panels	Ctrl 0-9 panel number	Cmd 0-9 panel number
	Open/Close All Panels	Ctrl-click on panel header	Cmd-click on panel header
	Toggle Solo Mode	Alt-click on panel header	Opt-click on panel header
	Open Additional Panel in Solo Mode	Shift-click on panel header	Shift-click on panel header
Screen Mode	Normal	Ctrl Alt F	Cmd Opt F
	Full Screen and Hide Panels	Ctrl Shift F	Cmd Shift F
	Full Screen Preview	F	F
	Next Screen Mode	Shift F	Shift F
Hide Lightroom			Cmd H
Hide Others			Cmd Opt H
	Close Window		Cmd W
	Close All		Cmd Opt W
	Minimize		Cmd M
	Minimize All		Cmd Opt M
Hide Lightroom			Cmd H
Hide Others			Cmd Opt H
	Close Window		Cmd W
	Close All		Cmd Opt W
	Minimize		Cmd M
	Minimize All		Cmd Opt M
Quit Lightroom		Ctrl Q	Cmd Q

VIEWING YOUR PHOTOS *6*

You'll browse and manage your photos in the Library module, where there are a number of different view modes.

If you've been exploring, select the Library module in the Module Picker, then go to the Catalog panel in the left panel group and select the *Previous Import* or *All Photographs* collection, or select a folder in the Folders panel, and we'll use these photos to explore the different view modes. **(Figure 6.1)**

VIEWING YOUR PHOTOS IN GRID VIEW

Much of the work you'll do in Lightroom will be in the Grid view, which can be accessed using the Grid icon on the Toolbar, by pressing the G key on your keyboard, or via the *View menu.* **(Figure 6.2)**

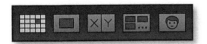

Figure 6.1 *The view modes buttons are on the Toolbar. From left to right, they are Grid, Loupe, Compare, Survey and People modes.*

Figure 6.2 *Enter Grid mode by clicking this button in the Toolbar or by pressing G.*

Grid view is a scrolling page of thumbnails **(Figure 6.3)**, and you can change the size of the thumbnails using the slider on the Toolbar. You can drag and drop these thumbnails into a different sort order in the Grid, or drag them onto other folders, collections or keywords to move or copy them. When dragging thumbnails, note that you have to pick them up by the thumbnail itself and not the border surrounding it, otherwise they'll become deselected.

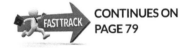

CONTINUES ON PAGE 79

On the right of the Grid view is a scrollbar which allows you to scroll through the thumbnails. My favorite trick is to Ctrl-click (Windows) / Opt-click (Mac) anywhere on that scrollbar to scroll directly to that point. It's much quicker than having to scroll a

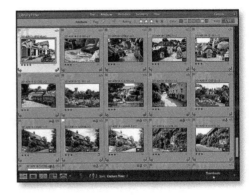

Figure 6.3 *Grid view*

line at a time and get dizzy watching the thumbnails pass before you!

If you swipe through photos on the Mac using a Magic Mouse, Trackpad or similar peripheral device, Lightroom scrolls very fast. To disable this "speed swiping", uncheck the *Preferences > Interface > **Swipe between images using mouse/trackpad*** checkbox.

In the Grid View, the thumbnails of the photos are contained within gray cells which hold additional information about the photos. There are three varieties of cell, which you cycle through using the J key or *View menu > Grid View Style*. First is a minimal view showing the thumbnail without any other distractions, then a compact cell view showing the icons and some file information, and finally an expanded cell view showing additional lines of information. **(Figure 6.4)**

Thumbnail Options

If you go to *View menu > View Options*, you can choose the information you want to show on the thumbnail cells. **(Figure 6.5)**

The view of the thumbnails updates in the background as you test various combinations of settings, to help you decide

which you like best. **(Figure 6.6)** Let's take a more detailed look at the thumbnail and its icons...

Thumbnail

In the center, of course, is a thumbnail preview of the photo. When you need to drag a photo, perhaps to another folder or collection, remember to click on the thumbnail itself rather than the cell border surrounding it, otherwise it won't move.

Cell Border

The cell border (or matte) surrounds the thumbnails and holds the extra metadata.

The color of the cell border changes through three different shades of gray, depending on the level of selection, and we'll come back to that in more detail on page 79. Clicking in the cell border deselects all other photos.

If you use color labels (which we'll come to in the Selecting the Best Photos chapter starting on page 93), the cell border can be tinted with the label color using *View Options > Tint grid cells with label color*.

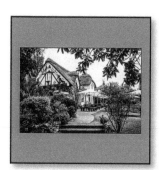 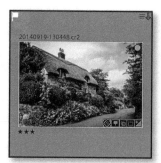 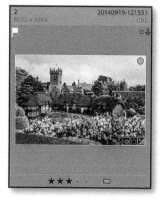

Figure 6.4 *The simplest cell style (left) just shows the thumbnail photo. The compact cell (center) and extended cell (right) show additional information of your choice.*

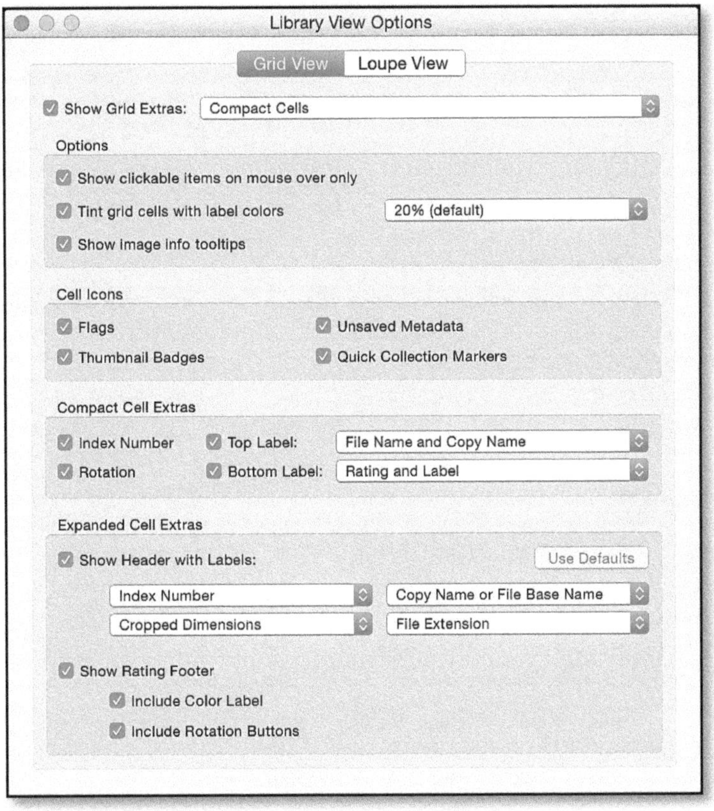

Figure 6.5 *Set the thumbnail options in the View Options dialog.*

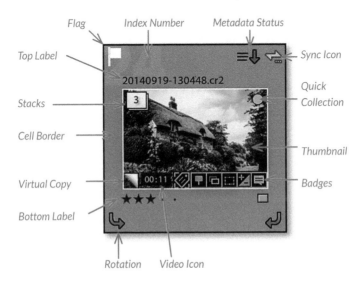

Figure 6.6 *A wide variety of information can be shown on the thumbnails.*

Top & Bottom Label

Metadata, such as the filename or capture date, can also be displayed within the cell border, above and below the thumbnail. By default, the top label is turned off and the bottom label displays the star ratings and color labels, but you can select which metadata to display on each cell using the View Options dialog. Right-clicking on the labels also displays a menu of available options. The Expanded Cells view has additional lines for file information.

Metadata Status

In the top right corner, the metadata status icons keep you informed of the status of the external files, for example, if the original file is missing or corrupted, or the file's metadata doesn't match the catalog records.

Lightroom primarily stores your image metadata in your catalog, but it's possible to store it with the files too. We'll discuss the XMP metadata in more detail starting on page 345. If you choose to write the metadata to the files, enable the *Unsaved Metadata* checkbox in the View Options dialog to display additional status icons. This is what all the different metadata status icons mean:

 Lightroom is checking the previews are current, building new previews, or waiting for a better quality thumbnail to load.

 The file is missing or is not where Lightroom is expecting, so click the icon to locate the missing file. More on that in the Missing Files section starting on page 435.

 The file is missing but a Smart Preview is available.

 The file is damaged or cannot be read, likely as a result of file corruption.

 Lightroom's catalog has updated metadata which hasn't been written to XMP.

 The file has updated metadata which hasn't been read into Lightroom's catalog.

 Metadata conflict—both the XMP data in the file and Lightroom's catalog have been changed. Click the icon to choose whether to accept Lightroom's version or the XMP version.

 This photo is included in a Sync collection.

 Lightroom is waiting to sync this photo.

Quick Collection Marker

In the top right corner of the thumbnail is a small circle, which you click to check (gray) or uncheck (transparent). The marker displays as a gray circle when the photo is in the Target Collection (usually the Quick Collection). The Quick Collection is a way of temporarily grouping photos, which we'll discuss in more detail in Selecting & Grouping the Best Photos. If you frequently accidentally hit the circular Quick Collection marker, you can disable it in the View Options dialog.

Badges

The square badges at the bottom of the thumbnails give you additional information about the settings applied to the selected photo, and clicking on them takes you to the related module or panel. They are Keywords,

Map Location, Collection Membership (only when not viewing the collection), Crop, Develop Adjustments and Comments (only when viewing a shared collection). **(Figure 6.7)**

Rotation

The rotation icons rotate your photo when you click on them. If **Show clickable items on mouse over only** is checked in View Options, the arrows disappear until you float over the photo.

Virtual Copy

A photo can have multiple versions of settings, whether that's metadata or Develop settings. These virtual copies are marked with a turned corner on the thumbnail. We'll come back to virtual copies in the Develop Module Tools chapter on page 305.

Stack

The Stack indicator shows how many photos are grouped together and the double lines on the left and right show the beginning and end of the visible stack. We'll discuss stacking in the Grouping Similar Photos section on page 99.

Flag

The flag state can be unflagged (invisible until you float over it), picked (white flag) or rejected (black flag). Clicking on it toggles between picked and unflagged, and Alt-click

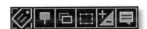

Figure 6.7 *On the thumbnails themselves, there are badges with additional information. From left to right, they are keywords, map locations, collection membership, crop, Develop settings and social comments.*

(Windows) / Opt-click (Mac) switches to a rejected flag. We'll come back to flagging in the next chapter, starting on page 93. **(Figure 6.8)**

Index Number

The index number counts the number of photos in the current view. For example, if you have 230 photos in your current folder or collection, the first is marked as 1 and the last as 230.

Video Icon

A video thumbnail icon displays the length of the video, and as you move your cursor horizontally across the thumbnail, it scrubs through the video, showing you the content. **(Figure 6.9)**

SELECTIONS

When you select multiple photos in Lightroom's Grid view or in the Filmstrip, you'll notice that the cell

Figure 6.8 *Photos can be flagged (left), unflagged (center) or rejected (right).*

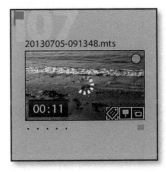

Figure 6.9 *Videos have an additional badge showing the length of the clip.*

border displays in three different shades of gray.

Because Lightroom allows you to synchronize settings across multiple photos, there needs to be a way of choosing the source of the settings as well as the target photos, so Lightroom has three different levels of selection (or two levels of selection plus a deselected state, depending on how you look at it). **(Figure 6.10)**

Active—The lightest shade of gray is the active photo. That's the single photo that would be shown in Loupe view or Develop module.

Selected—The mid gray is also selected, but it isn't the active photo.

Not Selected—The darkest shade of gray isn't selected.

Anything you do in Grid view on the primary monitor, such as adding star ratings or keywords, applies to all the selected photos, whereas other views only affect the active or most-selected photo.

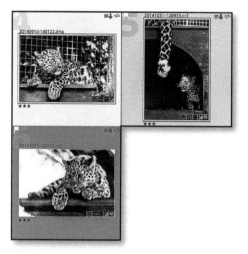

Figure 6.10 *There are three levels of selection—active (top left), selected (top right) and not selected (bottom).*

When applying settings, or especially when deleting photos, double check how many photos are selected, otherwise you could accidentally apply a command to all of them.

If you're synchronizing settings across multiple photos, Lightroom takes the settings from the active photo and applies it to the other selected photos.

To select a single photo, you simply click on it. To select non-contiguous photos—ones that aren't grouped together—click the first photo and then hold down the Ctrl key (Windows) / Cmd key (Mac) while clicking on the other photos. To select sequential photos, click on the first photo, but this time hold down the Shift key while you click on the last photo, and the photos in between will also be selected.

There's also a trick to deselecting photos. Clicking on the thumbnail itself retains your current selection and makes that the active photo, leaving the others selected too. But if you click on the cell border surrounding the thumbnail, the other photos are deselected, leaving just that single photo selected.

The thumbnails give you a good overview, but they're a little too small to see the detail in your photos, so Lightroom offers three further view modes—Loupe, Compare and Survey—each with different strengths.

Why aren't my actions applying to all of the selected photos?

Most of your actions only apply to the active photo, for example, pressing Delete only usually removes the active photo. To apply a setting to multiple photos, you must select Grid view on the primary window.

This protects you from applying a setting to multiple photos without realizing they're selected (perhaps because the Filmstrip is hidden) and accidentally undoing many hours of work.

With every rule, there are always exceptions. These are the main ones:

• If you right-click on the Filmstrip or Secondary Display Grid view, the menu command applies to all selected photos (because you're obviously looking at them at the time!).

• A few commands, such as Export and Build Previews, always apply to all selected photos, but they won't do any harm.

• You can change the default behavior by enabling *Metadata menu > Auto Sync*. This causes any metadata actions to apply to all selected photos, regardless of the current view mode.

Can I see a list view?

There isn't a list view built into Lightroom,

but there is an excellent plug-in by John Beardsworth called List View, available from https://www.Lrq.me/beardsworth-listview

VIEWING YOUR PHOTOS IN LOUPE VIEW

The Loupe view **(Figure 6.11)** displays a larger view of one photo at a time. To access Loupe view, click the Loupe button on the Toolbar **(Figure 6.12åœ)**, press the E key, or select Loupe in the *View menu*.

You can move from one photo to the next using the left and right arrows on the keyboard, by selecting another photo from the Filmstrip, or by turning on the arrows in the Toolbar.

Zooming In On Photos

To zoom in to check details, press the Z key or Spacebar, or click on the photo. By default, it zooms into 1:1 or 100% view, but there are additional zoom ratios at the top of the Navigator panel. **(Figure 6.13)**

The standard view is the **Fit** view which fits the whole photo within the preview area. **Fill** view fills the entire width or height,

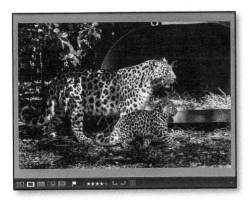

Figure 6.11   *Loupe view gives a detailed view on a single photo, allowing you to zoom in to check the detail.*

Figure 6.12   *Enter Loupe view by clicking this button in the Toolbar or by pressing E.*

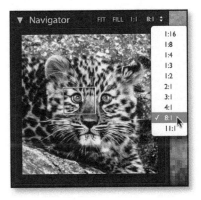

Figure 6.13   *The zoom ratios are on top of the Navigator panel. The last option is a pop-up of additional zoom ratios.*

hiding some of the photo. **1:1** is a 100% view, and the final option is a pop-up menu which allows you to switch through other zoom ratios. And yes, that last 11:1 option is a *This is Spinal Tap* movie reference!

Lightroom's zoom ratios are based on the ratio of screen pixels (first number) used to display image pixels (second number). If you're used to working in Photoshop, you might be more comfortable with zoom percentages, so here's how they translate on a standard resolution monitor:

1:16 = 6.25% (1 screen : 16 image px)
1:8 = 12.5% (1 screen : 8 image px)
1:4 = 25% (1 screen : 4 image px)
1:3 = 33% (1 screen : 3 image px)
1:2 = 50% (1 screen : 2 image px)
1:1 = 100% (1 screen : 1 image px)
2:1 = 200% (2 screen : 1 image px)
3:1 = 300% (3 screen : 1 image px)
4:1 = 400% (4 screen : 1 image px)
8:1 = 800% (8 screen : 1 image px)
11:1 = 1100% (11 screen : 1 image px)

Lightroom remembers your two most recent zoom settings and toggles between them, so to switch between Fit and 3:1 views, you'd click on *Fit* on the Navigator panel and then *3:1*.

Once you've zoomed in on the photo, the cursor becomes a hand tool and you can click and drag the photo around to view different areas, which is called panning. Alternatively, you can move the selection box on the Navigator preview.

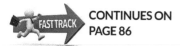

CONTINUES ON PAGE 86

Lightroom remembers the last-used zoom/pan position for each individual photo, and returns to that same position next time you zoom in. If you check *View menu > Lock Zoom*

Position, it ignores this saved position and uses the same image area for each photo. This is particularly useful if you're trying to compare the same spot on multiple photos, and you've previously zoomed into different areas on each photo.

Info Overlay

In the top left corner of the Loupe view (or Develop preview) is the Info Overlay, which displays information about the selected photo such as the filename or camera settings used. **(Figure 6.14)** Under *View menu > View Options > Loupe View tab*, you can store two different combinations of information to show in the Info Overlay, and then cycle through them using the I key.

Status Overlay

Whenever you use a keyboard shortcut to apply a setting, a status overlay message appears in the preview area, for example, *Set Rating to 3*.

A similar type of overlay is used in the Loupe or Develop preview when Lightroom is loading or building previews. **(Figure 6.15)** If you find the Loading Overlay distracting, you can turn it off by unchecking **Show message when loading or rendering photos** in

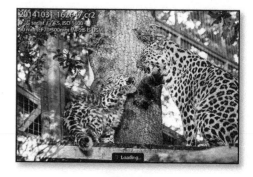

Figure 6.14 *The Info Overlay (top left) and Status Overlay (bottom center) appear in Loupe view.*

the View Options dialog. Personally, I leave it disabled in the Develop module, as you can start working on the photo long before it's finished loading.

If you're seeing the Loading overlay in the Library module, it's probably because you haven't built the previews you need in advance, or they need to be updated as you've made Develop changes. To solve this, select all (or none) of the photos in Grid view, choose *Library menu > Previews > Build Standard-Sized Previews or 1:1 Previews*, then go and make a drink while it works. **(Figure 6.16)**

We'll come back to previews in more detail in the Performance chapter starting on page 460.

Using Embedded Previews to Avoid the Loading Overlay

Building previews takes time, although it can be done when you're not using the computer. Most cameras embed a JPEG preview inside a raw file at the time of capture, and you can take advantage of these ready-made previews by selecting *Embedded & Sidecar* in the *Build Previews*

pop-up in the File Handling panel of the Import dialog (page 28).

When you come to view the photos in the Library module, the thumbnails have a small icon in the corner, and an overlay shown in the Loupe view, to remind you that you're viewing an embedded preview rather than one built by Lightroom. **(Figure 6.17)**

Embedded previews look like the camera JPEGs, with your in-camera settings applied. Develop presets selected in the Import dialog's *Apply During Import* panel are not applied to the embedded previews, so they won't show until you switch to the Develop module.

Lightroom still needs to build its own previews from the raw data eventually, so you can see your edits applied to the image. When you edit a photo using the Quick Develop panel or Develop module, Lightroom builds its own preview, replacing the embedded preview.

You can click on the Embedded Preview thumbnail icon or overlay to build a proper Lightroom preview at any time, or select the photos and go to *Library menu > Previews > Build Standard-Sized Previews or Build 1:1*

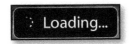

Figure 6.15   The Status Overlay keeps you informed about any changes being applied to the selected photo.

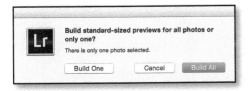

Figure 6.16   When one photo is selected, Lightroom asks whether to build previews for all the photos or just the selected photo.

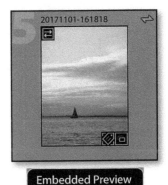

Figure 6.17   Embedded previews are marked with an icon (top left of thumbnail) and loupe overlay.

Previews when you're ready to convert them.

In *Preferences > General tab*, there's also a **Replace embedded previews with standard previews during idle time** checkbox, which does exactly as it suggests—it builds the previews when you're not using the computer. You're probably best to leave this unchecked because it only builds standard-sized previews, and if you needed to zoom in, you'd then have to wait for Lightroom to build a 1:1 size preview.

Once a Lightroom preview is rendered, you can't go back to the embedded preview, and you can't access embedded previews for photos that have already been imported into Lightroom. They're just designed as a fast import preview.

The size of the embedded previews varies, for example, most current Canon and Nikon DSLRs embed full size previews, whereas Fuji, Olympus and Sony embed smaller previews. To check the size of embedded preview that your camera creates, upload a raw file to http://exif.regex.info/exif.cgi and compare the pixel dimensions of the extracted preview on the right against the full resolution on the left. **(Figure 6.18)**

If you try to zoom in to 1:1 view on a photo that has a smaller embedded preview, it may look a little fuzzy. If an embedded preview is less than 50% of the full resolution original, Lightroom ignores it and renders a standard preview instead. In either of these cases, you can shoot raw+jpeg in camera and Lightroom will use the full-size sidecar JPEGs instead of the embedded previews.

Distraction Free Viewing—Lights Out and Full Screen Preview

While we're on the subject of distractions, let's talk about Lightroom's distraction free view modes. Lights Dimmed and Lights Out dim or black out the interface around the

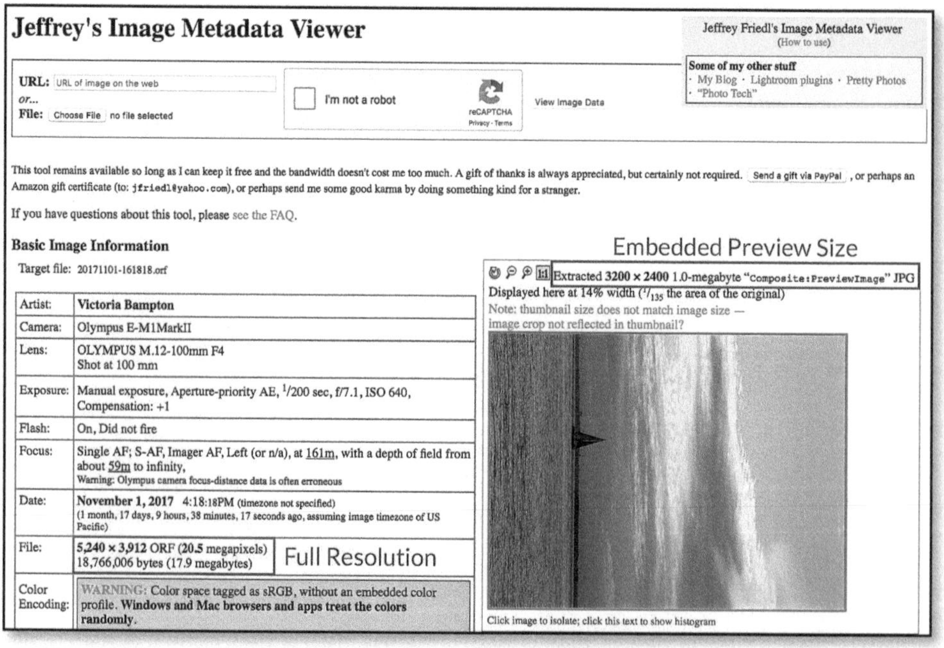

Figure 6.18 *Jeffrey's Image Metadata Viewer shows the size of the embedded preview.*

photo, allowing you to focus solely on the selected photos in the preview area. The photos are surrounded by a single white line. To cycle through the Lights Dimmed and Lights Out modes, and then return to normal Lights On mode, press the L key on your keyboard three times. You can adjust the color and dim level in the *Preferences dialog > Interface tab.*

To view a single larger photo in Full Screen Preview mode, press the F key to turn it on and off. Like Lights Out view, Full Screen Preview mode hides everything, displaying just the photo with a plain black background.

Loupe Overlay

If you're searching for a photo for a particular purpose—perhaps for a magazine cover or product shots for a catalog—then you may need to preview how the photo will look in its final layout. The Loupe Overlay allows you to preview your photo with an overlaid Grid, movable Guides, and a transparent layout image. **(Figure 6.19)**

The Loupe Overlay can be used on any photo in the Library or Develop module, but it's most useful when shooting tethered, allowing you to check that you're keeping the subject positioned correctly within the final frame. To activate the overlay, go to *View menu > Loupe Overlay* and add a checkmark to the *Grid, Guides* and/or the *Layout Image.*

If you select Layout Image, it asks you to choose a transparent PNG file. (You can change the overlay file again later by selecting *View menu > Loupe Overlay > Choose Image.*)

To adjust any of the overlays, hold down the Ctrl key (Windows) / Cmd key (Mac) to show the controls. When **Grid** is selected, the available options are size and opacity. When

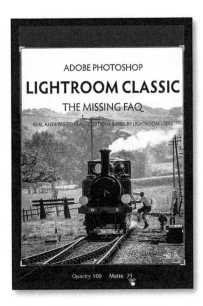

Figure 6.19 *The Loupe Overlay Layout Image allows you to preview how your photo will look in the final design, for example, for a book or magazine cover.*

Guides is selected, holding down the Ctrl key (Windows) / Cmd key (Mac) allows you to drag the crosshairs to move the guides, and double-clicking on the crosshairs resets them to center.

When you have a **Layout Image** selected, there are a few additional options. When the hand tool is showing, dragging the overlay moves it around on the photo. Dragging the corners resizes the overlay. The **Opacity** option affects the opacity of the overlay itself, and **Matte** affects the opacity of the black area surrounding the overlay. The matte works like Lights Out mode, hiding excess picture under a black matte.

Playing Videos in Loupe View

There's one final Loupe view overlay, which only appears when a video is selected. The playback controller overlay has a play/pause button, timeline, timestamp,

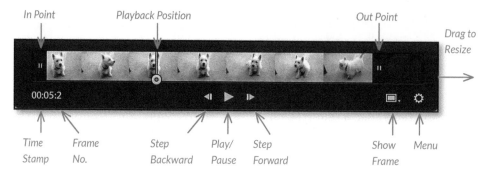

In Point   *Playback Position*   *Out Point*   *Drag to Resize*

00:05:2

Time Stamp   *Frame No.*   *Step Backward*   *Play/ Pause*   *Step Forward*   *Show Frame*   *Menu*

Figure 6.20 *The video controls appear when you float the cursor over the video in Loupe view.*

thumbnail button and editing button. Press the triangular button to play the video. **(Figure 6.20)** We'll come back to basic editing in the Video Editing section starting on page 222.

There are additional view options under *View menu > View Options > Loupe View* tab. **Show frame number when displaying video time** adds the frame number to the minutes:seconds display when the playback controller is expanded. *Play HD video at draft quality* uses a lower resolution for smoother playback on slower machines.

VIEWING YOUR PHOTOS IN SURVEY VIEW

Lightroom's Survey mode **(Figure 6.21)** allows you to view multiple photos at the same time, so it's particularly

useful when you have a series of similar photos to narrow down to your favorites.

Select the photos in Grid or Filmstrip. If they're consecutive photos, click on the first photo, then hold down the Shift key and click on the last one. If the photos are scattered, hold down the Ctrl (Windows) / Cmd (Mac) while clicking on their thumbnails. Once the photos are selected,

press the Survey button on the Toolbar **(Figure 6.22)**, the N key on your keyboard, or go to *View menu > Survey.*

Most of the shortcuts use quite logical letters, but there isn't even an N in the word 'survey.' As an interesting piece of trivia, and easier way of remembering the N shortcut, this view was initially called N-Up while it was being developed, which is where the shortcut originated.

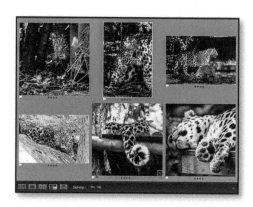

Figure 6.21 *Survey mode allows you to view multiple photos at the same time.*

Figure 6.22 *Enter Survey mode by clicking this button in the Toolbar or by pressing N.*

When you hover over a photo, the rating/flag/label icons appear, along with an X icon which removes the photo from the selection and from the Survey view. When you return to Grid view, only the leftover photos are still selected, so you can mark them using the ranking system of your choice.

VIEWING YOUR PHOTOS IN COMPARE VIEW

Compare view **(Figure 6.23)** is used to compare two similar photos, and unlike Survey view, it allows you to zoom in too. Select two photos and press the Compare button on the Toolbar **(Figure 6.24)**, the C key, or go to *View menu > Compare* to enter Compare mode.

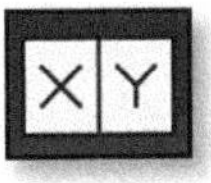

The active photo becomes the Select, shown on the left and marked with a white diamond icon. The other photo becomes the Candidate, shown on the right and marked with a black diamond icon. I struggle to remember which color diamond is the Select and which is the Candidate, but 'white for good and black for bad' is a handy memory prompt. **(Figure 6.25)**

The Select on the left is fixed in place, and as you use the left/right arrow keys on your keyboard to step through the photos, the Candidate on the right changes. When you find a photo you like better than the current Select, you can press the XY buttons on the Toolbar to switch them round, making your new favorite photo your new Select. **(Figure 6.26)**

As you upgrade a photo from a Candidate to a Select, the next photo becomes the new Candidate. Imagine you have a series of 5 similar photos, and you want to pick the best one. You start with number 1 as the Select and number 2 as the Candidate. **(Figures 6.27-6.30 overleaf)**

Figure 6.23 *Enter Compare mode by clicking this button in the Toolbar or by pressing C.*

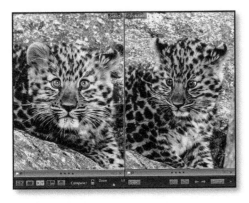

Figure 6.24 *Compare mode compares two photos in great detail, so you can choose your favorite before moving onto the next pair.*

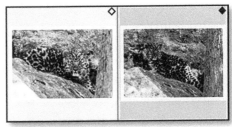

Figure 6.25 *When using Compare view, the white diamond is the Select and the black diamond is the Candidate.*

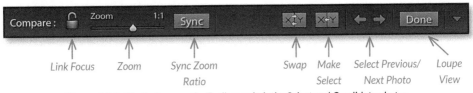

Link Focus   Zoom   Sync Zoom Ratio   Swap   Make Select   Select Previous/ Next Photo   Loupe View

Figure 6.26 *The buttons on the Toolbar switch the Select and Candidate photos.*

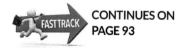

CONTINUES ON PAGE 93

The Link Focus icon (which looks like a lock) is particularly useful when checking that all the people in a group photo have their eyes open. If both photos are identically aligned, you can click the lock before zooming, and as you pan around the photo, both photos will pan. If they're not aligned, zoom in first and match up the alignment and then lock the position, so that the positioning follows you as you pan around both photos. With the lock unlocked (or while holding down the Shift key), the photos pan and zoom independently.

SECONDARY DISPLAY

When many users think of using dual monitors, they think of Photoshop and tear off panels. Lightroom's Secondary Display options don't allow you to tear off panels, but they do allow you to display the photos on a secondary display, whether that's on a second monitor or just another floating window on the same monitor.

The Display controls are on the top left of the Filmstrip. **(Figure 6.31)** A single click on the Secondary Display icon turns that display on or off, and a long click or right-click on each icon shows a context-sensitive menu with the View Options for that display.

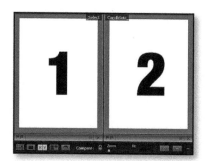

Figure 6.27 *Imagine you start with images 1 and 2. You decide you don't like number 2, so you move to the next photo by pressing the right arrow key.*

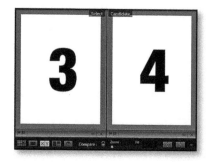

Figure 6.29 *You compare that against number 4, but you still like 3 better, so you press the right arrow key to compare 3 and 5.*

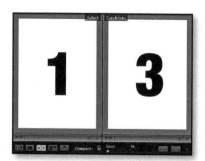

Figure 6.28 *You're now comparing photos 1 and 3, and you decide you like 3 better, so you press the X<Y button to make number 3 the new Select.*

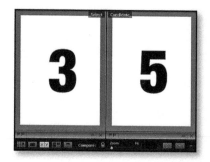

Figure 6.30 *In the end, number 3 is your favorite, so you mark it with a star rating.*

The Secondary Display offers a few different view options: **(Figure 6.32)**

Grid is particularly useful for selecting photos for use in the Map module or one of the output modules.

Loupe displays a large view of the photo currently selected on the main screen.

Live Loupe shows the photo currently under the cursor, and updates live as you float the mouse across different photos on the main screen.

Locked Loupe fixes your chosen photo to the Loupe view, which is useful as a point of comparison or reference photo. (You may also like to use Reference View for this purpose—see page 316 for more detail.)

Compare is the usual Compare view, but allows you to select and rearrange the photos in Grid view on the main screen while viewing Compare view on the secondary display.

Survey is the usual Survey view, but allows you to select and rearrange the photos in Grid view on the main screen while viewing Survey view on the secondary display. It's useful for checking consistency when editing a set of photos in Develop.

Slideshow is only available when the Secondary Display is in Full Screen mode, where it runs a slideshow of the current folder or collection, while you carry on working on the main screen. Just be aware that if you switch folder/collection on the main screen, the secondary slideshow will also follow that change.

Second Monitor Preview is useful if your second monitor is facing away from you, for example, facing a client on the opposite side of the table. **(Figure 6.33)** Using the pop-up in the corner of the preview, you can view and control what they see without repeatedly running round to the other side of the table. It only works when the Secondary Display is in full screen mode.

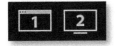

Figure 6.31 *The Secondary Display buttons change depending on whether they're set to full screen mode or window mode.*

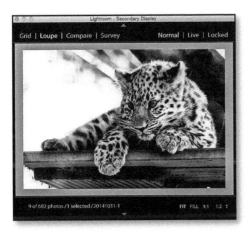

Figure 6.32 *The Secondary Display Main Window.*

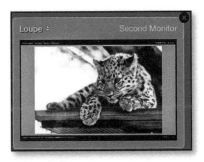

Figure 6.33 *The Second Monitor Preview is available when the Secondary Display is set to full screen view.*

Why do shortcuts and menu commands only apply to a single photo even though I have multiple photos selected on the Secondary Display Grid?

Lightroom doesn't know which screen you're looking at when you press a keyboard shortcut or menu command. For that reason, it always assumes that you're looking at the Primary Display (the main Lightroom window). Any shortcuts or menu commands will apply to the photo(s) shown on the Primary Display, unless you have *Metadata menu > Auto Sync* turned on, in which case it will apply to all selected photos.

The exception is the context-sensitive menu command on Grid on the Secondary Display, because if you've just clicked on the Secondary Display, you're obviously looking at it and realize that multiple photos are selected.

VIEWING PHOTOS SHORTCUTS

		Windows	Mac
Grid View	Go to Grid view	G	G
	Increase Grid Size	= or +	= or +
	Decrease Grid Size	-	-
	Show/Hide Extras	Ctrl Shift H	Cmd Shift H
	Show/Hide Badges	Ctrl Alt Shift H	Cmd Opt Shift H
	Cycle Grid View Style	J	J
	Show / Hide Toolbar	T	T
	Show / Hide Filter Bar	\	\
Grid/Loupe View	View Options	Ctrl J	Cmd J
Loupe View	Go to Loupe view	E	E
	Show Info Overlay	Ctrl I	Cmd I
	Cycle Info Display	I	I
	Show Loupe Overlay	Ctrl Alt O	Cmd Opt O
	Choose Layout Overlay Image	Ctrl Alt Shift O	Cmd Opt Shift O
	Loupe Overlay Options	Hold Ctrl key	Hold Cmd key
	Video Play / Pause	Spacebar	Spacebar

		Windows	Mac
Zoom	Toggle Zoom View	Z	Z
	Zoom In	Ctrl = or +	Cmd = or +
	Zoom In Some	Ctrl Alt = or +	Cmd Opt = or +
	Zoom Out	Ctrl -	Cmd -
	Zoom Out Some	Ctrl Alt -	Cmd Opt -
	Lock Zoom Position	Ctrl Shift =	Cmd Shift =
	Open in Loupe	Enter	Return
Compare View	Go to Compare view	C	C
	Switch Select and Candidate	Down arrow	Down arrow
	Mark next photos Select and Candidate	Up arrow	Up arrow
	Swap most-selected/active photo	\	\
Survey View	Go to Survey view	N	N
Selections	Select All	Ctrl A	Cmd A
	Select None	Ctrl D or Ctrl Shift A	Cmd D or Cmd Shift A
	Select Only Active Photo	Ctrl Shift D	Cmd Shift D
	Deselect Active Photo	/	/
	Select Multiple Contiguous Photos	Shift-click on photos	Shift-click on photos
	Select Multiple Non-Contiguous Photos	Ctrl-click on photos	Cmd-click on photos
	Add previous/next photo to selection	Shift left/right arrow	Shift left/right arrow
	Select Flagged Photos	Ctrl Alt A	Cmd Opt A
	Deselect Unflagged Photos	Ctrl Alt Shift D	Cmd Opt Shift D
	Select Rated/Labeled Photos	Ctrl-click on symbol in Filter bar	Cmd-click on symbol in Filter bar

		Windows	Mac
Moving between photos	Previous Selected Photo	Ctrl left arrow	Cmd left arrow
	Next Selected Photo	Ctrl right arrow	Cmd right arrow
Lights Out	Lights Dim	Ctrl Shift L	Cmd Shift L
	Next Light Mode	L	L
	Previous Light Mode	Shift L	Shift L
Secondary Display	Show Secondary Display	F11	F11
	Full Screen	Shift F11	Cmd Shift F11
	Show Second Monitor Preview	Ctrl Shift F11	Cmd Shift Opt F11
	Grid	Shift G	Shift G
	Increase Thumbnail Size	Shift = or +	Shift = or +
	Decrease Thumbnail Size	Shift -	Shift -
	Show Filter View	Shift \	Shift \
	Loupe - Normal	Shift E	Shift E
	Loupe - Locked	Ctrl Shift Enter	Cmd Shift Return
	Zoom In	Ctrl Shift = or +	Cmd Shift = or +
	Zoom In Some	Ctrl Shift Alt = or +	Cmd Shift Opt = or +
	Zoom Out	Ctrl Shift -	Cmd Shift -
	Zoom Out Some	Ctrl Shift Alt -	Cmd Shift Opt -
	Compare	Shift C	Shift C
	Survey	Shift N	Shift N
	Slideshow	Ctrl Alt Shift Enter	Cmd Opt Shift Return

SELECTING THE BEST PHOTOS

7

Having imported and viewed your photos, you're ready to start managing them— sorting through them and choosing your favorites, organizing them into groups, adding metadata to describe the photos, and then later going back to find specific photos using various filtering options.

RATING YOUR PHOTOS

Lightroom offers three different ways of ranking your photos.

Flags have three different states—flagged (picked), unflagged and rejected. It's a popular ranking system among Lightroom users. Note that flags can't be written to the files or shared with other software, so you may prefer to use them as a temporary ranking system, for example, when you're initially sorting through the photos and deciding which to keep. **(Figure 7.1)**

Star Ratings are used by photographers worldwide, with 5 stars being the best photos. Stars are standardized metadata so they can be understood by other software. Many photographers limit themselves to

using 1-3 stars when initially ranking their photos, and leave 4 and 5 stars for the best photos they've ever taken. **(Figure 7.2)**

Color Labels have no specific meaning, so you can decide how to use them. Many use them to mark photos that need further work in other editors, for example, photos that need retouching in Photoshop, sets of photos for merging into HDR, photos to be built into a panorama, etc. **(Figure 7.3)**

There are numerous ways to apply or remove star ratings, color labels and flags including clicking the icons on the thumbnails (or on the Toolbar if stars are enabled), selecting them from the *Photo menu* or right-click menu, or using their keyboard shortcuts.

On the keyboard, the 0-5 keys apply star ratings, with 1-5 obviously setting 1-5 stars, and 0 clearing your rating. The 6-9 keys apply or remove red, yellow, green and blue color labels. Flags use the P key for

Figure 7.2 *Star Ratings.*

Figure 7.1 *Flags (flagged, unflagged, rejected).*

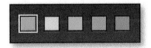

Figure 7.3 *Color Labels.*

Picked or Flagged, U for Unflagged, and X for rejected. The ` key (near the X) toggles between Flagged and Unflagged. If you change your mind, just tap a different key to assign a different rating.

If you're in a decisive mood, turn on Caps Lock, hold down Shift while using these keyboard shortcuts, or enable *Photo menu > Auto Advance.* When you press the keyboard shortcut, Lightroom applies the ranking and automatically advances to the next photo.

These keyboard shortcuts work in all view modes, but viewing photos in the Library module (Grid, Loupe, Compare & Survey views) is faster than the Develop module. Don't forget to build the correct size previews before you start (see page 460), otherwise you'll have to wait for Lightroom to load each photo.

How do I rank my photos?

Let's try ranking the photos you've just imported. If you haven't decided which system you prefer yet, keep it really simple and just use flags for now.

1. Select the first photo and switch to the Loupe mode using the E key or the Loupe button on the Toolbar.

2. Decide whether you like the photo on screen. Press the X key to mark it for deletion or P to mark it as a keeper. If you want to use stars, press the 1-5 keys to assign a star rating (but still use X to mark for deletion). If you prefer to use the mouse, click the triangle at the end of the Toolbar and select Flagging and Rating from the menu to display the icons, then click the icons on the Toolbar to apply your chosen ranking.

3. Use the left/right arrows on the keyboard to move between photos. Keep going until you get to the last photo. Remember, you can change your mind later!

4. If you find a group of similar photos, switch to Compare mode (C key) or Survey mode (N key) to view them together and then mark the best ones from the group.

Applying flags and star ratings to your photos is easy, but when you're faced with thousands of photos, where do you start? How do you decide which photos deserve which ratings... and how do you keep the meaning of the ratings consistent over time?

Which photos are worth keeping?

How you decide which photos are deserving of a specific ranking is a personal decision, but there are a few questions that may help:

• Does the photo immediately grab you?

• Does the photo trigger a strong emotion or a memory?

• Does the photo tell a story or capture a special moment?

• Do you have a similar photo that's better?

• Is the subject (person/animal) making eye contact? Does it capture their personality?

• Are there significant technical issues, for example, is it in focus?

Move fast and don't agonize over decisions. Your gut instinct is often right.

There are lots of different ways of sorting through photos. Some photographers use Grid view and others prefer Loupe. Some like to rate their photos in a single pass, and others like multiple passes. Some like flags

...continues on page 97

Rating Workflow

STEP 1

Start in Grid view with large thumbnails. It's easier to make decisions when you're not bogged down in the details. Just flag or reject the ones you really like or don't like. Leave the rest unflagged.

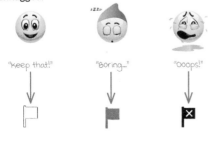

"keep that!"　　"Boring..."　　"Ooops!"

STEP 2

Go to *Photo menu* > *Delete Rejected Photos* to delete the really bad photos from the hard drive.

Use the Attribute Filters to show only Unflagged photos, then give them 1 star.

Filter: ◇◇◇

STEP 3

Use the Attribute Filters to show only Flagged photos. Go back through the Flagged photos again, occasionally switching to Detail view to check focus.

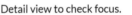
Filter: ◆◇◇

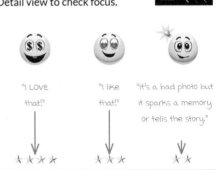

"I LOVE that!"　"I like that!"　"It's a bad photo but it sparks a memory or tells the story."

★★★★　★★★　★★

STEP 4

Some months later, go back through the 3 and 4 star photos and see if any need to be upgraded or downgraded. It's easier to make an objective decision when time has passed.

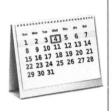

RESULT	Meaning	What's Next...
⚑	Really bad photo worthy of deletion.	Nothing (deleted)
★	Should be deleted really, but I'm a packrat. Never to be seen again!	Nothing (ignored)
★★	Triggers a memory, but not great as a photo. The hotel room, a meal out with friends, etc.	A fast edit and a few keywords. They might end up in a photo book or slideshow, but they'll never be great photos in their own right.
★★★	Decent photo I'd be willing to show someone.	
★★★★	Good photo, might end up on the wall or social media.	A careful edit, possibly some Photoshop work, titles/captions and more extensive keywords. These are the photos that will end up on the wall or on social media.
★★★★★	Best photos ever taken. Rare!	

Figure 7.4 *Need a tried & tested workflow for selecting your best photos? This is my personal workflow.*

More Rating Workflows

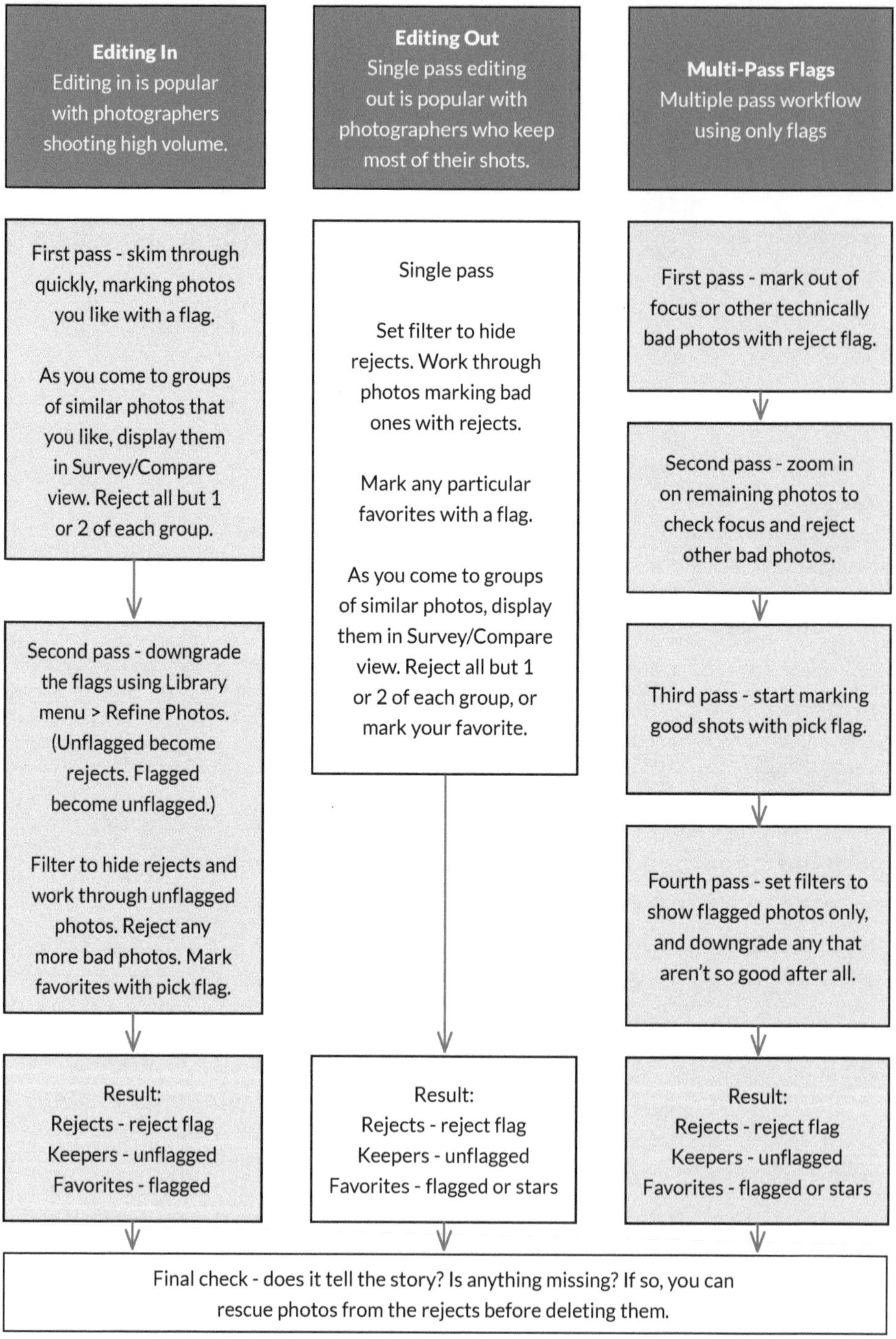

Editing In
Editing in is popular with photographers shooting high volume.

Editing Out
Single pass editing out is popular with photographers who keep most of their shots.

Multi-Pass Flags
Multiple pass workflow using only flags

First pass - skim through quickly, marking photos you like with a flag.

As you come to groups of similar photos that you like, display them in Survey/Compare view. Reject all but 1 or 2 of each group.

↓

Second pass - downgrade the flags using Library menu > Refine Photos. (Unflagged become rejects. Flagged become unflagged.)

Filter to hide rejects and work through unflagged photos. Reject any more bad photos. Mark favorites with pick flag.

↓

Result:
Rejects - reject flag
Keepers - unflagged
Favorites - flagged

Single pass

Set filter to hide rejects. Work through photos marking bad ones with rejects.

Mark any particular favorites with a flag.

As you come to groups of similar photos, display them in Survey/Compare view. Reject all but 1 or 2 of each group, or mark your favorite.

↓

Result:
Rejects - reject flag
Keepers - unflagged
Favorites - flagged or stars

First pass - mark out of focus or other technically bad photos with reject flag.

↓

Second pass - zoom in on remaining photos to check focus and reject other bad photos.

↓

Third pass - start marking good shots with pick flag.

↓

Fourth pass - set filters to show flagged photos only, and downgrade any that aren't so good after all.

↓

Result:
Rejects - reject flag
Keepers - unflagged
Favorites - flagged or stars

Final check - does it tell the story? Is anything missing? If so, you can rescue photos from the rejects before deleting them.

Figure 7.5 *Here's a few more popular workflows for selecting your best photos.*

and some prefer stars. Some only use 1-3 stars and some use all 5. Some pick out their favorite photos and others just reject the bad ones. It really is up to you.

Flexibility is a wonderful thing, but so much choice can be confusing, so here's my tried and tested rating workflow, which you're welcome to use. **(Figure 7.4)** A few more alternatives are shown in the following diagram **(Figure 7.5)**

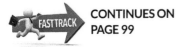

CONTINUES ON PAGE 99

What does Refine Photos do?

If you use Flags, you can select *Library menu > Refine Photos* to downgrade all of the flags at once. This command downgrades the un-flagged photos to rejects and flagged photos to unflagged.

It's little-used tool, but it works surprisingly well in a multi-pass workflow. Flag all of the photos you like, then select Refine Photos, so that the photo you didn't flag initially are marked as rejects. Go through the newly un-flagged photos again, marking the ones you still like with a flag, and repeat. In the end, only the best photos remain.

How do I use color labels?

Color labels are more flexible than star ratings and flags, because they're simple text metadata represented by a color. Add a red label to a photo using the 6 key, then look in the Metadata panel on the right-hand side of the Library module. You'll see the text *"Red"* listed next to the word Label, because the red label is associated with the word *"Red"* by default.

You can decide which color is used to represent which text using *Metadata menu >*

Color Label Set. **(Figure 7.6)** Preset groups of color assignments are listed, for example, if you select Bridge Default, the red label represents the word *"Select"*, the yellow label represents the word *"Second"*, and so forth. If you select *Edit*, you can create your own sets. **(Figure 7.7)**

I've heard some interesting ideas for using color labels. These are a few of my favorites:

What needs to be done to the photos— HDR/panorama sets, LR/PS retouching needed, finished photos

Output options—Facebook, Flickr, web galleries, email, print

Multiple cameras at the same shoot— each camera gets its own color, which helps identify them at a glance when developing

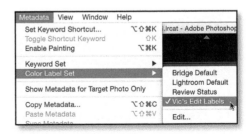

Figure 7.6 *Sets of color assignments can be saved as Color Label Sets.*

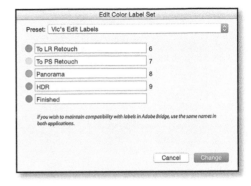

Figure 7.7 *You can decide which color is used to represent which text at any one time.*

Who took the photo—particularly useful in a family environment

Workflow—to flag/star, to be keyworded, to be developed, to output

Rating photos—some people skip flags and stars, and just use color labels

But how do you remember what each color represents? You could repeatedly go back to *Metadata menu > Color Label Set > Edit* to check. You could write them on a post-it note and stick it to the side of your computer. Or you could borrow my trick, and create a transparent PNG file in Photoshop and then add them as a panel end mark in Lightroom. **(Figure 7.8)**

You can even create lots of different sets, although that can get a bit confusing as a photo can only have a single color label at a time. If the label text doesn't match a color in the selected label set, it appears as a white label instead.

QUICK DEVELOP

While you're sorting through your photos and rating them, you may need to check whether some are worth keeping, for example, under-exposed photos. You could switch to the Develop module to make adjustments, but the Quick Develop panel (on the right in the Library module) offers easy access to the basic adjustments.

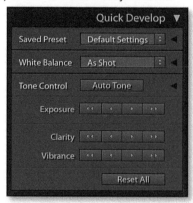

Figure 7.9 Quick Develop is collapsed by default.

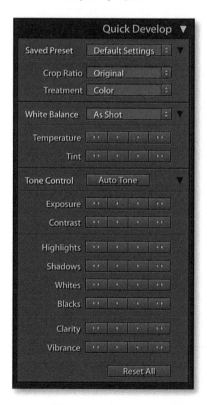

Figure 7.10 Click the Disclosure Triangles to expand the full Quick Develop panel.

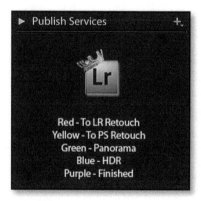

Figure 7.8 Panel end marks are great for reminding you what your color labels mean.

At first glance, the panel looks quite limited **(Figure 7.9)**, but if you click the disclosure triangles on the right, it expands to show a wider range of settings. **(Figure 7.10)** Two further adjustments are hiding—if you hold down the Alt (Win) / Opt (Mac) key, the *Clarity* buttons temporarily change to *Sharpening* and the *Vibrance* buttons temporarily change to *Saturation*.

To apply the adjustments to your photos, simply press the buttons. Single arrows make small adjustments and double arrows make larger adjustments. If you hold down the Shift key, the single arrows move in even smaller increments.

If you're viewing in Grid view, it applies to all the selected photos. If you're viewing Loupe, Compare or Survey, it only applies to the selected photo (unless Auto Sync is enabled and multiple photos are selected).

It's also handy for applying Develop corrections to photos you've already edited, as the adjustments are relative to the current settings, but we'll come back to that in the Editing chapters starting on page 181.

GROUPING SIMILAR PHOTOS USING STACKS

As you're sorting through the photos, you may also come across groups of photos that don't mean a lot

on their own. For example, groups of photos taken for a panorama or HDR often look awful as individual photos!

Lightroom offers stacking as a way to group photos. You can put your favorite photo on top of the stack and collapse the stack, hiding the other photos to clear some of the visual clutter.

To create a stack, select the photos and go to *Photo menu > Stacking > Group into Stack*, or press Ctrl-G (Windows) / Cmd-G (Mac). The photos automatically collapse into a stack, marked with double lines at the beginning and end. **(Figure 7.11)**

To open the stack, click the white number in the corner. The border surrounding the thumbnails is slightly different when the photos are in an open stack, but it's not always obvious as the thumbnail divide lines don't disappear until the photos are deselected. **(Figure 7.12)**

The photo on the left is the photo that shows when you view a collapsed stack. If the photo that best represents the stack—perhaps the finished panorama or the finished HDR photo—isn't currently at the top of the stack, click on its number to move it to the top of the stack. You can also go to *Photo menu > Stacking > Move to Top of Stack*.

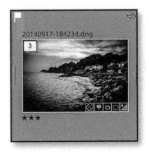

Figure 7.11 *Collapsed stacks show as a single photo.*

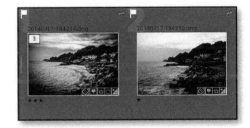

Figure 7.12 *When you click on the white rectangle, the stack opens to show the group of photos.*

To remove a photo from a stack, you can ungroup the whole stack using *Photo menu > Stacking > Unstack*, or you can drag the single photo out of the stack to a different place in the Grid view, leaving the rest of the stack intact.

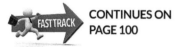

CONTINUES ON PAGE 100

There are a few 'quirks' with Lightroom's stacking that you need to be aware of.

Stacks only work when all the stacked photos are stored in a single folder or collection, so if the stacking options in the *Photo menu* are disabled, you're probably viewing a composite folder view and trying to stack photos which are in different folders, or you're viewing a smart collection. To solve it, either select a folder which doesn't have subfolders, deselect *Show Photos in Subfolders* in the *Library menu*, or group the photos in a collection.

Stacks are local to the folder or collection used to create them, so if you stack photos in a folder, they'll still appear as separate photos in their collections, and vice versa.

Also, if a stack is closed, adding metadata (such as keywords) to the stack only applies the metadata to the top photo. There's a trick, however, to make it a little quicker. If you double-click or Shift-click on the stack number, it opens the stack with the stacked photos already selected, so you can go ahead and add the metadata without having to pause to select them.

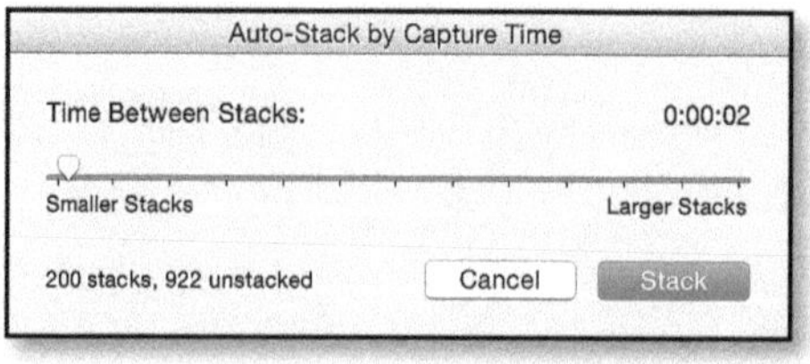

Finally, filtering doesn't search inside collapsed stacks, but you don't have to open all of the stacks individually. Instead, use the *Photo menu > Expand All Stacks* command to open them all in one go. *Collapse All Stacks*, of course, does the opposite!

Can I automatically stack sets of photos?

Stacking similar photos manually takes a long time, but Lightroom can automatically stack the photos based on their capture time. For example, you can automatically stack retouched files with their originals or group HDR/panorama sets.

Select the photos and choose *Photo menu > Stacking > Auto-Stack by Capture Time* and choose a 0 second time difference (0:00:00), or a little longer for panorama stacks. The number of stacks at the bottom of the dialog updates as you move the slider, showing how many stacks will be created automatically. **(Figure 7.13)** Once it completes, you may need to tidy up where you've shot in quick succession, but it does most of the work for you.

COLLECTIONS

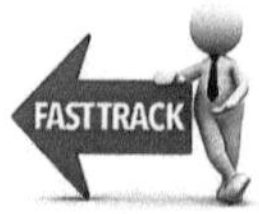

Collections are designed to group photos and videos for a specific purpose. Unlike folders, a single photo can be in multiple collections without taking up extra space on your hard drive, and these grouped photos can come from any number of different folders on the hard drive. Because they're virtual, they can only be viewed inside Lightroom.

Figure 7.13 *Auto-Stack by Capture Time can automatically stack photos shot in quick succession.*

So when might you want to create a collection?

• You prefer photos grouped by topic or genre. Perhaps you regularly view all of the photos of your grandchildren, or you want to group the photos from your vacations.

• You're gathering your best photos for your portfolio.

• You're working on a creative photo project over a long period of time.

• You want to share a collection of photos with friends and family using Lightroom Web.

• You want to sync photos to your phone or tablet.

• You're gathering photos for output – perhaps as prints, books, slideshows or web galleries.

To create a collection, scroll down to the Collections panel, which you'll find in the left panel group in all modules, click the + button at the top and select **Create**

Collection. Name the collection, and it appears in the Collections panel. **(Figure 7.14)** When you want to view a different collection of photos, just click on its name.

From the Grid view, select your chosen photos and drag them from the preview area onto the collection. Don't forget to grab the photos by their thumbnails, not the border surrounding them. If you don't like dragging, right-click on the collection and select *Add Selected Photos to this Collection* from the context-sensitive menu instead.

Removing photos from a collection is as simple as hitting the Delete key. When you're viewing a collection, the Delete key only removes the photo from the collection, rather than from the catalog or hard drive, and if the photo's synced, it remains in the *All Synced Photographs* collection too.

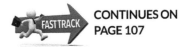

CONTINUES ON PAGE 107

That was easy, wasn't it! Collections are more powerful than they look at first glance

Create Collection	
Name: Holiday 2014-09	

Location
☐ Inside a Collection Set

⬦

Options
☑ Include selected photos
☐ Make new virtual copies
☐ Set as target collection
☑ Sync with Lightroom CC

[Cancel] [Create]

Figure 7.14 *To create a Collection, click the + button on the Collections panel and enter the name in the Create Collection dialog.*

though, so there's more to explore.

Collections aren't limited to containing photos—they store your chosen sort order, and they can also remember your filtering (depending on your preference setting). Special types of collections store Book, Slideshow, Print or Web module settings too.

You can also create Smart Collections, which are saved search criteria, smart folders or rules. We'll come back to these later with the filtering tools on page 177.

As well as creating an empty collection and adding the photos into it, you can first select the photos and then create the collection with *Include Selected Photos* checked in the New Collection dialog.

If you have a whole folder of photos that you'd like to turn into a collection, drag the folder from the Folders panel to the Collections panel. A collection of the same name is created, containing all the photos in

COLLECTION ICONS

Collection Set

Collection

Book

Slideshow

Print

Web Gallery

Smart Collection

Collection with Comments

the folder.

To duplicate a collection, hold down the Ctrl key (Windows) / Opt key (Mac) and drag the collection within the Collections panel. You can either drop it between existing collections (when the blue line appears) or drop it on a collection set. The same shortcut works for smart collections and even whole collection sets.

You can sync a collection to the cloud so it can be viewed on mobile devices and at https://lightroom.adobe.com Turn to the Cloud Sync chapter starting on page 483 for more information.

To delete a collection, select it and press the - button at the top of the Collections panel, or right-click on the collection and select *Delete*.

How do I delete photos from the hard drive while viewing a collection?

If you need to delete the photos from the hard drive while viewing a collection, use the wonderfully nicknamed 'splat-delete' or Ctrl-Alt-Shift-Delete (Windows) / Cmd-Opt-Shift-Delete (Mac). It deletes from the hard drive whether you're viewing a folder, collection or even a smart collection, but beware, it also bypasses the warning dialog, so use it with care!

How do I see which collections a photo belongs to?

If you need to check which collections a photo belongs to, right-click on the photo and choose *Go to Collection*, or click on the Collection badge in the corner of the thumbnail. Lightroom displays a list of collections containing that photo, and clicking on the collection name switches to the collection. **(Figure 7.15)**

If you're checking a large number of photos, switch to Grid view and hover the cursor over the collections in the Collections panel. All photos belonging to the collection under the cursor temporarily display a thin white border around the thumbnail, making them quick to identify.

How do I organize my collections into sets?

Using the + button on the Collections panel, you can choose whether to sort the Collections panel by name or collection type. **(Figure 7.16)** Changing the sort order works well until you have a large number of collections, at which point collection sets come into their own.

As your list of collections grows, it can become harder to find the right one. Collection Sets allow you to build a hierarchy of collections, just like you would with folders. For example, you may have a collection set called *Vacations*, and within that set, sets for each of your vacation destinations. These vacation destinations

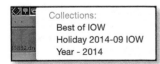

Figure 7.15 *When you click on the Collections badge on the thumbnail, the menu lists all of the standard collections which include that photo.*

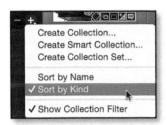

Figure 7.16 *You can change the collections sort order by clicking the + button on the Collections panel.*

might divide down further into sets for each year that you visited, and then individual collections for the long slideshow of all of your photos from each vacation, the web galleries or sync collections you created to show your friends, the book you created, and the individual pictures you printed. **(Figure 7.17)**

You can also include smart collections inside your collection sets too, so you might have additional smart collections for all the 5 star photos, all the photos of beaches, and so on. We'll come back to smart collections on page 177.

To create a Collection Set, press the + button on the Collections panel and select **New Collection Set**. Name it, and then drag existing collections onto the set to group them. When you're creating new collections, you can select which set to put them in using the pop-up in the New Collection dialog.

There's a notable difference between collections and collection sets. Collections can only usually contain photos and videos, whereas collection sets can contain collections or other collection sets but not

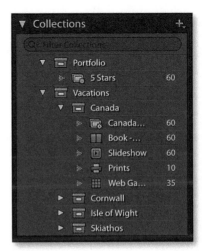

Figure 7.17 *Collections can be nested in Collection Sets to keep them organized.*

the photos or videos themselves.

(Although standard collections can't usually contain other collections, there's one exception. If you start with a standard collection, and then create a book, slideshow, print or web gallery, you can store it inside the first collection. This parent collection becomes a composite view of its children, showing all the photos you've used in those books, slideshows, prints and web galleries. If you add a photo to one of its children, it appears in the parent collection. If you remove a photo from the parent collection, it's also removed from any books/slideshows/prints/web galleries nested within.)

If you have a large number of collections, you can also search for them by name using the search bar at the top of the Collections panel. Type the name of the collection and press Enter to search. If you click on the magnifying glass to the left, you can decide whether to search all collections or just synced collections. Click the X at the end of the search field to clear the search. **(Figure 7.18)**

The one downside is collection sets don't sync with album folders in the Lightroom CC cloud. The collections show as a flat collections list in Lightroom mobile, which can become rather long if you're syncing a large number of collections, but you can manually replicate Lightroom Classic's collection set hierarchy using album folders in Lightroom CC.

What are the Quick Collection and Target Collection?

The Catalog panel holds a few more special and temporary collections, for example, *All Photographs* shows all of the photographs in your catalog, *All Synced Photographs* show all of the photos synced to the cloud, and *Previous Import* shows the last set of photos imported into your catalog. Other collections are added temporarily, for example, *Previous Export as Catalog, Added by Previous Export, Quick Collection* and more.

The **Quick Collection** is a special collection for temporarily holding photos of your choice. If you've added a group of photos to the Quick Collection and then you decide you would like to convert it into a permanent collection, you can right-click on it and select *Save Quick Collection* from the context-sensitive menu. **(Figure 7.19)**

The **Target Collection** isn't a collection in its own right—it's just a shortcut linking to another collection. It's marked by a + symbol next to the collection name. Pressing the shortcut key B or clicking the little circle icon on the thumbnail adds to (or removes the photo from) that Target Collection. By default, the Quick Collection is the Target Collection, but you can change the shortcut to the collection of your choice by right-clicking on your chosen collection and selecting *Set as Target Collection*.

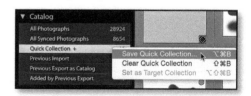

Figure 7.19 *The Quick Collection is a temporary collection which is always shown in the Catalog panel. The + next to the name indicates that it's also the Target Collection.*

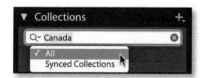

Figure 7.18 *Type in the Search bar at the top of the Collections panel to filter the collections.*

SELECTING PHOTOS SHORTCUTS

		Windows	Mac
Flags	Flagged	P	P
	Unflagged	U	U
	Rejected	X	X
	Toggle Flag	`	`
	Increase Flag Status	Ctrl up arrow	Cmd up arrow
	Decrease Flag Status	Ctrl down arrow	Cmd down arrow
	Auto Advance	Hold Shift while using P, U, X or turn on Caps Lock	Hold Shift while using P, U, X or turn on Caps Lock
	Refine Photos	Ctrl Alt R	Cmd Opt R
Star Ratings	0 - 5 stars	0, 1, 2, 3, 4, 5	0, 1, 2, 3, 4, 5
	Decrease Rating	[	[
	Increase Rating	]	]
	Auto Advance	Hold Shift while using 0-5 or turn on Caps Lock	Hold Shift while using 0-5 or turn on Caps Lock
Color Labels	Toggle Red	6	6-9
	Toggle Yellow	7	7
	Toggle Green	8	8
	Toggle Blue	9	9
	Auto Advance	Hold Shift while using 6-9 or turn on Caps Lock	Hold Shift while using 6-9 or turn on Caps Lock
Stacking	Group into Stack	Ctrl G	Cmd G
	Unstack	Ctrl Shift G	Cmd Shift G
	Collapse/Expand Stack	S	S
	Move to Top of Stack	Shift S	Shift S

		Windows	Mac
	Move Up in Stack	Shift [	Shift [
	Move Down in Stack	Shift]	Shift]
Collections	New Collection	Ctrl N	Cmd N
	Expand All SubCollections	Alt-Click on collection set disclosure triangle	Opt-Click on collection set disclosure triangle
Quick / Target Collection	Add to Quick / Target Collection	B	B
	Add to Quick Collection / Target and Next	Shift B	Shift B
	Show Quick / Target Collection	Ctrl B	Cmd B
	Save Quick / Target Collection	Ctrl Alt B	Cmd Opt B
	Clear Quick / Target Collection	Ctrl Shift B	Cmd Shift B
	Set Quick / Target Collection as Target	Ctrl Alt Shift B	Cmd Opt Shift B

MANAGING YOUR PHOTOS

8

As we've mentioned in earlier chapters, using a database to catalog photos is a new concept to many Lightroom users, so it's important to understand how the photos in Lightroom relate to the files on your hard drive.

So why have we waited until now to start discussing folders? Folders are primarily storage buckets. Lightroom offers other tools, such as collections and metadata, that are better suited to organizing your photos. (Remember we discussed that in "How should I organize my photos?" on page 36.)

You may, however, need to manage files at times, particularly if you start to run out of space on your hard drive. This is primarily done using the Folders panel (on the left in the Library module) and the Grid view.

MANAGING FOLDERS IN LIGHTROOM AND ON THE HARD DRIVE

The folders listed in the Folders panel are references to folders on your hard drive or optical discs. When you import photos into Lightroom, the folders containing these photos are automatically added to the Folders panel.

Anything you do in Lightroom's Folders panel is reflected on the hard drive. For example, creating or renaming folders in Lightroom does the same on your hard drive. You can drag photos and folders into other folders to reorganize them, just like you would in your file browser.

The reverse doesn't work in the same way— when you rename or move a file or folder on your hard drive using your file browser, Lightroom simply marks it as missing and leaves you to manually link it back up again. You'll save yourself a lot of time and frustration by only using Lightroom to manage your files once you've imported them.

We'll come back to moving, renaming and deleting the photos themselves in the following pages, but for the moment, let's concentrate on the Folders panel.

How do I set up a folder hierarchy?

If you've imported some photos, one or more folders will be listed in the Folders panel, but it probably won't match your hierarchical folder structure in Explorer (Windows) or Finder (Mac). Only folders that hold imported photos show in the Folders panel.

To make it easier to visualize where the photos are stored on your hard drive, we can display the same hierarchy. This also makes it easier to fix if you run into problems later.

We're going to talk about three levels of folders—top-level folders, parent folders and child folders—so it will help to define these first.

Child folders are folders that are inside another folder.

Parent folders are folders that have other folders inside them.

Top-level folders, otherwise known as root folders, are folders displayed without a parent folder.

Let's start tidying up...

1. Find a top-level folder. In **Figure 8.1**, this is one of the folders starting with 2013.

2. Right-click on this folder and choose *Show Parent Folder*. (**Figure 8.2**) (If this option doesn't appear in the menu, you've right-clicked on the wrong folder.) This doesn't import new photos. It just adds an additional hierarchy level to your Folders panel, and does a lot more behind the scenes.

3. In some cases, you'll only need to add a single parent folder, but if you have a deep nested hierarchy, you may want to repeat on the new top-level folders until you can visualize the whole tree.

4. In **Figure 8.3**, we're still missing some parent folders, so we right-click on the 2013-07 folder and choose *Show Parent Folder* and then right-click on the 2013 or 2014 folder to show the My Photos folder that contains all of the Lightroom photos.

5. We could go one step further and *Show*

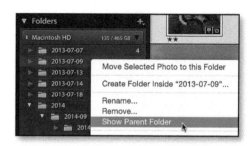

Figure 8.2 *Using Show Parent Folder to add additional parent folders to the Folders panel view makes it easier to visualize how Lightroom relates to the hard drive.*

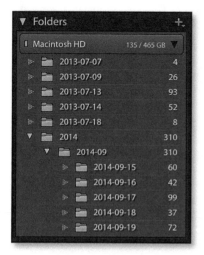

Figure 8.1 *The initial view of the Folders panel may not be easy to relate to the folders on the hard drive.*

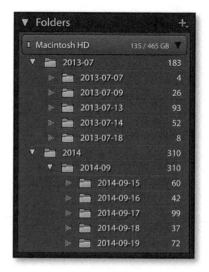

Figure 8.3 *In some cases, you'll need to use Show Parent Folder on multiple folders.*

Parent Folder on the My Photos folder to show the main Pictures folder too. **(Figure 8.4)**

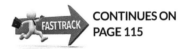
CONTINUES ON
PAGE 115

Once you've finished, you can see a hierarchy of folders that looks much more like the Explorer (Windows) / Finder (Mac) view. **(Figure 8.5)**

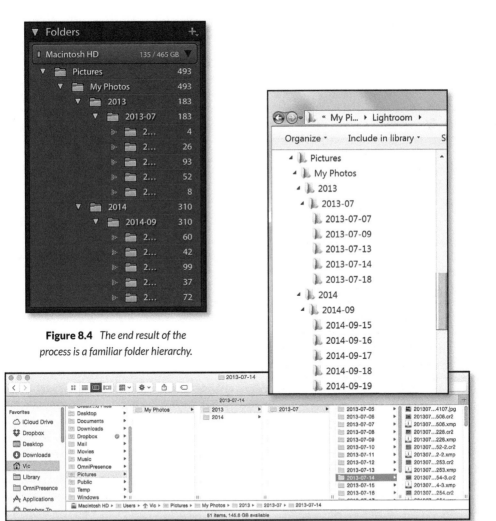

Figure 8.4 *The end result of the process is a familiar folder hierarchy.*

Figure 8.5 *The same folder hierarchy shown in Windows Explorer and Finder. There are more folders here than those showing in Lightroom's folder panel, as some of the folders haven't been imported into Lightroom.*

How do I hide parent folders?

If you go too far (perhaps showing your username or beyond), you can hide the top-level folder using **Hide This Parent**.

1. First, check whether there are any photos stored directly in the folders you're going to hide, as these photos would be removed from the catalog. To do so, uncheck *Library menu > Show Photos in Subfolders*.

2. In **Figure 8.6**, we see that the / folder, Users folder and Vic folder are empty, but the Pictures folder includes a photo, so we won't remove that one. (If you hide a folder containing imported photos, the photos are removed from the catalog, but it warns you first.)

3. Right-click on the top-level folder (shown as / in **Figure 8.6**) and choose *Hide This Parent*.

4. Select *Hide This Parent* on the Users folder, and then on the Vic folder (your folder will have another name, of course!).

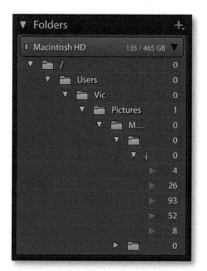

Figure 8.6 *If you show too many parent folders, it can be difficult to see the folder names.*

Once you've finished, your Folders panel should look like **Figure 8.4** again.

5. Once you've finished, you can check *Show Photos in Subfolders* again to put the folder counts back to normal.

That's the basics, but there are more Folder panel tricks and customizations to play with.

How do I switch between a composite folder view and a single folder view?

Now you have a folder hierarchy, Lightroom can show either the photos directly inside the selected folder, or it can show a composite view of all the photos in the selected folder and its subfolders. The folder counts are also affected by that setting, showing either the composite count, or the number of photos directly in each folder.

By default, **Show Photos in Subfolders** is enabled, showing a composite view. In many situations, it's useful to see a composite view of the subfolder contents, but there are a couple of restrictions. You can't apply a custom sort (user order) or stack photos across multiple folders in a composite view.

You can toggle this setting by going to *Library menu > Show Photos in Subfolders* and checking or unchecking it. You'll find the same option in the Folders panel menu, accessed via the + button.

Can I change the way the folders are displayed?

The Folders panel is divided into Volume Bars for each volume (drive) attached to your computer, whether they're internal or external hard drives, network attached storage, or optical discs.

Each of these Volume Bars can provide additional information about the drive—how many imported photos are on each volume, whether it's online or offline, and how much space is used or available. (**Figure 8.7**) You can choose which information to show by right-clicking on the Volume Bar. (**Figure 8.8**)

Click anywhere on a Volume Bar to expand it to show the folders contained in that drive, or to collapse it to hide the folders.

While you're exploring the Folders panel

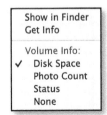

Figure 8.7 *The colored rectangle on the left of the Folders panel shows the amount of space available on the drive.*

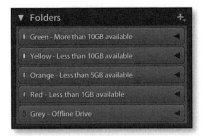

Figure 8.8 *You can choose the information shown on a Volume Bar by right-clicking on it.*

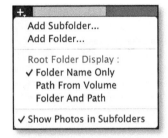

Figure 8.9 *Choose the Folder Path display format by clicking the + button in the Folders panel.*

view options, clicking on the Folders panel + button also gives additional path view options for the root folders. (**Figure 8.9**)

The options are *Folder Name Only*, *Path From Volume*, and *Folder And Path*. They simply display the path of the top level folders in different ways, as you can see from the screenshots in **Figure 8.10**.

If you're still confused about where to find a folder on your hard drive, just right-click on the folder and select *Show in Explorer* (Windows) / *Show in Finder* (Mac).

What are disclosure triangles?

Next to each folder name is a small triangle, which is officially called a disclosure triangle. You'll also find these triangles used throughout Lightroom's interface. When

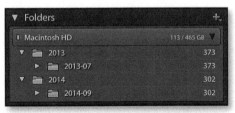

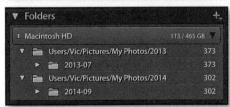

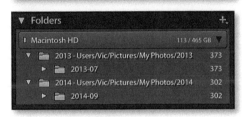

Figure 8.10 *The Folder Path can be shown in multiple formats. Folder Name Only, (top) Path From Volume (center), Folder And Path (bottom).*

you click on these triangles, they toggle to show or hide parts of the interface, such as sliders or buttons, or a hierarchy of folders, collections or keywords.

In the case of folders, collections, or keywords, a solid arrow indicates that it's a parent with subfolders/collections/keywords inside. Those marked with dotted arrows don't have any subfolders etc. inside. **(Figure 8.11)**

To expand or collapse the full hierarchy in one click, Alt-click (Windows) / Opt-click (Mac) on the parent folder's disclosure triangle.

CHANGING THE FOLDER STRUCTURE

Although Lightroom doesn't care how the photos are stored, you may want to reorganize folder structures or move photos to another drive.

Remember, if you start moving folders around in Explorer (Windows) / Finder (Mac) or other file browser software, Lightroom will complain that your folders have gone missing, and leave you to manually relink them. This can be a huge job if you've "tidied up", so it's usually simpler to manage the folders within Lightroom.

How do I create a new folder or subfolder?

To create a brand new folder, go to *Library menu > New Folder*, or press the + button on the Folders panel and select **Add Folder**. Navigate to the location of your choice.

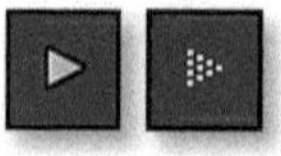

Figure 8.11 *Disclosure triangles hide part of the interface.*

On Windows, right-click and select *New* then *Folder* and type the name of the folder, then press Enter and select the new folder, then press *Select Folder*.

On a Mac, press the *New Folder* button in the operating system dialog. Give it a name and press *Create*. Your new folder is created on the hard drive and automatically selected in the operating system dialog, so press *Choose* to add it to Lightroom.

If the new folder already exists on the hard drive, but you want to add it to Lightroom, go to *Library menu > New Folder* and navigate to the folder, then press *Select Folder* (Windows) / *Choose* (Mac). If the folder is empty, it's added to the Folders panel. If there are already photos in the folder, Lightroom opens the Import dialog. In this case, you'll need to import at least one photo to add the folder to the Folders panel.

If you're creating a new subfolder, and the parent folder already exists in the Folders panel, it's even easier. Right-click on the parent folder and select **Create Folder Inside ***. Enter the subfolder name and press *Create*. If you have photos selected at the time, you can automatically move them to the new subfolder by checking the *Include Selected Photos* checkbox.

How do I move folders into other folders or drives?

Moving folders into other folders is simply a drag-and-drop operation, just like Explorer (Windows) / Finder (Mac). Select the folders in the Folders panel and drag them onto another folder in the Folders panel. The destination folder is highlighted in blue, showing where the folders will land when you release the mouse. **(Figure 8.12)**

Selecting a parent folder automatically moves all of its subfolders too. To move multiple separate folders, Ctrl-click (Windows) / Cmd-click (Mac) to select individual folders or Shift-click to select a series of folders, then drag and drop as normal.

If you're moving a large number of photos to a new drive, there's another option which is safer:

1. Follow the instructions on page 107 to show the folder hierarchy so you just have one or a few parent folders. This makes it easy to relink the folders/files that are marked as missing in this process.

2. Close Lightroom and use Explorer (Windows) / Finder (Mac) or file synchronization software to copy the folders/files to the new drive.

3. When the copy completes, rename the original folder (the one on the old hard drive) using Explorer (Windows) / Finder (Mac), or disconnect the old hard drive. This allows you to check everything is working correctly before deleting the files from the original location.

4. Open Lightroom and right-click on the parent folder. Select *Find Missing Folder* or *Update Folder Location* from the context-sensitive menu, depending on which option is available. Navigate to the new location of the folder and press *Select Folder* (Windows) / *Choose* (Mac). The folder disappears from the old volume (drive) in the Folders panel and reappears under the new volume bar.

5. If you have more than one parent folder, repeat the process for any other parent folders until the question marks have disappeared from all the folders.

6. Once you've confirmed that all the photos are available for editing within Lightroom, you can safely detach the old hard drive or delete the files from their original location using Explorer (Windows) / Finder (Mac).

How do I rename folders?

To rename a folder, simply right-click on the folder in the Folders panel and select **Rename**. When you enter the new folder name and press *Save*, it's not only updated in Lightroom but also on the hard drive.

How do I delete folders?

To delete a folder, right-click on the folder in the Folders panel and select **Remove**.

If the folder is empty in Lightroom, it's immediately removed.

If there are photos in the folder, Lightroom

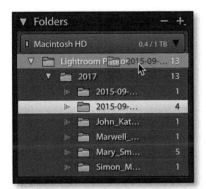

Figure 8.12 *Drag and drop folders onto other folders to move them on the hard drive as well as in Lightroom.*

PHOTOS ARE NOT 'IN' LIGHTROOM

Remember, photos are never IN Lightroom. Don't move, rename or delete files or folders using Explorer/Finder or other software after import, as Lightroom won't be able to find them.

requests confirmation because removing the folder will also remove these photos from Lightroom's catalog.

If there are no other files (e.g. text files) left inside the folder, the folder is also deleted from the hard drive.

I've added new photos to one of Lightroom's folders—why don't they show in my catalog?

If you import a folder into Lightroom's catalog and then later add additional photos to that folder using other software, Lightroom won't know about those additional photos until you choose to import them.

If you go back to the Import dialog and import that folder again, Lightroom just imports the new photos, skipping the existing ones. You can also use *Synchronize Folder* to automate the process.

How does the Synchronize Folder command work?

The main purpose of **Synchronize Folder** (found in the folders right-click menu) is to update Lightroom's catalog with changes made to the folder by other programs, for example, adding or deleting photos or updating the metadata. **(Figure 8.13)**

Synchronize Folder is one of the most misunderstood tools in Lightroom, and can cause all sorts of trouble if you don't read the dialog carefully, so let's run through the options...

Import new photos searches the folder and subfolders for any new photos not currently in this catalog and imports them. If you've dropped photos into the folder using other software, it saves you navigating to the folder in the Import dialog.

Show Import dialog before importing displays the photos in the Import dialog, to allow you to view the new photos and adjust the import options prior to import.

Remove missing photos from the catalog checks for photos that have been moved, renamed or deleted from the folder and removes the missing photos from the catalog.

Be very careful using this option because any metadata for those missing photos, such as Develop settings and ratings would

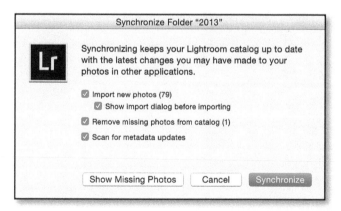

Figure 8.13 *Synchronize Folders is powerful, but can cause trouble if you've moved photos outside of Lightroom. Take care to make sure you understand exactly what will happen.*

be lost, even if the photos have simply been moved to another location. It doesn't intelligently relink the files. If in doubt, leave this option unchecked.

Scan for metadata updates checks the metadata in the catalog against the file, to see whether you've edited the file in any other programs, such as Bridge.

If you've only changed the metadata in Lightroom, it doesn't do anything.

If the metadata has changed in another program, but not in Lightroom, Lightroom reads the metadata from the file, overwriting Lightroom's settings.

If both Lightroom's catalog and the external file have changed, you'll see a *Metadata Conflict* badge on a thumbnail, and you'll have to click on that icon to choose which set of data to keep—the metadata in your catalog or the metadata in the file.

We'll come back to XMP metadata in more detail on page 345, including the use of the Metadata Conflict dialog.

The **Show Missing Photos** button searches for photos missing from the folder and creates a temporary collection in the Catalog panel. You can then decide whether to track them down and relink them, or whether to remove these photos from the catalog. If you want to check your entire catalog for missing photos, it's quicker to use the *Library menu > Find Missing Photos* command instead. Once you've finished with the temporary collection, you can right-click on it to remove it.

But stop! Before you press the *Synchronize* button, stop and think. If *Remove missing photos from the catalog* has a number next to it and you synchronize that folder, you may lose the work you've done in Lightroom.

It doesn't intelligently relink missing files. Instead, you need to cancel out of the *Synchronize Folder* dialog and manually relink the missing files, using the instructions on page 435.

Synchronize Folder is also the wrong tool to use when moving photos to a new hard drive, or moving to entirely new computer. See page 399 for the instructions.

So when is it useful? If you've dropped photos into a folder using other software (including Windows Explorer/Finder), or you've edited a photo in an external editor (e.g. Photoshop or OnOne) and it hasn't been automatically added to the catalog, then *Synchronize Folder* saves you navigating to the folder in the Import dialog.

Next time you need to use *Synchronize Folder*, don't forget to stop and read the options carefully before pressing OK.

MANAGING THE INDIVIDUAL PHOTOS

There are one or two more file management tasks you might need, such as deleting, renaming or moving individual photos, rather than whole folders.

How do I delete fuzzy photos?

Even the best photographers sometimes end up with photos that aren't worth keeping.

It's possible to delete photos while you're sorting through them, simply by pressing the Delete key on your keyboard, but it's quicker to mark them with a Reject flag (X key) and then delete them all in one go.

Photos marked as rejects show in the Grid

view as dimmed photos, so it's easy to check that you've marked the right ones. When you're ready to delete all the rejected photos, go to *Photo menu > Delete Rejected Photos.*

Before Lightroom deletes the photos, it asks whether to *Remove* or *Delete* them. **(Figure 8.14)** Note the difference. **Remove** just removes the reference to the photo from Lightroom's catalog, but the photo remains on the hard drive. **Delete** deletes the photo from your hard drive too (or sends it to the Recycle Bin/Trash if possible).

Before you select either option, double check the number of photos that it says will be deleted, just in case you've accidentally selected photos you want to keep. If you make a mistake with *Remove*, you can immediately use Ctrl-Z (Windows) / Cmd-Z (Mac) to undo it, but that won't work with *Delete.*

How do I rename one or more photos?

We've already learned how to rename

photos while Importing them, but you can also rename photos later in the Library module.

To do so, select the photos in Grid view, and then select *Library menu > **Rename**.* The Rename dialog options are almost identical to the Import dialog File Renaming panel, which we used in the Import chapter. **(Figure 8.15)** Select your chosen file naming template or select *Edit* to create your own template using tokens in the Filename Template Editor. Turn back to the File Renaming section of the Import chapter on page 30 if you need a refresher on the file renaming options.

That's great if you want to rename multiple photos, but to rename just a single photo, it's often quicker to open the Metadata panel on the right hand side of the Library module. If you click in the *Filename* field, you can edit the existing filename rather than having to use a template in the full Rename dialog. If you do decide to use a template after all, clicking the little icon at the end of the Filename field takes you directly to the

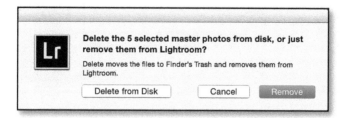

Figure 8.14 *In the Delete dialog, note the difference between Remove and Delete, and don't forget to check the number of photos that will be deleted.*

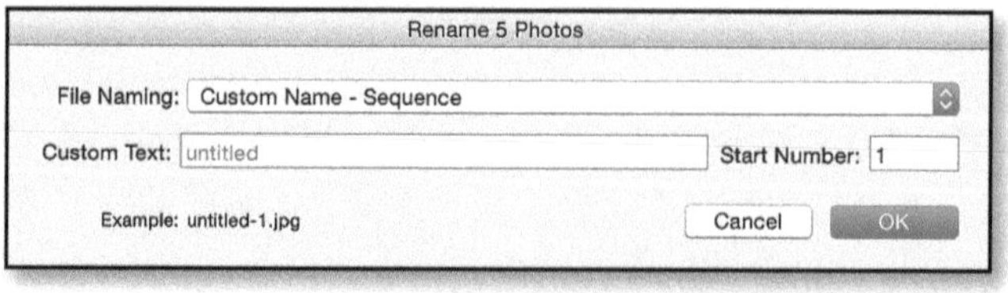

Figure 8.15 *You can rename photos in the Library Module using the same templates used in the Import dialog.*

full Rename dialog.

Why are some of the tokens missing?

The available tokens differ slightly between the Import dialog and the Library module. Import has a *Shoot Name* token, which isn't available in the Library module, but the Library module gains tokens such as *Folder Name, Original Filename, Copy Name,* slightly different sequence number options and additional IPTC metadata. The basic principles remain the same.

How do I rename photos back to their original filename?

There's another useful rename option which wasn't available in the Import dialog: *Original Filename.* **(Figure 8.16)**

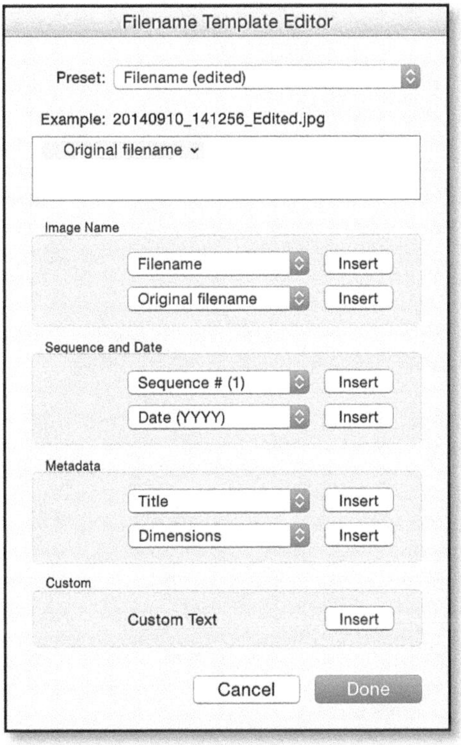

Filename Template Editor

Preset: Filename (edited)

Example: 20140910_141256_Edited.jpg

Original filename ⌄

Image Name

Filename — Insert

Original filename — Insert

Sequence and Date

Sequence # (1) — Insert

Date (YYYY) — Insert

Metadata

Title — Insert

Dimensions — Insert

Custom

Custom Text — Insert

Cancel   Done

Figure 8.16 *Original Filename is one of the tokens in the Filename Template Editor.*

If you've renamed a photo within Lightroom since you imported it into the current catalog, Lightroom may still have a record of the original filename. That *Original Filename* field would actually be better named *Import Filename,* as it's the name at the time of import, not necessarily the original name at the time of capture. If you want to check whether you have an original filename to revert to, select the *EXIF and IPTC* view at the top of the Metadata panel. **(Figure 8.17)** If the original filename is present in the database, you can go to the Rename dialog and select *Edit* in the pop-up to show the Filename Template Editor. You'll find the *Original Filename* token in the *Image Name* section.

Can I search and replace in filenames?

Lightroom's file naming allows for the creations of complex new filenames, but reusing part of the existing filename is not quite so simple. There's no way, for example, to remove –2 from the end of filenames, unless you can recreate the filename using metadata. It's one reason using a date/time filename is a particularly good choice!

There is a workaround, however, using John Beardsworth's Search Replace Transfer plug-in (https://www.Lrq.me/beardsworth-searchreplace). Taking the –2 scenario as an example, you'd use Search Replace Transfer to copy the filename to any unused IPTC field that Lightroom's renaming dialog can use—perhaps the Headline

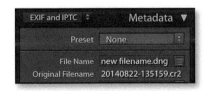

Figure 8.17 *If the original filename is stored in the catalog, you can view it by changing the Metadata panel to EXIF and IPTC view.*

field. Then you use the plug-in again, this time to remove –2 from the Headline field, and repeat to remove the file extension too. Finally, you'd use Lightroom's main Rename dialog, set to use the Headline token for the new filename. It's not for the faint-hearted, but it does come with excellent instructions.

How do I find out where a photo is stored on my hard drive?

If you ever need to find a photo on the hard drive, for example, to open in another program, you can right-click on a single photo and the context-sensitive menu gives you the choice of **Go to Folder in Library**, which selects the folder in the Folders panel, or **Show in Explorer** (Windows) / **Show in Finder** (Mac).

How do I move or copy photos between folders?

Although folders are primarily storage buckets, you may need to move individual photos at times. (Remember, we moved whole folders a little earlier in the chapter on page 112.) It's a simple drag-and-drop.

Select the photos you want to move, then click on the thumbnail of one of the photos (not the surrounding border) and drag it to the new folder location in the Folders panel, before releasing them. **(Figure 8.18)**

If you don't like to drag and drop, you can select the photos, then right-click on your chosen folder in the Folders panel and select *Move Selected Photos to this Folder* to get the same result.

Duplicating photos isn't quite so simple, because Lightroom's designed to use collections and virtual copies, rather than having multiple copies of the same physical file.

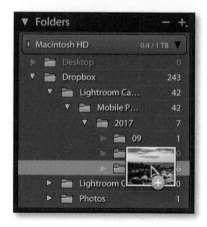

Figure 8.18 *If the original filename is stored in the catalog, you can view it by changing the Metadata panel to EXIF and IPTC view.*

If you only need a copy of the photo to try out some different Develop settings, or you want to apply different metadata, consider virtual copies instead. They don't create an additional copy on the hard drive, but they behave like separate photos within Lightroom. We'll come back to virtual copies in the Develop module chapter on page 317.

If you do need to create a physical copy on the hard drive, use *File menu > Export*, select the *Export Location* to the folder of your choice, check *Add to This Catalog* if you want to edit the duplicate in Lightroom, and select the *Original* file format setting.

How do I reorganize photos into dated folders?

Lightroom only automatically organizes photos (e.g. into dated folders) while importing. Any reorganization after import has to be done manually by creating, moving, renaming and deleting folders and photos, so it's best to get your folder structure right when importing.

1. Create your new dated folder structure in the Folders panel. Month folders inside of year folders is usually plenty—creating day folders inside each month takes a long time with minimal benefit. (You could create these as you need them, if you prefer.) **(Figure 8.19)**

2. Select *All Photographs* in the Catalog panel.

3. At the top of the Grid, select the Metadata Filters (discussed in more detail on page 171).

4. In the *Date* column, click an arrow to open a year and show the months of that year. Highlight a single month of photos, hiding photos/videos shot at other times. **(Figure 8.20)**

5. Select all of the photos in the Grid below and drag them to their month folder. As long as they're not marked as missing, they'll all be moved to the new month folder.

6. Repeat steps 4 and 5 until all of the photos are in the new dated folder structure.

7. There may be many leftover empty folders in the Folders panel—these can now be deleted.

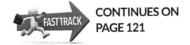

CONTINUES ON PAGE 121

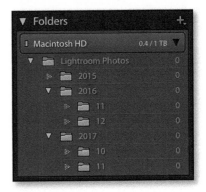

Figure 8.19 *Manually create a dated folder structure. Year/month folders work well.*

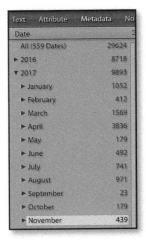

Figure 8.20 *Using the Metadata filters, select a month's photos at a time.*

MANAGING PHOTOS & FOLDERS SHORTCUTS

		Windows	Mac
Folders / Collections	New Folder	Ctrl Shift N	Cmd Shift N
	Expand all subfolders	Alt-click on folder disclosure triangle	Opt-click on folder disclosure triangle
	Show in Explorer/Finder	Ctrl R	Cmd R
Rename	Rename Photo	F2	F2
Delete	Delete Photo	Delete	Delete
	Delete Rejected Photos	Ctrl Delete	Cmd Delete
	Remove Photo from Catalog	Alt Delete	Opt Delete
	Remove and Trash Photo	Ctrl Alt Shift Delete	Cmd Opt Shift Delete

ADDING METADATA TO YOUR PHOTOS

9

Once you've finished selecting your favorite photos, it's time to add metadata to help you find them again later. Sorting through your photos first means you can focus your efforts on the best ones, which are the ones you're likely to want to find again.

First, we'll focus on the Metadata panel, then keywords, tagging people, and finally adding GPS location metadata using the Map module.

What is metadata?

Metadata is often defined as 'data describing data'.

As far as photos are concerned, metadata describes how the photo was taken (camera, shutter speed, aperture, lens, etc.), who took the photo (copyright) and descriptive data about the content of the photo (keywords, caption).

Lightroom also stores all of your Develop edits as metadata, which means that it records your changes as a set of text instructions (i.e. Exposure +0.33, Highlights −30, Shadows +25, etc.) instead of applying them directly to the image data. This means you can edit the photo again later without degrading the image quality.

EXIF data is technical information added

by the camera at the time of capture. It includes camera and lens information such as the make and model, and image information such as the capture date/time, shutter speed, aperture, ISO, and pixel dimensions. Apart from the capture date/time, Lightroom doesn't allow you to edit this EXIF data.

IPTC data is added by the photographer to describe the photo, for example, title, caption, keywords and the photographer's name and copyright. There are official definitions for the IPTC fields, and you can view the full IPTC specification at the IPTC website at http://www.iptc.org/ You can add IPTC data to your photos using Lightroom's Metadata panel.

ADDING METADATA USING THE METADATA PANEL

The Metadata panel, on the right-hand side of the Library module, allows you to view EXIF metadata added by the camera and add your own IPTC metadata.

How do I enter metadata for my photos?

Entering metadata in the Metadata panel is as simple as typing in the text fields. **(Figure 9.1)** For example, some photographers like to add descriptive text to the photos, perhaps for use as captions when posting to Flickr or Facebook, or in a slideshow or book.

The **Title** and **Caption** fields do have official IPTC definitions, but many photographers simply use *Title* for a short image title (e.g., Blue Eyes) and *Caption* for a more descriptive paragraph (e.g., Kanika, the Amur Leopard cub, has piercing blue eyes).

You'll also want to add your copyright information and contact details, if you didn't apply them using a preset while importing.

How do I add or change metadata for multiple photos at once?

Adding repetitive metadata would quickly become boring if you had to type that information into the Metadata panel one photo at a time, but there are a few ways to apply it to multiple photos in one go.

We said earlier that actions apply to all selected photos when in Grid view on the primary window, but usually only the selected photo in all other views. That applies in this case too, so the simplest option is to select multiple photos in Grid view (on the primary window) and type your metadata into the Metadata panel. If

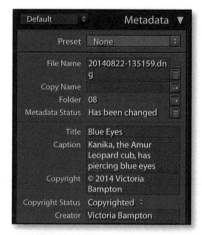

Figure 9.1 *Enter your Title, Caption and Copyright in the Metadata panel.*

it doesn't work, make sure that *Metadata menu > Show Metadata for Target Photo Only* is unchecked.

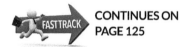

CONTINUES ON PAGE 125

If you prefer to select the photos in the Filmstrip with Compare, Survey or Loupe view on the primary window, or you have Grid on the secondary window, your metadata usually only applies to the active photo (with the lightest gray border). You can override this by enabling *Library menu > Auto Sync*.

When Auto Sync is enabled, your actions apply to all selected photos, so you can type in the Metadata panel and that metadata is applied to all the selected photos. Use it with caution if you work with the Filmstrip hidden, as you may not realize you have multiple photos selected.

There are two separate Auto Sync toggle switches—one under the *Library module > Metadata menu* and one under *Develop module > Settings menu*, and they both appear as switches on the *Sync* buttons at the bottom of the right-hand panel groups when multiple photos are selected. The Library switch applies to most metadata actions—assigning keywords, flags, labels, etc.—regardless of which module you're viewing, whereas the Develop switch only applies to Develop changes made in the Develop module.

Typing directly in the Metadata panel can be slow when working with a large selection of photos, as it updates all of the records each time you move between fields. In these cases, it's quicker to select the photos and press the *Sync Metadata* button (not the *Sync Settings* button) at the bottom of the right panel group. **(Figure 9.2)**

Sync Metadata

Figure 9.2 *The Sync Metadata button, at the bottom of the right panel group in Library module, allows you to copy metadata to all the selected photos.*

In the Synchronize Metadata dialog **(Figure 9.3)**, enter the details for any fields you want to update. Put a checkmark next to these fields or press the *Check Filled* button at the bottom of the dialog, as only checked fields are updated. Press *Synchronize* when you're finished to apply the metadata to all the selected photos.

Replacing existing metadata, perhaps because you've moved house and need to update the address on your photos, works in exactly the same way. To remove metadata from the selected photos, check the checkboxes in the Synchronize Metadata dialog, but don't type any replacement text.

How do I create and edit a Metadata preset?

If you find you're regularly applying the same metadata, you can save it as a Metadata preset. We used a Metadata Preset to add copyright information while importing the photos (page 35), so we'll quickly recap. At the top of the Metadata panel, choose *Edit Presets* from the *Presets* pop-up. **(Figure 9.4)**

The Edit Metadata Presets dialog

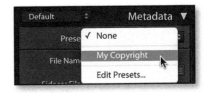

Figure 9.4 *Create a Metadata preset for metadata you add regularly, for example, your copyright information.*

Synchronize Metadata

▼ ☐ **IPTC Copyright**

Copyright	© 2015 Victoria Bampton	☑
Copyright Status	Copyrighted	☑
Rights Usage Terms		☐
Copyright Info URL		☐

▼ ☐ **IPTC Creator**

Creator	Victoria Bampton	☑
Creator Address		☐
Creator City	Southampton	☑
Creator State / Province		☐
Creator Postal Code		☐
Creator Country	UK	☑
Creator Phone	Type to add, leave blank to clear	☑
Creator E-Mail	mail@lightroomqueen.com	☑
Creator Website	http://www.lightroomqueen.com/	☑
Creator Job Title		☐

Check All | Check None | Check Filled | Cancel | **Synchronize**

Figure 9.3 *The Synchronize Metadata and Edit Metadata Preset dialogs are very similar. Only checked fields will be changed.*

automatically fills with the metadata from the selected photo, and then you can edit the information that you want to save in the preset. At the top of the dialog, select *Save Current Settings as New Preset* and name the preset before pressing *Done*. Remember, only checked fields are saved in the preset. Leaving fields blank but checked would clear any existing metadata saved in these fields.

If you've created a Metadata preset and want to update it, select *Edit Presets* to open the Edit Metadata Presets dialog. At the top of the dialog, select the preset you want to change, and then edit the metadata below. Finally, select *Update Preset* from the pop-up menu at the top of the dialog. To rename or delete a preset, select it at the top of the same dialog and then return to the pop-up and select *Rename Preset* or *Delete Preset*.

It's easy to accidentally save keywords in a Metadata preset, and then have these keywords mysteriously appear on all imported photos because you're applying the Metadata preset while importing, so it's usually worth excluding keywords from the preset.

How do I correct the information it's trying to autofill?

When you start typing metadata in the Metadata panel, Lightroom offers suggestions based on your recent entries. Click on a suggestion to accept it, or press the up/down arrow keys to select one of the suggestions and then press Enter to confirm.

To view all the available suggestions for a specific metadata field, click on the field label. That context-sensitive menu also allows you to clear the suggestions for that particular field or all fields.

To turn the Auto Fill feature off altogether, go to *Catalog Settings > Metadata tab* and

uncheck **Offer suggestions from recently entered values**. There's a *Clear All Suggestion Lists* button in the same location.

Where's the rest of my metadata?

Most of the available metadata fields are hidden by the default panel view. Using the pop-up menu on the Metadata panel header, select different metadata presets to view the additional metadata fields. The *Default* preset only shows the most frequently-used fields, whereas *EXIF and IPTC* displays most of the available fields.

To view additional metadata available to Lightroom, or create a custom view preset with information you most often use, try Jeffrey Friedl's Metadata Editor Preset Builder: https://www.Lrq.me/friedl-metadatapresets

How do I change the date format and units of measurement?

The metadata uses units and formats set by the operating system's regional settings. For example, the *Altitude* may display in feet or meters, and dates may display as day/month/year or month/day/year, depending on your locality. To change these settings go to *Control Panel > Region & Language > Additional Settings* (Windows) / *System Preferences > Language & Region > Advanced* (Mac).

What are the symbols at the ends of the fields?

At the end of some metadata fields are action buttons. For example, the button at the end of the filename opens the Rename Photo dialog, the button on the *Capture Time* field filters the photos taken on that date. Float over the button to display the action as a tooltip. **(Figure 9.5)**

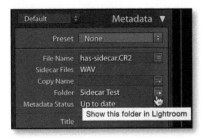

Figure 9.5 *At the end of some metadata fields are buttons. Float the cursor over the button to see what they do.*

Can I add notes to my photos?

Some photographers like to add notes to their photos, perhaps noting additional work that they need to do to the photo. Lightroom doesn't offer a notes field for this purpose, but you can use other metadata fields such as the *Workflow Instructions* field, (under the *EXIF & IPTC* view). These fields expand to fit larger quantities of text, and are included when you write to XMP or export the files.

Alternatively, for temporary notes that you don't want to write back to the files, the Big Note plug-in works as a handy scratch pad. https://www.Lrq.me/beardsworth-bignote

EDITING THE CAPTURE TIME

We've all done it... you go on vacation abroad, or Daylight Savings Time starts, and you forget to change the time stamp on the camera. It's not a problem though, as Lightroom makes it easy to correct the time stamp.

How do I fix the capture time?

1. Find a photo for which you know the correct time and note the time down—we'll call this the 'known time' photo for the

moment.

2. Select all the photos that need the time stamp changed by the same amount, for example, all those shot on the same vacation with the same camera.

3. Click on the thumbnail (not the border) of the 'known time' photo that we identified in step 1, making that photo the active (lightest gray) photo without deselecting the other photos.

4. Go to *Metadata menu > **Edit Capture Time*** to show the Edit Capture Time dialog. If you've selected the photos correctly, the preview photo on the left is your 'known time' photo. **(Figure 9.6)**

5. If you need to change the time by full hours, you can select *Shift by set number of hours* and enter the time difference, but otherwise, choose the first option, *Adjust to a specified date and time*, as this allows you to change by years, months, days, hours, minutes or seconds.

If you've selected the *Adjust to a specified date and time* option, enter the correct time—the time you noted down earlier for the 'known-time' photo. You can select each number (hours, minutes, etc.) individually, and change the value either using the arrows or by typing the time of your choice.

6. Click *Change All* to update all the selected photos.

If you make a mistake, don't panic, the original time stamp is stored in the catalog unless the photo is deleted, and you can return to the original time stamp by selecting the photos and going to *Metadata menu > Revert Capture Time to Original.*

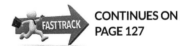

CONTINUES ON PAGE 127

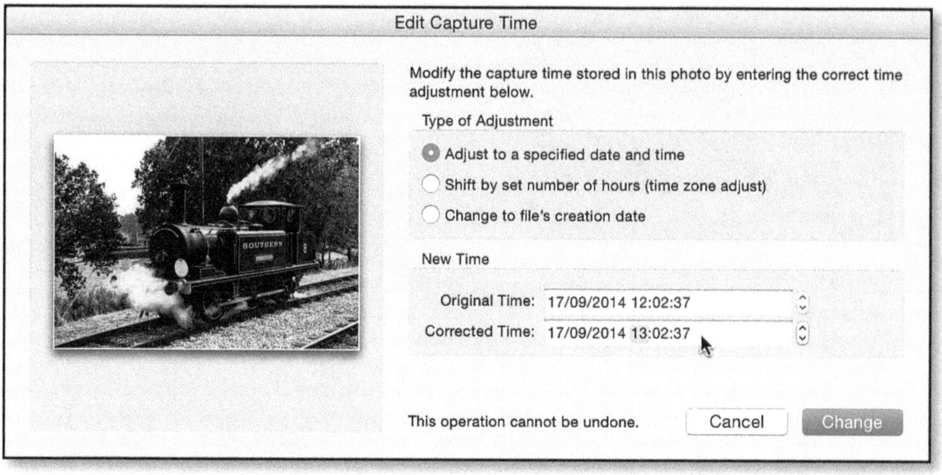

Figure 9.6 *The Edit Capture Time dialog allows you to correct the capture time on a group of photos in one go.*

Which Edit Capture Time option should I use?

There are three different options in the Edit Capture Time dialog:

Adjust to a specified date and time adjusts the active (lightest gray) photo to the time you choose, and adjusts all other photos by the same increment. It doesn't set them all to the same date and time. **(Figure 9.7)** This is the most useful option as you can use it to fix incorrect dates, correct capture times that are out by as little as a few seconds, or make half hour time zone adjustments.

Shift by set number of hours (time zone adjust) adjusts by full hours, which is useful when you've only forgotten to adjust the time zone on vacation.

Change to file creation date for each image sets the capture time to the file creation date. This is only usually used on scans that have no capture date, and even then, the file creation date is rarely the date the film photograph was captured.

	Original Time	New Time
Photo 1	08:57:38	09:57:38
Photo 2	**12:02:37**	**13:02:37**
Photo 3	16:20:46	17:20:46

Figure 9.7 *Capture Times all move incrementally, rather than setting all the photos to the same time.*

How do I sync the times on two or more cameras?

If you're shooting with two cameras, matching the capture times can be even more important, as the *Capture Time* sort order would also be incorrect, muddling up your photos. Of course, synchronizing the time stamps on the cameras before shooting would save you a job, but if you forget, all is not lost.

The principle remains the same as adjusting the time on a single camera, but you need to repeat the process for each camera with the wrong time stamp. It's easiest if you have a fixed point in the day for which you know the correct time and were shooting on all the cameras involved, for example, signing the register at a wedding.

First, separate each camera, so that you're working with one camera's photos at a time. You can do this easily using the Metadata filters, which we'll cover in more detail in the next chapter, starting on page 167. (In short, select *Metadata* from the Filter bar above the grid, select *Camera Model* or *Camera Serial* from the pop-up at the top of a column and then select the model or serial number of the first camera.) Then, using the instructions in the earlier question, change the capture time for these photos. Repeat the process on each additional camera until they all match, then disable the Metadata filter by clicking *None* in the Filter bar.

How do I change timestamps on scanned photos?

Lightroom's Edit Capture Time is designed for digital capture rather than scans, so it won't set all photos to a fixed date and time. John Beardsworth's CaptureTime to Exif plug-in, however, uses Exiftool to add your chosen date to TIFF, PSD, JPEG or DNG files. You can download it from https://www. Lrq.me/beardsworth-capturetimetoexif

KEYWORDS

It's worth spending a little time adding keywords to help you find specific photos again later, without having to scroll through your whole catalog. Keyword tags are text metadata used to describe the content of the photo, and they can be stored in the metadata of the files and understood by a wide range of software, so your efforts are not wasted, even if you later move to other software.

Image recognition software is already able to identify many subjects, reducing the need for keywords. However, it's likely to be some time before software can correctly name your friends and family, or tell the difference between a lesser spotted and great spotted woodpecker, so some keywords are still important.

What kind of keywords should I assign to my photos?

If you've never keyworded photos before, you may be wondering where to start. There are no hard and fast rules for keywording unless you're shooting for Stock Photography. Assuming you're shooting primarily for yourself, the main rule is simple—use keywords that will help you find the photos again later! For example, they can include:

Who is in the photo (people—we'll come back to Face Recognition in the next section starting on page 140)

What is in the photo (other subjects or objects)

Where the photo was taken (names of locations)

Why the photo was taken (what's happening)

When the photo was taken (sunrise/sunset, season, event)

How the photo was taken (HDR, tilt-shift, panoramic)

Before you start applying keywords to photos, think about the kinds of words you would use to search for your photos. Also think about consistency within your keyword list, otherwise you'll spend a lot of time tidying up your keyword list later, for example:

Grouping—as with folders and collections, you can use a hierarchical list of keywords instead of a long flat list. We'll consider the pros and cons shortly.

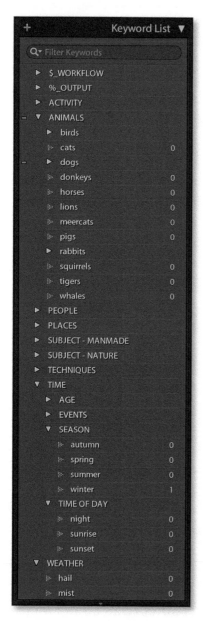

Figure 9.8 *This is a subset of the current keyword list from my personal catalog.*

Capitalization—stick to lower case for everything except names of people and places.

Quantity—either use singular or plural, but avoid mixing them. Either have bird, cat and dog or birds, cats and dogs. Where the plural spelling is different, for example, puppy vs. puppies, you can put the other spelling in the *Synonyms* field.

Verbs—stick to a single form, for example, running, playing, jumping rather than run, jumping, play.

Name formats—consider how you'll handle nicknames or last names for married women. Many use the married name followed by the maiden name (e.g., Mary Married née Maiden), while others choose to put previous names and nicknames in the *Synonyms* field.

Need some ideas? While controlled vocabularies are overkill for most amateur photographers, they can be a great place to get ideas for your own keywords and list structure. **(Figure 9.8)** It's possible to download these lists, covering just about every possible keyword you can imagine, and for Stock Photographers these lists are ideal. Many of the keywords you'll use may not appear on the downloadable lists, as they'll be names of friends, family and local places, but even if you decide to create your own keyword list, you may pick up some good ideas on how to structure your own list.

Should I use a flat or hierarchical keyword list?

On the left, we have a single long flat list of keywords, and on the right, a hierarchy of keywords nested inside other keywords. So which should you choose? **(Figure 9.9)**

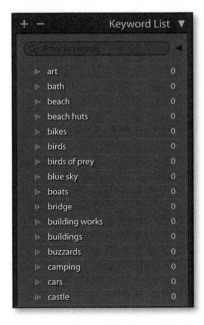 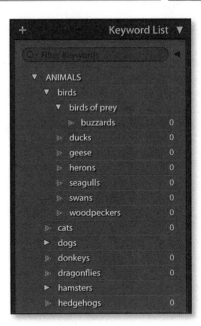

Figure 9.9 *Keyword List showing flat list (left) vs hierarchical list (right).*

There are a number of factors that might influence your decision. They include:

Simplicity—Adding new keywords to a hierarchy requires a little more forethought and logic, whereas adding random keywords to a flat list can be done on-the-fly.

Universally Understood—Flat keywords are understood by most photographic software. If you create a hierarchy in Lightroom, it writes out the keywords as both flat and hierarchical, so if you move to other software, your keywords will still go along for the ride, but probably as a flat list.

Editing in Other Programs—In addition to moving to other software in the future, you can also run into issues with keyword hierarchies when exporting photos to edit in other software and then adding them back into the catalog. If some keywords are set to *Don't Export* (often used for parent keywords like who, what, when), when the photos come back into Lightroom's catalog, their keywords will be listed as new root level keywords.

Scrolling—If you start adding a lot of keywords to your photos, a flat keyword list can become very long very quickly. If you're on Windows, you may even run into a bug/limitation, which prevents the Keyword List showing more than around 1600 keywords at one time. A keyword hierarchy allows you to collapse the list, so you're seeing fewer keywords at any time.

Automatic Entry—One of the major advantages to a hierarchy of keywords is that parent keywords are automatically added to the photos. For example, if I tagged a photo with *my house*, the parent keywords *Southampton, Hampshire, England, UK, Europe* would automatically be added to the photo too. This can save a lot of time.

Time Spent Reorganizing—If you don't start out with a clear idea of how you'll organize your keyword hierarchy, you can spend a lot of time organizing and reorganizing the keywords into a list you like.

Multiple Catalogs—If you use more than one catalog (pros and cons on page 428), and you reorganize a hierarchical keyword list in one catalog, you'll end up with a massive mess and duplicate keywords when you try to merge that back into another catalog. This can even apply to travel catalogs.

Your final decision will probably depend on how many keywords you think you're going to add. If you're shooting for stock photography, a hierarchy is the obvious choice. If you're shooting for your own use, a flat list may be a simpler choice.

There is, of course, a compromise. You could have a very simple hierarchy, with a few parent keywords and all of the other keywords nested directly inside, for example, your parent keywords might be who, what, where, when, why, how. These can also act as a prompt, to remind you to add at least one keyword for each.

If you decide on a hierarchical keyword list, draft your list in a text editor or spreadsheet, or even on a piece of paper. By doing so, you'll save yourself a lot of time rearranging your keyword list later. One more tip... when adding People keywords, don't try to create a family tree. Since most of us have more than one parent, it becomes messy fast!

Having decided how you'll keyword, you can either start by building your keyword list in the Keyword List panel and then apply these keywords to your photos, or you can start keywording the photos and allow your keyword list to build gradually.

How do I add my first keywords?

There are multiple ways to add and delete keywords, so we'll just describe one option using the Keywording panel to get you started and then we'll go into more detail.

1. Select the first photo, perhaps in Loupe view so you can see the contents clearly, and go to the Keywording panel in the right panel group in Library module.

2. Click in the keywords field that says *Click here to add keywords.*

3. Type your keywords, separating them with a comma (,). As you start to reuse keywords, Lightroom suggests existing keywords as you type, which helps to avoid creating additional keywords with different spellings.

4. When you've finished, press the Enter key. Your keywords then appear in the *Keywords* field above. If you make a mistake, click in that field and use the Delete/Backspace key to delete the incorrect keyword.

Don't go overboard, especially to start with. If you try to add 30 keywords to every photo you've ever taken, it can become an overwhelming job, so just start with a few significant keywords on your best photos.

That's the basics, but now let's do a deeper dive into keywording.

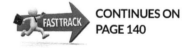

CONTINUES ON PAGE 140

What's the difference between the Keywording panel and the Keyword List panel?

You'll note that there are two panels for keywording photos—the Keywording panel and the Keyword List panel. The Keywording panel focuses on the keywords applied to the selected photos **(Figure 9.10)**, whereas the Keyword List panel focuses on managing the keywords themselves, organizing them and controlling how they're recorded in exported files. **(Figure 9.11)** There's overlap in basic functionality, for example, you can create and apply keywords using either panel.

How do I apply keywords to photos?

We said in the Fast Track that there are multiple ways to apply keywords to photos. The main options are:

Keywording panel—In the Keywording

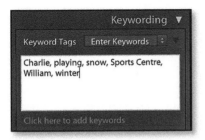

Figure 9.10 *You can add keyword tags to your photos by typing them directly into the Keywording panel.*

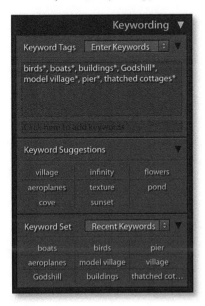

Figure 9.11 *You can type keywords directly into the main keyword field in the Keywording panel, or in the small keyword field below.*

panel, type the keywords directly into the main *Keywords* field, divided by commas (as long as the *Keyword Tags* pop-up above is set to *Enter Keywords*), or into the *Click here to add keywords* field below.

As you start to type, Lightroom offers autofill suggestions from your existing keywords. To select the keyword you want to apply, click on one of these suggestions or use the up/down arrow keys followed by tab, or ignore the suggestion and continue to type.

You can place a new keyword inside a new or existing keyword by separating them with a pipe character (|), for example, *Places|UK|London|Buckingham Palace*, or a greater than character (>) to type them in the opposite order, for example, *Buckingham Palace > London > UK > Places*.

If you're adding a keyword buried deep inside the hierarchy, for example, *pets > cats*, just type *cats*. If *cats* appears in your keyword list more than once, Lightroom displays the options with a less than character (*cats < pets*) so you can select the right one.

Keyword Suggestions—The *Keyword Suggestion* buttons intelligently suggest keywords based on your previous keyword combinations and the keywords already assigned to photos nearby. It's smarter than it looks! Clicking on any of those buttons assigns the selected keyword to the photo.

Keyword Sets—Using the pop-up menu in the *Keyword Sets* section, you can create multiple sets of keywords that you tend to apply to a single shoot. For example, you may have sets containing the names of your family members or kinds of animals that are usually found together. To apply the keywords, you can either click on them or use a keyboard shortcut. Hold down

Alt (Windows) / Opt (Mac) to see which numerical keys are assigned to each word. (That's why there are only 9 keywords in each set.)

Assign an existing keyword in the Keyword List panel—Click the square to the left of the keyword in the Keyword List panel to add a checkmark.

Click and drag to/from the Keyword List panel—Drag the keyword from the Keyword List panel to the photo or drag the photo to the keyword.

Create a new keyword in the Keyword List panel—If the keyword is new, and therefore doesn't appear in the Keyword List, press the + button on the Keyword List panel. Enter the keyword into the Create Keyword Tag dialog and ensure that *Add to selected photos* is checked, then press *Create*. We'll come back to the other options in this dialog a little later.

Painter Tool—Use the Painter tool to spray the keywords onto the photos. (See the next question.)

Keyword Shortcut—To assign a keyword to the keyboard shortcut, right-click on a keyword and choose *Set Keyword Shortcut* then press Shift-K to apply that keyword to selected photos.

Face Recognition—There's also Face Recognition for people keywords, but we'll come back to this in the next section, starting on page 140.

Stock Photography—To add a large number of keywords for stock agencies, try Tim Armes' Keyword Master plug-in from https://www.Lrq.me/armes-keywordmaster

Note that some stock agencies require keywords in a specific order, however

Lightroom always sorts in alphabetical order.

If you need to check how many keywords are applied, hover over the *Keywords* field in *Enter Keywords* view to view the Keyword Count in the tooltip.

How do I use the Painter tool to add metadata such as keywords?

If you like working in Grid view with the mouse (or touchpad, etc.), the Painter tool is a quick way to apply various settings to your photos without having to be too careful about where you click.

The Painter tool **(Figure 9.12)** can be used to assign color labels, ratings, flags, keywords, Metadata presets, settings (Develop presets), rotate photos or add to the Target Collection. It's particularly useful when you have a large number of interspersed photos that need the same settings, for example, a keyword for a particular animal while on safari.

To use it, click the spray can icon in the Grid view Toolbar (press T if you've hidden the Toolbar) to select the Painter tool and pick

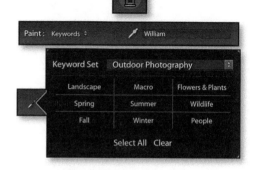

Figure 9.12 *The Painter tool (top) is stored on the Toolbar, and the options appear when the tool is selected (center). Hold down Shift to access the Keyword selector (bottom).*

the setting you want to apply from the pop-up. In this case, you'd select *Keywords* from the pop-up, and enter the keyword(s) in the text field to the right. Multiple keywords can be entered using a comma between each keyword.

Simply click on a thumbnail to apply the setting, or click-and-drag across a series of photos to apply the setting to all the photos the cursor touches.

Any photos that already have that setting applied display a thin white border around the thumbnail, making them easy to spot.

To use the Painter tool to remove a setting, hold down the Alt (Windows) / Opt (Mac) key. The cursor changes to an eraser, then you can click or click-and-drag across the photos to remove the selected setting.

There's also a Painter Tool Keyword Set pop-up. If you hold down the Shift key while the Painter tool is set to Keywords, a pop-up appears under the cursor. You can then click on any of the keywords to add them to the Painter tool (or remove them) without having to type them into the Keyword field. You can even add an entire Keyword Set in one go by clicking on the *Select All* button. It's a well-hidden feature, but it's useful if you regularly use the Painter tool to apply keywords.

How do I edit a keyword?

If you want to edit a keyword, perhaps to correct the spelling, simply right-click on the keyword in the Keyword List panel and select *Edit Keyword Tag*, type the correct name and press *Save*. When you rename a keyword, it's automatically updated on all of the tagged photos too.

How do I delete a keyword from a single photo or all photos?

If you add a keyword to a photo by mistake, you can remove it using either the Keywording or Keyword List panel. With the photo(s) selected, select the keyword in the *Keywords* field in the Keywording panel and press Delete/Backspace to delete the keyword, or remove the checkmark against the keyword in the Keyword List panel.

To delete the keyword from the keyword list as well as the tagged photos, select it and press the - button at the top of the Keyword List panel, or right-click and select *Delete*.

How do I merge keywords?

At some stage, you're sure to end up with duplicate keywords. Perhaps, before you decided on consistent capitalization, you added dog to some photos and Dog to others. Or perhaps you edited photos in another program and the photo came back into your catalog with new flat keywords. Merging them isn't as easy as it should be, but it is possible:

1. In the Keyword List, click the arrow to the right of the "wrong" keyword to show the photos tagged with that keyword. This filters the catalog to show only the photos tagged with the selected keyword.

2. Select all of the resulting photos in the Grid view and drag them onto the "right" keyword, or check the checkbox next to the "right" keyword. This assigns the "right" keyword to the photos.

3. Finally, go back and delete the "wrong" keyword.

Why aren't all of my keywords showing in the Keyword List?

Flat lists of keywords can run into a Windows limitation. There isn't a known limit to the number of keywords you can use, but part of a long flat list may be hidden (or showing but not accessible) in the Keyword List panel. It's possible to work around using the Filter Keywords field at the top of the Keywords panel, but it's far easier to avoid by using a hierarchy instead.

How do I create or change the keyword hierarchy?

By default, new keywords are added as a flat list, but you can change them into a hierarchy. You can have multiple levels of parent/child keywords, for example, your *Animal* keyword may be broken down into *Mammal, Reptile, Fish*, etc., with individual species within the sub-categories. Turn back to page 128 to consider the pros and cons.

As you drag a keyword onto another keyword, that new parent keyword is

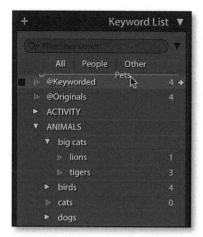

Figure 9.13 *To move a child keyword to root level, perhaps to turn a hierarchy into a flat keyword list, drag it to the top of the keyword list and wait for a line to appear.*

highlighted. **(Figure 9.13)** When you release the mouse, the keyword moves inside the new parent keyword, just as you would drag folders onto other folders to make them into subfolders.

If you want to do the opposite and change a child keyword into a top-level keyword, drag and drop the keyword between existing top-level level keywords instead. **(Figure 9.14)** As you drag, a thin blue line appears. Don't worry about dropping it in the right place in the list, as the Keyword List is automatically set to alpha-numeric sort.

Once your hierarchy is underway, you can place new keywords directly into the parent keyword of your choice. You can right-click on the parent keyword and select *Create Keyword Tag inside [keyword]*.

If you want to add a series of child keywords inside the same parent, select **Put New Keywords Inside this Keyword** from the right-click menu. Any new keywords are then added to that keyword as child keywords, unless you specifically choose otherwise. The keyword is marked with a small dot next to the keyword name to remind you. To

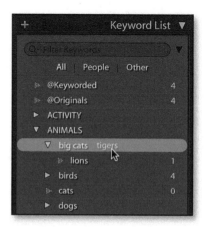

Figure 9.14 *To make an existing keyword into the child of another keyword, drag and drop it onto the new parent.*

remove it again, right-click on the keyword and uncheck *Put New Keywords Inside this Keyword*.

How do I clean up existing keywords?

If you've created a tangle of existing keywords in other software, and want to start from scratch, you can clear them automatically at the time of import. Create a Metadata preset with only the *Keywords* field checked, but leave the field empty. This clears any keywords as you import the photos.

Alternatively, once the photos are imported, select them all and delete the contents of the keyword field in the Keywording panel, and then go to *Metadata menu > Purge Unused Keywords* to remove the empty keywords from your Keyword List panel.

To avoid wasting all of the work you've already done, create a keyword called "To Sort" and drag the existing keywords into it. (We'll come back to creating keyword hierarchies shortly.) Then you can build your new keyword list and drag existing keywords into it or filter the photos using their old keywords and assign a new keyword.

Which options should I select when creating or editing a keyword?

In the Create Keyword Tag dialog **(Figure 9.15)**, there are additional options which create a fair amount of confusion. They are *Synonyms, Include on Export, Export Containing Keywords* and *Export Synonyms*. You can also access these options for existing keywords by right-clicking on the keyword in the Keyword List panel and selecting *Edit Keyword Tag*.

The **Synonyms** field allows you to add other words with a similar meaning. For example, you may add the latin name of a plant, or

nicknames of family members. Don't go overboard—you don't have to copy the whole thesaurus! These synonyms can be searched using Smart Collections and Text Filters without adding them as separate keywords. The **Export Synonyms** checkbox controls whether these synonyms are included in exported photos.

You might not want all of your keywords included with exported photos, particularly if they include private information, or they're just category heading keywords such as 'Places' or 'People.' They can be excluded by unchecking the **Include on Export** checkbox in the Create/Edit Keyword Tag dialogs. There's no indicator on the keyword list to show which keywords won't export, but using uppercase characters (PLACES, PEOPLE, etc.) can to help identify them.

When you assign a keyword to a photo, the parent keywords aren't directly applied, but they can be written to the file when you export the photos. For example, you may

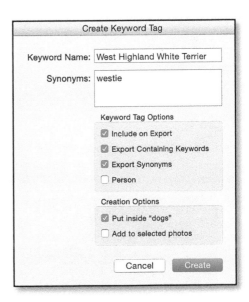

Figure 9.15 *You can enter synonyms in the Create Keyword Tag or Edit Keyword Tag dialogs.*

have a keyword 'dogs' and inside it you have 'Charlie'. The 'dogs' keyword isn't directly applied to the photo, but leaving **Export Containing Keywords** checked will include it at export. For simplicity, I'd suggest leaving it checked for all keywords, and then excluding specific parent keywords (i.e. PLACES) by unchecking the *Include on Export* checkbox on the parent keyword.

The interaction between these checkboxes is not as straight forward as you might hope, so I've illustrated it in the table below with a hierarchy of PLACES > UK > Southampton. I've added synonyms too. Southampton has Soton as a synonym, and UK has United Kingdom and Great Britain as synonyms. On **Figures 9.16 below & 9.18 opposite**, you can see the results of different checkbox combinations.

How do I see which keywords are applied to my photo?

Still confused about which keywords are applied to your photo? At the top of the Keywording panel is the **Keyword Tags** pop-up.

Enter Keywords is the normal view. It only displays keywords that are directly applied to the photo. In our example, it simply says Southampton.

Keywords & Containing Keywords shows the keywords directly applied to the photo and its parent keywords. In our example, it says

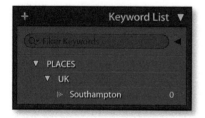

Figure 9.16 *This is the keyword hierarchy shown in **Figure 9.18**.*

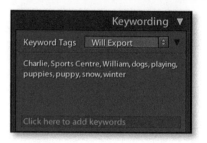

Figure 9.17 *The Keywording panel allows you to view the keywords directly assigned to the photo, the keywords that will be exported including synonyms, or the keywords including their parent keywords, as well as entering new keywords.*

PLACES, UK, Southampton.

Will Export shows all the keywords that will be included in an exported photo. In our example, it displays the results shown in the last column of the table, depending on which checkboxes are checked. **(Figure 9.17)**

If you have multiple photos selected, you may see an asterisk next to some of the keywords in that field. The asterisk indicates that the keyword is applied to some of the selected photos, but not all of them. If you delete the asterisk, the keyword's applied to all of the selected photos.

What do the symbols in the Keyword List panels mean?

There are a number of symbols displayed in the Keyword List to provide additional information. **(Figure 9.19)** They include:

A **check mark** indicates that all the selected photos have that keyword assigned.

An **empty square** indicates that the keyword isn't currently assigned to the selected photos. It only appears when you hover over the keyword.

Keywords (synonyms in brackets)	PLACES			UK (United Kingdom, Great Britain)			Southampton (Soton)			
Checkboxes	Include on Export	Export Containing Keywords	Export Synonyms	Include on Export	Export Containing Keywords	Export Synonyms	Include on Export	Export Containing Keywords	Export Synonyms	Results
Let's start with everything checked.	Yes	N/A	N/A	Yes	Yes	Yes	Yes	Yes	Yes	PLACES, UK, United Kingdom, Great Britain, Southampton, Soton
We don't want the PLACES category header to export, so we uncheck Include on Export for that keyword.	No	N/A	N/A	Yes	Yes	Yes	Yes	Yes	Yes	UK, United Kingdom, Great Britain, Southampton, Soton
The Export Synonyms checkbox controls whether that keyword's synonyms are included, so if you uncheck Export Synonyms for UK, UK's synonyms are excluded.	No	N/A	N/A	Yes	Yes	No	Yes	Yes	Yes	UK, Southampton, Soton
Export Containing Keywords controls whether the parent keywords are exported or not, but it won't override an unchecked Include on Export.	No	N/A	N/A	Yes	N/A	No	Yes	Yes	Yes	Southampton, Soton

The PLACES checkboxes marked N/A have no effect as the PLACES keyword has no parent keywords or synonyms.

This doesn't do anything as *Include on Export* is unchecked for PLACES.

Unchecking *Export Containing Keywords* for Southampton prevents UK and its synonyms from being included.

Figure 9.18 *The interaction between the different Keyword checkboxes.*

A **minus symbol** means that some of the photos you've selected have that keyword assigned, or a child of that keyword. If it's a parent keyword, it can also show that all of your selected photos have some, but not all, of its child keywords assigned.

A **plus sign** to the right of the keyword means that keyword is currently assigned to the Keyword shortcut or Painter tool.

A **dot** to the right of the keyword means that new keywords will be placed inside the selected keyword.

An **arrow** appears to the right of each keyword when you float over the keyword. It's a shortcut to filter the photos tagged with the selected keyword. We'll come back to filtering on page 167.

You'll notice that some of the keywords in the list are all capital letters. I do this to remind myself that *Include on Export* is unchecked, as these are just organizational keywords.

How can I keep certain keywords at the top of the list?

The list of keywords is displayed in standard alpha-numeric order, so adding a symbol to

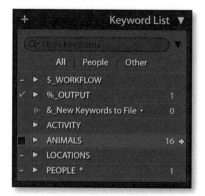

Figure 9.19 *Keyword symbols give additional information about the keyword.*

the beginning of the name, for example, the @ symbol, keeps these specific keywords at the top of the keywords list. It's particularly useful for workflow keywords, for example, I always add an @NotKeyworded keyword to all photos as they're imported, and remove it when I've finished keywording. If I get interrupted while applying keywords, any half-done photos might not show in the Without Keywords smart collection, but still appear in my @NotKeyworded filter.

Can I create my keyword list using a text editor?

Lightroom can import and export keywords from/to a text file. **(Figure 9.20)** This means that you can create your keyword list using a plain text editor or spreadsheet and then import it into Lightroom, but be warned, any formatting mistakes may block the import, and it can be a time-consuming job to figure out what's wrong.

If you want to try it, you'll need to save your list as a Tab Delimited .txt file rather than a Comma Separated .csv file. When creating the text file, only use a tab to show a parent-child hierarchy, and avoid other characters. Square brackets around a keyword unchecks the *Include on Export* checkbox, and curly brackets denote *Synonyms*. Back in Lightroom, go to *Metadata menu > Import Keywords* and navigate to the file. If it won't import, you've probably got some blank lines, extraneous spaces, return feeds, etc., or perhaps a child keyword without a parent.

You can also export the keywords to the text file using *Metadata menu > Export Keywords*. This allows you to view your keywords in a text editor to look for mistakes, and also transfer keyword lists between catalogs. Again, be warned, importing a keyword list from a text file won't remove or edit existing keywords, so you can't use it to tidy up your hierarchy externally.

Is there a quick way of finding a particular keyword in my long list?

If your keyword list becomes lengthy, or keywords are hidden under collapsed parent keywords, it can be difficult to find a

```
[ACTIVITY]
    eating
    jumping
    playing
    running
    sleeping
[ANIMALS]
    birds
        birds of prey
            buzzards
        ducks
        herons
        seagulls
        swans
    cats
    dogs
        {puppy}
        {puppies}
        Barney
        Charlie
        Maddie
        Nellie
        Rosie
        Tilly
        William
    donkeys
    dragonflies
        {dragonfly}
    fish
    goats
    guinea pigs
    hamsters
        Hercules
    horses
    kangaroos
    lions
    meercats
    pigs
    rabbits
        Rosie
        Smudge
        Wilbur
    seals
    squirrels
    tigers
    wallabies
        {wallaby}
    whales
    wildlife (unknown)
```

Figure 9.20 *Keyword Text File*

specific keyword quickly. Fortunately Adobe thought of this too, and there's a **Keywords Filter** at the top of the Keyword List panel, which instantly filters the keyword list to show matching keywords. **(Figure 9.21)** It's useful if you drop a keyword in the wrong place while making it a parent or child keyword, and then can't find it again. If you click on the magnifying glass to the left, you can choose to search *All* keywords, *People* keywords or *Other* keywords. If you select *Show All Keywords Inside Matches*, Lightroom also displays the sub keywords.

If you click the disclosure triangle to the right, Lightroom displays further filtering options to show **All** keywords, **People** keywords or **Other** keywords, but this time without searching for a specific keyword.

Is it possible to display all the photos in a catalog that aren't already keyworded?

If you want to find photos that haven't yet been keyworded, look in the Collections panel. There's a default smart collection called Without Keywords, or you can use a Text filter set to Keywords > Are Empty. **(Figure 9.22)**

We'll come back to filtering and smart collections in the next chapter (page 167). If you don't always complete your keywording in one session, you could also

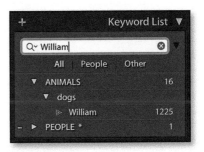

Figure 9.21 *Search for a keyword in the list by clicking in the Search field at the top of the Keyword List panel.*

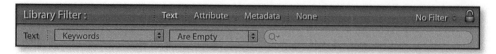

Figure 9.22 *A text search for Keywords Are Empty is a quick way to find all the photos you haven't keyworded yet. Add them to the Quick Collection rather than keywording them in the filtered view, otherwise they'll disappear when you add the first keyword.*

use my @NotKeyworded trick mentioned previously.

FACES

Face Recognition searches your photos for things that look like faces, and displays these faces as a grid, ready for you to identify the people. As you start naming people, Lightroom starts recognizing their facial features and suggesting their names for other faces that look similar, so it's ideal for tagging family and friends.

It gets smarter as you use it. Obviously it's not as smart as you are, and occasionally it identifies trees as people, suggests wrong names **(Figure 9.23)**, and misses incomplete or small faces, but the technology is improving, and even in its current state, it can save many hours of work.

The names are stored as a special type of keyword, so you can search and filter just like normal keywords, but there are a couple of differences. Whereas keywords apply to the whole photo, face recognition tags a specific region of the photo, like Facebook's face tagging. If there are multiple people in a photo, you may remember who's who now, but future generations are sure to appreciate the assistance!

Besides being quicker than keywording, confirming name suggestions can be quite funny, when you see some of the ridiculous suggestions. As the faces are all displayed at a similar size in the grid, it's also much quicker to find a specific expression on someone's face when searching.

So if you photograph family and friends, let's take it for a spin.

How do I face tag people?

1. Select a recent folder or collection containing people you can identify.

2. Open People view using the icon on the Toolbar **(Figure 9.24)** or by pressing the O key (O being round like a face).

3. Lightroom asks for permission to index your catalog. The indexing process scans your photos looking for faces and builds thumbnails to display in the People view. **(Figure 9.25)** Select **Only Find Faces As-Needed** for now, and leave the rest for later. If you select **Start Finding Faces in Entire**

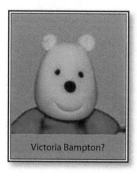

Victoria Bampton?

Figure 9.23 *No, that's definitely not me!*

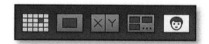

Figure 9.24 *Select the People icon in the Toolbar at the bottom.*

Catalog, it searches the entire catalog in the background.

Depending on the number of photos in the folder or collection, it may take quite some time and slow down your computer while it works. You can start exploring, but it's less frustrating to wait for this indexing stage to complete before you start tagging. You can check its progress in the Activity Center by clicking on the Identity Plate.

4. While you're waiting for the indexing to complete, think about how you'll name people. The names need to be unique, so *First Name Last Name* (e.g. Victoria Bampton) is an obvious choice.

If you've previously created keywords for names, select them in the Keyword List panel, right-click and choose *Convert Keywords to Person Keywords*. This makes the names available for use in the People view. **(Figure 9.26)**

5. Finished indexing? Good!

6. If it's your first time face tagging, click under a face and type the person's name. **(Figure 9.27)** When you add a new name, the person is added to the *Named People* section at the top of the People view.

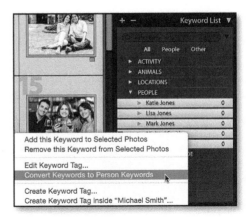

Figure 9.26 *If you previously used keywords to identify people, convert them to person keywords.*

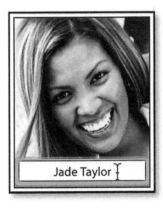

Figure 9.27 *Click below the thumbnail to add the person's name.*

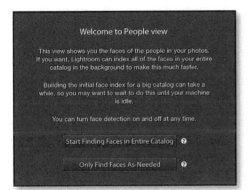

Figure 9.25 *Lightroom asks for permission to index your photos.*

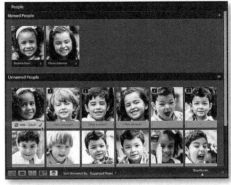

Figure 9.28 *As you add names, they're aded to the Named People section.*

(Figure 9.28) Press the Tab key to move to the next photo, or click under the next face, and type the name of the next person and repeat.

When Lightroom's pretty sure multiple faces are the same person, it stacks them so you can name the entire stack in one go.

7. Try to name one photo of each person who appears regularly in your photos. This gives Lightroom initial information to start suggesting names for the other photos.

8. Once you've given Lightroom a kick start, it's often quicker to switch to confirming Lightroom's guesses.

If Lightroom suggests a correct name, click the checkmark in the corner of the photo to confirm it, or hit Shift-Enter.

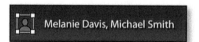

Figure 9.29 Select the Draw Faces tool in the Toolbar.

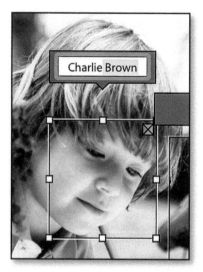

Figure 9.30 Draw around the face and add a name.

If you Ctrl-click (Windows) / Cmd-click (Mac) or Shift-click to select multiple faces, you can confirm them with a single checkmark click. It's quicker than clicking them all individually.

9. Select any photos that aren't people's faces (e.g., trees or animals), or faces that you'll never be able to name (e.g., unknown people in a crowd) and press the Delete key to delete the face region. This doesn't delete the photo itself—just the record of the face region.

10. Clicking the icon to reject a name suggestion just removes the suggestion. If Lightroom suggests an incorrect name or displays a question mark, type the correct name. It's quickest to confirm the most correct guessed names first and then fix the rest.

11. Once the Unnamed People section is empty, check the photos for any faces that Lightroom missed, perhaps because they were incomplete.

Switch to Loupe view and enable the Draw Faces tool in the Toolbar, if it's not already selected. (Figure 9.29)

Start on the first photo and use the right arrow to move through the photos to check for any missed faces.

If you find a face that Lightroom missed, click and drag a square around the face and type the name in the label above. (Figure 9.30)

That's the basics... now let's learn some extra tips and tricks.

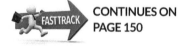

FASTTRACK CONTINUES ON PAGE 150

How do I index my whole catalog?

If you've experimented with face tagging and decided that you're going to use it, it's worth asking Lightroom to index your entire catalog at a time when you don't need to use the computer (e.g., overnight).

There are pros and cons to indexing the whole catalog. The biggest advantage is it saves you waiting for the indexing process each time you switch to People view for a new folder or collection. The downside is it takes a long time if you have a large number of photos and it may slow your computer down while it's indexing. It also takes up a little extra space in your catalog and previews, but it's only about 2 KB metadata per photo, plus a thumbnail of the face.

To start indexing the whole catalog, show the Activity Center by clicking the Identity Plate and click the triangle next to *Face Detection—Paused* label. **(Figure 9.31)** You can also go to *Edit menu* (Windows) / *Lightroom menu* (Mac) > *Catalog Settings > Metadata tab* and check the **Automatically detect faces in all photos** checkbox. (Figure 9.32)

Lightroom uses a couple of tricks to speed up the indexing process. If indexing is enabled for the entire catalog when you import new photos, Lightroom uses the embedded preview in the file (1024px or greater) rather than the full resolution data. For photos already in the catalog, Lightroom

makes use of any existing Smart Previews as these are quicker to load and provide all the information Lightroom needs.

If neither of these shortcuts are available, then Lightroom uses the original files to build the index. This can be a little slower, depending on the size of the originals and the drive speed. If the originals are offline, they're skipped until the photos are next available.

How do I stop indexing?

If you need to quit Lightroom, the indexing just carries on when you next open Lightroom.

If you need to pause the indexing process, perhaps because the computer's running too slowly and you need to do some other work, click the *Face Detection* pause button in the Activity Center to temporarily pause it, and click again to enable it later.

There isn't a way to disable it completely, but if you leave the indexing turned off for the catalog, never open People view and never select the Draw Face tool in Loupe view, Lightroom won't index the photos.

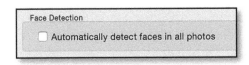

Figure 9.32 *You can also enable/disable indexing in Catalog Settings > Metadata.*

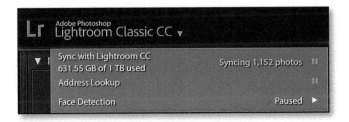

Figure 9.31 *In the Activity Center, you can pause or continue background detection of faces.*

How should I organize my people keywords?

In the Keywording section (page 127), we discussed different organizational methods for keywords, so we'll just summarize the main points to consider for your People keywords.

Unique Names—The names must be unique, even if they fall under different parent keywords in your keyword hierarchy.

Parent Keyword—If you decide to keep all of your People keywords together under a parent keyword (such as *PEOPLE*) right-click on the parent keyword and select **Put New Person Keywords Inside This Keyword** to automatically add new people to the group.

There are some occasions when you might want to leave people keywords in other locations, for example, if you visit a waxworks museum, you might want to nest these people's names under the name of the museum.

Family Hierarchies—You might choose to nest people keywords within a family/surname keyword. This works well for grouping, but you'll still need to use the person's whole name (e.g. *Victoria Bampton* rather than a *Victoria* keyword inside a *Bampton* keyword) as there may be more than one person with the same first name.

Consistency—Like other keywords, keep the formatting consistent. For example, you could use *First Name Last Name* or *Last Name—First Name*. (Note that you can't use a comma to separate *Last Name, First Name* as commas are used to separate keywords.)

Previous Names—Think about how you'll handle maiden names for married women, for example, *First Name Last Name née Maiden Name*.

If you already have keywords for people's names, you can convert them to people keywords. Right-click on the keywords and choose **Convert Keywords to Person Keywords** in the right-click menu. You can convert multiple photos in one go, and it also applies to any child keywords. Be careful, because there isn't a way to batch-convert them back to normal keywords if you select the wrong ones. If you do make a mistake, you must right-click on the keyword, select *Edit Keyword Tag* and uncheck the **Person** checkbox.

This is worth doing at the outset to avoid confusion. For example, if you have a keyword for Victoria (the State) in Australia, and then you type the name Victoria under a face, that Victoria keyword would be converted to a person keyword. That's not much help!

While you're converting the keywords, remember to make sure they're full names and unique, renaming them if necessary. If you have the name Victoria multiple times under different family surname keywords, all of the Victoria faces will end up tagged with the first keyword.

Can I convert existing keywords to People keywords?

Converting existing keywords doesn't automatically name all of the faces in the tagged photos because there may be more than one person in each photo. For example, if you have a photo tagged with John and Mary, Lightroom may automatically find their faces but it doesn't know who's who. All is not lost. This information can still help.

If you click the arrow to the right of the keyword, Lightroom filters the photos to only show the photos tagged with that keyword. When you switch back to People view, the *Unnamed People* section will still contain a number of different people (as the photos likely contain other people too), but the percentage of photos of the selected person will be much higher than the unfiltered view, making it easier to tag them all.

How do I navigate the People view?

The **People** view shows all of the people in the current selected source (e.g. folder, collection, *All Photographs*) and it's split into *Named People* at the top and *Unnamed People* at the bottom. **(Figure 9.33)** When you name a face, it moves from the *Unnamed People* to the *Named People* section.

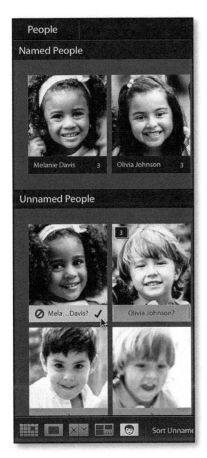

Figure 9.33 *When you confirm a face, it moves to the Named People section.*

In the **Named People** section, the name of the person shows below the thumbnail, and the number to the right shows how photos you have tagged with that name. When you hold down the Alt key (Windows) / Opt key (Mac) and float the cursor from left to right (or right to left) over the person's thumbnail, Lightroom scrubs through all of the thumbnails of that person. Unfortunately you can't select which photo to display for each person, because your chosen photo might not be in the current folder or collection. If you double-click on one of the faces, Lightroom switches to *Person View*, which we'll come back to shortly.

In the **Unnamed People** section at the bottom are all of the photos that haven't been identified yet. The label shows Lightroom's best guess, or if it can't guess the name, it just displays a question mark.

As you scroll through the photos, the dividers move to the top or bottom of the screen. If you click on one of the dividers, it immediately scrolls back to the beginning of the selected section. They also show the number of faces in each section.

Some of the thumbnails may be stacked, shown by a number in the top left corner. **(Figure 9.34)** This means that Lightroom's pretty sure the photos are all the same person.

Clicking on the stack number opens and closes the stack. If the face stack's closed, your actions apply to the entire stack (unlike normal stacks) so confirming or typing a name applies to all of the photos in the stack. When a stack's open, your actions only apply to the selected face.

You can quickly look inside the selected stack by holding down the S key (when the text field is inactive) but it's easier just to go ahead and name the stack and check the

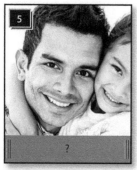

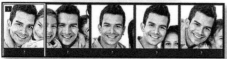

Figure 9.34 *When Lightroom's pretty sure the photos are all the same person, it stacks them.*

individual Person view for mistakes later.

Why are the thumbnails unavailable or too dark?

The thumbnails are based on the unedited file, so some may be too dark or light, but there's no way of fixing this at the moment.

They're automatically built at the same time as the indexing process, however if you quit Lightroom before it's finished, it might not have time to build all of the thumbnails. In this case, they'll build as you scroll through the photos (as long as the originals or smart previews are available).

The **Thumbnails** slider on the Toolbar changes the size of the face thumbnails. This makes it much easier to see who's in the photo.

How do I change the sort order?

Also on the Toolbar you'll see the **Sort Unnamed By** pop-up, which changes the sort order in the *Unnamed People* section.

Suggested Names is the default. It sorts all

of the suggested names into alphabetical order and puts the ones without guesses at the end.

Filmstrip Order puts them faces in the same order as the photos. It's most useful when naming people in photos taken over a long period of time, as the people progressively age!

Stack Size puts all of the stacks at the beginning, with the largest stacks first. This is handy for getting through the bulk of the photos in one go.

Popular Names puts your most frequently photographed people first. This is useful if you're most concerned with tagging close family and friends and you're not too concerned about people you see less frequently.

How do I add a name to a face?

Like keywording, there are multiple ways to assign a name to a face. They include:

Type under Face thumbnail—The obvious choice is typing the name directly under the photo in the *Unnamed People* section. The pop-up offers auto complete suggestions from the available People keywords.

Confirm suggestion—If Lightroom suggests the correct name, you can confirm it by clicking the checkmark or using the keyboard shortcut Shift-Enter. **(Figure 9.35)**

Drag to Named People—If the person already appears in the *Named People* section, you can drag the thumbnail and drop it on the correct person.

Drag to Keyword List—If the person's name already exists as a Person keyword, you can drag the thumbnail to the name in the Keyword List panel. This is easiest if you click the disclosure triangle to the right of the Filter Keywords field and then select *People* to only show the People keywords. **(Figure 9.36)**

Type on label in Loupe view—In Loupe view, with the Draw Face tool enabled, you can click in the name label and type the name.

You can also apply your changes to multiple faces in one go, which speeds the process up considerably. Hold down the Ctrl key (Windows) / Cmd key (Mac) while clicking on multiple faces to select them, then name,

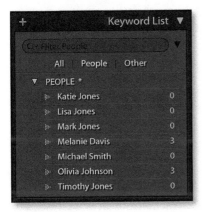

Figure 9.35 *You can reject an incorrect suggestion, but it's quicker just to correct it.*

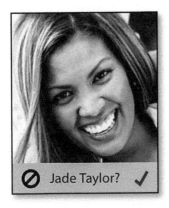

Figure 9.36 *You can filter the Keyword List to only show People keywords.*

confirm, reject or delete the faces all in one go. If the faces you want to select are contiguous (not interrupted), click on the first, hold down the Shift key and click on the last to select them.

I made a spelling mistake—how do I fix it?

If you make a spelling mistake, find the person in the *Named People* section and click on the name to correct it. You can also right-click on the name in the Keyword List panel and select *Edit Keyword Tag*.

Does rejecting a name suggestion take another guess?

If Lightroom suggests an incorrect name, you can press the icon to reject it, but it's quicker just to replace it with the correct name. Rejecting a name doesn't take another guess, and Lightroom doesn't learn from the photos you reject.

What do I do with people I don't recognize?

If you don't recognize the faces, look in Navigator panel in the top left corner to see whole picture or switch to Loupe view. The context can help to prompt your memory.

If there are children in the photos, use the Metadata Filters to face tag a year's photos at a time. Although the Filter Bar is hidden in People view, the photos remain filtered. Siblings often look very similar when they're little, so knowing that little Freddie was 6 months old and Johnny was 3 years old in the selected year can make them much easier to identify.

If you're still not sure who it is, but you expect to be able to find out (perhaps by asking another friend or family member), either leave them in the *Unnamed People* section, or give them a temporary name.

For example, you might call them *Unknown Bampton* or *Victoria Unknown* or even *Unknown Red Jacket Canada*. Using the word Unknown (or something similar) makes it easy to filter to find and name these people later. Be careful to uncheck *Include on Export* in the Edit Keyword Tag dialog for these keywords, as someone marked as *Unknown Big Nose* might be offended!

If don't think you're ever going to name the person, delete the face region by selecting the thumbnail and pressing the Delete key. **(Figure 9.37)** If you change your mind, you can draw it back later using the Draw Face tool, but there isn't a way to ask Lightroom to automatically reindex the photo once the regions have been deleted.

How do I access the photos of a single person?

When you double-click on a face in the *Named People* section (or right-click and select *Find Similar Faces*), it takes you to **Person View** and displays only the photos of the selected person in the **Confirmed** section. **(Figure 9.38)**

If you find a face in the *Confirmed* section that has the wrong name, perhaps because it was hidden in a collapsed stack, float over the face to show the label and type the correct name.

In the **Similar** section below, it displays additional photos that may or may not be the same person. The *Similar* section isn't as strict about suggesting faces, so there are a lot more incorrect guesses, but the best guesses are sorted to the top of the section, ready for confirmation. You can't reject suggestions in this section. It's particularly useful to select multiple thumbnails before clicking the checkmark, as the entire *Similar* section refreshes every time you confirm faces.

To switch back to People view, click on the People icon in the Toolbar or on the *People* link in the top left corner of the preview area. If you double-click on a face in *Person* view (or in the *Unnamed Person* section of the *People* view), Lightroom switches to Loupe view with the Draw Face tool enabled.

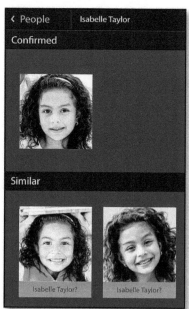

Figure 9.38 *In the Person view, you can see all of the confirmed faces of a single person and other similar faces.*

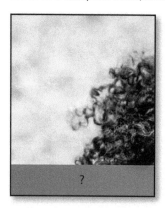

Figure 9.37 *Delete regions that aren't people you want to name.*

Why didn't the indexing find all of the faces?

Once you've cleared all of Lightroom's suggestions, you may want to check through the photos to find any extra faces that it missed. Face-on is relatively easy for Lightroom to find, but if it's the side of someone's head, Lightroom needs to be able to see both eyes to recognize it as a face. The faces also need to be big enough, so in a crowd of thousands, you'll be pleased to know it won't ask you to name every face!

How do I draw missing faces on the photo?

If Lightroom has missed some faces, you can use the Draw Face tool to add a face region to the photo. It's automatically selected when you switch to the Loupe view from a People view, or you can click on the icon in the Loupe view Toolbar to enable it. Simply drag a square around the face to add a face region. If you want to be really tidy, hold down the Shift key while dragging to constrain the bounding box to a square shape. If you draw a rectangle, Lightroom still creates a square thumbnail for the People views. **(Figure 9.39)**

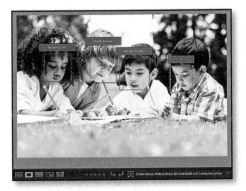

Figure 9.39 *Use the Draw Face tool to add any missing faces.*

Should I draw round the backs of people's heads?

While you're drawing face regions, you may come across photos of the back of a person's head. You could draw a face region around it. Lightroom won't recognize it as a face if it's missing eyes, so you won't harm the face recognition artificial intelligence, but the back of the head would appear in the Person view, which isn't very helpful. Instead, I'd recommend using the standard keyword tools (e.g., add a checkmark in the Keyword List panel or type the name in the Keywording panel) to tag using a standard keyword. You'll still be able to search and filter on the person's keyword to show all of the photos that include them.

How do I name people in Loupe view?

When you're in Loupe view with the Draw Face tool enabled, the face regions and labels show on the photo. Click on the label to enter or change the name. You can also confirm and reject name suggestions by clicking on the checkmark and reject icon that appear when you float over the label, and delete face regions by clicking the black X in the top right corner of the bounding box.

As a general rule, it's more efficient to do the bulk of the naming in the main People view, but the Loupe is useful for mopping up the ones it misses.

Can I add additional information about people, such as their birthday?

To take your People information to the next level, try Jeffrey's People Support plug-in. It allows you to enter the date of birth for each of your tagged people, and even tells you how old they were in a particular photo. https://www.Lrq.me/friedl-people

How do I delete face regions?

To remove all of the face regions from a single photo, open it in Loupe view, right-click on the photo and select *People > Remove All Face Regions*.

To remove all of the face regions from a larger number of photos—perhaps a series of crowd shots where you don't know anyone—select the photos and add them to the Quick Collection. Switch to the Quick Collection and then open People view. All of the faces will be from the photos in the Quick Collection, so you can easily select all of the faces and press the Delete key to remove them.

How do I keep my people keywords private?

When you come to export the photos, the names are included in the keywords and are also copied to the *Person Shown* IPTC field.

If you want the names to remain private, there's a **Remove Person Info** checkbox in the Metadata section of the Export dialog, however this only removes names attached to face regions, not those added as normal keywords.

You can also selectively excludes names by right-clicking on the keyword in the Keyword List panel, choosing *Edit Keyword Tag* and then unchecking *Include on Export*. **(Figure 9.40)**

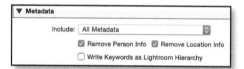

Figure 9.40   *To keep people keywords private when exporting photos, check the Remove Person Info checkbox.*

MAP LOCATIONS

Lightroom's Map module allows you to sort and manage your photos by location. Some photos, for example, those shot on mobile phones, automatically appear on the map as they include GPS (Global Positioning System) data. If you have a GPS device or smart phone app, Lightroom assists you in linking the tracklog with the photos. But you don't need any high-tech equipment to use the Map module, as Lightroom allows you to assign locations by dragging and dropping the photo directly onto the map.

How do I add my photos to the map?

First, we'll add location metadata to some of your photos using the map, and then we'll go into more detail on the other options.

1. Switch to the Map module by selecting *Map* in the Module Picker at the top of the screen, and make sure the Filmstrip is showing at the bottom of the screen. (If it's hidden, click the black bar at the bottom of the screen to unhide it.)

2. Initially the map displays whole world **(Figure 9.41)**, so you'll need to zoom in to the location your photos were shot. The quickest way to zoom in is to hold down the Alt (Windows) / Opt (Mac) key and drag a rectangle on the map, enclosing the area you want to view. **(Figure 9.42)** Once you've zoomed in most of the way, use the slider on the Toolbar to zoom in or out, and click and drag the map to pan around.

3. Using the Filmstrip, select photos shot in the same place and drag them onto the map, releasing them at that location. Lightroom displays a yellow marker where you drop the photos and adds the coordinates to the GPS field in the Metadata panel. If you make

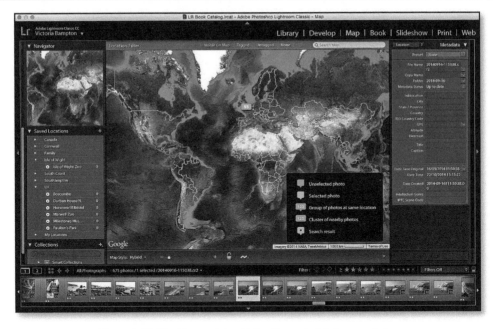

Figure 9.41   *The Map module adds location metadata to your photos.*

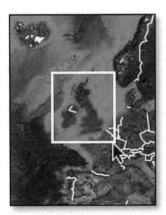

Figure 9.42   *Hold down Alt (Windows) / Opt (Mac) while dragging a rectangle to quickly zoom.*

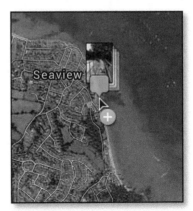

Figure 9.43   *Drag photos from the Filmstrip onto the map.*

a mistake, drag them from the Filmstrip to the correct location. **(Figure 9.43)**

4. At the top of the Map, select *Untagged* to dim the photos you've already tagged and repeat the process until all of the photos are dimmed.

5. To view the photos at a specific location,

click on the light or dark orange marker. The photos displayed are limited to those in current folder/collection.

Why is the map offline?

The Map module requires a current subscription and internet access to be able to view the maps, and Google's terms of service don't allow Adobe to cache this information. If your internet is offline or a firewall is blocking access to Google, it says *We have no imagery here* and then *Map is Offline*. When you reconnect to the internet, the Map module automatically reconnects.

That's the basics, but there's more to learn. Let's start with navigating the map and viewing the photos you've just tagged.

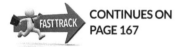

**CONTINUES ON
PAGE 167**

What do the different icons mean?

The color and style of marker depends on how many photos are tagged at a location, and whether they're selected or not. **(Figure 9.44)**

Photos are shown with a dark orange marker if they're not selected.

Selected Photos are shown with a light orange marker.

Groups of photos shot at the same location are shown using dark orange markers with numbers.

Clusters are shown using dark orange markers with no arrow. Cluster are groups of photos taken near to each other but not actually at the same location. The photos merge into clusters as you zoom out, and split into their individual markers again as you zoom in.

Search Results are marked using a light orange marker with a black spot. We'll come back to searching shortly.

When you roll over or select a single tagged photo in the Filmstrip, the marker bounces up and down to help you spot its location on the map, but it doesn't work for groups or clusters.

How do I view the photos attached to each location marker?

When you hover over a marker, a pop-up displays the photos under that pin. **(Figure 9.45)** If it's a group or cluster of photos, click on the left and right arrows or scroll the mouse wheel to scroll through the photos.

When you move away from the marker,

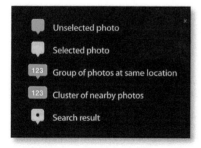

Figure 9.44 The Marker Key explains the meaning of each marker. Close the key by clicking the X in the corner. To bring it back, select View menu > Show Map Key.

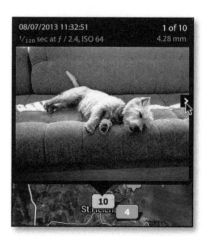

Figure 9.45 When you click on a marker, you can scroll through thumbnails of all the photos taken at that location.

the pop-up is automatically dismissed. If you'd like to fix the pop-up so that it remains on screen, click on the selected marker (a yellow one) or double-click on the unselected marker (an orange one). It then stays on screen until you click elsewhere.

How do I avoid accidentally moving a marker?

If you accidentally move a marker, you also change the location data for the photo, so there's a lock icon on the Toolbar to lock the markers in place. **(Figure 9.46)** Assuming you dropped the photos in the right place initially, you'll likely want to leave the markers locked most of the time.

Figure 9.46 *The Marker Lock prevents you accidentally moving a location marker.*

With the markers locked, you can still add new photos to the map, and also change the location of existing photos by dragging them from the Filmstrip to their correct location.

How do I select the map style?

The maps are powered by Google Maps because they offer detailed mapping of most of the planet. By default, Lightroom displays the *Hybrid* style, which is a combination of the *Road Map* and *Satellite* views, but you can select different map styles using the **Map Style** pop-up on the Toolbar. **(Figure 9.47)**

The maximum zoom depth is dependent on the map style—the *Hybrid*, *Road Map* and *Satellite* views offer more detail than the *Terrain* view. It also varies by location, with big cities showing more detail than less built-up areas. This is dependent on the information available from Google.

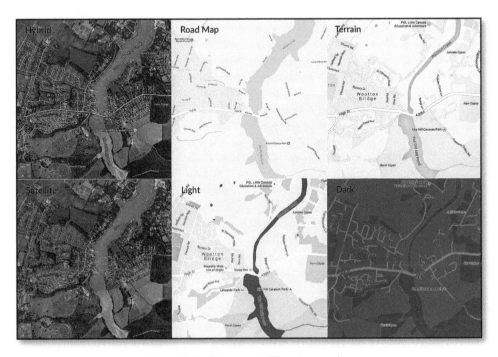

Figure 9.47 *There are six different map styles.*

How do I search for a specific location?

You can zoom in and out and pan around the map until you find the location you're looking for, but it's quicker to search for a specific location. To do so, type the location name or a zip/postal code in the Search Box at the top of the map and hit Enter. **(Figure 9.48)**

If there are multiple locations that meet your search criteria, Lightroom offers a choice if you search for the same term a second time. **(Figure 9.49)** The search results are weighted using your current map view, so if it doesn't offer the location you're expecting, zoom in to the general geographic region and try again. For example, if you are viewing the whole world when searching for *Windsor*, the search results offer a number of places in the United States and Canada. If, however, you zoom into the United

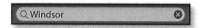

Figure 9.48 *Use the Search box at the top of the map to search for coordinates or place names.*

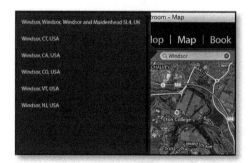

Figure 9.49 *If multiple locations match your search, Lightroom gives you a choice.*

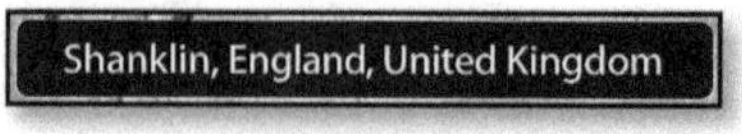

Shanklin, England, United Kingdom

Figure 9.50 *Press the I key to show and hide the Location Name overlay.*

Kingdom, the search results change to show Windsor in the UK first.

How do I show or hide the overlays?

In the top right corner of the Map, you'll see an overlay with the name of the current location or search results. **(Figure 9.50)** Like the Info overlay elsewhere, you can press the I key to show and hide it.

How do I use the Map Filter bar?

To the right of the search box is the Map Filter bar, offering three ways of filtering photos in the Filmstrip based on their location data **(Figure 9.51)**. Like the Filter bar in the Library module, press the \ key to show or hide it.

Visible On Map hides photos in the Filmstrip that aren't tagged with the current map location.

Tagged dims the untagged photos, making it easy to spot the tagged ones.

Untagged dims the tagged photos making it easy to spot the ones who haven't been tagged yet.

None clears the filtering.

You can also use the Library module Metadata Filter bar to filter for photos by location, using the Location, City, State/Province and Country IPTC fields or Saved Locations. **(Figure 9.52)** We'll come back to filtering in the Filtering Photos chapter starting on page 167.

Why use saved locations?

Many of the photos you take are likely at the same locations—perhaps at home, other places close to home, and favorite vacation destinations. You can save these locations for easy access.

Saved locations are like presets for maps, offering a number of benefits:

Shortcuts—They're shortcuts straight to a location, to save you having to search for it.

Photo Count—The count shows how many photos in the current folder or collection are tagged with this location.

Filtering—You can filter to find photos at saved locations using filters and smart collections.

Privacy—If you mark a saved location as private, you can selectively remove the location information when exporting photos, while retaining location information on other exported photos.

How do I create a saved location?

1. Navigate to the location on the map.

2. Click the + button on the Saved Locations panel.

3. In the New Location dialog **(Figure 9.53)**, give the location a name and set the radius in *Kilometers, Meters, Miles* or *Feet*. You can adjust the radius and location once the saved location is created.

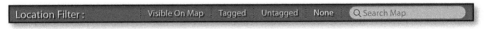

Figure 9.51   *The Map Filter bar allows you to hide photos based on their geocoding status.*

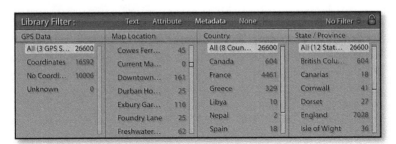

Figure 9.52   *The Metadata Filter columns in the Library module allow you to search the location data.*

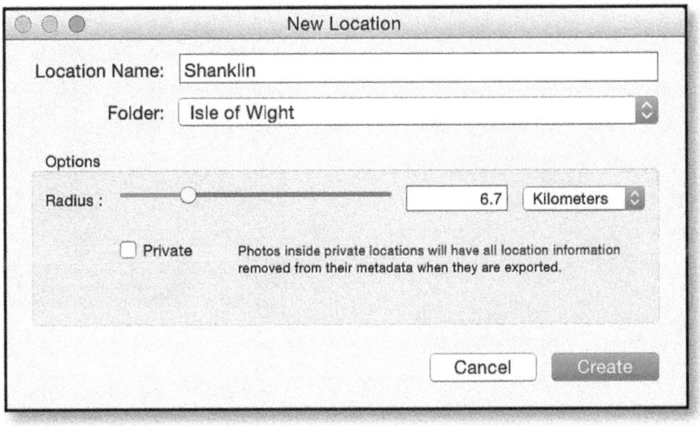

Figure 9.53   *Set the options for a saved location in the New Location dialog.*

4. Decide whether to make the location private. If *Private* is checked, any photos taken within the saved location have their location data automatically stripped on export. For example, you may want to mark the area surrounding your home as private, so that photos uploaded to the web are stripped of your home address.

5. Press *Create* to confirm the saved location.

6. The Saved Location appears on the map as a circle—black if it's private, white if it's not. **(Figure 9.54)** If it doesn't show, make sure your location is selected in the Saved Locations panel and press the O key to toggle the overlay (or go to *View menu > Show Saved Location Overlay*).

7. Move the circle to fine tune the location by dragging the dot in the center. The lock icon also indicates that it's a private location.

8. Change the radius of the saved location by dragging the dot on the outer circle to resize the circle.

To rename the location or change the privacy settings, right-click on the saved location in the Saved Locations panel and

select *Location Options* to access the Edit Location dialog.

To quickly return to a saved location, click the arrow at the end of the saved location name in the Saved Locations panel, or double-click on its name. **(Figure 9.55)** As you explore the map, you'll also notice that the names of saved locations within the current view light up.

You can have saved locations within other saved locations, for example, you may have a saved location which covers a whole country, and another saved location for a specific town or address.

We've already covered the basics of adding metadata using the map, but now let's learn some extra tricks.

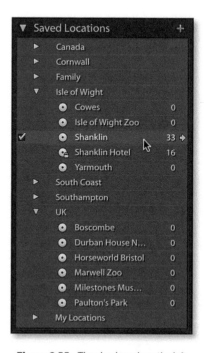

Figure 9.55 *The checkmark on the left shows that the selected photo was taken at the Saved Location, and the arrow on the right will take you to that area.*

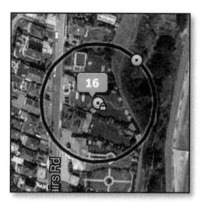

Figure 9.54 *Saved Locations show as circles on the map.*

How do I mark photos on the map?

There are numerous ways to add photos to the map and location metadata to the photo.

Drag onto the map—Simply dragging the photo from the Filmstrip or secondary window and dropping it on the map so a marker appears. This works equally well with multiple selected photos.

Right-click on the map—You can select the photos, right-click on the correct location on the map and select *Add GPS Coordinates to Selected Photos* from the context-sensitive menu.

Drag to/from a Saved Location—Select the photos and drag them onto a location in the Saved Locations panel, or drag the saved location onto the photos in the Filmstrip.

If you have a second screen or a large monitor, use the Grid view on the secondary window and drag the photos onto the map from the grid instead of the Filmstrip. It allows you to see and select more photos.

Check the Saved Location—Select the photos and go to the Saved Locations panel. As you float over the locations in that panel, a checkbox appears for each saved location. Click the checkbox to tag the selected photos with the central point of that saved location.

Manual Entry—Select the photos and type (or copy/paste from another photo) the GPS coordinates in the GPS field in the Metadata panel.

Sync from another photo—Select a group of untagged photos, plus a photo that already has coordinates. Click the thumbnail of the tagged photo to make that the active photo, then press the *Sync Metadata* button at the bottom of the right panel group. Check the

GPS field, leaving the others unchecked, and press *Synchronize* to copy that location to the other photos.

How do I find photos I haven't tagged yet?

If you're working through your entire back catalog and tagging photos with locations, it helps to narrow the photos down to the ones you haven't tagged yet.

The *Untagged* filter at the top of the map is useful, as it helps to identify photos that you haven't geocoded, but it can involve a lot of scrolling as the photos are only dimmed, rather than removed from view.

To hide the tagged photos, switch to the Grid view and select the Metadata Filter bar at the top of the grid. Using a pop-up at the top of a column, select *GPS Data* and then click on *No Coordinates* below. The tagged photos disappear from view. (We'll come back to filtering in more detail on page 167). Switch back to the Map module. As you drag additional photos onto the map, they also disappear from view. It works well as long as you drop them in the right place! If you drop them in the wrong place, press Ctrl-Z (Windows) / Cmd-Z (Mac) to undo and try again.

How do I move a photo or group of photos to a different location?

If you make a mistake when adding location metadata, you can easily move the photos to a new location.

To move photos that you've already added to the map, select them in the Filmstrip and drag them onto a different location, as if you were adding a location for the first time.

If a single marker is in the wrong place, you can also unlock the *Marker Lock* on the Toolbar and drag the single marker to a new location.

You can't drag group markers—it's a Google Maps API limitation. You can, however, click on the group marker to automatically select the photos, and then drag them from the Filmstrip to the new location, which moves the marker automatically.

How do I delete location information?

To completely remove location information from photos in the Map module, select the photos and go to the *Photo menu*, where you'll find two delete options. **Delete GPS Coordinates** removes the GPS data, removes the photo from the map, and removes any unconfirmed IPTC location data that was automatically added using address lookup. **Delete All Location Metadata** does the same, but also removes any IPTC Location data that you've added yourself. If you have multiple photos selected, a dialog checks whether you want to remove the data from all the photos or only the active photo.

How do I create a tracklog?

Once you start geocoding your photos, you may want to use a more automated solution, such as a dedicated GPS device. Some GPS devices attach directly to the camera, tagging the photos themselves at the time of shooting, so the photos automatically appear on the map. Other GPS devices create a tracklog, which is a series of GPS locations and timestamps, showing where you were at a specific time. Lightroom then helps you match the tracklog with the photos, showing where the photos were taken.

If you don't have a dedicated GPS device, but you want to use a tracklog rather than adding locations manually, you can use a smart phone app. For example, *Geotag Photos Pro* is an iPhone and Android app which can create a GPX tracklog. Learn more at their website: https://www.Lrq.me/geotagphotosapp Note that GPS tracking using a smart phone can drain your battery quickly, depending on your logging interval.

Which tracklog formats can Lightroom understand?

Lightroom imports GPX files, which is a standard format for the interchange of GPS data, used by many devices. Many devices, or the desktop applications that come with them, can create GPX files. If your device doesn't offer that facility, you can use GPSBabel (https://www.Lrq.me/gpsbabel) to convert the tracklog to a compatible GPX format. Simply select the correct format for the input file, and GPX XML as the output format.

How do I import my tracklog and match it with the photos?

Having a created a tracklog, upload it onto your computer (your device instructions will tell you how to do that) and switch to the Map module.

9. Click the *Tracklog* button on the Toolbar and select *Load Tracklog.* **(Figure 9.56)** (All of those options are also found under *Map menu > Tracklog.*)

10. Navigate to your tracklog on the hard

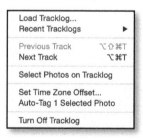

Figure 9.56 *The tracklog menu options are found on the Toolbar.*

drive and click *Choose*.

11. The tracklog is broken up into its individual sections, which are listed in the *Track* pop-up on the Toolbar. **(Figure 9.57)** Select *All Tracks* to see your entire route. The track displays as a blue line on your map. **(Figure 9.58)**

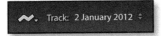

Figure 9.57 *Tracks may have multiple sections, which can be selected from the Track pop-up.*

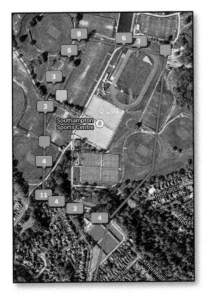

Figure 9.58 *The tracklog shows in Lightroom as a blue line, and the photos can be automatically added based on their timestamps.*

12. Select all the applicable photos in the Filmstrip and click the Tracklog button on the Toolbar, then select *Auto-Tag Photos*. Lightroom checks the photo timestamps against the tracklog timestamps and automatically drop the photos on the map. You may need to apply a timezone offset, which we'll come to shortly.

13. When you're finished, hide the tracks by selecting *Turn Off Tracklog* under the Tracklog button in the Toolbar. To view it again, select *Recent Tracks* from the menu.

How do I apply a timezone offset?

GPX logs, by definition, are time stamped in UTC (Coordinated Universal Time), whereas photos are usually stamped in local time. Rather than changing the photos to match the UTC time, you can apply a timezone offset to the tracklog.

1. Import the tracklog as before, and select the related photos as if you're going to apply the tracklog.

2. Under the *Tracklog* button on the Toolbar, you'll find *Set Time Zone Offset*.

3. Move the slider in the dialog to match the photo times to the tracklog times. **(Figure 9.59)** You don't even need to know what the time difference was, as the times for both the selected photos and tracklog are shown in the dialog, allowing you to match them. The text in the dialog turns

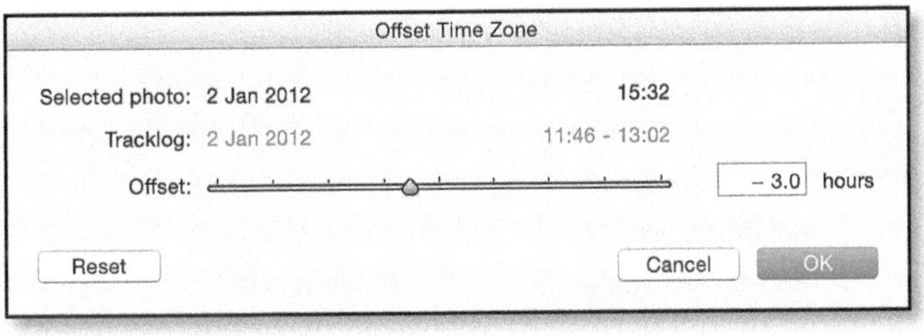

Figure 9.59 *Match photos tagged in local time with a UTC tracklog using the Offset Time Zone dialog.*

black when a likely match is found based on the selected photos, and turns red when the offset is wrong.

4. Press OK to confirm the time offset. You can then auto-tag the photos.

Why won't my tracklog import?

If your tracklog won't import, check that it's a supported file type. Lightroom only currently supports GPX files natively. If you used GPSBabel to convert the file, try reconverting from the original format, double checking your settings. There's a 10 MB tracklog file size limit on Mac, which could prevent the file from importing, but no equivalent limit on Windows. It may be possible to open the tracklog in a text editor and split it into multiple files, or Jeffrey Friedl's Geocoding plug-in can handle larger tracklogs. https://www.Lrq.me/friedl-geocoding

My camera time doesn't quite match the tracklog—how do I fix it?

If the photos don't land on quite the right spot because your camera timestamp was a few minutes off, there are two ways to fix it.

Fix the photo time stamps—Lightroom allows you to correct the camera timestamp using *Edit Capture Time*. Turn back to the Edit the Capture Time section (page 125) to learn more (and don't forget to correct the time on your camera for future shoots).

Shuffle the photos along the track—Lightroom allows you to manually move the photos along the track. Select all the photos you want to adjust, either in the Filmstrip or secondary window. Choose a photo for which you know the correct location, and click on its thumbnail to make it the active photo, shown by the lightest gray thumbnail border. Drag this photo from the Filmstrip to the correct position on the blue track line. Lightroom asks whether to adjust all the photos or just that photo. When you allow it to adjust all the photos, it shifts all the photos along the track using their relative timestamps to calculate their correct locations. **(Figure 9.60)**

What is Address Lookup?

Address lookup, previously called reverse geocoding, is the process of converting your GPS latitude/longitude data—your map location—into a readable address, which is then entered automatically into the IPTC Location fields. For example, if you drop a photo on Adobe's Headquarters, it would be entered as GPS coordinates of 37°19'52" N 121°53'36" W. From these coordinates Lightroom, in conjunction with Google Map's API, works out the San Jose address details.

Should I turn on address lookup in Catalog Settings?

When you import your first photo with GPS coordinates or drag your first photo onto

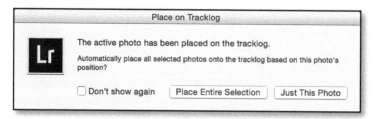

Figure 9.60 *If the timestamps are a few minutes off, you can drop a single photo in the right place on the track and Lightroom will use the relative times to place the other photos.*

the map in a new catalog, Lightroom asks for permission to enable address lookup. **(Figure 9.61)** If you decline, you can later enable it (or disable it) using the ***Look up city, state and country of GPS coordinates to provide address suggestions*** checkbox in *Catalog Settings > Metadata tab*, or by clicking the play button next to *Address Lookup* in the Activity Center. **(Figure 9.62)**

This permission is stored for each catalog individually, so you can have different settings for each catalog, and you can disable it again by going to *Catalog Settings > Metadata tab* and unchecking the *Address Lookup* checkboxes.

With address lookup enabled, Lightroom sends the GPS coordinates to Google, so that they can return the address. Only the coordinates are sent, without any personal information, but you must decide whether you're comfortable with this.

You can pause it at any time, perhaps because your bandwidth is limited or costly, by clicking the pause button in the Activity Center.

Will address lookup overwrite my existing location data?

Lightroom only calculates location data if the Location fields (*Sublocation, City, State/ Province, Country* or *Country Code*) are all empty. If you've already entered data in any of these fields, the address lookup is skipped.

If you want to replace manually entered data with reverse geocoded locations, you'll first need to clear the manual data. It's easiest to do as a batch process.

Select the photos in Grid view and press the *Sync Metadata* button at the bottom of the right panel group. Press *Check None*

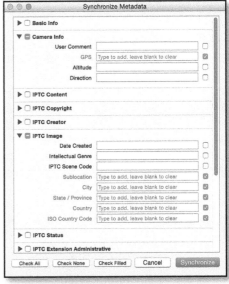

Figure 9.63 *To clear manually entered location metadata, check these fields in the Synchronize Metadata dialog but leave the fields blank.*

Figure 9.61 *As address lookup requires sending the coordinates to Google, Lightroom asks for permission.*

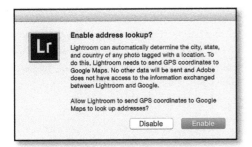

Figure 9.62 *You can disable address lookup in the Catalog Settings dialog.*

and then check the *Sublocation, City, State/ Province, Country* and *ISO Country Code* fields in the IPTC Image section. When you check these fields, the field names go red and the fields say *Type to add, leave blank to clear.* Leave them blank, then press *Synchronize* to remove the data. **(Figure 9.63)**

Why are the Location fields dimmed or italic?

You can view your reverse geocoded location metadata in the Metadata panel. The Location fields are dimmed and italicized to signify that the location metadata was generated using Google's maps, and may or may not be correct. **(Figure 9.64)** It's not permanent, so if you move the map marker to a new location, this data also updates.

Whether this metadata is included in exported photos depends on the status of the **Export address suggestions whenever address fields are empty** checkbox in *Catalog Settings > Metadata tab.* If it's unchecked, only confirmed (white) metadata is included in exported photos. (Note that it only applies to exported files, not writing metadata to XMP in the originals.) Why might you choose not to include Google's guesses? They have been known to be wrong on occasion!

How do I make the lookup data permanent?

If the location metadata is correct, you can commit it by clicking on the field label and then clicking on the menu that appears, or you can edit it manually. **(Figure 9.65)** Once you've done so, the metadata becomes white and no longer updates if you move the photo to a different map location. There isn't a way of committing the location data as a batch process, however.

If it's incorrect, you can type something different in the Location fields. Once you've done so, the metadata becomes white. It's then included when writing to XMP, as if you'd entered it all manually.

Why is address lookup not working?

If you're dropping photos on the map and nothing's appearing in the Metadata panel Location fields, there are a few possibilities to check:

• Go to *Catalog Settings > Metadata tab* and ensure that *Look up city, state and country of GPS coordinates to provide address suggestions* is checked, or click on the Identity Plate to show the Activity Center to check it's not paused. If you've only just turned it on, leave it for a while to catch up or restart Lightroom to trigger the lookups.

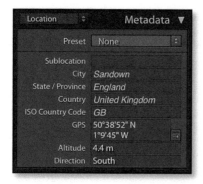

Figure 9.64 *Lightroom shows the reverse geocoded data in the Metadata panel.*

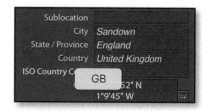

Figure 9.65 *The dark grey geocoded locations can be committed by clicking on the field label and clicking on the location in the pop-up menu.*

• Check that you have internet access and there isn't a firewall preventing Lightroom from accessing Google Maps. If you can navigate around the map in the Map module, that's probably fine.

• Check that you don't already have some user-entered location metadata. If any of the Location fields contain data, the address lookup for that photo is skipped.

• If Google sees the same IP address hit it for more than 100,000 requests per day, it stops sending responses until the next day.

Can I view the location in my web browser?

Alt-clicking (Windows) / Opt-clicking (Mac) on the GPS arrow in the Metadata panel opens Google Maps in your default web browser instead of Lightroom's Map module. Ctrl-Alt-clicking (Windows) / Cmd-Opt-clicking (Mac) goes to Yahoo Maps.

Can I use more advanced geocoding facilities?

If the Map module has whetted your appetite for geocoding, you may be interested in Jeffrey Friedl's Geocoding plug-in, which offers further options and features including altitude, enhancing Lightroom's own facilities. You can download it from https://www.Lrq.me/friedl-geocoding

METADATA SHORTCUTS

		Windows	Mac
Metadata	Copy Metadata	Ctrl Alt Shift C	Cmd Opt Shift C
	Paste Metadata	Ctrl Alt Shift V	Cmd Opt Shift V
	Enable Metadata Auto Sync	Ctrl Alt Shift A	Cmd Opt Shift A
	Save Metadata to File	Ctrl S	Cmd S
	Show Spelling and Grammar	Mac only	Cmd :
	Check Spelling	Mac only	Cmd ;
OS Copy/Paste within text fields	Cut	Ctrl X	Cmd X
	Copy	Ctrl C	Cmd C
	Paste	Ctrl V	Cmd V
Keywording	Go to Add Keywords field	Ctrl K	Cmd K
	Change Keywords	Ctrl Shift K	Cmd Shift K
	Set Keyword Shortcut	Ctrl Alt Shift K	Cmd Opt Shift K
	Toggle Keyword Shortcut	Shift K	Shift K
	Next Keyword Set	Alt 0	Opt 0
	Previous Keyword Set	Alt Shift 0	Opt Shift 0
	Apply Keyword from Set	Alt numberpad for 1 9	Opt numberpad for 1 9
Painter Tool	Enable Painter Tool	Ctrl Alt K	Cmd Opt K
	Show Keyword Painter Sets	Hold down Shift	Hold down Shift
	Add Keyword to Painter Tool	Hold Alt Shift and press 0-9	Hold Opt Shift and press 0-9
Face Recognition	Faces view	O	O
	Confirm Suggestion	Shift Enter	Shift Enter
	With text field inactive...		
	Delete Face Region	Delete (when text field inactive)	Delete (when text field inactive)

		Windows	Mac
	Expand/collapse stack	S	S
	Temporarily expand stack	Hold S	Hold S
	Show thumbnails inside stack	Hold Alt while mousing over stack	Hold Opt while mousing over stack
	Activate the text field	Shift O	Shift O
	With text field active...		
	Select Next Face text field	Tab	Tab
	Select Previous Face text field	Shift-Tab	Shift-Tab
	Confirm and select Next Photo	Enter	Enter
	Delete Name	Delete	Delete
	Cancel editing name	Escape	Escape
Map Module	Previous Photo	Ctrl left arrow	Cmd left arrow
	Next Photo	Ctrl right arrow	Cmd right arrow
	Search...	Ctrl F	Cmd F
	Tracklog - Previous Track	Ctrl Alt Shift T	Cmd Opt Shift T
	Tracklog - Next Track	Ctrl Alt T	Cmd Opt T
	Delete GPS Coordinates	Backspace	Delete
	Delete All Location Metadata	Ctrl Backspace	Cmd Delete
	Show Filter Bar	\	\
	Show Map Info	I	I
	Show Saved Location Overlay	O	O
	Lock Markers	Ctrl K	Cmd K
	Map Style - Hybrid	Ctrl 1	Cmd 1
	Map Style - Road Map	Ctrl 2	Cmd 2
	Map Style - Satellite	Ctrl 3	Cmd 3
	Map Style - Terrain	Ctrl 4	Cmd 4
	Map Style - Light	Ctrl 5	Cmd 5

		Windows	Mac
	Map Style - Dark	Ctrl 6	Cmd 6
	Zoom In	= or +	= or +
	Zoom Out	-	-
	Zoom to Selection	Alt-drag rectangle on map	Opt-drag rectangle on map

FINDING & FILTERING YOUR PHOTOS 10

Being able to add metadata to your photos is great, but the purpose of all this work is to be able to easily locate these photos again at a later date. Using the metadata automatically embedded by the camera, as well as the metadata you've added manually, you can search the database to easily find specific photos.

SORT ORDER

The most basic way of finding your photos is scrolling through the Grid view until you reach the photo you're looking for. If you know the approximate capture date or filename, you can sort the photos into a specific order.

How do I change the sort order?

The **Sort** options are on the Toolbar in Grid view **(Figure 10.1)** or under *View menu > Sort.*

The options are:

Capture Time sorts the photos from oldest to newest.

Added Order sorts the photos according to their import time, with the most recent imports first. It's the default for the *Previous/ Current Import* collection.

Edit Time sorts the photos according to how recently they were edited, including both Develop and metadata edits.

Edit Count sorts the photos according to how frequently you've edited that photo.

Rating groups the photos by their star ratings, with the 5 star photos first.

Pick groups the photos by their flags, with the flagged/picked photos first, then unflagged, then rejected.

Label Text groups the photos alphabetically based on their label text (e.g. Blue, Green, Purple, Red, Yellow)

Label Color groups the photos by their label color (i.e. Red, Yellow, Green, Blue, Purple) regardless of the label text

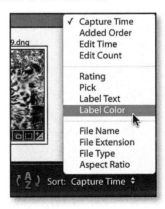

Figure 10.1 *The Sort Order controls are in the Toolbar below the Grid.*

File Name sorts the photos in alpha-numeric order from A to Z.

File Extension groups the photos by their extension (e.g. *.cr2, *.dng, *.jpg, *.nef, *.psd, *.tiff)

File Type groups the photos by their file type (e.g. Digital Negative Lossless, JPEG, PSD, Raw, TIFF, Video)

Aspect Ratio groups the portrait/vertical photos, then the square photos, then the landscape/horizontal photos, and finally the panoramic photos.

User Order allows you to drag and drop photos into a custom order as long as you're viewing a single folder or collection.

You can reverse the sort order using the **A-Z** button.

You can't change the default sort order, but when you change the sort order for a specific folder, that sort order is automatically selected again the next time you view that folder.

How do I drag and drop into a custom sort order?

To drag and drop photos into a custom sort order, or user order, pick up a photo by the thumbnail (not the gray border surrounding

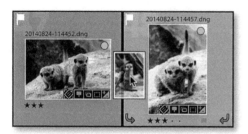

Figure 10.2 *When you drag and drop photos to change the sort order, a black line shows where the photo's going to drop.*

it), and drag it to its new location. As you drag the photo, a black line appears between two photos, showing where the photo will drop. **(Figure 10.2)** The sort order popup automatically changes to *User Order*.

Why can't I select User Order?

User Order isn't available when you're viewing a composite view (a folder with subfolders or a collection set with subcollections) or a smart collection. To solve that, either select a folder with no subfolders, or turn off *Library menu > Show Photos in Subfolders*, so you're only seeing photos directly in the selected folder or collection. If you need a custom sort across multiple folders, group the photos into a collection.

FILTERING YOUR PHOTOS

Scrolling through the photos works well if you only have a small number, but it becomes impractical as your photo library grows. That's where filtering comes in—it hides the photos that don't meet the criteria you choose. For example, you may only want to view the photos with 3 or more stars, or those taken with a specific camera, or even a combination of criteria, such as photos with two specific keywords shot on a particular date.

How do I filter my photos to show photos fitting certain criteria?

To search your whole catalog, switch to the Library module and select *All Photographs* in the Catalog panel on the left. **(Figure 10.3)** Filters apply to the photos or videos in the current source, so you can limit the search by selecting specific folders or collections in the Folders panel or Collections panel.

The Filter bar is a gray bar at the top of the Grid view. If it's missing, press the \ key or go to *View menu > Show Filter Bar*.

There are three types of filter that can be used separately or together: *Text, Attribute* and *Metadata*. **(Figure 10.4)**

Text filters search the metadata of each photo for the text of your choice. For example, you can search *All Photographs* for a filename (e.g. IMG_5493) to find that photo in your catalog.

Attribute filters search by flag status, star rating, color label, master/virtual copy status and file type (photo vs. video). For example, you can search for the videos with 3 or more stars.

The main Attribute filters can also be found on the Filmstrip for easy access. If your Filmstrip Filters are collapsed, click on the

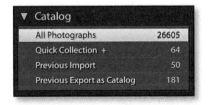

Figure 10.3 *To search the whole catalog, select All Photographs in the Catalog panel.*

word *Filter* to show the full range of options.

Metadata filters allow you to drill down through a series of criteria to find exactly the photos you're looking for, for example, photos taken of William last Thursday at home using a Sony RX100.

None temporarily disables the filters. If you want to clear them completely, select the *Filters Off* preset on the right of the Filter bar. You can save your own filters using that pop-up menu too.

To view the search options for each filter type, click on the filter label in the Filter bar. To open multiple filter types at the same time, hold down Shift while clicking on the filter labels or set the filter options in the first filter before clicking on another.

Let's try some simple filters before going into more detail.

1. Click on the word *Attribute* and then click on the 3rd star, highlighting it. All the 0, 1 and 2 star photos disappear from view, leaving only the 3, 4 or 5 star photos showing.

2. Click on the 3rd star again, and the other photos reappear.

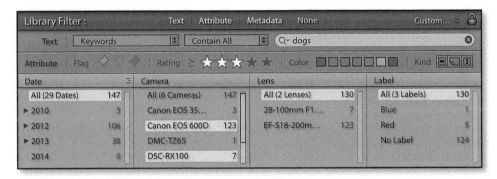

Figure 10.4 *The Text Filters (top), Attribute Filters (center) and Metadata Filters (bottom) can all be combined to drill down through a set of criteria and find the photo you need.*

3. Click on the red square, and only the red labeled photos show.

4. Click the 2nd star, while leaving the red square highlighted. Now the photos with 2 stars or greater and a red label are showing.

5. Click on the word *None* to close to Attribute filters, and then on *Metadata* to open the Metadata filters.

6. In the *Keyword* column, select a keyword of your choice. The other photos disappear from view, leaving only the photos tagged with that keyword.

7. Finally, click on the word *None* to disable the filters, so you're back where you started.

Now let's do a deeper dive to learn more filtering tips and tricks. We'll first look at Attribute filters, as those are most frequently used, then Metadata filters, then Text filters.

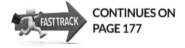

CONTINUES ON PAGE 177

How do I use Attribute filters?

We've already used Attribute filters in this simple example, but there are a couple more tricks to learn.

The options in the Attribute filter bar or on the Filmstrip Filters are toggle switches **(Figure 10.5)**, so they're highlighted when they're selected, and become a light gray when they're deselected.

The flags from left to right are flagged, unflagged and rejected. You can combine those, so to hide the rejected photos, click on the flagged and unflagged icons.

The symbol to the left of the stars allow greater control, so you can filter based on:

≥ rating is greater than or equal to

≤ rating is less than or equal to

= rating is equal to ()

For example, to display only photos with 0 stars, click on the symbol to the left of the stars and select the = icon, and leave the stars themselves deselected.

To show only photos with selected color labels, click on the colored icons, then click on them again to remove the filer. For example, to show the red and yellow labelled photos, click on the red and yellow boxes.

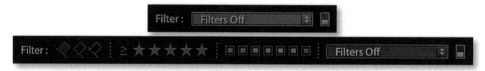

Figure 10.5 *The Attribute Filters on the Filmstrip are collapsed by default (top), but if you click on the word Filter, the other options will appear (bottom).*

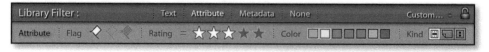

Figure 10.6 *You can combine the various attribute filters, for example, show red and yellow labeled master photos with exactly three stars and a flag.*

There are two additional color labels in the filters. The gray square displays photos that don't have a color label. White displays photos with a custom label, where the label name doesn't match a label color in the current Color Label Set.

The final icons are harder to differentiate, but if you float your cursor over the icons, the tooltip shows the button names. The first button shows all normal Master Photos, the second button filters for Virtual Copies and the final button finds Videos. **(Figure 10.6)**

If you Ctrl-click (Windows) / Cmd-click (Mac) on the flag, color label or star rating on the main Filter bar or on the Filmstrip, the cursor changes to show that you're selecting rather than filtering, and it selects all the photos in the current view with that flag, label or rating without changing the filtering. **(Figure 10.7)**

How do I use the Metadata filters?

We briefly used the Metadata filters in the Fast Track to search for a specific keyword, but the tool is far more powerful than that

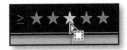

Figure 10.7 *Ctrl/Cmd clicking on the filters selects the photos without filtering.*

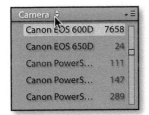

Figure 10.8 *Change the Metadata Filter columns by clicking on the pop-up at the top of the column.*

simple search.

The Metadata Filter bar has 4 columns by default, but you can have up to 8. To add and remove columns, click on the button which appears on the right as you float over the column header.

Using the pop-up at the top of each column, you can control which criteria you want to search. **(Figure 10.8)** By default, they're set to *Date, Camera, Lens* and *Label*, but there's a wide range of options.

Certain columns, such as the date and keyword columns, offer additional options, such as a *Flat* or *Hierarchical* view or *Ascending* or *Descending* sort order. Click on the button at the top right of the column to access these options. **(Figure 10.9)**

If you need a bit more vertical space to see a longer list of metadata, drag the bottom edge of the Filter bar to resize it.

How do I view only the photos with the parent keyword directly applied, without seeing the child keywords?

Let's expand the keyword example we used earlier. Imagine you've temporarily applied the parent keyword *Animals* to a group of photos, and now you want to go back and assign the individual child keywords such as *dogs, cats* or *mice* instead.

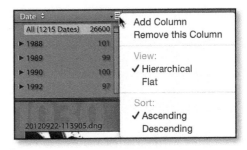

Figure 10.9 *Click on the icon at the top right of the column to view the menu.*

Click the arrow that appears at the right-hand end of the keyword in the Keyword List panel, which is a shortcut to the Metadata filters, or manually select *Animals* in the Keyword column.

By default, the keyword filter is set to **Hierarchical**, so it'll show all of the photos you've already assigned to *dogs*, *cats* and *mice*, as well as the photos you need to work on. That's not much help!

Click the button at the right-hand end of the column header and select the **Flat** view instead. Now the parents keywords are separated from the child keywords, as a long alphabetical list, so you can filter for photos with only the parent keyword *Animals* applied. **(Figure 10.10)**

Can I select multiple options from a single column, creating an OR filter?

But what if you need to find photos that

have either a cat or a dog or a mouse? Then you need an OR filter. To do so, hold down Ctrl (Windows) / Cmd (Mac) while clicking on multiple criteria in the same column. **(Figure 10.11)**

For example, to search for all photos with either a cat, a dog or a mouse, select a single keyword filter column, click on *cats*, then hold down the Ctrl (Windows) / Cmd (Mac) key while clicking on *dogs*, so that they're both selected.

To select a series of keywords, hold down Shift while clicking on the first and last in the series. For example, if your keyword column shows *cats*, *caterpillars*, *chipmunks*, *dogs*, click on *cats* and then shift-click on *dogs* to include *caterpillars* and *chipmunks* in your selection too.

How do I select multiple options within the Metadata filter columns, creating an AND filter?

Perhaps you need to do a complex search, drilling down through the catalog to find photos that match multiple criteria, such as photos with both a cat and a dog, taken at a specific location. That's where multiple columns come into their own.

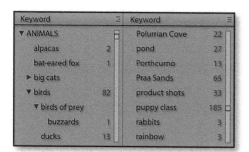

Figure 10.10 *Hierarchical (left) and Flat (right) column view.*

Selecting across multiple columns gives an AND filter, so to search for all photos with both a cat and a dog, select *Keywords* at the top of two filter columns and select *cats* in one column, and *dogs* in the other. **(Figure 10.12)**

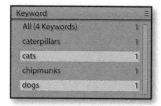

Figure 10.11 *Select multiple criteria in the same column to create an OR filter.*

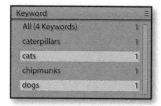

Figure 10.12 *Select criteria in multiple columns to create a complex AND filter.*

When you select *cats* in the first column, the second column updates to show only the keywords that are also assigned to cat photos, so if *dogs* doesn't appear in the second column, you don't have any photos with both keywords applied.

These multi-column AND filters aren't limited to keywords. You can add additional columns of criteria, for example, the *Map Location* option displays all of your Saved Locations. *Date*, *File Type* and *Camera* are other popular options, but there's a wide range to suit most scenarios. **(Figure 10.13)**

Let's try a complex search. We'll search for all the photos shot in 2014 at the Sports Center, using an iPhone, and containing the keyword *Charlie*. **(Figure 10.14)**

1. In the first column, which is set to *Date–Hierarchical*, click on *2014* to highlight it. The photos from other years disappear from the grid below.

2. In the second column, which is set to *Camera*, click on *iPhone*. Photos shot on other cameras also disappear from the grid view.

3. Select *Map Location* in the third column pop-up, and select *Sports Center* below. At this point it only shows photos shot in 2014 at the Sports Centre on an iPhone. Just Charlie left to find!

4. Select *Keyword* from the fourth column pop-up, and then select *Charlie* from the list below.

How do I use Text Filters?

There are certain types of metadata that you can't search using the Metadata filters, for example, the filename or the caption. The Text filter option allows you to search based on the text contents of these fields.

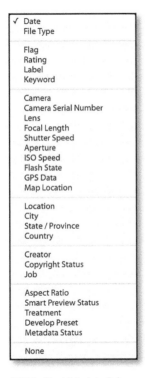

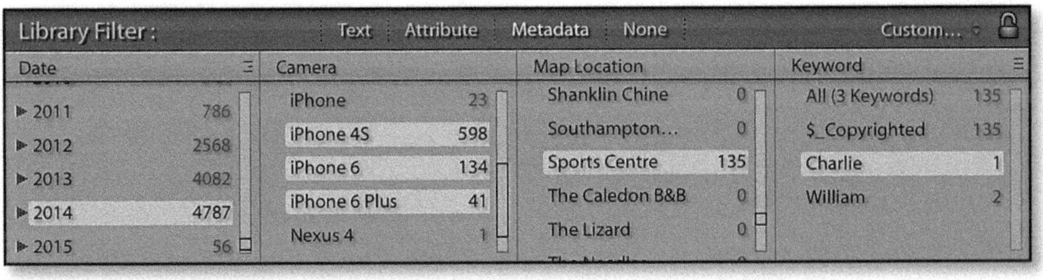

Figure 10.13 *The Metadata Column pop-up offers a wide range of searchable criteria.*

Figure 10.14 *Multiple types of criteria can be combined to narrow the photos down further.*

The first pop-up determines which metadata fields are searched. You can leave it set to *All Searchable Field*, or narrow it down to *Filename, Copy Name, Title, Caption, Keywords, Searchable Metadata, Searchable IPTC, Searchable EXIF* or *Any Searchable Plug-in Field*.

The next pop-up determines whether it has be an exact or partial match, and of course the text field contains the text you're looking for.

How can I use the Text filters to do AND or OR filters?

By default, the second pop-up **(Figure 10.15)** is set to *Contains All*, which means that only photos matching all the words (or part words) you type are included, but there are a few other options:

Contains runs an OR filter, such as photos with either *dogs* or *cats* keywords, including partial matches such as *hotdogs* or *tomcats*.

Contains All runs an AND filter, such as photos with both *dogs* and *cats* keywords, including partial matches such as *hotdogs* and *tomcats*.

Contains Words runs an AND filter, such as photos with both *dogs* and *cats* keywords, but only including whole matching words.

Doesn't Contain runs a NOT filter, such as photos without the keyword *dogs* or partial matches such as *hotdogs*.

Starts With runs an OR filter with photos starting with your chosen letters, for example, *dogs* would show photos with *dogs* or *dogsledding*, but not *hotdogs*.

Ends With runs an OR filter with photos ending with your chosen letters, for example, *dogs* would show photos with *dogs* or *hotdogs*, but not *dogsledding*.

To combine search types, you can add some special characters. A space is *AND*, ! is *NOT*, a leading + means *Starts With*, and a trailing + means *Ends With*. They only affect the adjacent word, so you can use *dogs !cats !mice* to find images with dogs but not cats or mice. **(Figure 10.16)**

Quotation marks don't work, so you can't search for "John Jack" to exclude photos of another man called "Jack John."

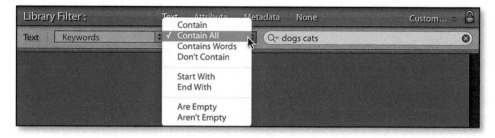

Figure 10.15 *The pop-up in the Text Filters controls whether it runs an AND, OR or NOT filter.*

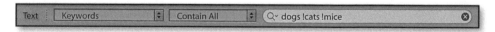

Figure 10.16 *Special characters can be used to create complex Text Filters.*

How do I search for a specific filename?

Let's try an example: you know the filename (e.g. IMG_2938.dng) but you don't know where the photo's stored.

1. Select *All Photographs* in the Catalog panel to search the whole catalog.

2. Select *Any Searchable Field* or *Filename* options in the pop-up menu.

3. Leave the next pop-up on *Contains All* to include partial matches, or *Contains Words* to match the entire filename.

4. Type the filename into the text field and press Enter to leave the field. If you've selected *Contains All*, you can just enter part of the filename (e.g. 2938) but if you've selected *Contains Words*, you'll need the entire filename including the extension (e.g. IMG_2938.dng). **(Figure 10.17)**

If you want to search for a series of filenames, enter them all into the search field with spaces or commas between the filenames, and change *Contains All* to *Contains*.

For longer lists of filenames—perhaps an order from a client, Tim Armes' LR/Transporter plug-in (https://www.Lrq.me/armes-lrtransporter) reads a text file and marks the related photos in your catalog automatically.

Can I combine Text filters, Attribute filters, and Metadata filters?

As with most tasks in Lightroom, there are multiple ways of combining features, and the filters are no exception. For example, if you want to find all the photos with the word 'dogs' somewhere in the metadata, with a red color label, shot in 2014, on a Canon 600D, with 18-200mm lens, and rated above 3 stars, you could combine all 3 filter types. **(Figure 10.18)**

To open multiple filter bars, simply enter your criteria in one filter before clicking on the next filter name. If you want to open all of the empty filters in one go, hold the Shift key while clicking on the filter names.

The criteria filters down in order, from top to bottom and from left to right, and it can be narrowed down further by first selecting a specific folder or collection view.

More complex filtering is available via smart

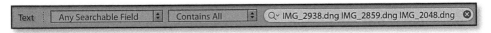

Figure 10.17 *Text Filters allow you to choose which metadata fields to search.*

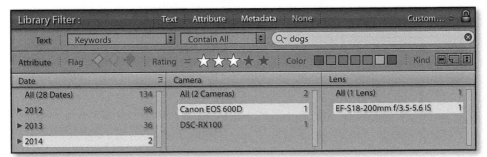

Figure 10.18 *Combining multiple filters allows you to drill down to specific photos.*

collections, which we'll cover in the next section, starting on page 177.

If you need even more complex search criteria, there are a few plug-ins that delve even deeper:

Lightroom Statistics
https://www.Lrq.me/lrstats

Jeffrey Friedl's Data Explorer
https://www.Lrq.me/friedl-dataexplorer

Jeffrey Friedl's Extended Search
https://www.Lrq.me/friedl-extendedsearch

John Ellis' Any Filter
https://www.Lrq.me/ellis-anyfilter

How do I lock filters, so they don't disappear when I switch to another folder?

When you switch to another folder or collection, any filters are automatically disabled.

In most cases, that's useful behavior, but there may be occasions when you want your filter to remain enabled, for example, browsing all of the 5 star photos across different folders.

To the right of the Filter bar is a small **Filter Lock** icon. **(Figure 10.19)** By default, it's unlocked but if you click to lock it, the current filter remains enabled as you browse different folders or collections.

If the Filter Lock remains unlocked, you can

enable the previous filter by pressing Ctrl-L (Windows) / Cmd-L (Mac), or using the switch at the end of the Filmstrip Filters.

This only turns back on the last filter that you used, not the last filter used on that specific folder. If you prefer to remember the filter settings used on each individual folder/collection, rather than a single global filter, go to *File menu > Library Filters* and select *Lock Filters*, and then return to that same menu and select **Remember Each Source's Filters Separately**.

Can I save the filters I use regularly as presets?

The pop-up on the right of the Filter bar holds filter presets with different combinations of criteria. The same pop-up appears in the Quick Filters on the Filmstrip, which makes your presets accessible from any module.

There are a few presets built in, but you can also save your own frequently used filters for easy access. Select your filter options and then select *Save Current Settings as New Preset* from the preset pop-up. **(Figure 10.20)**

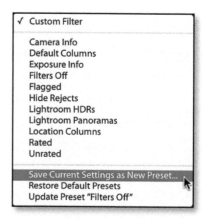

Figure 10.19 *The Filter Lock keeps the filter enabled when you switch folders. The pop-up contains Filter Presets.*

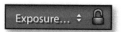

Figure 10.20 *Select your filter criteria and then select Save Current Settings as New Preset to save them for quick access in future.*

USING SMART COLLECTIONS

As well as filter presets, you can use Smart Collections to save filter criteria. They're like saved searches, smart folders or rules in other programs, and they live in the Collections panel. **(Figure 10.21)**

Unlike standard collections (page 100), where you manually add or remove photos from the collection, smart collections update themselves without any user-intervention

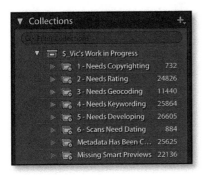

Figure 10.21 *Smart Collections are stored in the Collections panel.*

Photos automatically appear in the Smart Collection when they meet the criteria you choose, and they disappear again when they stop meeting that criteria. For example, you can create a Smart Collection to show your 3+ star photos, so you can quickly view your best work without having to go to *All Photographs* and set up a filter. Smart Collections automatically search your entire catalog unless you specify a folder or collection as part of the criteria.

Smart Collections also allow you to do more extensive filtering than the Filter bar, as some criteria is only available for Smart Collections.

Let's try a simple example.

1. Press the + button on the Collections panel and select **Create Smart Collection**.

2. Enter a name for your Smart Collection at the top of the dialog.

3. Enter one or more rows, selecting the metadata type in the pop-up and the criteria

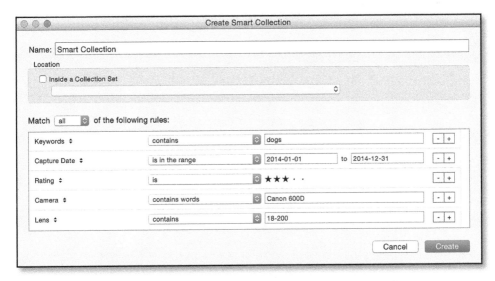

Figure 10.22 *Smart Collections are like Saved Searches, automatically updating as photos meet, or stop meeting, the criteria you choose.*

to the right. The + button at the end of the row creates an additional row. Our earlier example of photos with the keyword 'dog', shot in 2014, on a Canon 600D, with 18-200mm lens, and rated above 3 stars, is shown in **Figure 10.22**.

4. Press *Create* to finalize your Smart Collection. Your new Smart Collection appears in the Collections panel and you can click to view it again at any time, or double-click to edit the criteria.

Smart Collections are far more powerful than they look at first glance though, so let's learn some power-user tricks...

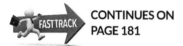

CONTINUES ON PAGE 181

How do I create complex smart collections?

There are additional conditions you can apply to your smart collections to make them even smarter.

Above the rows of search criteria, you can choose whether to include photos that *Match All* of the criteria (AND query), *Any* of the criteria (OR query) or *None* of the

criteria (NOT query).

If you hold down Alt (Windows) / Opt (Mac) while clicking on the + button at the end of a row, you can fine tune your criteria further with conditional rules, which show as indented rows. Each of those conditional rules has its own *All/Any/None* pop-up, so the combinations are endless.

Smart collections, particularly with conditional rules, are ideal for workflow collections. For example, I have an 'Unfinished' smart collection **(Figure 10.23)**, in case I don't get to finish adding metadata when selecting my favorite photos. It contains any photos that are either rated, labelled or flagged, but are either missing keywords or are missing my copyright information.

As an excellent example of the workflow benefits of Smart Collections, download John Beardworth's complete set of workflow smart collections from https://www.Lrq.me/beardsworth-workflowsc

How do I duplicate a smart collection?

If you're creating a set of smart collections with similar criteria, for example, 5 star photos taken in 2012 and tagged with

Match all ◆ of the following rules:				
Any of the following are true ◆				− +
Rating ◆	is greater than or equal to ◆	★ · · · ·		− +
Pick Flag ◆	is not ◆	flagged ◆		− +
Any of the following are true ◆				− +
Keywords ◆	are empty ◆			− +
Copyright Status ◆	is not ◆	copyrighted ◆		− +
Creator ◆	is not ◆	Victoria Bampton		− +

Figure 10.23 Criteria can be nested to create complex searches.

names of family members, you may want to set up the first person's smart collection, duplicate it and edit the duplicates. To do so, hold down the Ctrl key (Windows) / Opt key (Mac) and drag the smart collection to a new location in the Collections panel. You can either drag onto a collection set, in which case a + icon appears, or you can drag between existing root-level collections, so that a line appears.

How do I transfer smart collection criteria between catalogs?

Smart collections, like other collections, are stored within the catalog, so if you want to use them in other catalogs, you need to create them in each catalog. If they use complicated criteria, that could take a while. Instead, right-click on the smart collection and select *Export Smart Collection Settings* to export them to individual template files.

If you have many smart collections, even importing and exporting them individually can take a long time. The quickest solution is to select a single photo, go to *File menu > Export as Catalog* to create a catalog of the single photo, switch to the target catalog, go to *File menu > Import from Another Catalog* to pull that tiny catalog into your open catalog. All of your smart collections are automatically imported at the same time, and then you can remove the temporary photo. We'll go into importing and exporting catalogs in more detail in the Multi-Catalog chapter starting on page 419.

FILTERING SHORTCUTS

		Windows	Mac
Filtering	Enable/Disable Filters	Ctrl L	Cmd L
	Show Filter Bar	\	\
Text Filters	Select Text Filter	Ctrl F	Cmd F
	Starts with	+ at beginning of word	+ at beginning of word
	Ends with	+ at end of word	+ at end of word
	Doesn't Contain	! at beginning of word	! at beginning of word
Smart Collections	Add nested smart collection line	Alt-click on + button	Opt-click on + button

DEVELOP
BASIC EDITING

11

Most photographers choose Lightroom for its industry-standard photo editing tools. Most of your image adjustments will be performed using the Basic panel on the right side of the Develop module. Just because there are a lot of sliders in the Develop module doesn't mean you have to adjust every single one!

Lightroom's editing tools are non-destructive. This means you can move the sliders as many times as you like. It doesn't degrade the image quality because the adjustments are saved as text instructions and only applied to the on-screen preview until you export the finished photo.

First, we'll consider basic tutorials to help you get started, then we'll investigate the Basic panel in more detail. **(Figure 11.1)** In the following chapters, we'll explore selective or local edits, more advanced adjustments and finally Develop module tools that make your life easier.

ANALYZE THE PHOTO

Before we start randomly moving sliders, take a few moments to analyze the photo. What are your first impressions of your photo? We're going to consider three main factors:

1. The brightness of the photo overall as well as in specific tonal ranges, such as the highlights or shadows.

2. The dynamic range and contrast of the photo.

3. The color of the photo.

How's the exposure?

In the real world, our eyes don't care whether something is light or dark, as they automatically adjust to see detail in both

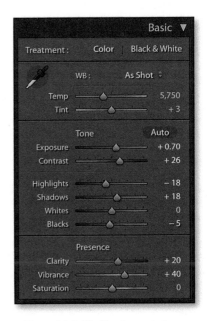

Figure 11.1 *You'll make most of your image adjustments using the Basic panel in the Develop module.*

the highlights and shadows, even in high contrast situations such as midday sun.

A photo (and especially a print) is unable to hold that wide a range of tones while still looking natural. Something has to give. Editing photos is a balancing act, determining which tones are most important and where you're willing to sacrifice detail.

There is no such thing as "correct" exposure, but the human visual system (the combination of our eyes and brain) expects to see an image in a specific way. If your photo looks too light or too dark to you, it probably is too light or too dark.

Our eyes are most comfortable when the main focus of interest is in the midtones, so the aim of your adjustments is usually to move the most important tones toward the midtones. For example, you may need to darken the clouds or lighten the shadows to move these tones toward the midtones. **(Figures 11.2 & 11.3)**

How's the dynamic range?

The difference between the brightest and darkest tones in the photo is called the dynamic range. The histogram is the easiest way to determine the range of tones.

AHistogram is a bar graph showing the distribution of tonal values. You'll find the Histogram panel in the top right corner of the Library and Develop modules. If you can't see it, go to *Window menu > Panels > Histogram.*

The brightness of each pixel is measured from 0% (black) to 100% (white). Along the X axis, the histogram runs from the blackest shadow on the left to the brightest highlight on the right. Each vertical bar shows the number of pixels with that specific tonal value. **(Figure 11.4)**

A color photo is made up of three channels— red, green and blue—so the histogram has a series for each channel (all overlapping each other) as well as a white series showing the overall luminance (or brightness).

Analyzing the histogram is just an information-gathering exercise. There's no such thing as a 'correct' histogram, so don't get too hung up on it. We're trying to make

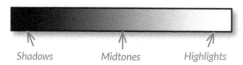

Shadows   Midtones   Highlights

Figure 11.2 *Our eyes are most sensitive in the midtones.*

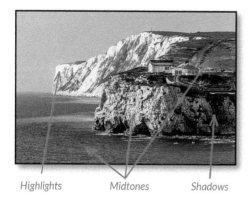

Highlights   Midtones   Shadows

Figure 11.3 *Note which areas of the photo are considered highlights, midtones and shadows.*

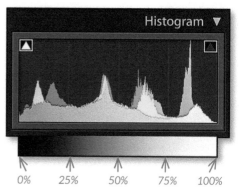

0%   25%   50%   75%   100%

Figure 11.4 *The histogram shows the number of pixels with each brightness value.*

great photos, not great histograms! The aim is to identify whether the photo has a high dynamic range (spikes at the ends), a low dynamic range (no true white or black) or a full dynamic range (reaches the ends without clipping). In most cases, you'll want to stretch or compress the data to fill the entire tonal range without significant clipping.

Low Dynamic Range—A histogram stuck in the middle of the range, without reaching the ends is a narrow or low dynamic range. In most cases, these photos benefit from stretching to create real white and black points because they lack contrast. **(Figures 11.5 & 11.6)** However some photos, such as those shot in thick fog, may not have any true white or black details, so you wouldn't expect these to reach the ends.

High Dynamic Range—The histogram of a scene that has a much wider dynamic range than the camera could capture shows spikes at both ends. **(Figures 11.7 & 11.8)** These are pixels that are currently clipped to pure white or pure black, but if it's a raw file, there may be detail that can be recovered with careful editing.

Clipping—If the last pixel on the left or the right of the histogram spikes, it means that some of pixels in your photo are solid white or black without any detail. These are called clipped highlights or shadows, or you may hear them referred to as blown highlights and blocked shadows.

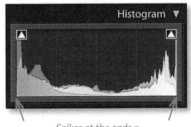

*Spikes at the ends =
dynamic range too wide*

Figure 11.7 *The histogram of a photo with a high dynamic range may spike at the ends.*

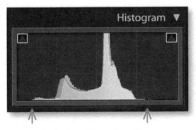

*Data doesn't reach ends
= low dynamic range*

Figure 11.5 *A histogram of a photo with a low dynamic range doesn't stretch to the ends.*

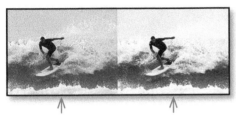

*Low dynamic range   Stretched to full
                          dynamic range*

Figure 11.6 *A photo with low dynamic range lacks contrast (left), but the tones can be stretched to give a true white and black (right).*

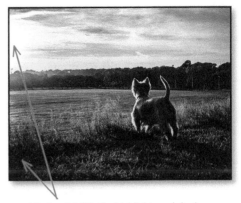

Missing detail in the highlights and shadows

Figure 11.8 *A photo with too a high dynamic range loses detail in the brightest highlights and darkest shadows.*

Clipping on skin looks unnatural and is worth avoiding at all costs. (**Figure 11.9**)

Clipping isn't always bad though, as long as there's a smooth transition to image detail and you haven't lost important detail.

In some areas of the photo, such as bright spots on shiny objects, clipping is expected. Small areas of clipping on a light source, (such as a light bulb or the sun) can also look fine, but ideally you don't want large clipped areas, such as a window with no detail.

Some studio or product photographers like to clip their backgrounds to pure white or black. Intentionally blocking the shadows to gain contrast elsewhere can be a creative choice.

To check whether the clipped pixels are in areas of important image detail, hold down the Alt key (Windows) / Opt key (Mac) while dragging the *Exposure*, *Highlights*, *Shadows*, *Whites* or *Blacks* sliders to view the clipping warnings. You can also show/hide the clipping warnings by clicking the triangles in the corners of the histogram or by pressing the J key. (**Figure 11.10**)

How's the color?

A color cast is an unwanted tint in the image, often caused by an incorrect White Balance setting. It makes the photo look muddy and hazy, like you're viewing it through a colored film. When you remove the tint, the other colors usually fall into place. (**Figure 11.11**)

ADJUST FROM THE TOP... MOSTLY

Once you've roughly analyzed the photo, then you can start editing.

You may have read articles and watched videos by numerous Lightroom users on editing photos, and they all have different opinions.

Some will tell you to start at the top and always work down. Others will tell you to always set *Whites* and *Blacks* first. Some will

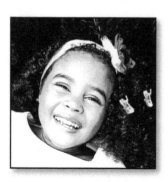

Figure 11.9 *Avoid clipping skin tones.*

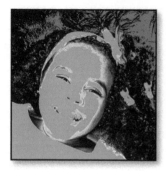

Figure 11.10 *Clipping warnings help you to identify which areas of the photo have clipped pixels, so you can see whether you're losing important detail.*

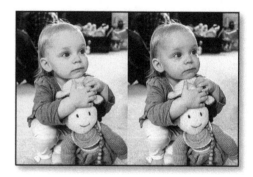

Figure 11.11 *A color cast (left) makes the photo look muddy.*

tell you skip the Basic panel and use a Tone Curve instead. So who is right?

They're all right—and they're all wrong. It's impossible to set hard and fast rules because Lightroom's Basic panel Tone sliders are image-adaptive (intelligent). The range and effect of the sliders changes based on the content of the photo and the values of the other Basic panel sliders.

In this book, we'll discuss how the sliders were *designed* to work, as explained by the engineers who created them, because they know the tools better than anyone.

Work Top Down... Sort Of

The Basic panel's Tone sliders (*Exposure, Highlights, Shadows, Whites, Blacks*) were designed to be used top down, because the first few Tone sliders affect the range of the lower Tone sliders. For example, if you change *Highlights* and *Shadows* before *Exposure*, the sliders won't move far enough. It'll be ok for little tweaks, but you'll want to get them in the right ballpark first.

The *Contrast* slider is the exception to the top-down rule. It can be used at any time as it doesn't affect slider range, and it's usually easiest to set it you've set the other Tone sliders.

However, the top-down rule doesn't mean you have to adjust every slider. For example, a photo with a low dynamic range (one that doesn't stretch to pure white/black but should do so) is still best adjusted from top to bottom, but goes straight from *Exposure* to *Whites/Blacks*, bypassing the *Highlights/Shadows* sliders. **(Figure 11.12)**

We're going to look at the principles behind the "normal" use of each slider, as well as examples of when you might want to break the general rules for a specific effect.

Auto

If you just need a quick way to improve photos, try the **Auto** button in the Basic panel. Like your camera's exposure meter, it's not as intelligent as you, so it doesn't know what's in the photo or how you want it to look, but it's often a reasonable starting point.

Auto was completely redesigned in Lightroom Classic CC version 7.1 (December 2017 release), using artificial intelligence trained by professional editors editing of tens of thousands of photos, so it works a lot better than previous versions.

If you hold down the Shift key and double-click on a Tone slider label, Lightroom automatically adjusts that single slider. This is particularly useful for the *Whites* and *Blacks* sliders, where the automatic adjustments are usually quite accurate.

Fix the Biggest Problem First

In the Basic panel, you'll also find the White Balance *Temp* & *Tint* sliders, and eyedropper. These compensate for the color of the light, and are used to remove a color cast in the photo.

If the White Balance is way off, roughly fix it before making tonal adjustments. Likewise, if the photo is very under or over exposed, fix the brightness before trying to adjust white balance.

Basic Panel Workflow

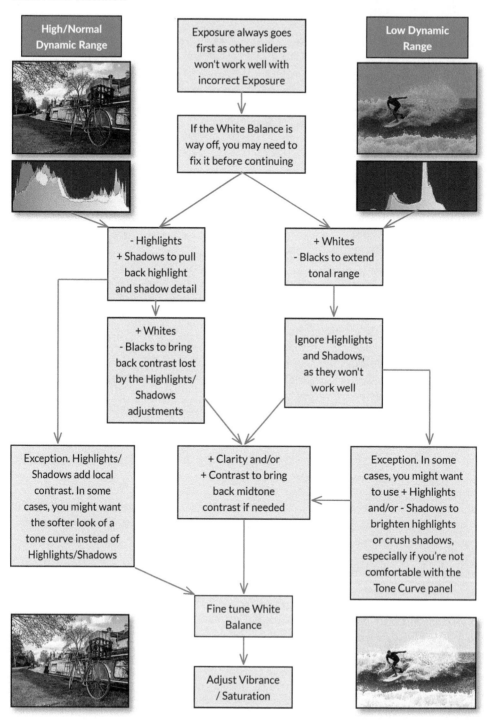

Figure 11.12 *Lightroom's Basic panel is designed to be used top-down... mostly.*

INTRODUCTION TO EDITING

Let's work on some simple examples before going into more detail on how the sliders interact.

Thatched Cottage

1. Start by analyzing the photo and its histogram. We want to bring out the blue sky, the detail in the bushes and the colors of the flowers. The histogram shows a good tonal range, with only a few clipped blacks,

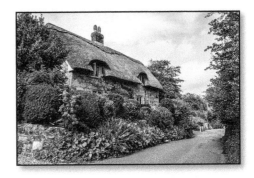

Figure 11.15 *Use the Clarity slider to bring out the contrast in the bushes and stone wall.*

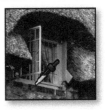

Figure 11.16 *Click on something that should be neutral using the White Balance Eyedropper.*

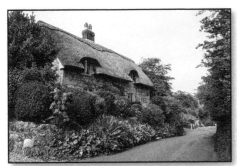

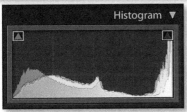

Figure 11.13 *Start by analyzing the photo and the histogram.*

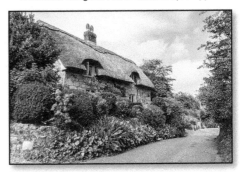

Figure 11.17 *After the white balance adjustment, the photo is much warmer.*

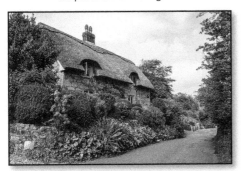

Figure 11.14 *Auto hasn't done a bad job with this photo.*

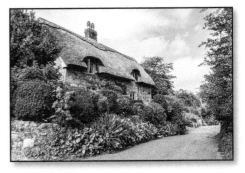

Figure 11.18 *The slight increase in contrast just finishes it off.*

but the blue sky is clipping. **(Figure 11.13)**

2. You could try pressing the *Auto* button in the Basic panel. Sometimes it does a great job and other times it's wildly wrong. If you don't like the result, press Ctrl-Z (Windows) / Cmd-Z (Mac) to undo, or use it as a starting point for further adjustments. It doesn't do a bad job with this photo, setting the photo to *Exposure* +0.01, *Contrast* -16, *Highlights* -85, *Shadows* +41, *Whites* +22, *Blacks* -19, *Vibrance* +17 and *Saturation* +4. **(Figure 11.14)**

3. The overall brightness, and the detail in the sky and bushes are good, but it's just flat. We'll add some local contrast or 'punch' using the *Clarity* slider. Since there are no people in this photo, we can afford to push it right up to +50. **(Figure 11.15)**

4. It's looking better, but it's a bit cold (blue). The quickest way to set the white balance is to select the White Balance Selector tool (it looks like an eyedropper) and click on something that should be light gray. In this case, we'll use the white window frame. It selects *Temp* 5800 and *Tint* +20, which looks good. **(Figures 11.16 & 11.17)**

5. It still looks a little flat, and I'm willing to sacrifice a little highlight and shadow detail, so I'm going to finish it off by increasing the *Contrast* slider to +10. **(Figure 11.18)**

TRY IT WITH ME

If you've registered your paperback book or bought this book direct from my website, you can download the following sample photos from the Members Area and follow along using your own copy of Lightroom.

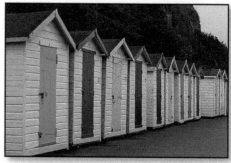

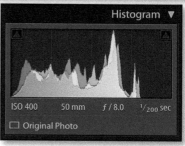

Figure 11.19 *Start by analyzing the photo and histogram.*

Beach Huts

1. As before, start with analyzing the photo. It's underexposed and we can tell from the histogram that it has no true white because it was shot at dusk. **(Figure 11.19)**

2. It's too dark overall, so we'll increase the *Exposure* to +0.5. We could go further, but we're more interested in the highlights (the white wooden boards) than the shadow tones (the bushes in the background). **(Figure 11.20)**

3. The photo has a low dynamic range, so we'll skip the *Highlights* and *Shadows* sliders.

4. Shift-double click on the *Whites* and *Blacks* slider labels to automatically set their values. They come out at *Whites* +56 and *Blacks* -16. **(Figure 11.21)**

5. The overall brightness is better, and there's good shadow and highlight detail,

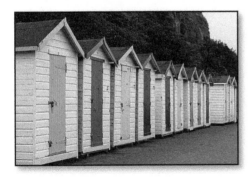

Figure 11.20 *Increase the exposure first.*

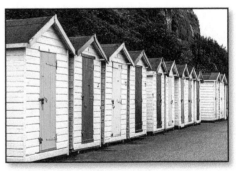

Figure 11.22 *Adding Clarity makes it much more punchy.*

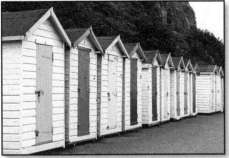

Figure 11.21 *The Auto settings for Whites and Blacks stretch the tonal range.*

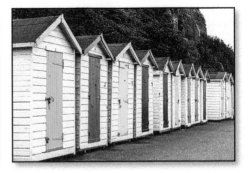

Figure 11.23 *Adding Saturation makes the colors bright and punchy.*

but it just looks flat, so we'll add *Clarity* +40. **(Figure 11.22)**

6. Finally, we want to highlight the bright colors of the beach huts, so we'll bump *Saturation* to +40. **(Figure 11.23)**

Sunset Cove

1. As usual, start by analyzing the photo. The coastline's too dark, but if we just increase *Exposure*, we'll blow out the sky. **(Figure 11.24)**

2. We'll use *Highlights* -100 to recover and enhance the detail in the sky, and *Shadows* +80 to bring out detail in rocks and houses.

3. These adjustments have compressed the tonal range, so let's pull the histogram back

to the ends. We'll use *Whites* +17, so the sun is just short of clipping, and *Blacks* -40, which blocks the darkest shadows in the rocks. I'm willing to sacrifice the detail in those rocks to increase the overall contrast. **(Figure 11.25)**

4. *Clarity* +100 is an unusually extreme adjustment, but the photo is just flat and boring, and using too much *Contrast* would lose the detail in the sky and rocks.

5. Next, we'll push *Saturation* to +100 to make it much more colorful. *Vibrance* would have enhanced the blues on the building and protected the yellows, whereas I want to pump up the yellow tones. Increasing the *Saturation* before the white balance will help me set the *Temp* & *Tint* sliders to taste. **(Figure 11.26)**

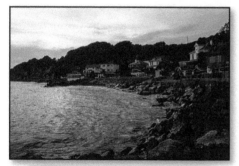

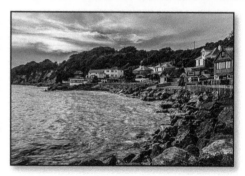

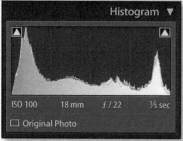

Figure 11.24 *Start by analyzing the photo and histogram.*

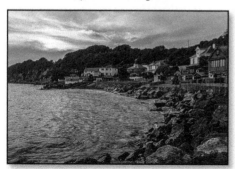

Figure 11.25 *The Highlights, Shadows, Whites and Blacks adjustments bring out the detail, but the photo looks very flat.*

6. The photo is still quite cold, and this was shot at sunset, so we'll warm it up from *Temp* 4850 and *Tint* +13 to *Temp* 5450 and *Tint* +18. **(Figure 11.27)**

7. Finally, it's still a little flat and dark, and we can afford to sacrifice some of the highlight and shadow detail, so we'll bump *Contrast* to +40 and *Exposure* to +0.30 to finish. **(Figure 11.28)**

Figure 11.26 *To bring back some punch, we've used Clarity and Saturation.*

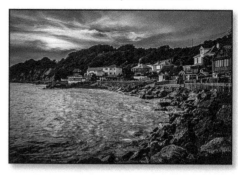

Figure 11.27 *Using the White Balance controls to warm the photo enhances the sunset vibe.*

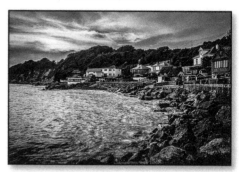

Figure 11.28 *A increase of Contrast and Exposure finishes it off.*

Further tweaks

Although the major adjustments are made in the Basic panel, you probably won't stop there. For example, if you want to try the photo in B&W, select *B&W* at the top of the Basic panel or press the V key.

WORKING WITH SLIDERS

Drag—The obvious thing to do with a slider is to grab the marker and move it, and of course that works, but there are also other options which may suit your workflow better.

Lengthen—If you like dragging sliders, but find it difficult to make fine adjustments, drag the edge of the panel to make the panel wider. It makes the sliders longer and easier to adjust.

Float—If you hover over the slider without clicking, you can use the up and down keys to move the slider. Adding Shift moves in larger increments or Alt (Windows) / Opt (Mac) decreases the increments.

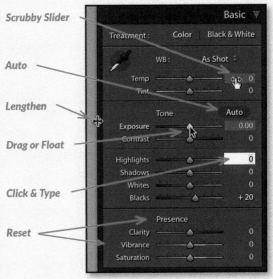

Figure 11.29 *There are multiple ways to adjust the sliders.*

Scrubby Sliders—Scrubby sliders, such as those used in Photoshop, also work in Lightroom. As you float over the numeric value field at the end of the slider, the cursor changes to a hand with a double arrow, and clicking and dragging to the left or right moves the slider.

Click & Type—While we're looking at the numeric value fields, you can click directly in one of these fields and either type the number that you're aiming for, or use the up/down arrow keys to move in smaller increments. If you've activated a field to type directly, don't forget to hit Enter or click elsewhere to complete your adjustment.

Shortcuts—If you click on a slider label, that slider becomes highlighted, and using the + / – keys on the numberpad adjusts that slider. Adding modifier keys changes the increments, so adding Shift again moves in larger increments, and Opt (Mac only) moves in smaller increments. The ; key selects the Exposure slider, and the , and . keys move up and down through the sliders, selecting each in turn.

Reset—To reset a single slider, you can double-click on the slider label. Within many panels, you'll also find a panel label, such as *Presence* in the screenshot, and double-clicking or Alt-clicking (Windows) / Opt-clicking (Mac) on that label resets that whole panel section.

Auto—Holding down Shift and double-clicking on the slider label sets the slider to its Auto position without adjusting the other sliders. Unlike the main Auto button, the slide's Auto setting is based on the existing slider settings, including the crop.

You might also want to crop/straighten the photo, remove red eye and sensor dust spots or apply adjustments to specific areas of the photo—we'll come back to these adjustments in the Selective Editing chapter starting on page 227.

You may then want to apply sharpening, noise reduction and lens corrections to your photo—we'll come back to these adjustments in the Advanced Editing chapter starting on page 263.

And finally, you can also copy your settings to other photos and apply special effect presets to your photos—we'll come back to these tools in the Develop Tools starting on page 305.

At the end of the chapter, there's also a diagram demonstrating a typical editing workflow. (**Figure 11.77** on page 226)

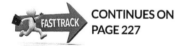

CONTINUES ON PAGE 227

SHOOTING RAW, SRAW OR JPEG

Having gained a quick overview of the Basic panel, let's go back and start right at the beginning of your workflow. Some of the camera settings at the time of capture can affect your options when you later come to edit the photos. These include the file format, picture style, crop ratio and high dynamic range camera settings. Most other camera settings are ignored by raw editors such as Lightroom.

Should I shoot raw or JPEG?

The most important camera setting is the file format. Shooting in your camera's raw file format offers a lot more flexibility than JPEG, especially if your exposure or white balance aren't perfect, or if you're shooting

at high ISO or in a high contrast situation.

Lightroom's Develop tools are primarily designed for raw image processing, giving you the greatest latitude, but Lightroom also works with rendered files (JPEG, TIFF, PSD, PNG), giving you an easy way to edit batches of photos. So if you can use Lightroom with JPEGs, which take up less hard drive space, why would you want to consider shooting raw? Well, think of it this way... did you ever play with colored modeling clay when you were a child? **(Figure 11.30)**

Imagine you have a ready-made model made of a mixture of different colors, and you also have separate pots of the different colors that have never been used. You can push the ready-made model around a bit and make

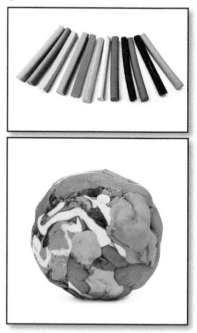

Figure 11.30 *When using modeling clay, you get a better result starting from the raw material than trying to reuse an existing model. In the same way, you'll have more flexibility when working with raw files than you will with ready-made JPEGs.*

something different, but the colors smudge into each other and it's never quite as good as it would have been if you'd used the individual colors and started from scratch.

A JPEG is like that ready-made model: it's already been made into a photo by the camera before you start editing it. You can change its appearance, but if you try to change it too much, it's going to end up a distorted mess. Your raw file is like having the separate pots of clay—you're starting off with the raw material, and you choose what to make with it.

When you come to edit JPEG photos in the Develop module, you'll notice that some of Lightroom's controls are more limited when working with rendered files (JPEG, TIFF, PSD, PNG). They include:

White Balance—White Balance sliders change from Kelvin values to fixed values, as you're adjusting from a fixed color rather than adjusting white balance. Incorrect white balance is much harder to fix on rendered files.

Exposure Latitude—If photos are under or over exposed or very high contrast, there's a lot more information to work with in a raw file. JPEGs start to fall apart a lot more quickly than raw files. (**Figure 11.31**)

Camera Profiles—Camera profiles are only available for raw files as they emulate the look of the camera's picture styles.

Lens Profiles—Most lens correction profiles are built for raw files as the camera may have already applied additional processing (e.g. vignette correction) to JPEGs.

Sharpening and Noise Reduction—Sharpening and noise reduction are turned off by default as these may have already been applied by the camera. Lightroom's sharpening and noise reduction controls work better on raw files, as they have more information to work with.

Which file format you choose is your decision. If you shoot raw, there are a couple of additional settings to watch out for...

Why doesn't the photo look the same as it did on the camera?

When you shoot in your camera's raw file format, the data isn't fully processed by the camera. The mosaic sensor data is recorded in the raw file, and this sensor data must be converted into an image using raw processing software.

Each raw processor interprets the raw data in a slightly different way. As a result, the photo won't look exactly the

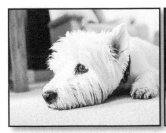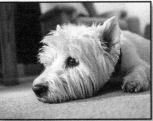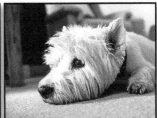

Figure 11.31 *If your file is overexposed or has the wrong white balance (left), the detail is much more recoverable from a raw (center) file than a JPEG (right). The highlight detail on William's nose is missing on the JPEG and it's very difficult to adjust the white balance.*

same in Lightroom as it did on the back of the camera. There isn't a right or wrong rendering—they're just different.

Adobe could use the camera manufacturer's SDKs (Software Development Kits) to convert the raw data and the rendering would be the same as the camera JPEG, but then they couldn't improve the processing or add additional features to Lightroom, such as local adjustments. It's all or nothing. One of the major benefits of the raw file format is the ability to tweak the photo to your own taste rather than being tied to the manufacturer's rendering.

The initial preview you see in Lightroom is the JPEG preview embedded by the camera, so it has the manufacturer's own processing applied. Lightroom then renders its own preview, ready for you to start editing. This is why it looks like Lightroom is changing the image.

I shot in B&W—why is Lightroom changing the photos back to color?

The same principles apply to the camera's B&W or monotone setting. The sensor data in the raw file remains in color, and Lightroom doesn't know that you were shooting B&W, so it displays the full color photo. You can then use Lightroom to convert the photo to B&W, with full control over the color mix used to convert the file.

If you want to remember which ones you shot in B&W (or any other picture style), enable RAW + JPEG in the camera and import both files into Lightroom. The JPEG will remind you of what you were thinking at the time of shooting, so you can select the matching raw files and convert them all to B&W or a matching picture style in one go.

Can I emulate the camera's own color?

If you prefer the camera's manufacturer's rendering, there are special camera profiles which emulate the camera style settings for the most popular cameras. These are found in the **Profile** pop-up in the Camera Calibration panel. **(Figure 11.32)**

Adobe Standard is Adobe's default profile for your camera, and it's available for all camera raw files. It's designed to be as consistent as possible across a range of different cameras.

Camera Standard emulates the camera's default style.

Camera Portrait, Camera Neutral, Camera Landscape and others with similar names emulate other camera styles offered by your camera.

Embedded is a profile embedded/applied by the camera. This is the only option for rendered files (JPEG, TIFF, PSD, PNG) but can also be found on DNG files, which can contain embedded custom profiles.

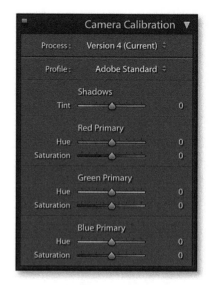

Figure 11.32 *The Profile pop-up is found in the Camera Calibration panel.*

Although the profiles have generic names in the pop-up, they intelligently select the correct profile for your camera model behind the scenes. For example, the *Adobe Standard* profile applied to a Canon EOS 5D Mark III is not the same profile as the one applied to a Nikon D810. They use these standard names so that you can save them in presets to apply to multiple different camera models.

If you're going to use a non-default profile, select it before making your Basic panel adjustments, as the profiles significantly change the appearance of the photos. Lightroom doesn't automatically select the correct profile based on your camera settings, and it doesn't know about any other customizations applied in the camera, such as added contrast or sharpening.

If you use a camera emulation profile on most photos, for example, *Camera Standard*, you can set it as the default setting so it's automatically selected for new imports. We'll discuss custom defaults on page 311.

In addition to the included camera profiles, you can build your own profiles using the free DNG Profile Editor. This is particularly useful for extreme white balances, infrared photography and tweaking existing profiles to your own taste. You can learn more in The Geeky Bits Appendix on page E-14.

Why are my photos so dark?

Certain camera settings can affect the exposure of your raw file directly or indirectly. Most of the settings you can change on your camera only apply to the manufacturer's own JPEG processing. For example, contrast, sharpening, picture styles and color space don't affect the raw data, however these settings do affect the JPEG preview you see on the back of the camera and the resulting histogram and clipping warnings, which can cause you to change your exposure. There are some specific ones to look out for...

Canon's Highlight Tone Priority automatically underexposes the raw data by one stop to ensure you retain the highlights, leaves a tag in the file noting that this setting was applied, and applies its own special processing to the JPEG preview that you see on the back of the camera. Lightroom also understands this tag and increases the exposure by one stop behind the scenes to compensate, but if you accidentally underexpose the image with HTP turned on too, you can end up with a very noisy file. When shooting raw for use in Lightroom, there's no advantage to using this setting instead of changing the exposure compensation yourself, so you may wish to turn off HTP and set your exposure to retain the highlights manually.

Canon's Auto Lighting Optimizer and Nikon's Active D-Lighting don't affect the raw data itself, but Lightroom has no idea that you've used these settings, and even if it did, the processing applied by the camera is variable. When ALO or ADL are turned on, that special processing is applied to the JPEG preview that you see on the back of the camera, as well as to the resulting histogram. Seeing this false brighter preview could cause you to unknowingly underexpose the image. You'd then be disappointed to find it's underexposed when you view the unedited photo in Lightroom, so it's a good idea to turn these settings off unless you're shooting JPEG or only using the manufacturer's own software.

Other camera manufacturers have similar settings, so check your camera manual for similar highlight priority and high dynamic range settings. They include Dynamic Range Optimization (Sony), Shadow Adjustment Technology (Olympus) and Intelligent

Exposure (Panasonic).

Are there any other camera settings that Lightroom understands?

There are a couple of other settings that Lightroom does understand. The White Balance setting is understood by most raw converters. For example, if you set your camera to *Cloudy* and Lightroom is set to *As Shot*, Lightroom uses the white balance values set by the camera (although it's still an interpretation by the software programmers). The Kelvin numbers may not match as the values are stored in a different format behind the scenes.

Lightroom also respects the in-camera crop ratio, for example, if you have your camera set to a 1:1 (square) crop, it's also 1:1 in Lightroom. For cameras produced since the end of 2012, you can access the full sensor data using the pop-up in the Crop Options panel in Develop, but older cameras must use the DNG Recover Edges plug-in to access the extra data.

If I shoot sRAW format, can Lightroom apply all the usual adjustments?

While we're talking about raw files, there's also a hybrid file type to consider. Canon and Nikon's reduced resolution formats work slightly differently to standard raw formats. Full raw files are demosaiced by the raw processor, whereas sRAW/mRAW files are demosaiced by the camera and some of the data is discarded to create a lower resolution file. (The demosaic is the process of turning the raw sensor data into image data.)

You still have access to all the controls that are available for raw files, however there are a few things which are usually part of the demosaic processing which are not applied to your sRAW files. Artifacts may also be present, for example, Lightroom maps out hot pixels (bright pixels that appear on long exposures) on full raw files, but can't do so on sRAW files. On some cameras, for example, the Canon 7D, the highlight recovery potential is reduced when shooting in sRAW. Other settings may also behave differently, for example, the sharpening and noise reduction may need slightly different settings.

If you convert to DNG (except Lossy DNG), you'll notice that Canon's sRAW files get bigger instead of smaller because the way the sRAW data is stored is specific to the manufacturer and not covered by the DNG specification.

CALIBRATE YOUR MONITOR

Before you start editing seriously, it's also worth taking the time to calibrate your monitor.

Why should I calibrate my monitor?

When you walk into a TV store and look around, you'll notice that all of the screens are slightly different. Some are a little brighter, some are a little darker, some are more contrasty, others have less contrast, some are more colorful, some are warm, some are cool... the differences go on.

If you display the same image on all of these screens, they'll all look slightly different. The same applies to computer monitors. The same photo will look different, depending on the screen you're using.

The aim of monitor calibration is to adjust all of these different screens to a standard, so the photo looks similar regardless of the screen you're viewing at the time.

Trying to edit your photos on an

uncalibrated monitor is like trying to edit with your eyes closed. You'll be guessing what they look like.

Your surroundings also influence your perception of brightness and color. Ideally, it's best to edit your photos in dim light, with the light source no brighter than the screen. This may be as simple as closing the curtains and turning on a small desk lamp holding a daylight bulb.

When you put your photos out into the world, you can't control exactly how they'll look, because most people don't calibrate their monitors, but editing your photos on a standardized system gives you the best shot at getting your prints to match the screen.

How do I calibrate my monitor?

Monitor calibration isn't complicated. You simply need a monitor calibration tool and the software that comes with it. The main players are X-Rite's ColorMunki and i1 Display Pro devices, and Datacolor's range of Spyder devices. The software will differ slightly, but the principles remain the same. Let's use the i1 Display Pro to illustrate:

1. Install the software and drivers that come with the calibration device.

2. Follow the instructions in the software. **(Figure 11.33)** Most ask you to make a few decisions:

Monitor Technology—Newer monitors are probably *White LED*, while older ones are mainly *CCFL*. The software often selects the right one automatically.

White Point—select *D65* or *6500*.

Luminance—select *120 cd/m2* as a starting point. (You may increase/decrease it later, if your prints are a little darker/lighter than you see on screen.)

Contrast Ratio—select *Native*.

3. Place the calibration device on the

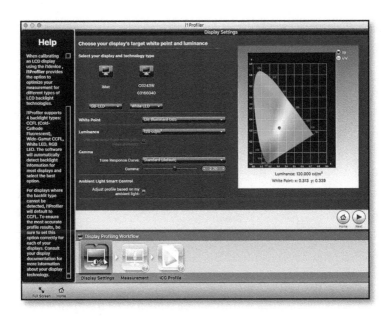

Figure 11.33 *Calibration software asks you a few basic questions.*

screen, ensuring that it's flat against the screen with no ambient light creeping in the sides, and start measuring. **(Figure 11.34)**

4. The software measures the brightness of the screen, and tells you how bright it is currently. Use the monitor buttons (or *System Preferences > Display* on a Mac with a built-in screen) to increase or decrease the monitor brightness until the line is in the green 'optimum' area. Most monitors are way too bright, so don't be surprised if you have to make a big adjustment.

Some high-end monitors make these adjustments automatically. Other monitors may also ask you to adjust contrast or RGB values to match the target values.

5. The calibration software then flashes a series of colors on the screen, measuring each in turn, so it can build a profile.

6. When the calibration finishes, give the profile a sensible name (perhaps include the date) and click the *Save* button, then close the software. You'll need to recalibrate periodically, as monitors drift over time.

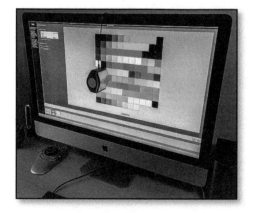

Figure 11.34 *The calibration puck is placed on the monitor, where it reads a series of swatches displayed on the screen.*

WHITE BALANCE

Having gained an overview of the Basic panel and set up your camera and editing environment, let's take a more detailed look at the individual sliders and understand what's going on behind the scenes. We'll work from the top down for easy reference, starting with White Balance.

The color of light varies depending on its source. It can range from cool (blue sky) to warm (candlelight or tungsten), and the color temperature is measured using the Kelvin scale.

Our eyes and brain automatically compensate for different lighting conditions, which is why a white object looks white to us whether it's viewed in sunlight, shade or indoors using artificial lighting.

Cameras aren't quite so smart. A camera's auto white balance works fairly well in a narrow range of daylight with "average" image content, but it doesn't take much to confuse it. Capture a scene of autumn leaves, and the camera's likely to make the photo a little cold and blue. Capture a snow scene, and the camera will probably try to warm it up.

Lightroom's White Balance sliders are designed to compensate for the color of the light in which the photo was taken. When you get the white tones right, everything else falls into place. **(Figure 11.35)**

Most of the time, you'll want the colors in the scene to be rendered as accurately as possible, but sometimes you'll want to warm or cool the scene to suit the mood of the photo.

If you look outside on a cold winters day, the light is cool and blue, but during a beautiful sunset, it may be warm and orange. If

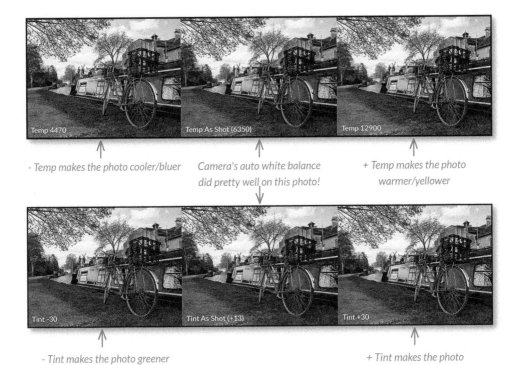

- Temp makes the photo cooler/bluer

Camera's auto white balance did pretty well on this photo!

+ Temp makes the photo warmer/yellower

- Tint makes the photo greener

+ Tint makes the photo more magenta (pinker)

Figure 11.35 *The white balance adjustments compensate for the color of the light.*

you neutralize these colors, you lose the atmosphere.

How do I set the white balance?

White balance adjustments are made using the **Temp** *(Temperature)* and **Tint** sliders in the Basic panel. **(Figure 11.36)**

There are a few ways of deciding on the best values:

Auto—In the *White Balance* pop-up, select **Auto**. It attempts to neutralize the photo, but like the camera's auto white balance, it's not as intelligent as your eyes, so the results may not be perfect.

Presets—If you're working on a raw file, the **White Balance** pop-up includes presets for standard lighting conditions. They

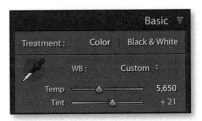

Figure 11.36 *The White Balance Eyedropper and sliders are at the top of the Basic panel.*

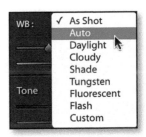

Figure 11.37 *White balance presets are available for standard lighting conditions.*

include *As Shot, Daylight, Cloudy, Shade, Tungsten, Fluorescent and Flash* settings. Select the right preset for the lighting conditions, for example, if the photo was captured on a cloudy day, select the *Cloudy* preset. (Rendered files—JPEG, TIFF, PSD, PNG— only have *As Shot, Auto* and *Custom*.) **(Figure 11.37)**

Eyedropper—For more control, the White Balance Selector allows you to click in the photo to automatically neutralize any color cast.

Click the eyedropper icon in the Color panel or press the W key, then click on something in the photo that *should* be neutral, for

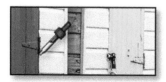

Figure 11.38 *Select the White Balance eyedropper and click on something that SHOULD be white or light gray, like this white beach hut.*

Figure 11.39 *The easiest way to correct the white balance is to start with the eyedropper and tweak from there.*

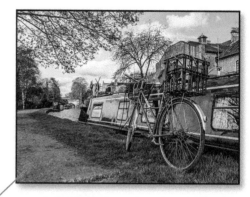

Oooops, clicking on the stone path turned the photo too blue

Clicking on the window made it a bit too warm and pink because it's reflecting the surroundings

What else might be neutral in this picture?

Darker areas of clouds may work if they weren't partially clipped (white with no detail), but results can vary depending on where you click

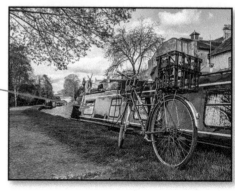

The satellite dish gave the best result, but it's still a bit cold, so try an extra 200K-400K on Temp

Paintwork and white fabrics often yellow over time

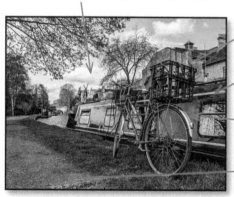

Shiny objects are no good, as they'll reflect surroundings

Stone sometimes works, but it's rarely perfectly neutral

example, the shadows on a white t-shirt. Using white or light gray subjects gives a more accurate result than darker shades, but avoid whites that are too bright, as some of the color data may be clipped. **(Figures 11.38 & 11.39)**

When you click with eyedropper, the pop-up changes to *Custom* and the sliders automatically adjust. If it still doesn't look right, click somewhere else to try again or tweak the sliders by eye. The eyedropper's often a good way to get the white balance in the right ballpark before tweaking.

If you regularly shoot in difficult lighting or you struggle to select the right white balance, a WhiBal, ColorChecker or other calibrated neutral light gray card is an easy way to guarantee correct white balance. Simply shoot a photo of the card in the same lighting conditions as the subject and click the eyedropper on that photo to get an accurate white balance setting. You can then copy these values to other photos shot in the same conditions.

Adjust Sliders By Eye—As you gain experience, you can go straight to the *Temp* and *Tint* sliders. If the photo's too yellow or warm, move the *Temp* slider to the left to compensate, and if it's too blue or cold, move the slider to the right. Likewise, the *Tint* slider adjusts from green on the left to magenta on the right.

If you're working on a raw file, the *Temp* slider uses the Kelvin scale to measure the color of the light. For JPEGs and other image formats, the slider runs from -100 to 100, because the white balance compensation has already been applied to the image data (e.g., by the camera), and now you're simply warming or cooling the photo.

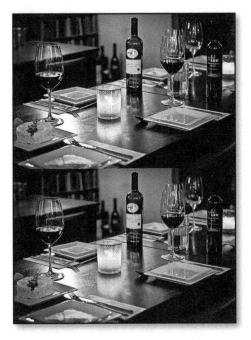

Figure 11.40 *Candlelit photos look better warm. Some photos just aren't meant to be perfectly neutral!*

How do I adjust for mood?

Once you've made the photo neutral, you can tweak the white balance sliders to enhance the mood. For example, indoor photos often look better with a *Temp* value 200-400K higher than neutral, to bring back a pleasant warmth. Or a sunset shot may need warming up to reflect the lovely warm light usually seen at that time of day. **(Figure 11.40)**

How do I keep the White Balance eyedropper turned on?

While you have the White Balance eyedropper active, there's an **Auto Dismiss** checkbox in the Toolbar. **(Figure 11.41)** With this checkbox unchecked, the Eyedropper remains on screen until you intentionally dismiss it by pressing W, clicking the *Done* button in the Toolbar or returning the Eyedropper to its base. This can be useful if you're trying a number of different areas of the photo to find the best click white balance. If you can't see the Toolbar beneath the photo, press T.

Can I change the eyedropper averaging?

When the Eyedropper is selected, the White Balance Loupe appears next to it. It displays an enlarged view of the area you're sampling, so you can make sure you're selecting the best set of pixels without any other colored areas that might influence the white balance calculation. **(Figure 11.42)**

The Eyedropper averages the pixel values you can see in its loupe, so there are two ways you can affect the sampling area. When you zoom out, you're sampling a larger area than when you're zoomed in, which is particularly useful for noisy photos. Also, you can change the loupe scale using

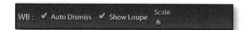

Figure 11.41 *The White Balance Eyedropper options are on the Toolbar.*

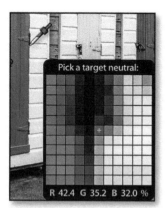

Figure 11.42 *The White Balance Loupe shows a zoomed view of the area under the Eyedropper, so you can check that you're not polluting your selection with pixels that aren't meant to be neutral, like this red door.*

the **Scale** slider on the Toolbar, to change from a 5x5 pixel area up to a 17x17 pixel area, so it averages over a smaller or larger number of pixels.

If you find the Loupe distracting, you can disable it using the **Show Loupe** checkbox on the Toolbar.

How do I handle mixed lighting?

Sometimes your photos will be shot with light from two or more sources. For example, a photo shot at night may have moonlight and street lighting, a photo shot near a window may have warm tungsten light and cooler daylight, or a photo shot outdoors may have bright sunlight and shade. **(Figure 11.43)**

In this case, you have three choices:

• Pick a white balance in the middle that looks ok for both.

• Get the lighting right for one light source and don't worry about the other.

• Use Lightroom's Selective Editing tools to apply a different white balance to each area of the photo (page 255).

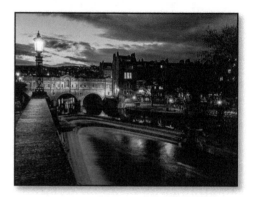

Figure 11.43 *Photos shot in mixed lighting are notoriously difficult to correct.*

How do I adjust white balance for infrared photos?

Lightroom's White Balance sliders only run from 2000K to 50000K Temp and -150 to 150 Tint. That covers most lighting conditions, but some extreme lighting or infrared shots or photographs of film negatives can fall outside of this range. To solve this issue, you can create custom profiles for these extreme white balances. For example, open an infrared DNG file of a landscape using the DNG Profile Editor and on the *Color Matrices* tab, move the *Temp* slider to around -75 to -100, making the foliage as neutral as possible. Export the profile, then restart Lightroom and select the new profile in the Camera Calibration panel. Use the white balance eyedropper to click on foliage (or something else that should be white), then edit as usual. You can learn more about the DNG Profile Editor in the Appendix starting on page E-14.

TONE & PRESENCE

In the Fast Track, we learned roughly how to use the Basic sliders, but now let's take a closer look at how each slider affects the tones of the photo and how they interact.

As everyone learns differently, we're going to demonstrate the effect of the sliders in four ways: **(Figure 11.44)**

1. A raw photo.

2. A gray 21 step wedge, created in Photoshop to illustrate the effect on the full range of tones.

3. The histogram showing the effect of the sliders on the 21 step wedge. Each spike on the histogram is one of the gray squares on the step wedge. As the spikes move to the left, the tones are getting darker. As they move to the right, the tones are getting lighter. As the spikes move further apart, there's greater contrast in that range of tones, and as they move closer together, the contrast is reduced.

4. A curve based on sRGB measurements from the 21 step wedge. If you're comfortable reading curves, it makes it easy to see the amount of contrast introduced to different tones. (If you've never used curves, we'll discuss them in more detail in the Advanced Editing chapter starting on page 263).

Baseline Photos for Comparison

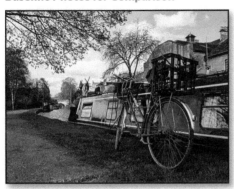

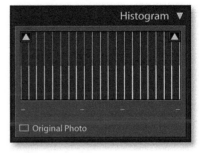

Figure 11.44 *As a baseline for comparison, these are the images with everything set to 0.*

PRINTING PRESS & EREADER LIMITATIONS

The limitations of printing presses and eReaders affects the reproduction in printed form, so if you're reading this in a paperback book, do check the examples in the complimentary PDF version on a calibrated monitor. Better still, if you'd like to try some of these tests for yourself, you can download these files from the Members Area.

Bear in mind that the histogram and curve are only guides showing the effect of each slider. The actual measurements and slider values vary depending on the content of each photo, as the processing is image-adaptive. This means that the values you use for each photo will vary. +50 on a slider has a different effect on different photos, depending on the image content and the other settings, so don't focus too much on the numerical values—focus on the photo itself.

EXPOSURE

Near the top of the Basic panel, the **Exposure** slider sets the overall image brightness, and it uses the same f-stop increments as your camera, so +2.0 of *Exposure* is the equivalent of opening the aperture on your camera by 2 stops. The *Exposure* slider attempts to maintain a gentle transition to pure white to avoid harsh digital clipping. **(Figures 11.45 & 11.46)**

It's important to get the *Exposure* setting about right before moving on to the other Basic tone panel sliders, as the range of other sliders are affected and they won't work well if your *Exposure* slider is set incorrectly.

How do I set the *Exposure* slider?

So how do you know where to set the *Exposure* slider? Try these tips:

Squint Your Eyes—If you screw your eyes up or watch the small Navigator panel preview, you won't be able to see the detail in the photo, and you'll be left with the overall impression of how bright it is. You're aiming for a mid-gray.

The Only Slider—Pretend it's the only control you have available. If there weren't any other sliders, how bright would you make the photo?

Confuse Your Brain—Your eyes adjust to the original camera exposure, making it difficult to judge the correct exposure. It can help to confuse your brain by swinging the *Exposure* slider to the left and right like a pendulum and then settle somewhere in the middle, wherever it looks right.

Focus on the Midtones—Don't worry if the highlights are a bit bright or the shadows a bit dark, or if there are clipped highlights or shadows at this stage (white/black areas with no detail), as you'll pull them back using the *Highlights* and *Shadows* sliders.

You can hold down the Alt key (Windows) / Opt key (Mac) to view the clipping warnings, but don't worry about them at this stage.

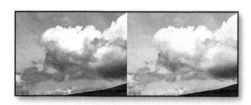

Figure 11.45 *Harsh clipping (left) vs. gentle transition (right).*

Exposure Slider

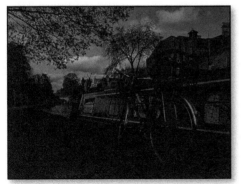

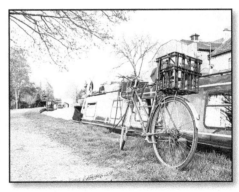

Exposure -2 shows there's loads of detail available even in the brightest clouds, which can be pulled back using the Highlights slider, but the change makes it way too dark overall.

Exposure +2 makes it way too bright and loses all the detail in the clouds, but shows there's loads of detail in the dark areas, which can be pulled back using the Shadows slider.

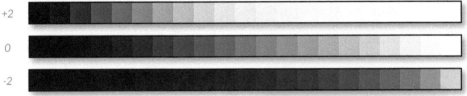

+2

0

-2

Figure 11.46 *The Exposure slider brightens or darkens the photo overall, and attempts to protect the highlights from clipping.*

The stepwedge, histogram and curves are all based on rendered data, however on a raw file, there may be more hidden highlight detail that can be recovered, like the clouds in the photo.

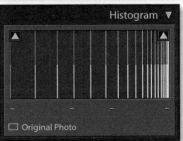

Exposure +2 moves the histogram to the right. The shadows increase in contrast (spikes move apart) but highlights are compressed.

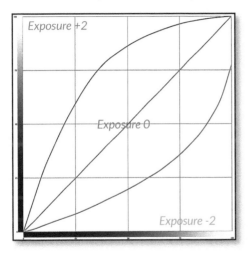

Exposure +2

Exposure 0

Exposure -2

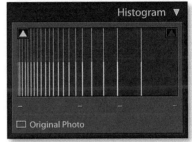

Exposure -2 moves the histogram to the left. The highlights increase in contrast (spikes move apart) but shadows are compressed.

GLOBAL VS. LOCAL CONTRAST

The next slider in the Basic panel is the **Contrast** slider. It's a bit of a blunt instrument, so it usually works better when you adjust other sliders first. But why?

How do I increase contrast?

To increase midtone contrast globally, you have to make light pixels lighter and dark pixels darker. That's what the *Contrast* slider does. The problem is, you lose highlight and shadow detail in the process. **(Figure 11.47)**

Fortunately, our eyes are more interested in local contrast—small contrasts in similar tones—than they are in big global contrast. Local contrast adjustments look for small changes in contrast and enhances them. This adds contrast without sacrificing as much detail in the highlights and shadows. Lightroom mainly adjusts local contrast using the *Clarity* slider, but it's also affected by the *Highlights*, *Shadows* and *Dehaze* sliders.

It can sound complicated, so let's illustrate the difference using the stepwedges and photos. The stepwedge's 21 blocks of gray, ranging from pure black to pure white, make it easier to see the differences. **(Figure 11.48)**

Once you've adjusted all of the other Basic tone sliders and added local contrast where needed using *Clarity*, you can tweak the midtone contrast using the *Contrast* slider or Tone Curve, but in many cases, it won't need adjusting at all.

How do I decrease contrast?

But what if you have the opposite problem? If a photo has too much contrast (too wide a dynamic range), you can darken highlights and lighten the shadows using—*Contrast* to

see more detail in those tones, but then you lose midtone contrast, making the photo look really flat. The *Highlights/Shadows* sliders are usually better at reducing dynamic range as they add local contrast at the same time, so it's often best to skip the *Contrast* slider altogether.

There may be exceptions, however. On a soft dreamy image, the extra local contrast may not be desirable, so you might want to use a negative *Contrast* adjustment or Tone Curve in that case. Or if the *Highlights/ Shadows* sliders don't go far enough, some negative *Contrast* can be useful to compress the tones. **(Figure 11.49)**

HIGHLIGHTS AND SHADOWS

We've skipped *Contrast*, and in many cases, *Clarity* is best left for later, so after setting *Exposure*, the *Highlights* and *Shadows* sliders are next in line for adjustment.

The **Highlights** slider only adjusts the brighter tones in the photo and barely touches the darker tones. It's generally intended to be dragged to the left (-) to recover highlight details, such as fluffy clouds in the sky or detail on a bride's dress. **(Figure 11.50)**

Shadows does the opposite, mainly affecting the darker tones in the photo. It's generally intended to be moved to the right (+) to lighten shadow details, such as shadowed areas on people's faces or detail in a groom's suit. **(Figure 11.51)**

How do I set Highlights and Shadows?

Here's a few tips to help you decide where to set the *Highlights* and *Shadows* sliders:

Local Contrast—Brightening shadows and darkening highlights usually comes at the

Increasing Contrast or Clarity Sliders

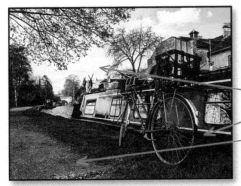

**+ Global Contrast
(using the Contrast slider)**

Lost highlight & shadow detail

Added midtone contrast

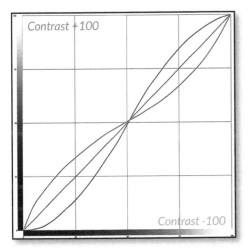

**+ Local Contrast
(using the Clarity slider)**

Still plenty of highlight & shadow detail

Added midtone contrast

Figure 11.47 *The Contrast slider adds global contrast by compressing the highlights and shadows (top), whereas the Clarity slider looks for areas of local contrast and enhances them (second from top).*

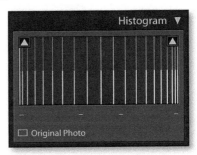

Contrast +100 increases contrast in the midtones (spikes move apart) but highlights and shadows are compressed.

Contrast +100

Contrast -100

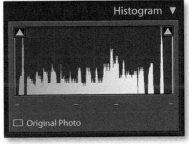

Clarity +100 increases local contrast but without changing brightness. Note that the spikes have spread due to the gradients.

Contrast vs. Clarity Sliders

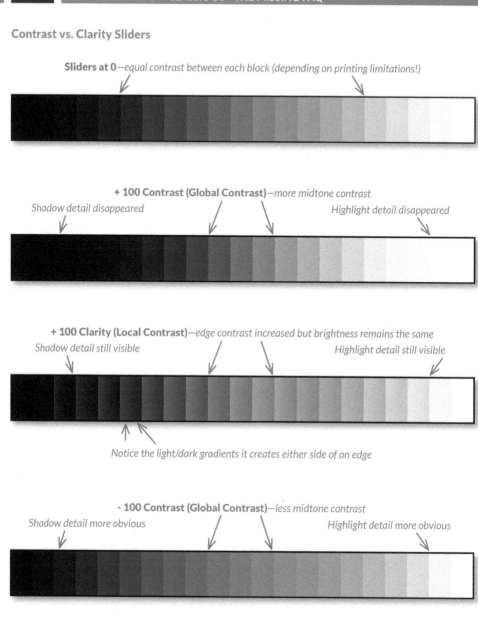

Figure 11.48 *The Contrast slider adds global contrast by compressing the highlights and shadows, whereas the Clarity slider looks for areas of local contrast and enhances them.*

Decreasing Contrast or Clarity Sliders

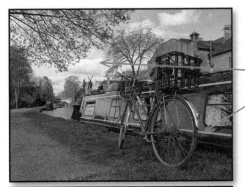

- Contrast (Global Contrast)

Reducing contrast recovers the highlight and shadow detail

Whole photo ends up really dull and flat

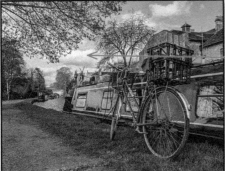

- Highlights / + Shadows (with Local Contrast)

- Highlight brings back the cloud detail

+ Shadows brings back the shadow details

Photo still retains its punch thanks to the local contrast enhancement

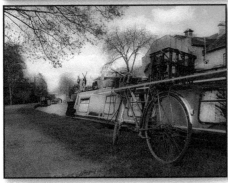

- Clarity (reduces Local Contrast)

The edges in the photo are softened, but the overall brightness of each tone remains about the same.

Figure 11.49 *If there's too much contrast, the Contrast slider can make the photo flat, whereas Highlights & Shadows darkens the highlights and lightens the shadows while adding local contrast.*

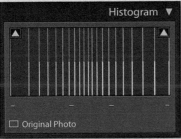

Contrast -100 decreases the contrast in the midtones (spikes move closer) but highlights and shadows gain contrast.

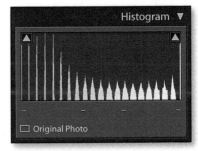

Clarity -100 retains the overall contrast between tones but softens the edges.

Highlights Slider

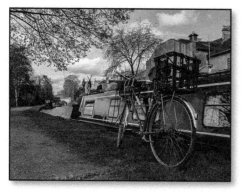 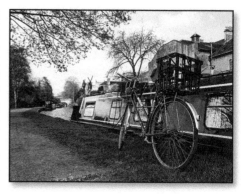

- Highlights brings back cloud detail without darkening the shadows

+ Highlights lightens the highlight tones without affecting the shadows

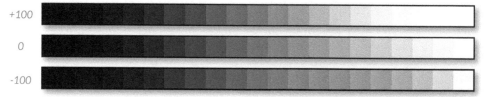

+100

0

-100

Figure 11.50 *The Highlights slider lightens or darkens the highlight tones. The slider is usually pulled to the left, bringing back highlight detail in the clouds.*

The stepwedge, histogram and curves are all based on rendered data, however on a raw file, there may be more hidden highlight detail that can be recovered, like the clouds in the photo.

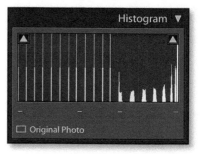

Highlights +100 lightens just the highlight tones. The highlight spikes spread due to the local contrast gradients.

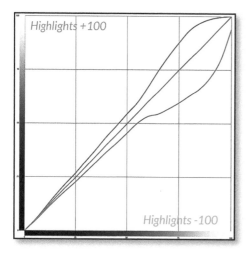

Highlights +100

Highlights -100

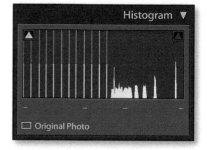

Highlights -100 darkens just the highlight tones. The highlight spikes have spread out due to the local contrast gradients.

Shadows Slider

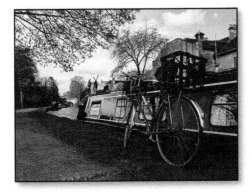
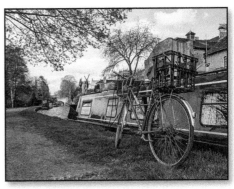

- Shadows darkens the shadows without affecting the highlights

+ Shadows lightens the shadow tones without lightening the highlights

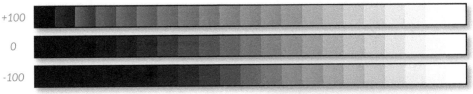

+100

0

-100

Figure 11.51 *The Shadows slider lightens or darkens the shadow tones. The slider is usually pulled to the right, bringing back detail back into the darkest tones.*

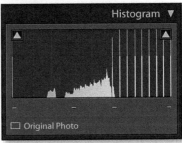

Shadows +100 lightens just the shadow tones. The shadow spikes spread out due to the local contrast gradients.

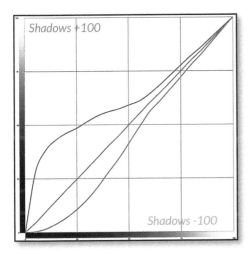

Shadows +100

Shadows -100

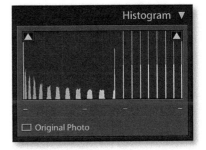

Shadows -100 darkens just the shadow tones. The shadow spikes have spread out due to the local contrast gradients.

cost of midtone contrast. Unlike a simple highlights or shadows control, *Highlights* and *Shadows* also adds local contrast (like *Clarity*) to help compensate for the loss of global contrast, and it also affects saturation. (Figure 11.52)

Amount—How much highlight and shadow detail you recover will depend on the results of your photo analysis. For example, if the photo is of a stormy beach, the detail in the clouds will be essential, so you'll use more highlight recovery. Likewise, if the photo is a woodland scene, you'll need more shadow detail in the leaves and bark, but you won't need as much if the bushes are unimportant in the background of a wedding photo.

While you're moving the *Highlights* slider, hold down the Alt key (Windows) / Opt key (Mac) to see the clipping warnings, to ensure your adjustment is recovering any clipped highlights.

The effect on local contrast (like *Clarity*) gets stronger as you move the sliders further. Both sliders look fairly natural up to 50%, but beyond that, the effect becomes more surreal, which can make photos look over-processed if not used carefully.

Symmetrical Sliders—Due to the local contrast and saturation changes included with the *Highlights/Shadows* sliders, they usually work best when they're fairly symmetrical, for example, -50 *Highlights* and +50 *Shadows*. There are always exceptions, for example, you may only want local contrast in the clouds but softer shadows.

Add Global Contrast with Whites/Blacks—Darkening highlights and lightening shadows decreases the midtone (global) contrast, so you'll usually need to adjust the *Whites/Blacks* sliders after *Highlights/Shadows*. We'll look at these sliders next.

Opposite Directions—If you need to swing both sliders in the same direction, it's usually (but not always) a sign that the *Exposure* slider needs moving in that direction.

There are some exceptions, when you might choose to break these general rules:

The "Wrong" Way—Occasionally, you may want to swing the sliders in the opposite direction to darken shadows and lighten highlights. This adds global contrast, but with more control than just using the *Contrast* slider, however it also affects local contrast. Traditionally you'd use a Tone Curve for this purpose.

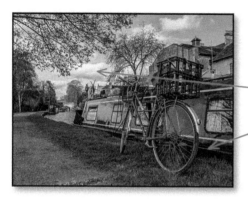

- Highlights / + Shadows
(adds Local Contrast)

- Highlights brings back the cloud detail

+ Shadows brings back the shadow details

Photo still retains its punch thanks to the local contrast enhancement

Figure 11.52 *Highlights and Shadows bring back detail without making the photo too flat, due to their local contrast enhancement.*

Local Contrast Control—You don't have any control over how much local contrast (*Clarity*) is added with *Highlights/Shadows*, and you can't remove the effect using the *Clarity* slider either. For average photos, that's not a problem, but for some photos you may want a softer look, so you might prefer to use the Tone Curve.

WHITES AND BLACKS

The **Whites** and **Blacks** sliders affect the clipping point and roll off at the extreme ends of the tonal range. If you've used other image editing software, they're similar to the black and white points in Levels. **(Figures 11.54 & 11.55)**

In most cases, the *Whites* slider is pulled to

the right (+) and *Blacks* is pulled to the left (-) to expand the tonal range.

How do I set Whites and Blacks?

Here's a few tips to help you decide where to set the *Whites* and *Blacks* sliders:

After Highlights / Shadows—If you've used -*Highlights* and +*Shadows*, pulling *Whites* and *Blacks* in the opposite direction (+*Whites* and -*Blacks*) brings back some contrast by clipping a few of the lightest and darkest pixels. **(Figure 11.53)**

Try Auto—The *Auto* values for the *Whites* and *Blacks* sliders are usually accurate, so try holding down the Shift key while double-clicking on the slider labels.

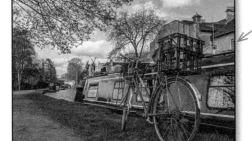

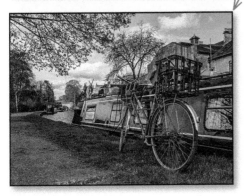

Whites/Blacks After Highlights/Shadows

After -100 Highlights and + 100 Shadows, the full range of detail is back but the photo looks very flat

If we use +21 Whites and -61 Blacks (below left), we can add back contrast without losing it anywhere important

Using the Blacks clipping warning (black areas) we can see we're just clipping the blacks in areas where the detail doesn't matter

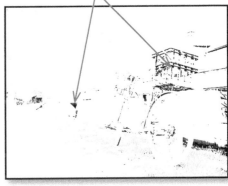

Figure 11.53 *Use Whites and Blacks after Highlights and Shadows to bring back some contrast.*

Whites Slider

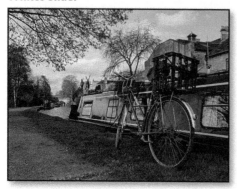

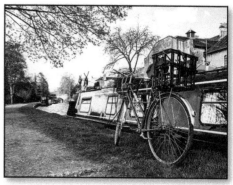

- Whites darkens the entire photo, but especially the lightest tones.

+ Whites clips light pixels to pure white, but we've pushed it too far and lost detail in the clouds. Try to only clip small specular highlights.

+100

0

-100

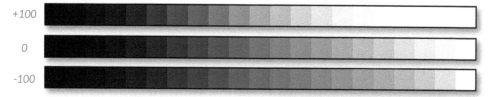

Figure 11.54 *The Whites slider lightens or darkens the photo allowing you to clip the whites.*

The stepwedge, histogram and curves are all based on rendered data, however on a raw file, there may be more hidden highlight detail that can be recovered, such as the detail in the clouds.

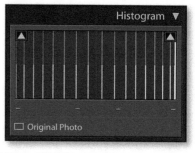

Whites +100 lightens the entire photo, clipping the lightest tones. Note the increase in contrast (spikes slightly further apart) in the midtones.

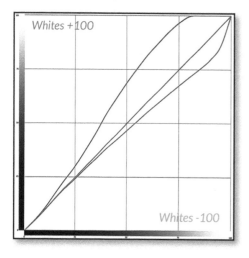

Whites +100

Whites -100

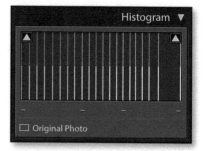

Whites -100 darkens the entire photo. Note the increase in contrast in the very lightest tones, but other tones lose contrast.

Blacks Slider

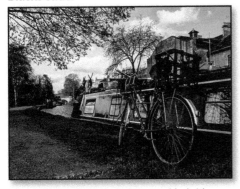

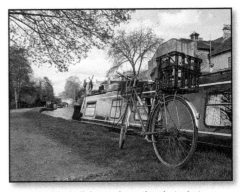

- Blacks clips dark pixels to pure black. It's ok to clip dark pixels to black, but avoid creating large areas of solid black like this.

+ Blacks lightens the entire photo, but especially the darkest tones.

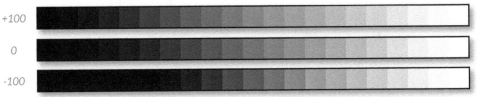

+100

0

-100

Figure 11.55 The Blacks slider lightens or darkens the photo allowing you to clip the blacks.

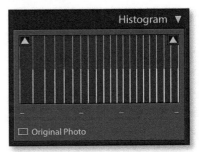

Blacks +100 lightens the entire photo. Note the increase in contrast in the very darkest tones, but other tones lose contrast.

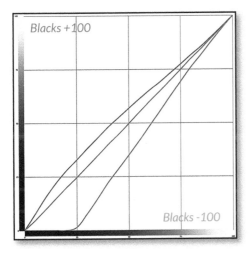

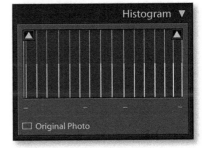

Blacks -100 darkens the entire photo, clipping the darkest tones. Note the increase in contrast (spikes slightly further apart) in the midtones.

Low Dynamic Range—If a photo was captured in flat light, and therefore has a low dynamic range , use +*Whites* and -*Blacks* to stretch image data to fill the entire histogram, making a few pixels black and a few pure white. **(Figures 11.56 & 11.57)**

Adaptive Range—The sliders adapt to the range of the photo, so even a foggy white photo can be stretched to fill the entire tonal range. This becomes even more useful when working with scans of old faded photos, as it allows you to create a bright white and deep black point in even the lowest contrast photos if you need to do so. **(Figure 11.58)**

Check the Clipping Warnings—Hold down the Alt key (Windows) / Opt key (Mac) while dragging the *Whites* or *Blacks* sliders to view the clipping warnings, so you can check you're not clipping important details (making large areas pure white or pure black). The colored overlay shows whether the clipping only affects one channel, multiple channels, or all channels. **(Figure 11.59)**

Mind the Skin—Clipping any channel on someone's skin looks really bad and is worth avoiding at all costs.

Specular Highlights—Some areas of the photo, called specular highlights, are meant to be pure white and we don't expect to see detail. These include the sun, reflections on shiny objects and similar. It's fine to clip these areas, but you don't want large areas of pure white (such as a window). **(Figure 11.60)**

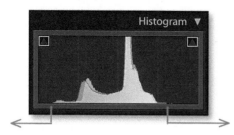

Figure 11.56 *A histogram of a photo with a low dynamic range doesn't stretch to the ends, but can be stretched using the +Whites and -Blacks sliders.*

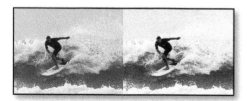

Figure 11.57 *A photo with a low dynamic range may be dull and flat (left) but expanding the dynamic range using the Whites and Blacks sliders sets a true white and black point (right).*

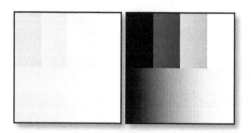

Figure 11.58 *The sliders adapt to the range of the photo, so even a foggy white photo (left) can be stretched to fill the entire tonal range (right).*

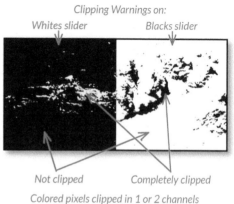

Clipping Warnings on:
Whites slider   *Blacks slider*

Not clipped   Completely clipped
Colored pixels clipped in 1 or 2 channels

Figure 11.59 *The clipping warnings show which areas of the photo have lost detail.*

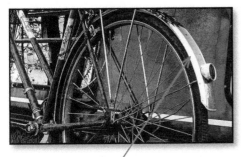

Pure white clipped highlights don't look out of place on shiny objects

Figure 11.60 *The clipping warnings show which areas of the photo have lost detail.*

Deep Blacks—Deep blacks, caused by clipping larger numbers of dark pixels, is a popular choice to enhance contrast. Just be careful not clip too far and lose important shadow detail. This is more frequently done with a tone curve, as it compresses the dark tones with gentler transitions.

Clipping Studio Backgrounds—If you're shooting against a white studio background, which you want to keep pure white, the *Whites* slider allows you to clip highlights that would otherwise be protected by the *Exposure* slider's gentle roll off. If the photo was correctly exposed, with the whites close to clipping, a small value such as +15-25 is enough to blow the white background without having a noticeable impact on the overall exposure. The same principle applies using the *Blacks* slider with a black studio background.

CLARITY

The **Clarity** slider creates local contrast in the midtones by searching for edges and other areas of local contrast and enhancing that contrast. As we learned on page 206, local contrast helps to lift the photo off the page or screen, adding depth and drawing

you into the photo, without losing too much highlight or shadow detail. You might also use words like definition, punch, pop or texture.

How do I set *Clarity*?

As a general rule, it's best to use a very low setting for portraits, if you use it at all, as it can accentuate lines and wrinkles. **(Figure 11.61)**

It's very good at emphasizing texture, so it works well on architecture and landscapes, adding a distinctive crisp feel, and it can also look great on high contrast B&W photos. Although the slider goes to 100, that's usually too strong. **(Figure 11.62)**

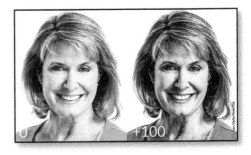

Figure 11.61 *Wrinkles on faces create local contrast, so avoid adding more. I know of very few women who appreciate having their wrinkles exaggerated!*

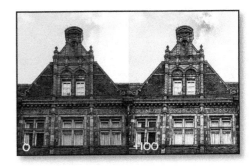

Figure 11.62 *The Clarity slider helps to add 'pop' to buildings, landscapes and other textured scenes, which naturally have small contrasts between similar tones.*

Clarity doesn't increase saturation, so if you use high *Clarity* values, you may find that the colors start to look a little muted. Adding a little *Vibrance* or *Saturation* can make the effect look more natural.

Set to a negative amount, it creates a diffuse soft-focus effect. It gives a gentle glow to the photo, so it can look good on B&W, vintage style or infrared photos. On faces, it softens the eyes too much when applied using the main slider, but it works well for skin softening when applied using a brush (page 241). **(Figure 11.63)**

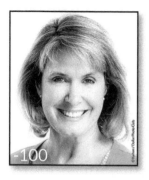

Figure 11.63 *Negative Clarity has softened everything in this example, but applying it using the brush protects the eyes/hair.*

DEHAZE

The **Dehaze** slider is found in the Effects panel, but since it affects the color and tone, we'll discuss it here, with the other tonal controls.

Dehaze is designed to remove (or add) haze, for example, atmospheric haze over a landscape or city smog. It also works well on photos of the night sky, backlit photos, underwater photos, reflections, scans/ photographs of old faded photos, and more. It's also brilliant for adding a high contrast gritty feel to B&W photos. **(Figure 11.64)**

It runs complex calculations to adapt to the content of the image to get a good result as quickly as possible.

How do I set *Dehaze*?

To get the best result, adjust the white balance first (page 198), as it uses the air light color and light transmission in its calculations, then adjust the *Dehaze* slider until your photo looks great.

It's best used in combination with the

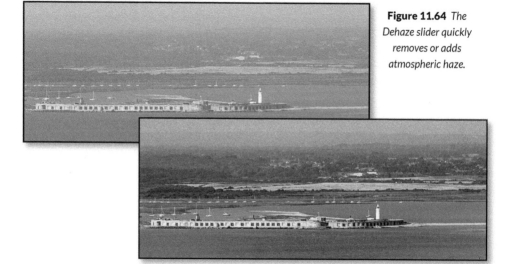

Figure 11.64 *The Dehaze slider quickly removes or adds atmospheric haze.*

normal adjustment sliders. Use *Dehaze* to remove the worst of the haze, and then use the other sliders as normal to finish editing the photo.

Dehaze is a magical slider, but it can have negative side effects such as unwanted color shifts, halos, stronger noise, enhanced sensor dust and enhanced lens defects. As a result, you may need to adjust the Light panel sliders, *Vibrance* or *Saturation*, *Noise Reduction*, *Vignette* and tweak any spot removal after applying the *Dehaze* slider.

Because *Dehaze* adapts to the content of each photo, it's best avoided when doing timelapse photography.

VIBRANCE VS. SATURATION

Saturation describes the intensity or purity of a color. Lightroom offers two different global saturation controls, with slightly different behaviors. **(Figure 11.65)**

Saturation is quite a blunt instrument which adjusts the saturation of all colors equally. This can result in some colors clipping as they reach full saturation.

Vibrance is often more useful as it adjusts the saturation on a non-linear scale, increasing the saturation of lower-saturated colors more than highly saturated colors. It also aims to protect skin tones from becoming over-saturated. **(Figures 11.66 & 11.67)**

Understanding these differences is important, for example, if you want to boost the yellows, oranges and reds in a sunset, *Saturation* may be a better choice than *Vibrance*, but on skin tones, the opposite would be true.

How do I set the saturation?

Our eyes are drawn to vivid saturated colors, but if you go too far, it becomes garish and cartoon-like. This is particularly true on skin tones, which look ridiculous when heavily saturated.

The saturation of colors also affects the mood of the photo. You may want bright, saturated colors for a kid's party, but calm, muted colors may be better suited to a newborn photo.

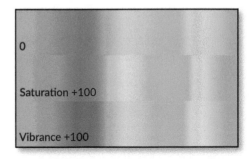

Figure 11.66 *Vibrance enhances the blue tones more than Saturation, and keeps the reds/oranges looking more natural.*

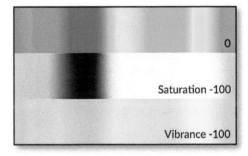

Figure 11.67 *Saturation completely desaturates to B&W whereas Vibrance is more gentle.*

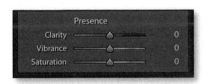

Figure 11.65 *The Vibrance and Saturation sliders affect saturation in different ways.*

If you need even more control over the saturation of specific tones, you can use the HSL tools (page 274) or selective editing (page 241).

PROCESS VERSIONS

Over Lightroom's lifetime, there have been significant changes in Lightroom's processing algorithms to improve the image quality that it can produce.

As Lightroom's edits are stored non-destructively as text instructions, simply removing the old sliders or changing the effect of existing sliders would change the appearance of existing photos. All of your photos would need editing again whenever major changes were made to Lightroom.

To avoid this situation of significantly different rendering, Lightroom uses a concept called Process Versions. This tells Lightroom which set of algorithms to use when rendering a photo.

PV1 (2003) is the original rendering from ACR 1. New sliders were added over time, but existing ones remained constantâ. **(Figure 11.68)**

PV2 (2010) was added in Lightroom 3. It changed *Sharpening*, *Noise Reduction* and *Fill Light*.

PV3 (2012) was added in Lightroom 4. It changed most of the Basic panel sliders, resulting in a completely different rendering, as well as adding RGB point curves and new local adjustment sliders. **(Figure 11.69)**

PV4 (2017) was added in Lightroom Classic 7, for the the new range mask and updated auto mask for local adjustments.

How do I know which process version I'm using?

To check which process version a photo is using, check the Histogram panel. If you're using an older version, a lightning bolt appears, and floating over the icon displays the process version number. **(Figure 11.70)**

You can also check the ***Process*** pop-up in the Camera Calibration panel. **(Figure 11.71)**

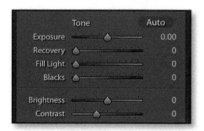

Figure 11.68 *PV1/PV2 used the original Basic panel Tone sliders.*

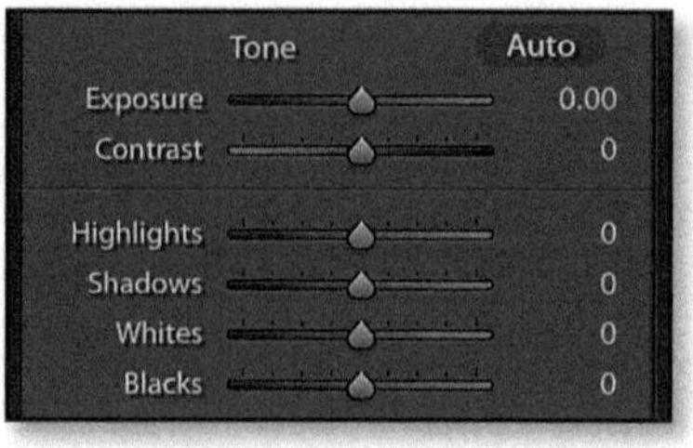

Figure 11.69 *PV3/PV4 use the newest set of Basic panel Tone sliders.*

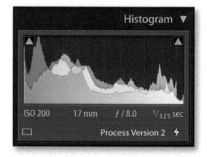

Figure 11.70 *A lightning bolt appears under the Histogram if your photo uses an older process version.*

Which process version should I use?

The most recent process version—currently PV4—offers the best image quality and latest technology, so it's generally the best choice.

That said, if you upgrade photos from PV1/2 to PV4, you'll generally need to edit them again, so don't upgrade all of your old photos.

How do I update the process version?

New photos default to PV4 unless you apply an old Develop preset, or they already have settings stored in their metadata, so for most new imports, you won't need to do anything.

For existing photos, you may want to update the process version.

Photos set to PV3 are automatically upgraded to PV4 when you start editing, unless you've already used auto mask, in which case they don't update themselves

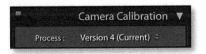

Figure 11.71 *The Process Version is found at the top of the Camera Calibration panel.*

until you use Range Mask in the Adjustment Brush or Linear/Radial Gradients (page 249).

Photos that use much older process versions can be upgraded by selecting *Version 4 (Current)* in the *Process* popup in the Camera Calibration panel or via *Settings menu > Process*.

To update to the latest process version, you can also click on the lightning bolt in the Histogram panel. In the resulting dialog **(Figure 11.72)**, choose:

Review Changes via Before/After displays the before/after side-by-side so you can decide whether to go ahead. If you decide not to update, use Ctrl-Z (Windows) / Cmd-Z (Mac) or select the previous state in the History panel to revert to the earlier setting.

Update just updates the selected photo. If you're going to select this option, it's quicker to hold down the Alt (Windows) / Opt (Mac) while clicking on the lightning bolt, as this skips the dialog.

Update All Filmstrip Photos updates all of the photos in the current view. Be careful, because if the photos were set to PV1/2, you'll likely have to edit all of the photos again using the new sliders.

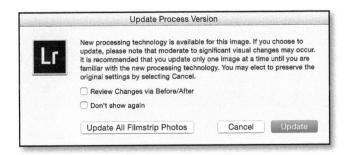

Figure 11.72 *If you click on the lightning bolt in the Histogram panel, Lightroom asks whether you'd like to update just that photo or multiple photos.*

How do I update my presets to the new process version?

Some of your Develop presets may include an old process version, so when you apply the preset, the photo reverts to PV3 or earlier.

We'll come back to creating and updating presets on page 311. If you have lots of presets to update and you're an advanced user, it's quicker to open the presets in a text editor and remove the entire Process Version line (e.g., *ProcessVersion = "6.7",*) or update the version number to 10.0 for PV4.

What do the other Camera Calibration panel sliders do?

We already discussed the *Profile* pop-up on page 194 . The rest of the sliders (**Shadows, Red Primary, Green Primary** and **Blue Primary**) in the Camera Calibration panel are primarily legacy sliders. They were used for adjusting camera calibration before the detailed camera profiles were invented, so

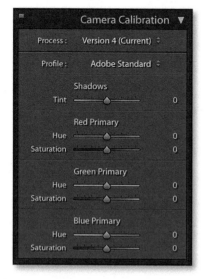

Figure 11.73 *The Camera Calibration panel contains legacy calibration sliders, which preceeded the Profile pop-up.*

they're rarely needed now. That said, they can be useful for creative effects. **(Figure 11.73)**

EDITING VIDEOS

Many digital cameras now produce, not only still photographs, but also video. We've already used the Loupe view to play your videos, so before we move on to more advanced stills editing, let's take a quick look at Lightroom's basic video editing tools.

How do I trim videos?

In the Loupe view, click on the cog button on the video overlay to show the individual video frames. If the overlay isn't wide enough to accurately scrub through the video, you can drag both ends to enlarge it.

The trim handles are shown at the left and right ends of the overlay, and dragging these toward the center trims the ends from the video. The easiest way to select the best trim position is to drag the position marker or pause the video in the right spot. When you drag the trim handles, they snap to the selected frame.

The trimmed sections of video aren't removed from the original file, but they're hidden when playing the video in Lightroom, and are excluded when you export the video to a new file.

You can't clip sections out of the middle of the video, as it only allows you to trim the ends, however you could create virtual copies of your video, allowing you to trim a different section from each. **(Figure 11.74)**

Can I join videos together?

There isn't officially a way of merging video clips together into a single video within

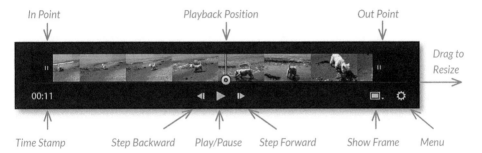

In Point   Playback Position   Out Point

Drag to
Resize

00:11

Time Stamp   Step Backward   Play/Pause   Step Forward   Show Frame   Menu

Figure 11.74 *Video playback and editing options.*

Lightroom, but there is a workaround... Add the videos to the Slideshow module, remove the extraneous overlays and background and then go to *Slideshow menu > Export Video Slideshow* to create a merged video.

What do Capture Frame and Set Poster Frame do?

Under the rectangular thumbnail button on the video overlay are two additional options:

Capture Frame extracts the current frame as a JPEG and automatically adds it to the folder. If you're viewing a folder or standard collection, the captured frame should appear next to the video, but it may be hidden if you're working in *Previous Import, Quick Collection* or if you set a filter or smart collection to only show videos.

Set Poster Frame allows you to select which frame is shown as the video thumbnail in the Grid view, and as the preview in other modules.

If you're trying to select a specific frame for the Capture Frame or Poster Frame, it can be difficult to drag the position marker to exactly the right spot. If you drag it to approximately the right spot, you can use the arrow buttons either side of the play button to step through one frame at a time.

Can I view video metadata such as Frame Rate?

If you select the *Video* preset at the top of the Metadata panel, you'll be able to see additional video metadata, such as the *Frame Rate, Dimensions* and *Audio Sample Rate.* **(Figure 11.75)**

You will note that there's limited metadata included in most video files. Details that we're used to seeing in digital image EXIF data, such as the camera and lens used, are not usually present. If this data is important to you, consider taking a photo just before recording, so that you have a permanent record.

You can add or edit the capture time for videos, just as you can for photos, which can help if the capture time wasn't initially recorded with the video.

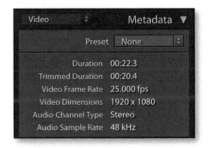

Figure 11.75 *The Video preset in the Metadata panel shows additional information such as Frame Rate.*

Can I edit the color and exposure of my videos in the Develop module?

Video isn't supported in the Develop module, however you can make Develop changes using the Quick Develop panel or Develop presets. Any changes you make apply to the whole video, not just the selected frame.

The Quick Develop panel in the Library module gives you quick access to basic Develop controls—*Treatment (Color or B&W)*, *White Balance*, *Auto Tone*, *Exposure*, *Contrast*, *White Clipping*, *Black Clipping*, *Vibrance*, and also *Saturation* when holding down the Alt (Windows) / Opt (Mac) key.

Additional adjustments can be made to Tone Curve, Split Toning, Process Version & Camera Calibration by including them in a Develop preset. This enables you to make your videos sepia or apply other effects, in addition to basic exposure and white balance corrections.

The easiest way to make the adjustments is to use *Capture Frame* to create a JPEG from the video. You can edit this JPEG in the Develop module and then save it as a preset or sync the changes to the video. It allows you to preview your adjustments before applying them to the whole video, rather than using trial and error. When syncing the settings, you'll note that only settings that can be applied to videos are available in the Sync dialog. **(Figure 11.76)** (We'll come back to creating presets and synchronizing settings in the Develop Tools chapter starting on page 305.)

Can I open my video into specialist video editing software?

Lightroom doesn't make it easy to open your videos into editing software such as Adobe Premiere, but you can right-click and choose *Show in Explorer* (Windows) / *Show in Finder* (Mac) and then open into the editor of your choice.

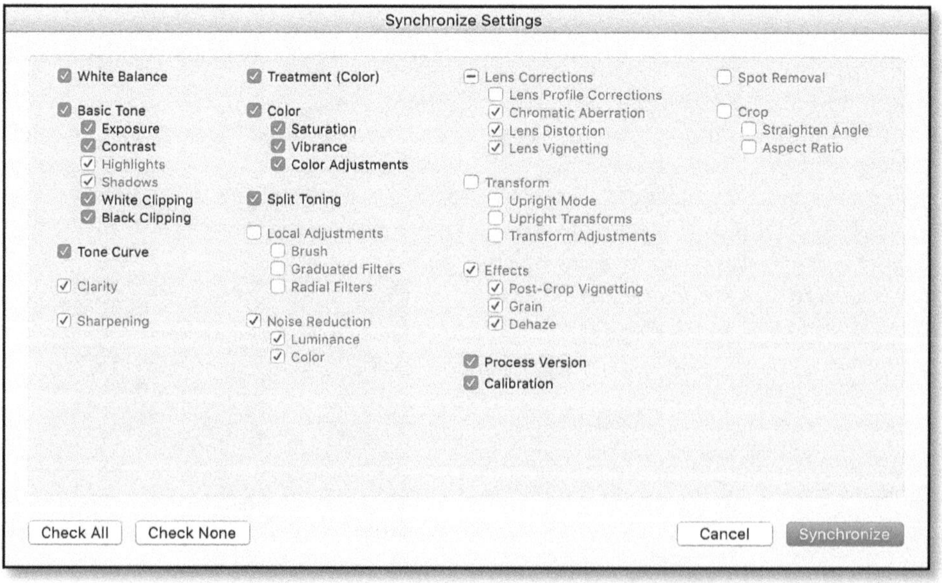

Figure 11.76 *Only some Develop settings can be synchronized when working with videos. The other checkboxes are disabled.*

Alternatively, John Beardsworth's Open Directly plug-in allows you to open the original video into the

software of your choice, including video editing software: https://www.Lrq.me/beardsworth-opendirectly

DEVELOP BASIC SHORTCUTS

		Windows	Mac
Go to Develop		D	D
Sliders	Select next Basic panel slider	.	.
	Select previous Basic panel slider	,	,
	Increase slider value	= or +	= or +
	Decrease slider value	-	-
	Move slider value by larger increment	Shift while using = or + or -	Shift while using = or + or -
	Move slider value by smaller increment		Opt while using = or + or -
White Balance	Select White Balance Eyedropper	W	W
Auto	Auto White Balance	Ctrl Shift U	Cmd Shift U
	Auto Settings	Ctrl U	Cmd U
	Auto Slider Value	Shift double-click on slider label	Shift double-click on slider label
Clipping Indicators	Show Clipping	J	J
	Temporarily Show Clipping	Hold Alt while moving slider	Hold Opt while moving slider
Reset	Reset Slider	Double-click on slider label	Double-click on slider label
	Reset Group of Sliders	Double-click on group name	Double-click on group name
	Reset All Settings	Ctrl Shift R	Cmd Shift R
Video	Toggle Play/Pause	Space	Space
Video Trimming	Set In Point	Shift I	Shift I
	Set Out Point	Shift O	Shift O

Typical Develop Workflow

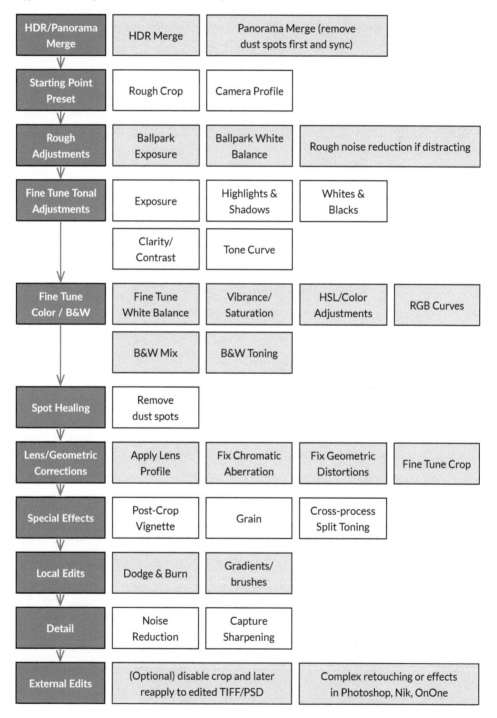

Figure 11.77 *A typical editing workflow.*

DEVELOP SELECTIVE EDITING

12

Once you've made basic tonal adjustments to your photos, you can make more selective adjustments. These include cropping the photo, removing dust spots, fixing red eye and applying tonal adjustments to specific areas of the photo using gradients and brush masks. These tools are found in the Tool Strip directly beneath the Histogram panel. We'll investigate each in turn. **(Figure 12.1)**

CROPPING & STRAIGHTENING

In an ideal world, you would have the time to make sure a photo was perfectly composed in the camera at the time of shooting. Unfortunately, few of us live in an ideal world, and by the time you've perfected the shot, you've missed the moment.

Most photos benefit from cropping, whether to remove distracting objects, straighten horizons, for artistic effect, or simply to fit your chosen ratio.

When you're cropping in Lightroom, you're deciding which bits of the photo will be cropped, rather than setting a fixed size. When you come to export, you then define

the size of the exported photo, either as pixel dimensions or as inches/cm combined with a resolution setting. Let's give it a try...

1. To open the Crop tool, select the first icon in the Develop Tool Strip below the Histogram or press the R key. The Crop Options display below. **(Figure 12.2)**

2. First, straighten your horizon by pressing the *Auto* button.

3. If Auto doesn't work well, select the Straighten tool in the Crop Options panel, and click and drag a line along the horizon. Lightroom automatically rotates the photo to make it horizontal.

4. Select your crop ratio in the *Aspect* pop-up. (You don't choose the size until

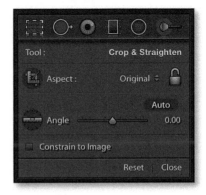

Figure 12.2 *To open the Crop tool, select the first icon in the Tool Strip. The options appear below.*

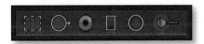

Figure 12.1 *The Tool Strip.*

you export the photo.) To switch the crop orientation, for example, to make a vertical crop from a horizontal photo, press the X key.

5. Adjust the crop by dragging the corners or the edges of the bounding box.

6. Move the photo around under the crop overlay by clicking within the bounding box and dragging the photo into position. Rotate the photo by clicking and dragging around the outside of the bounding box. Think of it as moving the photo underneath the crop overlay, rather than moving the crop.

7. Once you've finished cropping, press the Enter key or the *Done* button on the Toolbar.

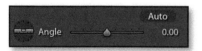

CONTINUES ON PAGE 234

That's the basics, but now let's do a deeper dive into the crop options.

How do I straighten or rotate a photo?

As well as clicking on the Straighten tool icon in the Crop Options panel, you can quickly access the tool by holding down the Ctrl key (Windows) / Cmd key (Mac) while

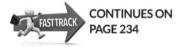

Figure 12.3 *The Straighten tool is stored in the Crop Options panel, next to the Angle slider.*

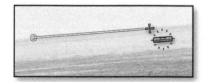

Figure 12.4 *Straighten the photo by selecting the Straighten tool and dragging a line along the horizon.*

you drag along the horizon line on the photo. **(Figures 12.3 & 12.4)**

If you prefer to straighten by eye, hover outside of the crop boundary, so that the cursor changes to a double-headed arrow **(Figure 12.5)**, then click and drag to rotate the photo up to 45 degrees in either direction. Or you can manually adjust the degree of rotation using the **Angle** slider.

As you rotate the crop, the photo remains level so you don't have to turn your head to see how the photo will look once it's cropped. **(Figure 12.6)**

To get a better view of the cropped photo as you adjust the crop, try enabling Lights Out mode by pressing the L key twice. Press L again to switch back to the normal view.

Figure 12.5 *To rotate a crop, float the mouse around the outside of the crop area until the double-headed arrow appears.*

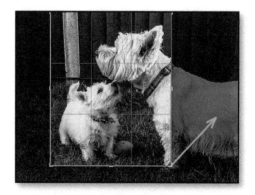

Figure 12.6 *Reverse the crop orientation by dragging a corner at a 45 degree angle or pressing the X key.*

How do I resize the crop?

To resize the crop, drag the edges of the photo. If you drag the corners, you can adjust two sides in one go.

You can also move the photo around under the crop overlay by dragging the center of the photo.

How do I draw a freeform crop?

For a free form or non-standard crop ratio, unlock the Lock icon and click and drag a rectangle on the photo or drag the edges of the bounding box.

How do I crop a vertical portion from a horizontal photo?

To change the crop orientation, drag the corner of the crop diagonally until the long edge becomes shorter than the short edge and the grid flips over (it gets easier with practice!), or just press the X key to flip the crop overlay.

Alternatively, unlock the ratio lock in the Crop options panel and adjust to the crop of your choice. You can also drag a crop freehand, by dragging a rectangle on the photo, but if you already have a crop applied, you have to press the *Reset* button in the Crop Options panel first.

What is Aspect Ratio?

Images on screen can be any shape you like, but if you're printing or framing a photo, you'll be limited by the aspect ratio of the paper or frame.

The aspect ratio is simply the proportional relationship between width and height of a photo—it's the shape of the photo. You'll often see it written with a colon (2:3) or with an x (2x3).

Some aspect ratios are long and thin, whereas others are closer to square. To illustrate, we'll overlay a few different aspect ratios over each other, all aligned to the left edge, so we can compare them. The white square on top is 1x1—the height and width are equal. At the bottom of the stack, the red 2x3 shape is a long and thin rectangle. **(Figure 12.7)**

How do I change the crop ratio?

If you're planning on printing the photo, you may want to restrict your crop to a standard aspect ratio. As Lightroom never throws away pixels, it doesn't crop to a specific size—just a ratio. This enables you to reuse the same crop for multiple different sizes, for example, a 4x5 ratio crop can be output as 800x1000 pixels, 4"x5", 8"x10", etc.

By default, the crop ratio is set to *Original* (or *As Shot* for photos that have an in-camera crop). If you'd prefer a different ratio, select it from the **Aspect** pop-up.

When you change the crop ratio on an existing crop in the Develop module (not Quick Develop), Lightroom applies the new ratio to the existing crop instead of resetting the crop to maximum size. If you'd like it to reset the crop to the largest possible size, hold

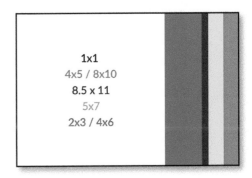

Figure 12.7 *The shape of standard print ratios varies. For example, 4x5 (blue) is quite square, whereas 2x3 (red) is longer and thinner.*

down the Alt (Windows) / Opt (Mac) key while selecting a ratio.

What's the difference between *As Shot* and *Original*?

Some cameras allow you to crop the photos to a specific ratio at the time of shooting, or display crop lines on the screen. Some photographers want their in-camera crop (i.e. 3:2, 16:9, 1:1) applied in Lightroom and others want the full raw file.

In cameras added to Lightroom 4.2 or later, the *As Shot* crop ratio displays the photo with the in-camera crop applied, but changing to *Original* in the *Aspect* pop-up displays all the available sensor data.

For older cameras (those released before mid-2012), you'll need to use the free DNG Recover Edges plug-in (see page E-13 in the Appendix).

How do I set a custom crop aspect ratio?

The standard ratios are: *As Shot, Original, Custom,* 1x1, 4x5/8x10, 8.5x11, 5x7, 2x3/4x6, 4x3, 16x9 and 16x10.

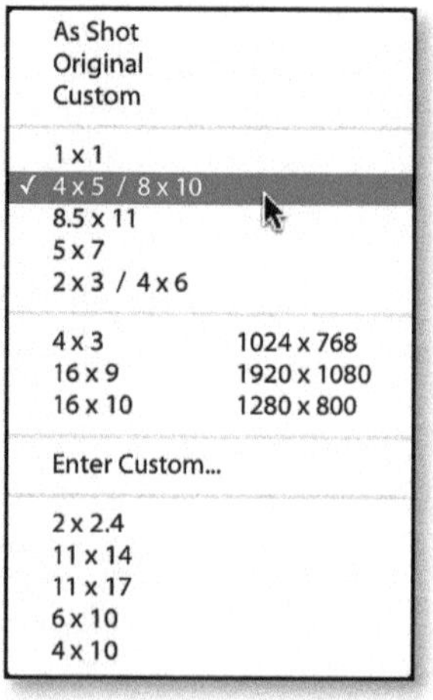

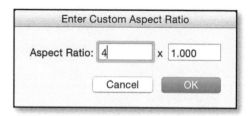

Figure 12.8 *Select the ratio from the list or create a custom one.*

(Figure 12.8) If your chosen crop ratio isn't on this list, you can create your own custom crop ratio.

In the *Aspect* pop-up, select *Enter Custom* and type your own crop ratio. **(Figure 12.9)** It'll automatically be added to the bottom of the list. You can't delete custom crop ratios manually, but they work on a rolling list of 5, so only your most recent custom ratios remain in the list. As you add a new one, the oldest one is removed from the list.

How do I lock my crop ratio?

When you select a crop ratio from the pop-up, the lock icon to the right automatically locks. **(Figure 12.10)** As you drag the edges of the crop bounding box, the nearest three edges move, retaining your chosen crop ratio. To allow the crop edges to move freely, one at a time, click the crop ratio lock icon to unlock it.

Can I set a default crop ratio?

If you always crop your photos to a specific ratio, for example, 8x10, you may want to apply this ratio automatically instead of selecting 8x10 from the *Aspect* pop-up on each photo. You can't change the

Figure 12.9 *Create your own custom ratios by selecting Enter Custom from the Aspect pop-up.*

Figure 12.10 *The lock icon fixes your crop to your chosen aspect ratio.*

default crop ratio, but there are two easy workarounds.

Return to the Grid view and select all of the photos. In the Quick Develop panel **(Figure 12.11)**, click the disclosure triangle to the right of the *Saved Preset* pop-up to show the *Crop Ratio* pop-up, then select your chosen ratio.

Alternatively, crop the first photo in the normal Crop mode, and synchronize or copy/paste that crop to all the other photos. (We'll come to Synchronize in the Develop Module Tools chapter on page 305.)

Once you've done this, your chosen ratio will already be selected in the Crop options panel and you can go through the photos and adjust the crop to taste.

Either way, it's intelligent enough to rotate the crop for the opposite orientation photos,

but beware, it also resets any existing crops.

Why do I need to select the right ratio for prints?

Imagine you have a rectangular photo and a square frame. **(Figure 12.12)**

Clearly it doesn't fit, so what are your options? **(Figure 12.13)**

1. Squash/squeeze the photo to fit. This never looks good, so Lightroom doesn't let you do it.

2. Keep the rectangular shape, but add white borders along the other edges.

3. Crop the top and bottom (or sides), so

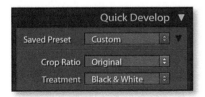

Figure 12.11 *Crop ratios can also be accessed from the Quick Develop panel in the Library module.*

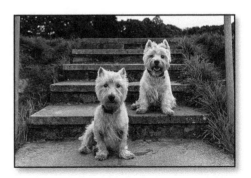

Figure 12.12 *Imagine you need to make this rectangular photo fit a square frame.*

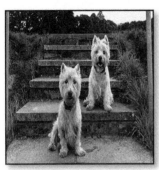

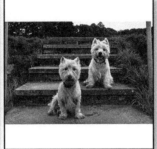

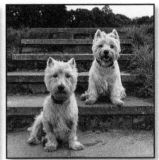

Squash/squeeze it   *Add white borders*   *Crop it*

Figure 12.13 *To make a rectangular photo fit a square frame, you must squash it, add borders or crop it.*

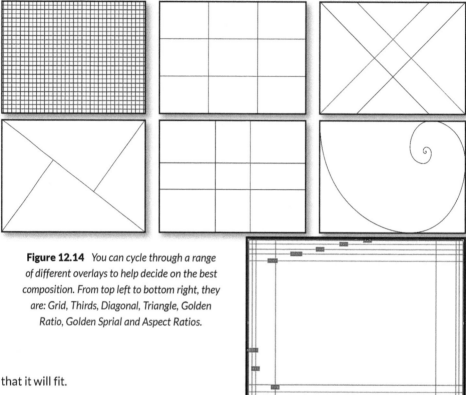

Figure 12.14 *You can cycle through a range of different overlays to help decide on the best composition. From top left to bottom right, they are: Grid, Thirds, Diagonal, Triangle, Golden Ratio, Golden Sprial and Aspect Ratios.*

that it will fit.

4. Buy another frame that's closer to the aspect ratio of the photo, so you don't need to crop as much.

The same principle applies to other aspect ratios, not just cropping to square. Imagine trying to fit a panoramic photo into a normal rectangular frame, and you'll have the same choices to make.

How do I change the Crop Overlay?

When you first enter the Crop mode, gray grid lines are overlaid over the photo. This is called the Crop Overlay and it's useful as a composition guide. It's set to *Thirds* by default, named after the Rule of Thirds, but there's a variety of different overlays to choose from: *Grid, Thirds, Diagonal, Triangle, Golden Ratio, Golden Spiral and Aspect Ratio.*

Press the O key to cycle through a variety of

overlays **(Figure 12.14)**, and Shift-O changes the orientation of these overlays. You may only use some of the overlays so you can hide the others by selecting *Tools menu > Crop Guide Overlay > Choose Overlays to Cycle.* **(Figure 12.15)**

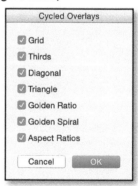

Figure 12.15 *You can choose which overlays to display.*

The *Aspect Ratio* overlay displays a number of different ratio lines to help envisage how it'll look at different ratios. You can choose which ratios to display using the *Tools menu > Crop Guide Overlay > Choose Aspect Ratios* dialog. **(Figure 12.16)**

You can't change the Crop Overlay color but if you find the overlays distracting, press the H key to hide them, or select *Never* from the pop-up on the Toolbar. If the pop-up's set to *Auto*, the Grid overlay only displays when you're rotating the photo.

Is there a way to see what the new pixel dimensions will be without interpolation?

If you go to *View menu > View Options*, you can set the Info Overlay to show *Cropped Dimensions*, which is the cropped pixel dimensions without any resampling. Every time you let go of the edge of the bounding box, these dimensions update. You'll also find the original and cropped dimensions in the Metadata panel in the Library module.

Should I check *Constrain to Image*?

Finally, there's a **Constrain to Image**

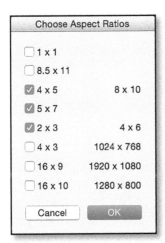

Figure 12.16 *You can choose which aspect ratios to display in the Aspect Ratio overlay.*

checkbox in the Crop Options panel. It prevents you from including blank white pixels in your crop, which may be caused by lens corrections. It means that you can crop your photo without having to be too careful to avoid including blank areas, so it's usually worth leaving checked. There's a *Constrain Crop* checkbox in the Transform panel which does the same thing.

How do I flip photos?

Occasionally you may want to flip a photo horizontally or vertically, so they look good as a group on the wall, or to lead the viewer's eye from left to right. To flip the photo, go to *Photo menu > Flip Horizontal* or *Flip Vertical*.

When you're in the Library module, there's also a temporary flipped view under *View menu > Enable Mirror Image Mode*. It affects all of the photos you're viewing, but only while it's enabled. It's useful when viewing photos of yourself (or showing other people photos of themselves), because it's the same view we see in the mirror every day.

How do I reset the crop?

If you change your mind about the crop setting, you can cancel it at any time by pressing the **Reset** button at the bottom of the Crop Options panel.

How do I zoom in while cropping?

You can't zoom while in Crop mode, but if you need a larger preview, select the Crop tool and then press Shift-Tab to hide all the side panels. It's particularly useful when straightening a photo.

If you need even more space, Shift-F hides the window title bar and T hides the Toolbar.

SPOT REMOVAL—CLONE & HEAL TOOLS

The second icon in the Tool Strip beneath the Histogram is the Spot Removal tool, also known as the Advanced
Healing Brush. **(Figure 12.17)** It's not intended to replace Photoshop or other pixel editors, but it allows you to quickly remove dust spots and other small distractions.

Let's try removing a small spot **(Figure 12.18)** before we go into more detail.

1. Select the second icon in the Tool Strip beneath the Histogram, or press the Q key.

2. Adjust the brush size using the slider in the Options panel and then click on the spot in the photo, or click and drag to remove a line or non-circular shape. **(Figure 12.19)**

3. The spot overlay appears on the screen, showing the outline of the retouched area

and the source of the new pixels. The circular black and white pin allows you to move or reselect the spot overlay. Lightroom automatically tries to find a good source, but you can click and drag the circular pins to fine tune the correction. **(Figure 12.20)**

4. To delete a spot correction, hold down the Alt key (Windows) / Opt key (Mac) to change the cursor into a pair of scissors, and then click on the spot again.

What's the difference between clicking and dragging?

There are two kinds of spot—circle spots and brush spots (non-circular healing).

Circle spots are created by a single click. They display as single round spots and they can be moved and resized. **(Figure 12.21)**

Brush spots are created by clicking and dragging. As you paint across the photo, a white brush stroke appears, and it's then replaced by two white outlines showing the source and target. Brush spots can have an arbitrary shape but they can't be resized later. **(Figure 12.22)**

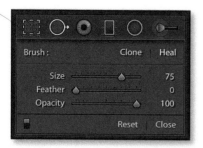

Figure 12.17 *Select the Spot Removal tool from the Tool Strip under the histogram.*

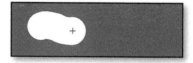

Figure 12.19 *Click and drag to paint over the distraction.*

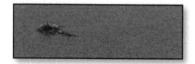

Figure 12.18 *Find a spot or distraction in the photo, such as this piece of seaweed on the sand.*

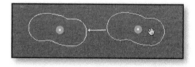

Figure 12.20 *Lightroom finds some new pixels to cover the distraction, but you can click and drag the overlay to choose a different source.*

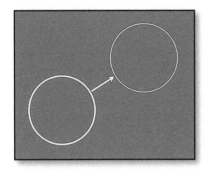

Figure 12.21 *Click on the dust spot to create a circle spot.*

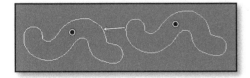

Figure 12.22 *Click and drag over a non-circular shape to create a brush spot.*

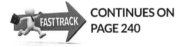

CONTINUES ON PAGE 240

How do I draw a straight line?

Holding down the Shift key while you're drawing a brush spot constrains it to a horizontal or vertical line, which is rarely helpful. However the Shift key can be used to create straight lines at other angles, which is particularly use for power or telephone lines. Click at the beginning of the line to create a circle spot, and then hold down the Shift key and click at the end of the line. Lightroom joins the spots using a straight brush spot.

How do I move or delete an existing spot?

Spots have circular pins in the center, which mark their location and allow you to reselect or move the spot correction. The pins have two states—selected or not selected, or active and inactive. Not selected is shown by a white pin, and clicking on the pin selects that spot, turning the pin black.

When you hover over the center of an existing selected (black) spot, the cursor changes to a hand, and you can then drag to move the spot to a new location. **(Figure 12.23)**

To delete a spot, click on it to make it active, and then press the Delete key on your keyboard. Alternatively, if you hold down the Alt key (Windows) / Opt key (Mac), the cursor changes to a pair of scissors, and then clicking on the individual spots or dragging a rectangular marquee selection around the spots deletes them. **(Figure 12.24)** To remove all spots, press the **Reset** button.

Spot Removal is the one tool in Lightroom that's sensitive to the order in which the

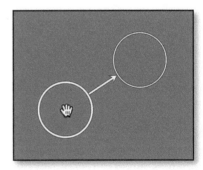

Figure 12.23 *To move a spot, click and drag the center of the spot.*

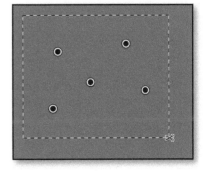

Figure 12.24 *To delete spots, hold down the Alt (Windows) / Opt (Mac) key and click on the spots or drag a marquee around them.*

corrections are applied. The target for one spot can become the source for another spot, and if you then delete the first spot, the latter spot is affected too.

How do I choose the source of the replacement pixels?

When you create a circle or brush spot, Lightroom intelligently searches for the most suitable source of replacement pixels, even if that's outside of the current crop boundary. You can then pick up the source spot's pin, and drag it to a better source.

If you're creating a circle spot, you can select the source while you're creating it. Hold down the Ctrl (Windows) / Cmd (Mac) key while clicking on the spot and drag to your chosen source without letting go of the mouse button.

This does have implications when copying/ synchronizing the spot removal to other photos. If Lightroom automatically finds the source, and then you copy the spot removal to other photos, Lightroom will check for the best source on each of the photos. If you select a source manually, Lightroom copies from the same location on each of the photos. This is particularly useful when using the spot tools to remove sensor dust in a clear area of sky, as it's intelligent enough to adjust for orientation.

How do I adjust the brush size or the size of an existing spot?

In the Spot Removal Options panel under the Tool Strip is a brush **Size** slider, which affects the size of the circle spot or brush stroke. You can also use the [and] keyboard shortcuts or your mouse scroll wheel to adjust the size. Holding down the Ctrl+Alt keys (Windows) / Cmd+Opt keys (Mac) while clicking and dragging on a spot, sets the spot size on-the-fly, overriding the Size

slider.

You can readjust an existing circle spot by clicking on the pin to make it active and then adjusting these same controls. Alternatively, if you hover over the edge of an existing circle spot, the cursor changes and you can then drag the edge to adjust the size. **(Figure 12.25)** You can't resize brush spots, which are the non-circular strokes.

What's the difference between *Clone* mode and *Heal* mode?

While you're in the Spot Removal Options panel, you'll note that you have a choice of *Clone* or *Heal*.

Heal works like the Healing Brush in Photoshop, intelligently blending the edge pixels.

Clone works like Photoshop's Clone tool, picking up the pixels and dropping them in another location.

For most spots, the *Heal* option works best, particularly in clean areas such as sky. If you're trying to retouch a spot along an edge in the photo, for example, a roofline against the sky, the *Heal* tool can smudge, in which case the *Clone* option may work better. We'll come back to some tricky retouching examples later in this section.

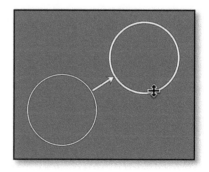

Figure 12.25 *To resize a circle spot, drag the edge of the spot.*

The **Feather** slider is particularly useful when combined with the *Clone* mode. The *Heal* mode works best with *Feathering* set to 0 as it automatically attempts to blend the edges. *Clone* mode stands out if it has hard edges, so a higher value, such as 90, works better. **(Figures 12.26 & 12.27)**

The **Opacity** slider allows you to fade the retouching, for example, you may not want to completely remove the lines on a person's face, but just fade them slightly. If you want

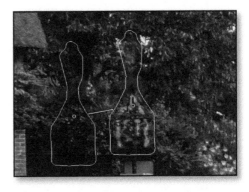

Figure 12.27 *Avoid using the Feathering slider with Heal mode, because you may end up with transparent patches, such as the red triangular sign which is still visible in this photo.*

to remove the blemish completely, leave it set to 100.

How do I use *Visualize Spots* to quickly find dust spots?

When the Spot Removal tool is selected, there's a checkbox and slider in the Toolbar (below the photo) marked **Visualize Spots**. **(Figure 12.28)** When you check its checkbox or press the A key, Lightroom displays a black and white mask of your photo. **(Figure 12.29)**

If you drag the slider to the right, more dust spots are revealed, and dragging it to the left hides them. It's similar to the mask used for the sharpening *Masking* slider, which we'll come to on page 276. You can retouch the spots with the mask active, or you can turn it off again once you've found them.

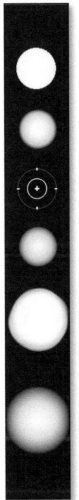

Figure 12.26 *The difference between feathering on circle spots and brush spots. From top to bottom:*

1. Circle spot size 80, feather 0, results in hard edges.

2. Circle spot size 80, feather 100, results in soft edges.

3. Spot removal cursor, size 80. Note the inner and outer circles showing the range of the feathering.

4. Brush spot size 80, feather 100, results in soft edges. The edges are much softer than the second circle spot of the same size, as brush spots have greater feathering range.

5. Brush spot drawn with a small size 75 brush has minimal feathering as the feathering is relative to the size of the brush tip.

6. Brush spot drawn with a larger size 90 brush has much greater feather as it's relative to the size of the brush tip and this brush is much larger.

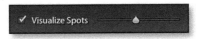

Figure 12.28 *The Visualize Spots checkbox shows in the Toolbar when Spot Removal is selected.*

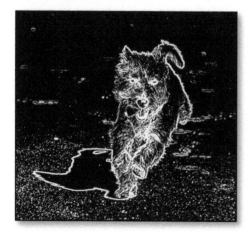

Figure 12.29 *Visualize Spots makes it easier to spot distractions, such as the stones and seaweed in the sand.*

How do I ensure I don't miss a spot?

If you zoom into 1:1 view to retouch dust spots, start in the top left corner and then press the Page Down key (Windows) / Fn + down arrow (Mac) to work through the photo. It divides the photo up into an imaginary grid, so when you reach the bottom of the first column, it automatically returns to the top of the photo and starts on the next column. By the time you reach the bottom right corner, you'll have retouched the entire photo without missing any spots. If you prefer to work left to right, hold down the Shift key too. **(Figure 12.30)**

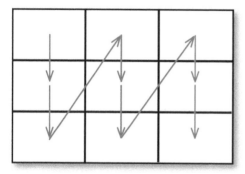

Figure 12.30 *Page Down divides the photo into imaginary sections.*

What are the limitations of the Lightroom's Spot Removal tools?

It's possible to do fairly complex retouching using Lightroom's Spot Removal tools, however, as Lightroom is a metadata editor, it has to constantly re-run text instructions, so it gets slower with the more adjustments that you add.

The tools are ideal for removing distractions such as sensor dust, power cables in the sky, leaves on the grass, etc., but detailed retouching is still quicker and easier in a pixel editing program, such as Photoshop or Photoshop Elements. The point where a pixel editor becomes more efficient than Lightroom depends on your computer hardware, as well as the retouching you're trying to do. When it gets frustrating, stop and switch to Photoshop! **(Figure 12.31)**

Let's try a more complex example combining Clone and Heal modes... **(Figure 12.32-36)**

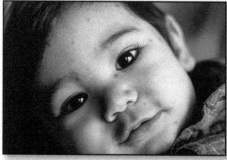

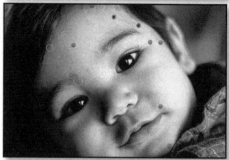

Figure 12.31 *Chickenpox spots or acne can be removed using Circle Spots.*

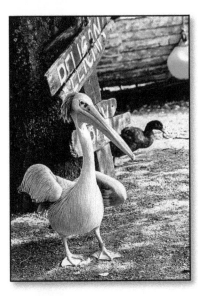

Figure 12.32 *(left) The duck photobombed this photo, so we want to remove him.*

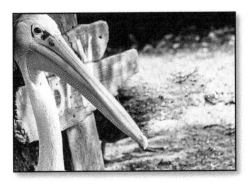

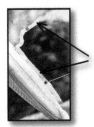

Figure 12.33 *(left) To avoid the smudging, we use two thin Clone lines along the edge of the beak and sign. When we then paint a large Heal stroke over the duck's head and body, and slightly overlap the earlier Clone strokes, we can get a much cleaner result.*

Figure 12.34 *(above) If we just paint up to the edge of the beak and sign in Heal mode, it leaves a dark smudge, and Clone mode leaves harsh edges.*

Figure 12.35 *(left) In this case, there's only one suitable small clone source to the right of the duck's head, which isn't big enough to clone over his whole head and body. To solve this, we divide him up using additional Clone strokes, and add multiple smaller heal chunks, slightly overlapping the clone dividers to clone over the duck.*

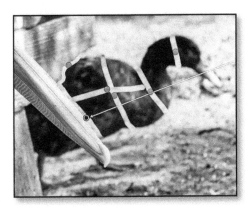

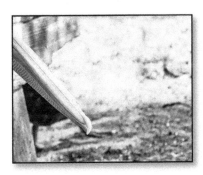

Figure 12.36 *(right) Additional strokes could be used to heal any leftover artifacts. Repeat the process for the rest of the duck.*

RED EYE & PET EYE CORRECTION TOOLS

Red eye in photography— or green eye, in the case of pets—is caused by light from a flash bouncing off the inside of a person's eye. Although many cameras now come with red eye reduction, their pre-flashes tend to warn people that you're about to take a photograph, and can lose any spontaneity. If you turn it off, you can use Lightroom's Red Eye tool to fix red eye in post-processing.

To remove red eye or pet's green eye:

1. Select the third icon in the Tool Strip beneath the Histogram.

2. Select **Red Eye** or **Pet Eye** from the Options panel below.

3. Drag from the centre of the eye, to encompass the whole eye. Lightroom automatically searches for the red/green eye within the selected area, and then makes the other options available in the Options panel. **(Figure 12.37)**

4. Once it locks, you'll see a dark gray spot

Figure 12.37 Drag from the center of the eye.

Figure 12.38 Once the pupil has been detected, adjust the size and darkness of the pupil.

which replaces the red eye. **(Figure 12.38)**

5. Using the **Pupil Size** slider, adjust the size of the spot to cover the pupil, then adjust the **Darken** slider to darken or lighten the pupil. **(Figure 12.39)**

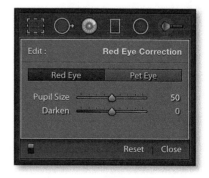

Figure 12.39 Once the circles are in place, edit the Pupil Size and Darken settings.

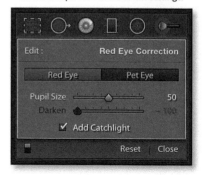

Figure 12.40 Using the Pet Eye Correction, you can add a white catchlight by clicking the Add Catchlight checkbox.

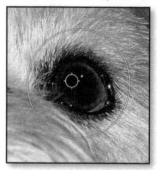

Figure 12.41 Adjust the catchlight position by moving the inner circle.

6. If you're adjusting a pet eye, check the **Add Catchlight** checkbox to add a small white catchlight spot on the pupil. **(Figure 12.40-41)**

Lightroom's Red Eye Correction tool can't lock on to the red eye—is there anything I can do to help it?

If the Red Eye Correction tool can't lock on to the red eye, scroll down to the HSL panel, select the *Saturation* tab and increase the *Red* slider (or *Green* for Pet Eye), then try again. Once it locks, you can set the HSL panel back to its previous settings (0 by default).

LOCAL ADJUSTMENTS— GRADIENTS & BRUSHES

Most of Lightroom's sliders apply to the whole photo, but the local adjustment tools allow you to apply settings to specific areas, either using a gradient or a brush.

How do I use the Graduated or Radial Filter?

The linear (or straight) Graduated Filter is particularly useful for darkening the sky in a sunset photo, but it can also be useful if the lighting on one side of the photo is different

to the other side. **(Figure 12.42)** Let's try it...

1. Select the Linear Graduated Filter—the fourth icon—in the Tool Strip, just below the

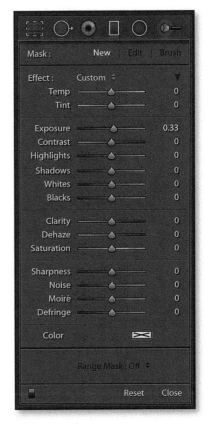

Figure 12.43 *Adjust the settings using the Graduated Filter Options panel.*

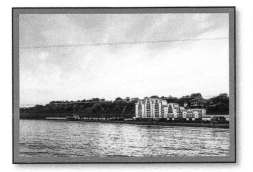
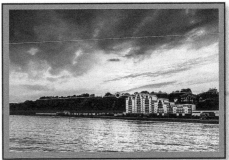

Figure 12.42 *The Graduated Filter is ideal for darkening skies. The central line rotates and the outer lines show the limits of the gradient.*

Histogram. **(Figure 12.43)**

2. In the Options section below, select the settings that you want to apply selectively. It can help to select more extreme settings when creating the gradient, for example, *Exposure +1*, so you can easily see the effect. You can go back and change the settings later.

3. Click on the photo and drag to create your gradient, for example, drag from the top down to darken the sky.

4. Lines appear on screen, showing the limits of the gradient. The outer lines show where the gradient starts (0% of settings applied) and stops (100% of settings applied). Drag the lines to increase or decrease the range. The center line rotates the gradient.

5. Once you're happy with the gradient, you can fine tune the sliders in the Options panel to get the effect you desire.

The same principle applies for the Radial Filter—the fifth icon—except the Radial Filter creates a circular or oval gradient, so you drag out from the center of the photo towards the edges. It's particularly useful for off-center vignettes, but it can also be used to lighten faces in photos and blur backgrounds, amongst other things.

How do I use the Adjustment Brush?

The Adjustment Brush allows you to paint on the photo, perhaps to lighten dark shadows, sharpen eyes, or apply a different white balance to a specific area of the photo.

1. Select the Adjustment Brush—the sixth icon—in the Tool Strip.

2. Select your chosen slider values in the Options panel below. **(Figure 12.44)** As with

the Graduated and Radial Filters, you can go back and fine tune these settings later.

3. There's a selection of presets in the *Effects* pop-up to help you get started. They include basic presets for each of the sliders, plus presets for *Burn (darken)*, *Dodge (lighten)*, *Iris Enhance*, *Soften Skin* and *Teeth Whitening*.

4. The presets just move the sliders to specific values, but they can be helpful if you're not sure which sliders to adjust.

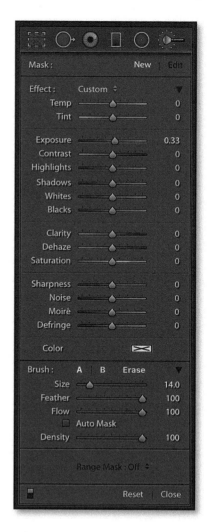

Figure 12.44 *Adjust the brush settings using the Adjustment Brush Options panel.*

For example, the *Teeth Whitening* preset increases the exposure to lighten the teeth and reduces saturation to desaturate the yellow.

5. Select your brush size at the bottom of the Options panel.

6. Click and drag on the photo to paint your brush strokes. If you make a mistake, hold down the Alt key (Windows) / Opt key (Mac) to turn the brush into an eraser, and click and drag over the mistake to remove the brush stroke.

In the Options panel, you can select a mixture of slider settings to apply to your masked area. For example, the *Exposure* adjustment is similar to dodging and burning in Photoshop or in a traditional darkroom. Settings such as *Sharpness*, *Clarity* and *Noise Reduction* can be used for softening skin on portraits. *White Balance* or *Color* are useful when adjusting for mixed lighting situations. Settings can be combined, so a combination of perhaps *Exposure*, *Highlights*, *Saturation*, *Clarity* and a blue tint can make a dull sky much more interesting.

When you've finished making local adjustments, press the *Done* button on the Toolbar or click the icon in the Tool Strip to close the tool.

If you can't find certain controls, such as the *Done* button for Develop tools, your Toolbar may be missing. Press the T key to make it reappear.

We'll work on some more examples at the end of this chapter, but first, let's explore the tools in more detail, starting with the different types of gradient, then the brush, then questions that apply to editing both types of local adjustments.

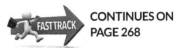

FAST TRACK **CONTINUES ON PAGE 268**

How do I create a new Graduated or Radial Filter mask?

When you select the Graduated or Radial Filter tool, it's automatically ready to start a new mask. The word *New* is highlighted at the top of the Options panel.

Click at your gradient starting point, and drag to your gradient end point before releasing the mouse button. **(Figure 12.45)** If you prefer to work from a central point, rather than selecting your gradient start and end points, hold down the Alt (Windows) / Opt (Mac) key while dragging. The gradient then expands equally from both sides of your starting point. You can hold down the Shift key while creating the gradient to constrain it to a 90 degree angle.

For a radial filter, click in the center of your new circle/oval, and drag out towards the edge of the photo before releasing the mouse button. **(Figure 12.46)** Holding down the Shift key constrains it to a circle instead of an oval. There's a multitude of other shortcuts and modifier keys for the Radial Filter, which are listed in the Keyboard Shortcuts sheet in the Members Area.

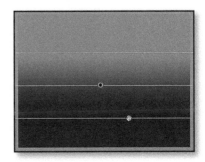

Figure 12.45 *Graduated Filters use three lines to control the distance and rotation of the gradient.*

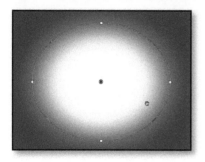

Figure 12.46 *The Radial Filter has a single circle/oval overlay which controls the size, shape and rotation of the gradient.*

How do I edit an existing Graduated Filter?

The local adjustments are marked with small gray circles called Pins. To select an existing local adjustment, click on the pin. The center of the pin turns black, the word *Edit* is highlighted at the top of the Options panel, and the overlay lines for this adjustment appear on the screen.

A **Graduated Filter** mask is controlled by three lines, which allow you to adjust the size, rotation and position of the gradient.

Feather/stretch the gradient—When you float over the outer lines—the ones without the pin—the cursor changes to a hand tool, enabling you to adjust how far the gradient stretches. Moving the outside lines further apart increases the feathering, and moving them closer together reduces the feathering.

Rotate the gradient—When you float over the central line—the one with the pin—the cursor changes to a double-headed arrow, enabling you to adjust the rotation of the gradient. You'll have more control if you drag the outer ends of the lines. (Figure 12.47)

Invert the gradient—If the gradient is the wrong way round, you could drag both

outer lines, swapping their positions, but it's quicker to simply press the ' key to invert it.

Move the gradient—If you need to move the whole mask, click and drag the central pin itself. **(Figure 12.48)**

How do I edit an existing Radial Filter?

A **Radial Filter** is controlled by the circular bounding box and the 4 square markers.

Resize the radial filter—When you float over the square markers, the cursor changes to a straight double-headed arrow, enabling you to adjust how far the gradient stretches. To automatically expand the mask to the edges of the photo, double-click inside the oval bounding box.

Feather the radial filter—The feathering on the Radial Filter is controlled using the *Feather* slider in the Options panel.

Rotate the radial filter—When you float over the line itself, the cursor changes to a curved double-headed arrow, enabling you to click and drag to adjust the rotation of the

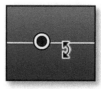

Figure 12.47 *Rotate the gradient using the double-headed arrow which appears when you float over the central line.*

Figure 12.48 *Drag the pin to move the gradient.*

gradient. **(Figure 12.49)**

Invert the radial filter—If the gradient is the wrong way round, you can press the **Invert Mask** checkbox in the Options panel, but it's quicker to simply press the ' key to invert it.

The Radial Filter was primarily designed in response to requests for off-center vignettes, so by default it affects the outside of the circle. If that's not the way you expect it to behave though, it's simple to change the default behavior. To do so, select the Radial Filter and make sure the Options panel is set to *New* rather than *Edit*. Check the *Invert Mask* checkbox, and that, along with any other slider settings in the Options panel, is set as the new defaults.

Move the radial filter—If you need to move the whole mask, click and drag the central pin itself.

How do I create an additional gradient?

To start a new gradient, in order to apply different adjustments to another area of the photo, press the **New** button at the top of the Options panel and start painting. You can have multiple adjustments (pins), on an image, and they can overlap.

How do I delete a gradient?

To delete a gradient, select the pin then press the Delete key or right-click on the pin and select **Delete**. To delete all gradients, press the **Reset** button.

How do I brush away part of the gradient?

At times you may want to prevent parts of the photo being affected by a gradient. For example, if you're darkening the sky, you may not want to darken the building on the horizon at the same time. In this case, you can brush away part of the gradient. **(Figure 12.50)**

To do so, create your gradient, then select **Brush** at the top of the Graduated Filter or Radial Filter Options panel and set the brush options to *Erase* at the bottom of the panel. **(Figure 12.51)** Select the **Size** and **Feather** (softness) for the brush and click and drag across the photo to remove areas of the gradient. (The Brush options in the Graduated Filter or Radial Filter work like the main Adjustment Brush tool, so we'll investigate these next.)

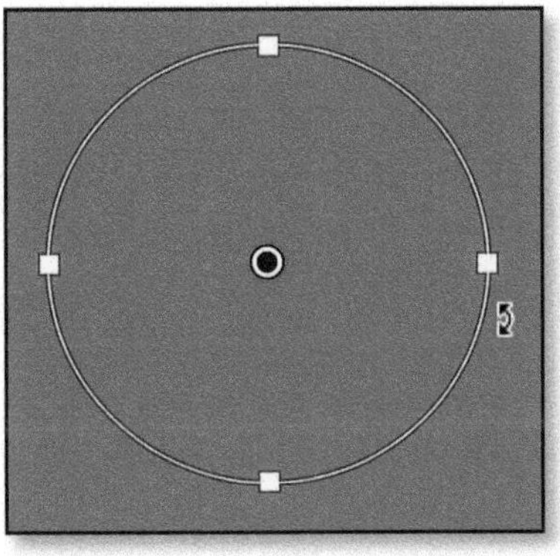

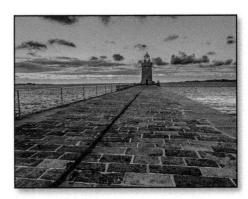

Figure 12.49 *Rotate the Radial Filter using the double-headed arrow, and change the shape by dragging the squares on the overlay.*

Figure 12.50 *If there's a building on the horizon, you may want to brush away that part of the gradient so it's not affected.*

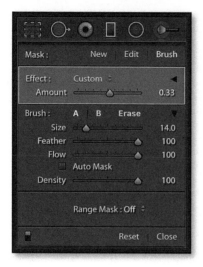

Figure 12.51 *You can remove parts of a gradient using a brush.*

Likewise, by selecting the *A* or *B* brush instead of *Erase*, you can add the same adjustments to another area of the photo. Note that it doesn't brush back the gradient that you've removed. It acts like a standard brush stroke.

To delete the brush strokes without resetting the entire gradient, hold down Alt (Windows) / Opt (Mac) and press the **Reset Brushes** button which replaces the *Reset* button.

There's another tool called Range Mask, which can create even more complex masks. We'll come back to Range Mask on page 249.

Why would I use the Adjustment Brush rather than editing a photo in Photoshop?

The Adjustment Brush tool allows you to paint local adjustments onto the photo, so you can easily lighten shadow areas, pull back highlight detail in other areas, and selectively soften skin on faces.

Photoshop's traditionally been used for localized adjustments, so why would you use Lightroom's Adjustment Brush? Two simple reasons—non-destructive editing and raw data.

When you edit a photo in Photoshop, you have yet another large photo file to store, and if you want to edit it without degrading the original image data, you have to retain multiple layers, which increases the file size further. Lightroom's Local Adjustments store the local adjustment information as metadata in the catalog, so you can safely go back and change your adjustments repeatedly.

Also, when you're using the adjustment brush in Lightroom, you have access to the full raw data, whereas Photoshop uses rendered data (unless you use the raw file as a smart object). For example, if you're using a masked area to lighten shadow areas, there's a much wider range of data available in the raw file, so you can pull back greater detail.

This doesn't mean that Lightroom entirely replaces Photoshop. There are still many pixel based adjustments that require Photoshop, and sometimes it's simply more efficient to use Photoshop for localized adjustments. Because Lightroom has to constantly re-run text instructions, rather than immediately applying them to the original pixels, it can become quite slow when there are lots of local adjustments, so the practicality depends largely on your computer hardware.

How do I create a new brush mask?

When you select the Adjustment Brush, it's automatically ready to start a new mask. The word *New* is highlighted at the top of the Options panel. Select the size and feathering of the brush using the controls at the bottom of the Options panel, and select the effect you're going to apply. **(Figure 12.52)**

When you're ready to start painting on the photo, hold down the mouse button and drag the cursor across the photo. Holding down the Shift key while you paint draws the stroke in a straight vertical or horizontal line. In some cases, you may find it helpful to paint with the effects sliders turned up higher than your intended result, or with the mask overlay turned on (press O), in order to clearly see where you're painting. You can then adjust the sliders again when you've finished painting.

Like the gradients, your brush masks are marked with small gray circles called Pins. To select an existing adjustment, click on the pin. The center of the pin turns black, the word *Edit* is highlighted at the top of the Options panel, and you can continue painting on the same brush mask, or switch to the eraser to remove some of the mask.

To start a new brush mask, in order to apply different adjustments to another area of the photo, press the *New* button at the top of the Adjustment Brush Options panel and start painting. You can have multiple adjustments (pins) on an image, and they can overlap.

How do I choose the size and softness of my brush?

At bottom of the Adjustment Brush Options panel are the brush settings. The **Size** slider runs from 0.1, which is a tiny brush, to a maximum size of 100. **Feather** runs from 1, which is a hard edged brush, to 100 which is soft. **(Figure 12.53)**

You can also use the [and] keys or scroll the mouse wheel to increase and decrease the size of the brush, and Shift-[and Shift-] keys or Shift/scroll to increase and decrease the feathering.

There are two brushes, plus an eraser, all accessed from this panel. This allows you to quickly switch between a hard and soft brush or a large and small brush, without having to constantly adjust the sliders.

To store the settings for each brush, click on **A**, adjust your brush settings for your A brush, and then click on **B** and adjust your settings for that brush too. You can quickly switch between them by clicking on the A or B button, or by using the / key.

You set the size and softness of the **Erase** brush in the same way, except Lightroom won't allow you to select the eraser brush until you've added a brush stroke to the photo.

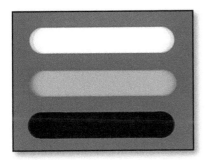

Figure 12.52 *Exposure. +4.0 brightens the exposure by +4.0 (top), +1.0 brightens the exposure by +1.0 (center), and -4.0 darkens the exposure by -4.0 (bottom).*

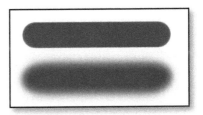

Figure 12.53 *Feathering set to 0 (top) and 100 (bottom).*

What's the difference between *Flow & Density?*

The **Flow** slider controls the rate at which the adjustment is applied.

With *Flow* at 100, the brush behaves like a paintbrush, laying down the maximum

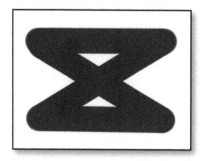

Figure 12.54 *Flow at 100 creates solid lines.*

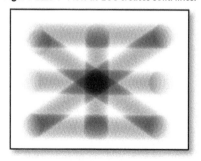

Figure 12.55 *Flow at 25 builds up the effect gradually.*

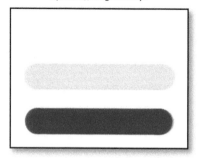

Figure 12.56 *Density 0 (top), 25 (center) and 100 (bottom). The Density slider prevents the brush strokes getting any stronger than the maximum setting, regardless of how many times you paint over it.*

effect with each stroke. The effect is applied equally with each stroke.

With *Flow* at a lower value such as 25, the brush behaves more like an airbrush, building up the effect gradually. Each stroke adds to the effect of the previous strokes. Areas that have multiple brushstrokes are stronger than those with a single stroke.

Density limits the maximum strength of the stroke. Regardless of how many times you paint using those brush settings, the mask can never be stronger than the maximum density setting. Unless you need the Density control for a specific purpose, I would suggest leaving it set at 100.

To fully understand the difference, try creating a white or grey image and testing different combinations of sliders. It's easier to see the differences when you're not distracted by an image. **(Figures 12.54-12.56)**

How do I erase brush strokes?

If you make a mistake when brushing, it's not a problem. Simply select the *Eraser* in the Adjustment Brush Options panel or hold down the Alt (Windows) / Opt (Mac) key to select it temporarily, and then you can erase all or part of the existing stroke. Of course, if you've just painted a stroke, Ctrl-Z (Windows) / Cmd-Z (Mac) will also undo your last action.

To delete the whole brush stroke, select the pin then press the Delete key or right-click on the pin and select **Delete**. To delete all brush strokes, press the **Reset** button.

How do I move brush strokes?

You can now move Adjustment Brush strokes by dragging the pin, just like the Graduated and Radial Filter pins.

Can I invert the mask?

You can't invert a brush mask, however you can use a large brush to paint over everything, and then use a small brush to erase from that mask. For example, you can paint the entire photo using a -100 Saturation brush to make it Black & White and then erase to show a small amount of the original color photo below.

What does Auto Mask do?

The **Auto Mask** checkbox confines your brush strokes to areas of similar color, based on the tones that the center of the brush passes over, helping to prevent your mask spilling over into other areas of the photo. For example, you can paint over a child's shirt to selectively adjust the color, without having to carefully brush around the edges.

It's very performance intensive so it may slow Lightroom down, and it can also result in some halos, for example, trying to darken a bright sky with a silhouette of a tree in the foreground may leave a halo around the edge of the tree. **(Figure 12.57)**

Auto Mask actually works better in reverse—use a large brush without Auto Mask to paint a large area first, and then enable Auto Mask while erasing areas of your mask.

Why are there small dots or speckles on my photo?

If you're editing a noisy photo, you may find speckles or dots in the brushed area. To avoid this issue, apply noise reduction before painting your mask with *Auto Mask* enabled. The photo must be set to PV4 or later (page 220) for this trick to work.

How do I use Range Mask?

The Range Mask tools allow you to build complex masks for local edits. The Color Range Mask selects an area based on sampled colors, and the Luminance Range Mask selects pixels based on their brightness. This means you can mask detailed areas, such as trees, or make localized HSL-type adjustments.

Since Range Mask is a way of fine-tuning a mask, first add a gradient or brush mask over the approximate area you want to adjust. If you want to adjust the whole image, create a narrow linear gradient that both begins and ends outside of the image

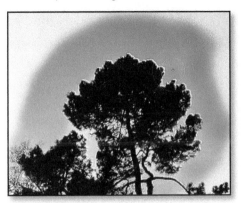

Figure 12.57 *Auto Mask may leave a halo if you don't use it carefully.*

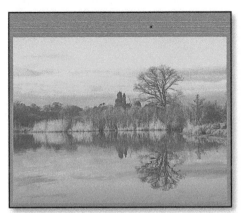

Figure 12.58 *Create a linear gradient outside of the photo area to affect the entire photo, or select a much smaller area to refine.*

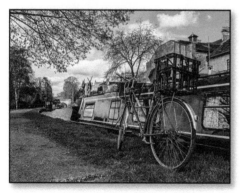

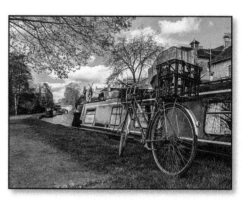

Figure 12.59 *The Color Range Mask is useful for selecting specific colors. For example, buy brushing roughly over the tree in the top left corner, we can then add Color Samplers to select only the leaves, and make them more yellow and saturated.*

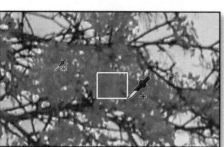

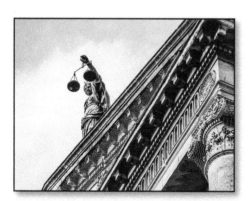

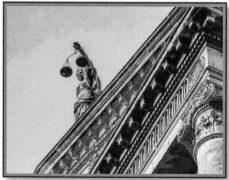

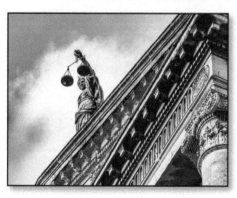

Figure 12.60 *The Luminance Range mask is useful for creating complex selections based on the brightness. For example, we could darken and add Clarity to the sky using a Linear Gradient, but it would also affect the statue. The Luminance Range Mask allows you to primarily select the sky with minimal effect on the statue, with a gentle fall off so it looks natural.*

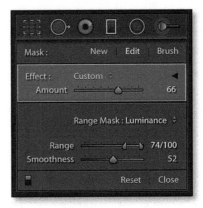

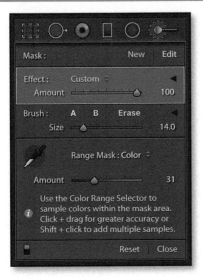

Figure 12.61 For the Color Range Mask, select the Color Range Selector and then adjust the threshold using the Amount slider in the Brous Options panel.

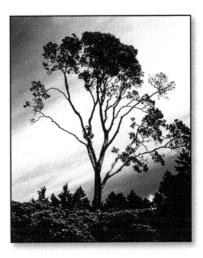

Figure 12.62 For the Luminance Range Mask, adjust the Range and Smoothness in the Brush Options panel.

area. **(Figure 12.58)**

To use the Color Range Mask, select **Color** from the Range Mask pop-up, then select the **Color Range Selector** (it looks like an eyedropper) and click on your chosen color in the photo, or for greater accuracy, click and drag rectangles around the colors you want to adjust. By holding down the Shift key, you can add up to five samples. If you make a mistake and need to remove a sample point, hold down the Alt key (Windows) / Opt key (Mac) and click on the sample icons. Once you've selected the right color ranges, adjust the **Amount** slider to adjust the threshold. **(Figures 12.59 & 12.61)**

The Color Range Mask can be used to make local HSL type adjustments. Select the color range you wish to adjust, then move the *Temp/Tint* sliders or *Color* adjustment to adjust the hue, the *Saturation* slider to affect the saturation, or the *Exposure* slider to make luminance adjustments.

Figure 12.63 Hold down the Alt/ Opt key while moving the sliders to see a greyscale preview.

To use the Luminance Range Mask, select **Luminance** from the *Range Mask* pop-up. Adjust the **Range** slider to set the endpoints of the selected luminance range, then use the **Smoothness** slider to adjust how smooth the falloff is at either end of the selected luminance range. **(Figures 12.60 & 12.62)**

In either case, hold down the Alt key (Windows) / Opt key (Mac) while moving the sliders to display the mask as grayscale. **(Figure 12.63)** This makes it much easier to see the selected area.

Why is nothing happening when I brush over the photo?

If you're brushing over the photo and nothing seems to be happening, it's usually because either the *Flow* or *Density* sliders are set too low. If those are both set to 100, try turning on the mask overlay by pressing the O key, or move one of the sliders to an extreme value such as *Exposure +4* so you can see where you're brushing.

How do I use the pins?

Earlier in the chapter, we mentioned that your gradient or brush masks are each marked with small circles called Pins. The mask pins have two states—selected or not selected, or active and inactive. Not selected is shown by a gray pin, and clicking on the pin selects that mask, turning the pins black with a white border. **(Figure 12.64)** Once your existing mask is reselected, you can adjust the sliders to change the effect, or go back and edit the mask itself.

If you find the pins and the gradient lines distracting, you can change their view options. Under *Tools menu > Tool Overlay*, you have the option to *Auto Show* which only shows the pin when you float the mouse nearby, as well as *Always Show*, *Show Selected* and *Never Show*. You'll also find those options in the **Show Edit Pins** pop-up on the Toolbar while the local adjustment tools are active. **(Figure 12.65)**

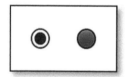

Figure 12.64 The pins have a black center when the mask is selected (left) and a gray center when the mask is not selected (right).

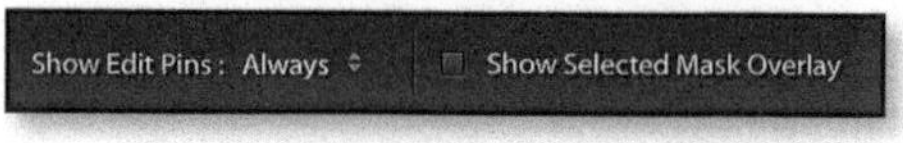

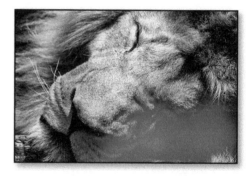

Show Edit Pins : Always ◆   ☐ Show Selected Mask Overlay

Figure 12.65 The pins and mask overlay can be turned on and off using the controls in the Toolbar.

How do I use the mask overlay?

The adjustment mask overlay is a colored mask that shows the location and opacity of your brush strokes or gradient.

To show the mask, check the **Show Selected Mask Overlay** checkbox on the Toolbar (or under *Tools menu > Adjustment Mask Overlay*) or press the O key to toggle it on and off. If the pin's deselected (gray), you can just hover the cursor over the pin to view the mask. **(Figure 12.66)**

By default, it's a red mask, but you can select red, green, lighten or darken using the *Tools menu > Adjustment Mask Overlay* or by pressing Shift-O to cycle through the options. There's a choice because some colors are more visible on specific photos than others. For example, the lighten mode isn't much help on a snow scene!

How do I fade the effect of an existing mask?

When you come to edit a mask, you may

Figure 12.66 The red Mask Overlay highlights the masked area.

want to increase or fade the effect of your adjustments. You can adjust each of the individual sliders separately, but if you've applied a lot of different adjustments, you may prefer to use the *Amount* slider to adjust them all in one go.

Click the disclosure triangle to the right of the *Presets* pop-up menu to switch between a combined **Amount** slider and the more advanced slider mode. The *Amount* slider increases or decreases the strength of all the adjustments on the selected mask, with all the sliders being adjusted by the same percentage of change. **(Figure 12.67)**

You can access the same *Amount* control without having to click on the disclosure triangle, by holding down the Alt (Windows) / Opt (Mac) key while floating over the active pin. The cursor changes to a double headed arrow, and clicking and dragging left and right increases and decreases the *Amount* slider. **(Figure 12.68)**

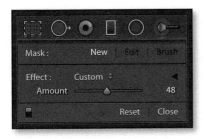

Figure 12.67 *The disclosure triangle hides the individual sliders and shows a single Amount slider.*

Figure 12.68 *Hold down the Alt or Opt key and drag over the mask pin to change the Amount without visiting the Options panel.*

Hold down the Alt/Opt key while floating over the pin to adjust all of the slider amounts in one go.

Can I duplicate the masks? And layer the effect of multiple masks?

If you've reached the limit of a slider, you may want to duplicate the mask. To do so, right-click on the pin and select **Duplicate**. You can then edit the new pin's settings separately.

You can create as many different masks as you like, and they can be overlapped and layered, with the effect being cumulative.

How do I set default slider settings?

If you're editing a set of photos that need the same adjustments, it can be irritating to have to reselect the slider values for each new photo and pin, but to save time, you can save the settings as new defaults. To do so, select one of the local adjustment tools, make sure the Options panel is set to *New* rather than *Edit* mode, and adjust the sliders to your new chosen defaults. Lightroom remembers these settings and uses them for any new Graduated Filters, Radial Filters or Adjustment Brush strokes, until you next repeat the process.

How do I save sets of slider settings as a preset?

In the Fast Track, we also mentioned local adjustment presets, which simply move the sliders to preset positions. Lightroom ships with some built in presets. If the default presets disappear, select *Restore Default Presets* from the **Effect** pop-up.

You can also save your own presets of settings you use regularly. To do so, set your chosen slider settings, and then select *Save Current Settings as New Preset* from the *Effect* pop-up menu. Your new preset appears in the pop-up, ready to select. Like the other pop-up menus through the program, you have to select the preset in the pop-up to show the *Rename, Update* and *Delete* options.

Can I save brush strokes or gradients as presets?

If you've created your ideal off-center vignette, or another Graduated or Radial Filter, you can save it as a Develop Preset for use on other photos. To do so, click on the + button on the Presets panel and press *Check None* to clear the checkboxes. Check the *Graduated Filter* and/or *Radial Filter* checkboxes and give the preset a name, then press *Create*. Your preset appears in the Presets panel. We'll come back to Presets in more detail in the Develop Module Tools chapter on page 308.

Lightroom doesn't allow you to save brush strokes in a preset, although you can sync or copy/paste the masks across multiple photos.

Let's explore the sliders and some practical applications...

How do I reduce bloodshot eyes?

To brighten the eyes, select the *Iris Enhance* preset from the *Effect* pop-up and brush over the iris of the eye. The blood shot look can be reduced using the adjustment brush set to positive *Exposure*, positive *Shadows* and negative *Saturation*. **(Figure 12.69)**

How do I soften skin?

The *Soften Skin* preset allows you to soften the skin without affecting the rest of the photo. Brush it over the face, avoiding the eyes, eyebrows, nose, mouth, hair and clothing. **(Figure 12.70)**

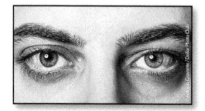
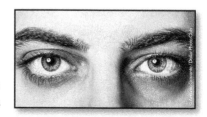

Figure 12.69
Brighten the iris and reduce redness using the adjustment brush.

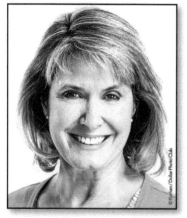
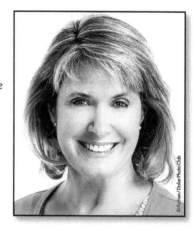

Figure 12.70 *The Soften Skin preset allows you to soften the skin without affecting the eyes, nose, mouth, hair or clothing.*

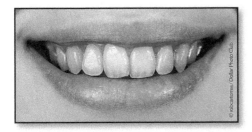 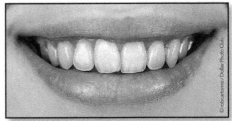

Figure 12.71 *Clean up yellowing teeth using the Teeth Whitening preset.*

How do I whiten teeth?

The *Teeth Whitening* preset in the *Effect* pop-up whitens yellowing teeth, although you may need to increase or decrease the *Exposure* slider to suit the photo. **(Figure 12.71)**

How do I fix mixed lighting?

The *Temp* and *Tint* sliders allow you to apply different white balance settings to different areas of the photo. This is particularly useful when correcting photos shot in mixed lighting.

How do I add a specific color tint?

To select a color tint, click on the *Color* icon to bring up the Color Picker. Select your chosen color from the gradient.

To select a color from the photo, click in the Color Picker and while holding the mouse button down, drag the cursor onto the photo. As you drag across the photo, the Color Picker updates live to reflect the color beneath your cursor. When you release the mouse button, the color under the cursor is selected in the Color Picker.

To clear the tint, double-click on the *Color* label and the *Color* box changes to a white box with a cross in it to show it's disabled.

Black and white aren't available in the color

tint section, but you can set the *Exposure* to +4 for white or −4 for *Black*. If the effect isn't strong enough, you can duplicate the mask by right-clicking on the pin.

How do I dodge and burn?

One of the most logical uses for local adjustments are tonal changes—*Exposure, Contrast, Highlights, Shadows, Whites & Blacks*. They can use for darkening skies, off center vignettes, brightening shadows, reducing bright highlights and many other adjustments. **(Figures 12.72, 12.73 & 12.74)**

How do I add local contrast?

The *Clarity* slider allows you to add local midtone contrast, which is particularly useful for the clouds in the sky.

Dehaze is particularly useful when used selectively. When applied globally, it can create halos and color shifts, so either paint *Dehaze* onto selected areas, oreduce the *Dehaze* effect if it's too strong. It also works surprisingly well on reflections on glasses!

Can I adjust Vibrance instead of Saturation?

The *Saturation* slider is a cross between intelligent *Vibrance* and linear *Saturation*. Positive values behave like + *Vibrance* in the Basic panel, but negative values behave

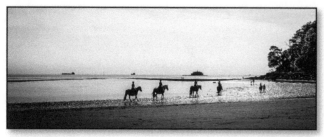

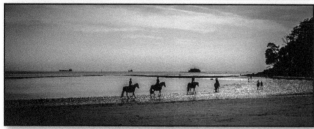

Figure 12.72 *The Graduated Filter is great for darkening skies. In this case we've used negative Exposure to reduce the brightness, positive Clarity to make the clouds stand out, slightly increased Saturation plus a slight blue Color tint.*

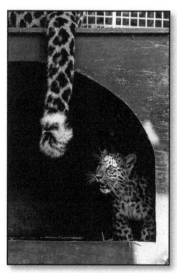
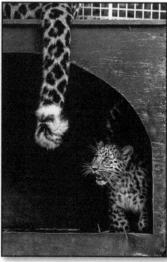

Figure 12.73 *The light falling through the trees is distracting on the kennel walls. An adjustment brush set to negative Exposure helps to remove the distraction.*

The light on the leopard cub's face is also uneven. A mixture of Exposure, Highlights and Saturation pulls back the light and dark areas to even it out.

like - *Saturation*, completely desaturating the photo. Negative *Saturation* is useful for creating B&W photos with spot color.

Can I sharpen selective?

The *Sharpening* slider can be used to selecting increase or decrease the sharpening applied to specific areas of the photo, for example, the eyes of a portrait often benefit from a little extra sharpening.

The local adjustments only affect the *Amount* of sharpening, and the *Radius*, *Detail* and *Masking* settings remain identical across the photo, using the settings selected in the Detail panel.

Can I add a lens blur effect?

If you set the *Sharpening* slider to between -50 and -100, it applies a blur similar to a lens blur, allowing you to blur the

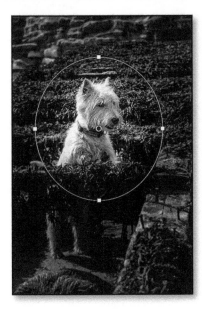

Figure 12.74 *The Radial Filter is ideal for off-center vignettes. In this case we've used negative Exposure, negative Highlights and negative Sharpening.*

background of a photo. It's very processor intensive, so it can be slow. Negative *Clarity* gives a slightly different softening effect.

How do I reduce noise in a smaller area, or only in the shadows?

The *Noise* slider in the Local Adjustments panels should be called Noise Reduction, but there's not enough space, particularly in some languages. When you paint with a negative noise value, it doesn't add noise, but it reduces or removes any global noise reduction that you've applied or other noise reduction brushstrokes.

If you add a linear gradient outside of the photo boundary, then use a luminosity range mask to only target the shadow tones, you can limit your noise reduction to the darker areas of the photo. This helps to avoid softening detail in the highlights.

How do I reduce Moiré?

Moiré is a rainbow-like pattern which is often seen when photographing fabrics. It's caused by two patterns combining—in

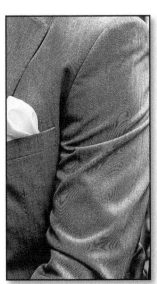
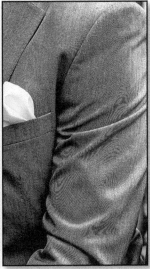

Figure 12.75 *Moiré causes a colored pattern on the image (left) but it can be fixed using the Moiré slider and the Adjustment Brush (right).*

this case, the weave in fabric and the grid of the camera sensor—which creates a new pattern. **(Figure 12.75)**

The *Moiré* removal slider in the Adjustment Brush allows you to paint the moiré rainbow away. It can only usually remove the color rainbow, not any luminosity changes, but it works very well. It works on both raw and rendered photos, although the additional data in a raw file means that it is far more effective on raw files.

To use it, select a plus value on the *Moiré* slider, ensure that you've turned off *Auto Mask*, and brush over the pattern. If you cross a boundary of another color in the photo, it can blur or smudge, so it's best to use a hard edged brush (*Feather*=0) and be careful where you brush. This gives the cleanest result without any side effects. It can help to temporarily increase *Saturation* in the Basic panel while brushing, and then reduce it again when you're done. If you set the *Moiré* slider to a negative value, it won't do anything—it's only used to reduce the effect of another brush stroke which already has positive moiré removal applied.

How do I remove local color fringing?

The *Defringe* sliders remove color fringing. We'll come back to these in the Lens Corrections section starting on page 281.

DEVELOP SELECTIVE EDITING SHORTCUTS

		Windows	Mac
Cropping	Go to Crop Tool	R	R
	Reset Crop	Ctrl Alt R	Cmd Opt R
	Crop As Shot	Ctrl Alt Shift R	Cmd Opt Shift R
	Constrain Aspect Ratio	A	A
	Crop to Same Aspect Ratio	Shift A	Shift A
	Rotate Crop Aspect	X	X
	Reset Crop to Maximum for new Aspect Ratio	Alt while changing aspect ratio	Opt while changing aspect ratio
	Crop from Center of Photo	Alt while dragging	Opt while dragging
	Rotate Left 90° CCW	Ctrl [	Cmd [
	Rotate Right 90° CW	Ctrl]	Cmd]
	Rotation Angle Ruler	Ctrl-click on start and end points	Cmd-click on start and end points
	Cycle Guide Overlay	O	O
	Cycle Guide Overlay Orientation	Shift O	Shift O
Spot Removal	Go to Spot Removal	Q	Q
	Create New Circle Spot with auto source	Click	Click
	Create New Circle Spot scale from center	Ctrl Alt while clicking	Cmd Opt while clicking
	Create New Circle Spot scale from starting point	Ctrl Shift while clicking	Cmd Shift while clicking
	Create New Circle Spot with manual source	Ctrl while click spot and drag to chosen source	Cmd while click spot and drag to chosen source
	Create New Brush Spot	Click and drag	Click and drag
	Create New Brush Spot constrain to horizontal/vertical axis	Shift and drag	Shift and drag

		Windows	Mac
	Edit Existing connect existing circle spot to new spot, changing to brush spot	Select existing circle spot then Shift and click	Select existing circle spot then Shift and click
	Toggle Clone/Heal	Shift Q	Shift Q
	Select new auto source	/	/
	Increase circle spot size	]	]
	Decrease circle spot size	[	[
	Increase feather	Shift [	Shift [
	Decrease feather	Shift]	Shift]
	Visualize Spots	A	A
	Hide Spot Overlays	H	H
	Delete Spot	Select Spot then Delete or hold Alt while clicking	Select Spot then Delete or hold Opt while clicking
	When zoomed in, go to top left corner	Home	Fn Left Arrow
	When zoomed in, move down	Page Down	Fn Down Arrow
	When zoomed in, move to the right	Page Up	Fn Right Arrow
	Delete Multiple Spots	Hold Alt and drag marquee to surround spots	Hold Opt and drag marquee to surround spots
Local Adjustments Brush/Graduated Filter/Radial Filter	Show Overlay	O	O
	Cycle Overlay Color	Shift O	Shift O
	Hide Pins and Bounding Boxes/Lines	H	H
	Duplicate Pin	Ctrl Alt while dragging pin	Cmd Opt while dragging pin
	Delete Pin	Select pin then Delete	Select pin then Delete

		Windows	Mac
	Increase or decrease Amount slider	Alt click and drag horizontally on pin	Opt click and drag horizontally on pin
	Apply & dismiss Radial Filter tool	Double-click	Double-click
Adjustment Brush	Go to Adjustment Brush	K	K
	Paint brush stroke	Click and drag	Click and drag
	Switch brush A / B	/	/
	Temporary Eraser	Hold Alt	Hold Opt
	Increase brush size	]	]
	Decrease brush size	[	[
	Increase brush feathering	Shift]	Shift]
	Decrease brush feathering	Shift {	Shift {
	Toggle Auto Mask	A	A
	Set Flow value	0-9	0-9
	Constrain Brush to Straight Line	Shift while clicking or dragging	Shift while clicking or dragging
	Delete Color Range Mask samples	Hold Alt and drag marquee to surround spots	Hold Opt and drag marquee to surround spots
	Confirm brush stroke	Enter	Return
Graduated Filters	Go to Graduated Filter	M	M
	Create New Graduated Filter	Click and drag	Click and drag
	Edit Existing extend/contract	Click and drag outer lines	Click and drag outer lines
	Edit Existing rotate	Click and drag center line	Click and drag center line
	Edit Existing move	Click and drag pin	Click and drag pin
	Constrain Gradient to 90 degrees	Shift while dragging	Shift while dragging

		Windows	Mac
	Graduated Filter Brush	Shift T	Shift T
	Invert Graduated Filter Mask	' (apostrophe)	' (apostrophe)
Radial Filter	Go to Radial Filter	Shift M	Shift M
	Create New scaled from center	Click and drag	Click and drag
	Create New scale from starting point	Alt while dragging	Opt while dragging
	Create New constrain to circle	Shift while dragging	Shift while dragging
	Create New scale from starting point and constain to circle	Alt Shift while dragging	Opt Shift while dragging
	Create New constrain to crop bounds	Ctrl double click	Cmd double click
	Edit Existing opposite sides move	Click and drag edge	Click and drag edge
	Edit Existing selected side moves	Alt while dragging edge	Opt while dragging edge
	Edit Existing constrain to existing aspect ratio	Shift while dragging edge	Shift while dragging edge
	Edit Existing expands 3 nearest sides	Alt Shift while dragging edge	Opt Shift while dragging edge
	Edit Existing maximize to crop bounds	Ctrl double click within ellipsis	Cmd double click within ellipsis
	Edit Existing move	Click and drag pin	Click and drag pin
	Radial Filter Brush	Shift T	Shift T
	Invert Radial Filter Mask	' (apostrophe)	' (apostrophe)

DEVELOP ADVANCED EDITING

13

We've explored the Basic panel and selective adjustments, but there are plenty of extra panels with advanced controls yet to investigate. They include selective color and contrast adjustments, advanced sharpening and noise reduction, lens and perspective corrections, and special effects.

TONE CURVES

Below the Basic panel is the Tone Curve panel. Like the Basic panel, it allows you to lighten or darken the tones in your photo. The sliders even have similar names: *Highlights, Lights, Darks* and *Shadows*. That's where the similarities end, as the behavior can be quite different.

How do I read a tone curve?

The first thing you'll see when you look at the Tone Curve panel is the 4x4 grid which holds the tone curve. You'll spot the histogram showing faintly in the background.

Along each axis are all the possible tones, with pure black (0%) on the left/bottom and pure white (100%) on the right/top. The horizontal (x) axis is the pixel brightness before adjustment, and the vertical (y) axis represents the adjustments you make using the Tone Curve. **(Figure 13.1)**

The tone curve starts as a straight 45°

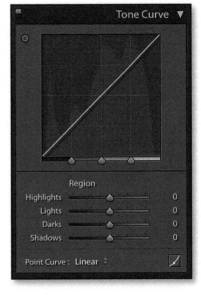

Figure 13.1 *Before adjustment, the Tone Curve is a straight line.*

diagonal line, with no changes being applied to the photo. Moving the line up makes the tones lighter, and moving down makes the tones darker. The line getting steeper means contrast is increased, and getting flatter means contrast is reduced. **(Figure 13.2)**

Why use curves?

Tone Curves are primarily used for controlling brightness and contrast in specific tonal ranges. The steeper the angle of the curve, the higher the contrast becomes. When the curve gets steeper, increasing the contrast in one range of

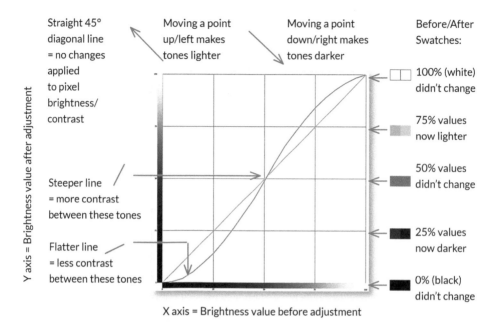

Straight 45°
diagonal line
= no changes
applied
to pixel
brightness/
contrast

Moving a point
up/left makes
tones lighter

Moving a point
down/right makes
tones darker

Before/After
Swatches:

100% (white)
didn't change

75% values
now lighter

50% values
didn't change

Steeper line
= more contrast
between these tones

25% values
now darker

Flatter line
= less contrast
between these tones

0% (black)
didn't change

Y axis = Brightness value after adjustment

X axis = Brightness value before adjustment

Figure 13.2 *A typical S shaped tone curve adds contrast by making the light tones lighter and the dark tones darker.*

tones (e.g. the shadows), it gets shallower in another range of tones (e.g. the highlights), decreasing the contrast in that range. It allows you to control where you're willing to sacrifice contrast to gain it in other areas.

The most frequently used curve is an S shape, which increases midtone contrast by lightening the highlights and darkening the shadows. The middle of the curve becomes steeper, giving the midtones greater contrast, while the highlights and shadows become shallower with less contrast. **(Figure 13.3)**

How are Tone Curves different to the Basic panel?

So you might be wondering how that's different to the Basic panel. After all, you can lighten the highlights using the *Highlights* sliders and darken the shadows using the *Shadows* slider.

Remember we said that the *Highlights* and

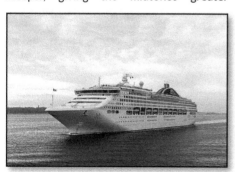
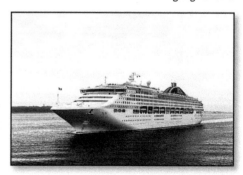

Figure 13.3 *Before (left) and after (right) a standard S curve contrast adjustment.*

Shadows sliders in the Basic panel build a mask to limit the effect of the slider to part of the tonal range. This means that brightening the shadows has the greatest effect on the darkest shadows, tapering off to a minimal effect on the highlights and vice versa. **(Figure 13.4)**

The tone curve doesn't build a mask. There's always a trade-off. If you increase the shadows to see more detail, you also brighten the highlights. If you then pull the the highlights back down, you flatten the contrast in the midtones. **(Figure 13.5)** This doesn't mean it's a bad tool to use, but it's different.

You might also compare the tone curve to the *Contrast* slider in the Basic panel, which creates a simple S curve behind the scenes.

You can create an identical S curve using the Tone Curve panel, but the tone curve gives you much greater control. Depending on the content of the photo, you can decide which range of tones need more contrast and which tones can be safely compressed.

As a rule of thumb, the Basic panel does the heavy-lifting—the major adjustments—and the Tone Curve is usually used for fine tuning. (Rules are, of course, made to be broken, so feel free to experiment!)

What's the difference between the parametric curve and the point curve?

Lightroom offers two different tone curves:

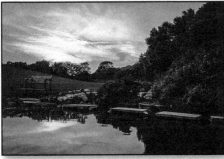

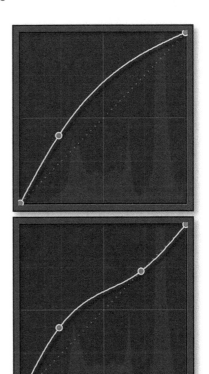

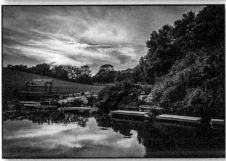

Figure 13.4 *Using the Tone Curve to pull back highlight and shadow detail reduces the midtone contrast (top), whereas the Highlights and Shadows sliders retain the contrast (bottom).*

Figure 13.5 *If we increase the shadows (top), the highlights are also lightened. If we pull the highlights back down to compensate (bottom), the midtones become flattened, losing contrast.*

a parametric curve and a point curve.

The parametric tone curve is the default view, and it allows you to adjust sections of the curve rather than individual points. It protects the photo from extreme adjustments, so it's generally considered the easier option.

The point curve interface is usually used by advanced users, or those familiar with Photoshop's curves dialog. It gives you full control over the curve, including the individual RGB channels. **(Figure 13.6)**

Point curves aren't necessarily an alternative to the parametric curves. You may be more comfortable with one or the other, but both curves are active at the same time and the effect is cumulative.

How do I adjust the standard parametric tone curve?

To adjust the parametric tone curve, click and drag up and down on the curve itself or adjust the sliders below. For example, to darken the darker midtones tones in a photo, you'd click between the 25% and 50% gridlines and drag downwards. You could also drag the *Darks* slider to the left to get the same result. The gray highlighted section shows the maximum range of movement for that slider.

Why are the sliders missing?

If you're missing the Tone Curve sliders, you're viewing the point curve interface, so press the point curve button to return to the parametric curves.

How do I use the Targeted Adjustment Tool?

Appearing in the Tone Curve, Hue, Saturation, Luminance and B&W panels, the Targeted Adjustment tool, or TAT for short, allows you to directly control the sliders by dragging on the photo itself. It means you can concentrate on the actual photo rather than the sliders, and saves you having to work out which sliders you need to adjust for a specific color or tone. This rather unobtrusive little tool is a real gem! **(Figure 13.7)**

The easiest and most intuitive option is to use the TAT tool, which stands for Targeted Adjustment Tool. It's available for both the parametric and point curve.

1. Click the circle icon in the top left corner of the panel to select it.

2. Float the cursor over the photo. As you float, a small circle displays on the curve, showing which section of the curve you'll be adjusting, but you don't need to take too much notice of the curve. Just focus on the photo itself. **(Figure 13.8)**

3. Click on the image and drag up to make the tones lighter or down to make the tones darker. For example, to darken the shadows, click and drag downwards on a shadowy area of the photo until you're happy with the result.

Figure 13.7 *The TAT, or Targeted Adjustment tool, appears in the top left corner of the Tone Curve, HSL, Color & B&W panels.*

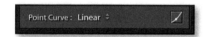

Figure 13.6 *The point curve is accessed using the button in the bottom right corner of the Tone Curve panel.*

Alternatively, you can hover the TAT cursor over the shadows in the photo and press the Up/Down keys on your keyboard to adjust it.

4. Repeat on other tones in the image, for example, drag upwards on a light area to make the highlights lighter.

5. Once you've finished, just press Escape or return the tool to its base in the corner of the panel.

What are the triangles at the bottom of the parametric tone curve?

At the bottom of the parametric tone curve are three triangles called split points. **(Figure 13.9)** They define the tonal range for each of the sliders. For example, if you've used the *Lights* and *Darks* sliders to create strong midtone contrast, you may move the 25% and 75% split points out to restrict the flattened contrast to the lightest highlights and the deepest shadows. Double-clicking

on any of those triangles resets it to the default position.

How do I use the point curve?

To adjust the point curve, click the small button to the right of the *Point Curve* pop-up menu to switch to the point curve interface. The sliders disappear and you're left with a basic point curve. **(Figure 13.10)**

Click anywhere on the curve line to add a control point, and then drag it up or down to adjust the photo.

Like the parametric curve, the TAT tool makes it easy to work out where on the curve to place an additional point. Be careful not to place too many points as extreme twists and turns in the curve can create posterization (banding) in the photo.

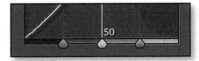

Figure 13.9 *The split point triangles at the bottom of the curve control how much of the tonal range is affected by each slider.*

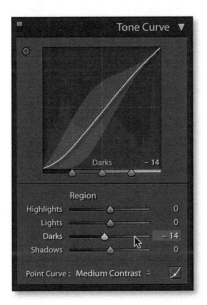

Figure 13.8 *When you float over a slider, the maximum adjustment limits are highlighted on the curve.*

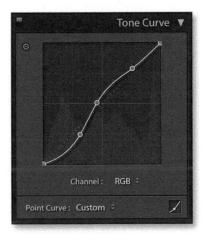

Figure 13.10 *The point curve allows you to create a freeform curve.*

Unlike Photoshop, you can't use the keyboard to adjust the points, but holding down the Alt (Windows) / Opt (Mac) key while dragging slows the movement.

To remove a point, right-click on it and choose *Delete Control Point*. To reset the entire curve, remove all of the individual points or right-click and select *Flatten Curve*.

You can also access RGB curves in the same point curve interface (PV3/4 photos only) using **Channel** pop-up. The individual red, green and blue curves are particularly useful for adjusting colors in rendered files such as scans. Where color casts differ between the highlights and shadows—perhaps where the overall color is correct but the shadows have a magenta tinge—normal white balance adjustments would be unable to fix it, but RGB curves allow you detailed control over each channel.

The **Point Curve** pop-up holds point curve presets which are shared with Camera Raw (ACR) in Photoshop. *Linear* is the default for PV3/4 photos, but two more legacy presets—*Medium Contrast* and *Strong Contrast*—also add a slight S curve. To save your own point curve as a preset, select *Save* from the pop-up. (You can also save it as a normal Develop preset.) Unlike most of the preset pop-ups, you can't update, rename or delete the point curve presets from within Lightroom. Instead, you must find them in the Camera Raw user folder (page 455) using Explorer (Windows) / Finder (Mac) and delete them manually.

How do I invert a negative photo?

To invert the photo, perhaps because you've scanned a negative, select the point curve and drag the left point to the top left corner and the right point to the bottom right corner. It's handy for negative scans as well as special effects. Don't forget to save it as a preset, as it's tricky to get the points in the right place.

B&W & SPLIT TONES

Black and white photography is an art in its own right. Some photographers consider it more creative than color photography, because it doesn't match the reality we see around us.

In the days of film, you generally had to make the decision at the time of capture, and add filters to change the appearance. For example, you'd use a red filter to create a dark dramatic sky. Today, you can make the decisions while editing the photos.

Lightroom offers great control over the contrast between light and dark, and between the different colors that made up the original scene, but first, you need to decide which photos to convert.

How do I decide which photos to convert to B&W?

A good color photo usually also makes a good B&W photo, so how do you decide which photos to convert? Do you have to test a B&W conversion on every single photo? There are a few questions you can ask yourself...

• Is the photo lacking color? For example, the drab colors captured in bad weather may be better removed altogether. **(Figure 13.11)**

• Does color add anything to the photo? (Hint - if the photo's of a sunset, the answer's probably yes, but in bad weather, the photo may be better without color.)

- Is the color distracting? For example, is the color drawing your eye to the wrong spot?

- How would conversion to B&W affect the story and mood of the photo? The way we respond emotionally to color may conflict with the story we're trying to tell. **(Figure 13.12)**

You can also look out for elements in the photos that look great in B&W, for example:

- Contrasts of brightness, especially the beams of light and strong shadows caused by directional light.

- Contrasts of color (light vs. dark, saturated vs. unsaturated, warm vs. cold.)

- Shapes, textures, patterns and compositional features like leading lines. By removing the color, you concentrate more on the lines, textures and contrasts in the photo.

But remember, these are just a guide - rules are made to be broken!

How do I convert photos to B&W?

Before you convert a photo to B&W, first adjust the photo in color. This will remove any color cast or other problems, so you can accurately judge the best B&W settings. You may even want to create a virtual copy or snapshot (page 317), so you retain your color version as well as the B&W rendition.

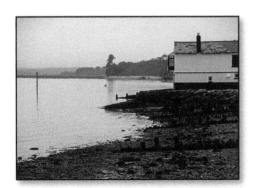
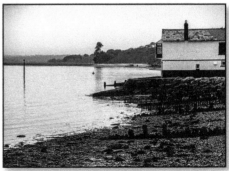

Figure 13.11 *Photos that lack color can look better in B&W.*

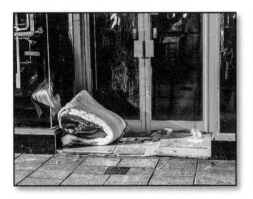
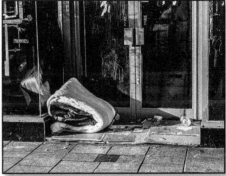

Figure 13.12 *Color may add to or detract from the story you're trying to tell.*

Next, press the V key or select **Treatment: Black & White** at the top of the Basic panel. **(Figure 13.13)** Lightroom creates a basic black & white photo, which you can then fine tune by adjusting the way the colors are mixed and tweaking the contrast. Don't just move the *Saturation* slider to -100, as you won't have so much control.

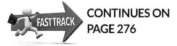

CONTINUES ON PAGE 276

How do I the change the color mix for a black & white photo?

Before you switch the photo to B&W (or switch it back to color briefly using the V key), take a close look at the contrasts between the different colors in your photo. These different shades become varying levels of brightness in the B&W photo, and by mixing the colors to make some colors lighter and others darker, you can control the contrast (or tonal separation) in your B&W photo.

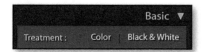

Figure 13.13 *Convert to B&W using the button at the top of the Basic panel.*

Notice in the color wheel in **Figure 13.14**, the first conversion makes all of the tones a similar brightness, and the first B&W color wheel lacks contrast as a result. However, when adjusting the brightness of the different colors, we can create some interesting contrasts.

Now let's put this into a simple real world situation. If you look at a landscape on a sunny day, the sky may be vibrant blue and the grass and bushes a vibrant green, so there's an interesting contrast, however the default conversion may make them a similar shade of grey. Using the B&W Mix tools, you can darken the sky to contrast with the white fluffy clouds, and lighten the greens and yellows to draw your eye around the photo. **(Figure 13.15)**

Likewise, on a portrait, lightening the skin tones (especially red tones) can make the skin seem smoother, whereas darkening it enhances wrinkles.

In the B&W panel **(Figure 13.16)**, you'll notice that Lightroom automatically mixes the color channels to create a result it thinks is pleasing. If you don't like the result, either adjust the mix from the existing settings, or double-click on the *Black & White Mix* heading to reset them to 0.

You can simply move the sliders to the left

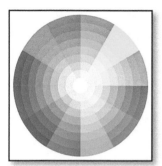
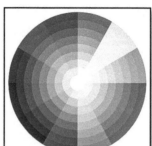
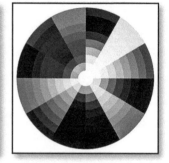

Figure 13.14 *The default conversion (center) lacks contrast, but adjusting the B&W mix (right) allows you to lighten some colors and darken others.*

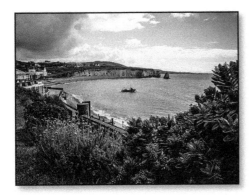
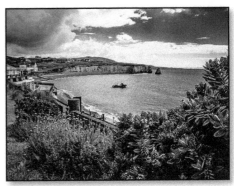

Figure 13.15 *The way you mix the colors can add contrast and draw your eye to different areas of the photo.*

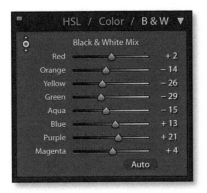

Figure 13.16 *Fine tune the B&W channel mix using the B&W panel.*

green and yellow tones lighten.

There isn't a right or a wrong way to convert to B&W. There are other things you can play with, for example, try different white balance values, or while still in Color mode, set all of the HSL *Saturation* sliders to -100 and then increase one or two sliders.

How do I finish off the B&W photo?

Most B&W photos need a full range of tones, from a deep black with detail to a bright white with detail, and all the shades in between, so once you've adjusted the B&W mix, you'll likely need to fine tune the overall contrast using the Basic panel sliders or Tone Curve. You may also want to adjust the contrast to better suit the B&W version of the photo using the Basic or Tone Curve panel.

The Linear Gradient (page 241) can be useful for darkening the sky in a B&W photo, like an ND Grad filter, and you can add *Clarity* to bring out contrast in the clouds. A Radial Gradient can darken the edges of the photo to draw your eye into the center, especially if there are bright areas around the edge that draw the viewer's eye out of the photo.

to make the color darker, or to the right to make the color lighter, but it's even easier to use the Targeted Adjustment tool, as you don't need to know exactly which color channels are affecting a specific area of the photo. Click on the TAT tool icon in the top left corner of the panel. The TAT tool allows you to adjust the B&W mix visually by dragging directly on the photo, while it figures out which sliders to move. Find an area of the photo that you'd like to be darker—perhaps the blue sky—and click and drag down on that area. As you drag, the blue tones get darker and the sliders in the B&W panel move. Find another color in the photo that you'd like to be lighter—perhaps the grass—and as you click and drag up the

You may also want to use the Adjustment Brush (page 241) to dodge and burn to add emphasis, or add local contrast. Be careful not to go overboard, or the changes will stand out. You can also damp down the contrast in some areas to draw the viewer's eye away from distractions.

Many people love the grain inherent in many popular B&W film stocks, so turn to page 296 to learn to add grain to your B&W photos.

You can also try adding a Sepia or Selenium tint to the photo, like many monochrome photos from years ago. In the Split Toning panel set the *Hue* sliders to around 40 to 50 for Sepia or around 215-225 for Selenium, and then adjust the *Saturation* sliders to increase or decrease the strength of the effect. You can create your own mix of colors if you prefer, and even have different

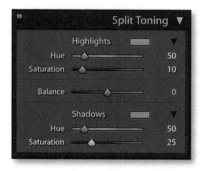

Figure 13.17 *The Split Toning panel creates sepia or other toned photos, or even cross-processed effects.*

tints in the highlights and shadows. Let's take a closer look at the Split Toning panel.

How do I use the Split Toning panel?

The Split Toning panel is primarily designed for effects such as toned monochrome photos and cross-processed color. **(Figure 13.17)** There are two pairs of **Hue** and **Saturation** sliders. The first pair affect the color of the highlights in the photo and the second pair affect the shadows. The **Balance** slider in the center balances the effect between the highlights and the shadows.

You can manually adjust the *Hue* and *Saturation* sliders to choose the tone, but it's easier to click on the color swatch rectangle and select your chosen color using the Color Picker. **(Figure 13.18)**

The Color Picker is used throughout Lightroom. The main gradient shows a full range of colors, and the eyedropper selects your chosen color. You can also select a color from the photo or anywhere else on the screen by clicking in the gradient and dragging the eyedropper onto the photo. Along the top of the Color Picker are swatches or presets. When you find a color you like, you can save it as a swatch by Alt-clicking (Windows) / Opt-clicking (Mac) on one of the swatches.

Once you've got the color about right, you

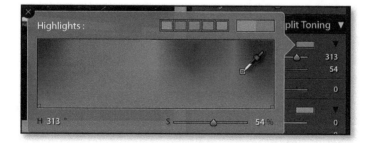

Figure 13.18 *Click on the color rectangle for Highlights or Shadows to access the Color Picker.*

tweak the *Hue* slider to fine tune it. Holding down the Alt key (Windows) / Opt key (Mac) displays a heavily saturated version to help you decide on the perfect color. Holding it down while moving the *Balance* slider displays a red and green mix, so you can see which areas of the photo are affected by the *Highlights* sliders and which are affected by the *Shadows* sliders.

The number of combinations are almost endless, although some look better than others! If you're just starting to experiment with cross-processing and toned black & whites, there are many free presets to give you ideas. **(Figure 13.19)** There are some built in to Lightroom, for example, those in the Lightroom B&W Toned Presets and Lightroom Color Presets sets in the Presets panel.

How do I create a B&W photo with some areas in color?

There's a technique which is often called B&W with Spot Color. It's a B&W photo with a small area of the photo in its original color. It's possible to reproduce this in Lightroom using the Adjustment Brush, although you have little control over the B&W conversion. First, make Develop adjustments to create a good color version. Then select a large adjustment brush set to −100 *Saturation*, and paint over the entire photo to make it all

B&W. Finally, switch the brush to a smaller eraser and erase the B&W brush stroke to bring back the spot color. You can also start/stop a linear gradient outside of the image area and paint away part of the gradient to get the same result.

How do I create an infrared effect?

If you don't own an infrared-converted camera, you can create some infrared-style effects using Lightroom. There are many styles of infrared photography, but the most popular has three main traits: blue sky is very dark, green foliage is white, and it has a slight glow.

To create something similar in Lightroom, try this:

1. Switch to *B&W* at the top of the Basic panel.

2. In the B&W panel, increase *Yellow* and *Green* to +100 and reduce *Blue* to -100.

3. In the Basic panel, move the *Temp* and *Tint* sliders to the left. The exact value depends on each individual photo.

4. Set *Clarity* to a negative value to create the glow, for example, -40.

5. Save it as a preset for use on other

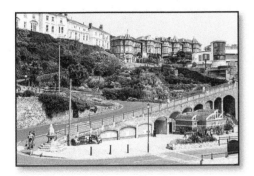
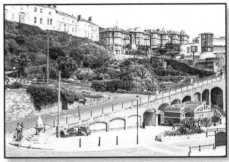

Figure 13.19 *The Split Toning panel is used for cross-processing effects.*

photos. (But note that they're extreme adjustments, so they work better on raw files than JPEGs).

HSL & COLOR

The HSL and Color panels can look slightly daunting to start with, as there is a multitude of sliders divided into separate tabs. They allow for much finer adjustments of specific colors in your photos. **(Figure 13.20)**

What are the HSL and Color panels used for?

They allow you to adjust the individual colors in your photo.

H stands for **Hue**, which is the color.

S stands for **Saturation**, which is the purity or intensity of the color.

L stands for **Luminance**, which is the brightness of the color.

The tabs at the top of the HSL panel change the view, displaying the *Hue* sliders, *Saturation* sliders, *Luminance* sliders or all of the sliders in a single view.

The sliders are tinted to help you remember how the color will change, for example, moving the *Red Saturation* slider to the left reduces the saturation of the reds in the photo.

The Color panel works in exactly the same way. **(Figure 13.21)** They're the same tools laid out differently. The *Hue, Saturation* and *Luminance* sliders are grouped for each color, with the color options along the top.

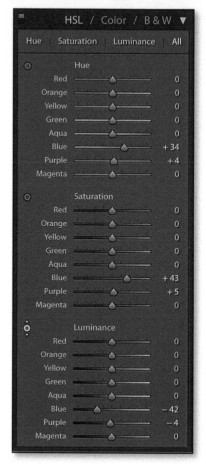

Figure 13.20 *HSL adjustments target specific colors.*

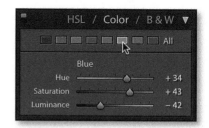

Figure 13.21 *The Color panel shows the HSL sliders in a different format.*

When would I use HSL and Color?

HSL is particularly useful when your white balance is perfect but you want to change or enhance particular colors. **(Figure 13.22)** For

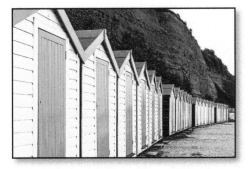
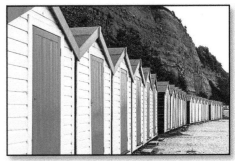

Figure 13.22 *HSL Hue adjustments can be used to change colors, such as the blue/purple color in these beach huts.*

example, if you have some grass in your photo, moving the *Green* slider to the left makes that grass more yellow, without affecting the reds significantly. If someone's skin is too pink, you may need to adjust a few of these sliders, including the *Magenta* and *Red* sliders.

How do I use the HSL/Color TAT tool?

In the top left corner of the panel is the TAT tool, like the one used in the Tone Curve panel. It's particularly useful when working with HSL, as color in your photo is usually affected by more than one slider. The grass may not be green, but a mix of green and yellow. **(Figure 13.23)**

The ***Target Group*** pop-up in the Toolbar controls whether the TAT tool affects the hue, saturation or luminance slider for that color.

My favorite use of the TAT tool and the HSL panel is for a quick blue sky fix. **(Figure 13.24)** When brightening a photo causes those beautiful blue skies and white fluffy clouds to become too light, select the TAT tool, set it to *Luminance* in the pop-up (or select the *Luminance* tab in the HSL panel), and click on the blue sky and drag downwards to darken the sky. You may want to switch to *Saturation* and drag upwards

Figure 13.23 *The HSL TAT tool is the easiest way to select the right mix of sliders.*

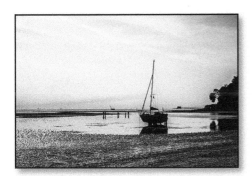
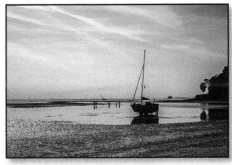

Figure 13.24 *HSL adjustments are a quick way to create deeper blue skies.*

to increase the blue too. Don't go too far, as you'll start to introduce noise, but it's a quick fix.

DETAIL—SHARPENING & NOISE REDUCTION

Most digital photographs require some degree of sharpening, and although camera sensors are improving, most high ISO photos also benefit from noise reduction. Some even say that the quality of the sharpening can make or break an image. Lightroom's Detail panel contains advanced tools to improve your photos. **(Figure 13.25)**

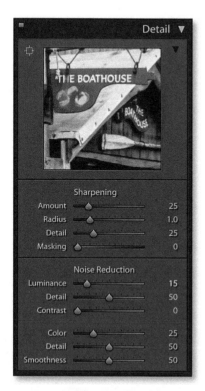

Figure 13.25 *Sharpening and Noise Reduction are applied using the Detail panel.*

How do I fix noisy or soft photos?

In the *Sharpening* section of the Detail panel, the *Amount* slider controls the amount of sharpening applied. The default settings are an excellent starting point and you may be satisfied with these settings. If you want to experiment further, try the sharpening presets found in the Presets panel. We'll come back to the other sliders in more detail shortly.

Noise in your photos can be distracting. You'll particularly notice it in photos shot at high ISO, for example, shot without flash in a darkened room. If you've increased the exposure considerably within Lightroom, it can also increase the appearance of noise. Fortunately, Lightroom's Noise Reduction tools are excellent.

If you're working on raw files, try a setting of around 15-20 *Luminance* as a starting point. This reduces the noise without losing too much image detail. The aim is to reduce the noise, rather than making the subject look like plastic, so don't push it too far. JPEGs may have already had some noise reduction applied by the camera, so you'll need a lower value for these.

When adjusting the sharpening or noise reduction on your photos, it's important to zoom into 1:1 view by clicking the 1:1 icon on the top of the Navigator panel. Other zoom ratios aren't as accurate. If do you need to assess noise reduction or sharpening in Fit view, switch to the Library module, zoom into 1:1 view and then zoom back out. The result is closer than the other non-1:1 views.

The Detail Preview, which can be hidden using the disclosure triangle to its right, always displays a 1:1 view. If you select on the square spiky icon to the left of the preview and then click on the photo, you can choose which section of the photo to preview.

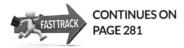

CONTINUES ON PAGE 281

What is multiple pass sharpening?

Lightroom's sharpening is based on Bruce Fraser's multiple pass sharpening techniques. The sharpening is done in stages:

Capture sharpening is intended to offset the inherent softness caused by digital capture and the demosaicing that's done by the raw converter, and it's done using the sliders in the Detail panel.

Creative sharpening is usually applied to specific parts of the photo, for example, the eyes in a portrait. Clarity and the sharpening in the Local Adjustments would be classed as creative sharpening.

Output sharpening is the last stage, depending on whether the photos are viewed on screen, inkjet print, photographic print or a variety of other presentation options. The sharpening applied in the Export dialog or Print module would be classed as output sharpening, as it's calculated based on the output size and type.

How do the sharpening sliders interact?

Let's take a closer look at the individual sharpening sliders and how they interact...

Digital image sharpening works in two ways.

USM, or unsharp mask, works by creating small halos along edges to make them appear sharper. On the dark side of an edge it creates a darker halo, and on the light side

of an edge it makes a lighter halo. (Figure 13.26)

Deconvolution sharpening attempts to calculate and reverse the cause of the blurring.

Lightroom uses both kinds of sharpening, balanced using the *Detail* slider.

Amount works like a volume control. It runs from 0-150, with a default of 25 for raw files or 0 for JPEGs, as the JPEGs may have been sharpened in the camera. The higher the value, the more sharpening applied. You won't usually want to use it at 150 unless you're combining it with the masking or detail sliders which suppress the sharpening.

Radius affects the width of the sharpening halo. It runs from 0.5-3, with a default of 1.0. Photos with fine detail need a smaller radius, as do landscapes, but a slightly higher radius can look good on portraits.

Detail and *Masking* are dampening controls, allowing you to control which areas get the most sharpening applied and which areas are protected, but there's a difference in the way they behave.

Detail is very good at controlling sharpening of textures. Low values use the USM sharpening methods, and as you increase the slider, it gradually switches to

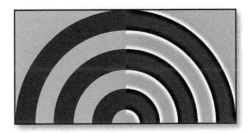

Figure 13.26 *USM sharpening creates halos either side of edges.*

deconvolution methods. The default of 25 is a good general sharpening setting. A low setting is ideal for large smooth areas, such as portraits or sky. Try a high setting for landscapes or other shots with lots of fine detail, where you want to sharpen details like the leaves on the trees. As you increase *Detail*, it also starts to amplify the noise in the image, so you may need to reduce the *Amount* slider and increase the *Masking* and *Luminance* noise reduction to compensate.

Masking creates a soft edge mask from the image, protecting pixels from sharpening. It runs from 0-100, with a default of 0 (no masking). Higher values are particularly good for close-up portraits, allowing higher sharpening settings for the eyes, but still protecting the skin from over-sharpening.

Holding down the Alt key (Windows) / Opt key (Mac) while moving the sharpening sliders shows a grayscale mask of the effect, which can help you determine the best value for each slider individually, for example, when using the *Masking* slider, the white areas of the mask are sharpened and the black areas aren't. **(Figure 13.27)**

So how do you know where to set the sliders to get a crisp result, without over sharpening? Try this:

1. Zoom out to Fit view so you see the entire photo.

2. Hold down the Alt key (Windows) / Opt key (Mac) and drag the *Masking* slider to the right. You're aiming to make areas of low detail, such as the sky, turn black so that that'll be protected from sharpening.

3. Zoom into 1:1 view to accurately preview your further adjustments.

4. Increase the *Amount* slider to easily preview the effect of your adjustments. Try

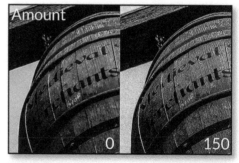

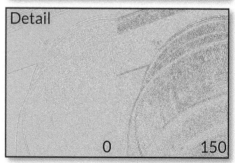

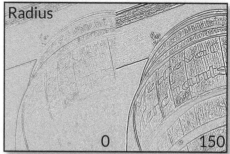

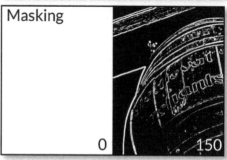

Figure 13.27 *Holding down the Alt key (Windows) / Opt key (Mac) while moving a slider shows a mask to make it easier to select the right slider value. Amount mask (first), Radius mask (second), Detail mask (third), Masking mask (fourth).*

around 75-100 temporarily.

5. Hold down the Alt key (Windows) / Opt key (Mac) and drag the *Detail* slider slightly to the left for portraits or slightly to the right for detailed shots such as landscapes. The aim is to enhance the detail, shown in white, without sharpening the noise, protected in gray.

6. Hold down the Alt key (Windows) / Opt key (Mac) and drag the *Radius* slider slightly to the left for detailed shots such as landscapes or slightly to the right for portraits. Watch the width of the black and white halos you're creating along the edges, and note where these halos are most visible. A value around 1 is usually perfect.

7. Hold down the Alt key (Windows) / Opt key (Mac) and drag the *Amount* slider to the left until the halos almost disappear.

8. Check over the photo for any areas that appear over sharpened. Select the Adjustment Brush, set to *Sharpening* 0 to -50 (no further, as that starts to blur) and brush over the over sharpened areas to reduce the sharpening. Don't remove it entirely, as it may look too smooth in comparison with the rest of the photos.

9. Finally, you may want to go back to the Basic panel and adjust the *Clarity* slider to increase midtone contrast slightly.

Why are my photos softer and noisier in Lightroom than in other software?

When Lightroom's sharpening and noise reduction sliders are at 0, these tools are disabled, whereas many other programs apply additional sharpening and noise reduction behind the scenes, even with their tools set to 0.

How do the noise reduction sliders interact?

There's also an array of noise reduction sliders, but just because they exist doesn't mean you need to use them on every photo. Most photos only require the *Luminance* and *Color* sliders. **(Figure 13.28)** The other sliders are there for more extreme cases, and can be left at their default settings most of the time.

The **Luminance** slider controls the amount of luminance noise reduction applied, moving from 0, which doesn't apply any noise reduction, through to 100 where the photo has an almost painted effect. **(Figure 13.29)**

The **Color** slider tries to suppress single pixels of random noise without losing the edge detail. **(Figure 13.30)** By default, it's set to 25 for raw files, which is usually plenty. It's set to 0 for JPEGs, but if there's still colored noise in your photo, particularly in the dark shadows, try increasing it slightly.

The other sliders only make a noticeable difference to extremely noisy images, such as those produced by the highest ISO rating that your camera offers, or where a high ISO file is extremely underexposed. You're unlikely to see a difference at lower

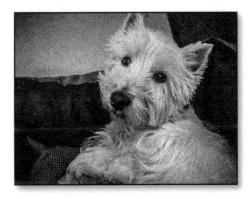

Figure 13.28 *A high ISO photo shows a lot of noise.*

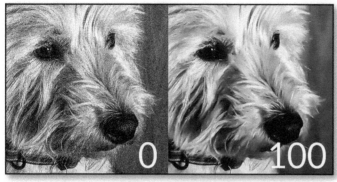

Figure 13.29 *Luminance Noise Reduction at 0 doesn't apply noise reduction, but 100 removes the noise, turning the detail into a painted or smooth plastic effect.*

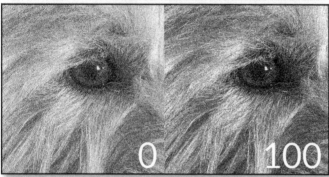

Figure 13.30 *Color Noise Reduction set to 0 doesn't apply color noise reduction, but 100 can create color bleed. The default of 25 is often about right.*

ISO ratings, for better or for worse, so in most cases you won't need to change these settings from their defaults.

The **Luminance Detail** slider sets the noise threshold, so higher values preserve more detail but some noise may incorrectly be identified as detail.

The **Luminance Contrast** slider at 0 is a much finer grain than 100. Higher values help to preserve texture, but can introduce a mottling effect, so lower values are usually a better choice.

The **Color Detail** slider refines any fine color edges. At low values it reduces the number of color speckles in these edges but may slightly desaturate them, whereas at high values, it tries to retain the color detail but may introduce color speckles in the process.

The **Color Smoothness** slider is similar to the *Color* slider, but it aims to remove larger

areas of color mottling or splotchiness. You're most likely to see this on very underexposed images, where you've brightened an area considerably, or extreme contrast images that you're tone-mapping. The default is 50, which works very well on most images. Moving the slider to the right increases the smoothing at the cost of performance.

Can I apply or remove sharpening or noise reduction selectively?

The sliders in the Detail panel apply to the whole photo, but the Adjustment Brush allows you to apply or remove sharpening and noise reduction in specific areas of the photo. You can 'paint in' increased sharpening over a selected area, such as the eyes in a portrait, or selectively reduce global sharpening on large smooth areas of sky. Local noise reduction allows you to selectively increase or decrease the global noise reduction, perhaps because the noise is more noticeable where you've lightened the shadows. (Turn back to the Local Adjustments section on starting on page 241 for more information on using the Adjustment Brush.)

The Local Adjustment Sharpening is directly tied to the sharpening sliders in the Detail panel, so the *Radius, Detail* and *Masking* settings from the Detail panel are combined with the amount set in the Brush options panel. This also gives you the ability to remove sharpening that's been applied by the main sharpening *Amount* slider in the Detail panel.

0 to -50 on the Local Adjustment sharpening reduces the amount of sharpening applied by that global sharpening. Beyond -50 starts blurring the photo with an effect similar to a lens blur, but that's very processor intensive, so don't be surprised if Lightroom starts to slow down.

The Local Adjustment noise reduction applies luminance noise reduction only. You'll need to use the global *Color* noise slider in the Detail panel to reduce color noise.

LENS & PERSPECTIVE (TRANSFORM) CORRECTIONS

You may notice some distortion in your photos, either because of defects in the lens itself or because of the shooting angle. Fixing these issues is as simple as clicking the checkboxes in the **Profile** tab of the Lens Corrections panel. **(Figure 13.31)**

These lens and perspective corrections interact, so it's best to work from the top down. Upright, particularly, works much

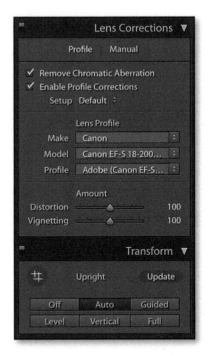

Figure 13.31 *The basic lens and perspective corrections are found in the Lens Correction and Transform panels.*

better when a Lens Profile has been applied first.

1. First, check the **Remove Chromatic Aberration** checkbox. It removes specific types of fringing in the photo, particularly around high-contrast edges or in the corners of the photo.

2. Next, check the **Enable Profile Corrections** checkbox to apply the default lens profile.

If the profile isn't automatically selected in the pop-ups below, manually select the correct lens profile.

If the file was shot using a recent compact or mirrorless camera, a lens profile may have already been applied behind the scenes so you don't need to do anything. If so, it'll say *Built-in Lens Profile applied* at the bottom of the panel.

3. Finally, you can press the **Upright Auto** button in the Transform panel to apply automatic perspective adjustments. Most of the time, *Auto* is the best choice, but you can try the other *Upright* buttons to see if you prefer the result.

There are additional lens and perspective controls, so now let's take a closer look at the options. Since the lens correction controls jump between different panels and tabs, we'll cover them in the order you're likely to need them.

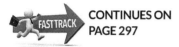

CONTINUES ON PAGE 297

How do I select the correct profile for my lens?

When you check the **Enable Profile Corrections** checkbox, Lightroom checks the EXIF data in the file to identify the lens. If it finds a matching profile, the pop-up menus below automatically populate, and you're done. If Lightroom can't find the correct profile, then you can help by selecting the correct lens profile in the **Make, Model** and **Profile** pop-up menus in the **Profile** tab of the Lens Corrections panel. (If there isn't a suitable profile listed, we'll come back to your options shortly.)

Why is the lens profile not selected automatically?

The EXIF 2.3 official standard for recording lens information in the metadata is only just starting to come into effect, and therefore it isn't always clear which lens was used. Lightroom uses all the information available to make an educated guess, but if it's not sure, it leaves you to select the profile. Once you've chosen the lens, you can set this as a default for that camera/lens combination, so you don't have to select it on every photo in

future.

How do I set a default lens profile?

If your lens isn't automatically recognized by Lightroom, you can set a default lens profile to save manually selecting it each time. This default includes the lens details selected in the pop-up menus and the *Amount* sliders below.

1. Open a photo taken with the camera/lens combination.

2. Go to the Lens Correction panel and check the *Enable Profile Corrections* checkbox.

3. Select the lens make, model and profile from the pop-up menus.

4. (Optional) Adjust the *Amount* sliders to increase or decrease the effect of the profile.

5. Go to the *Setup* pop-up menu and select *Save New Lens Profile Defaults*. **(Figure 13.32)**

In the *Setup* pop-up menu, what's the difference between *Default*, *Auto* & *Custom*?

In the **Setup** pop-up, you'll note three other options:

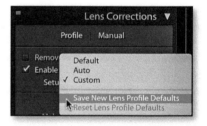

Figure 13.32 *If Lightroom doesn't recognize your lens correctly, you can update the default settings.*

Auto leaves Lightroom to search for a matching profile automatically. If it can't find a matching profile, either because the profile doesn't exist yet, or because it doesn't have enough information in the photo's EXIF data, the pop-ups remain blank.

Default does the same, but also allows you to customize the settings for specific lenses. For example, if *Auto* can't find a lens because it doesn't have enough information, you can select the correct profile from the pop-up menus below and save it as a default for the future. From then on, whenever you select *Default* for a photo with that camera/lens combination, it applies your new default lens setting. It's also useful if you have multiple profiles for a lens—perhaps one provided by Adobe and one you've created yourself—and you want to automatically select one of these profiles.

Custom means that you've manually selected a profile or changed one of the *Amount* sliders and you haven't saved it as a new default setting.

How do I apply lens corrections to new photos by default?

To automatically enable lens corrections for all new imports, first set your photo to its normal default settings (e.g. press *Reset*), and then check the *Enable Profile Corrections* checkbox and make sure the *Setup* pop-up menu is set to *Default* (this is crucial). Finally, go to *Develop menu > Set Default Settings* to set the default for that camera. We'll come to setting defaults in the Develop Module Tools section on page 273.

How do the Amount sliders interact with the profile?

There are some situations where you might want to use some of the profiled correction,

but not all of it. The **Amount** sliders at the bottom of the *Profile* tab act as a volume control, increasing or decreasing the amount of profiled correction that's being applied. 0 doesn't apply the correction at all, 100 applies the profile as it was created, and higher values increase the effect of the correction. For example, with a fisheye lens, you might want to remove the vignette automatically, but keep the fisheye effect. To do so, reduce the **Distortion Amount** slider to 0 but leave the **Vignetting Amount** slider at 100.

Why is the lens profile available for some photos and not others, using the same lens?

Many of the lens profiles are for raw files only, so if a profile is usually available for your lens, check the format of your selected photo. It may be a JPEG or TIFF/PSD.

The processing applied by the camera to non-raw formats can affect the corrections needed, for example, some cameras apply distortion correction and many apply processing that reduces the lens vignetting and chromatic aberration.

If you apply a raw profile to a rendered file (i.e. a JPEG), you may get an unexpected result as it tries to correct for a defect which has already been corrected. There are unofficial ways of making a raw profile available for use with JPEGs by editing the profile with a text editor, but creating your own profile or downloading one created using JPEGs gives a more accurate result.

How do I know whether my lens profile's built in?

Many recent cameras have lens profile information embedded in the raw file and applied automatically by Lightroom. These include many compact cameras and newer mirrorless cameras, and identical lens corrections are usually applied to JPEGs by the camera.

To check whether your camera is affected, look for information at the bottom of the Lens Corrections panel > *Profile* tab. **(Figure 13.33)** If it says *Built-in Lens Profile applied*, click on the *i* button to view additional information about the automatic fixes. **(Figure 13.34)** The built-in profile can apply corrections for distortion, chromatic aberration and/or vignetting. For example, the Sony RX100 applies corrections for distortion and chromatic aberration behind the scenes, but you might still want to check *Enable Profile Corrections* to apply a profile that removes the vignetting.

What are my options if my lens profile isn't available?

If your lens doesn't appear in the Lens Profile pop-up menus and isn't built in, you have a number of different options:

• Wait for Adobe to create a profile for that lens. Lens profiles are being added

gradually in each dot release. You can check the list of supported lenses at https://www.Lrq.me/lensprofiles

• Switch to the *Manual* tab and adjust the sliders manually.

What's the difference between the Distortion/Vignetting sliders on the Profile tab and the Manual tab?

You'll notice that there are also *Distortion* and *Vignetting* sliders on the **Manual** tab of the Lens Correction panel **(Figure 13.35)**. Although they have the same name, they're not completely interchangeable.

The sliders at the bottom of the *Profile* tab are used in conjunction with a lens profile, increasing or decreasing its effect, whereas the sliders on the *Manual* tab are used when you don't have a profile for the lens and need to make manual corrections for distortion, colored fringing and lens vignetting.

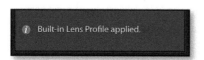

Figure 13.33 *Many recent cameras have the lens profile information built-in and applied automatically.*

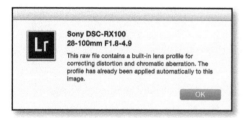

Figure 13.34 *If a built-in profile has been applied, click on the i icon to see which corrections are included.*

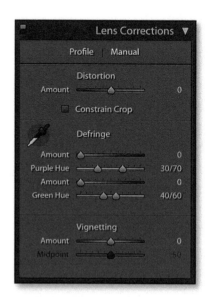

Figure 13.35 *The Manual tab of the Lens Corrections panel offers manual distortion, vignetting and chromatic aberration correction.*

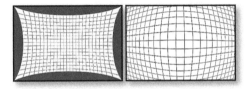

Figure 13.36 *Distortion in the Manual tab +100 (left) and -100 (right).*

The **Distortion** slider corrects for barrel or pincushion distortion **(Figure 13.36)**, and the **Vignetting Amount** and **Midpoint** sliders correct lens vignetting. Unlike the *Post-Crop Vignette* in the Effects panel, these *Vignetting* sliders are not affected by cropping.

How do I fix Chromatic Aberration or colored fringes?

Chromatic aberration, or CA, refers to the little fringes of color that can appear along high contrast edges, where the red, green and blue light wavelengths are unable to focus at the same point. There are two different kinds of chromatic aberration, which require different treatment.

Type 1—Lateral/Transverse Chromatic Aberration

Lateral or transverse chromatic aberration results from color wavelengths hitting the focal plane next to each other. **(Figure 13.37)** It's most noticeable around the corners of photos taken with a lower quality wide angle lens, and doesn't appear in the center of the image. You'll recognize the two different colored fringes appearing on opposite sides of your image details.

This type of chromatic aberration is fixed using the **Remove Chromatic Aberration** checkbox in the *Profile* tab of the Lens Corrections panel. It's disabled by default as it can slow Lightroom down slightly, and in rare cases may introduce new fringing.

Type 2 – Axial/Longitudinal Chromatic Aberration

The second type of chromatic aberration is called axial or longitudinal chromatic aberration, which results from the color wavelengths focusing at different lengths. **(Figure 13.38)** Unlike lateral CA, with its pairs of opposing colors, axial CA causes a halo of a single color – purple in front of the focal plane or green behind it—which can be present anywhere on the image.

Axial CA isn't the only cause of purple fringing. Flare and sensor issues can also cause it, usually along high contrast backlit edges, but the treatment of these purple fringes is the same regardless of the cause.

This type of chromatic aberration is fixed

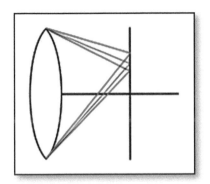

Figure 13.37 *Lateral/Transverse Chromatic Aberration.*

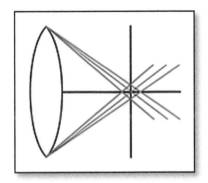

Figure 13.38 *Axial/Longitudinal Chromatic Aberration*

using the **Defringe** sliders and eyedropper in the *Manual* tab. **(Figure 13.39)** These allow you to target specific hues to remove the fringing.

To demonstrate how to use these tools, let's correct this example image **(Figure 13.40)**, which exhibits both types of chromatic aberration.

1. Develop the image, working from the top down as normal.

2. Correct lens distortion by checking the *Enable Profile Corrections* checkbox in the *Profile* tab of the Lens Corrections panel, as the distortion corrections can affect the chromatic aberration.

3. The green and magenta fringes caused by lateral chromatic aberration are still visible

(Figure 13.41) so enable the **Remove Chromatic Aberration** checkbox in the *Profile* tab.

4. After removing the lateral chromatic aberration, this photo still exhibits purple fringing along the backlit edges. Zoom in to 1:1 or greater magnification in order to clearly see the fringe pixels. **(Figure 13.42)**

If the leftover chromatic aberration is limited to a small area, it's quicker and safer to use the local brush or gradient rather than the global lens corrections, so skip the next 2 steps. Otherwise continue to the next step to apply global corrections.

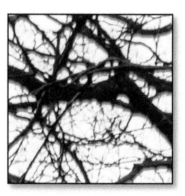

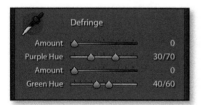

Figure 13.39   *The Defringe controls allow you to fix chromatic aberration and other fringing.*

Figure 13.41   *Even with the lens profile applied, the purple and green fringes are still visible.*

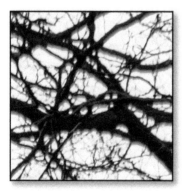

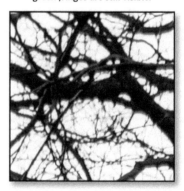

Figure 13.40   *Chromatic aberration refers to little fringes of color.*

Figure 13.42   *After checking the Remove Chromatic Aberration checkbox, the photo still shows some purple fringing.*

5. Select the eyedropper tool from the *Manual* tab of the Lens Corrections panel and float over the fringes. The end of the eyedropper becomes purple or green, depending on the color of the fringe you're sampling. **(Figure 13.43)** If the end is white, it won't work. Click on the purple fringe to automatically remove it. If there's any green fringing, click to sample the green fringe too.

For many photos, that's all you need to do. When you sample the fringe using the eyedropper, the *Defringe* sliders in the *Manual* tab of the Lens Corrections panel are automatically adjusted.

6. If you need to fine tune the corrections further, you can adjust the **Defringe** sliders manually.

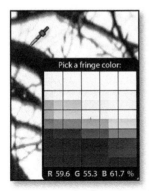

Figure 13.43 *The tip of the Fringe Color Selector changes color based on the color of the pixels.*

There are two pairs of sliders for correcting purple and green fringes. The **Amount** sliders affects the strength of the adjustment, and the **Hue** sliders affects the range of colors being corrected. As you move the *Hue* sliders further apart, the fringe removal affects a wider range of colors.

At first glance, it may appear easiest to set the amount to 20 with the widest hue range possible, but doing so would also desaturate the edges of other objects in your image. To avoid this, use the lowest amount and narrowest hue range possible, while still removing the fringing.

The easiest way to check that you've captured all the fringe pixels is to hold down the Alt key (Windows) / Opt key (Mac) while dragging the slider.

For the *Amount* sliders, only the affected area is shown, with the rest of the image being masked in white. This enables you to check that the fringe pixels have been completely desaturated. **(Figure 13.44)**

Used with the *Hue* sliders, the affected fringes turn black, allowing you to check that there are no stray colored fringe pixels. **(Figure 13.45)**

7. Finally, once you've removed the fringing using the global controls, you may want to increase or decrease the fringe removal in some areas.

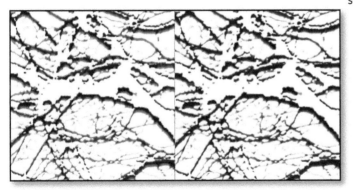

Figure 13.44 *When you hold down the Alt (Windows) / Opt (Mac) key and drag the Amount slider, the photo shows a B&W mask with your fringe highlighted (left). Drag the slider until the fringe disappears (right).*

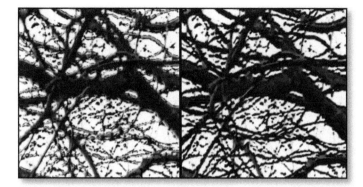

Figure 13.45 *The same Alt/Opt mask applies with the Hue slider, with the colored fringes (left) turning black (right) as you move the slider, showing that you've captured all the stray colored pixels.*

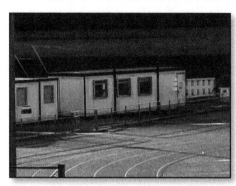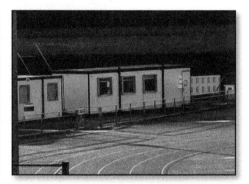

Figure 13.46 *The global defringe may affect other edges in the photo (note the gray desaturated areas along the black edges in the left photo) but setting the Adjustment Brush to -100 Defringe and painting over the area brings back the color (right).*

How do I remove localized fringing?

As long as your photo is set to PV3/PV4, you can use the adjustment brush or gradient tool to apply defringe to specific areas, or to protect objects from the global fringe removal.

For example, you may find that global defringe adjustments have unavoidably affected the edges of other objects, such as this building. **(Figure 13.46)**

Select the adjustment brush, set the *Defringe* slider in the adjustment brush settings to a negative slider value (i.e., -100) and brush over the areas you want to protect from the global adjustment. (Turn back to page 241 for general information on the local adjustments)

You can also use a positive *Defringe* value (i.e., +100) on the adjustment brush to remove any leftover fringing that wasn't removed by the global adjustment, or to apply small amounts of fringe removal on photos that don't require a global adjustment.

The positive values on the local adjustment *Defringe* slider are not tied to the global sliders, so it removes fringing of any color, such as the red fringe shown in **Figure 13.47**.

How do I fix the perspective?

Moving on to the Transform panel, the **Upright** tool can fix perspective

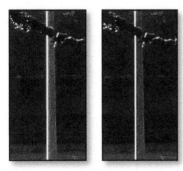

Figure 13.47 *The Adjustment Brush Defringe slider set to positive values removes fringing of any color, such as the red fringe in this photo.*

The ***Guided*** button allows you to draw lines directly on the image to show Lightroom which lines should be horizontal or vertical. We'll come back to this tool in more detail in a moment.

The ***Full*** button is the most extreme option. It levels the photos and fixes converging horizontal and vertical lines, even if that means using very strong 3D corrections which distort image features.

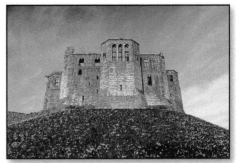

automatically by analyzing the straight edges in your photo. **(Figure 13.48)** For example, it attempts to automatically fix tilted horizons and straighten buildings. You can then tweak the results to get the exact correction you desire.

What do the different Upright buttons do? Which one should I use?

The ***Off*** button is simple—Upright is disabled, so no adjustments are made.

The ***Auto*** button is the most intelligent option. It not only tries to level the photo and correct converging horizontal and vertical lines, but it also takes into account the amount of distortion that's created by the correction. It aims to get the best visual result, even if that's not perfectly straight. **(Figure 13.49)**

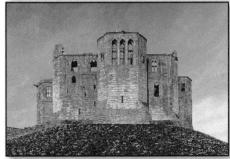

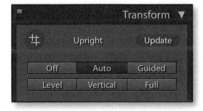

Figure 13.48 *The Upright buttons are found in the Transform panel.*

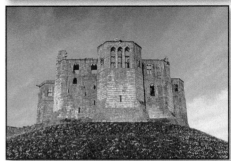

Figure 13.49 *Upright corrects perspective distortion, but a full correction may look unnatural. Original (first), Full (second), Auto (third).*

The **Level** button only tries to level the photo, fixing tilted horizons and verticals. It's similar to straightening the photo when cropping. It doesn't try to adjust for converging lines.

The **Vertical** button levels the photo, like the *Level* button, but also fixes converging verticals.

There's a little bit of trial and error involved in picking the right one for each photo, but more often than not, the *Auto* button gives the best result.

How do I use Guided Upright?

Upright's Guided mode allows you to draw lines on the image, showing which lines should be vertical or horizontal.

1. First, enable the lens profile or make manual lens corrections in the Lens Corrections panel.

2. In the Transform panel, click the **Guided** button. This automatically selects the Guided Upright tool, which lives in the corner of the panel. **(Figure 13.50)**

3. Click at the beginning of your vertical or horizontal line (for example, the wall of a building) and drag to the end of the line. Hold down the Alt (Windows) / Opt (Mac) key to slow down the cursor for greater accuracy. **(Figure 13.51)**

4. Repeat to add additional lines—up to two horizontal and two vertical. If you add more than two lines in each direction, an error message displays at the bottom of the Transform panel. When you add the second, third and fourth line, Lightroom updates the perspective of the image so you can preview the effect.

As you float over the image, the floating Loupe tool displays a zoomed section of the photo, which aids in making an accurate selection, but if you find it distracting, uncheck *Show Loupe* in the toolbar. **(Figure 13.52)**

To adjust an existing line, click on the square at the end of the line and move it to a new position. If the lines aren't showing on the

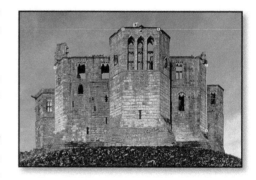

Figure 13.51 *Using the Guided Upright tool, draw up to 4 lines on the image to show which parts of the photo should be vertical or horizontal.*

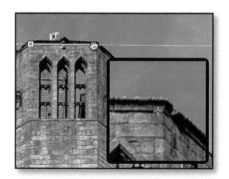

Figure 13.52 *The Loupe displays a zoomed section of the photo, which aids in making an accurate selection.*

Figure 13.50 *The Guided Upright tool lives in the corner of the Transform panel.*

image, select the Guided Upright tool in the corner of the Transform panel. By default, the lines show on the image whenever the Guided Upright tool is enabled, but you can set the *Tool Overlay* pop-up in the Toolbar to *Always*, *Auto* (hides the lines when you move the cursor away from the image) or *Never*.

To delete a line, click on it to select it and press the Delete key on the keyboard. To remove all of the lines, double-click on the word *Upright* in the Transform panel.

When do I need to press *Update*?

The **Update** button is only available when the adjustments need to recalculated, usually because you've checked or unchecked the *Enable Profile Corrections* checkbox in the Lens Corrections panel, or occasionally because Adobe have improved the automated calculations.

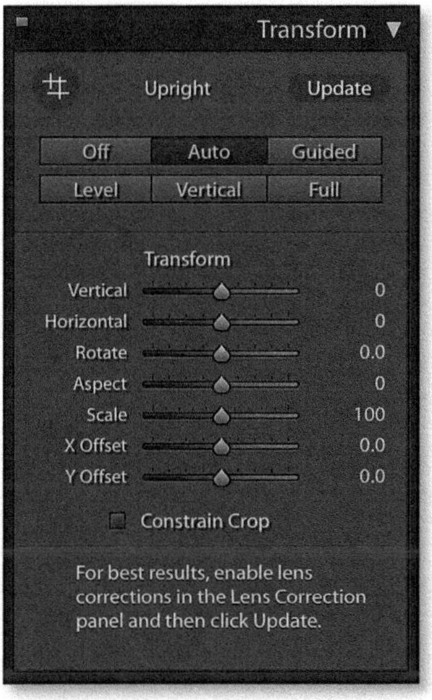

How do I reduce the effect of the Upright correction?

You'll notice that the **Transform** sliders below aren't adjusted automatically when using Upright. **(Figure 13.53)** This is because the complex calculations would require numerous extra sliders, so it's all done behind the scenes. These manual sliders are still useful for reducing the effect of the Upright corrections.

We're used to seeing converging verticals in everyday life, so full correction can look unnatural. Using the *Transform* sliders, you can adjust individual axes of rotation, reducing their effect. For example, setting the *Vertical* slider to +10 reintroduces some converging verticals, giving a more natural appearance.

What do each of the *Transform* Lens Corrections sliders do?

As well as reducing the effect of Upright, the *Transform* sliders are particularly useful for slimming people and recovering pixels pushed out of the frame by other lens and perspective corrections. Let's take each in turn...

The **Vertical** and **Horizontal** sliders adjust for perspective. It's most useful for reducing the effect of Upright corrections. **(Figure 13.54)**

The **Rotate** slider adjusts for camera tilt. It's applied at a much earlier stage in the processing than the crop, with a different

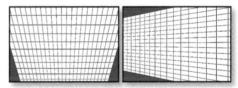

Figure 13.53 *The Transform sliders manually rotate and turn the image.*

Figure 13.54 *Vertical -100 (left) and Horizontal +100 (right).*

result. *Rotate* pivots on the center of the uncropped photo instead of the center of the crop.

If you're using the *Transform* sliders to correct perspective, and your camera wasn't level, it's better to use the *Upright* buttons or the *Rotate* slider in the Transform panel to level the camera, rather than *Angle* in the Crop tool. **(Figure 13.55)**

The **Aspect** slider squashes or stretches the photo to improve the appearance. Strong keystone corrections can make a photo look unnatural, especially when they include people. The slider direction is sensitive to the image rotation, but in most cases, dragging the slider to the left makes things look wider, and dragging the slider to the right makes them look taller and thinner. **(Figure 13.56)**

Even if you haven't used the other perspective corrections, moving the *Aspect*

slider slightly (usually to the right) slims down the subject, reversing "the camera adds 10lbs!" **(Figure 13.57)**

The **Scale** slider interpolates the data to recover pixels which have been pushed out of the frame by other lens or perspective corrections, which the Crop tool can't do.

Scale can also remove blank areas of the photo caused by the lens and perspective corrections, but it interpolates the data (creates new pixels) in the process, so cropping these blank areas is usually a better choice. **(Figure 13.58)**

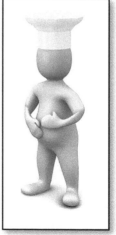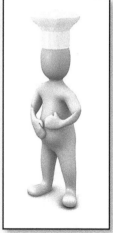

Figure 13.57 *The Aspect slider can make anyone look slimmer!*

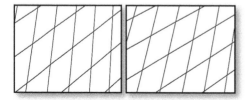

Figure 13.55 *The same grid was rotated using the Crop Angle slider (left) and the Rotate slider (right) followed by an identical -100 Vertical transform. This small crop was taken from the corner of each photo, so you can see there's a difference in the slider behavior.*

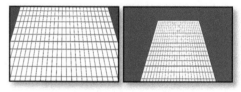

Figure 13.58 *With Scale at 0 (left), some of the image is being lost from the corners, whereas Scale -50 (right) shows the extra image data.*

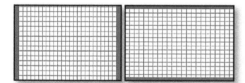

Figure 13.56 *Aspect set to +100 (left) and- 100 (right).*

The **X Offset** and **Y Offset** sliders shift the photo left/right/up/down, which is useful when an adjustment has pushed the important section of the photo out of the frame, as it moves it back into range without interpolating the data. **(Figure 13.59)**

Finally, the **Constrain Crop** checkbox crops the photo to remove any gaps around the edge, which can be caused by lens or perspective corrections. It's identical to the *Constrain to Image* checkbox in the Crop Options panel (page 233).

How do I hide the grid?

By default, the grid overlay appears when you float over the Transform sliders, to help you make adjustments by eye. You can turn the overlay off or on permanently using *View menu > Loupe Overlay > Grid* or by selecting the Guided Upright tool (in the corner of the Transform panel) and adjusting the *Grid Overlay* options in the toolbar.

What's the difference between syncing Upright Mode vs. Transforms?

We'll come to synchronizing settings in the Develop Tools chapter on page 305, but it's worth noting that the wording on some of the Upright Sync options isn't entirely clear. **Transform Adjustments** refers to the *Manual*

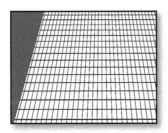

Figure 13.59 *If some of the data is pushed out of the frame by the lens corrections, the X Offset and Y Offset sliders can shift the data without interpolation.*

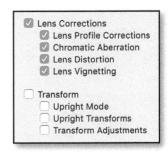

Figure 13.60 *Note the difference between Upright Mode and Upright Transforms when syncing settings to other photos.*

sliders (*Vertical, Horizontal,* etc). **Upright Mode** uses the same Upright button (*Auto, Level,* etc.) but analyzes each photo individually, whereas **Upright Transforms** uses exactly the same settings behind the scenes, without adjusting for each photo. In most cases, *Upright Mode* is the option you'll choose. If you're syncing across photos that are almost identical, then *Upright Transforms* gives a more consistent result. **(Figure 13.60)**

EFFECTS—POST-CROP VIGNETTE & GRAIN

Vignetting is the darkening or lightening of the corners of a photo. **(Figure 13.61)**

Although traditionally it's caused by the camera lens, it's become popular as a photographic effect, so the controls are found in the Effects panel. **(Figure 13.62)** There's also a grain effect, designed to simulate traditional film grain, which feels more natural than digital noise.

What's the difference between Highlight Priority, Color Priority and Paint Overlay?

The **Style** pop-up in the Effects panel gives a choice of three different post-crop vignettes, which all fit within the crop

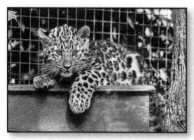
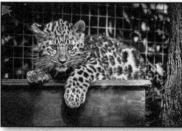

Figure 13.61 A vignette can help to draw your eye into a photo and focus on the main subject.

boundary, rather than the original lens correction vignette which is designed for correcting lens problems.

Highlight Priority is the default and imitates a traditional lens vignette with the colors remaining heavily saturated throughout.

Color Priority retains more natural colors into the vignette, with smoother shadow transitions.

Paint Overlay adds a plain black or white overlay.

Figure 13.62 The Effects panel contains the Post-Crop Vignetting and Grain controls.

How do the Post-Crop Vignette sliders interact?

The **Amount** slider controls how dark or light the vignette should be, with 0 not applying a vignette at all. Most photos look better with a dark vignette, rather than a white one. **(Figure 13.63)**

For many photos, the main *Vignette* slider is the only one you'll need to adjust, but if you want more control, click the arrow to the right to show additional sliders.

The **Midpoint** slider controls how close to the center of the photo the vignette affects. The vignette created by the Effects panel is always centered within the crop boundaries, but if you need an off-center vignette, you can use the Radial Gradient instead (page 241). **(Figure 13.64)**

The **Roundness** slider controls how round or square the vignette is. -100 is almost rectangular and barely visible whereas +100 is circular. Most vignettes look great with the default of 0, which matches the ratio of the photo. **(Figure 13.65)**

The **Feather** slider runs from 0 to 100, with 0 showing a hard edge, and 100 being so soft it almost disappears. The default of 50 is a great starting point, with most vignettes ranging from 35 to 65. **(Figure 13.66)**

The **Highlights** sliders runs from 0, which has no effect, to 100, which makes the highlights

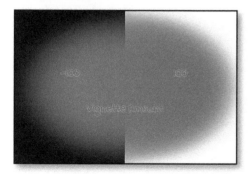

Figure 13.63 *The effect of the Vignette Amount slider.*

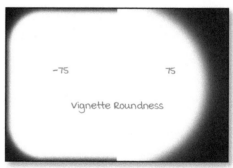

Figure 13.65 *The effect of the Vignette Roundness slider.*

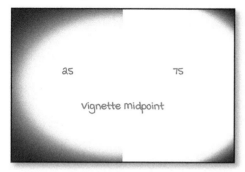

Figure 13.64 *The effect of the Vignette Midpoint slider.*

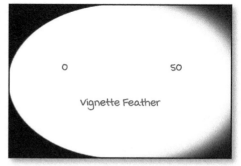

Figure 13.66 *The effect of the Vignette Feather slider.*

under a dark vignette brighter. This allows you to darken the edges without the photo becoming too flat and lacking in contrast. **(Figure 13.67)**

How do I decide on the best vignette settings?

Ready to give it a try? You can use the sliders in any order, but this works well:

1. Move the *Amount* slider to -100, so you can easily see the effect of the other sliders.

2. Adjust the *Midpoint* slider, so the vignette doesn't cover important areas of the photo.

3. Adjust the *Feather* slider so the edge of the vignette disappears.

4. Move the *Amount* slider back towards 0,

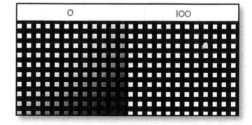

Figure 13.67 *The effect of the Vignette Highlights slider.*

until you're drawn into the photo, but the vignette isn't immediately obvious.

5. Adjust the *Highlights* slider if the corners look too flat and lack contrast.

How do I move the vignette off-center?

The Post-Crop Vignette is always centered

within the Crop boundaries, but the Radial Filter allows you to create your own off-center vignettes. Turn back to page 227 to learn how.

How do the Grain sliders interact?

We spend a lot of time trying to reduce the noise in our photos... and then put grain back! However, some photos look great with a little extra grain, particularly if they're B&W or sepia. **(Figure 13.68)**

It can also help to hide the plasticky look that results from high noise reduction.

Lightroom's **Grain** sliders aim to emulate a traditional film grain, which looks a little different to digital noise.

The **Amount** slider in the Detail panel affects the amount of grain applied. The noise is applied equally across the photo, giving a much more film-like quality than digital noise, which tends to be heavier in the shadows. **(Figure 13.69)**

Size affects the size of the grain, just as grain on film came in different sizes, and it gets softer as it gets larger. More expensive film usually had smaller grain. **(Figure 13.70)**

Roughness affects the consistency of the grain, so 0 is uniform across the photo, whereas higher values become rougher. **(Figure 13.71)**

Like sharpening and noise reduction, you'll need to zoom into 1:1 view to get an accurate preview. Grain is very sensitive to resizing, sharpening and compression, so if

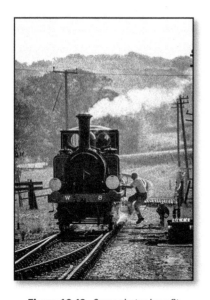

Figure 13.68 Some photos benefit from added grain for effect.

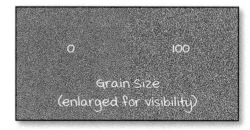

Figure 13.70 The effect of the Grain Size slider.

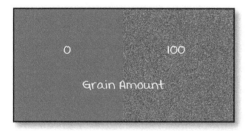

Figure 13.69 The effect of the Grain Amount slider.

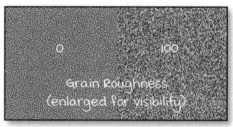

Figure 13.71 The effect of the Grain Roughness slider.

you're going to downsize the photo when exporting, you'll need stronger grain. It won't reproduce well in this book, so try it on some of your own photos too.

PHOTO MERGE

The Photo Merge feature allows you to stitch together multiple photos into a panorama or create a high dynamic range (HDR) file from multiple images.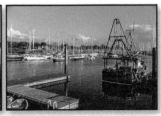

How do I stitch a panorama?

1. Select a series of photos. The order of the photos in the Filmstrip doesn't matter, as Lightroom matches the photos visually. This means you can even stitch multi-row panoramas. **(Figure 13.72)**

2. Go to *Photo menu* > *Photo Merge* > *Panorama*.

3. Select a projection mode that looks good.

4. Check the *Auto Crop* checkbox to remove the blank white space, or drag the *Boundary Warp* slider to warp the photo to fill the white space.

5. Press *Merge*. **(Figure 13.73)**

6. The resulting photo is stored in the same folder as the originals and automatically imported into Lightroom, where you can edit it in Develop as a normal photo.

How do I create an HDR file?

When the camera's sensor isn't capable of capturing detail in both the lightest and darkest tones, you can take a series of shots with bracketed exposures and blend them in Lightroom.

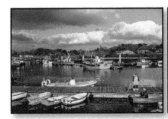
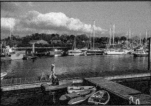

Figure 13.72 *Select multiple photos to merge into a panorama.*

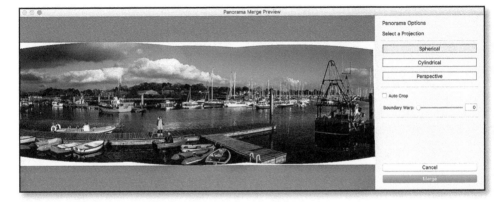

Figure 13.73 *Select the merge options in the dialog.*

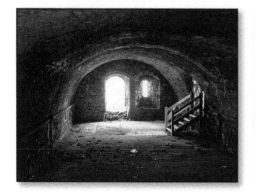
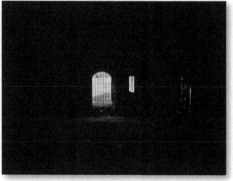

Figure 13.74 *Select two photos to merge into an HDR file.*

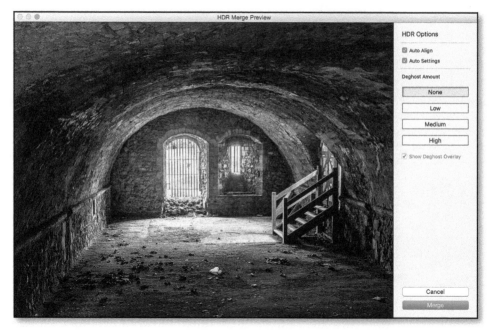

Figure 13.75 *Select the merge options in the dialog.*

1. Select a series of bracketed photos. In most cases, select just two photos—one for the highlights and one for the shadows. **(Figure 13.74)**

2. Go to *Photo menu > Photo Merge > HDR.*

3. Check the *Auto Align* and *Auto Tone* checkboxes.

4. If there's movement in the photo (e.g. water), try the *Deghost* options until you find the one that gets the best result. If there's no movement, leave it set to *None.*

5. Press *Merge.* **(Figure 13.75)**

6. The resulting HDR photo is stored in the same folder as the originals and automatically imported into Lightroom, where you can edit it in the Develop module. You'll note that the *Exposure* slider now runs from -10 to +10 instead of -5 to +5.

The Photo Merge options also appear in the right-click menu in the Grid and Filmstrip, which is useful when you're working in the Develop module. They're only available when you have two or more photos or a collapsed stack selected. If you want to use the same settings as your last merge, hold down the Shift key while selecting the Merge option to bypass the dialog.

The Merge preview is low resolution for speed, so you can resize the dialog or zoom in slightly, but you can't zoom in to a full 1:1 view.

When you press **Merge**, the merge happens in the background so you can continue working on other photos. If your computer is a high enough specification, you can run multiple merges at the same time, however it's very memory intensive. The **Cancel** button cancels without merging, of course.

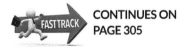

CONTINUES ON PAGE 305

Why use Lightroom for merging instead of Photoshop or other software?

In External Editors, we'll briefly discuss the Edit In > Merge to HDR Pro and Merge to Panorama using Photoshop, which was Adobe's older merge method. Photoshop's Merge to Panorama is still useful for merging rendered files (e.g. JPEGs) as it gives you greater control over the blending, but Lightroom's new merge has a distinct advantage when working with raw files.

Photoshop and other software have to partially convert the raw data before merging, reducing the possible dynamic range and applying the white balance. This affects the image quality.

When the merge is performed on the raw image data, as Lightroom now offers, the resulting file has all the editing flexibility of the original raw files. It is demosaiced, so it's no longer in the original sensor format, but it's still scene-referred data so you have full control over the white balance as well as a much wider dynamic range.

There are still some cases where you might want to use other software. For example, for tricky panoramas, dedicated software such as Hugin may get a better result. Also, Lightroom creates fairly natural looking HDR files, but you may prefer the surreal HDR style that dedicated HDR software produces.

What type of files do I need for merging?

There are a few requirements for the source files. The files must be:

• All the same file type (raw or rendered). Raw files get significantly better results.

• All original files (required for HDR. Smart previews work for panorama merge, but the resulting merge is smaller).

• All shot on the same camera (required for HDR, but best for panoramas too).

• All the same size and orientation (vertical or horizontal).

• All shot using the same focal length.

• Metadata containing at least the exposure time for HDR.

There are a couple of shooting tips that can help you get the best merge result:

• For the best results, use a tripod to ensure the photos are correctly aligned, especially when shooting HDR sets.

• Overlap panorama sections by around 30% so they blend smoothly, and shoot panoramas with a 20mm-50mm lens in Manual mode to avoid significant lens distortion and exposure differences (although Lightroom does attempt to normalize the exposure for raw files).

What format are the merged files?

The merged files are stored as 16-bit DNG files. Lightroom automatically names the merged file using the name of the active photo and it adds -Pano or -HDR to the end of the filename to help identify them. (Make sure you keep this Pano/HDR ending, as it's currently the only way to filter for these files.)

In the case of HDR images, the files don't need the full 32-bit depth used for Photoshop HDR merges as the pixel data is stored as floating-point data. This makes it possible to store the image values accurately across a huge contrast range without such a huge file size.

Panoramic images have to be no more than 65000 pixels along the longest edge or 512 megapixels (whichever is smaller) to fit within ACR/Lightroom's maximum, so Lightroom automatically downsizes any panoramas that would fall outside these limits when creating them.

Should I edit the photos before I merge them?

There's no need to edit the photos before you merge them as the data remains scene-referred (assuming it's a raw file in the first place). This means you can edit the file after it's merged without any loss of quality.

There are two things to look out for when merging panoramas - lens corrections and sensor dust.

Lightroom applies the default lens profile and chromatic aberration correction to the raw data before merging the panorama to get the best result, whether you've enabled it for the selected files or not. If Lightroom doesn't automatically select the right profile for your lens, turn back to page 282 and save a default profile before merging.

Dust or sensor spots appear in the same place on every image, and retouching them individually can take a long time on a huge panorama. You can fix your dust spots on one photo, sync the corrections to the other photos, and they'll be applied during the merge process.

One thing to note is that these spot corrections are 'baked in' to the resulting merged image data, so you can't go back and edit them in the finished panorama. Other spots that only need to be removed on a single image are best left until the finished merged image is available.

If you do choose to edit the photos before merging, Lightroom automatically copies some of the Develop settings from the active photo onto the merged photo. It skips things like the crop, lens corrections and local adjustments as they may not end up in the right place on the merged photo.

Let's take a closer look at some of the merge options.

What's the difference between the Panorama projection options?

There are three projection options: **(Figures 13.76 & 13.77)**

Spherical aligns and transforms the photos

as if they were mapping the inside of a sphere. If you've taken a 360° panorama, this is usually the best choice.

Cylindrical displays the images as if they're on an unfolded cylinder, using the middle image as the reference point and transforming the photos where they overlap. It reduces the bow-tie type distortion you can get with Perspective. It works well on wide panoramas.

Perspective uses the middle image as the reference point and transforms the other images where they overlap, but it can result in a bow-tie type distortion.

How do I fill in the white areas around the edges?

When you create a panorama, you end up with blank areas around the edges. You have a few options:

1. Crop the photo to remove the white areas. To do so automatically, check the *Auto Crop* checkbox. All of the pixel detail is retained and you can use the Crop tool to reset or edit the crop later in the Develop module.

2. Use Content Aware Fill in Photoshop to create new pixels.

3. Use *Boundary Warp* to analyze the image and warp it to fill the empty space. It has a slider ranging from 0-100, so you can choose how far to warp the image.

4. Use a combination of all three, perhaps warping the photo slightly and then cropping off the rest.

As with any tool, Boundary Warp has pros and cons. Unlike Content Aware Fill, Boundary Warp doesn't require an additional rendered file, so doesn't take up additional disc space and it retains the editing flexibility of the original raw files. Also, because it's warping the existing data,

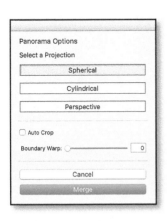

Figure 13.76 *Panorama Options.*

Figure 13.77 *There are three projection options—Spherical (top), Cyclindrical (center) and Perspective (bottom).*

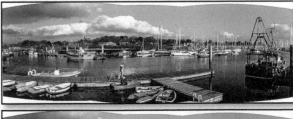

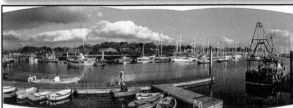

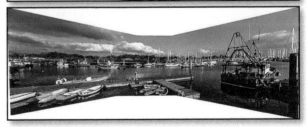

it doesn't create additional artifacts. On the other hand, because it's warping the data, it can make straight lines a little wavy, so you'll want to avoid using it with Perspective mode, which is designed to keep lines straight! **(Figure 13.78)**

Where are the HDR editing options?

Many photographers use the term HDR to describe a specific surreal style of editing, but think about the letters HDR... they stand for high dynamic range.

There are two stages to the process:

1. Merging multiple source files to create a single image with a much higher dynamic range. The result is an HDR file.

2. Manipulating the high dynamic range data to compress it into a lower dynamic range suitable for viewing on a screen or print. The result is a normal photo with a specific style of editing applied.

Most HDR software combines these two steps, allowing you to merge the files into

an HDR image, apply your chosen style and output that photo with a low dynamic range.

Lightroom splits this process into its separate stages, first merging the photos into an HDR image, and then tone-mapping this image in the Develop module before outputting the photo. This allows you to go back and change the look of the photo non-destructively at a later date without having to merge the original images all over again.

How many photos should I select for an HDR file?

Unlike most HDR software, Lightroom works best with as few source images as possible. In most cases, this is only two raw files—one correctly exposed for the highlights and one correctly exposed for the shadows. As Lightroom's working with the raw data, it doesn't need the images in between, and additional images actually increase the risk of misalignment and ghosting.

If the images are more than 3 stops apart, add one or more additional images in

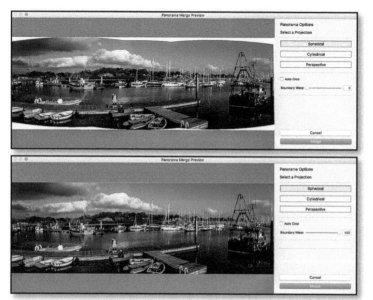

Figure 13.78 *The content of the photo may determine whether you crop the image, use Content Aware Fill in Photoshop or use Boundary Warp in the Merge dialog.*

between to reduce noise, ideally shot on a tripod to avoid introducing ghosting, for example:

-1.5 to 1.5 = 2 exposure (-1.5, 1.5)
-3.0 to 3.0 = 3 exposure (-3, 0, 3)
-4.5 to 4.5 = 4 exposure (-4.5, -1.5, 1.5, 4.5)
-6.0 to 6.0 = 5 exposure (-6, -3, 0, 3, 6)

There's no point trying to do a 'fake HDR' using a single file, because you won't gain any additional dynamic range.

Should I check *Auto Align* and enable *Deghost*?

There are a couple of options available in the HDR Preview dialog. **(Figure 13.79)**

Auto Align is worth checking if the photos were shot handheld and may not be perfectly aligned. If the photos were shot using a tripod and remote release, with no risk of movement, you can leave it unchecked.

The **Deghost** options are needed if there's a moving subject in the photo, for example, water or trees, as these can creates ghosts when photos are merged. There are three levels to choose from—*Low*, *Medium* or *High*—and they control how sensitive Lightroom is to movement in the photo. The *High* setting is much more aggressive, whereas *Low* just picks up significant ghosting.

Check the **Show Deghost Overlay** checkbox to see which areas are affected by the deghosting, and remember to check them in the finished photo to ensure the deghosting hasn't introduced additional noise or sharp edges. **(Figure 13.80)**

How do I edit the HDR file after merging?

Auto Tone is applied to the preview to give you an idea of the tonal range before merging. Once the photo's merged, you can edit it in the Develop module. The resulting file has a much greater range of data with more highlight headroom and shadows with less noise. The *Exposure* slider runs to +10/-10 instead of +5/-5, and the *Highlights* and *Shadows* sliders have a greater range. If you need to push the *Highlights* or *Shadows* further than +/- 100, you can paint on greater values using the local adjustments such as the Adjustment Brush or Graduated Filter.

HDR Options

☑ Auto Align
☑ Auto Settings

Deghost Amount

None

Low

Medium

High

☑ Show Deghost Overlay

Cancel

Merge

Figure 13.79 *HDR options*

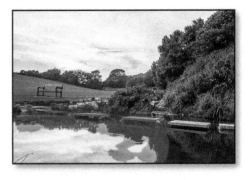

Figure 13.80 *Check the Deghost Overlay to see which areas are being taken from a single photo to minimize ghosting.*

DEVELOP ADVANCED SHORTCUTS

		Windows	Mac
Tone Curve	Constrain drag to vertical only	Hold Shift while dragging up/down	Hold Shift while dragging up/down
	Slow down movement	Hold Alt while dragging point	Hold Opt while dragging point
Black & White	Toggle Color / Black & White	V	V
Targeted Adjustment Tool	Tone Curve	Ctrl Alt Shift T	Cmd Opt Shift T
	Hue	Ctrl Alt Shift H	Cmd Opt Shift H
	Saturation	Ctrl Alt Shift S	Cmd Opt Shift S
	Luminance	Ctrl Alt Shift L	Cmd Opt Shift L
	Black & White Mix	Ctrl Alt Shift G	Cmd Opt Shift G
	Deselect TAT tool	Ctrl Alt Shift N	Cmd Opt Shift N
Sharpening/Noise Reduction	Show Mask	Hold Alt while moving sliders	Hold Opt while moving sliders
Lens Corrections	Apply Upright without clearing Crop/Manual Transforms	Hold Alt while clicking Upright button	Hold Opt while clicking Upright button
	Cycle Upright options	Ctrl Tab	Ctrl Tab
	Cycle Upright options without clearing Crop/Manual Transforms	Ctrl Alt Tab	Ctrl Opt Tab
Soft Proofing	Show/Hide Soft Proof	S	S
	Destination Gamut Warning	Shift S	Shift S
Merge to HDR	with HDR dialog	Ctrl H	Ctrl H
	without HDR dialog	Ctrl Shift H	Ctrl Shift H
	Show overlay	O	O
	Cycle overlay colors	Shift O	Shift O
Merge to Panorama	with Panorama dialog	Ctrl M	Ctrl M
	without Panorama dialog	Ctrl Shift M	Ctrl Shift M

DEVELOP MODULE TOOLS

14

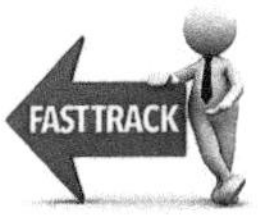

In the previous chapters, we've covered the types of changes you can make to your photos, but the Develop module also includes a range of tools to make your editing quicker and easier. For example, you can sync your settings across multiple photos, save settings as presets to apply to other photos, update the default settings that are applied to new imports, undo changes that you've made and compare your edits against other versions of the photo.

COPYING SETTINGS TO SIMILAR PHOTOS

Lightroom is a workflow tool, so it's designed to work with multiple photos. If you shoot a series of photos in similar light, you may want to copy settings from one photo to the other similar photos. There are multiple ways to do that...

Sync

Sync uses the data from the active (lightest gray) photo, and pastes it onto all the other selected (mid-gray) photos. That's why there are three different levels of selection.

1. Adjust the first photo, which is the source of the settings.

2. Keeping this photo active, also select

the other photos by holding down Ctrl (Windows) / Cmd (Mac) or Shift key while clicking directly on their thumbnails, rather than the cell borders.

3. Click the *Sync* button in the Develop module **(Figure 14.1)**, or *Sync Settings* in the Library module, to show the Sync Develop Settings dialog.

Holding down the Alt (Windows) / Opt (Mac) button while pressing the *Sync* button synchronizes the settings but bypasses the dialog. It remembers which checkboxes were checked last time you accessed the dialog.

4. Select the checkboxes for the slider settings that you want to copy to the other selected photos, and then press *Synchronize* to transfer the settings.

Copy and Paste

The Copy and Paste buttons allow you to copy settings into memory, and then paste them onto individual photos.

1. Adjust the first photo, which is the source of your settings.

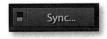

Figure 14.1 *The Sync button is at the bottom of the right panel group.*

2. Click the **Copy** button in the Develop module. **(Figure 14.2)**

3. Select the checkboxes for the slider settings that you want to copy.

4. Press the arrow key on your keyboard to move to the next photo, or select a different photo in the Filmstrip.

5. Click the **Paste** button to paste the settings onto the selected photo.

You don't have to copy all the settings. *Sync* and *Copy/Paste* both have dialogs allowing you to choose specific settings to transfer, so you may just sync *Noise Reduction* or *White Balance*, for example, without copying the *Exposure* settings. You may want to exclude things like Crop, Red Eye and Spot Removal that are specific to the photo.

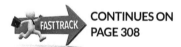

FAST TRACK **CONTINUES ON PAGE 308**

Previous

The Previous option copies all the settings from the most recently selected photo to the next photo you select.

1. Adjust the first photo.

2. Press the arrow key on your keyboard to move to the next photo, or select a different photo in the Filmstrip. (Don't view any photos in between, as it takes the settings from the previously selected photo).

3. Press the **Previous** button to paste the

settings onto the selected photo. **(Figure 14.3)**

There's one exception—if you're moving from a photo with no crop, to a photo with an existing crop, the crop is not reset.

Auto Sync

When you have multiple photos selected, any slider adjustments are applied to all the selected photos. (This matches the behavior of ACR in Photoshop/Bridge.) It can be slow for large numbers of photos, particularly when used with the crop or local adjustment tools.

1. Select multiple photos.

2. Toggle the switch next to the Sync button so that the label changes to **Auto Sync**. **(Figure 14.4)**

3. As you adjust the photos, all the selected photos update with any slider adjustment at the same time.

Auto Sync is powerful but dangerous, as it's easy to accidentally apply a setting to multiple photos without realizing that they're all selected. It gets particularly confusing if you often switch between standard Sync and Auto Sync, so you may find it easiest to leave it turned on at all times, or at least leave the Filmstrip visible

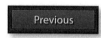

Figure 14.3 *The Previous button only shows at the bottom of the right panel group when a single photo is selected.*

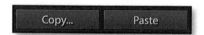

Figure 14.2 *The Copy and Paste buttons are at the bottom of the left panel group.*

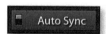

Figure 14.4 *Auto Sync can be enabled by clicking the switch to the left of the Sync button.*

so you can see the number of photos that are selected.

When you have Auto Sync turned on, you can still use the keyboard shortcuts for the other sync options such as Previous, Paste or standard Sync, but they apply to ALL selected photos, not just active (most-selected) photo, as Auto Sync is still active.

Why won't my white balance sync?

There's one quirk that trips everybody up when syncing settings. Your white balance is perfect on photo A, so you sync the settings to photo B... but it doesn't change. So you try it again... and it still doesn't change. Why?

As Shot is the key. If photo A is set to *As Shot* white balance, photo B is also then set to As Shot, not the same numerical values. To solve it, select *Custom* from the white balance pop-up, or shift the values slightly, and then sync with photo B, and your numerical values will be copied.

Can I make relative adjustments, for example, brighten all selected photos by 1 stop?

Imagine you've processed a series of photos, each with different settings, and then you decide you would like them all 1 stop brighter than their current settings. The first photo is set to -0.5 exposure, the next is 0 exposure, and the third is +1 exposure.

You could use Synchronize Settings, but that would move the sliders of the selected photos to the same fixed value as the active (most-selected) photo. Instead, you need relative adjustments, relative to their current settings.

You can't make relative adjustments directly within the Develop module, but you can do so using the Quick Develop panel in the

Library module.

Select the photos and make sure you're viewing the Grid view, so that your changes apply to all selected photos.

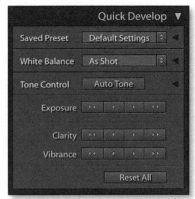

Figure 14.5 *The Quick Develop panel is collapsed by default.*

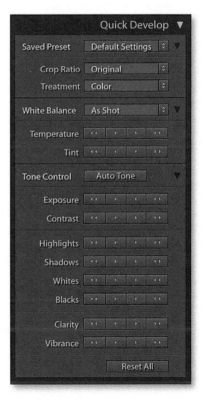

Figure 14.6 *Click the disclosure triangles to view additional buttons.*

By default, the Quick Develop is collapsed, so only a few of the buttons are available. Click the disclosure triangles to expand the full panel, then press the buttons to adjust the sliders. **(Figures 14.5 & 14.6)**

The double-arrow buttons move in large increments, and the single-arrow buttons move in smaller increments. For even smaller adjustments, hold the Shift key while pressing the single-arrow buttons. *Sharpening* and *Saturation* don't have buttons of their own, but they appear when you hold down the Alt key (Windows) / Opt key (Mac).

If some of the buttons are unavailable, your selected photos include a video or a mix of process versions.

What does Match Total Exposures in the Settings menu do?

While we're on the subject of synchronizing settings, let me introduce you to **Match Total Exposures**. It's a little known command found under the *Settings menu* in Develop, and it's very useful. It intelligently adjusts the exposure value to compensate for variations in camera settings.

Where photos are shot in the same lighting, but on Aperture Priority/AV, Shutter Priority/TV or Program, it results in varying exposure values. This clever command calculates and adjusts the exposure on all selected photos to end up with the same overall exposure. It doesn't adjust for the sun going behind a cloud though!

To use it, correct the exposure on a single photo, then select other photos taken at the same time in the same light. In the Develop module, go to *Settings menu > Match Total Exposures*. The photos are automatically adjusted to match the overall exposure of the active photo, taking into account the

variation in camera settings. You'll also find it in the Library module under *Photo menu > Develop Settings*, so you can apply it from Grid view.

PRESETS—SAVING SETTINGS TO APPLY TO OTHER PHOTOS

Presets save sets of settings to apply to other photos over and over again. They simply move sliders to preset positions.

Some presets ship with Lightroom, so you can experiment with them before creating your own presets.

How do I apply a preset?

1. Go to the Presets panel on the left in Develop **(Figure 14.7)**. As you float over the preset names, it displays a preview in the Navigator panel above. **(Figure 14.8)**

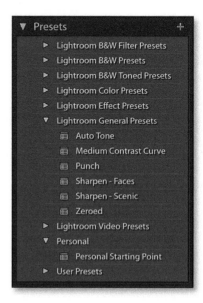

Figure 14.7 *Develop presets are stored in the Presets panel.*

2. To apply the preset to your photo, simply click on the preset name.

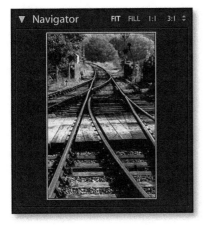

Figure 14.8 *When you float the cursor over a preset name, it's previewed in the Navigator panel.*

How do I create my own preset?

1. Adjust a photo to the settings that you want to save as your preset.

2. Press the + button on the Presets panel to show the New Develop Preset dialog. **(Figure 14.9)**

3. Check or uncheck the sliders you want to save in your preset. If a checkbox is unchecked, that slider won't be adjusted when you apply your preset to another photo. For example, if your preset is just for Sharpening settings, uncheck the other checkboxes and only leave the *Sharpening* checkbox checked.

4. Give your new preset a name, and you can also create folders to group similar presets together.

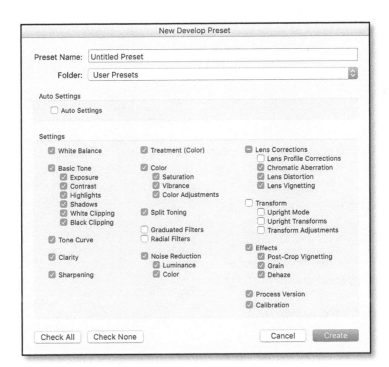

Figure 14.9 *Create a new preset by pressing the + button on the Presets panel and checking the sliders you want to include in the preset.*

5. Press the *Create* button. Your preset now appears in the Presets panel for use on any photos.

Where do I download new presets?

A whole community has sprung up, sharing and selling Lightroom Develop presets. They can offer a good starting point for your post-processing, or more often, some weird and wonderful effects.

How do I install downloaded Develop presets?

If you're installing presets from a single folder, the automatic method is quick and easy. If you're installing lots of presets in one go, perhaps because you've bought a whole set, and they're organized into multiple folders, then the manual installation may be quicker.

Automatic installation:

1. Unzip the presets if they're zipped.

2. Go to Develop module Presets panel, right-click the *User Presets* folder and choose *Import*.

3. Navigate to the folder of presets, select them and press the *Import* button.

Manual installation:

1. Unzip the presets if they're zipped.

2. Find the Develop Presets folder in Explorer (Windows) / Finder (Mac) by going to *Preferences > Presets tab* and pressing the **Show Lightroom Presets Folder** button.

3. Drag (or copy/paste) the presets into that folder, still in their folders if you'd like to keep them organized in the same way.

4. Restart Lightroom.

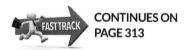

CONTINUES ON PAGE 313

How can I organize my presets into folders or groups?

Many users are now overflowing with presets that they've created or downloaded, and it can be difficult to find the one you're looking for. You can create folders for the presets by right-clicking on any existing user preset or preset folder and choosing **New Folder**. Once you've created folders, you can drag and drop the presets into logical groups. If you have hundreds of presets, you might find it useful to group your most often used presets in a single folder, rather than having to scroll through them all.

How do I apply presets to multiple photos?

To apply your preset in the Develop module to the currently selected photo, you can just click on the preset in the Presets panel.

To apply it to multiple photos, it's easiest to select all the photos in Grid view and choose your preset from the pop-up in the Quick Develop panel or from the right-click > *Develop Settings menu*. Anything you do in Grid view applies to all the selected photos. If you want to stay in Develop module, you can apply the preset with Auto Sync enabled, or you can apply to one photo and then use Sync to copy the settings to the rest of the photos.

Can I apply multiple presets to the same photo, layering the effects?

Presets only move a slider to a new position. They don't calculate new settings relative to the current slider settings.

If Preset A only adjusts, for example, the Exposure and Contrast sliders, and Preset B only adjusts the Vibrance slider, all of the settings are applied to the photo.

If the presets change the same sliders, for example, Preset A sets the Exposure to -1 and then Preset B sets the Exposure to 0, then the changes made by the first preset are overwritten by the second preset.

Can I fade presets?

Lightroom doesn't offer a fade or opacity control for presets. You could create multiple versions of your presets, with different strengths of settings. Alternatively there is a plug-in which offers allows you to fade your presets on the fly. You can download it from https://www.Lrq.me/presetfader

How do I update, rename or delete Develop Presets?

To edit or update a preset, set the photo to the settings of your choice (as you did when creating it) and then right-click on a preset in the Presets panel and choose **Update with Current Settings**. Check or uncheck the sliders you want to save in your updated preset. If a checkbox is unchecked, the slider value isn't saved with the preset.

To rename a preset, right-click on it and select **Rename**. Renaming the preset file manually in Explorer (Windows) / Finder (Mac) doesn't work because the preset name is embedded in the file itself. It's possible to edit the preset with a text editor, but a minor error could corrupt the preset, so be careful!

To delete a preset, right-click on the preset and choose **Delete**. You can also navigate directly to the Develop Presets folder via the *Show Lightroom Presets Folder* button in the *Preferences dialog > Presets tab*, and

delete/move multiple presets in one go, and then restart Lightroom. I keep a 'Spare Develop Presets' folder next to the main Develop Presets folder for the presets I uninstall but may want to reinstall in future, which helps to reduce the clutter.

The default presets included with Lightroom are embedded in the program files, so you can't remove them.

How do I share my presets?

If you've created a really good Develop preset, you may want to share it with other Lightroom users. To do so, right-click on the preset and select **Export**, then select a folder on your hard drive. Alternatively, you can right-click on a preset and select *Show in Explorer* (Windows) / *Show in Finder* (Mac). That takes you directly to the current template location, ready to copy to another computer. Showing the whole folder is particularly useful when copying a larger number of templates.

Where have my presets gone?

If your presets suddenly disappear, go to *Preferences dialog > Presets tab* and try toggling the *Store presets with this catalog* checkbox to see if they reappear. You can learn more about this checkbox in the Multi-Computer chapter on page 425. In most cases, it's best to leave it unchecked.

DEFAULTS

Default settings are automatically applied whenever you import photos. Adobe sets the original default settings, but you can change them to suit your own taste. The defaults you set in Lightroom are also used by ACR (Camera Raw) in Photoshop/Bridge, and vice versa.

Why would I change the default settings instead of using a preset?

You could apply a Develop preset in the Import dialog instead of changing the defaults, but the defaults have a couple of additional benefits:

• The default settings only apply to newly imported photos that don't have existing settings stored in XMP, whereas a preset would override these existing settings.

• The default settings also apply any time you press the *Reset* button, whereas the resetting a photo imported with a preset resets to Adobe's defaults.

• The defaults can be set for specific camera models or ISO values, whereas presets apply to all of the photos in the import.

Why would I want different defaults for each ISO and serial number combination?

The default settings only apply to the specific camera model and file type combination used to create the default. For example, your Canon 5D Mk2 raw photos may require a little more contrast than your Nikon D800 JPEG files.

In the *Preferences dialog > Presets tab*, there are additional checkboxes to apply the defaults to specific files. **(Figure 14.10)**

Make defaults specific to camera serial

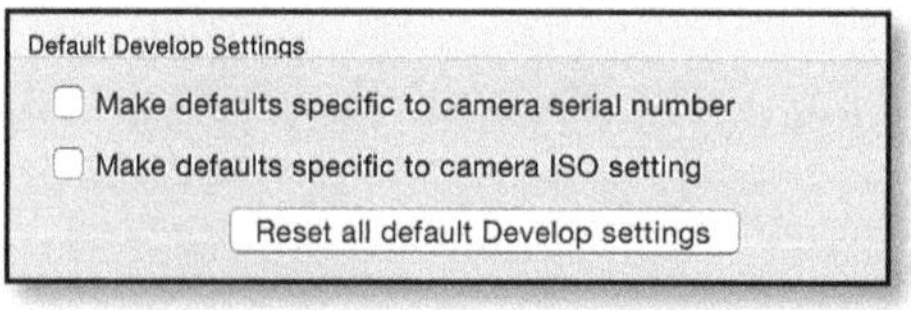

Figure 14.10 *In the Preferences dialog, you can choose whether the defaults should be specific to a camera body or ISO rating.*

number is useful if you have multiple camera bodies of the same model, for example, with one set up for infrared photography requiring a different camera profile.

Make defaults specific to camera ISO setting

is useful for applying additional noise reduction at high ISO ratings.

Which settings should I use as the defaults?

Your default settings are a matter of personal taste, but Adobe's own defaults are a good starting point for most people. You might prefer a different camera profile, slightly more clarity or vibrance, or a higher contrast or sharpening setting. It's up to you, and if you change your mind, you can change your defaults again.

How do I change the default settings?

First go to *Preferences dialog > Presets tab* and decide whether you want *Make defaults specific to camera serial number* and *Make defaults specific to camera ISO setting* turned on or off. Then you're ready to change your default settings:

1. Open a photo in the Develop module and set your new settings. It's a good idea to press *Reset* first, to ensure that you only change the defaults that you intend to change.

2. Go to *Develop menu > Set Default Settings*.

3. Press *Update to Current Settings*. Although the dialog gives the warning that the changes aren't undoable, you can return to the dialog at any time to restore the Adobe's own default settings or set new ones. **(Figure 14.11)**

4. Repeat with a sample photo from each camera, and each combination of ISO/Serial

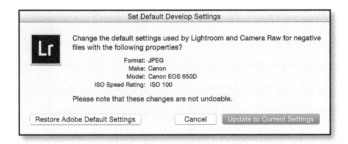

Figure 14.11 *The Restore Adobe Default Settings button in the Set Default Develop Settings dialog resets the defaults.*

Number if these options were selected in Preferences.

Your new default settings apply to new imports, and any photos that you reset. To apply your new defaults to a group of existing photos, select them in Grid view and press *Reset* in the Quick Develop panel or in the right-click context-sensitive menu.

HISTORY & RESET

Because Lightroom's edits are stored as metadata, you can easily undo any of the adjustments.

As in most programs, Ctrl-Z (Windows) / Cmd-Z (Mac) is the Undo command. When pressed repeatedly, it steps back through your recent actions, whether that's slider movements, star ratings, or simply switching between modules. There are a few actions that can't be undone using these shortcuts, such as deleting photos from the hard drive, but the dialogs always warn if an action is not undoable using this shortcut.

Lightroom also keeps a record of all the Develop changes made to each photo. You can see this list in the History panel on the left in the Develop module. **(Figure 14.12)** You can try different settings without worrying, and then return to your

earlier state if you don't like the result of your experiment.

To go back to an earlier version, click on an earlier history state in the History panel. If you make further changes, a new history is written from that point on, replacing the

▼ History		✕
Temperature	-50	5.3K
Black Clipping	+10	-10
Temperature	-200	5.3K
White Balance: Custom		
Tint	+45	4
Tint	-65	-41
Tint	+20	24
Temperature	-1.8K	5.1K
Temperature	+1.8K	6.9K
Post-Crop Vignette Hig...	+100	100
Post-Crop Vignette Am...	-15	-15
Clarity	-40	10
Contrast	+20	90
Shadows	0	40
Shadows	+20	40
Contrast	+20	70
Exposure	-0.10	0.43
Exposure	+0.40	0.53
Exposure	-0.20	0.13
Shadows	+20	20
Contrast	+20	50
Highlights	-20	-40

Figure 14.12 *The History panel keeps track of the Develop changes you make, as well as any exports.*

steps that followed.

Finally, if you don't like the results of your edits and want to start again, press the *Reset* button at the bottom of the right-hand panel group to reset the photo's settings back to their defaults. There are reset options for individual panels and sliders too. Let's explore further...

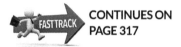

CONTINUES ON
PAGE 317

CONTINUES ON PAGE 317

How long do the adjustments stay in the History panel?

Thanks to its database, Lightroom keep a per-photo list of the Develop steps you've taken to get to the current settings. Unlike Photoshop, the history remains in the catalog indefinitely, even if you close Lightroom. As long as you don't remove the photo from the catalog, you can come back months later and pick up where you left off, or go back to an earlier history state and carry on processing from there.

The *X button* at the top of the History panel clears the list of History states from the list, but it doesn't reset the Develop settings for the photo. It's useful if you've used a large number brush strokes, which are taking up a huge amount of space in the catalog and can increase RAM usage, but it's not usually necessary.

To clear the history states for multiple photos, select the photos and then go to *Develop menu > Clear History*. If more than one photo is selected, Lightroom asks whether to clear the history for the active photo or all of the selected photos.

The Develop History is linear, so you can't remove a single earlier history state. If you look at the numbers to the right, it tells you

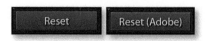

Figure 14.13 *The Reset button sets the sliders back to your current default settings, which may be different to Adobe's default settings.*

how far you moved the slider, and you can manually move the slider back by the same amount.

How do I reset Develop settings?

To reset a photo back to default, press the **Reset** button at the bottom of the right-hand panel in the Develop module. If you've changed the default settings, you can reset the photo to Adobe's default settings by holding down the Shift key. This changes the *Reset* button to **Reset (Adobe)**. (Figure 14.13)

To reset multiple photos back to your default settings, it's easier to switch to the Grid view in the Library module and press the *Reset All* button in the Quick Develop panel (or select it in the right-click menu > *Develop Settings*).

To reset a single slider to its default setting, double-click on the slider label. To reset a whole section within a panel, hold down Alt (Windows) / Opt (Mac) and the panel label changes to a *Reset* button for that section (e.g. *Reset Tone*), or double-clicking on that same panel label without holding down the Alt (Windows) / Opt (Mac) buttons does the same.

BEFORE / AFTER PREVIEW

Once you've edited your photos, you'll want to see the results of your hard work. The Before/After Preview allows you to compare your current Develop settings with an earlier version, using your current crop settings. **(Figure 14.14)**

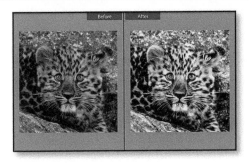

Figure 14.14 *The Before and After views allow you to compare the results of your Develop adjustments.*

Press the \ key to toggle back and forth between before/after, or the Y key to see them side-by-side. The Y button on the Toolbar offers further options.

The Before/After preview excludes the crop settings, as different crops make it difficult to compare the other Develop adjustments.

How do I change the preview options?

By default, the Before/After preview displays side-by-side, but if you click the *Before / After Previews* button in the Toolbar (the one with Y's on it)—you'll see other options, such as side-by-side, top-and-bottom and split-view previews.

When would you use each option? Vertical side by side is useful for vertical photos, but hopeless for viewing wide panoramas, so click on the arrow to the left of the YY button and select *Before/After Top/Bottom* instead. **(Figure 14.15)** If you're comparing something like noise reduction or sharpening, one of the split options is more useful, as it splits the photo down the middle.

How do I select a different history state for the Before view?

By default, the Before view is the last time you read settings from the file's metadata

state which is usually when the photo was imported.

You can choose any history step or snapshot to be the Before view. To do so, right-click on the history step or snapshot, and choose *Copy History Step Settings to Before* or *Copy Snapshot Settings to Before*. (**Figure 14.16**)

If you have the *Before* view on screen, you can also drag a history state from the History panel directly onto the *Before* preview, rather than going through the right-click menu. The key is dragging, rather than just clicking on the history state, as clicking would change the *After* view instead of the *Before* view. The arrowed buttons on the Toolbar allow you to swap the views currently on screen.

To revert the photo's settings to the *Before* state, because you liked the old settings better, click the first arrow icon.

To update the *Before* state to match the current *After* state, perhaps because you want to make further adjustments to the photo and compare them against the current state, click the second arrow icon.

To swap the *Before* state and the *After* state, click the icon with two arrows.

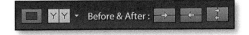

Figure 14.15 *The YY button on the Toolbar allows you to change the display layout of the Before/After views.*

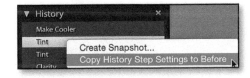

Figure 14.16 *Select a different Before view by right-clicking in the History panel.*

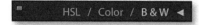

Figure 14.17 *Use the toggle switch on panel headers to preview the image with and without that panel's adjustments.*

Can I turn off the effect of a whole panel's settings, to see the preview with and without these settings?

On the end of most panel headers in the Develop module, such as the Tone Curve panel, there's a toggle switch. **(Figure 14.17)** This switch temporarily enables or disables the sliders in the section, so you can preview the photo with and without the effect of panel's sliders. It not only affects the preview but also any photos you export. This also applies to the selective editing tools in the Tool Strip, which have a switch at the bottom left of their Options panel.

COMPARING PHOTOS IN REFERENCE VIEW

Like the Library module's Compare view,

Reference View allows you to display two photos side-by-side, but it also allows you to edit one of the photos at the same time. **(Figure 14.18)**

This can be useful for:

• Matching photos shot at the same time using different cameras.

• Trying to match a raw file to its in-camera jpeg.

• Trying to match photos that will be displayed together, perhaps on the wall or in an album.

• Replicating a "look" of a different photo.

• A skin tone reference shot (like an old-fashioned Kodak Shirley card).

You can use a Locked Secondary Window (page 88) for the same purpose, but Reference View is more useful if you're on a single monitor.

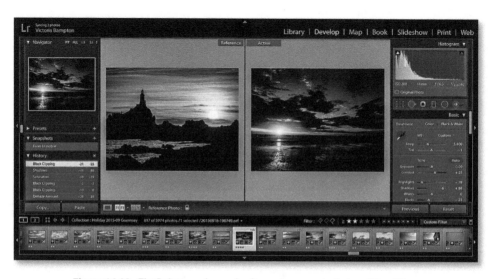

Figure 14.18 *The Reference view makes it easy to compare photos while editing.*

How do I display a photo in Reference view?

1. Click the **R/A** button in the Develop module toolbar or press Shift-R to open Reference view. If you can't see the toolbar, press the T key to show it. (Clicking the R/A button again switches between side-by-side and top-and-bottom views.)

2. Drag and drop the reference photo onto the left pane from the filmstrip, or right-click on a thumbnail in Grid view or the Filmstrip and select **Set as Reference Photo**.

3. Go ahead and edit the active photo as you normally would.

4. To switch back to normal single image view, click the Loupe icon in the toolbar or press D.

Why does the Reference photo keep disappearing?

The reference photo disappears when you switch modules, but if you lock the lock icon in the toolbar, the reference photo remains selected until you quit Lightroom.

VERSIONS—SNAPSHOTS & VIRTUAL COPIES

The before/after preview is great if you only want to compare two history states, but what do you do when you want to compare multiple versions of a photo? You could keep switching between history states, but there's an easier option... snapshots and virtual copies.

If you want to experiment with different settings without overwriting your current version, you can create a virtual copy.

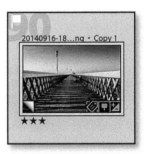

Figure 14.19 Virtual Copies can be identified by the triangular page turn icon in the corner of the thumbnail.

Virtual copies show up in Lightroom as duplicate photos, and they have their own metadata and settings. They don't take up much more space on your hard drive as Lightroom doesn't need to duplicate the original image file.

To create a virtual copy, right-click and choose **Create Virtual Copy** or use the shortcut Ctrl-' (Windows) / Cmd-' (Mac). An additional copy appears next to the Master (the original file), and it has a small triangle in the corner of the thumbnail indicating that it's a virtual copy. It's automatically stacked with the original in the folder view. **(Figure 14.19)**

If you no longer want a virtual copy, you can delete it like any other photo. Deleting a virtual copy won't remove the original photo from the hard drive—only a Master can do that. It just removes that version of the metadata.

A snapshot is a special history state, which captures the slider settings at the moment of its creation. You can make changes to your photo, save it as a snapshot, make more adjustments, and then easily go back to the earlier snapshot state, even if you clear the History panel.

To create a snapshot, click the + button on the Snapshots panel. **(Figure 14.20)** By

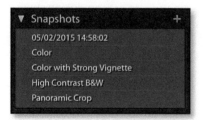

Figure 14.20 *Snapshots capture the slider settings at the time of creation.*

default, it names the snapshot using the current date/time, but you might prefer to give it a more useful name such as "4x5 crop." To update, rename or delete it, right-click on it. To reselect a snapshot, just click on its name (but remember that any Develop changes will overwrite your history).

Virtual copies and snapshots are particularly useful for keeping different versions of your photos, for example, a color version, a black & white version, a special effect version, and different crops.

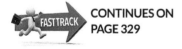

CONTINUES ON PAGE 329

How do I choose whether to use a virtual copy or a snapshot?

There's a crossover in the two concepts, so you can decide which works best for you.

Both options are virtual, so they don't take up additional space on the hard drive, with the exception of the metadata, and also the preview for a virtual copy.

A virtual copy is treated like a separate photo, so they show in Grid view alongside the master and any other virtual copies. This means you can compare the different versions side by side in the Compare or Survey views.

You can do almost anything to a virtual copy that you can do to a master photo. For example, you can give it a different star rating, label, keywords, or other metadata. A new virtual copy starts off with a copy of most of the metadata and Develop settings from the original photo, but the History panel only shows a single History state. (Just remember that if you edit the original image file in other software, such as Photoshop, your edits apply to all versions of the photo.)

A snapshot is more like a bookmarked history state. A photo can only be in a single snapshot state at any one time. A photo with multiple snapshots only appears as one photo in Grid view, and there's no way of telling that there are multiple versions from the Grid view unless you use the Metadata Filters or a Smart Collection.

If you write metadata to the files, as well as the catalog (we'll come back to this in the XMP section on page 345), there's one more deciding factor: information about virtual copies is only stored in the catalog and can't be written to the files, whereas snapshot information can be written back to the files.

Can I rename virtual copies?

If you rename a virtual copy, the name of the master photo changes too—after all, it's virtual. When you export the virtual copies, they can have different names from the originals as if they're individual photos, and you have some control over this naming while still in the Library module.

In the Metadata panel of a virtual copy is a *Copy Name* field which defaults to Copy 1. You can change it to an alternative name of your choice, for example, Sepia. **(Figure 14.21)**

You can display the copy name on the

thumbnails or Info Overlay using the *View menu > View Options* dialog. For example, *File Name and Copy Name* displays both the master file name and the copy name, whereas *Copy Name or File Base Name* displays the copy name unless it's blank, in which case it displays the existing filename.

You can also use the copy name to rename the photos when you export them, by selecting the *Copy Name* token in the Filename Template Editor. For example, if you've set the copy name to *Sepia*, you can use *Original Filename_Copy Name* tokens to create IMG_003_Sepia.jpg. **(Figures 14.22 & 14.23)**

Can I convert snapshots to virtual copies and vice versa?

If you're viewing a snapshot when you create a virtual copy, the virtual copy uses the current settings, and if you're viewing a virtual copy when you create a snapshot, the snapshots use the current settings.

Snapshots are available to all of the virtual copies, which is a really handy feature. It means you can use virtual copies when you're experimenting with different

versions, and then save the final state of each virtual copy as a snapshot. You can then delete the virtual copies to clear the clutter when you've finished comparing them, without losing your Develop adjustments.

If you need to create snapshots for lots of photos, Matt Dawson's Snapshotter plug-in can automate the process. https://www.Lrq.me/photogeek-snapshotter

Can I promote virtual copies and delete the master?

If you need to swap a virtual copy for its master, perhaps because you want to keep the virtual copy's settings and delete the other, select the virtual copy and then select **Set Copy as Master** from the *Photo menu*. If you want to do a whole batch of photos, it's not quite so simple. There are two options.

Export the virtual copies to another folder, with the file format set to *Original*, and then import the new files into your catalog.

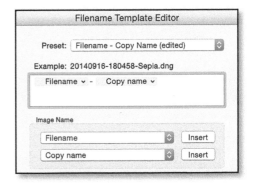

Figure 14.23 *Rename the photos when exporting, using their Copy Name as part of the new filename.*

Figure 14.21 *Set the Copy Name of virtual copies in the Metadata panel.*

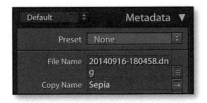

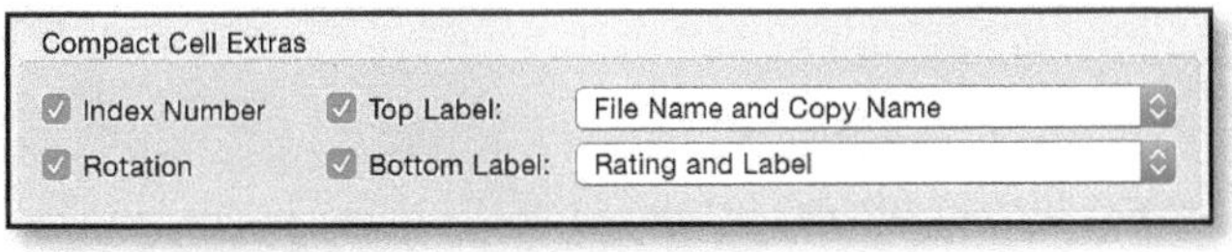

Figure 14.22 *In the View Options dialog, you can set the thumbnail cell options to include the Copy Name.*

You'd only have data that's stored in XMP, but it may be a good compromise in some circumstances.

Use the Syncomatic plug-in to sync settings from virtual copies to their master photos. It can sync flags, star ratings, labels, keywords and most Develop settings, but the crop is not copied. https://www.Lrq.me/beardsworth-syncomatic

What do Sync Copies and Sync Snapshots do?

Earlier in the chapter (on page 305) we used Sync to copy settings between photos. Under the *Settings menu*, there are two additional sync options which apply to virtual copies and snapshots. **Sync Copies** and **Sync Snapshots** allow you to sync settings from your current rendering to all of that photo's virtual copies or snapshots in one go. For example, if you've created different versions for different crop ratios, and then you brighten the photos or change the sharpening, you might want to update all of your other versions of that photo too.

HISTOGRAM AND RGB VALUES

We introduced the Histogram on page 182, but there's a few extra tricks.

As you hover over the *Exposure*, *Highlights*, *Shadows*, *Whites* or *Blacks* slider in the Basic panel, the approximate range affected by slider is highlighted on the histogram. You can click and drag directly on the Histogram to lighten or darken the affected tones, and the highlighted slider moves. **(Figure 14.24)**

Can I view the RGB values?

As you hover the cursor over the photo, Lightroom displays the RGB values for these pixels. **(Figure 14.25)** 0 0 0 % is pure black and 100 100 100 % is pure white. Matching numbers in between are neutral, for example, 50 50 50% is mid gray.

Can I view the RGB values using a 0-255 scale?

If you've used Photoshop or other photographic software, you might be used to seeing the RGB values displayed using a 0-255 scale, for example, 128 128 128. In Lightroom, the RGB values are shown in percentages (0-100%) because 0-255 is an 8-bit scale and Lightroom works in 16-bit. When you turn on Soft Proofing, the RGB values switch to the 0-255 scale, as you're simulating an 8-bit output color space. We'll come back to soft proofing in the Develop Tools chapter starting on page 321, and bit depth in the External Editors chapter on page 191.

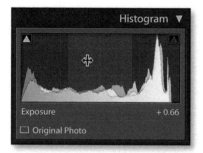

Figure 14.24 *You can adjust the Basic tone sliders by dragging left <> right on the histogram.*

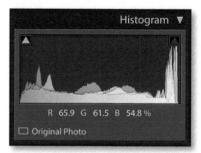

Figure 14.25 *Lightroom displays the RGB values of the selected pixel as you float over the photo.*

Can I display L*a*b* values instead of RGB?

You can also display L*a*b* values under the Histogram, as an alternative to the normal RGB values. To switch from RGB to L*a*b*, right-click on the Histogram and select *Show Lab Color Values*.

L*a*b* values are primarily used in scientific and reproduction environments, but they can also be useful for correcting skintones. For 'average' skintones, if there is any such thing, keep the a* and b* values close, often with the b* value slightly higher.

COLOR MANAGEMENT & SOFT PROOFING

When it comes to color management, there's lots of confusion. Should you choose sRGB because it's commonly used? But you've heard ProPhoto RGB is better because it's bigger, so maybe you should choose this one?

Lightroom is internally color-managed, so as long as your monitor is properly calibrated, the only time you need to worry about color spaces is when you're outputting the photos. This may be passing the data to Photoshop or other software for further editing, passing the data to a printer driver for printing, or exporting the photos for other purposes, such as email or web.

So why are we talking about color management in Develop? There's a tool in Develop called Soft Proofing, which helps you to visualize the limitations of the output color spaces. Before we can dive into that though, we need a basic understanding of color management. Color management is a huge subject that could fill a separate book, so we'll just cover the bits you need to know.

If you'd like to learn more about color management, Jeffrey Friedl wrote an excellent article on color spaces at: https://www.Lrq.me/friedl-colorspace

Which color space should I use?

In the Histogram section on page 198, we said that photos are made up of pixels, and each pixel has a number value for each of the color channels (red, green and blue). For example, 0-0-0 is pure black. 255-255-255 is pure white. The numbers in between are open to interpretation. Who decides exactly which shade of green 10-190-10 equates to? That's where color profiles come into play: they define how these numbers should translate to colors.

There are two main groups of profiles—working profiles and output profiles—and they each cover different ranges of colors. Some color spaces contain a larger number of colors than others, so we refer to the 'size' of the color space.

Working profiles are standardized, so they can be used in a wide range of situations, whereas output profiles are designed for specific outputs, for example, a particular printer/paper/ink combination.

The most popular working spaces are:

sRGB is a small color space, but fairly universal. It can't contain all the colors that your camera can capture, which results in some clipping, so it's not great as a working space. However, as it's a common color space, it's a good choice for photos that you're outputting for screen use (web, slideshow, digital photo frame), and many non-pro digital print labs expect sRGB files too.

Adobe RGB is a slightly bigger color space, which contains more of the colors that your camera can capture, but still can't contain the full range. Many pro digital print labs accept Adobe RGB files. It's also a good choice for setting on your camera if you choose to shoot JPEG rather than the raw file format, if your camera can't capture in ProPhoto RGB.

ProPhoto RGB is the largest color space that Lightroom offers, and it's designed for digital photographers. It can contain all the colors that today's cameras can capture, with room to spare. The disadvantage is that putting an Adobe RGB or ProPhoto RGB file in a non-color-managed program, such as most web browsers, give a flat desaturated result. This makes it an excellent choice for editing and archiving 16-bit photos, but a poor choice when sending photos to anyone else.

Display P3 is a wide gamut color space used on the latest Apple devices. It's a similar size to Adobe RGB, but it's shifted slightly towards reds/oranges and loses some of the greens/blues. It's primarily useful when exporting photos for display on the latest Apple devices.

Output profiles are specific to the device, whether they're inkjet printers or huge photo labs.

So the right color space depends on the situation. You don't need to worry while the photo stays in Lightroom, as all the internal editing is done in a large color space which Lightroom manages. When the photo leaves Lightroom, then you need to make a choice. When you edit in an External Editor such as Photoshop, you'll want to stick with a large working space. Once you've finished your editing, and you want to export the finished photo for a specific purpose, then you can choose a smaller color space which defines the characteristics of your output device (i.e. printer).

Whichever color space you choose to use, always embed the profile. A digital photo is just a collection of numbers, and the profile defines how the numbers should be displayed. If there's no profile, the program has to guess—and often guesses incorrectly. Lightroom always embeds the profile, but Photoshop offers a checkbox in the Save As dialog, which you must leave checked.

We'll discuss color spaces for editing in the External Editors chapter starting on page 331, and output profiles for editing in the Export and Print chapters (page 358 and page C-20), but for now let's focus on soft proofing the finished result.

What is soft proofing?

Soft proofing attempts to simulate, on your calibrated monitor, how the photo will look with your chosen printer/paper/ink combination. You can then adjust the photo for that specific output without creating numerous test prints.

If you don't print to a locally attached printer, such as an inkjet printer, soft proofing can still be useful. If you send prints to an offsite lab, they may be able to provide their printer profile for soft proofing purposes.

Even if you only ever show your photos on a screen—perhaps on the web—soft proofing can show how your photos will look when exported to the smaller sRGB color space. Colors that are within Lightroom's working space may clip when converting to sRGB, for example, highly saturated reds become much less colorful when exported as sRGB. Soft proofing allows you to preview that effect and compensate if needed.

Let's illustrate with these flowers... the saturated colors make it clear to see the difference. We'll look at the histogram and

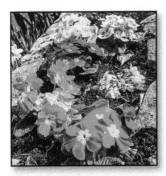

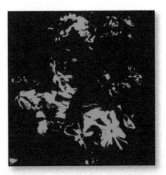

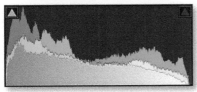

Figure 14.26 *Lightroom's working space can contain the full range of colors that the camera captured.*

Figure 14.27 *In sRGB, the highly saturated colors clip (shown as red highlights) because they fall outside of the small sRGB gamut.*

clipping, in addition to the photo.

In the first photo **(Figure 14.26)**, the histogram doesn't spike at either end and the clipping warnings aren't showing, which means that all of of the colors can be contained in Lightroom's working color space.

And then we have the sRGB version **(Figure 14.27)**, with clipping warnings turned on, and it's clear to see, both from the clipping warning and the histogram, that the red channel is clipped in the smaller color space.

How do I enable soft proofing?

To turn on soft proofing, check the **Soft Proofing** checkbox in the Toolbar. (Figure 14.28)

The Histogram panel changes to a Soft Proofing panel with additional options, and the background surrounding the photo changes from mid-gray to paper white. **(Figure 14.29)**

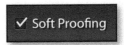

Figure 14.28 *Soft Proofing is enabled using the checkbox on the Toolbar.*

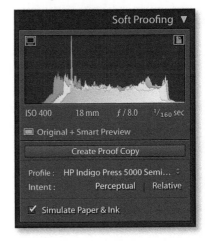

Figure 14.29 *The Histogram panel changes to a Soft Proofing panel.*

Select your output profile from the **Profile** pop-up menu. If your profile doesn't appear in the pop-up, select *Other* at the bottom of the *Profile* pop-up and put a checkmark next to your output profile in the Choose Profiles dialog. It then appears in the *Profile* pop-up, ready for selection. **(Figure 14.30)**

Why is my profile not available for selection?

If your profile is correctly installed in the operating system, but it still doesn't appear in the Choose Profiles dialog, then it may be an unsupported profile. Lightroom's limited to RGB, so it won't work with grayscale profiles, or some other non-standard profiles designed for Printer RIPs (Raster Image Processor).

Some profiles don't conform to the ICC Specification, and they're ignored too. Running *Profile First Aid* in ColorSync Utility on a Mac can often repair these profiles, making them available in Lightroom. I'm not aware of any free Windows software that can run an ICC profile repair.

Should I select Perceptual or Relative Colorimetric?

When you've selected your profile, the **Intent** options become available. The rendering intent options only apply to output spaces such as printer profiles, not working spaces like sRGB, Adobe RGB and ProPhoto RGB.

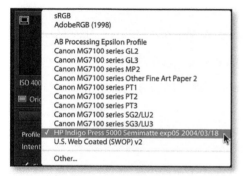

Figure 14.30 *Select the profile you want to use for soft proofing.*

Perceptual squeezes all the colors into the smaller color space while trying to retain their relationship to each other. That means that all the color values shift but it should still look natural. Perceptual rendering intent is good for highly saturated photos with a lot of out-of-gamut colors.

Relative Colorimetric leaves most of the colors alone, and just clips the out-of-gamut colors to the closest reproducible colors. It's usually a better choice if a photo is mostly within gamut, as it only shifts the out-of-gamut colors.

So which should you choose? If you're exporting the photo using the Export dialog, use *Relative Colorimetric*, as the Export dialog doesn't give you a choice of rendering intent. If you're printing through Lightroom, the Print module does give you a choice. In this case, it depends on the photo, so try both and see which looks best.

Should I check Simulate Paper & Ink when viewing my soft proof?

Simulate Paper & Ink simulates the reduction in contrast caused by dull white paper and dark gray black ink, so it's also known as the *Make the Photo Look Rubbish* checkbox. Your eyes adapt to the color and brightness of the whitest object in your view, making the soft proof look dark and flat.

To solve this, remove all other white/light reference points from your view and switch to Lights Out mode by pressing the L key. Your eyes then adjust to the soft proof version and you can adjust the photo accordingly.

With Lights Out, however, it's obviously impossible to adjust the photo, so when you're ready to start making adjustments, you'll need to disable Lights Out by pressing the L key again.

The 1:8 and 1:16 zoom ratios on top of the Navigator panel allow you to zoom out further, surrounding the photo with a larger area of paper white, while still being able to adjust the photo using the Develop controls.

Can I change the background color surrounding the photo while soft proofing?

By default, the background surrounding the photo shows a paper white, but the accuracy of that paper white depends on the quality of the profile. Some profiles show a bright yellow background which looks nothing like the paper. If it's wrong, you can switch to an alternative background by right-clicking in the background area. There's a range of shades of white and gray available, so you can select one which more closely matches the paper. Your chosen color is also used for the background when using Lights Out mode.

What's the difference between the Monitor Gamut and Destination Gamut warnings?

In the top corners of the histogram, the clipping warning buttons are replaced by gamut warning buttons. **(Figure 14.31)** (The gamut is the complete subset of colors that can be reproduced in your chosen color space or by a specific device.)

When you click to enable them, out of gamut areas of your photo are highlighted in blue, red or purple. If either out of gamut warning is showing, it's simply telling you that you're not seeing an accurate preview of those colors. **(Figure 14.32)**

Blue indicates that a color is outside of the monitor gamut, which means that even if the color is printable, you won't get a good print-to-screen match because the monitor can't display that particular color accurately.

Red means that a color is outside of the destination gamut, which means that it's not printable and will be remapped by the output profile.

Purple is out of both gamuts.

What should I do if some colors are out of gamut?

If the colors are showing as out of gamut, it doesn't necessarily mean that you need to do anything about it. It's simply information. It tells you that the final print won't exactly match the screen preview in those areas.

Desaturating the photo, or locally desaturating the out-of-gamut colors, is traditionally suggested as a solution, however a good quality profile usually does a far better job of pulling these colors back into gamut without you having to adjust anything.

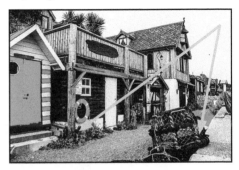

Figure 14.32 *Colors that are out of gamut are highlighted to warn you that they may not print as expected.*

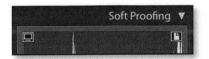

Figure 14.31 *The Monitor Gamut (left) and Destination Gamut (right) triangles take the place of the clipping warning buttons in the corner of the histogram.*

How should I adjust the photo while viewing the soft proof?

So if you're not going to reduce the saturation of the out of gamut colors, what's the point of soft proofing?

The main aim is to compensate for the losses in printing, to make the print look closer to the original. Often that's a difference in contrast and brightness, rather than color.

We discussed the Before/After views earlier in the chapter (starting on page 314), but they become particularly useful when soft proofing, as they allow you to compare your original intended rendering with the soft proofed copy. To turn it on, press the *Before/After Preview* button (the one with the Y's on it) in the Toolbar. Other views are also available when you click on the arrow next to the *Before/After Preview* button.

With the original photo on screen next to the soft proof preview, adjust the sliders to make the soft proof more closely match the original. You're simply trying to make the soft proof—and therefore the finished print—look better. (**Figure 14.33**)

How do I compare my proof adjusted photo with the original?

There's an additional **Before** pop-up in the Toolbar which allows you to select which version of the photo you want to compare against.

Current State shows the current settings for the photo, without the soft proof applied. This allows you to see the effect that the output profile is having on the photo.

Before State shows the normal 'before' state of the photo, without the soft proof applied. You can update this Before State by right-clicking on your chosen History state and selecting *Copy History Step Settings to Before* or by dragging the History state onto the Before view.

Master State shows the current settings of the Master photo, without the soft proof applied. This allows you to see how well your profile-specific adjustments on the virtual copy match the general edits for that photo. You also have the option to compare with other virtual copies of the photo.

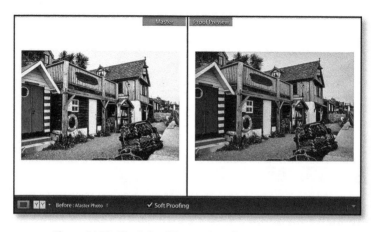

Figure 14.33 *The Before/After preview allows you to compare your proofed version with your original rendering.*

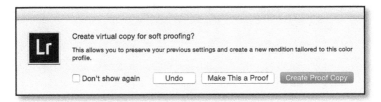

Figure 14.34 *When you edit a photo with soft proofing enabled, Lightroom offers to create a virtual copy.*

How do I save my photo after adjusting it for a specific profile?

Just below the histogram, there's a **Create Proof Copy** button, which creates a virtual copy of your photo for soft proofing. It means that your original settings, which were suitable for any kind of output, remain untouched, and your profile-specific adjustments are stored separately in a virtual copy.

If you start editing a photo without first creating a proof copy, Lightroom asks if you want to create a virtual copy for the soft proof, or whether you want to edit the original photo. **(Figure 14.34)**

If you select *Make This a Proof*, your current photo is marked as a proof under the *Settings menu*, and your adjustments apply to the master photo. It's not a bad choice if you're editing for sRGB use, but if you're adjusting for an output profile, it's better to select *Create Proof Copy*.

How can I tell which profile I used for a particular photo?

If you allow Lightroom to create a virtual copy for the soft proof, it enters the name of the profile in the *Copy Name* metadata field, and it updates if you switch to a different profile. You can view the Copy Name in the Metadata panel, the Grid view thumbnails, the Info Overlay or along the top of the Filmstrip. **(Figure 14.35)**

Any snapshots you create in Soft Proof mode also automatically include the profile in the Snapshot name.

When exporting the file, you can include the *Copy Name* field in the new filename for reference. *Filename-CopyName* tokens will result in a filename such as IMG_003-sRGB.jpg. Remember that Export always uses Relative Colorimetric as the rendering intent.

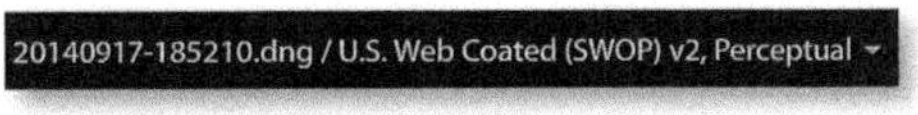

20140917-185210.dng / U.S. Web Coated (SWOP) v2, Perceptual ▾

Figure 14.35 *If you create a virtual copy for the soft proof, the name of the profile appears in the breadcrumb bar.*

DEVELOP TOOL SHORTCUTS

		Windows	Mac
Copy, Paste & Sync	Copy Settings	Ctrl Shift C	Cmd Shift C
	Paste Settings	Ctrl Shift V	Cmd Shift V
	Paste Settings from Previous	Ctrl Alt V	Cmd Opt V

		Windows	Mac
	Sync Settings	Ctrl Shift S	Cmd Shift S
	Sync Settings (bypass dialog)	Ctrl Alt S	Cmd Opt S
	Enable Develop Auto Sync	Ctrl Alt Shift A	Cmd Opt Shift A
	Match Total Exposures	Ctrl Alt Shift M	Cmd Opt Shift M
Presets	New Preset	Ctrl Shift N	Cmd Shift N
	New Preset Folder	Ctrl Alt N	Cmd Opt N
Undo/Redo	Undo	Ctrl Z	Cmd Z
	Redo	Ctrl Y	Cmd Shift Z
Reset	Reset Slider	Double-click on slider label	Double-click on slider label
	Reset Group of Sliders	Double-click on group name	Double-click on group name
	Reset All Settings	Ctrl Shift R	Cmd Shift R
Before / After View	Toggle Before/After	\	\
	Left / Right	Y	Y
	Top / Bottom	Alt Y	Opt Y
	Split Screen	Shift Y	Shift Y
	Copy After's Settings to Before	Ctrl Alt Shift left arrow	Cmd Opt Shift left arrow
	Copy Before's Settings to After	Ctrl Alt Shift right arrow	Cmd Opt Shift right arrow
	Swap Before and After Settings	Ctrl Alt Shift up arrow	Cmd Opt Shift up arrow
Reference View	Open Reference View	Shift R	Shift R
Snapshots & Virtual Copies	Create Snapshot	Ctrl N	Cmd N
	Create Virtual Copy	Ctrl '	Cmd '
Soft Proofing	Show / Hide Soft Proof	S	S
	Destination Gamut Warning	Shift S	Shift S

FURTHER EDITING IN OTHER PROGRAMS

15

Lightroom is a brilliant workflow tool but there are still some tasks, such as detailed retouching, that require a pixel editor such as Photoshop. Lightroom can pass your edited photo over to your pixel editor and automatically add the resulting photo back into the catalog.

Integration with Photoshop

If a full version of Photoshop is installed on your computer, it appears in *Photo menu > Edit In* or the right-click menu. **(Figure 15.1)** You can also press Ctrl-E (Windows) / Cmd-E (Mac) to open the photo into Photoshop.

If the photo is a raw file and you're using ACR 9 in CS6 or CC, Lightroom opens the photo directly into Photoshop. Older ACR

Edit In	▶	Edit in Adobe Photoshop CC 2014...
Photo Merge	▶	Edit in Other Application...
Set Flag	▶	Color Efex Pro 4
Set Rating	▶	Dfine 2.0
Set Color Label	▶	Perfect B&W 8
Add Keyword "William"		Perfect Batch 8
		Perfect Effects 8
Remove from Quick Collection	B	Perfect Enhance 8
		Perfect Portrait 8
Stacking	▶	Perfect Resize 8
Create Virtual Copies		Photoshop CS6
Develop Settings	▶	Photoshop Elements 11
Metadata Presets	▶	Pixelmator
		Sharpener Pro 3.0: (1) RAW Presharpener
Rotate Left (CCW)		Sharpener Pro 3.0: (2) Output Sharpener
Rotate Right (CW)		Silver Efex Pro 2
Metadata	▶	Viveza 2
Export	▶	Open as Smart Object in Photoshop...
Email Photos...		Merge to Panorama in Photoshop...
		Merge to HDR Pro in Photoshop...
Use as Cover Photo		Open as Layers in Photoshop...

Figure 15.1 *Lightroom can pass your photos to Photoshop and other external pixel editors.*

versions ask how to handle the file, so press *Render Using Lightroom* in order to ensure the file renders correctly.

If you're working with a JPEG, TIFF, PSD or PNG file, a dialog asks how to handle the file. Select *Edit a Copy with Lightroom Adjustments* to open your photo with your Develop adjustments applied.

Once you've finished editing the photo in Photoshop, go to *File menu > Save* and then close the photo and switch back to Lightroom. Your edited photo is updated in your catalog automatically.

Integration with Photoshop Elements

Not everyone needs the power of full Photoshop. Elements can do many of the tasks photographers require. Like Photoshop, Lightroom recognizes when a recent version of Elements is installed, and *Photo menu > Edit In > Edit in Photoshop Elements* or Ctrl-E (Windows) / Cmd-E (Mac) opens the photo into Photoshop Elements. Once you've finished editing the photo, save (don't change the filename or file type) and close the file before returning to Lightroom.

Opening Photos in Other Editors

Lightroom can also send files to other external editors, such as On1 software, Nik software, Pixelmator or PaintShop Pro.

Some of these editors come with their own Lightroom plug-ins and presets which are installed automatically. If your editor doesn't install its own connection, you can set it up manually. We'll come back to that a little later on page 342.

Why might I use an external editor?

But can't you do everything in Lightroom? Lightroom does offer a wide range of tools to cater for most of your editing needs, but that doesn't always make it the best tool for the job.

It's a parametric editor, which means that it runs text instructions rather than directly editing the pixels.

The benefit is it's non-destructive, so you don't need to save multiple versions of the file, taking up masses of hard drive space, and you can go back and change your edits again later.

The downside is that running text instructions over and over again is slower than making a single change to the pixels themselves. For global edits, that's barely noticeable, but Lightroom can start to drag when using multiple local adjustments and retouching multiple spots. For this reason, pixel editors such as Photoshop and Elements are still better suited to more detailed retouching.

There may also be times when you want to do more specialized edits. For example, Lightroom can do great B&W conversions but Nik Silver Efex is designed purely for that purpose.

When in my workflow should I use Edit in Photoshop or other External Editors?

You may be wondering when to use your external editor. Is it better to edit your photo in the Develop module first, or wait until you've finished the retouching in the external editor?

Lightroom's Develop adjustments work best on raw files, because they have the largest amount of data available. For this reason, it's usually best to do most, if not all, of your Lightroom adjustments in Lightroom before using Edit in Photoshop to do your retouching. The same would apply to most other External Editors.

There are a couple of exceptions:

• You may prefer to leave cropping until after your external edits, leaving you the flexibility to non-destructively crop to multiple different ratios without having to repeat your retouching and other edits.

• If the photo is going to be in both B&W and color, you may also want to retouch the color version and then convert the resulting photo to B&W so that you only have to do the retouching once.

• If your photo was shot in JPEG, or it's a scan, the workflow order isn't as important. For example, you may decide to retouch dust on negative scans in Photoshop before editing them in Lightroom.

Having covered the basics, let's do a deeper dive into the settings.

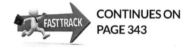

CONTINUES ON
PAGE 343

SETTING EXTERNAL EDITOR PREFERENCES

We'll go into more detail on specific programs, but first, let's consider the settings that apply to all external editors. The file type, color space, bit depth, resolution and compression are all set in *Preferences > External Editing*. The top half of the dialog sets the primary editor's settings—the most recent version of Photoshop or Photoshop Elements—and the lower half creates presets for all other external editors. **(Figure 15.2)**

Which file format should I use?

The first pop-up, ***File Format***, determines the file type that's passed to the external editor.

TIFF is publicly documented, more efficient when updating metadata, compatible with a wide range of software, and can contain almost everything that PSD's do. It's generally considered the best choice for external edits. We'll come back to the various ***compression*** options in the Export chapter on page 356, but ZIP compression is a good choice for most external editors.

PSD is Adobe's proprietary format. It's well supported by other applications, as long as you check *Maximize Compatibility* but it's generally considered an older format now, so even Adobe are recommending TIFFs instead of PSD files now. Some plug-ins, such as OnOne software, prefer PSD format.

JPEG is only available for secondary external editors, as some (rare!) editing programs are unable to work with TIFF or PSD files. It's a lossy format, so it's not a great choice for external edits.

Which color space should I select?

Files are automatically color managed in Lightroom, but when you pass them to

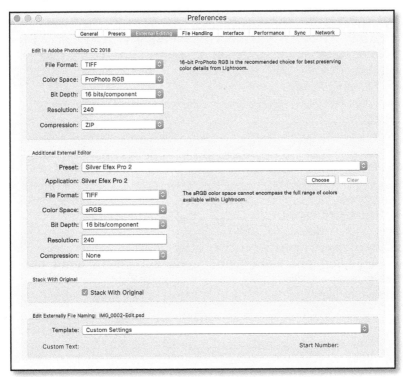

Figure 15.2 *Set the default settings for Photoshop and other external editors using the Preferences dialog.*

another editor, you'll need to choose a working space using the **Color Space** pop-up. We've already discussed color spaces in the previous chapter (starting on page 321), but as a reminder:

ProPhoto RGB is the best choice if your external editor is color managed, as it preserves the widest range of color information. ProPhoto RGB doesn't play well with 8-bit though, because you'd be trying to jam a large gamut into a small bit depth, which can lead to banding, so stick with 16-bit while using ProPhoto RGB.

Adobe RGB is a smaller color space, but it's a good choice if your external editor can only handle 8-bit files (or you're saving as JPEG).

sRGB is the smallest color space available, so it's not ideal for external editors.

Display P3 is a wide gamut color space used on the latest Apple devices. It's a similar size to Adobe RGB, but it's shifted slightly towards reds/oranges and loses some of the greens/blues. It's primarily useful when exporting photos for display on the latest Apple devices.

Why use a big color space when nothing can print that wide a range?

Now it's true, not all of these possible ProPhoto RGB colors can be reproduced on screen or print at this point in time, but that's not a good reason for throwing data away and using a smaller space. Even now, some printers can print some colors that can't currently be displayed on the best screens.

Remember when computer monitors were only B&W or 256 colors? Photographers still created full color images even though they couldn't see the full range of colors. If they'd limited themselves to what they could see,

they'd have kicked themselves when the current monitors became available. So in the future, when even more advanced monitors are released, you'll be able to see your full range of image data.

There can be a little bit of guesswork involved when working with extremely saturated colors, but that's where the gamut warnings on the soft proof start to help. These give you information, telling you which colors may not match what you're seeing on screen. Unless you're pushing the saturation/vibrance really high, you won't run into issues on most images, and even when you do, profiles do an excellent job of pulling colors back into gamut without you having to change anything. But it helps to understand what's happening.

Whichever color space you choose, it's important that it's selected in both programs. We'll come back to settings the color space in Photoshop and Photoshop Elements in the next section (starting on page 335).

Should I choose 8-bit or 16-bit?

The next pop-up is **Bit Depth**. To the right, you'll notice a note that says 16-bit ProPhoto RGB is the officially recommended choice for best preserving color details from Lightroom, but what does that actually mean?

Every photo is made up of pixels. In an RGB photo, each pixel has a Red, a Green and a Blue channel, and in an 8-bit photo, each of those channels has a value from 0-255.

If you need to make any significant tonal changes, you only have a maximum of 256 levels per channel to play with. For example, if you've significantly underexposed the photo, all the detail may be in the first 128 levels (on the left of the histogram). As you correct the exposure, you stretch the detail out to fill the full 0-255 range, but you can't create new data. The missing data displays as gaps in the histogram. **(Figure 15.3)**

The gaps may not be visible on an average photo, but they display as banding (or steps) on photos with smooth gradients, such as a sky at sunset. **(Figure 15.4)** A 16-bit photo, on the other hand, has 65,536 levels per channel, so you can manipulate and stretch it without worrying about losing too much data.

The downside to 16-bit is that all that extra data takes up more space on your hard drive, so in the real world, it's not always quite so clear cut. 16-bit files can only be saved as TIFF or PSD, not JPEG, and the file sizes are much bigger than an 8-bit high quality JPEG, often with very little, if any, visible difference to the untrained eye on a small print. A Canon 5D Mk2 file is around 126 MB for a 16-bit TIFF, 63 MB for an 8-bit TIFF, but less than 15 MB for a maximum quality 8-bit JPEG. That's a big difference on a large volume of files!

So the reality is you may want to weigh it up on a case-by-case basis. Everything's a trade-off. If you're producing a fine art print, 16-bit would be an excellent choice to preserve as much detail as possible. Or if you're going to take a file into Photoshop and make massive tonal changes, 16-bit would be an excellent choice, giving greater latitude for adjustments. But if you're just doing light retouching on a large volume of files, 8-bit JPEG could be a far more efficient choice. You can always re-export from Lightroom as a 16-bit file if you find a photo which would benefit, such as a photo exhibiting banding in the sky, or suchlike.

Which resolution should I select?

We'll come back to the concept of **Resolution** in the Export chapter (page 359). While editing the photos in external editors, your choice of resolution doesn't really matter,

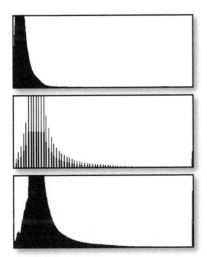

Figure 15.3 *If you take an underexposed photo (top) and stretch the 8-bit data, you'll get gaps in the histogram (center) whereas 16-bit has more data to stretch (bottom).*

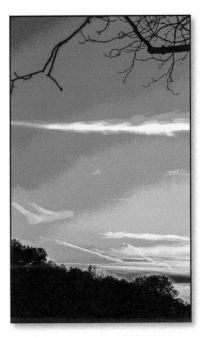

Figure 15.4 *This 8-bit image shows significant banding in the sky.*

as all of the pixels (less any cropped pixels) are passed to the external editor. There are a few cases where you might want to select a specific resolution, for example, when you're running a Photoshop action that uses specific measurements.

How do I change the file name and location?

By default, Lightroom saves the edited file in the same folder as the original, and simply adds -Edit to the end of the filename to show that it's a derivative file. You can change -Edit to another file naming template of your choice at the bottom of the Preferences dialog > External Editing tab.

As long as you simply save the file when you've finished editing it in Photoshop or another editor, the edited file is also returned to your catalog. If you choose to Save As a different filename, file type or location, the behavior changes, depending on the type of external editor you're using. (Figure 15.5)

Can I create different filenames for different editors?

The single filename template in the External Editor preferences applies to all external editors, so you can't apply a different filename to each editor (e.g. 201503092100-NikSilverEfex.tiff).   The edited photos are also saved in the same

	Edit In...	Save	Save As	Close (No Save)
File Created by Photoshop	• Edit in Photoshop with (matching ACR version) • Edit in Photoshop (outdated ACR version set to Open Anyway) • Open as Smart Object in Photoshop or Merge to Panorama/HDR using Photoshop or Open as Layers in Photoshop	**Folder:** same as original **File Type:** as preferences **Filename:** as preferences **Catalog:** adds edited file on save	**Folder:** your choice **File Type:** your choice **Filename:** your choice **Catalog:** if you select a new filename, file type or location, file is not added to the catalog.	File not saved
File Created by Lightroom	• Edit in Additional External Editor • Edit in Photoshop (outdated ACR version set to Render Using Lightroom)	**Folder:** same as original **File Type:** as preferences **Filename:** as preferences **Catalog:** adds new file at time of creation and updates when saving	**Folder:** your choice **File Type:** your choice **Filename:** your choice **Catalog:** adds unedited file at time of creation but catalog doesn't know about the new edited file	**Folder:** same as original **File Type:** as preferences **Filename:** as preferences **Catalog:** adds new file at time of creation

Figure 15.5 *The Save / Save As / Close behavior varies depending on whether Photoshop or Lightroom renders the file.*

folder as the original, rather than a folder you specify.

You can work around this limitation by using Export presets instead. We'll come back to the options in more detail in the Export chapter (starting on page 351), but in short, go to the Export dialog and select the options of your choice, for example:

Export Location—Set to the location of your choice, for example, *Same folder as original photo* and select *Put in Subfolder* called *Edited*. Check *Add to this Catalog* if you want the resulting photo imported automatically, as it would be with standard External Editors.

Rename to—Set to *Filename-Custom Text* with the custom text set to *NikSilverEfex* (or your editor's name)

Image Format—TIFF 16-bit or another rendered file format of your choice.

Post-Processing—Set it to *After Export: Open in Other Application* and navigate to the program. Select the exe file (Windows) / application (Mac).

Finally, save your settings as a preset and cancel out of the Export dialog. To use the preset, right-click on a photo, scroll down to *Export* and click on your preset.

Can I automatically stack the files?

The final option in preferences is a **Stack with Original** checkbox that stacks the edited photo with the original, putting the edited version on top. Some photographers like to apply a color label to their finished photos to help quickly identify them.

Why does Lightroom keep putting the photos at the end of the current folder/ collection?

If your sort order is set to *User Order, Edit Time*, etc., Lightroom puts the edited file at the end of the series of photos, and if you have it set to *Stack with Original* in Preferences, it also moves the original photo to the end. If you don't want to have to keep scrolling back again, use a sort order such as *Capture Time* or *Filename* that won't automatically be updated.

EDITING IN PHOTOSHOP OR PHOTOSHOP ELEMENTS

As you'd expect, Lightroom has greater interaction with Adobe software than it does with other pixel editors. In the case of Photoshop CS6 or CC, this includes the ability to pass the raw data, without first needing to create a TIFF/PSD file. It uses Adobe Camera Raw (ACR) to render the file, which we'll discuss in more detail in the next section, starting on page 340.

Why isn't Lightroom opening my photo as a TIFF or PSD file according to my preferences?

If Photoshop is set as the Primary External Editor (the first choice), the photo is opened directly into Photoshop and rendered using Adobe Camera Raw (ACR), so it's not saved as a TIFF or PSD until you choose to save it.

When you press Ctrl-S (Windows) / Cmd-S (Mac) in Photoshop, or go to *File menu > Save*, Photoshop creates the TIFF or PSD file according to your Lightroom preferences. You don't need to use *Save As* to create the TIFF/PSD file (in fact, it causes more complications if you do use *Save As!*)

That's a great feature, as if you're just

experimenting and you decide not to keep your edited file, you can just close without saving and don't have to worry about going back to delete the TIFF or PSD. (Note that this only works with matching ACR versions, or when you select *Open Anyway* in the ACR mismatch dialog. We'll come back to ACR mismatches in the next section on page 340.)

What's the difference between Edit Original, Edit a Copy, or Edit a Copy with Lightroom Adjustments?

If you're passing a rendered file to Photoshop or Elements—a TIFF, a PSD, or a JPEG—then Lightroom first asks how you want to handle the file. **(Figure 15.6)** (It doesn't ask for raw files.)

Edit a Copy with Lightroom Adjustments passes the image data and the settings to ACR to open directly into Photoshop, or creates a TIFF/PSD if you're using Elements. Any layers are flattened in the process. If there's a mismatch in ACR versions, it displays the same ACR Mismatch dialog as a raw file, with the same results.

Edit a Copy creates a copy of the original file, in the same format, and opens this into Photoshop without any of your Lightroom edits. It allows you to edit the photo without overwriting your previous file, and also retains any layers in the file.

Edit Original opens the original file into Photoshop without any of your Lightroom edits. It's useful if you want to continue editing a photo that you've previously edited in Photoshop, as it retains any layers in the file.

If you need to open the photo back into Photoshop to make further adjustments to the layers, perhaps for additional retouching, choose the *Edit Original* or *Edit a Copy* options, rather than *Edit a Copy with Lightroom Adjustments*. This opens the layered file into Photoshop without your Develop adjustments, and when you bring the file back into Lightroom, your Develop adjustments are still laid non-destructively over the top.

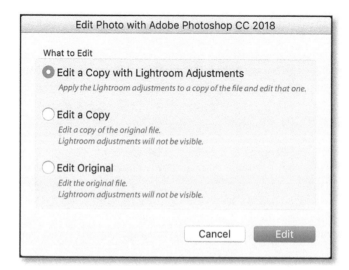

Figure 15.6 *When you send rendered files to Photoshop, it asks you how to handle the file. This dialog is skipped for raw files.*

What do the other options in the Edit In menu do?

Using Edit in Photoshop as the primary External Editor, you can open the file or multiple files directly into Photoshop CS3 10.0.1 or later without first saving an interim TIFF or PSD file (**Figure 15.7**), although you may get unexpected results if you're not using a fully compatible version of ACR. The older the Photoshop version, the more unexpected the results will be.

Open as Smart Object in Photoshop allows you to edit the Develop settings in the ACR dialog while in Photoshop, although these Develop settings won't then be updated on the original file in your Lightroom catalog, but remain with the edited copy.

Merge to Panorama, Merge to HDR Pro and *Open as Layers in Photoshop* only become available when you have multiple photos selected.

Merge to Panorama in Photoshop opens the files directly into the Photomerge dialog in Photoshop, allowing you to create panoramic photos with more control over the layout and blending than Lightroom's own *Photo Merge > Panorama* tool.

Merge to HDR Pro in Photoshop opens the files directly into the Merge to HDR Pro dialog in Photoshop to create HDR photos. Lightroom's own *Photo Merge > HDR* is a better choice as it works on the unprocessed

raw data.

Using *Merge to Panorama* or *HDR Pro* automatically adds the resulting photos to your Lightroom catalog when you save them.

Open as Layers in Photoshop opens the files directly into Photoshop and places the photos into a single document as multiple layers, which is particularly useful if you need to merge multiple photos in Photoshop.

Should I still use Merge to HDR Pro or Merge to Panorama in Photoshop?

Lightroom now has its own HDR and Panorama merge tools, but there are occasions when you might want to use Photoshop's version of these tools.

If Lightroom has trouble with ghosting in an HDR file, Photoshop can occasionally do a better job. To try it, select the files, right-click and choose *Edit In > Merge to HDR Pro in Photoshop*. In the HDR Pro dialog, select 32-bit mode and press *OK*. The White Point Preview slider only affects the preview. When you save the resulting photo as a 32-bit floating-point TIFF, Lightroom allows you to import and edit the photo with an extended slider range.

If you're merging photos into a panorama and you want to control the blending yourself, or you want another perspective that Lightroom doesn't offer, you can use Photoshop instead.

When creating a panoramic photo using Photoshop, first edit your photos in the Develop module. Make sure they match, otherwise you'll find join lines in the finished panorama. Pay particular attention to the exposure, especially if you weren't shooting in Manual mode. It's also a good time to

```
Open as Smart Object in Photoshop...
Merge to Panorama in Photoshop...
Merge to HDR Pro in Photoshop...
Open as Layers in Photoshop...
```

Figure 15.7 *If you're using a recent full version of Photoshop, additional options will be available, such as Merge to Panorama and Merge to HDR Pro.*

apply lens corrections, noise reduction, etc. The photo that comes back from Photoshop will be a rendered file (TIFF or PSD) with less editing flexibility, unlike Lightroom's own panorama merge.

Select the files, right-click and choose *Edit In > Merge to Panorama in Photoshop*. Select the merge options in Photoshop's Photomerge dialog and press *OK*.

Why do my photos look different in Photoshop?

If you open your files into Photoshop and they're a different color, it's usually due to incorrect color space settings. For example, a ProPhoto RGB photo mistakenly rendered as sRGB displays as desaturated and flat. **(Figure 15.8)**

1. In Lightroom, go to the *Preferences dialog > External Editing tab*.

2. Make a note of the *Color Space* setting for Photoshop. **(Figure 15.9)**

3. Switch to Photoshop or Elements and go to *Edit menu > Color Settings* to view the Color Settings dialog.

4. Set the **RGB Working Space** to the same color space that you selected in Lightroom's External Editor preferences. **(Figure 15.10)**

Selecting *Preserve Embedded Profiles* and/or checking the *Ask When Opening for Profile Mismatches* in that same dialog helps to prevent any profile mismatches.

Preserve Embedded Profiles tells Photoshop to use the profile embedded in the file regardless of whether it matches your usual working space.

Ask When Opening for Profile Mismatches displays a warning dialog when the embedded profile doesn't match your usual working space, and asks you what to do. If *Preserve Embedded Profile* is selected, you can safely leave the profile mismatch checkboxes unchecked. **(Figure 15.11)**

As long as your Photoshop and Lightroom color settings match, or you have Photoshop set to use the embedded profile, your photos should match between both programs.

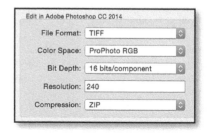

Figure 15.9 *Lightroom's External Editor Settings need to match Photoshop's Color Settings.*

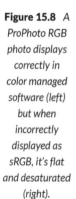

Figure 15.8 *A ProPhoto RGB photo displays correctly in color managed software (left) but when incorrectly displayed as sRGB, it's flat and desaturated (right).*

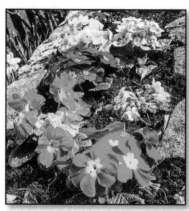

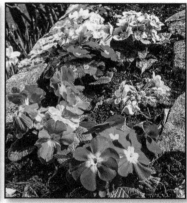

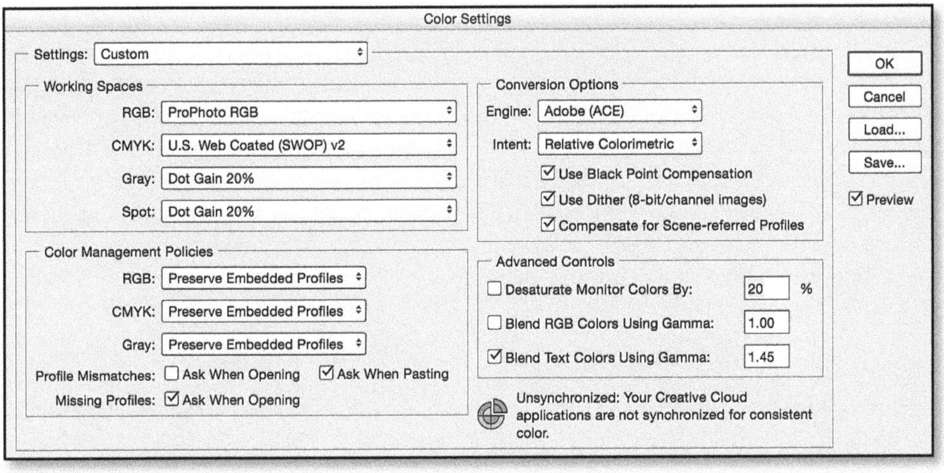

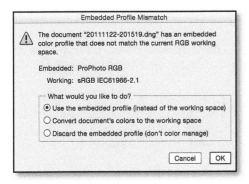

Figure 15.10 *Photoshop's Color Settings need to match Lightroom's External Editor Settings.*

Figure 15.11 *Checking the Ask When Opening checkbox in Photoshop's Color Settings dialog displays the Embedded Profile Mismatch dialog when the color spaces don't match.*

The same principles also apply to opening photos in other software, or when opening photos exported from Lightroom using the Export dialog.

If your color space settings are correct, a color mismatch can also be caused by a corrupted monitor profile. That's easy to check using the instructions on page 446 of the Troubleshooting chapter.

Lightroom can't find Photoshop to use Edit in Photoshop—how do I fix it?

When Lightroom starts up, it checks to see whether Photoshop or Photoshop Elements are installed, and if it can't find them, then the *Edit in Photoshop* menu command is disabled.

If you install a new version of Photoshop, and then uninstall an earlier version, the link can get broken by the uninstall. Uninstalling and reinstalling Photoshop usually solves it, or you can fix it by editing the registry key (Windows) or deleting Photoshop's plist file (Mac). There's more information on the official Adobe tech note at: https://www.Lrq.me/fixphotoshoplink

Of course, you may be able to take the easy course and add it as an *Additional External Editor*, however you would be missing out on some of the direct integration which comes with matching ACR versions.

ADOBE CAMERA RAW COMPATIBILITY FOR PHOTOSHOP

ACR, or Adobe Camera Raw, is the processing engine which allows Adobe programs to read raw file formats and convert them into image files. It's available as a plug-in for Adobe Bridge, Photoshop and Elements, and the same engine is built directly into Lightroom itself.

Updates are released every 3-4 months to add new camera and lens support and bug fixes.

Lightroom runs as a standalone program, without any need for Photoshop. If you do want to use the two together, it's important to update both at the same time to make sure the ACR versions are fully compatible, or at least ensure that you understand the implications of a mismatch.

If you're using Photoshop CC, use the Adobe Creative Cloud app to install the updates. If you're using Photoshop CS6 or Elements 13, go to *Help menu > Updates* to launch the Adobe Application Manager instead.

If you're using the most recent version of Lightroom and the most recent ACR plug-in in Photoshop CC, everything's perfectly matched.

If you're using the most recent version of Lightroom and the most recent ACR plug-in in Photoshop CS6 or Elements 13, Edit in Photoshop works correctly, but some of the controls are missing from the ACR dialog if you edit a raw file directly in CS6/Elements.

What happens if I'm still using an older version of ACR and Photoshop?

With older versions of ACR or Photoshop, it gets a little more complicated.

Usually, when you open a photo into Photoshop from Lightroom, Lightroom passes the original raw data and instructions over to the ACR plug-in hosted by Photoshop, and ACR performs the conversion and opens the image into Photoshop. **(Figures 15.13)**

If you're using an older version of ACR, it may not understand all of Lightroom's instructions, resulting in a completely different rendering. When the ACR version doesn't match, Lightroom displays the ACR Mismatch dialog mentioned on page 340. This allows you to choose how to handle the file.

What's the difference between *Render Using Lightroom* and *Open Anyway* in the ACR mismatch dialog?

The ACR Mismatch dialog **(Figure 15.12)** gives you two choices:

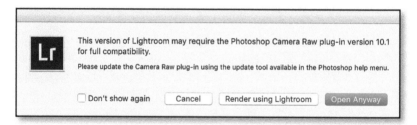

This version of Lightroom may require the Photoshop Camera Raw plug-in version 10.1 for full compatibility.

Please update the Camera Raw plug-in using the update tool available in the Photoshop help menu.

☐ Don't show again   Cancel   Render using Lightroom   Open Anyway

Figure 15.12   If your ACR version isn't fully compatible, Lightroom will ask whether to Render Using Lightroom, creating a TIFF/PSD and passing that to Photoshop, or Open Anyway, taking a chance that the rendering may be different.

Edit In Photoshop Logic Tree

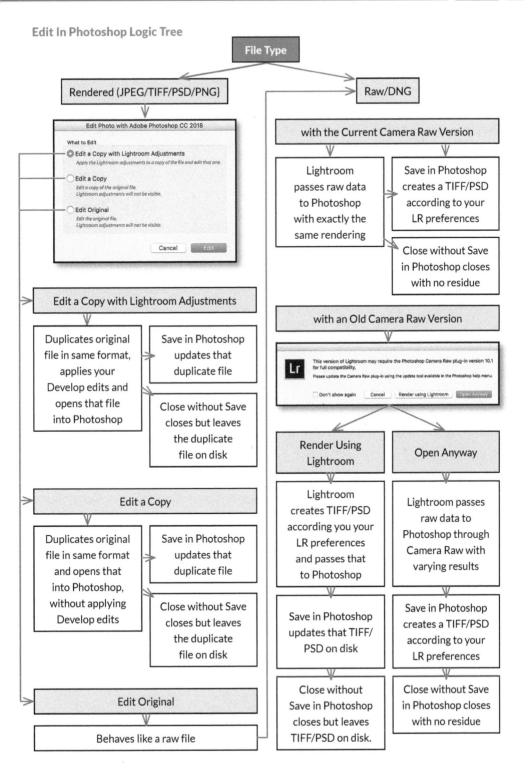

Figure 15.13 *The Edit in Photoshop logic, depending on whether they're raw or rendered.*

Render using Lightroom uses Lightroom's own processing engine to render the TIFF or PSD file, which is then automatically opened into Photoshop. All of your Lightroom adjustments are applied correctly.

Open Anyway ignores the mismatch and passes the image data and settings to Photoshop for ACR to process, which may produce something close to the correct rendering or may be completely different. It doesn't save the TIFF/PSD until you choose to save the changes.

If you try to open a proprietary raw file from a camera that wasn't supported by your old ACR version, the file won't even open as ACR won't know what to do with it.

If your ACR version is recent, for example, you've just upgraded to Lightroom Classic 7.4 but ACR is still on the previous version (e.g. Camera Raw 10.3), *Open Anyway* is a fairly safe choice. If your ACR version is older, select *Render using Lightroom* to ensure it renders correctly.

SETTING UP ADDITIONAL EXTERNAL EDITORS

Although Photoshop or Elements are the obvious choice for use with Lightroom, they're not the only choice. Many photographers use Nik Software or OnOne software with Lightroom, among others.

Some programs automatically install plug-ins, external editor settings or export presets, which you can access from the *File menu > Plug-in Extras, Photo menu > Edit in* or *File menu > Export as Preset* respectively. You'll also find those options in the right-click menu. Check with the developer for each individual program.

How do I create my own external editor preset?

If you have a program that doesn't automatically link with Lightroom, you can create your own external editor preset.

1. Go to Lightroom's Preferences dialog, under the *Edit menu* (Windows) / *Lightroom menu* (Mac) and select the *External Editors* tab.

2. In the bottom half of the dialog, press *Choose* and navigate to the program's exe file (Windows) / app (Mac). **(Figure 15.14)**

3. Select other preferences below—TIFF is a good choice for file format, and 8-bit vs. 16-bit depends on your specific editor. If your software is fully color-managed, select ProPhoto RGB. Otherwise select sRGB.

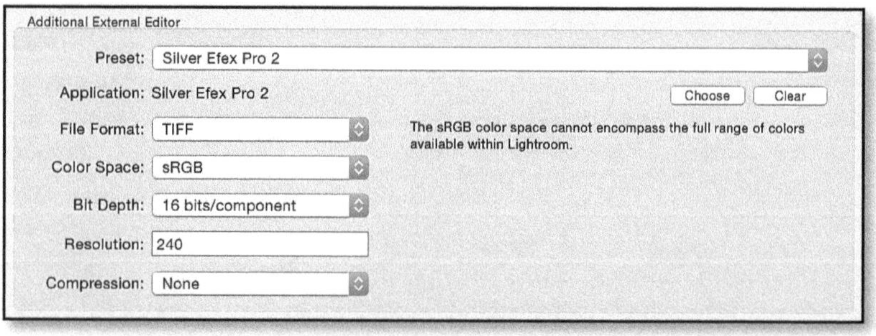

Additional External Editor	
Preset:	Silver Efex Pro 2
Application: Silver Efex Pro 2	Choose Clear
File Format:	TIFF
Color Space:	sRGB
Bit Depth:	16 bits/component
Resolution:	240
Compression:	None

The sRGB color space cannot encompass the full range of colors available within Lightroom.

Figure 15.14 *You can set up multiple additional external editors using the External Editing tab in the Preferences dialog.*

4. In the Preset pop-up, select *Save Settings as New Preset* and give your editor a name.

You can use the same steps to create as many external editors presets as you like.

When you close the dialog, the preset selected in the Preset pop-up becomes the main Additional External Editor shown at the top of the list, and it's assigned the secondary keyboard shortcut, which is Ctrl-Alt-E (Windows) / Cmd-Opt-E (Mac).

5. To open a photo into your external editor, go to *Photo menu > Edit In* or access it from the right-click menu. **(Figure 15.15)**

How do I edit an external editor preset?

If you need to change one of your External Editors, return to the *Preferences dialog > External Editing tab* and select the preset from the pop-up menu. You can then edit the settings, perhaps changing the file format or

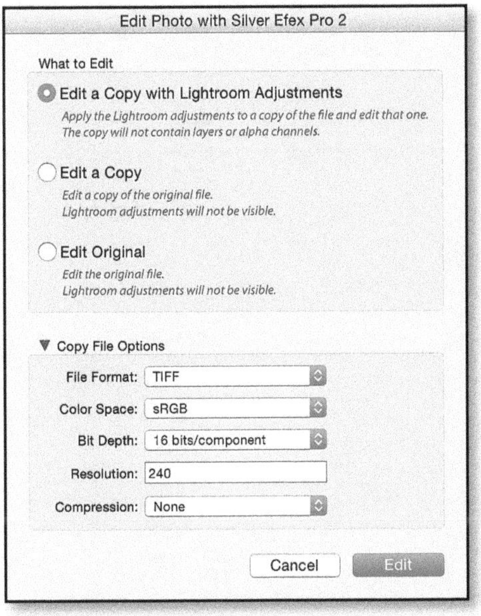

color space, and go back to the pop-up and select *Update Preset* from the listed options. To rename or delete a preset, select it in the pop-up and then select *Rename preset* or *Delete preset*.

Where have my external editors gone?

If some external editor presets go missing, toggle the *Store presets with this catalog* checkbox in Lightroom's Preferences > Presets tab to see if they reappear. To learn more about this checkbox, turn to page 425.

Can I open the raw file into another raw processor?

Lightroom sends TIFF/PSD files to its Additional External Editors, rather than the raw data, which is ideal for most pixel editing software, but there may be occasions when you want to open a photo into another raw processor (or a video into video editing software). On these occasions, right-click on the photo, choose *Show in Explorer* (Windows) / *Show in Finder* (Mac) and then open into your raw processor.

Alternatively, John Beardsworth's Open Directly plug-in takes the original file and passes it to the software of your choice. https://www.Lrq.me/beardsworth-opendirectly

INSTALLING PLUG-INS

Plug-ins allow third-party developers to add additional functionality to Lightroom, with greater integration than simple External Editors. They're written in Lua, and the SDK (Software Development Kit) is freely available from: https://www.Lrq.me/sdkdownload

There's a wide variety of plug-ins available,

Edit Photo with Silver Efex Pro 2

What to Edit

◉ Edit a Copy with Lightroom Adjustments
Apply the Lightroom adjustments to a copy of the file and edit that one. The copy will not contain layers or alpha channels.

○ Edit a Copy
Edit a copy of the original file. Lightroom adjustments will not be visible.

○ Edit Original
Edit the original file. Lightroom adjustments will not be visible.

▼ Copy File Options

File Format:	TIFF
Color Space:	sRGB
Bit Depth:	16 bits/component
Resolution:	240
Compression:	None

Cancel   Edit

Figure 15.15 *If you open a file into a secondary external editor, it allows you to change the file preferences on-the-fly.*

doing everything from adding a List view to the Library module, to adding borders while exporting photos, to automatically uploading photos to various websites. I've mentioned my favorites throughout the book, but you can find a longer list at https://www.Lrq.me/links/plugins

How do I install a plug-in?

Some plug-ins automatically install themselves, but if your downloaded doesn't automatically install:

1. If the plug-in has a .zip extension, double-click to unzip it, and store it somewhere safe.

It's a good idea to keep all of your plug-ins in one place, to make them easy to find, update, transfer, back up or delete. Creating a *Plug-ins* folder alongside the other presets folders would be an ideal place, and you can find that folder easily by going to *Preferences dialog > Presets tab* and clicking the *Show Lightroom Presets Folder* button.

2. Go to *File menu > Plug-in Manager* to show the Plug-in Manager dialog. (**Figure 15.16**)

3. Click on the *Add* button in the lower-left corner.

4. Navigate to the *.lrplugin* or *.lrdevplugin* folder/file for the plug-in you would like to install. On Windows, you need to select the folder, rather than its contents, whereas .lrplugin files are a single package file on Mac.

5. Some plug-ins have additional instructions, for example, the LR/Mogrify plug-in also needs you to install the Mogrify application. Most developers include full installation instructions.

How do I uninstall a plug-in?

To remove any plug-ins that you've installed by means of the *Add* button, simply select the plug-in in the Plug-in Manager dialog and press the *Remove* button. The *Remove* button isn't available for plug-ins stored in Lightroom's own Modules folder, such as plug-ins that use an installer.

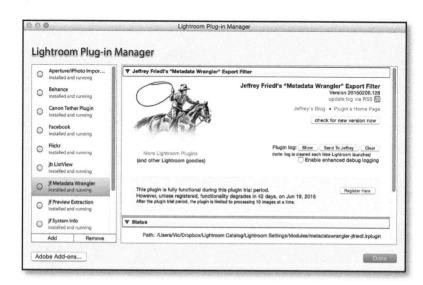

Figure 15.16 *Plug-ins are installed and uninstalled using the Plug-in Manager dialog.*

How do I use a plug-in?

Once you've installed the plug-in, it's ready to use. The way you access it depends on the individual plug-in, but each developer should provide instructions.

Some plug-ins that export directly to a different destination, such as LR/TreeExporter, show in the pop-up menu at the top of the Export dialog, where it usually says *Hard Drive*. They may also create their own panels in the Export dialog. **(Figure 15.17)**

Some plug-ins, such as LR/Mogrify and Metadata Wrangler, appear in the Post-Process Actions section of the Export dialog, below the Export Presets. From there, you can choose which options you want to

make available for your current export, for example, on LR/Mogrify, a single border. The plug-in panels that you choose then appear beneath the normal export panels.

Publish Service plug-ins appear in the Publish Services panel, like the built in Facebook and Flickr plug-ins. **(Figure 15.18)**

Most other Export Plug-ins have a menu listing under the *File menu* or *Library menu* in the Plug-in Extras section instead (yes, there are two different menus with the same name!).

SAVING METADATA TO THE FILES

While we're on the subject of editing photos in other programs, let's also talk about sharing metadata with other programs.

Because Lightroom is designed around a database, any changes you make in Lightroom are stored within Lightroom's catalog. This means that the changes aren't available to other programs such as Bridge. To make the metadata available to other programs, you need to store it in/with the files using a format called XMP.

Figure 15.17 *Some Export plug-ins appear in the pop-up at the top of the Export dialog. Other plug-ins create their own section in the bottom left corner of the Export dialog.*

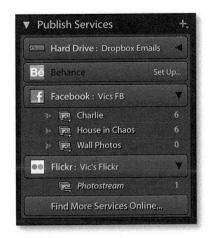

Figure 15.18 *Plug-ins for Publish Services appear in the Publish Services panel.*

XMP stands for Extensible Metadata Platform. It's simply a way of storing text metadata, such as Develop settings, star ratings, color labels and keywords, among other things, with the photos themselves. XMP is based on open standards and the SDK is freely available, which means that other companies can also write and understand that same format, making your metadata available to other image management software.

The XMP for most file types (e.g. JPEG, TIFF, PSD, DNG) is written to a section in the header of the file. These changes don't affect the image data, and therefore never degrade the quality of the photo. The metadata's written to a sidecar file for proprietary raw files because writing back to these file formats can prevent some other software from reading them.

Should I write to XMP?

Writing the metadata back to the files has pros and cons:

Sharing metadata—To edit or view metadata using other software, it has to be written to the files.

Belt-and-braces backup—Many use XMP data as an additional backup of settings in case their Lightroom catalog and backups become corrupted or they remove photos from the catalog by accident.

Transferring between catalogs—Some use XMP to transfer photos between catalogs (but only some of the metadata can be stored in XMP so Import from Catalog is a better choice... we'll come back to that on page 432).

Corruption—On the downside, writing changes back to the original files does slightly increase the risk of file corruption for JPEG, TIFF, PSD and DNG files, even though it's only updating the header of the file.

Big backups—Updating the metadata in the original JPEG, TIFF, PSD or DNG files means they're seen as changed by your backup software. If you use online backups, that could mean all the adjusted photos being re-uploaded each time you make a change.

Lots of little files—If you write metadata to proprietary raw files, it's written to sidecar files. You may like or dislike all those extra little files!

Limited data—Only some of your Lightroom settings can be written to the files, due to limits in the XMP specification. It's not a complete backup.

Sync Bandwidth—When metadata is written back to the file, it's seen as changed and therefore uploaded again. This can use a lot of bandwidth quickly.

Which of Lightroom's data isn't stored in XMP?

Flags, virtual copies, collection membership, uncommitted location data, Develop history, stacks, Develop module panel switches and zoomed image pan positions are currently only stored in the catalog itself, and not the XMP sections of the files.

How do I write settings to XMP?

To write settings to XMP, select the files in Grid view and press Ctrl-S (Windows) / Cmd-S (Mac) or go to *Metadata menu > Save Metadata to Files*.

When you're manually writing metadata to DNG files, you'll note that the Metadata menu offers two options:

Save Metadata to File just updates the XMP metadata, as it would with any other kind of file.

Update DNG Preview & Metadata does the same, but it also updates the embedded preview in any DNG files to include your Develop edits.

You can also turn on ***Automatically write changes into XMP*** in *Catalog Settings > Metadata tab* (**Figure 15.19**), which updates the XMP every time a change is made to the photo (although it's smart enough to wait a few seconds for you to stop editing).

If you're considering enabling automatic writing, there are a few points to be aware of:

• Think about how it will affect your backups—XMP sidecars for proprietary raw files are tiny to back up, but updating XMP embedded in DNG, JPEG, PSD, TIFF or PNG files may trigger your backup system to back up the whole file again. Even something as simple as correcting the spelling of a keyword triggers an update.

• Making changes to large numbers of photos (i.e., thousands) may be noticeably slower with auto-write turned on, due to the sheer volume of individual files that need to be written. This is especially noticeable when reorganizing your keyword list.

• When you first turn auto-write on, performance may drop considerably while it writes to XMP for all the photos in the catalog. Once it's finished doing so, performance improves, so you're best just to leave it to work for a while.

• Avoid turning auto-write off and on again too often, as every time you turn it on, it has to update the files with all the changes.

Should I allow Lightroom to update the capture time in raw files rather than XMP sidecar files?

There's an exception to the sidecar rule for proprietary raw files. If you edit the capture time, the new capture time can be updated in the original file. It's written to a documented portion of the metadata file header, so it's relatively safe. Some people feel that their raw files should never be touched in any way, so there's a ***Write date or time changes into proprietary raw files*** checkbox in *Catalog Settings > Metadata tab* which allows you to choose whether the updated date/time is stored only in the catalog, exported files and XMP sidecar files, or whether it can be updated in the original raw files too.

Should I check or uncheck *Include Develop settings in metadata inside JPEG, TIFF, PNG and PSD files*?

There's an extra option in *Catalog Settings >*

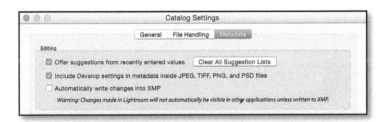

Figure 15.19 *Automatically write changes into XMP saves the metadata with the files as well as in the catalog.*

Metadata tab with regard to XMP, marked **Include Develop settings in metadata inside JPEG, TIFF, PNG and PSD files**. It controls whether Lightroom includes your Develop settings when it writes the other metadata. Personally, I leave it checked to include Develop settings when I write to XMP, but these text instructions can increase the file size if you've used lots of local adjustments or spot removal.

How do I read the metadata from the files?

Having written the metadata to the files, Lightroom essentially ignores it. The adjustments you make in Lightroom are still stored in the catalog, and that database is always assumed to be correct, whether XMP metadata exists or not.

The external metadata is only read at the time of import, or when you choose to read the metadata using *Metadata menu > Read Metadata from Files*. If you read the metadata

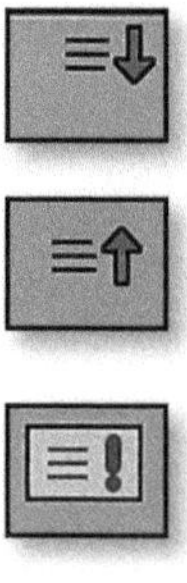

The metadata in the catalog is newer than the metadata in the file.

The metadata in the file is newer than in Lightroom.

The metadata has changed both in Lightroom and externally, resulting in a conflict.

Figure 15.20   *The Metadata Status icons shows the external metadata.*

from the files, it overwrites the information stored in the catalog for that photo.

Lightroom uses the metadata icons to show whether Lightroom's metadata or the external metadata was most recently updated (although it can take a few minutes before Lightroom notices an external change). **(Figure 15.20)**

Clicking on this icon requests confirmation: **(Figure 15.21)**

Import Settings from Disk—If you've intentionally changed the metadata using another program, this reads the metadata from the file and replacing the information in the catalog.

Cancel—don't do anything.

Overwrite Settings—If you're comfortable that everything looks correct in Lightroom, this replaces the external XMP metadata with Lightroom's data, clearing the warning icon.

When resolving metadata conflicts, is there a way to preview what will happen?

If Lightroom tells you there's a metadata conflict, you have to decide which set of data to keep. The problem is, it doesn't tell you which data is different in each version, so you have to either remember which you last updated, or take a guess. The good news is there's a workaround, although it would be time-consuming if you have a large

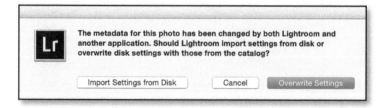

Figure 15.21   *If there's a metadata conflict, clicking on the icon will ask how to handle it.*

number of conflicts.

If you create a virtual copy before reading the metadata, the virtual copy retains the Lightroom metadata and the master is updated with the external metadata. You can then flick back and forth, comparing metadata and Develop settings, and decide which to keep. If you want to keep the data on the virtual copy, select *Photo menu > Set Copy as Master* before removing the other copy.

If the conflicted file is raw file, you can also open the XMP file using a XML or text editor to manually compare the contents with the information in the catalog.

How do I avoid metadata conflicts?

If you're going to make changes to the metadata in another program, save Lightroom's settings out to the files before editing in the other software. When you read the metadata again later, Lightroom's Develop settings are simply read back again, along with your new metadata edits, rather than being reset to default.

EDIT IN... SHORTCUTS

		Windows	Mac
Edit in	Edit in Photoshop	Ctrl E	Cmd E
	Edit in Other Application	Ctrl Alt E	Cmd Opt E
XMP	Write Metadata to Files	Ctrl S	Cmd S

EXPORT, EMAIL & PUBLISH SERVICES

Lightroom is non-destructive, which means that it doesn't save over your original image data. To apply your settings to your photos, you use *Export*, which is like a *Save As* in other programs.

When you export photos, it's usually for a specific purpose, such as posting on the web, giving them to someone else, or sending them away to be printed. Most exports can be deleted after use, as the photos can be exported again in future using the original image data and the settings saved in the catalog.

You can also email photos from within Lightroom, and publish photos to social media websites, but we'll come back to these a little later in the chapter (page 369 and page 373). First, let's cover the basics of export.

'SAVE AS' A COPY ON THE HARD DRIVE USING EXPORT

To export your finished photos, select them and then go to *File menu > Export* or press the *Export* button at the bottom of the left panel group in Library module.

These are the main settings you'll need to check: (**Figure 16.1**)

Export Location—decide where on the hard

drive to save the exported photos.

File Name—you can rename on export, for example, creating a template for Sequence #(001)-Filename puts a sequence number before your existing filename to ensure that they sort correctly in other software. It doesn't affect the names of the original files.

File Format—JPEG is an excellent choice for web, email, etc. TIFF is best for pixel editors such as Photoshop.

Color Space—select sRGB for screen/web use or ProPhoto RGB for color managed pixel editors such as Photoshop.

Size—refers to the pixel dimensions of the photo. There are some sample sizes in the sidebar.

Output Sharpening—select *Screen* for screen/web use, and the type of paper for prints.

If you're just starting out, here are some sample export settings for different uses:

Email or small web photo—*Longest Edge* 800px, and you can ignore the resolution as we're specifying the size in pixels. Format JPEG, quality 60. sRGB.

4" x 6" digital print—*Dimensions* 4" x 6" at 300ppi. Format JPEG, quality 70. sRGB.

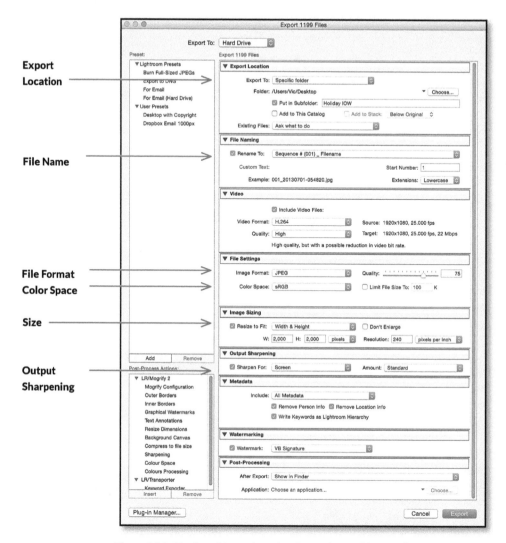

Figure 16.1 *Use Export to create copies of your photos with your adjustments applied.*

8" x 10" digital print—*Dimensions* 8" x 10" at 300ppi. Format JPEG, quality 80. sRGB (unless your lab requests another profile).

Full resolution file—uncheck the *Resize to Fit* checkbox. Format JPEG, quality 90-100. (There's a significant reduction in file size by dropping from 100 to 90, with minimal visible changes). sRGB.

Edit in another color managed program—uncheck the *Resize to Fit* checkbox. Format

TIFF, no compression, 16-bit, ProPhoto RGB.

Now let's start exploring these settings in more detail, starting at the top of the Export dialog and working down.

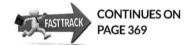

CONTINUES ON PAGE 369

EXPORT TO

At the top of the Export dialog is the **Export To** menu that's usually set to *Hard Drive* for normal exports. The other options include writing the exported files to *CD/DVD*, creating photos to *Email*, or exporting to specific plug-ins. **(Figure 16.2)**

To burn exported photos to CD/DVD directly from Lightroom (Blu-ray burning not available), change the pop-up menu at the top of the Export dialog to *CD/DVD*. When you press the *Export* button, it prompts you to insert a disc. If there's too much data for a single disc, Lightroom calculates how many discs are needed and spans the data without splitting any individual files. Alternatively, you can export to the hard drive and use specialized software to burn instead.

If you're exporting to a USB stick, select *Hard Drive* at the top, and then select the USB stick in the Export Location panel, as if you're selecting another external hard drive.

On the left of the dialog are Export Presets and then space for plug-in options. We'll come back to these later (page 368). The right-hand side of the Export dialog is made up of a series of collapsible sections which

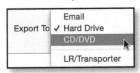

Figure 16.2 *Set the export type in the Export To pop-up.*

hold all the export options, so we'll start exploring these.

EXPORT LOCATION & FILE NAMING

The first pop-up in the **Export Location** section **(Figure 16.3)** determines the destination folder for the exported files. You have three choices:

Specific folder groups all the exported photos in a single folder. Select the location by pressing the *Choose* button and navigating to a folder. The chosen folder path then displays below the pop-up. Clicking on the arrow to the right displays the other folders you've recently used for exports.

Select folder later also groups all the exported photos in a single folder, but it pops up asking for a folder location just before the export begins. It's useful if you're creating a preset that will export to a different location each time you use it.

Same folder as original photo stores the exported photos with their original files, so they may be spread across a variety of different locations. It's particularly useful when combined with the *Put in Subfolder* checkbox.

The **Put in Subfolder** checkbox creates a new subfolder inside your chosen destination folder, using the name you enter in the field. For example, you might select an *Exported*

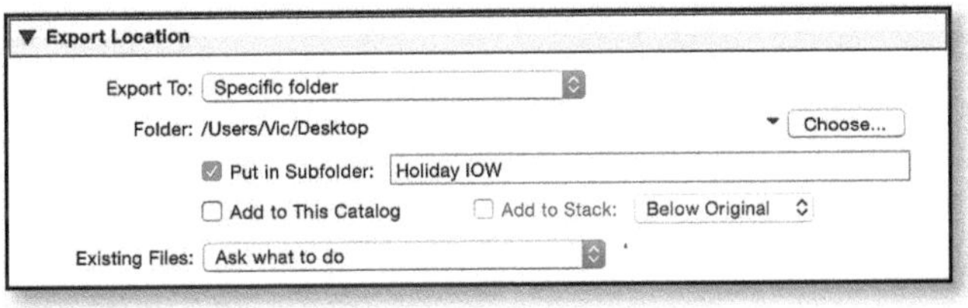

Figure 16.3 *In the Export Location section, select the Destination folder for the exported photos.*

Photos folder on your desktop, inside which you create a named subfolder for each export you run, or you might want to create *Finished JPEGs* folders inside the original image folders.

Lightroom can't reproduce the folder hierarchy natively, for example, a wedding that's grouped into folders for each stage of the day, LR/TreeExporter plug-in can save you doing so manually. https://www.Lrq.me/armes-lrtreeexporter

You can do the same using Publish Services (we'll come back to these on page 373) for both folder hierarchies and collection hierarchies, using Jeffrey Friedl's Folder Manager and Collection Manager plug-ins. https://www.Lrq.me/friedl-folpub and https://www.Lrq.me/friedl-colpub

Can Lightroom automatically re-import the exported files?

In most cases, you won't need to import the exported photos into your catalog, as they're exported for a specific purpose and can then be deleted. If, however, you're exporting photos ready to be retouched in an external editor, you may want these retouched versions to be catalogued along with the originals.

You could use the Import dialog to manually import the exported photos into the catalog, but it's quicker to check the **Add to This Catalog** checkbox to add them automatically.

At the same time, the exported photos can be automatically stacked above or below the original photos using the **Add to Stack** checkbox. Remember, stacking is a way of grouping photos in the grid so they appear as a single photo. To make this option available, you must have the *Export To* pop-up set to *Same folder as original photo* (because stacked photos have to be in the

same folder) and *Put in Subfolder* must be unchecked.

Of course, to add the exported photos to the same folder in order to stack them, they must have different filenames or file formats, otherwise they could overwrite the originals. The simplest solution is to add an additional word such as -Edit to the end of the filename. You can rename the photos while exporting—we'll come to that in a moment (page 355).

How do I handle existing photos with the same names?

If there are already photos with the same names in your destination folder, perhaps because you forgot to rename while exporting, Lightroom needs to know how to handle them. It can skip exporting these photos, overwrite them (only if they're not the original photos you're exporting) or automatically use unique names. Unique names just adds a -2 (or similar) to the end of the filename. You can select the default behavior in the Export dialog, or you can leave the **Existing Files** pop-up set to *Ask what to do* so it gives you the choice when those circumstances arise. **(Figure 16.4)**

Can I overwrite the original photos?

Lightroom won't allow you to save over the original file that you're exporting, as it goes against its philosophy of non-destructive editing. Overwriting the originals is like

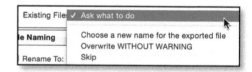

Figure 16.4 *If files with the same name exist in the Destination folder, Lightroom asks you what to do. You can pre-empt the decision using the pop-up in the Export dialog.*

throwing away the negatives once you've made a print that you like!

How do I change the filename while exporting?

Beneath the Export Locations section is **File Naming**. Photos are only renamed if the **Rename To** checkbox is checked. The options should be familiar by now, as they're the same options used in the Import dialog (page 30) and Rename Photo dialog (page 116). To create a filename template, select *Edit* from the pop-up, add your chosen tokens and save it using the pop-up at the top of the Filename Template Editor dialog.

The *File Naming* section in the Export dialog **(Figure 16.5)** renames the exported photos, but it doesn't affect the original photos in your catalog, so there are a number of situations where it's helpful.

We've already mentioned the example of adding a word such as -Edit to the end of a filename, to distinguish a retouched photo from the original. To create this template, insert a filename token, then click in the white field and type -Edit (or use a custom text field if you want to change it regularly).

(Figure 16.6)

If the photos you're exporting are to be viewed in other software, adding a sequence number with leading zeros to the beginning (i.e. 003-myfile.jpg) forces them to sort in the same order as the Grid view. Remember, in the *Sequence* pop-up, there's a variety of different sequence numbers, with varying numbers of leading zeros. If you're exporting 100 to 999 photos, you'll need 3 digits. **(Figure 16.7)**

When renaming exported photos, consider whether you'll later need to match them up with their originals. For example, if you export as wedding001.jpg to wedding300.jpg (custom name—sequence template), but your originals in Lightroom are still called IMG_3948 to IMG_8574, how are you going to match them up when the client brings back a list of orders?

VIDEO & FILE SETTINGS

The next sections in the Export dialog are **Video** and **File Settings**, where you select the file format, quality and color space.

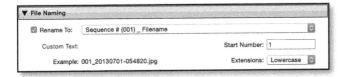

Figure 16.5 *Set the filename in the File Naming section. If the Rename checkbox is unchecked, the files retain their existing names.*

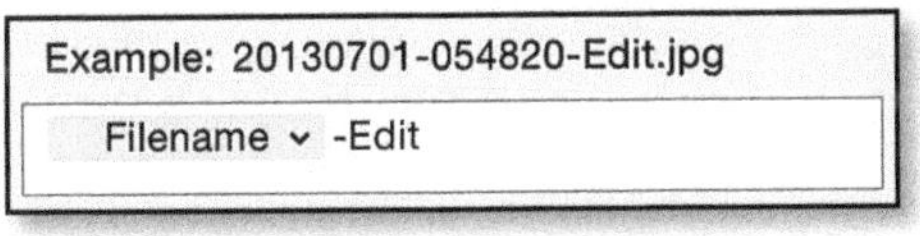

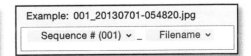

Figure 16.6 *You can automatically add -Edit to the end of filenames.*

Figure 16.7 *Use a Sequence # (001) token, then a hyphen (-) or underscore (_) and then a Filename token, to ensure that photos sort correctly in other software.*

The file format you select depends on the purpose of the photo or video. **(Figure 16.8)**

We'll come back to video formats in a moment (page 358), but for photos you have four *Image Format* choices:

JPEG is an excellent choice for emailing photos or posting them on the web. It's a lossy format so there is a trade-off between smaller file sizes and artifacts, but these artifacts are often invisible at medium-high quality settings. JPEGs can only hold 8 bits of data per channel, so stick with smaller color spaces such as Adobe RGB and sRGB.

TIFF is a lossless format, so it's great for storing working files and high-value edited photos. TIFFs can hold 16 bits of data (or even 32 bits for HDR photos) as well as Photoshop layers and transparency. Compression usually reduces the file size, although it takes a little longer to save.

PSD is also lossless and allows you to save less frequently used Photoshop color modes such as duotone, but TIFF is more widely supported.

DNG is the digital negative format. It wraps the raw data in a standardized format, along with the metadata. It's a good choice when sending raw data along with your Lightroom settings to another Lightroom or Photoshop user. You can learn more about DNG in the Geeky Bits Appendix starting on page E-1.

Original exports in the original format, creating a duplicate of the original file but with updated metadata. Your Develop edits are not applied to the image data when selecting *Original* format, but may be visible if the photo's imported into Lightroom or opened in Bridge/Photoshop.

Should I apply compression to the photos?

There are two main kinds of compression: lossless and lossy.

Lossless compression, as the name suggests, compresses the files, but they can be put back together perfectly, without any loss of quality.

Lossy compression works by throwing away some of the data. It can significantly reduce file size but at the expense of image quality and detail.

Because compressed files require more processing to open and close them, they can be a little slower to work with, but the space saving can be substantial.

The PSD format automatically compresses the files using lossless compression.

The TIFF format gives you a choice of compression, between *None, LZW* and *ZIP*.

None applies no compression, so the file sizes are large.

ZIP applies ZIP compression. It's a good all-round choice.

LZW is only available for 8-bit files, because LZW compression doesn't work well with 16-bit files and often makes them larger.

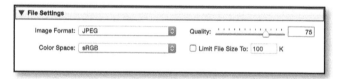

Figure 16.8 *Set the image format and color space in the File Settings section.*

It's still available for compatibility with some programs that don't understand ZIP compression, although such programs are rare now.

The JPEG format has a **Quality** slider, which controls the amount of compression applied to the photo. The resulting file sizes vary depending on the content of the photo, and therefore how much they can be compressed. Photos with large flat areas of color compress much more than detailed or noisy photos.

As a rule of thumb, Lightroom's default setting of 75 is a good all-round choice. 60 creates smaller for photos for the web/email, without significant loss of quality. For 'master' images that aren't important enough to require lossless compression, try using 90 instead of 100. There's a substantial reduction in file size without visible degradation.

Visit https://www.Lrq.me/friedl-jpegquality for interactive examples showing the effect of different quality settings.

Can I export to a specific file size?

If you're uploading the JPEGs to a website with a specific file size limit (e.g. 70 KB), it can be time-consuming to repeatedly export the photos, changing the quality setting until the file falls inside the limit. If you check the **Limit File Size To** checkbox and enter a limit, Lightroom does that for you, however the export can take longer than a standard export. It also removes the embedded thumbnail to improve the reliability and

reduce the file size.

Lightroom only adjusts the JPEG quality setting automatically, and not the pixel dimensions, so you'll need to select reasonable pixel dimensions for the file size. It's only intended to work for small web-size photos, so if you enter 8000K (i.e. just under 8 MB), it may well fall over.

Which bit depth should I select?

We also discussed the subject of **Bit Depth** in the Edit in External Editors chapter on page 332. As a reminder:

8-bit—saves hard drive space but may introduce banding in smooth gradients. It's a reasonable compromise for most finished files.

16-bit retains a larger amount of image data, so it's a better choice for working files (e.g., to send to external editors) and important master images.

JPEGs are always 8-bit. PSD and TIFF files give you the choice.

What is *Save Transparency*?

There's one final option in the TIFF settings, marked **Save Transparency**. TIFF's the only format that offers the choice as PSD and DNG include transparency automatically, and JPG can't contain transparency. **(Figure 16.9)**

A PNG, TIFF or PSD file may have already included transparent areas before the

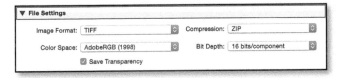

Figure 16.9   *The TIFF format also allows you to select the Bit Depth and Save Transparency.*

photo was imported, Lightroom's manual lens corrections can create transparent areas where you've corrected for distortion or rotation, or a panorama may have transparent areas around the edge. In most cases, you'll want to save the transparency.

Which color space should I select?

While you're working in Lightroom, it manages the colors for you, however when you take the photos outside of Lightroom (such as when you're exporting), you're in charge of selecting the best color space using the *Color Space* pop-up. We discussed the pros and cons of different color spaces in the Soft Proofing section starting on page 321, but as a quick reminder, here are your options.

ProPhoto RGB retains the most data, so it's the best choice when transferring photos to Photoshop or other external editors. ProPhoto RGB photos look odd in programs that aren't color managed, such as web browsers. Because the space is so wide, it's not appropriate for 8-bit images.

Adobe RGB is a good all-round choice, as long as you're working in a fully color-managed environment (for example, you're sending the files to a print lab that accepts Adobe RGB files).

sRGB is a smaller color space, but it's the most widely used. It's a great choice for screen output, emailing or uploading to the web. It's also the safest choice if you don't know where the photos will end up.

Display P3 is a wide gamut color space used on the latest Apple devices. It's a similar size to Adobe RGB, but it's shifted slightly towards reds/oranges and loses some of the greens/blues. It's primarily useful when exporting photos for display on the latest Apple devices.

Other allows you to select other RGB ICC profiles installed on your system. For example, some professional labs may request that you convert the photos to their own custom ICC profile. To do so, select *Other* from the *Color Space* pop-up, add a checkmark next to your custom profile and then press OK. Your custom profile is automatically selected in the pop-up.

How do I export or save my edited videos?

If you've edited a video, you likely want to apply the changes before sending it to someone else, just as you would for an image file. Using Export, you can create a duplicate of the original unedited video, or output to DPX or H.264 mp4 format. The options in the **Video Format** pop-up **(Figure 16.10)** are:

DPX is a lossless format used for editing in some professional video editing programs, such as Adobe Premiere.

H.264 is the best option for compressing your final videos, and it offers multiple quality settings.

Maximum quality uses a bit rate as close to the source file as possible, to prevent any

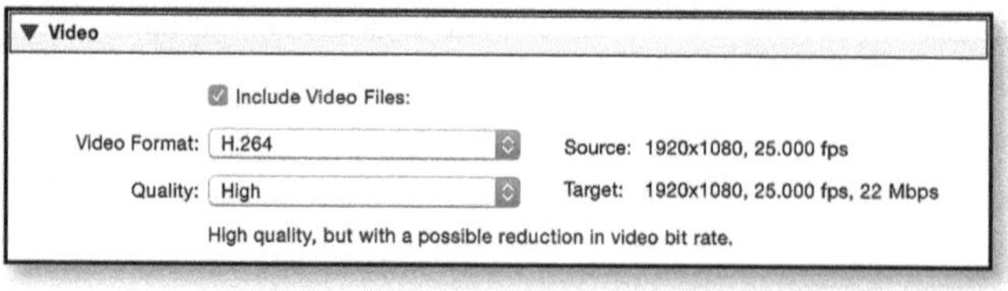

Figure 16.10 *Set the file format and quality in the Video section.*

loss of quality.

High quality retains the resolution but may reduce the file size slightly.

Medium quality is useful for sharing on the web, as it's a lower resolution and bit rate.

Low quality is intended for mobile devices such as mobile phones, with a much lower resolution and bit rate resulting in a much smaller file size.

Original, as with photos, is a duplicate of the original file.

As a guide, a 10 second clip from a Canon 600d resulted in the following file sizes:

Original file: 155 MB for 27 seconds, so around 51 MB for 10 seconds

DPX—2.07 GB

H264 Max—29.7 MB, 1920x1080, 22 Mbps approx.

H264 High—29.7 MB, 1920x1080, 22 Mbps approx. (in this case it didn't make a difference)

H264 Medium—11.3 MB, 1280x720, 8 Mbps approx.

H264 Low—1.5 MB, 480x270, 1 Mbps approx.

IMAGE SIZING & RESOLUTION

If you leave the **Resize to Fit** checkbox

unchecked in the Image Sizing panel, the photos remain at their native resolution, (less any cropped pixels). If you check it, you can resize the exported copies to the right size for your intended purpose. Remember, Lightroom doesn't resize the original photos while cropping, as this would go against it's non-destructive design. After all, there's nothing more destructive than deleting original pixels! Instead, you crop to a specific ratio in the Develop module and then set the size (or more accurately, the number of pixels) you require in the Export dialog. **(Figure 16.11)**

Pixels don't have a fixed physical size. They expand or contract to fill the space available. If you expand them too far, the photo appears blurry and pixelated (you can see the squares), so the aim is to keep the pixels smaller than or equal to the monitor pixels or printer dots. **(Figure 16.12)**

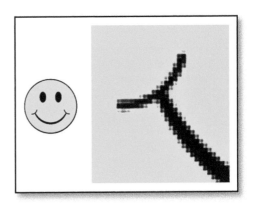

Figure 16.12 *The smiley face looks sharp when it's printed small, but the individual pixels show when it's enlarged too far.*

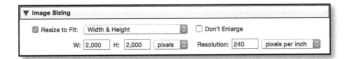

Figure 16.11 *Set the new pixel dimensions in the Image Sizing section of the Export dialog.*

How big can I print my photo without visible pixelation?

Most current cameras capture large files suitable for most purposes, but if you've cropped the photo heavily, you may have cropped many of the pixels away. You can check the original and cropped dimensions in the Metadata panel. In **Figure 16.13**, the 4032x3024 pixel file has been cropped to 1187x1008.

To check how big a high-quality print you can create, simply take the number of pixels along each edge and divide them by the desired print resolution.

$$1187px \; / \; 300ppi = 4"$$

$$1008px \; / \; 300ppi = 3.4"$$

Why 300ppi? Most printers output high quality prints at 250-360dpi, or dots per inch. You can often get away with a lower value (e.g., 200-240ppi), especially for large prints, as you'll view them from a distance, but they won't be quite as sharp. Some printers and papers are also more forgiving than others, for example, a print on canvas doesn't notice if it's a little soft or pixelated.

How do I calculate the number of pixels I need for a specific print size?

To work out how many pixels you need for a specific print size, it's another simple calculation. Let's use a 8" x 10" print. Simply multiply the length of the edge in inches by 300ppi, and you'll end up with the pixel dimensions.

$$10" \times 300ppi = 3000px$$

$$8" \times 300ppi = 2400px$$

The good news is Lightroom can do most of the math for you. You just have to enter the *Size* and *Resolution*.

Print sizes are usually defined in inches or cm, so enter your print size and select *inches* or *cm* from the pop-up, for example, 4" x 6". We said the *Resolution* setting is only useful when combined with units of measurements. If you enter the PPI required by your print lab (usually between 250ppi and 360ppi), Lightroom automatically calculates the right number of pixels for that size print. This process of creating new pixels or selectively throwing away pixels is called resampling.

Screen sizes are usually defined in pixels, so they're easy. You just enter the pixel dimensions you require and select *pixels* in the pop-up, for example, you may email a file that is 1024px along the longest edge. There's no point sending a huge file when it's only going to be viewed on screen. When you're defining the image size in pixels, the *Resolution* setting is irrelevant.

What's the difference between *Width & Height, Dimensions, Longest Edge, Shortest Edge, Megapixels & Percentage?*

The differences between the *Width & Height, Dimensions, Longest Edge* and *Shortest Edge* options are more easily illustrated using diagrams. The red lines mark the dimensions entered into Lightroom's Export dialog, and the black rectangle shows the resulting photo size and orientation. **(Figures 16.14)**

Width & Height fits the photos within a

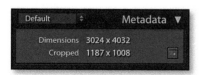

Figure 16.13 *Check the pixel dimensions in the Metadata panel.*

bounding box in their current orientation. This setting is width/height sensitive—settings of 400 wide by 600 high produces a 400×600 vertical photo, but only a 400×267 horizontal photo, assuming it's a 4x6 ratio.

Dimensions fits your photo within a bounding box, but it's a little more intelligent than *Width & Height*. It takes into account the rotation of the photo, and it makes the photo as big as it can within your bounding box, even if it has to turn the bounding box round to do so. The *Dimensions* setting isn't width/height sensitive, so settings of 400 wide by 600 high produces a 400×600 or 600x400 photo, if the photo has a 4x6 ratio.

Longest Edge sets the length of the longest edge, as the name suggests. A setting of 10 inches long would give photos of varying sizes such as 3"×10", 5"×10", 7"×10", 8"×10",

10"×10", depending on the ratio of the photo.

Shortest Edge sets the length of the shortest edge, again as the name suggests. A setting of 5 inches along the shortest edge would give varying sizes such as 5"×5", 5"×8", 5"×10", 5"×12", depending on the ratio of the photo.

Megapixels sets the dimensions automatically, based on your chosen pixel count. For example, selecting 24MP (24,000,000 pixels) would result in files of 4000x6000 and panoramas of 2400x10000, depending on their crop ratio. (Note that megapixels aren't the same as megabytes, so a 24MP file won't be 24 MB when saved.)

These measurements must still fall within the ACR limits of 65,000 pixels along the

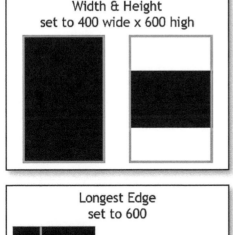

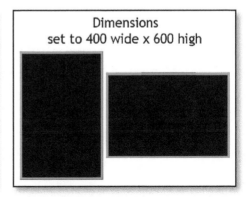

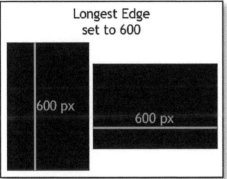

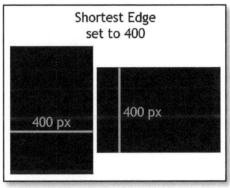

Figure 16.14 *The Resize to Fit options in the Export dialog.*

longest edge and 512MP, so if your photo falls outside of this range according to the measurements you've set, Lightroom simply makes the photo as big as it can.

There's also a **Percentage** option, so you can create files that are 50% of the original pixel dimensions, and so forth.

It's generally easiest to use *Longest Edge* and a pixel dimension for screen/email files and *Dimensions* with inches/cm and PPI for prints.

What's the difference between DPI, PPI, pixels per inch and pixels per cm?

Many people mix up PPI and DPI. DPI refers to Dots Per Inch. It doesn't apply to digital images until they're dots on a piece of paper. While they remain as pixels, the resolution is measured in PPI, or pixels per inch.

Pixels per cm is also available in the Export dialog, but it's rarely used, even if the print dimensions are measured in cm.

What does the *Don't Enlarge* checkbox do?

The **Don't Enlarge** checkbox prevents small photos from being upsized to meet the dimensions you've set, while still downsizing photos which are too large to fit your chosen dimensions.

Is it better to upsize in Lightroom or in Photoshop?

When Lightroom resizes, you don't have a choice of interpolation method, unlike Photoshop which offers *Nearest Neighbor, Bilinear, Bicubic, Bicubic Smoother* and *Bicubic Sharper*. Instead, Lightroom uses an intelligent adaptive bicubic algorithm which automatically adjusts for the increase or decrease in size. In theory, because Lightroom is working with the raw data and isn't limited to one specific resizing algorithm, it should give the best results. Either program can do a good job though.

OUTPUT SHARPENING

Once you've set the sizing, the **Sharpening** option are is next in line. The output sharpening may only have two pop-up menus, but it's far more powerful than it looks. **(Figure 16.15)**

The complex output sharpening algorithms were created by the team at Pixel Genius, who also created the well-known Photoshop plug-in PhotoKit Sharpener. Based on the size of the original file, the output size and resolution, the type of paper, and the strength of sharpening you prefer, it automatically adjusts the sharpening to create the optimal result.

Which Export Sharpening setting applies more sharpening—*screen, matte* or *glossy*?

The difference between *Matte* and *Glossy* is barely noticeable on screen, but there is a difference between each of the settings. At a glance, you'll see that the *Screen* setting sharpens the high-frequency details less than the *Matte* or *Glossy* settings, but there are a lot more technicalities behind that.

As a general rule, pick the right paper type, and you'll be about right. Sending matte sharpening to a glossy paper looks worse

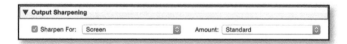

Figure 16.15 *Output Sharpening complements the Capture Sharpening applied in the Develop module.*

than sending glossy sharpening to matte paper, because the matte sharpening is compensating for the softer appearance of matte paper. Screen sharpening may look a little soft on old CRT monitors as it's optimized for LCD screens.

The **Amount** pop-up controls the amount of sharpening applied to the photo, and this decision is a question of personal taste. To get the best out of the automated output sharpening, you do need a properly capture-sharpened photo, so the sharpening settings in the Develop module are still essential. Avoid over-sharpening in the Develop module though, as the Export Sharpening makes it look a lot worse.

If you have no idea how the photos will be used, perhaps because you're giving them to a friend or client, *Glossy Standard* is a reasonable default.

METADATA & WATERMARKING

As soon as you release your photos, whether on the web or in printed form, they're at risk of being stolen. While you can't control that, ensuring that you have copyright metadata stored in the files, and possibly adding a watermark, can help to deter would-be thieves. On the other hand, you might want to strip some metadata from your files to protect your privacy.

How do I select which metadata to include in my files?

The **Metadata** section of the Export dialog (**Figure 16.16**) allows you to decide how much of the photo's metadata to **include** in the exported file. The basic options are self-explanatory. From the most retained metadata to the least, they are: *All, All Except Camera & Camera Raw Info, All Except Camera Raw Info, Copyright & Contact Info Only* or *Copyright Only.*

If you've added Map locations to your photos, you may want to strip the location data to protect your privacy. The **Remove Location Info** checkbox removes both the GPS coordinates and the IPTC Location data. You can also selectively remove specific locations, for example, your home address, by encircling these locations in a Saved Location using the Map module and marking it as private.

For the same privacy reasons, you may want to check the **Remove Person Info** to automatically exclude people's names from the exported keywords. Like the location data, you can right-click on the individual keywords in the Keyword List panel, select *Edit Keyword Tag* and uncheck *Include in Export* to only exclude specific people.

There's also a **Write Keywords as Lightroom Hierarchy** checkbox in the *Metadata* section. When it's checked, Lightroom uses the pipe character (|) to show parent/child relationships for your keywords, for example, *Animals | Pets | William.* It's useful if you'll be importing the photos back into the catalog, or into other software that understands keyword hierarchies. If you uncheck it, the keywords assigned to the photo are only recorded individually,

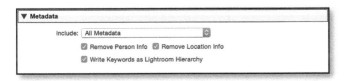

Figure 16.16 *You can remove specific metadata from exported photos using the Metadata section.*

resulting in separate keywords for *Animals*, *Pets*, and *William*.

If you want to be even more selective, Jeffrey Friedl's Metadata Wrangler Export Plug-in allows you to choose which metadata to remove and which to keep. You can download it from: https://www.Lrq.me/friedl-metadatawrangler

How do I add a watermark to my photos?

In the **Watermarking** section **(Figure 16.17)**, you can select a watermark to apply to your photos.

Check the **Watermark** checkbox and then select your watermark from the pop-up.

The most basic form of watermark is a small text watermark in the lower left corner of the photo, aptly named the *Simple Copyright Watermark*. It takes its text from the Copyright metadata field in the Metadata panel, and it's so simple you can't even change the font or size.

If you'd like something a little more decorative, select *Edit Watermarks* to design your own text or graphical watermark using the Watermark Editor dialog. **(Figure 16.18)**

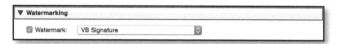

Figure 16.17 *Select your watermark in the Watermarking section.*

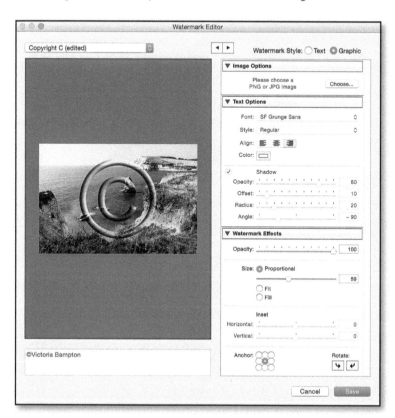

Figure 16.18 *In the Watermark Editor dialog, you can design your own watermarks.*

How do I create a text watermark?

Let's first create a text watermark. Select the *Text Style* option at the top of the dialog, and then enter your text in the text field beneath the preview image. To add a © copyright symbol, hold down Alt while typing 0169 on the number pad (Windows) or type Opt-G (Mac).

Using the options in the **Text Options** section (Figure 16.19), choose the **Font**, **Style** and **Color** of your watermark text. The *alignment* buttons apply to the text alignment within the bounding box and they only come into effect when you have multiple lines of copyright text. You can also add a **Shadow** behind the text.

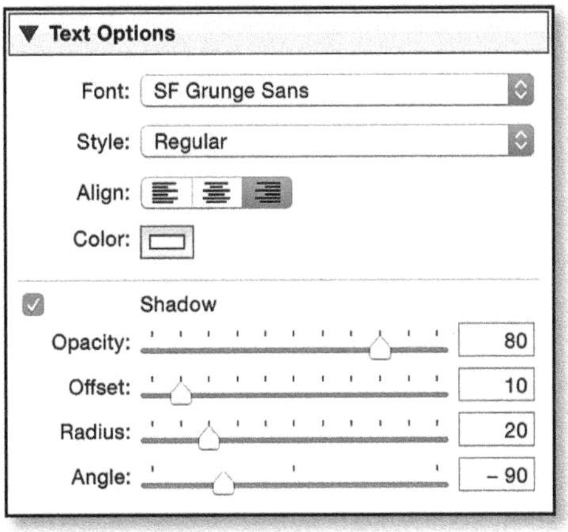

Figure 16.19 *Set the options for your text watermark.*

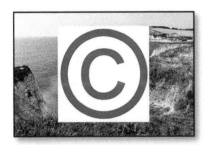

Figure 16.20 *A graphical watermark without transparency won't work!*

How do I create a graphical watermark?

If you'd prefer a graphical watermark, press the *Choose* button in the **Image Options** section and navigate to the PNG or JPEG file of your choice.

The PNG format has the advantage of allowing transparency, or semi-transparency—for example, you may want a large © symbol across your photo, but you don't want a large white square showing. (Figure 16.20)

You can download some of my favorite watermarks from: https://www.Lrq.me/resources

How do I set the size and placement on the photo?

The **Watermark Effects** section (Figure 16.21) allows you to set the size and placement of the watermark.

The **Size** is proportional to the size and orientation of the exported photo, and you can decide whether to *Fit* the watermark

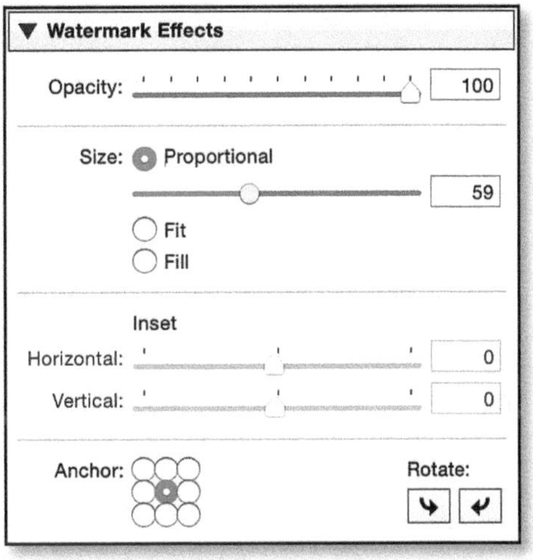

Figure 16.21 *Set the position and size of the watermark using the Watermark Effects section.*

within the short edge, *Fill* the long edge, or keep it *Proportional* to the current orientation. If it's set to *Proportional*, you can adjust the size using the slider or the small square in the corner of the bounding box on the preview. **(Figure 16.22)** Remember to consider how it'll look on horizontal, vertical, square and panoramic photos.

To move the watermark around on the image, you can't drag it, but you can use the 9-way **Anchor** buttons to lock it to the center, a corner, or an edge of the photo. Once it's anchored, you add additional spacing to distance it from the edge of the photo using the **Inset** sliders. If, for some reason, you've saved the graphic the wrong way round, you can also use the arrows to **rotate** the watermark.

If you haven't adjusted the opacity of the graphic, or you're using text, use the **Opacity** slider to reduce the opacity of the watermark, fading it into the photo.

Can I place the watermark in a different place on each photo?

The Watermark tool's purpose is to apply a watermark to large numbers of photos in the same size and position, so there isn't an interface for moving the watermark on individual photos, unless you want to keep returning to the Edit Watermark dialog every time you export. You could save multiple versions of a watermark preset, with the watermark in different positions, however you'd still have to select the photos to use with each preset. Using the Identity Plate and Print to JPEG, which we'll cover in the Print module, is a partial workaround if you need to carefully position a watermark on each individual photo.

How do I save my watermarks?

Once you're happy with your watermark, use the pop-up menu at the top of the dialog to *Save Current Settings as New Preset* ready for use on your photos. **(Figure 16.23)**

To edit a preset you've already saved, first select the preset in the pop-up, edit it, and

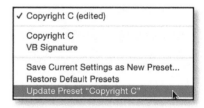

Figure 16.23 *To overwrite an existing Watermark preset, select it, make your changes, and then Update appears in the pop-up.*

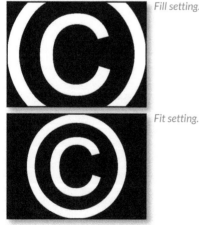

Fill setting.

Fit setting.

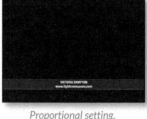

Proportional setting.

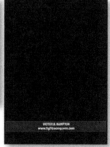

Figure 16.22 *The size of the watermark is always relative to the size of the photo.*

then return to the pop-up and select *Update Preset*. To rename or delete, first select the preset in the pop-up and then the *Delete Preset* and *Rename Preset* options become available.

Can I add metadata to my watermark?

Using Lightroom's watermark feature, you can add either a text or a graphical watermark, but not both. If you want greater control over the watermarking and you're willing to experiment to get your ideal result, the LR/Mogrify plug-in offers extensive options for adding multiple lines of text, metadata, multiple graphics and borders. You can download it as donationware from: https://www.Lrq.me/armes-lrmogrify2

POST-PROCESSING & OTHER EXPORT QUESTIONS

The final **Post-Processing** section (**Figure 16.24**) of the export dialog focuses on what happens to the photos after they're exported.

The **After Export** pop-up is set to *Do Nothing* by default, but *Show in Explorer* (Windows) / *Show in Finder* (Mac) is a useful alternative, taking you directly to the exported photos.

If you're exporting photos for editing in another program, select the *Open in Other Application* option and press the *Choose* button below to select the program.

If you choose the *Go to Export Actions Folder Now* option, it opens an Explorer (Windows)

/ Finder (Mac) window. Placing shortcuts/ aliases to applications or even Photoshop Droplets in this folder adds them to the main *After Export* pop-up for easy access.

What are Post-Process Actions?

If you've installed certain plug-ins, such as LR/Mogrify 2, there may be an additional section in the Export dialog marked **Post-Process Actions**. (**Figure 16.25**) To use one of these actions, select it and press the *Insert* button. The action options become available as additional panels on the right of the Export dialog.

OTHER EXPORT QUESTIONS

Before we move on to email and Publish Services, there are a few other questions that often arise when exporting photos.

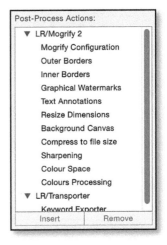

Figure 16.25 *The Post-Process Actions section may be added by a plug-in.*

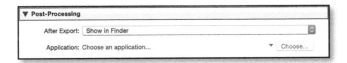

Figure 16.24 *In the Post-Processing section, select the action to take once the export has completed.*

Can I save my Export settings as a preset?

Having chosen all of your settings in the Export dialog, you can save them as a preset for easy access next time. A few Export presets are already included by default, but it's useful to save your own settings too. You might choose to create presets for regular exports, such as email, blog, printing at a lab, archiving full resolution, and so forth.

To create an Export preset, set your Export options, and then press the *Add* button in the **Presets** panel of the Export dialog. **(Figure 16.26)**

Your presets are stored in the User Presets folder by default, but you can organize them into folders by right-clicking in the Presets panel and choosing *New Folder*, and then dragging the presets into your folders. To rename, delete or update them when your

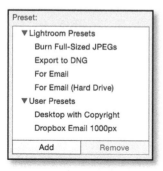

Figure 16.26 *Export presets show on the left hand side of the Export dialog, and you can group them into folders to keep them organized.*

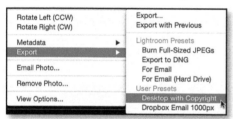

Figure 16.27 *Export presets can be accessed from the photo's right-click menu.*

settings change, right-click on the preset. To share the presets with others, use the *Import* and *Export* options in that same right-click menu.

Having set up Export presets, you can easily access these through *File menu > Export with Preset*, or through the right-click context-sensitive menu for any photo. **(Figure 16.27)** This is particularly useful if you're using the Export preset to open the files in an external editor.

Why are my adjustments not being applied to my exported file?

If you choose *Original* as the File Format in the Export dialog, you'll create a duplicate of the original file, without your Develop settings applied. The file size may be slightly different as Lightroom updates the metadata, unlike an operating system duplication, but it won't re-compress the image data, so the quality won't be reduced.

It gives an error message—*Some export operations were not performed. The file could not be written.* or *The file could not be found.* What went wrong?

If Lightroom says it couldn't export the files **(Figure 16.28)**, press the *Show in Library* button to view an *Error Photos* temporary

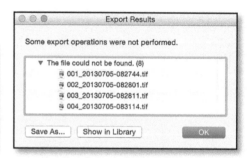

Figure 16.28 *If an export fails, Lightroom displays an error dialog listing which photos failed and the reason for the failure.*

collection, so you can see the photos in question.

If the error says *The file could not be found*, then some of the selected photos are missing because you've moved or renamed them with other software, or the drive is offline. Click on the exclamation point on the thumbnail and locate the original file, and run the export again. We'll come back to locating missing files in more detail in the Troubleshooting chapter starting on page 435.

If the error says *The file could not be written*, check the permissions on the export folder or parents of that folder, because they're probably read-only, or you're running out of disc space on that drive.

EMAILING YOUR PHOTOS

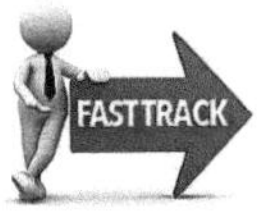

You could export your photos to a folder on your hard drive and then attach them to an email, but Lightroom makes even easier to email the

photos direct.

Select the photos (no more than 100) and then go to *File menu > Email Photos.*

Which mail clients are supported?

On Windows, most email clients are supported, using standard Windows APIs to pass the images. This includes Windows Live Mail, Thunderbird, Eudora, Microsoft Outlook, etc.

On Mac, only Apple Mail, Microsoft Outlook, Microsoft Entourage and Eudora are supported, as each is coded separately.

How do I set up email if my email client is supported?

1. Lightroom displays the Email dialog. **(Figure 16.29)** Your email software is automatically selected in the *From* pop-up.

2. Select the photo size using the **Preset** pop-up in the bottom left corner.

3. Leave the address and the rest of the

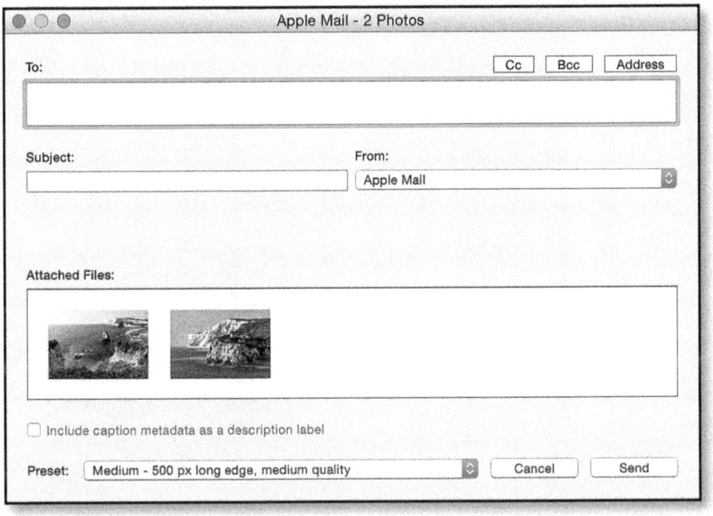

Figure 16.29 *If your email client is supported, you can select it in the From pop-up.*

email blank and press **Send**. The email message opens into your email software, where you can type your message and access your address book.

4. Alternatively, you can type the recipient's email address and your message into the Email dialog and send it directly.

How do I set up email if I use webmail or an unsupported email client?

1. Lightroom first asks you for your email account SMTP settings. **(Figure 16.30)** (These are the settings you'd use to set up your email in a desktop email program.) You'll only need to add them once, as they're stored for future emails.

2. In the New Account dialog, select your email Service Provider—AOL, Gmail, Windows Live Hotmail or Yahoo Mail. Enter a name for the account to help you identify it,

and enter your email address and password, and press OK.

3. If you use another email host, select Other from the Service Provider pop-up, enter the basic account details and press OK. In the Email Account Manager dialog **(Figure 16.31)**, enter the rest of your email SMTP server settings. Once you've finished entering the details, press Validate to confirm that you've set up the account correctly, and press Done to confirm.

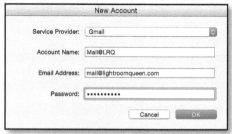

Figure 16.30 If your default email client isn't supported, Lightroom asks for your server details.

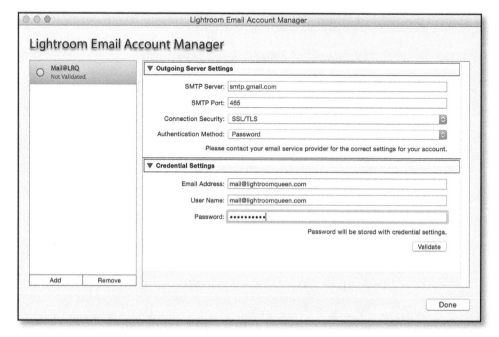

Figure 16.31 If your email client isn't supported, enter your email server SMTP details into the Email Account Manager dialog.

If you're not sure of your SMTP details, google the name of the provider and SMTP (e.g. "iCloud SMTP") or ask your email provider. When the Port is 465, the Security setting is usually SSL/TLS. When the port is 587, it's usually STARTTLS.

If you're using Gmail, Google may block Lightroom from validating. You can solve this without lowing Gmail's security settings by enabling 2-step verification and then following the instructions at https://www.Lrq.me/gmailpw

4. Select your new account in the **From** pop-up in the Email dialog **(Figure 16.32)**, and you'll be ready to send your first email.

5. Enter the address of the recipient, a subject for your email, and the message to include with your photos. Select the size of photos from the *Preset* pop-up in the lower left corner of the dialog, and finally press *Send*. To send an email to multiple email addresses, separate them with a ; and a space.

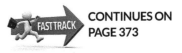

CONTINUES ON PAGE 373

Can I have multiple email accounts?

If you're manually setting up email accounts using the Email Account Manager dialog, you can store settings for multiple accounts. To add additional accounts, select *Go to Email Account Manager* in the *From* pop-up, and click the *Add* button to add accounts. The accounts are then listed in the *From* pop-up as presets. (You can also delete accounts using the *Remove* button in the same dialog.)

How do I set the size of the photos I want to email?

In the bottom left corner of the Email dialog is the *Preset* pop-up. **(Figure 16.33)** Lightroom comes with 4 email presets by default, with different sizes and JPEG quality settings. They are: 300px low quality, 500px medium quality, 800px high

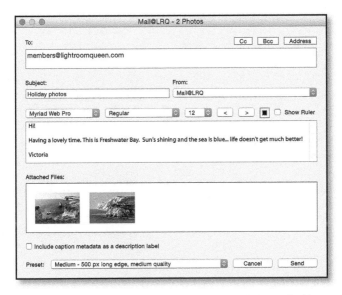

Figure 16.32 *Enter the recipient's email address in the To field, the email subject, and your email message below. Set the image size using the pop-up in the bottom left corner.*

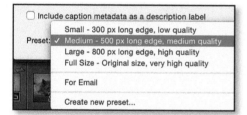

Figure 16.33 *There are four image sizes available by default, or you can create a custom one for this email.*

quality, and full resolution very high quality.

Bear in mind the overall email size if you're sending lots of photos, or you're sending a few full resolution photos. Many email accounts have a 10mb-per-email limit, both for sending and receiving email, although Gmail/Yahoo have increased this to 25mb. A few full resolution photos can quickly reach this limit and cause the email to bounce.

If you need to send many photos to the same person, consider creating a web gallery or uploading them to a photo sharing website instead of attaching them to an email. Lightroom web is ideal for sharing galleries of photos and it's included in any Adobe Creative Cloud subscription. See the Cloud Sync chapter starting on page 483 for more information.

If the recipients need to download a large number of photos, export them to a Dropbox folder (https://www.Lrq.me/dropbox) and email the download link, or use WeTransfer (https://www.Lrq.me/wetransfer) to send the files. It's more efficient for both you and the email recipient, and avoids clogging their email inbox.

If your emailed photos don't match the size you've selected in the Email dialog, check that your email software isn't downsizing the photos further. For example, Apple Mail

has an *Image Size* pop-up that must be set to *Original Size*.

Can I save a custom email preset including extra settings, such as a watermark or a different file format?

If you'd like to specify your own export settings for the photos, perhaps to include a watermark, or a different sharpening setting, you can create your own preset using the Export dialog.

If you're viewing the Email dialog, select *Create New Preset* from the *Preset* pop-up in the bottom left corner to open the Export dialog. If you're already viewing the Export dialog, select *Email* at the top of the dialog to save an email Export preset. When you've selected your export settings, don't forget to save it as a preset. Turn back to Saving Presets (page 368) for a quick reminder.

How do I use Lightroom's address book?

If you use a supported desktop mail client, Lightroom passes the photos over to the mail client, so you can use your standard email address book.

If you send emails direct from Lightroom, you won't have access to your main address book. Instead, Lightroom allows you to save email addresses in a Lightroom address book. **(Figure 16.34)** To access Lightroom's address book, press the ***Address*** button in the Email dialog.

To save a new address, press the *New Address* button and enter the details. The new address is listed in the main Address Book.

If you regularly send emails to the same group of people—perhaps family members—you may want to create a group of their email addresses for easy access. In the

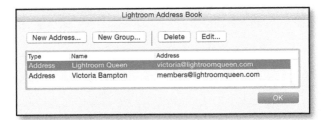

Figure 16.34 *You can store email addresses in Lightroom's own address book.*

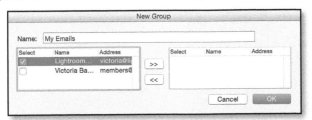

Figure 16.35 *Add users to a group using the New Group dialog.*

Address Book dialog, press *New Group* and click to put a checkmark against their email addresses in the left column. **(Figure 16.35)** Press the >> button to send them to the group, shown in the right column. Give your group a name and press *OK*. Your group is then listed in the Address Book dialog.

To use saved addresses in your email, press the *Address* button to return to the Address Book dialog and put a checkmark next to the individual or group, and their email addresses is automatically added to the *To* field. For individuals, rather than returning to the Address Book dialog, you can simply start to type the name of the recipient or the beginning of the email address in the *To*, *CC* or *BCC* fields, and it autofills. The autofill doesn't work for group names.

How do I keep a copy of my sent email?

If you send through your default email client, the sent email storage depends on the preferences for that software—if it usually saves your sent emails, it continues to do so for emails initiated by Lightroom.

If you send through Lightroom directly, saving the sent email depends on the email host. Some, for example, Gmail/Google Apps, automatically keep all outgoing as well as incoming emails, whether they're sent via SMTP or directly through webmail. Most other hosts do not keep all email, but pressing the *BCC* button in the Email dialog and typing your own email address would send the email to your own inbox, as well as the primary recipient's inbox.

PUBLISH SERVICES

Publish Services is another way of sharing your photos. You could consider it a 'managed export' as it keeps tracks of the photos exported to specific locations, and when you update the photos within Lightroom, it offers you the opportunity to update them at their exported location too. Depending on the service used, some updates such as comments made on websites can also be transferred back to your catalog.

How do I set up a Publish Services account?

We'll use Facebook for the step-by-step instructions, and then go into more detail.

1. Go to the Publish Services panel

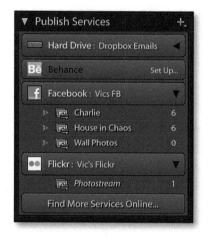

Figure 16.36 *Publish Services have their own panel in the left panel group in the Library module.*

(Figure 16.36), on the left in the Library module. There may also be others, depending on the plug-ins you've installed, but these four plug-ins ship with Lightroom.

2. Click on the **Facebook Set Up** button to show the Lightroom Publishing Manager dialog. (Figure 16.37)

3. At the top of the dialog, give your account a name and then press the **Authorize on Facebook** button. Lightroom asks for confirmation and then opens Facebook's website.

4. Log in using your normal account details and confirm that you want to allow Lightroom access to your Facebook account. If you've previously authorized Lightroom access, it may skip the authorization page.

5. Switch back to Lightroom. In the **Facebook Album** section, use the pop-up to select a default album to hold the photos, or

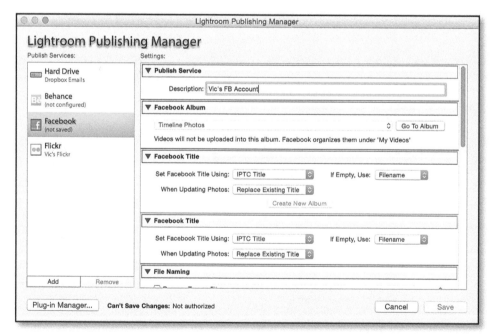

Figure 16.37 *Authorize your account in the Publishing Manager dialog.*

create a new album.

6. In the **Facebook Title** section, select the title/caption to display with the photo.

7. Set your normal export preferences below, for example, file name, size, sharpening and watermark. The options should be familiar from the standard Export dialog, which we discussed earlier in the chapter.

8. Press *Save* to store the settings. The dialog closes and in the Publish Services panel, you'll see your new Facebook connection, with your chosen album displayed underneath.

9. Drag photos from the grid to the Facebook album/collection.

10. Click on the Facebook album/collection to display the photos. The grid is divided into sections, showing the current status of the photos.

11. Click on the **Publish** button at the bottom of the left panel group, or right-click on the Facebook album and select *Publish Now*.

12. Go to the Facebook website to view your uploaded photos.

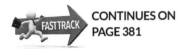

CONTINUES ON PAGE 381

How do I set up other publish services?

The basic principles of Publish Services setup are the same regardless of which service you're using. Some just offer additional features.

For example, you can organize your photos into collections, creating photosets for Flickr, albums for Facebook, or a hierarchy of folders and subfolders for the Hard Drive.

Let's take a look at some of these differences...

Facebook-specific details

There's one primary difference to note with Facebook. Most Publish Services can update existing photos when you make changes in Lightroom, but the Facebook Publish Service can't do that due to Facebook's API. If you republish photos to Facebook, it simply uploads a new one and leaves you to delete the old one in your web browser. Comments and likes aren't transferred to the updated photo either.

You can have multiple Facebook albums under a single Facebook connection. To create additional collections, right-click on a collection within your Facebook Publish Service in Lightroom and choose *Create Collection* from the context-sensitive menu. **(Figure 16.38)** This dialog gives you the option of creating a new album, or using an album which already exists at Facebook. If you're using an existing album, I'd recommend using the same name within Lightroom, otherwise it can easily get confusing. You only need to create separate Facebook connections if you want to change the size of the images, or other settings such as the watermark.

What size photos should I send to Facebook?

Facebook recommend uploading photos that are 720, 960 or 2048 pixels along the longest edge. Lightroom automatically converts the photos to sRGB. Facebook recompresses the photo and strips the metadata too.

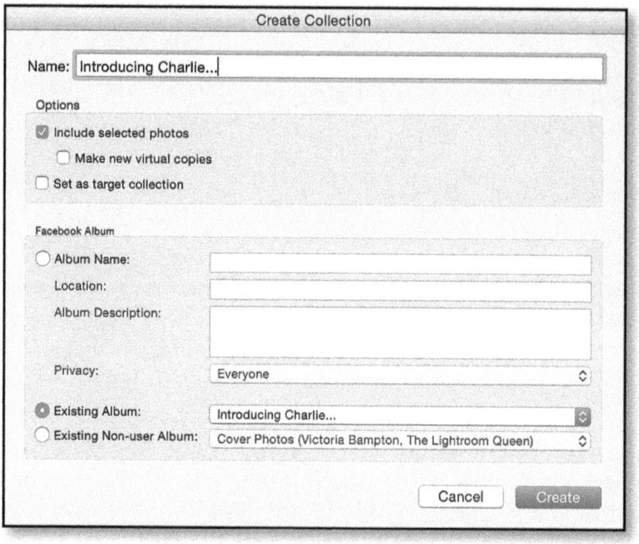

Figure 16.38 *Create additional collections by right-clicking on the existing collection, selecting Create Collection, and then deciding whether to create a new album at Facebook or photoset at Flickr, or whether to link your new Lightroom collection to an existing album/photoset.*

Flickr-specific details

The Flickr Photostream automatically appears in the Flickr section of the Publish Services panel when you create a Flickr connection. You can add photos to that collection as if it was a standard collection, or you can right-click to create another collection (except here they're called photosets to match with Flickr's name). To add additional photos to existing photosets, create a collection with precisely the same name.

Unlike Facebook, when you republish updated photos, the existing photo is updated.

The Flickr Publish Service also offers additional privacy settings at the bottom of the setup dialog. **(Figure 16.39)** These settings control who can view your photos, so they can be set to *Public* to be visible to everyone or limited to your friends and family. *Safety* controls Flickr's own content

filters, rating the photos as safe for anyone to view through to restricted which are unsuitable for some age groups, like movie parental guidance ratings.

What can I use the Hard Drive option for?

One of the most useful Publish Services is the Hard Drive service, as it manages photos exported to a folder on your computer. If you create additional collections, they become subfolders.

Any changes you make to these photos within your catalog after the initial export are tracked, allowing you to selectively export only the photos that have changed or are not yet published, without re-exporting

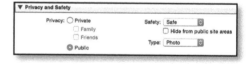

Figure 16.39 *Flickr's Privacy and Safety settings control who can view the photos.*

the whole set.

For example, maybe you like to keep photos on your iPad, so you could have an iPad collection which updates the photos in a folder ready to be transferred by iTunes next time you sync your iPad.

Perhaps you like to have your screensaver showing your latest photos, so a smart collection sending your last month's photos to your screensaver folder would be useful.

If you're using album design software, it's also a convenient way of making changes to the individual photos in Lightroom, and then being able to keep the exported versions updated in the album design.

If you need to export different sizes of photos, you'll need to set up two separate Publish Services connections as the settings are per-connection.

There are a couple of things to be aware of. If you move to a new computer, you can't change the location of the folder. Also, if you rename the files in Lightroom after the initial export, the exported photos aren't renamed to match. For a more advanced plug-in, try Jeffrey's Collection Publisher https://www.Lrq.me/friedl-colpub

Third Party Plug-ins

The built-in plug-ins are just a starting point—a sample to show what can be done with Publish Services. Third-party developers use Adobe's SDK (software development kit) to build Publish Service plug-ins to add additional photo sharing websites.

If you're using the built-in Flickr and Facebook plug-ins, consider upgrading to Jeffrey's more advanced and more regularly updated versions which can

be downloaded as donationware from https://www.Lrq.me/friedl-plugins

Third-party developers have also created Publish Service plug-ins for many other popular photo sharing websites, including Zenfolio, SmugMug and Picasa. Each of the services have slightly different limitations, dependent on the photo sharing website facilities and API, but the basic setup is the same. There's a list of the most popular Publish Service plug-ins at https://www.Lrq.me/links/plugins

Lightroom Sync

Lightroom Sync isn't technically a Publish Service, but there are similarities. It allows you to select collections to sync to the cloud, and these web galleries can then be shared publicly. Any likes or comments that friends or family add to the photos are automatically synced back to your catalog. As you edit the photos in Lightroom, your changes are updated on the web and mobile devices, and when you edit the photos on your mobile device, they're updated in your desktop catalog. See the Cloud Sync chapter starting on page 483 for more detail.

SYNCHRONIZING CHANGES

Once you've set up your Publish Service, chosen your photos, and grouped them, you're then ready to synchronize it with the other service, whether that's a website or a hard drive location.

How do I publish my photos?

We've already used the **Publish** button to publish a single collection. To publish multiple collections in one go, Ctrl-click (Windows) / Cmd-click (Mac) or Shift-click on the collections to select them all before pressing *Publish*. The photos start to upload which, depending on the dimensions chosen and your internet connection upload speed, could take a while!

To temporarily limit your upload to specific photos, hold down the Alt (Windows) / Opt (Mac) key. The *Publish* button at the bottom of the left-hand panel changes into a *Publish Selected* button which only uploads the selected photos.

Does it automatically publish changes I make to my photos?

Publish Services tracks the changes you make to the photos, but it doesn't upload the updated photos automatically. Lightroom waits for you to click on the collection and choose *Publish*, otherwise it would be constantly uploading every time you made a change to a photo and you could end up accidentally publishing photos that you're part-way through editing.

How do I update my service with the changes I've made to my photos?

Lightroom divides the Grid view into different sections—**New Photos to Publish, Deleted Photos to Remove, Modified Photos to Republish** and **Published Photos**. (Figure 16.40) To update your service with your changes, right-click on the collection and choose *Publish Now* or press the *Publish* button below. To update multiple collections in one go, select them all before pressing the *Publish* button.

If photos are in the *Deleted Photos to Remove* section, they're removed from most services. Facebook is the main exception, as Facebook's API doesn't allow you to remove photos using other programs. To remove a photo from Facebook, delete it on the Facebook website (and from Lightroom's published collection, if you don't want to republish it).

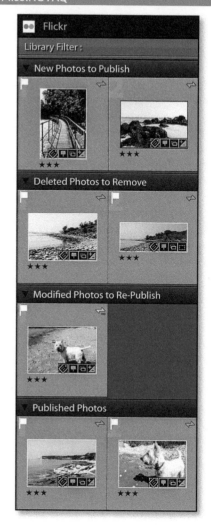

Figure 16.40 *Lightroom keeps track of the changes you make and groups the photos into New Photos to Publish, Deleted Photos to Remove, Modified Photos to Re-Publish and Published Photos.*

How do I mark photos as already published, so they don't upload again?

If you make a change to a photo, such as changing some metadata, it moves to the *Modified Photos to Re-Publish* section. If you don't want to republish it, perhaps because the change was minor or you don't want to upload it as a new photo on Facebook, right-click on the photo and choose **Mark** *as Up-To-Date* to move it back into the *Published Photos* section.

I didn't mean to remove a photo from a collection—how do I restore it?

If you accidentally remove a photo from a collection, just drag it back again. If you pressed *Publish*, nothing will have changed on the service (Flickr/Facebook, etc.) and it moves straight back into the *Published Photos* section. If the photo has been deleted from the service, it's uploaded again.

I accidentally revoked the authorization on the website—how do I fix it?

While we're on the subject of accidents, you may accidentally revoke the authorization on the website (e.g. Facebook), preventing Lightroom from publishing your photos. To fix it, right-click on the Publish Service in Lightroom and choose *Edit Settings* to access the Publishing Manager dialog. There you can log in again and re-authorize Lightroom's access.

Can I have the same account connected to multiple catalogs?

The same Flickr or Facebook account can be connected to multiple catalogs, but there are limitations. You can't easily transfer your collections/photosets between catalogs, even using Export as Catalog, and Lightroom won't know about anything that's already on the website or in your other catalog. Some advanced plug-ins, such as those created by Jeffrey Friedl, attempt to match up photos in your catalog against existing photos on the website, but it's a situation best avoided.

There is a plug-in which can transfer Publish Services information between catalogs, although it does have some limitations. You can find more information about the Lightroom Voyager plug-in at https://www.Lrq.me/alloy-lrvoyager

How do I view people's comments?

The Comments panel is designed to work with Publish Services and Lightroom CC, synchronizing comments with supported photo sharing services, so it's only available when you have a Publish collection or Synced collection selected. If someone comments on one of your photos on the website, their comments are retrieved when you next publish/sync that collection. **(Figure 16.41)**

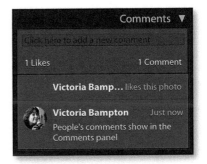

Figure 16.41 *People's comments show in the Comments panel.*

EXPORT SHORTCUTS

		Windows	Mac
Export	Export dialog	Ctrl Shift E	Cmd Shift E
	Export with Previous	Ctrl Alt Shift E	Cmd Opt Shift E
Email Photo		(no shortcut)	Cmd Shift M
Plug in Manager		Ctrl Alt Shift ,	Cmd Opt Shift ,

OUTPUT MODULES 17

Lightroom's primary focus is organizing and editing photos, but it also includes tools for creating
basic photobooks, slideshows, prints and web galleries. They're more limited than dedicated software, but they're adequate for most photographers. We'll introduce these less frequently used modules in this chapter, and then go into much greater detail in the bonus chapters at the end of the eBook formats.

BOOK MODULE

The Book module **(Figure 17.1)**, as its name suggests, assists you in creating photo books without the need for external software. Using a template-based system and drag-and-drop interface, you can create a beautiful book complete with text, and then easily upload it to Blurb for printing. Blurb are a well known photobook company who print and ship high quality books to photographers worldwide.

We'll go into detail in the Appendix (starting

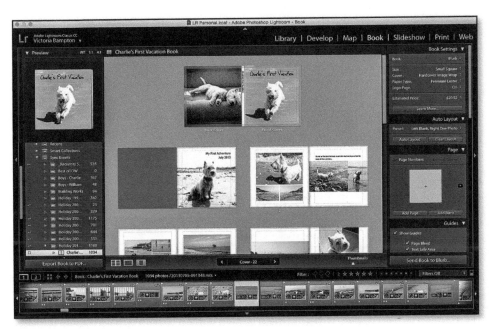

Figure 17.1 *The Book module.*

on page A-1), but let's just run through the basics so you can start to create your first photo book.

1. In Library module's Grid view, decide which photos you want to include in your book. This might be a folder or a collection of photos. If the photos are spread across multiple folders or collections, use the Quick Collection to group them together.

2. Switch to the Book module by selecting it in the Module Picker.

3. The first time you switch to the Book module, Lightroom takes the photos from your current view and creates a book using Auto Layout. This gives you opportunity to explore before starting on your first book project.

4. There are three different view modes in the Book module, all accessed using the buttons on the Toolbar. **(Figure 17.2)** (If you can't see the Toolbar, press T.)

5. Select each in turn, then return to the Multi-Page view. **(Figure 17.3)**

Multi-Page view is like the Library module Grid view, complete with the thumbnail size slider on the Toolbar.

Spread view fills the preview area with facing pages and the buttons on the Toolbar move from one page to the next. **(Figure 17.4)**

Single Page view is particularly useful when working with text, as it allows you to zoom in closer. You'll find the zoom options on the top of the Preview panel, just as they'd be on the Navigator panel in Library module.

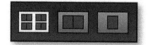

Figure 17.2 *The view modes are found on the Toolbar—Multi-Page view (left), Spread view (center) and Single Page view (right).*

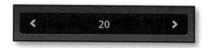

Figure 17.4 *In Spread or Single Page view, you can move between photos using the arrows on the Toolbar.*

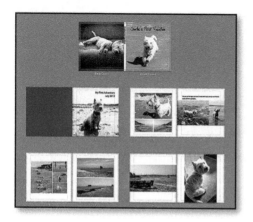

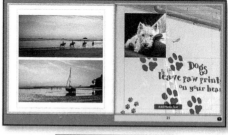

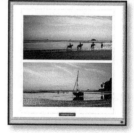

Figure 17.3 *Multi-Page view (top left), Spread view (top right), Single Page view (bottom right).*

6. In the Auto Layout panel, press *Clear Layout* to start with a clean slate.

7. At the top of the Preview Area, press the *Create Saved Book* button and give your empty book a name. **(Figure 17.5)** Saving the book before you start means you won't accidentally lose your work. The saved book appears in the Collections panel, and it remembers the photos you're using as well as the book layout.

8. Select your book size and orientation using the *Size* pop-up in the Book Settings panel and ignore the other options for now. **(Figure 17.6)**

9. The first pair of pages in the book are the front and back cover. You can change the template and photos and add text, just as

you would with a page inside the book. Let's work on the inside of the book first...

10. In the Page panel, click on the template preview to display the Page Template Picker. **(Figure 17.7)**

11. The templates are grouped into sets based on the number of photos or template style. Click on the set names at the top of the Page Template Picker to view the templates

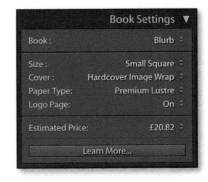

Figure 17.6 *Select your book size and orientation.*

Figure 17.5 *Save your book before you start on the design.*

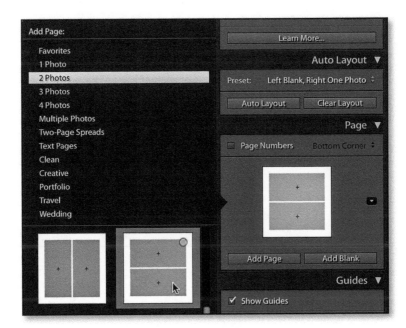

Figure 17.7 *Select a template for the page layout.*

below. The gray cells are photo cells and the lines are text cells.

When you find a template you like, click on it to add a new page.

12. Select a photo from the Filmstrip at the bottom of the screen, and drag its thumbnail onto a gray photo cell on the page in the main Preview Area. If you can't see the Filmstrip, click the black bar at the bottom of the screen.

13. Return to the Page panel and repeat the process to add additional pages and photos.

14. To change a page template, click on the page to select it, shown by a large orange border, then click on the template in the Page panel to display the Page Template Picker, and select a different template.

15. To move a photo to a different photo cell, click on it and drag to the new location.

16. Switch to Single Page view by clicking on the third icon in the Toolbar. Press T if the Toolbar is missing.

17. In the Text panel, check the *Page Text* checkbox and start typing in the text field that displays on the page. **(Figure 17.8)**

18. You can adjust the colors and design of the pages, as well as the text overlays, using the panels on the right. We'll come back to these settings in more detail in the following pages.

19. Scroll back to the beginning and click on the words *Front Cover* to highlight the cover pages, then change the template, add photos and text.

20. At the bottom of the left panel group, press the *Export Book to PDF* button to create a PDF preview of your finished book.

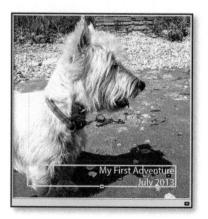

Figure 17.8 *Select Single Page view before entering text.*

You can then upload the book to Blurb for printing using the *Send Book to Blurb* button at the bottom of the right panel group.

Having learned the basics, it's time to begin fine-tuning your book. We'll consider how to use the pages and templates first, before going on to add photos, text and decoration.

SLIDESHOW MODULE

Lightroom's Slideshow module **(Figure 17.9)** isn't designed to replace specialized software, but it's an easy way to create a simple slideshow. You can design the slides yourself, add branding and text overlays to personalize your slideshow, and add audio backing tracks. The finished slideshow can be played in Lightroom, or it can be exported as video, PDF or JPEG format.

We'll go into detail in the Appendix (starting on page B-1), but let's just run through the basics so you can start to create your first slideshow.

1. In Library module's Grid view, decide which photos you want to include in your slideshow. This might be a folder or

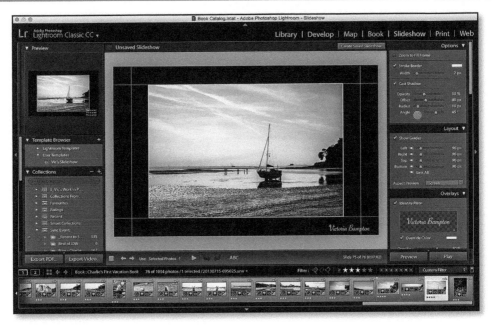

Figure 17.9 *The Slideshow module.*

a collection of photos. If the photos are spread across multiple folders or collections, use the Quick Collection to group them together.

2. Switch to the Slideshow module by selecting it in the Module Picker.

3. At the top of the Preview Area, press the *Create Saved Slideshow* button and give your slideshow a name. Saving the slideshow at the beginning means you won't accidentally lose your work. The saved slideshow appears in the Collections panel, and it remembers the photos you're using as well as the slideshow settings.

4. In the Template Browser panel on the left, click on the different templates to apply them to your slideshow until you find a design that you like.

5. You can adjust the colors and design of the slides, as well as the text overlays, using the panels on the right. We'll come back to these settings in the following pages.

6. (Optional) Add a musical backing track by going to the Music panel and press the + button. Navigate to your music on the hard drive, and choose a DRM-free MP3 or AAC music file.

7. (Optional) Check the *Sync Slides to Music* checkbox in the Playback panel to align the slide timings with the music tracks.

8. Preview your slideshow in the Preview Area by pressing the *Preview* button at the bottom of the right panel group. Press the Escape key or the square stop button on the Toolbar to stop the slideshow and adjust settings, and then preview again until you're happy.

9. Finally, you're ready to play your slideshow full screen. Press the *Play* button, which is next to the *Preview* button. It's worth doing a dry run before showing it to someone else, as Lightroom builds slide

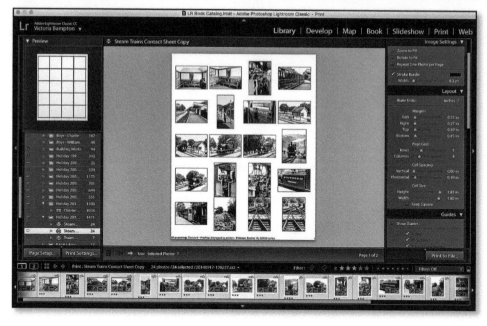

Figure 17.10 *The Print module.*

previews before playing the first time.

PRINT MODULE

Although most photos today start out as digital files, at some stage you may to want to print them. Exporting the photos and sending them to an online lab is an easy option but Lightroom also includes a Print module. **(Figure 17.10)** You can print single prints on a local printer, or build contact sheets and lay out multiple photos on a page to print on a local printer or send away.

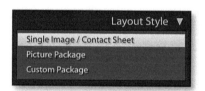

Figure 17.11 *The Layout Style panel allows you to choose whether to create a print with single or multiple photos.*

Lightroom offers three different layout options for printing, which you select in the Layout Style panel. **(Figures 17.11 & 17.12)**

Single Image/Contact Sheet is a single photo on a page, or different photos all the same size, laid out as a contact sheet grid.

Picture Package is the same photo in different sizes, laid out free-form on the page.

Custom Package is different photos in different sizes, laid out free-form on the page.

We'll cover all of the various options in the Appendix (starting on page C-1), but in this chapter, we'll run through the basics of setting up each style of print and how to print your design.

How do I create a 4" x 6" borderless print?

First, let's create a simple 4"x6" borderless

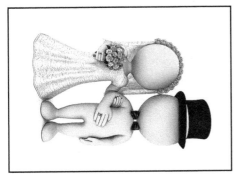

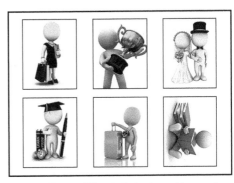

Single Image - one photo per page.   *Contact Sheet - different photos in a grid, same size.*

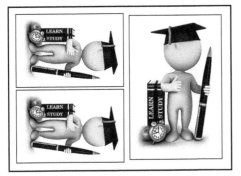

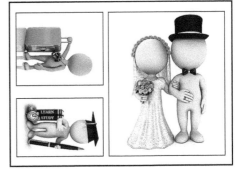

Picture package - same photo, different sizes.   *Custom Package - different photos, different sizes.*

Figure 17.12 *There are multiple different layout styles.*

print (assuming your printer can print borderless!). If you're just sending individual photos to an online or local lab to be printed, it's quicker to turn back to the Export chapter (starting on page 351) and export JPEGs instead.

1. Select the photo or photos you want to print, and then switch to the Print module using the Module Picker at the top of the screen.

2. At the bottom of the left panel group, click the *Page Setup* button to display your printer's dialog. (The options vary depending on the operating system and printer.)

3. Select your paper size, for example, if you're using 4x6 borderless paper, you'll need to select the 4" x 6" borderless setting.

Close the *Page* Setup dialog. **(Figure 17.13)**

4. In the Layout Style panel at the top of the right panel group, select *Single Image/ Contact Sheet.*

5. In the Image Settings panel, check *Zoom to Fill* and *Rotate to Fit.* This fills the cell with the photo.

6. In the Layout panel, set all the margins to 0 for borderless printing. If they won't go down to 0, the Page Setup isn't set to borderless or your printer can't print

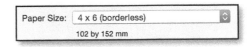

Figure 17.13 *Set the paper size to 4" x 6" borderless in the Page Setup dialog.*

borderless, in which case you'll need to use a larger piece of paper and cut it down after printing.

7. Still in the Layout panel, set the *Rows* and *Columns* sliders to 1 to place a single photo on the page, and set the *Cell Size* to 6x4 for a 6" x 4" print. **(Figure 17.14)**

8. In the Toolbar underneath the preview, choose *Selected Photos* from the *Use* pop-up to print the selected photo(s) or *All Filmstrip Photos* to print all of them. Try a single print to double check your settings before

printing a large number of photos.

How do I print it?

Once you've finished designing your layout, whether that's a single print or a complex design, it's time to print.

1. Scroll down to the Print Job panel. **(Figure 17.15)** As a default, set the *Print Resolution* field to 360ppi for Epson or 300ppi for Canon/HP.

2. Enable the *Print Sharpening* checkbox, selecting the amount in the first pop-up (*Low*, *Standard* or *High*) and the paper type (*Glossy/Matte*) in the second pop-up. If in doubt, select *Standard Glossy*.

3. If you have a profile for your printer,

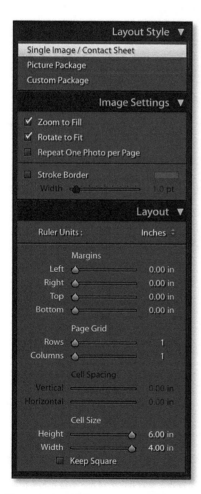

Figure 17.14 *These are layout settings you'll need to create a 4"x6" borderless print.*

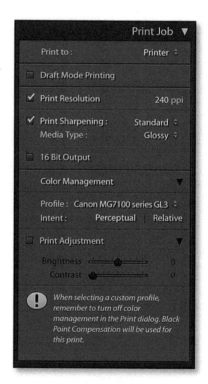

Figure 17.15 *Select the Resolution, Sharpening and Color Profile for the print in the Print Job panel.*

select *Other* from the *Color Management Profile* pop-up and choose the profile. Press *OK* and select the profile in the pop-up. If you don't have a profile, select *Managed by Printer* so that the printer cares for the color management.

4. Press the *Printer* button to view the Print dialog. Like the Page Setup dialog, this dialog varies depending on the operating system and printer driver. If you're using a Mac, you may need to press the *Show Details* button to access the printer driver options. **(Figure 17.16)**

Select your paper type, quality settings and any other settings specific to your printer driver. (If these options aren't available, ensure that you've installed the printer driver direct from the manufacturer rather than the default driver provided by the operating system.) If you've selected a profile in the *Color Management Profile* pop-up, select *No Color Adjustment* or *ColorSync* in the printer dialog.

5. Finally, press *Print* and wait with bated breath!

How do I create a contact sheet?

A contact sheet is a selection of photos laid out as a grid, often with a filename underneath. **(Figure 17.17)** They're often used by photographers to help clients select their photos or as an index page in an album. Others use contact sheets to check their prints will turn out as expected, without wasting ink on full size test prints.

1. In Library module's Grid view, decide which photos you want to include in your contact sheet. This might be a folder or a collection of photos. If the photos are spread across multiple folders or collections, use the Quick Collection to group them.

2. Switch to the Print module using the Module Picker at the top of the screen.

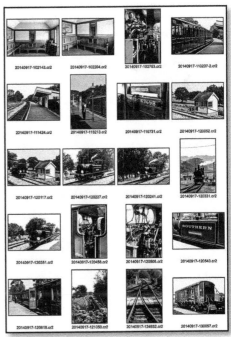

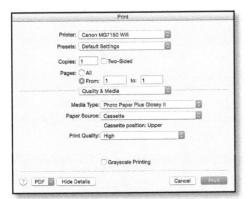

Figure 17.16 After setting up the print layout in Lightroom, press the Printer button and select the correct paper and quality settings.

Figure 17.17 Contact sheets were traditionally used for selecting the best photos, but are still useful for test prints today.

3. In the Toolbar underneath the preview, choose *All Filmstrip Photos* from the *Use* pop-up.

4. At the bottom of the left panel group, press the *Page Setup* button and select your paper size (e.g. Letter or A4 size) in the printer dialog before returning to Lightroom.

5. In the Layout Style panel at the top of the right panel group, select *Single Image/ Contact Sheet*.

6. In the Layout panel, choose the numbers of rows and columns for your contact sheet using the *Page Grid* sliders, and adjust the spacing between the cells using the *Cell Spacing* sliders. As you adjust the slider, the preview updates live. **(Figure 17.18)**

7. If you have a mixture of horizontal and vertical photos, toggle the *Rotate to Fit* checkbox in the Image Settings panel to enable or disable rotation.

8. To display the filename beneath each photo thumbnail, check *Photo Info* in the Page panel and select *Filename* in the pop-up to the right.

9. Then turn back to page 388 to send it to your printer.

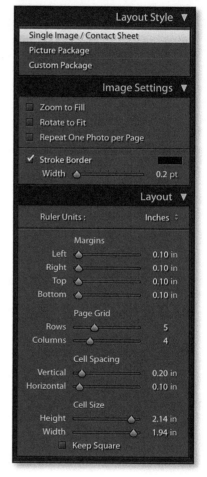

Figure 17.18 *Select your page layout settings in the right panel group in the Print module. These are the settings for a contact sheet.*

How do I create a picture package?

The Picture Package enables you to print multiple versions of the same photo in varying sizes on the same piece of paper, for example, printing two small copies for your wallet, and a larger copy for a frame.

1. Select the photo, and then switch to the Print module using the Module Picker at the top of the screen.

2. In the Toolbar underneath the preview, choose *Selected Photos* from the *Use* pop-up.

3. At the bottom of the left panel group, press the *Page Setup* button and select your paper size (e.g. Letter or A4 size) in the printer dialog before returning to Lightroom.

4. In the Layout Style panel, select *Picture Package*.

5. In the Ruler, Grid & Guides panel, select cm or inches from the *Ruler Units* pop-up, depending on your preference.

6. Click a button in the Cells panel to add a cell of that size, for example, press the 4x6 button to add a 4" x 6" cell to the page. Repeat to add additional photo cells. To delete a cell, click on it and then press the Delete key. Press *Clear Layout* if you want to start again. **(Figure 17.19)**

7. Once you've added the cells, click the *Auto Layout* button to automatically arrange the cells on the page or drag and drop them into a layout that you like.

8. In the Image Settings panel, check the *Zoom to Fill* and *Rotate to Fit* checkboxes to fill the cells you've created.

9. Turn back to page 388 to send your design to your printer.

How do I create a custom package?

The Custom Package enables you to print any photos in a mixture of sizes to avoid wasting paper, so you have two choices: either you place the cells first and then drop the photos into those cells, or you drop the photos directly onto the page and their cells are automatically created, ready for you to resize. In this example, we'll drop the photos onto the page.

1. In Library module's Grid view, decide which photos you want to include in your design. This might be a folder or a collection of photos. If the photos are spread across multiple folders or collections, use the Quick Collection to group them for easy access.

2. Switch to the Print module using the Module Picker at the top of the screen.

3. In the Layout Style panel, select *Custom Package*.

4. Select a photo in the Filmstrip, drag it to the page and drop it.

5. Using the squares in the corners of the bounding box, adjust the size of the cell. To move it, click in the center of the cell and drag it. **(Figure 17.20)**

6. To add an additional photo, drag it from the Filmstrip and drop it on a blank area of the page. If you drop a new photo on an existing cell, the photo is replaced. To delete a cell, click to select it (shown by the bounding box) and press the Delete key.

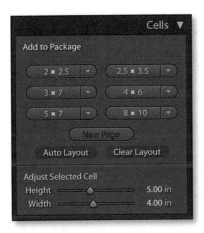

Figure 17.19 *Add cells to the page using the Cells panel.*

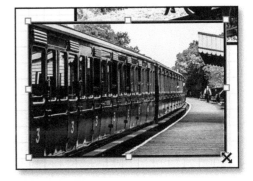

Figure 17.20 *Drag the bounding box handles to resize the cells and drag the center of the cell to arrange the cells on the page.*

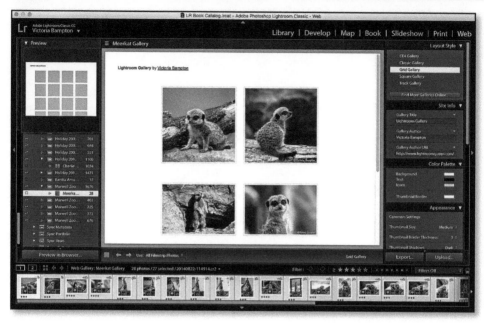

Figure 17.21 *The Web module.*

7. Turn back to page 388 to send your design to your printer.

WEB MODULE

The Web module **(Figure 17.21)** makes it easy to create static galleries. Lightroom offers multiple ways of publishing your photos online, and it can be difficult to figure out which is best suited to your needs. There are, of course, a huge number of alternative photo sharing websites, and today, they're generally a better option.

However, if you're looking for a simple static web gallery, let's just run through the basics. We'll cover all of the various options in the Appendix (starting on page D-1).

1. In Library module's Grid view, decide which photos you want to include in your web gallery. This might be a folder or a collection of photos. If the photos are spread across multiple folders or collections,

use the Quick Collection to group them together.

2. Switch to the Web module by selecting it in the Module Picker.

3. At the top of the Preview Area, press the *Create Saved Web Gallery* button and give your gallery a name. Saving the web gallery at the beginning means you won't accidentally lose your work. The saved web gallery appears in the Collections panel, and it remembers the photos you're using as well as the gallery settings.

4. In the Template Browser panel on the left, click on the different templates to select a design (or float over them to preview in the Preview panel above). Lightroom ships with four different web gallery styles. **(Figure 17.22)**

5. (Optional) You can adjust the colors and design of the gallery, as well as the text overlays, using the panels on the right. We'll

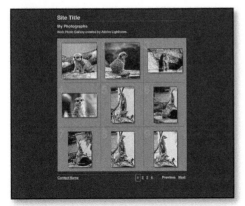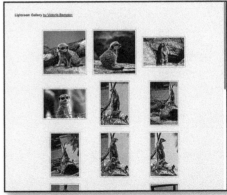

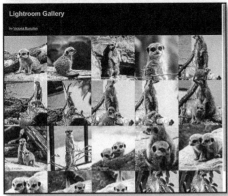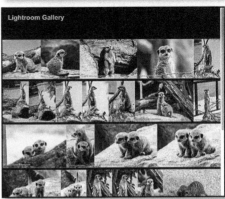

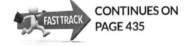

Figure 17.22 *There are four default layouts: Classic (top left), Grid (top right), Square (bottom left) and Track (bottom right).*

come back to these settings in the following pages.

If you customize any of the settings, click + button on Template Browser to save your design as a new template. This allows you to apply the same settings to other groups of photos.

6. Once you're happy with the preview in the Web module, click *Preview in Browser* at the bottom of the left panel group to open it in your default web browser.

7. Finally, to export your web gallery, click the *Export* button at the bottom of the right panel group. This saves the web gallery on your hard drive, ready to upload to your website using FTP software (such as FileZilla).

It's also possible to upload the gallery directly from Lightroom by entering the FTP server details in the Upload Settings panel, however the built-in FTP is not as robust as dedicated FTP software.

FASTTRACK CONTINUES ON PAGE 435

MULTIPLE COMPUTERS OR CATALOGS

18

At the beginning of the book, we talked about creating a database called a catalog. The catalog contains records of all the photos you've imported, plus metadata and other settings you've applied to these photos in Lightroom.

In this chapter, we'll consider how to look after that catalog, then how to move your Lightroom files, whether that's on the same computer or to a new computer. We'll also explore the options for working on multiple computers, and the pros and cons of using more than one catalog.

Some people ask whether they have to use a catalog. Why not just browse the photos on the hard drive instead? Quite simply, many of Lightroom's features are dependent on its database backbone, and wouldn't be possible using a simple file browser. For example, Lightroom can create virtual copies, store extensive edit history for each image, and track information on settings for books, slideshows, prints and web galleries and their associated photos, all of which depend on the database. Searching image metadata (EXIF, keywords, etc.) is much faster as a result of the database, and Lightroom can also search for photos that are offline, as well as those currently accessible.

MANAGING CATALOGS

Let's start off with some catalog basics—finding, renaming and maintaining your catalog.

How do I find my catalog on the hard drive?

When you opened Lightroom the very first time, using the information in the Before You Start section (page 11), Lightroom created a catalog to store the information about your photos.

By default, Lightroom places the catalog in your user account *Pictures* folder and calls it *Lightroom Catalog.lrcat*, but you may have chosen a different name or location.

If you don't remember where you stored your catalog, go to *Edit menu* (Windows) / *Lightroom menu* (Mac) > *Catalog Settings*. The name and location of your open catalog is displayed on the *General* tab of the Catalog Settings dialog. Press the *Show* button to open an Explorer (Windows) / Finder (Mac) window at that location.

If you can't open Lightroom, perhaps due to catalog corruption, then you'll need to use your operating system's search facility to search for files with a *.lrcat file extension (that's LRCAT).

What do the catalog files contain?

When you view the catalog location in your file browser, you'll note there are a variety of different Lightroom files. **(Figure 18.1)**

*.lrcat is the catalog (SQLite database) which holds all of your settings. This stands for LightRoom CATalog. (Version 1.0 catalogs used *.lrdb and prerelease beta catalogs were *.aglib files.) The catalog contains a note of where the images are stored on the hard drive plus other metadata—that's information about the photos, including the EXIF data from the camera, any IPTC data, keywords and other metadata you add in Lightroom, any Develop changes you make in Lightroom, and any book, print, slideshow and web gallery settings, all of which are stored as text records. **(Figure 18.2)**

*Previews.lrdata and ***Smart Previews. lrdata** contain your standard and smart previews. On Windows, the individual previews are contained in a hierarchy of folders and subfolders, and on a Mac, they're wrapped up in a package file. The individual previews inside the lrdata folder/ file are *.lrprev files for standard previews, and *.dng files for smart previews.

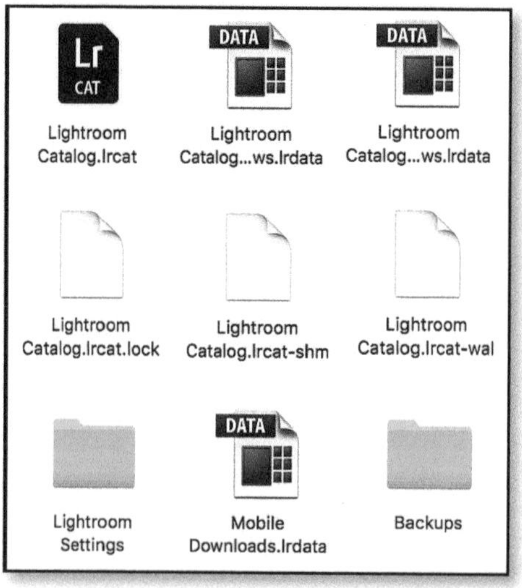

If Lightroom is open, you may have a couple of additional files:

*.lrcat.lock is a lock file that is created whenever you open the catalog. It protects the database from being corrupted by multiple users attempting to use it at the same time. If Lightroom is closed and the lock file remains, you can safely delete it. It can sometimes get left behind if Lightroom crashes, and may prevent you from opening the catalog again.

*.lrcat-shm and *.lrcat-wal files contain blocks of data that are in the middle of being written to the catalog. They should automatically disappear when you close Lightroom, but if Lightroom quits abnormally, they'll get removed at the next startup.

Additional temporary files may sometimes appear, such as Temporary Import Data.db-journal. If they're still there after closing Lightroom, and they're more than a few days old, you can safely delete them.

There may also be a few folders created by Lightroom with the catalog:

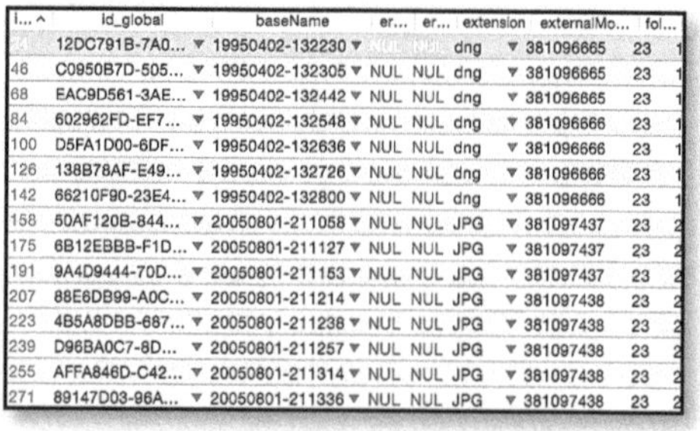

Figure 18.1 *Lightroom uses a few different files and folders, in addition to the main catalog file.*

Figure 18.2 *A Lightroom catalog is a SQLite database.*

Images folders may contain some or all of your photos. They're stored on your hard drives as normal image files, so they may be stored anywhere, but the default Destination folder selected in the Import dialog is an Images folder next to the catalog.

Backups folder may contain catalog backups, if you haven't changed the default backup location.

Lightroom Settings folder may contain some of your presets if you have *Store Presets with Catalog* checked in the Preferences dialog.

How much space does Lightroom's catalog take up on my hard drive?

That's a long list of files, so you may wonder how much space they take up on your hard drive. You can check this using the same Catalog Settings dialog. **(Figure 18.3)**

The catalog file size is listed under the *General* tab. The size depends on the number of photos and the amount of data stored for each photo. For example, local adjustments, spot healing and large numbers of history states increase the catalog size significantly.

Preview and Smart Preview cache sizes are noted under the *File Handling* tab.

Standard Preview size depends on the image content and your preview size and quality settings, as well as the presence of any 1:1 previews. Smart Previews also vary depending on the image content, averaging 0.5-1.5 MB each regardless of the original raw file size.

As a guide, a catalog that contains 25000 photos may be:

Catalog—1 GB (with zipped backups of around 250 MB)

Previews (1680px, medium quality, discard 1:1 after 1 day)—16 GB

Smart Previews—25 GB

Original Files—300 GB

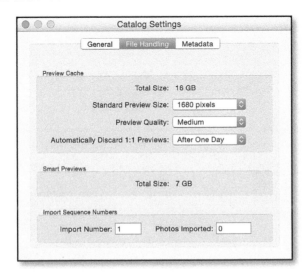

Figure 18.3 *In the Catalog Settings dialog, you can check how much space your catalog and previews are using.*

How do I rename my catalog?

Lightroom doesn't offer a catalog renaming tool, but you can rename the catalog in Explorer (Windows) / Finder (Mac) as if you were renaming any other file. Just make sure you close Lightroom first.

When you rename the catalog file, you should also rename the preview folders/files to match. For example:

Lightroom Catalog.lrcat > New Name.lrcat

Lightroom Catalog Previews.lrdata > New Name Previews.lrdata

Lightroom Catalog Smart Previews.lrdata > New Name Smart Previews.lrdata

After renaming, double-click on the catalog file (*.lrcat) to open it into Lightroom.

If you don't rename the previews correctly, Lightroom simply recreates them all. There's no harm done except for the time involved. If you have offline files, previews for these photos won't be recreated until they're next online. If this happens, delete the old previews file to regain the drive space once your previews have been recreated.

After opening the renamed catalog, go to *Preferences > General > Default Catalog pop-up* and ensure the correct catalog is selected.

Do I need to do any regular maintenance?

We've already discussed how important the catalog is, so how do you look after it? Under the *File menu*, the **Optimize Catalog** command checks through your catalog, reorganizing your database to make it run faster and more smoothly. **(Figure 18.4)**

For the more technically minded, over the course of time, with many imports and deletes, the data can become fragmented and spread across the whole database, making Lightroom jump around to find the information it needs. *Optimize Catalog* runs a SQLite VACUUM command to sort it all back into the correct order, bringing it back up to speed.

It's worth running the catalog optimization whenever you've made significant database changes, such as removing or importing a large number of photos, or any time you feel that Lightroom has slowed down.

There's also a checkbox in the Back Up Catalog dialog to automatically run the optimization each time you back up your catalog.

And most importantly, don't forget to back up regularly!

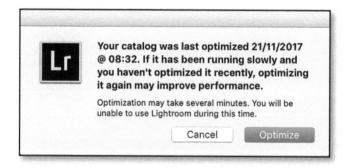

Figure 18.4 *Catalog optimization 'tidies up' to make Lightroom run faster.*

MOVING LIGHTROOM

The time may come when you run out of space on your hard drive and need to move Lightroom to a new home on a bigger hard drive, or you may need to move to a new computer or reinstall your operating system. Lightroom uses files in so many different locations, the move may look daunting at first, but it's surprisingly straightforward if you follow my step by step instructions carefully.

We'll cover four different scenarios:

- Moving just the catalog to a new location.

- Moving just the photos to a new location.

- Moving the catalog and the photos to a new location.

- Moving to a completely new computer or reinstalling the operating system.

How do I move only my catalog to another hard drive, leaving the photos where they are?

If only your catalog is moving, and the photos are remaining in their existing locations, the process is very simple:

1. Quit Lightroom.

2. Move your catalog (and any extra files such as the previews) to the new location using Explorer (Windows) / Finder (Mac). It's usually easiest to move the entire folder containing your catalog and other related files.

3. Double click on the catalog (*.lrcat file) to open it. After opening the catalog at its new location, go to *Preferences > General > Default Catalog pop-up* and ensure the correct catalog is selected.

As none of the photos moved, you can continue working without further issues. When the backup next runs, double check the location of the backups. (Instructions on page 54.)

How do I move only my photos to another hard drive, leaving the catalog where it is?

If you need to move photos to another hard drive, perhaps because you've outgrown your existing hard drive, there are two main options. As a rule of thumb, you can use option two for moving a few photos/folders, but option one is safer when moving larger numbers of photos.

Option One—move in Explorer/Finder and update Lightroom's links

1. Follow the instructions in the Library chapter (page 107) to show the folder hierarchy. This makes it easy to relink the folders/files that are marked as missing in the process.

2. Close Lightroom and use Explorer (Windows) / Finder (Mac) to copy the folders/files to the new drive.

Most file corruption happens while moving/copying photos between hard drives. To ensure that the files gets to the new drive safely, I prefer to use file synchronization or other software with byte-for-byte/checksum verification. Consider using:

TeraCopy https://www.Lrq.me/teracopy

Vice Versa (Windows)
https://www.Lrq.me/viceversa

Chronosync (Mac)
https://www.Lrq.me/chronosync

3. When the copy completes, rename the original folder (the one on the old hard drive) using Explorer (Windows) / Finder (Mac), or disconnect the old hard drive. This allows you to check everything is working correctly before deleting the files from the original location.

4. Open Lightroom and right-click on the parent folder. Select *Find Missing Folder* or *Update Folder Location* from the list, depending on which option is available. Navigate to the new location and press *Select Folder* (Windows) / *Choose* (Mac). The folder disappears from the old volume (drive) in the Folders panel and reappears under the new volume bar.

Don't Re-import! Using these instructions to update the location in the catalog is essential. Don't import the photos at the new location, or use *Synchronize Folder* to update the folder references, as you'll lose all of the work you've done in Lightroom.

5. If you have more than one parent folder, repeat the process for any other parent folders until the question marks have disappeared from all the folders.

6. Once you've confirmed that all the photos are available for editing within Lightroom, you can safely detach the old hard drive or delete the files from their original location using Explorer (Windows) / Finder (Mac).

Option Two—move the photos using Lightroom's Folders panel

1. If you can't see the new folder in the Folders panel, go to *Library menu > New Folder*. Navigate to the new location and create a new folder, or select an existing folder where you plan to place the photos. (Existing folders can only be selected if they're empty, or by importing one of the photos in that folder.)

2. Within the Folders panel, drag the folders to their new location. One warning—don't press the X in the Activity Center to cancel this move. There have been (rare!) reports of problems caused by canceling the transfer, so it's best to let it complete uninterrupted.

3. Check that the entire folder contents have copied correctly before deleting the originals. If you drag individual photos to the new location, rather than whole folders, remember that files that aren't currently in the catalog (e.g. text files) won't be copied as Lightroom doesn't know that they exist.

How do I archive photos to offline hard drives?

As your collection of photos grows, your working hard drives may eventually start to overflow, but Lightroom can continue to track photos held in offline storage. The easiest solutions for the working copy of your offline archives are external hard drives or NAS units, as they hold large amounts of data. Optical media (DVD/Blu-ray) can be used, but they have a comparatively short lifespan and limited space.

If you move the photos to offline storage using the instructions in the previous question, the archived photos remain referenced in your main catalog. They are marked as missing when the drive is offline, but you can search through those offline photos along with the rest of your current photos, and Lightroom remembers where the photos are stored.

Ensure you have standard previews before you disconnect the hard drive, so you can still browse with the photos offline. To access the original file, perhaps to export a copy, plug that drive back into the computer and carry on working as normal.

How do I move my complete catalog & photos to another hard drive on the same computer?

If you need to move both the catalog and the photos to a new hard drive, use the same steps as moving each individually (instructions on previous pages).

There's another option which has been recommended in the past, which involves using Export as Catalog to create a new catalog and duplicate photos on the other hard drive, and then deleting the existing catalog and photos. There are, however, a few risks in using that option, as not all data is included when using Export as Catalog, so I can no longer recommend it.

Export as Catalog is better suited to exporting work temporarily to another computer and then importing back into the main catalog later, rather than moving whole catalogs. We'll come back to Export as Catalog in more detail later in the chapter on page 419.

How do I move my catalog, photos and other Lightroom files to a new computer?

Moving Lightroom to a new computer can appear daunting at first, especially if you're moving cross-platform, but rest assured, it's straightforward as long as you follow these simple steps.

Note that these instructions are for a one-way move, for example, moving from an old computer to a new one, or reinstalling the operating system. Working on multiple computers, for example, transferring between a desktop and a laptop, requires a slightly different process that we'll consider in the next section (page 404).

1. Preparation – set up your folder hierarchy

It's a good idea to make sure that Lightroom's Folders panel shows a tidy hierarchy before you back up the catalog. You may need relink the files if the relative folder location, or the drive letter for an external drive, changes as a result of the move. Doing so using a hierarchy (right) is much easier than a flat list of folders (left). **(Figure 18.5)** There are instructions on

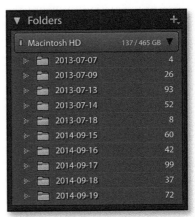

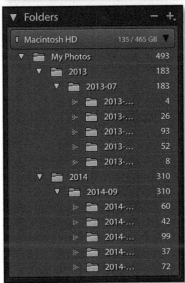

Figure 18.5 *A flat folder list (top) is much harder to reconnect compared with a folder hierarchy (bottom).*

setting up a folder hierarchy starting on page 107. It's especially important if you're moving to a different operating system.

2. Check your backups

Next, you need to make sure that all the essentials are backed up—the catalogs, photos, preferences, presets, profiles, defaults, plug-ins and any other related files. Turn back to the backup chapter for a full list of all the Lightroom files you need to include in your backups (page 61). If you're wiping the hard drive in the process, rather than running both machines at the same time, it's even more important to make sure that you don't miss anything.

3. Install Lightroom on the new machine

Once everything's safely backed up, we're ready to set Lightroom up on the new computer. Turn back to the installation instructions for more details (page 9).

It's possible to upgrade Lightroom at the same time as transferring to a new computer, for example, from Lightroom 5 on the old computer to Lightroom CC on the new one. I would, however, suggest that you do the upgrade and transfer as separate processes to minimize the risk of mistakes.

For example, either install Lightroom Classic on the old machine, allow it to upgrade the catalog, check everything's working

---

CROSS-PLATFORM MOVE

The process of moving your catalog cross-platform is exactly the same as moving to a new machine of the same platform. If you're transferring between platforms, it's even more important that you set Lightroom to show the folder hierarchy (step 1) to make it easy to relink missing files, as Windows works with drive letters and macOS works with drive names.

If you're moving from Windows to Mac or vice versa, some of the file locations are different, especially for preferences and presets. The locations of those files on both platforms are listed in the Backup chapter on page 61.

The subscription is cross-platform, so Lightroom will work on both Windows and Mac, although there are separate downloads for the Windows and Mac versions.

There's just one other main thing to look out for if you're moving cross-platform—the Mac OS can read Windows NTFS formatted drives, but can't write to them, and Windows can't read or write to Mac HFS/APFS formatted drives. If you're going to use your external drives with a different operating system, you may need to reformat them at some stage, after having copied the data off safely to another drive, of course.

If you're constantly moving between Mac and Windows, consider formatting transfer drives as exFAT, or using additional software such as NTFS for Mac (https://www.Lrq. me/ntfsmac) that allow either operating system to have read/write access regardless of drive format, but be aware that it may be slower than using a native drive format.

as expected and then move to the new computer, or install Lightroom 5 on the new computer, follow all of the instructions to move to the new computer and check everything's working, and then install Lightroom Classic and allow it to upgrade the catalog.

4. Transfer the files

Transfer the files to the new computer—the catalog, the photos, preferences and so forth—and if possible, place them in the same locations as they were on the old computer. Most people copy the files to an external hard drive for the transfer, or copy them over a wired network connection.

5. Open the catalog on the new computer

Now it's time to open the catalog, which you've already transferred. Double-click on the *.lrcat catalog file to open it, or hold down Ctrl (Windows) / Opt (Mac) while launching Lightroom to show the Select Catalog dialog and navigate to the catalog.

6. Relink any missing files

You might find that there are question marks all over the folders **(Figure 18.6)** or there are rectangular icons containing exclamation points in the corners of the thumbnails. These warnings appear if the

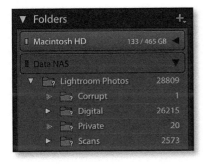

Figure 18.6   *The hard drive or photos may be marked as missing.*

original photos can no longer be found at the previous known location. STOP! Don't be tempted to remove the missing photos and re-import, or try to synchronize a folder, and don't try to relocate individual files by clicking on a thumbnail icon, as you'll create a bigger job.

Instead, right-click on the parent folder that we created in step 1, and choose *Find Missing Folder* from the context-sensitive menu, and navigate to the new location of that folder. Relocate any other top level folders (you should have one for each drive), until all the photos are online. There are more details on reconnecting missing files starting on page 435. If you get stuck at this stage, please ask and I'll be pleased to help.

7. Check your preferences and presets

Double check that all of your presets and templates appear correctly, for example, all of your Develop presets are available in the Develop module, to confirm that you copied all the files correctly. If they don't show up, you may need to toggle the *Preferences > Presets > Store presets with this catalog* checkbox. (See page 425 for more detail.)

8. Reload any disabled plug-ins

Finally, you might find your plug-ins need reloading as the locations may have changed in the move. Go to *File menu > Plug-in Manager* and check whether all the plug-ins

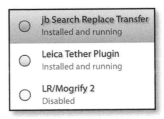

Figure 18.7   *Plug-ins are marked with a green circle if they're enabled. Yellow, red or gray circles warn of problems with the plug-in.*

have green circles. **(Figure 18.7)** If any plug-ins are incorrectly loaded or missing, add them again at their new locations. Turn back to the Before You Start chapter for a refresher (page 5).

That's it! It's as simple as that. The main things to remember are to transfer all the applicable files onto the new computer, don't try importing anything, don't use Synchronize Folder, and ideally don't wipe the old machine until you've checked that everything's up and running.

WORKING WITH MULTIPLE MACHINES

Many photographers today are working between multiple computers, for example, a laptop and a desktop.

You can have Lightroom activated on two computers at a time, for example, your desktop and your laptop. It can be installed on additional machines, but you would need to deactivate and reactivate when switching machines. Using the same catalog on multiple computers is a little trickier, so let's investigate...

Can I use Lightroom over a network?

Lightroom doesn't have network or multi-user capabilities, other than accessing photos that are stored on a network drive. The SQLite database format that Lightroom uses isn't well suited to being accessed across a network; the file would be too easily corrupted beyond repair by something as simple as the network connection dropping at the wrong moment. That's not just an oversight—SQLite was chosen for its other benefits, such as the simplicity for the user, cost, and most importantly, speed of access.

There are some 'solutions' posted on the web, suggesting that it's possible to trick Lightroom's network blocking by using a subst command on Windows or mounting a disc image stored on a network drive on a Mac. Take care! The network blocking is there for good reason. SQLite, which is the database used for Lightroom's catalog, depends on a guarantee from the operating system that what it thinks has been written to disk has actually been written to disk. Network volumes are notorious for lying about that to improve perceived performance. Adobe strongly discourages these workarounds because they can corrupt your catalog beyond repair, so I can't recommend it either. It's a risky hack.

You could, of course, store your catalog on a NAS and copy it to a local drive every time you want to work on it, and then copy it back again. The process can be automated using File Synchronization software, but it's still a lot of data to constantly move around the network. Alternatively, using software like Dropbox to keep the same catalog on multiple machines can work well, and although it's not supported by Adobe, it doesn't attempt to circumvent any of Lightroom's features, so the risks are limited.

The photos can be on your NAS or other network drive, but if you're putting the photos on your NAS, be aware that NAS file access can be slower than internal or even external drives, depending on the connection speed, so this may slow Lightroom down too.

If I can't use Lightroom over a network, how can I use it on multiple computers?

There are solutions, however. For example, Lightroom allows you to split and merge catalogs to move parts of catalogs easily between computers, and Lightroom can work with offline photos on the road too.

If you need to work on multiple machines or even with multiple users, there are many different options. We're going on concentrate on six primary options, each with their own variations. Later in the section, on page 425, we'll also look at ways of keeping your presets up to date on each computer.

The simplest option gives you partial access to your catalog via the Lightroom Cloud:

Lightroom Sync—sync your photos from your 'main' computer to the cloud, then access them using the new simpler Lightroom CC cloud-native apps on other computers or mobile devices or using a web browser.

The next three options give you access to your entire catalog and the full power of Lightroom Classic on each machine, with or without the image files.

Self-Contained—place your catalog and photos on an external hard drive, and plug it into whichever machine you're going to use at the time.

Semi-Portable—place your catalog and previews on an external drive and plug it into whichever machine you're going to use at the time, but the photos remain on the main computer or on network accessible storage.

Copy/Sync (e.g. Dropbox)—copy your catalog back and forth, using synchronization software such as Dropbox to keep both copies updated.

The final two options involve splitting and merging catalogs, so they're a little more complicated.

Import from a Temporary Catalog—create a new catalog for the photos on the secondary machine and merge them back into the primary machine.

Split and Merge—use one computer as a base (usually the desktop) and export chunks of work out as a smaller catalog out for use on the secondary computer (usually the laptop), then merge it back into the primary catalog on your return.

Lightroom CC Cloud Sync

Summary: Using the new Lightroom CC cloud-native app on your secondary computer or mobile devices, you can view your photos, flag & star them, add titles and captions, manage collections, search for photos using image-analysis, do a wide range of Develop edits, as well as uploading photos. (Details are correct at the time of writing but change frequently!) **(Figure 18.8)**

For whom: You primarily work on a single machine, where you need all of the features that Lightroom Classic offers, but sometimes you need to view/edit your photos or add new photos from another computer or mobile device.

Difficulty Rating: 1/4

Pros:

• Very easy to set up – just select the collections to sync.

• There's nothing to worry about when you get back to your main computer as the changes automatically sync.

• Works well if multiple people need access to the photos, even at the same time.

Cons:

• Requires an internet connection, both

Sample "Lightroom CC Cloud Sync" Workflow

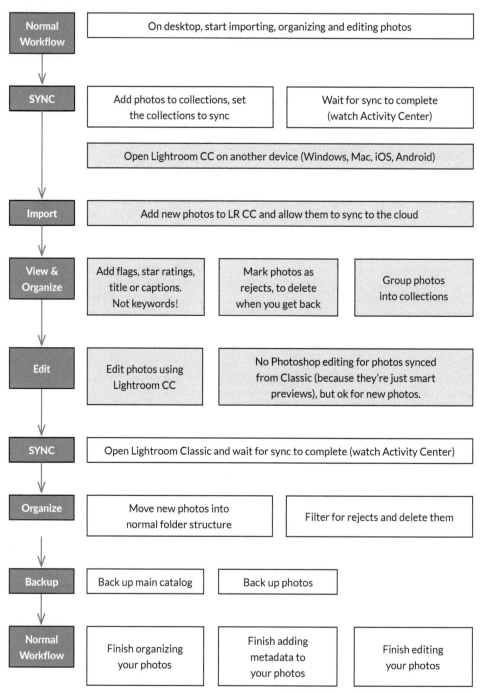

Figure 18.8 *Lightroom Sync is an easy way of accessing your photos on other devices and doing limited edits, without having to import and export catalogs.*

for the initial upload and while downloading on the other computer. If new photos are added to the Lightroom CC apps, these are uploaded to the cloud as full resolution files, so a fast connection and unlimited bandwidth are beneficial.

• Features in Lightroom CC are more limited than Lightroom Classic.

• Keywords, stacks, album folders and a growing list of features don't sync back to Lightroom Classic, although Develop edits are fully compatible. (See the Cloud Sync chapter for full details, starting on page 483.)

• Lightroom CC may not have access to full resolution original photos, although lower resolution smart previews work fine for most editing.

• Only one Lightroom Classic catalog can be synced with the cloud.

Storage—Catalog: Stays on your main computer, synced to the cloud.

Storage—Photos: Stay on your main computer, synced to the cloud as smart previews.

Storage—Presets: Stay on your main computer. Can be copied to Lightroom CC Windows/Mac but not iOS/Android at the time of writing.

Other Considerations:

• Think about what you'll actually need to do on the other computer, and whether Lightroom CC has all the features you need. To double check, see https://www.Lrq. me/lightroom-cc-vs-classic-features/ If it doesn't fill your needs yet, check back again regularly, as they're constantly adding new features.

• If you're allowing someone else access to your photos using this method (by giving them your login details), consider how much of a mess they could make of your existing ratings and edits!

Setup Instructions:

1. In Lightroom Classic on the primary machine, enable sync in the Activity Center.

2. Add the photos to Collections (not Smart Collections), and enable Sync for the collections. (You could simply drag them to the *All Synced Photographs* collection in the Catalog panel, but they're more easily managed when broken down into smaller groups.)

3. Wait for the photos to upload. You can check the status in the Activity Center.

4. Specify a local folder for originals added using Lightroom CC (page 491).

Switching Computers:

1. Open Lightroom CC on another computer or mobile device, and wait for it to sync.

2. Work on the photos in Lightroom CC, and add any new photos. Lightroom CC uploads changes whenever it has an internet connection.

3. When you return to your primary machine, open Lightroom and simply wait for Lightroom to sync the changes and download new photos. Again, you can watch the progress in the Activity Center.

4. Filter for rejected photos in Lightroom Classic and delete them if desired. This will also delete them from the cloud sync (whereas photos deleted from the Lightroom CC apps may not be deleted from

Lightroom Classic).

Self-Contained Catalog

Summary: Other than cloud sync, the simplest solution is to place the entire catalog and all of your photos on a portable external hard drive, which you can then plug into whichever computer you want to use at the time.

For whom: You regularly work on different computers and your entire collection of photos is small enough to fit on a portable hard drive. You need the full power of Lightroom Classic on both computers. **(Figure 18.9)**

Difficulty Rating: 1/4

Pros:

• Your entire catalog is available.

• As the original photos are on the same drive, Lightroom's functionality is not limited.

Cons:

• External hard drive speeds are usually slower than internal drives, so you'd want to choose a fast connection such as a Thunderbolt, eSATA or USB 3.0 connection if possible.

• Slightly greater risk of corruption when the catalog is stored on an external drive, as they're more likely to become disconnected while you're working.

• Small external drives are at a higher risk of being lost, stolen, or dropped.

Storage—Catalog: Portable drive.

Storage—Photos: Portable drive.

Storage—Presets: Store Presets with Catalog or Dropbox Sync.

Other Considerations:

• Think about your backup strategy, as your portable drive may be excluded from your normal backups.

Sample "Self-Contained Catalog" Workflow

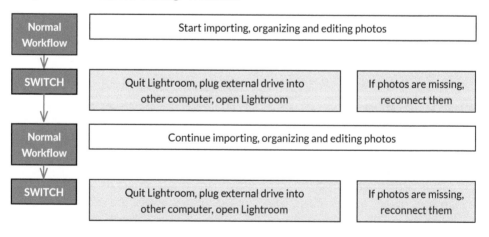

Figure 18.9 *Storing the catalogs and photos on an external works well for multiple computers.*

• If you work on multiple platforms, you may need to relink the files each time you switch computers, as Windows uses drive letters whereas macOS uses drive names. You'll also need to use an ExFAT formatted drive or translation software.

Setup Instructions:

1. Turn back to page 399 and follow the instructions for moving the photos to another drive.

2. Turn back to page 399 and follow the instructions for moving the catalog to another drive.

3. Turn to page 425 and follow the instructions for sharing your presets with both computers.

Switch Instructions:

1. Quit Lightroom on Computer A.

2. Safely disconnect the portable hard drive.

3. Plug portable the hard drive into Computer B.

4. Open Lightroom on Computer B. If the photos are marked as missing, perhaps because the drive letter has changed or you're moving cross-platform, turn to page 435 to fix the broken links.

Semi-Portable Catalog

Summary: Place the entire catalog on a portable external hard drive, which you can then plug into whichever computer you want to use at the time. Store most photos on one computer or network storage. Your current photos may fit on the portable drive with the catalog. **(Figure 18.10)**

For whom: You regularly work on different computers but your entire collection of photos is too large to fit on an external

Sample "Semi-Portable Catalog" or "Copy/Sync" Workflow

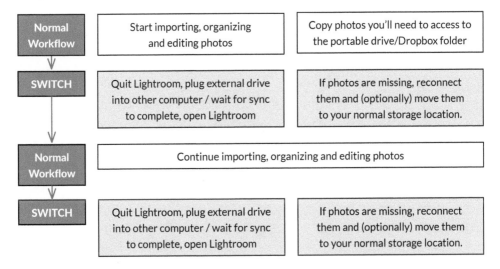

Figure 18.10 *A semi-portable catalog workflow places the catalog on an external drive or syncs it to other other computer using software like Dropbox, but leaves most files at home.*

drive. You need the full power of Lightroom Classic on both computers.

Difficulty Rating: 2/4

Pros:

• Your entire catalog is available.

Cons:

• Access to the original files varies, depending on where they're stored.

• External hard drive speeds are usually slower than internal drives, so you'd want to choose a fast connection such as a Thunderbolt, eSATA or USB 3.0 connection if possible.

• Slightly greater risk of corruption when the catalog is stored on an external drive, as they're more likely to become disconnected while you're working.

• Small external drives are at a higher risk of being lost, stolen, or dropped.

Storage—Catalog: Portable drive.

Storage—Photos:

• Store photos on network storage (i.e. NAS) or shared drive. This allows you to access the photos from any computer on the network, but the data transfer rate may be slower.

• Store photos on main computer (internal/external drives). This has the benefit of faster data transfer on the main machine, with more limited edits from other computers.

• A mixture—store specific photos on the portable drive with the catalog (e.g. the ones you're currently working on), and store the rest on the main computer or NAS. This gives access to specific files from any computer, even when you're offline, with more limited access to the rest.

Variations:

When the original files are offline (e.g. you're not connected to the network

Options	with standard previews	with 1:1 previews	with smart previews	with selected originals
Add new photos	Yes (move later)	Yes (move later)	Yes (move later)	Yes (move later)
View & search	Yes	Yes	Yes	Yes
View 1:1 (e.g. check focus)	No	Yes (if 1:1)	No	Yes (if original)
Edit in Develop	No	No	Yes (if smart)	Yes (if original)
Edit in PS	No	No	No	Yes (if original)
Rename/Delete Files	No	No	No	Yes (if original)
Export	No	No	Yes (up to 2560px)	Yes (if original)

Figure 18.11 *If you're using a Semi-Portable Catalog, the available Lightroom features depend on which previews or files you have available at the time.*

storage), you can still work on those photos using Lightroom's previews. The kind of work you can do depends on the type of previews. **Figure 18.11** summarizes the main limitations. For the full list, turn to page 420.

Storage—Presets: Store Presets with Catalog or Dropbox Sync.

Other Considerations:

• Think about your backup strategy, as your portable drive may be excluded from your normal backups.

• If you work on multiple platforms, you may need to relink the files each time you switch computers, as Windows uses drive letters whereas macOS uses drive names.

Setup Instructions:

1. Turn back to page 399 and follow the instructions for moving the catalog to another drive.

2. Turn to page 425 and follow the instructions for sharing your presets with both computers.

Switch Instructions:

1. Quit Lightroom on Computer A.

2. Safely disconnect the portable hard drive.

3. Plug the portable hard drive into Computer B.

4. Open Lightroom on Computer B.

5. (Optional) If the photos are available on network storage, but marked as missing, turn to page 435 to fix the broken links.

Portable Originals:

If you want to transfer some originals to your portable drive, or you shoot some new photos while you're away from your main storage and need to transfer them into your primary archives, turn back to page 112 and follow the instructions for safely moving those photos between hard drives.

Copy/Sync (e.g. Dropbox)

Summary: The catalog, the previews, smart previews and even the photos themselves can be automatically copied to multiple computers using Dropbox, or file synchronization software such as Vice Versa (Windows) / Chronosync (Mac). You can also copy the files manually, but that introduces more room for user error. (The workflow is the same as **Figure 18.10**).

For whom: You regularly work on different computers but you don't like the idea of a portable hard drive. You need the full power of Lightroom Classic on both computers.

Difficulty Rating: 3/4

Pros:

• Your entire catalog is available.

• The catalog is stored on internal hard drives, so it's not limited by portable hard drive speeds.

• There's no portable hard drive to drop or lose.

Cons:

• Access to the original files varies, depending on where they're stored.

• You have to be very careful to avoid creating conflicts when switching computers.

• Using Dropbox uses significant bandwidth as the previews are updated when you make Develop changes. File synchronization software uses the local network, but requires a little more tracking.

• Sync services such as Dropbox are not officially supported by Adobe. (I've used Dropbox for my own personal catalog for years, but I haven't tested other sync services.)

Storage—Catalog: Copied to both computers using Dropbox/file sync software.

Storage—Photos:

• Store photos on network storage (i.e. NAS) or shared drive. This allows you to access the photos from any computer on the network, but the data transfer rate may be slower.

• Store photos on portable drive. This allows you to access the photos from any

computer, but only if the portable drive is plugged in.

• Store photos on main computer (internal/external drives). This has the benefit of faster data transfer on the main machine, with more limited edits from other computers.

• Sync photos to both computers (e.g. using Dropbox or file sync software). This allows you to access the photos from any computer, but may use lots of bandwidth and storage space.

• A mixture—sync specific photos to both computers (e.g. the ones you're currently working on, using Dropbox or file sync software), and store the rest on the main computer or NAS. This gives access to specific files from any computer, with more limited access to the rest.

Variations:

When the original files are offline (e.g. you're not connected to the network storage), you can still work on those photos

Options	with previews	with 1:1 previews	with smart previews	with some/all originals
Add new photos	Yes (move later)	Yes (move later)	Yes (move later)	Yes (move later)
View & search	Yes	Yes	Yes	Yes
View 1:1 (e.g. check focus)	No	Yes	No	Yes (if original)
Edit in Develop	No	No	Yes (if smart)	Yes (if original)
Edit in PS	No	No	No	Yes (if original)
Rename/Delete Files	No	No	No	Yes (if original)
Export	No	No	Yes (up to 2560px)	Yes (if original)

Figure 18.12 If you're copying your catalog back and forth, the available Lightroom features depend on which previews or files you have available at the time.

using Lightroom's previews. The kind of work you can do depends on the type of previews. **Figure 18.12** summarizes the main limitations. For the full list, turn to page 420.

Storage—Presets: Store Presets with Catalog or Dropbox Sync.

Other Considerations:

• Make sure that the catalog isn't changed on both computers at once, as one of the catalogs would become a 'conflicted copy' in Dropbox. You must allow time for the catalog to be completely uploaded and downloaded before you open it on the other computer.

• There's more potential for things to go wrong when using File Sync software or services, whether due to bugs or user error, so make more frequent catalog backups (ideally every time you quit Lightroom).

• If you have performance problems with Dropbox running at the same time as Lightroom, pause Dropbox sync while you're working in Lightroom. If you don't, Dropbox runs constantly, trying to stay up to date with all the preview changes.

Setup Instructions:

1. Turn back to page 399 and follow the instructions for moving the catalog. Move it to your Dropbox folder (or other sync folder).

2. Turn to page 425 and follow the instructions for sharing your presets with both computers.

Switch Instructions:

1. Quit Lightroom on Computer A.

2. Wait for the sync to complete on Computer A and Computer B. This is VERY important.

3. Open Lightroom on Computer B.

4. (Optional) If the photos are marked as missing, turn to page 435 to fix the broken links.

Import from a Temporary Catalog

Summary: Create a new catalog for the shoot on the secondary machine (or a portable hard drive) and later merge it into the main catalog on the primary machine. **(Figure 18.13)**

For whom: You want to keep your new shoot separate (e.g. a location shoot or vacation photos) until you're ready to transfer it back to your main computer. You don't need access to your existing photos on the secondary machine.

Difficulty Rating: 3/4

Pros:

• It's relatively simple, especially if it's a one-off.

Cons:

• No access to existing photos.

• Keyword list isn't available in the new catalog, so you may end up with duplicates or different spellings.

• Face recognition data isn't available in the new catalog.

• Publish Services (e.g. Facebook, Flickr) and Lightroom mobile sync information isn't transferred between catalogs.

Sample "Import from a Temporary Catalog" Workflow

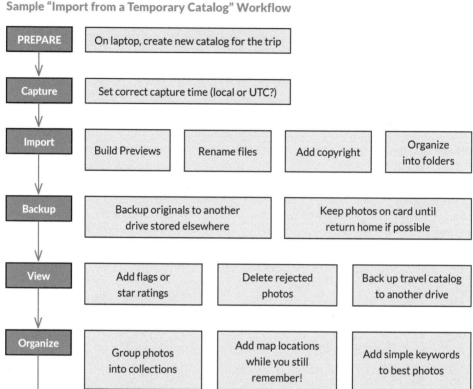

Figure 18.13 *If you create a temporary catalog while travelling, you can merge it into your main catalog when you return.*

Storage—Catalog: Main catalog on main computer, new catalog on secondary computer.

Storage—Photos: Main photos on main computer, external hard drive or NAS. New photos on secondary computer or portable hard drive.

Storage—Presets: Leave on main machine or Dropbox Sync.

Other Considerations:

• Think about your backup strategy, as your secondary computer or portable drive may be excluded from your normal backups.

Setup Instructions:

1. On the secondary computer, go to *File menu > New Catalog* and create a catalog.

2. Import your photos as normal.

Switch Instructions:

1. Upon your return, copy the catalog and photos to the main computer, or transfer the portable hard drive.

2. Double-click on the temporary catalog to open it, then relink any files that are marked as missing, using the instructions on page 435.

3. Open the main catalog (*File menu > Open Recent*) and select *File menu > Import from Another Catalog*.

4. Navigate to the folder containing the temporary catalog, select the lrcat file and press *Choose*.

5. In the Import from Catalog dialog, check the folders at the top. In the *File Handling* pop-up, decide whether to *Add new photos to*

catalog without moving or *Copy new photos to a new location and import* as shown in **Figure 18.14**. Since this was a new catalog, the *Changed Existing Photos* section is unavailable.

6. Click *Import*.

7. When you're happy that everything's transferred correctly and backed up, delete the temporary catalog and photos from the secondary computer or portable drive.

Split and Merge

Summary: Use one computer as a base (your main workstation, often a desktop) and export chunks of work out as a smaller catalog out for use on the secondary computer, then merge it back into the primary catalog on your return. **(Figure 18.15)**

For whom: Someone else needs to work on some of the photos while you're working in the main catalog.

Difficulty Rating: 4/4

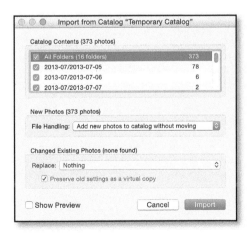

Figure 18.14 *Use Import from Another Catalog to merge the travel catalog into your main catalog.*

Sample "Split & Merge" Workflow

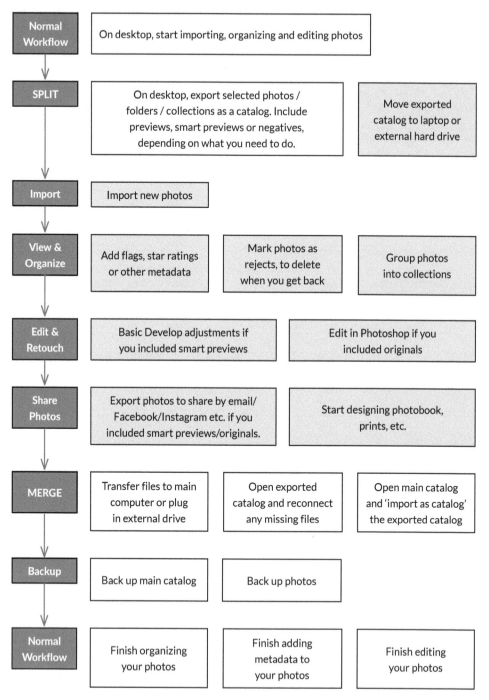

Figure 18.15 *Use Export as Catalog and Import from Another Catalog to take part of your catalog offsite.*

Pros:

• Multiple people can work on the photos.

• The photos are still primarily stored in a single searchable catalog.

Cons:

• You must keep track of who is working on each chunk of photos, as the latest edits win when merging catalogs.

• It can quickly become complicated if you're not careful.

• The exported catalog only has access to the selected photos.

• Face recognition data isn't available in the new catalog.

• Publish Services (e.g. Facebook, Flickr) and Lightroom mobile sync information isn't transferred between catalogs.

Storage—Catalog: Main catalog on main computer, exported chunks on other computers or portable drive.

Storage—Photos: Main photos on main computer, external hard drive or NAS. Selected photos on secondary computer or portable hard drive.

Variations:

When the original files are offline (e.g. you're not connected to the network storage), you can still work on the photos using Lightroom's previews. The kind of work you can do depends on the type of previews. **Figure 18.16** summarizes the main limitations. For the full list, turn to page 420.

Storage—Presets: None or Dropbox Sync.

Other Considerations:

• Think about how you'll track which photos you've exported, for example, add

Options	with selected previews	with selected 1:1 previews	with selected smart previews	with selected originals
Add new photos	Yes (move later)	Yes (move later)	Yes (move later)	Yes (move later)
View & search	Yes (only selected photos)	Yes (only selected photos)	Yes (only selected photos)	Yes (only selected photos)
View 1:1 (e.g. check focus)	No	Yes (if 1:1)	No	Yes (if original)
Edit in Develop	No	No	Yes (if smart)	Yes (if original)
Edit in PS	No	No	No	Yes (if original)
Rename/Delete Files	No	No	No	Yes (if original)
Export	No	No	Yes (up to 2560px)	Yes (if original)

Figure 18.16 *If you're using Export as Catalog to take part of your catalog offsite, the available Lightroom features depend on which previews or files you include when creating the exported catalog.*

them to a special collection or apply a color label to remind you not to edit the photos in the main catalog while the exported catalog is 'checked out'.

Setup Instructions:

1. In the main catalog, select the photos, folder or collections that you want to transfer.

2. Go to *File menu > Export as Catalog* and navigate to a location for the exported catalog (e.g. a portable hard drive). **(Figure 18.17)**

3. Depending on the kind of work you need to do, include only the previews and either the smart previews or originals. Check the table above to work out which you checkboxes you need.

4. On the secondary computer, double-click to open the exported catalog, and work as normal.

Switch Instructions:

1. When you return to the main computer, connect the portable hard drive or copy the

catalog and any new/edited originals from the secondary computer (you don't need to copy the originals if you haven't changed them).

2. Select *File menu > Import from Another Catalog.* **(Figure 18.18)**

3. Navigate to the folder containing the exported catalog, select the lrcat file and press *Choose.*

4. As the photos are already in your main working catalog, the Import from Catalog dialog asks how to handle the new settings:

In the *Changed Existing Photos* section, select *Metadata, develop settings and negative files* from the pop-up and check the *Replace non-raw files only (TIFF, PSD, JPEG, PNG)* checkbox below. (For more detail on the available options, turn to page 423.)

If you've accidentally edited the photos in both catalogs, check the *Preserve old settings as a virtual copy* checkbox. To overwrite the main catalog with the settings from the exported catalog, leave it unchecked.

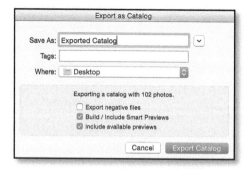

Figure 18.17 *Use Export as Catalog to take a chunk of your catalog to another machine (or send it to another person). The checkbox settings depend on what you need to do with the files. See* **Figure 18.12** *to help you choose the right options.*

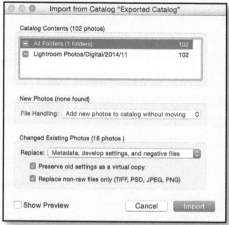

Figure 18.18 *Use Import from Another Catalog to merge the exported catalog back into your main catalog.*

Check the *All Folders* checkbox at the top of the dialog. If you've only edited some of the files, it displays a line instead of a checkmark.

5. Click *Import*.

6. When you're happy that everything's transferred correctly and backed up, delete the temporary catalog and photos from the secondary computer or portable drive.

Can multiple users use a Lightroom catalog?

Lightroom isn't designed for multi-user workflows, but some solutions are available. They include:

• Split and Merge workflow on page 415.

• Write the second user's settings to XMP and read them back into the main catalog (learn about XMP on page 345).

• Use Lightroom mobile to apply star ratings or flags on a mobile device such as a tablet.

How does Export as Catalog work?

We've used Export as Catalog and Import from Catalog in the last couple of multi-computer examples, but let's take a closer look at the options so you can apply it in a wider range of situations.

Export as Catalog allows you to take a subset of your catalog—perhaps a folder or collection—and create another catalog from these photos, complete with your metadata, the previews and smart previews, and the original files too if you wish. You can then take this catalog to another computer, and merge it back in to your main catalog later.

1. Decide which photos you want to include

in the export. You can export any selected photos using *File menu > Export as Catalog*, or right-click on a folder or collection and select *Export Folder/Collection as Catalog*.

2. Navigate to a folder that will hold your newly exported catalog, such as a portable hard drive. **(Figure 18.19)**

3. Decide which previews or files to include:

Include available previews exports the previews that have already been rendered. This is important if you're exporting a catalog subset to take to another computer and you won't be taking the original files with you, otherwise you'll just have a catalog full of gray thumbnails.

Build/Include Smart Previews exports the smart previews, or builds them if they don't already exist. This allows you to edit your photos in the Develop module without the negative files (full size original images).

Export negative files copies the original photos along with the catalog, you edit the photos in Photoshop or export full resolution photos.

The resulting catalog is a normal catalog, just like any other. If you've chosen to *Export negative files*, there are also one or more subfolders containing copies of your original

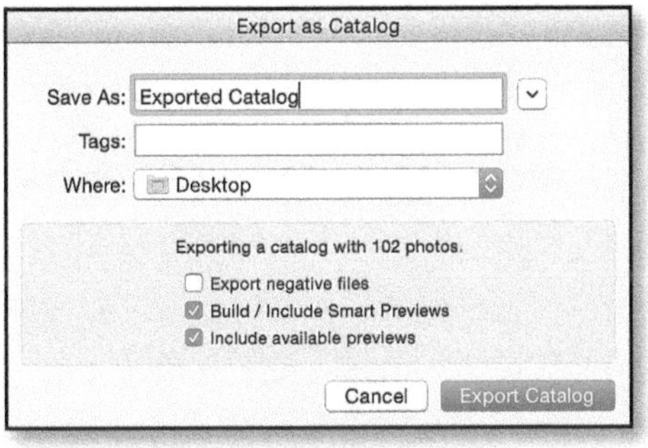

Figure 18.19 *Export as Catalog allows you to take part of your catalog to another computer.*

files, in folders reflecting their original folder structure.

You can transfer this catalog to any computer with the same version of Lightroom Classic installed, and either double-click on it, hold down Ctrl (Windows) / Opt (Mac) on starting Lightroom, or use the *File menu > Open Catalog* command to open it.

Note that some data is excluded when exporting catalogs. This includes Publish Services and Sync, as well as potentially some plug-in metadata.

Having finished working on that catalog, you can later use Import from Catalog to merge it back into your main catalog again. First, though, let's look at the limitations resulting for each checkbox setting in more detail.

What are the limitations of offline files, with standard or smart previews?

When the original files are offline, perhaps because you're working on another machine or the drive containing your original photos is disconnected, you'll still be able to do some work in Lightroom.

As long as you have standard-sized previews, you'll still be able to do Library tasks—labeling, rating, keywording, creating collections, etc. You can also view slideshows, design books, and export web galleries. If you've built 1:1 size previews, you'll also be able to zoom in to check focus in the Library Loupe view.

With Smart Previews, you can go one stage further—editing in the Develop module, and exporting medium resolution photos.

The Smart Previews have been designed to behave as much like the originals as possible, so Develop adjustments applied

to the smart previews should look almost identical when applied to the original files. Noise reduction and sharpening know the size of the smart preview compared to the size of the original and scale the settings appropriately behind the scenes. You may choose to fine tune them later, but this won't be necessary in most cases.

There are exceptional cases where you might see a difference between the Smart Previews and the original files. For example, if you make extreme adjustments, it may be possible to see artifacts in the smart previews, caused by the 8-bit lossy compression. The artifacts disappear when you reconnect the original raw files.

The Smart Previews are only up to 2560px along the long edge, so if you zoom into 1:1 view when the originals are offline, it won't truly be a 1:1 view. (There's one exception— if you've created 1:1 standard previews and you have made any Develop changes, the Library Loupe 1:1 view is true 1:1.) They average around 1 MB each.

Of course with the originals offline, you can't do anything that requires the original files— moving files between folders, renaming, writing to XMP, deleting files, creating HDR or full size panoramic photos, editing the photos in Photoshop, and other similar tasks—until the original files are available again. **(Figure 18.20)**

How do I check which photos have previews or smart previews?

Under the Histogram is a file status area. **(Figure 18.21)**

When a single photo is selected, it says:

Original Photo—the original is available, but there's no smart preview

	Standard Previews	Smart Previews	Original Files
Import			
Import from Catalog			✓
File Management			
Move			✓
Rename			✓
Remove from Catalog	✓	✓	✓
Delete from Hard Drive			✓
Metadata			
Add Stars, Labels, Flags	✓	✓	✓
Add Keywords	✓	✓	✓
Create Faces Index		✓	✓
Add Names to Faces	✓	✓	✓
Add Map Locations	✓	✓	✓
Add other Metadata	✓	✓	✓
Create Virtual Copies	✓	✓	✓
Work with Videos			✓
Create & Edit Collections	✓	✓	✓
Previews			
Build Standard Sized Previews		✓	✓
Build 1:1 Sized Previews			✓
Build Smart Previews			✓
Export as Catalog			
Export as Catalog with Standard Previews	✓	✓	✓

	Standard Previews	Smart Previews	Original Files
Export as Catalog with Smart Previews		✓	✓
Export as Catalog with Originals			✓
Import from Catalog with Standard Previews	✓	✓	✓
Import from Catalog with Smart Previews		✓	✓
Import from Catalog with Originals			✓
Develop			
Global Develop Adjustments		✓	✓
Local Develop Adjustments		✓	✓
Merge to Panorama		✓	✓
Merge to HDR			✓
Soft-proof photos		✓	✓
Export			
Export best quality full resolution photos			✓
Export to any size photos		larger than 2560 px will be upsampled	✓
Email photos		✓	✓
Publish Services			
Publish photos (as Export)		✓	✓

Figure 18.20 *A quick summary of which previews you can use for each task.*

	Standard Previews	Smart Previews	Original Files
Book			
Design Book	✓	✓	✓
Export Book to PDF			✓
Export Book to JPEG			✓
Export Book to Blurb			✓
Slideshow			
Design Slideshow	✓	✓	✓
Preview Slideshow	✓	✓	✓
Play Slideshow on Computer	✓	✓	✓
Export Slideshow to PDF			✓
Export Slideshow to JPEG			✓
Export Slideshow to Video	✓	✓	✓
Print			
Set up Print	✓	✓	✓
Print to JPEG			✓
Print to Printer			✓
Web			
Design Web Gallery	✓	✓	✓
Export Web Gallery to Hard Drive	✓	✓	✓
Export Web Gallery to FTP	✓	✓	✓

Figure 18.20 continued

Original + Smart Preview—the original is available, but a smart preview is available if the originals go offline

Smart Preview—the original is offline, but a smart preview is available

Photo is Missing—the original is offline and there's no smart preview

If multiple photos are selected, it just displays the icons and photo counts. When more than 1000 photos are selected, a + symbol appears next to the photo counts, showing that it stopped counting for performance reasons. **(Figure 18.22)**

You can also create a Smart Collection for *Has Smart Previews* is True or False, which makes it easy to keep track of which Smart Previews you need to build.

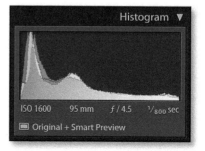

Figure 18.21 *File status shows in the Histogram panel.*

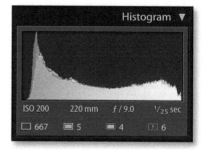

Figure 18.22 *When multiple photos are selected, the file status switches to icons.*

How do I build or discard smart previews?

You can build smart previews while you're importing photos by checking the Build Smart Previews in the Import dialog's File Handling panel, or later, select all (or none) of the photos in Grid view and choose *Library menu > Previews > Build Smart Previews*. It skips any photos that already have smart previews. Likewise, you can discard smart previews that you no longer need by selecting the photos and using the *Library menu > Previews > Discard Smart Previews* command.

How does Import from Catalog work?

The Import from Catalog command is used to merge multiple catalogs into a single catalog, or transfer photos between catalogs without losing all the work you've done.

1. Open the source catalog and reconnect any photos that are marked as missing, using the instructions on page 435. This helps to prevent duplicate records in the merged catalog.

2. Open the target catalog that you want the photos to end up in. If you're merging multiple catalogs into one catalog, you might want to create a new catalog.

3. Select *File menu > Import from Another Catalog*, and navigate to the source catalog, from which you want to pull the metadata.

4. Lightroom reads the source catalog and checks it against the target catalog, resulting in the Import from Catalog dialog. **(Figure 18.23)**

If you select an older catalog in the Import from Catalog dialog, Lightroom automatically upgrades the catalog before

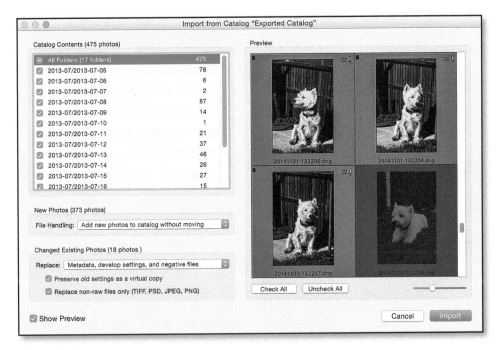

Figure 18.23 *Import from Catalog allows you to merge catalogs together. You can select specific folders or photos to copy into the target catalog.*

importing. You can save the upgraded catalog, as if you had opened the catalog normally and run the upgrade, or discard the upgraded catalog. Either way, the original catalog is left untouched.

Depending on the choices you make, new photos are imported into the target catalog and existing photos are updated. The main options are:

The **Catalog Contents** section lists all of the folders in the source catalog, and allows you to check the folders that you want to include in the import. It's particularly useful when you want to import selected folders.

The **Show Preview** checkbox displays a thumbnail area to the right. Each thumbnail has a checkbox, allowing you to include or exclude specific photos. If you click on a folder in the *Catalog Contents* section, the thumbnail preview area updates to show only the photos in the selected folder. Dimmed photos are unavailable for import as they already exist in the target catalog with the same settings.

New Photos controls how new photos are handled. These are photos that don't exist in the target catalog in a matching folder hierarchy.

File Handling offers a choice of *Add new photos to catalog without moving, Copy new photos to a new location and import* or *Don't import new photos.*

Changed Existing Photos controls how photos that already exist in the target catalog are handled. Photos that are identical in both catalogs are skipped, as you won't need to update these.

The **Replace** pop-up offers a choice of *Metadata and develop settings only, Metadata, develop settings and negative files* or *Nothing*

from the pop-up. Unless you've edited the files themselves in another program, for example, retouching in Photoshop, then you can usually just copy the metadata and settings.

If you select *Metadata, develop settings and negative files*, the **Replace non-raw files only (TIFF, PSD, JPEG, PNG)** checkbox becomes available. This saves time by only replacing files that may have been edited, for example, photos edited in Photoshop. Unless you've worked on the files themselves in another program, for example, retouching in Photoshop, then you can usually just copy the settings.

Preserve old settings as a virtual copy is useful if you've accidentally edited the photos in both catalogs. It creates a virtual copy of the target catalog's settings and imports the source catalog's settings as the master photo. Once the import completes, you can check through the photos and determine which version to keep

Are there any limitations when importing and exporting catalogs?

I should give one word of warning about the catalog import/export process: some data is excluded. This includes:

Extra Files—Any files that are stored in the selected folders but aren't referenced in Lightroom's catalog, such as text documents, are not included in the exported catalog/folder.

Keywords—Your keyword list in the exported catalog only includes keywords that have been applied to the selected photos. You can work around this by using *Metadata menu > Export Keywords* in the main catalog, and *Metadata menu > Import Keywords* in the exported catalog to add your full keyword list.

Publish Services—Publish Services settings and collections are tied directly to their original catalog and are not transferred by Export as Catalog. (Although Publish Services data is excluded when using Import/Export Catalogs, it's possible to work around this limitation using the LRVoyager plug-in. https://www.Lrq.me/alloy-lrvoyager)

Lightroom mobile—Lightroom mobile only syncs with a single catalog, and switching catalogs involves wiping all of the cloud data and re-uploading.

Plug-ins—Some plug-ins store data in undefined areas of the catalog, which may not be transferred by Export as Catalog.

Sync—Lightroom CC sync can only be tied to one catalog.

As with many things, it's simply a case of weighing the pros and cons.

It's also worth noting that Import from Catalog merges complete photo records, so if you've changed a photo's star rating in the source catalog and Develop settings in the target catalog, all of the photo's metadata in the the source catalog overwrites the same photo's metadata in the target catalog. You can choose to create virtual copies, retaining both sets of settings at the expense of additional clutter in your catalog.

Can I share my catalog with multiple users on the same machine?

We've discussed using Lightroom on multiple computers, but what happens if you have multiple user accounts on the same computer and you want to share the same photos? All of the same options apply. Only one user can have the catalog open at a time, so if both users are logged in to the computer at the same time using Fast User Switching, the previous user needs to close Lightroom before the next user can open it.

How can I use my presets on both computers?

By default, your presets are stored in your user account on your computer, but if you're using your catalog with multiple computers, you can choose to store them with the catalog by checking the *Preferences dialog > Presets tab > **Store presets with this catalog*** checkbox. **(Figure 18.24)**

This option allows you to store the presets alongside the catalog itself, for use with that specific catalog on any machine. It does, however, mean that the presets are not available to other catalogs on either computer.

Before you rush off to check the checkbox, there are a few warnings to note, as this checkbox causes as much confusion as it solves:

• Lightroom doesn't move the presets to the new location automatically, so we'll step through how to do that in a moment.

• If your presets ever seem to have 'gone missing,' this checkbox is probably to blame.

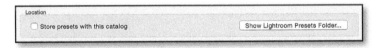

Figure 18.24 *If you work with a single catalog and use it on multiple computers, perhaps on an external drive or synced via Dropbox, consider checking Store presets with this catalog. Otherwise, it's best left unchecked.*

• When checked, the presets are only available to that specific catalog, so don't check it if you need to use multiple catalogs (unless you want different presets with each catalog).

• Some settings are always stored in the user account, regardless of the *Store presets with this catalog* checkbox state. These include default Develop settings, custom point curves, lens and camera profiles, and email account settings, which are always tied to a single machine. (There is an alternative way of using Symbolic Links and Dropbox or similar sync software to sync presets between computers, described in the next question.)

• In most situations, this checkbox causes unnecessary confusion, so I'd recommend leaving it unchecked unless you have a specific reason for using it (such as using a single catalog on multiple computers or requiring different presets in different catalogs).

Checking or unchecking the *Store presets with this catalog* only changes where Lightroom looks for presets and stores new ones. It doesn't copy any existing presets to the new location, so you need to manually copy them. To do so:

1. Go to *Preferences > Presets tab* and uncheck *Store presets with this catalog* and press the **Show Lightroom Presets Folder** button.

2. An Explorer (Windows) / Finder (Mac) window opens, showing the presets in their global location. Keep it open in the background.

3. Check the *Store presets with this catalog* checkbox and press the *Show Lightroom Presets Folder* button again.

4. A second Explorer (Windows) / Finder (Mac) window opens, showing the catalog-specific Lightroom Settings folder.

5. Drag (or copy/paste) your presets from the global folder to the catalog-specific one.

If you have the opposite problem, and the presets are stored with the catalog, just swap the steps around. If you have multiple catalogs with multiples sets of presets, you can copy and paste them all into the global location to make them available to all catalogs.

How do I synchronize my presets using Dropbox?

The more technical (but more flexible) workaround for keeping presets updated on multiple computers involves using Dropbox (https://www.Lrq.me/dropbox) and junctions (Windows) / symlinks (Mac). It works well, particularly if the computers aren't on the same local network. You can also apply the same principle to the camera raw shared folders, such as camera and lens profiles, allowing these to be kept updated everywhere too. The computers can even run different platforms, for example, a Windows machine and a Mac.

Having installed Dropbox according to the instructions on their website, you first need to copy the presets and profiles into the Dropbox folder. Personally I keep a *Sync* subfolder in Dropbox, as I use this same principle for many different programs.

For both operating systems:

1. Close Lightroom.

2. Go to the application data folders at:

Windows—C: \ Users \ [your username]\ AppData \ Roaming \ Adobe \

Mac—Macintosh HD / Users / [your username] / Library / Application Support / Adobe /

(Note that these are hidden OS folders)

3. Copy the Lightroom folder and the CameraRaw subfolders (e.g. Defaults, CameraProfiles - but exclude the GPU folder as it crashes Lightroom) to your Dropbox folder.

4. Move, rename or delete the original folders in the Application Support folder.

Having copied the presets and other folders, it's time to create the symbolic links, so the instructions depend on your operating system...

Windows:

1. Download Symlink Creator (https://www.Lrq.me/winsymlink). It's a small free program which creates a symbolic link without needing to understand DOS and the mklink command.

2. There's no installation needed other than unzipping the download (or just selecting the .exe download in the first place). To avoid permissions issues, you'll need to right-click

on the Symlink Creator.exe file and select *Run as Administrator*.

3. In the dialog, working from the top, select *Folder symbolic link* as the type of link. **(Figure 18.25)**

4. In the *Link Folder* section, browse for the C:\Users\[your username]\AppData\ Roaming\Adobe\Lightroom folder (this may be a hidden folder) and call the link *Lightroom*.

5. In the Destination Folder section, browse to the Lightroom folder you created in your Dropbox folder.

6. Select *Symbolic Link* as the type of link, and press *Create Link*.

7. Repeat steps 3-6 using the Camera Raw subfolders instead of the Lightroom folder.

8. Now restart Lightroom and check that it has found your presets and camera raw settings correctly.

9. Switch to the other computer and repeat steps 1-8. If you had different presets on the other computer, you may want to merge them into your Dropbox folders so that they're available on all computers.

Mac:

1. Download SymbolicLinker (https://www.Lrq.me/macsymlink). It's a small free program which creates a symbolic link without needing to visit Terminal.

2. Install it according to the instructions included with the app.

3. Right-click on the Lightroom folder in Dropbox and select *Make Symbolic Link*. **(Figure 18.26)**

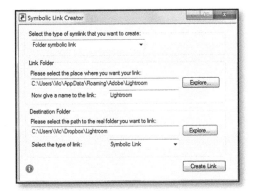

Figure 18.25 *Symbolic Link Creator is an easy way to create symbolic links on Windows.*

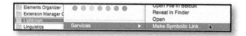

Figure 18.26 *SymbolicLinker is an easy way to create symbolic links on Mac.*

4. The new symbolic link appears next to the Lightroom folder, and is called *Lightroom symlink*.

5. Drag the new Lightroom symlink to the Macintosh HD/Users/[your username]/Library/Application Support/Adobe/ folder, where the original folder was stored.

6. Rename the Lightroom symlink to remove the word symlink—you want to match the original name (Lightroom) so that Lightroom follows your link.

7. Repeat steps 3-6 using the Camera Raw subfolders instead of the Lightroom folder.

8. Now restart Lightroom and check that it has found your presets and camera raw settings correctly.

9. Switch to the other computer and repeat steps 1-8. If you had different presets on the other computer, you may want to merge them into your Dropbox folders so that they're available on all computers.

Once the setup is complete, Lightroom looks at the presets in the Dropbox folder, which should be updated whenever you add or edit a preset. If Lightroom is open on both computers at the same time, changes may not appear on the other computer until Lightroom is restarted.

SINGLE OR MULTIPLE CATALOGS

Until now, we've been working on the assumption that you have a single master catalog. Since version 1.1, Lightroom has made it easy to create and use multiple catalogs, but the question is, just because you can, should you? We'll consider some of the pros and cons, and how to make it work if you do decide that multiple catalogs are right for you.

Should I use one big catalog, or multiple smaller catalogs?

There's no 'right' number of catalogs. As with the rest of your Lightroom workflow, it depends on how you work. So should you use multiple catalogs for your main working catalog, or should you split your photos into multiple catalogs? We're not referring to temporary catalogs which are created for a purpose, for example, to take a subset of photos to another machine before later merging them back in, but more specifically your main working or master catalog.

The main benefit of keeping all of your photos in a DAM (Digital Asset Management) system is being able to easily search through them and find specific photos, but there are a few other pros and cons to consider:

<u>Pros of Multiple Catalogs</u>

• Smaller catalogs may be slightly faster on very low spec hardware. (Although even 50,000 photos counts as a small catalog!)

• Backups are faster than a single big catalog.

• Multiple catalogs give a clear distinction between types of photography, i.e., work vs home.

• You can't accidentally drag photos into the wrong folder (e.g. wedding photos can't end up with the wrong client).

• If your catalog becomes corrupted, you have less to lose (although frequent backups will avoid this issue).

• If multiple users need to be working on photos at the same time, it's easier to track individual catalogs.

Cons of Multiple Catalogs

• Can't search across multiple catalogs (e.g. to find the best photos from multiple shoots).

• Cloud sync only works with one catalog.

• You can end up with variations in metadata and keyword spellings.

• It's harder to keep track of backups.

• You have to keep switching catalogs.

• You can't switch catalogs while a process is running (e.g. if you're running an export in one catalog, you have to wait for it to complete before switching to another catalog).

• Some photos may be forgotten and not included in any catalog.

• You can end up with duplicate photos in multiple catalogs by accident.

There are few questions to ask yourself:

• How many photos are you working on at any one time? And how many do you have altogether?

• Do you want to be able to search through all of your photos to find a specific photo? Or do you have another DAM system that you prefer to use for cataloging your photos?

• If you decide to work across multiple catalogs, how are you going to make sure your keyword lists are the same in all of

your catalogs?

• If you use multiple catalogs, is there going to be any crossover, with the same photos appearing in more than one catalog?

• How would you keep track of which photos are in which catalog?

• Do you want to keep the photos in your catalog indefinitely or just while you're working on them, treating Lightroom more like a basic raw processor?

• How will you keep track of catalogs and their backups?

Your answers likely depend on your reasons for using Lightroom. For some people, using multiple catalogs isn't a problem—they already have another system they use for DAM (digital asset management), and they want to use Lightroom for the other tools it offers. For example, some wedding photographers may decide to have a catalog for each wedding, and if they know that a photo from Mark & Kate's wedding is going to be in Mark & Kate's catalog, finding it really isn't a problem. But then, if you had to find a photo from a specific venue, or to use for publicity, you'd have to search through multiple catalogs.

Many high-volume photographers choose the best of both worlds: a small catalog for working on their current photos, and then transferring them into a large searchable archive catalog for storing completed photos. That's certainly another viable option, and a good compromise for many.

There are some easy distinctions, for example, you may also decide to keep personal photos entirely separate from work photos. These kind of clear-cut distinctions work well, as long as there's never any crossover between the two.

Keeping the same photo in multiple catalogs is best avoided, as it becomes very confusing! The more catalogs you have, the harder they become to track.

As a simple rule of thumb, use the fewest catalogs you can and no fewer. For most photographers, that's just one catalog.

Is there a maximum number of photos a catalog can hold?

So you might be wondering, how big is too big? There's no known maximum number of photos you can store in a Lightroom catalog. At the last count, the largest known catalog contained 7 million photos, and it's likely much larger now!

If your catalog's stored on a FAT32 formatted hard drive, 2 GB is the maximum file size allowable on that drive format, so your catalog could hit that limit, but then you could always move the catalog onto a drive formatted as NTFS on Windows or HFS/APFS on Mac.

How do I create a new catalog and open catalogs?

Assuming you've decided to create a new catalog, you'll need to understand some basic catalog management, such as how to create new catalogs and switch between them.

If Lightroom's already running, you can create a new catalog using *File menu > New Catalog*, or open an existing catalog using *File menu > Open Catalog*.

If Lightroom's closed, hold down the Ctrl key (Windows) / Opt key (Mac) while opening Lightroom. In the Select Catalog dialog, it lists your recently used catalogs, or you can open another existing catalog or create a new catalog. **(Figure 18.27)**

How do I set or change my default catalog?

By default, Lightroom opens your last used catalog when it launches, however you can change this behavior in Lightroom's *Preferences > General tab*. **(Figure 18.28)** You can choose to open a specific catalog, open the most recent catalog, or be prompted each time Lightroom starts.

How do I set default Catalog Settings to use for all new catalogs?

Certain settings are catalog-specific, for example, anything set in the Catalog Settings dialog, Identity Plates, smart

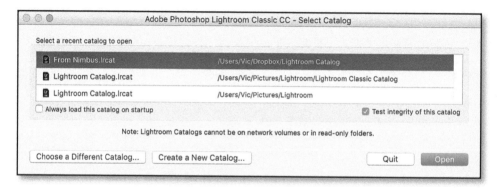

Figure 18.27 *If you hold down Ctrl (Windows) / Opt (Mac) while starting Lightroom, it asks which catalog to open.*

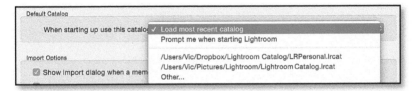

Figure 18.28 *Set your default catalog in Lightroom's Preferences dialog.*

collections and keyword lists. Lightroom doesn't currently provide a way of making these settings available to new catalogs as templates, however there is a workaround. Set up a new empty catalog with the settings of your choice and save it somewhere safe. Whenever you need a new catalog with all of your favorite settings, simply duplicate the template catalog using Explorer (Windows) / Finder (Mac) instead of using *File menu > New Catalog*.

If you only need to import your smart collections into each new catalog, there's another handy trick. Export the existing smart collections (right-click > *Export Smart Collection Settings*) and change their file extension from ".lrmscol" to ".lrtemplate" Then go to *Preferences dialog > Presets tab* and press the *Show Lightroom Presets Folder* button. There you'll find a folder call *Smart Collection Templates*. If you add your renamed smart collections to that folder, they'll automatically be added to any new catalogs.

How do I delete a spare catalog?

If you've ended up with too many catalogs, you may want to delete any unused catalogs. It's probably a good idea to open it before you delete it, to check that you definitely don't want to keep it. To do so, either use *File menu > Open Catalog* or double-click on the catalog in Explorer (Windows) / Finder (Mac). You can safely delete the spare catalog and its previews files as long as you're sure there are no settings in it that catalog that you need. If in doubt, delete the

previews (*.lrdata), zip the catalog (*.lrcat) and keep it somewhere safe.

How do I merge multiple catalogs into one larger catalog?

To merge your existing separate catalogs into one large catalog, it's simply a case of using Import from Catalog to pull the data into a new combined catalog. If you've accidentally ended up working in a backup catalog or created a new catalog by mistake, this process also allows you to fix your mistake without losing any data.

1. Open each individual catalog by double-clicking on it. If any folders or photos are marked as missing, turn to page 435 and fix the broken links before merging catalogs. You'll save a lot of time later.

2. Select *File menu > New Catalog* and create a clean catalog which will become your new master catalog.

3. Go to *File menu > Import from Another Catalog* and select one of the smaller catalogs (the *.lrcat file). Ideally you should work through in date order, from the oldest catalog to the newest. Note that we're importing the metadata from the existing catalog rather than importing the photos using the standard Import dialog. There's a big difference!

Assuming that your photos are remaining in their current location, you'll need to select:

New Photos > File Handling set to *Add new*

photos to catalog without moving.

Changed Existing Photos > Replace set to *Metadata and develop settings only.*

If photos appear in more than one catalog, and you're not sure which settings are the most recent, check *Preserve old settings as a virtual copy.* This creates virtual copies of each of the different sets of settings, so you can go back through later and decide which to keep.

For more information on the available options, turn back to page 423.

4. Repeat the Import from Catalog process for each of the other smaller catalogs until you've imported them all.

5. Keep the individual catalogs at least until you're sure that everything's transferred correctly and you have a current backup.

6. If some photos were duplicated in more than one catalog and you checked *Preserve old settings as a virtual copy,* sort through the photos and delete any virtual copies you don't need to keep. If the version you want to keep is a virtual copy, promote it to master status using *Photo menu > Set Copy As Master* and then delete the other version.

If you merge multiple catalogs, especially from multiple computers, you may end up with duplicate photos. The Duplicate Finder plug-in can help to identify them, although there's still some manual cleanup involved. https://www.Lrq.me/duplicatefinder

How do I split a catalog into multiple catalogs?

To split an existing catalog into smaller catalogs, use the Export as Catalog command discussed on page 419. (There are few occasions when I'd recommend this,

as using a single large catalog is usually a better choice. However there are occasions when it's useful, for example, you may need to take part of the catalog to another computer or have someone else work on part of the catalog.)

How do I transfer photos between catalogs?

If you do decide to use a small working catalog and a large archive catalog, you'll need to transfer photos between catalogs. Using Import from Another Catalog is essential when transferring photos between catalogs. Simply importing the photos instead of the catalog would lose all of the work you've previously done in Lightroom.

1. Open your Archive catalog, or create one if you haven't done so already.

2. Select *File menu > Import from Another Catalog,* and navigate to the Working catalog. In the Import from Catalog dialog that follows, select the folders that you want to transfer into your Archive catalog, deselecting the others.

Assuming that your photos are remaining in their current location, you'll need to select:

• *New Photos > File Handling* set to *Add new photos to catalog without moving.*

• *Changed Existing Photos > Replace* set to *Metadata and develop settings only* if it's available.

• For more information on the available options, turn back to page 423.

3. Import these folders into your Archive catalog and check that they've imported as expected.

4. Close your Archive catalog and reopen

your Working catalog.

5. Make sure you have a current backup, before you start removing photos from a catalog, just in case you make a mistake.

6. Select the photos that you've just transferred.

7. Press the Delete key to remove these files from the Working catalog, being careful to choose *Remove from the catalog* rather than *Delete from the hard drive.*

8. Repeat the process whenever you want to transfer more photos into the Archive catalog.

CATALOG SHORTCUTS

		Windows	Mac
Open Catalog		Ctrl O	Cmd Shift O
	Open Specific Catalog when opening Lightroom	Hold down Ctrl while opening Lightroom	Hold down Opt while opening Lightroom

TROUBLESHOOTING

19

It's a computer—they don't always work the way you expect! Hiccups do occur, so let's explore some of the most frequent troubleshooting steps.

First, we'll look at the most frequent problems and their solutions, and then general troubleshooting steps you can try, if none of these fit. The most frequent problems are:

• Missing photos, marked with question marks or exclamation points.

• Missing toolbar.

• Missing panels and dialogs.

• Catalogs that won't open, perhaps due to corruption.

• Corrupted photos.

• Preview problems, including odd colors, gray thumbnails and corruption.

MISSING FILES

At some stage, most people run into worrying exclamation points or question marks denoting missing files. Those warnings appear when Lightroom can no longer find the photos at their last known location.

Usually, it's because you've used other software such as Explorer (Windows) or Finder (Mac) to:

• Delete the photos or folders.

• Move the photos or folders.

• Rename the photos or folders.

It can also happen when something's happened to the drive, such as:

• The external or network drive holding the photos is unplugged/disconnected.

• The drive letter has changed (Windows) or drive mount point has changed (Mac).

• You've moved to a new computer.

How do I know that Lightroom can't find my photos?

Missing files are identified by a rectangular icon in the corner of the Grid thumbnail, with or without an exclamation point. **(Figure 19.1)** (In earlier versions, it displayed a question mark icon instead.)

If you've previously built Smart Previews, it says *Smart Preview* under the Histogram, to indicate that the original file is unavailable. You can continue working in Lightroom using those lower quality proxy files even though the original files are offline, with

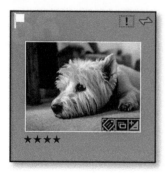

Figure 19.1 *Missing photos have an exclamation point icon.*

some limitations that we discussed in the Multi-computer chapter on page 395.

If there are no Smart Previews, the rectangular icon on the thumbnail contains an exclamation point, and when you check the histogram, you'll find it's blank and says *Photo is missing.* **(Figure 19.2)** When you switch to the Develop module, the sliders are unavailable, as you can't edit a photo that's completely missing.

If the entire folder is missing, the folder name in the Folders panel goes gray with a question mark folder icon. **(Figure 19.3)**

If an entire drive is offline, the volume name in the Folders panel and the small rectangular icon on the left turn gray.

What else can cause photos to disappear?

There's a couple of other things that can make it look like your photos have disappeared. They include:

Opening the Wrong Catalog—Go to *File menu > Open Recent* and see if another catalog is listed. If it's not, search your hard drives for **.lrcat* files and double click to open.

Collapsed Stacks— Go to *Photo menu > Stacking > Expand All Stacks.*

Filters—Uncheck *Library menu > Enable Filters.*

Show Photos in Subfolders— Check *Library menu > Show Photos in Subfolders.*

STOP!

If you have missing photos or folders, don't be tempted to synchronize the folder or re-import the photos until you've explored every other possibility. If you do so, you may lose the work you've done in Lightroom.

Lightroom thinks my photos are missing— how do I fix it?

If Lightroom tells you that files are missing,

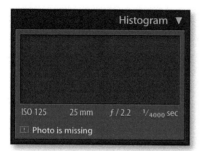

Figure 19.2 *Missing Photo status also shows in the Histogram panel.*

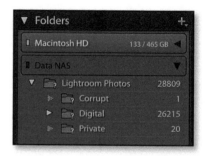

Figure 19.3 *Missing folders have question mark icons. If the whole volume's offline, the drive goes gray.*

don't panic. First, stop and work out the extent of the problem, and if you can, why it's happened. Then fix it as soon as you can, using the instructions below, as problems tend to snowball if you ignore them.

The quickest way to fix the missing files is to follow these instructions in order. If you start relinking missing photos before you relink missing folders and drives, you can create a bigger job.

1. First, you must **find the files on your hard drive**. Lightroom can't tell you where you've put the files, if you've moved/renamed/deleted them using other software, so you first need to locate the missing files on your hard drives.

Once you've found them on your hard drive using Explorer (Windows) / Finder (Mac), you can move on to step 2. If you get stuck, try using Windows Search or Mac Spotlight to search for one of the filenames.

2. Look in the Folders panel. **Is the whole drive offline**, shown by dark gray text and a gray rectangle on the left?

If the answer's no, skip on to step 3.

If the answer's yes, why is the drive offline? Is it disconnected? If you're on Windows, has the drive letter changed? If you're on a Mac, has the drive name changed?

If the drive is disconnected, plug it back in or reconnect to the network storage.

If the drive letter/name has changed, you can change it back (page 439), or you can move on to step 3 and reconnect the individual folders.

3. Look in the Folders panel. **Are some of the folders marked as missing**, with gray text and a question mark on the folder icon?

If the answer's no, skip on to step 4.

If the answer's yes, why are the folders missing? Did you delete, rename or move a folder?

If you deleted the folders, restore from the Recycle Bin/Trash or from a backup.

If you renamed or moved the folder, you could move/rename it back and then redo the move/rename within Lightroom.

If you can't put them back as they were, you can link Lightroom to the new name/location. That's the next step...

4. If you set up the folders as a hierarchy using the instructions earlier in the book (page 107), is a **whole folder hierarchy of parent/child folders** marked as missing? Or is it a single folder (or a few folders) that's marked as missing?

If it's a whole folder hierarchy that's missing, right-click on the parent folder (rather than the individual subfolders) and select *Find Missing Folder* from the context-sensitive menu, then navigate to the new location of that parent folder. As long as the names and structure of the subfolders hasn't changed, all of the subfolders are fixed at the same time.

If it's a single missing folder, right-click on the missing folder and select *Find Missing Folder* from the context-sensitive menu, then navigate to the new location of that single folder. Lightroom then updates its records to the new location and the question marks disappear.

If there are multiple missing folders, that aren't in a folder hierarchy, do the same for each of these folders.

5. Are individual photos still marked as

missing, with an exclamation point inside a rectangle on each of the thumbnail borders?

If the answer's no, your work is done. Go to *Library menu > Find Missing Photos*, just to double-check you haven't missed any photos.

If the answer's yes, why are those photos missing? Do you remember moving or renaming them? Or deleting them?

If you deleted them, you'll need to restore the photos to their previous location from the Recycle Bin/Trash or from a recent backup. Remember, the photos are never IN Lightroom, and most of Lightroom's tools won't work without the original photos. (We'll come back to worst case scenarios in a moment).

If you moved the photos without renaming, you can either move them back, or you can link Lightroom's records to the new location of the photos.

To link Lightroom to the new name/location, click on the rectangle in the corner of the thumbnail. Lightroom displays the last known location of the photo. Click **Locate** and navigate to the new location of that photo. Check the ***Find nearby missing photos*** checkbox to allow Lightroom to try to automatically relink other files in the same folder. Lightroom updates its records to the new location and the rectangular icons disappear. **(Figure 19.4)**

If you renamed the photos outside of Lightroom, the quickest solution is to restore the photos with the old names from your backups and then redo the rename within Lightroom. If there are only a few photos, you can link Lightroom to the new name/location (using the previous instructions), however every renamed photo must be relinked individually.

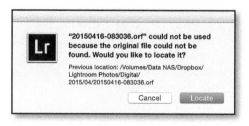

Figure 19.4 *Click on the exclamation point and navigate to the new location of the photo. Lightroom doesn't find them automatically, but it does display the last known location.*

How do I prevent missing files?

Prevention is better than cure, and preventing missing files will save you some additional work, so there are a few things to look out for...

• Don't delete the original files from your hard drive. Photos are not stored IN Lightroom.

• Move any files or folders within Lightroom's own interface, simply by dragging and dropping around the Folders panel. Don't "tidy up" using other software or the operating system (or if you do, fix Lightroom's links immediately).

• Rename any files before importing into Lightroom, or use Lightroom to rename them. Whatever you do, don't rename in other software once they're imported.

• Don't use *Synchronize Folder* to remove missing files and import them again at their new location as you'll lose all of your Lightroom settings.

Set Lightroom's Folders panel to show the full folder hierarchy to a single root level folder. If a folder is moved from its previous location, or the drive letter changes, it can be fixed more easily than individual folders.

How do I change drive letters on Windows?

When using external drives, Lightroom doesn't change the drive letters, but Windows often does. That can confuse Lightroom, requiring you to relink missing files on a regular basis. Leaving the drives plugged in to your computer, or always reattaching them in the same order can help avoid the drive letter changing.

To set the drive letter a little more permanently, or reset them if they change, you can go into Windows Disk Management and assign a specific drive letter. You'll need to be logged in as an Administrator. On Windows 7/10, go to *Start menu > Control Panel > Administrative Tools > Computer Management* or use the Search charm on Windows 8. Disk Management is listed in the left-hand panel under *Storage*. Selecting this connects to the Virtual Disk Service and displays the drives seen in the main panel.

Find the relevant drive in the list, right-click and there's an option to *Change Drive Letter and Paths*. Be careful to ensure you have the correct drive! Selecting Change displays a list of available letters to select from. Selecting a letter outside the range Windows would usually assign automatically helps to reduce the possibility of it changing, so a letter from the latter half of the alphabet is a good choice. When you've finished, press *OK*, and select *Yes* when prompted to confirm the drive letter change.

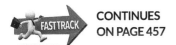

CONTINUES ON PAGE 457

It says *The selected folder or one of its subfolders is already in Lightroom. Do you want to combine these folders?* Do I say yes or no?

If a folder has been marked as missing for a while, and you've since imported photos from the new location, when you select *Find Missing Folder*, it might say *The selected folder or one of its subfolders is already in Lightroom. Do you want to combine these folders?* If you're sure you've selected the correct folder, press the *Merge* button to combine them.

It says *The file is associated with another photo in the catalog.* How do I fix it?

There's another problem that can arise if you reimport the photos at their new location instead of fixing the broken links. This creates duplicate records, and prevents you from fixing the links.

How might you get into this state? Imagine your photos hard drive is originally called Drive D, and you import your photos and edit them. Then, at some point, Windows changes the drive letter to Drive F (or you rename a Mac drive). Later, you want to edit one of these old photos but it's marked as missing, so you import it again (big mistake!). Time passes, and you're reading this chapter, so you decide to relink all of the missing files. When you try to relink some of the files, Lightroom says "The file is associated with another photo in the catalog" and won't let you continue.

So how do you fix it? Let's work through it step by step:

1. Back up your catalog, just in case you make a mistake.

2. First, you have to determine which of the duplicates to keep. The original one that's marked as missing? Or the newer one? In most cases, you'll choose to keep the version that you've edited.

3. When you've decided which record you're going to remove from the catalog, make sure you have a folder selected (not a collection) then select the photo and press the Delete key. When Lightroom asks whether to *Remove* or *Delete*, make sure you select *Remove*.

4. Once that duplicate record has been removed from the catalog, check the photo you've decided to keep. If it was marked as missing, click the rectangle in the corner and navigate to the new location. Lightroom now allows you to select the photo.

5. Repeat for each of the photos with the same problem. If you have the same problem on a large number of photos, you may be able to check and delete a whole folder at a time, rather than fixing each photo individually.

It can be a time consuming job, so it's yet another good reason to fix missing photos at the earliest opportunity.

How do I check my catalog for missing files?

If you go to *Library menu > Find Missing Photos*, Lightroom creates a temporary collection of the missing photos so that you can relink them. It doesn't update live, so even after you've located the missing photo, it still appears in that collection. To remove this temporary collection from the Catalog panel, right-click on it and select *Delete this Temporary Collection*. **(Figure 19.5)**

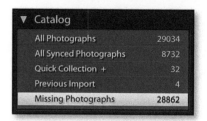

Figure 19.5 *If you go to Library menu > Find Missing Photos, Lightroom creates a collection in the Catalog panel.*

I accidentally deleted my photos from my hard drive and I don't have backups! Can I recover them using Lightroom's previews or smart previews?

If you've deleted your original files, you don't have backups, and they're not in the Recycle Bin (Windows) / Trash (Mac), the next thing to check is whether the photos are still on the memory card. If you haven't reshot the entire card, it may be possible to rescue some of the original photos using recovery software. You could also try recovery software on the hard drive, to see if they can be rescued from there.

If that's not possible, before you do anything else, close Lightroom, find the catalog on the hard drive, and duplicate the catalog and previews, just in case you make a mistake.

It's possible to convert Lightroom's previews into files. It's not ideal as the quality isn't as high as the original files, but they're not bad as a last-ditch rescue attempt.

First, check under the Histogram in the Library module to see whether you have Smart Previews for the missing photos. You're looking for the words *Smart Preview*. If there are Smart Previews, select the photos and go to *File menu > Export*. Choose *DNG* as the File Format (leave the checkboxes unchecked) and export them to a folder on the hard drive. They're only 2560px along the longest edge and they're lossy compressed, but they're better than nothing. (Turn back to the Export chapter starting on page 351 for more information on exporting).

Next, we'll save your standard previews as JPEGs. If you don't have smart previews, these standard previews are the only files you have left. Even if you did have smart previews, the standard previews may be larger (i.e. 1:1 size) so it's worth trying both options.

Adobe released a script that retrieves Lightroom's previews and saves them as image files, however there are also a couple of free plug-ins which make the process easier. The resulting JPEGs are only the size and quality of the previews, but they're better than nothing. In these instructions, we'll use a plug-in by Jeffrey Friedl.

1. Download Jeffrey's plug-in from https://www.Lrq.me/friedl-extractpreviews

2. Double click to unzip the plug-in.

3. Go to *File menu > Plug-in Manager* and press the *Add* button. Navigate to the plug-in you've just unzipped.

4. Back in Lightroom's Grid view, select the photos you need to rescue.

5. Go to *File menu > Plugin Extras > Extract Preview Images* to show the dialog.

6. Select the location for the extracted previews and press *Begin Extraction*.

7. In the results dialog, the plug-in reports on the size and quality of the extracted previews. **(Figure 19.6)**

Finally, import the new DNG files and/or JPEG files into your Lightroom catalog. You may need to reorganize them into folders while importing, and then sort them into collections again and reapply flags, but they're better than nothing. Once you're happy that your replacement files are sorted out, you can remove the old missing files from the catalog.

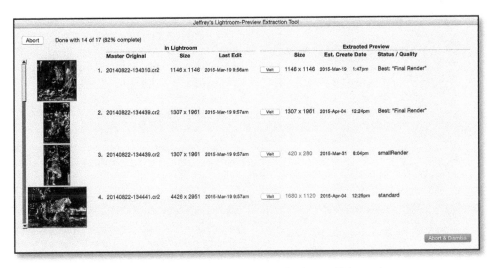

Figure 19.6 *Jeffrey's Extract Previews plug-in turns Lightroom's previews into normal JPEGs, if you've lost the originals.*

THE CAT WALKED OVER THE KEYBOARD

There are some other problems that frequently crop up on the forums, so here are the quick fixes for your reference...

My Toolbar's disappeared—where's it gone?

The Toolbar usually appears between the photos in the Preview Area and the Filmstrip. It holds buttons such as view options and the *Done* button in the Develop module. Flip back to the Workspace chapter on page 71 for more detail. If your Toolbar disappears, press T—you've hidden it!

Where have my panels gone?

If a panel goes missing, for example, the Basic panel in the Develop module, go to *Window menu > Panels* and click on the name of the panel to enable it. You can also right-click on a panel header (in the gray space next to the panel name) to show the context-sensitive menu and put a checkmark against the name of the missing panel. **(Figure 19.7)**

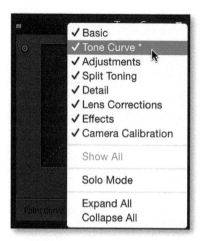

Figure 19.7 *If a panel goes missing, right-click on one of the other panel headers and reselect it from the menu.*

How do I show missing dialogs?

If you've hidden some of the dialogs by checking a *Don't Show Again* checkbox, you can bring them all back by pressing the *Reset all warning dialogs* button in the *Preferences dialog > General tab*.

Dialogs can also go missing if you use dual monitors. Lightroom remembers which monitor you last used to display each dialog. If you then unplug one of those monitors, Lightroom may still try to show the dialog on the detached monitor, resulting in an error beep when you try to press anything else. To solve it, press the Escape key to close the imaginary dialog, and either plug the second monitor back so you can see the dialog to move it back, or reset Lightroom's Preferences file. We'll come to these instructions a little later in the chapter on page 451.

CATALOG CORRUPTION

Lightroom's catalogs are basic databases, so it's possible for them to become corrupted, even though it's relatively rare. Don't worry, you have nothing to fear from keeping all of your work in a single catalog, as long as you take regular backups. But what do you do if you have problems with your catalog? Let's investigate.

Why can't I open my catalog?

If you can't open your catalog, there are a few possible reasons, and the error message offers a few clues.

Lightroom may say: *The Lightroom catalog cannot be opened because another application already has it open. Quit the other copy of Lightroom before trying to relaunch.* If so, check the catalog's folder for a *.lrcat.lock file. If Lightroom's closed, it shouldn't be there, so you can safely delete it. They sometimes get left behind if Lightroom crashes. Remember, if there's a *.lrcat-journal file, don't delete this journal as it contains data that hasn't been written back to the catalog yet.

Lightroom requires read and write access to the catalog file, so it may show an error message that says: *The Lightroom catalog cannot be used because the parent folder ... does not allow files to be created within it* or *Lightroom cannot launch with this catalog. It is either on a network volume or on a volume on which Lightroom cannot save changes.*

If you see either of these errors, check your operating system's folder and file permissions as they're probably set to read-only. It may not be the catalog folder itself that has the wrong permissions, but perhaps a parent folder. On Windows, there are additional security layers which can cause similar issues. (You might need to Google how to do that, as these are operating system settings.)

Also check your catalog location—it can't stored be on a network drive, or on read-only media such as a DVD, or on an incorrectly formatted drive (e.g. an NTFS drive on a Mac).

Finally, Lightroom might give a warning about the catalog being corrupted. This can be more serious, so we'll cover it in more detail.

How do catalogs become corrupted?

In almost all cases, corruption results from a hardware problem. This can include the computer crashing due to a hardware fault, kernel panics, or power outages, any of which can prevent Lightroom from finishing writing to the catalog safely.

Catalogs also become corrupted if the connection to the drive cuts out while Lightroom is writing to the catalog, for example, as a result of an external drive being accidentally disconnected or the catalog being stored on a network drive (via an unsupported hack). Some external drives drop their connection intermittently for no known reason, so it's safest to keep your catalog on an internal drive if possible.

Lightroom says that my catalog is corrupted—can I fix it?

If Lightroom warns you that your catalog is corrupted, it also offers to try to repair it for you. **(Figure 19.8)** In many cases, the corruption can be repaired automatically, but it depends on how it's happened. **(Figure 19.9)**

If the catalog repair fails, restoring a backup is your next step, which we covered in detail in the Backup chapter on page 58. **(Figure 19.10)** You can also try moving the catalog to a different drive, which can solve some false corruption warnings.

If you don't have a current backup catalog, there may be another way of rescuing your data. It involves using Import from Catalog to transfer the uncorrupted data into a new catalog. Usually the corruption is confined to one or two folders that were being accessed when the catalog became corrupted, so working through methodically can sometimes rescue almost all of your data. It's worth a shot!

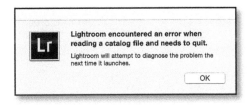

Figure 19.8 *If Lightroom can't open the catalog, it warns you before quitting.*

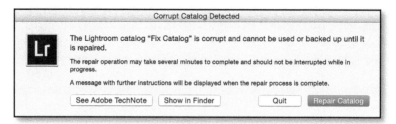

Figure 19.9 *If Lightroom confirms that the catalog is corrupted, it offers to repair it.*

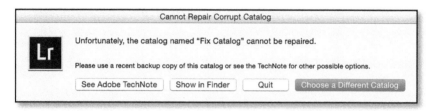

Figure 19.10 *If the catalog can't be repaired, you'll need to restore a backup.*

To attempt recovery:

1. Close Lightroom and duplicate the corrupted catalog using Explorer (Windows) / Finder (Mac) before you proceed with rescue attempts, just in case you make it worse.

2. Create a new catalog (by going to *File menu > New Catalog*) and then go to the Catalog Settings dialog and set the backup interval to *Every time Lightroom exits*. You can change this back again later, but it saves you starting this process again from the beginning if you pull some corrupted data into the new catalog.

3. Go to *File menu > Import from Another Catalog* and navigate to the corrupted catalog. If it gets as far as the Import from Catalog dialog box, select just a few folders in the *Catalog Contents* section. In the pop-ups below, select *File Handling > Add new photos to catalog without moving*.

4. Repeat the Import from Catalog, each time selecting a few folders to transfer. Between imports, close and reopen Lightroom, so that a new backup is created, and the integrity check runs to ensure that your new catalog hasn't become corrupted.

5. Keep repeating the process until all of the folders are imported from the corrupted catalog. If you hit another corruption warning, go back a step, restore the previous backup, and make a note of the folders you had just imported, skipping them. In the process, you may be able to narrow the corruption down to a single folder or even specific photos.

6. Once you've finished, and you have a working catalog again, select all the photos and go to *File menu > Export as Catalog*. Give the exported catalog a new name, and uncheck the checkboxes at the bottom. This extra step helps to remove any orphaned data.

7. Open the newly exported catalog. This now becomes your main working catalog.

8. After a significant corruption, it's also worth rebuilding the previews. To do so, select all the photos and go to *Library menu > Previews > Render Standard-Sized Previews*. This process takes a long time if you have a large number of photos, so you might choose to leave it running overnight.

9. Finally, if everything's working as expected, you can archive or delete the backups created in step 4, the temporary catalog created in step 2, and the corrupted catalog.

Of course, having current backups would have prevented all of this work, so you'll want to make sure that your backups are current in future!

How do I prevent catalog corruption?

A little bit of common sense goes a long way in protecting your work.

• Back up regularly, and keep older catalog backups.

• Always shut your computer down properly.

• Don't disconnect an external drive while Lightroom is open.

• Keep the catalog on an internal drive if possible.

• Turn on *Test integrity* and *Optimize catalog* in the Backup dialog to run each time you back up. If they have trouble running, it'll give you a clue that something's going wrong.

IMAGE & PREVIEW PROBLEMS

Viewing accurate previews of your photos is essential. Problems do sometimes occur, so you'll need to know how to fix them, even if they're not Lightroom's fault.

Why do I just get gray boxes instead of previews?

If Lightroom's showing gray thumbnails **(Figure 19.11)** instead of image previews in the Grid view, there are a few possibilities...

Previews don't exist—If there's an exclamation point in the corner of the thumbnail in Grid view as well as gray thumbnails, Lightroom simply hasn't been able to build the previews yet. The original file may have been renamed or moved outside of Lightroom, or the drive was disconnected before Lightroom was able to create the previews. If you reconnect the drive or find the missing files, the previews can be created. (Turn back to the Missing Files section starting on page 435 for more information.)

Previews can't display—If there are no exclamation points in the corner of the thumbnails in Grid view, a corrupted monitor profile is the most likely cause, or the graphics card driver may need updating. We'll discuss corrupted monitor profiles in more detail in the next question.

Corrupted preview cache—It's also possible that the preview cache is corrupted, particularly if your catalog has been upgraded from an earlier version. We'll

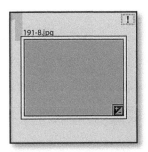

Figure 19.11 *Gray thumbnails may be caused by a corrupted monitor profile, graphics card drivers, or missing files.*

come back to that on page 446.

Everything in Lightroom is a funny color, but the original photos look perfect in other programs, and the exported photos don't look like they do in Lightroom either. What could be wrong?

In addition to previews that are completely missing, your previews may be displayed in the wrong color.

Strange colored previews that don't match the exported photos in color managed programs are usually caused by a corrupted monitor profile. Lightroom uses the profile differently to other programs (perceptual rendering rather than relative colorimetric), so corruption in that part of the profile shows up in Lightroom even though it appears correct in other programs. It often happens with the manufacturer's profiles that come with most monitors.

To confirm that the corrupted monitor profile is the mostly likely cause, select a B&W photo (or turn a photo B&W by pressing the V key). The B&W photo and its histogram should be neutral shades of gray, but you may see a color cast (likely brown) if your profile's corrupted. **(Figure 19.12)**

Ideally you should recalibrate your monitor using a hardware calibration device, such

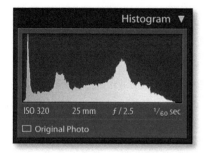

Histogram ▼

ISO 320   25 mm   f / 2.5   ¹/₆₀ sec
☐ Original Photo

Figure 19.12 *A color cast on the Histogram panel is a clear indication that the monitor profile is corrupted.*

as a Spyder, i1Display Pro or ColorMunki. If you don't have such a tool, put it on your shopping list, and in the meantime, remove the corrupted monitor profile as a temporary solution.

How do I remove my monitor profile to check whether it's corrupted?

Windows

1. Close Lightroom.

2. On Windows 7/10, go to *Start menu > Control Panel > Color Management* or type *color management* in the Start menu search box. On Windows 8, use the Search charm to search for 'color management' and then select *Settings > Color Management*.

3. Click the *Devices* tab if it's not already selected. **(Figure 19.13)**

4. From the *Device* pop-up, select your monitor. If you have more than 1 monitor connected, pressing the Identify monitors button displays a large number on screen for identification.

5. Check the *Use my settings for this device* checkbox.

6. Make a note of the currently selected profile, which is marked as (default). If there isn't an existing profile, you can skip this step.

7. Click the *Add* button.

8. In the Associate Color Profile dialog, select *sRGB IE61966-2.1* (sRGB Color Space Profile.icm) and press *OK*.

9. Back in the Color Management dialog, select the sRGB profile and click *Set as Default Profile*, and then close the dialog.

macOS

1. Close Lightroom.

2. Go to *System Preferences > Displays.*

3. Select the *Color* tab.

4. Press the *Calibrate* button and follow the instructions. **(Figure 19.14)**

5. Turn on the *Expert Options* and calibrate to gamma 2.2.

Finally, restart Lightroom and check whether everything looks correct. If it does, you've confirmed that the previous monitor profile was the cause of the problem. You can temporarily leave sRGB as the monitor profile, as it's better than a corrupted one, but it would then be wise to calibrate your monitor accurately using a hardware calibration device.

The only real way of calibrating a monitor is with a hardware calibration device. Software calibration is only ever as good

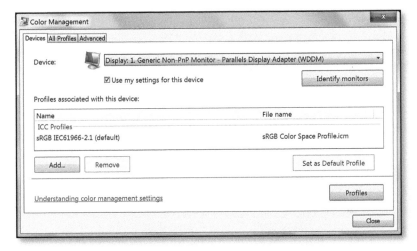

Figure 19.13 *Setting the monitor profile to sRGB using the Windows Color Management dialog confirms or rules out a corrupted monitor profile.*

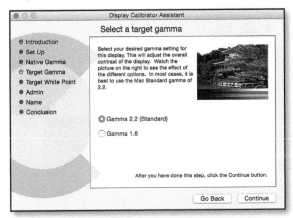

Figure 19.14 *The basic Mac Calibration tool is ok for testing, but it's only as good as your eyes, so you'll still need calibration hardware.*

as your eyes, and everyone sees color differently, but calibration hardware, such as the ColorMunki, i1 Display Pro or Spyder devices are now inexpensive, and an essential part of every keen digital photographer's toolkit.

Most calibration software offers an advanced setting, so if it gives you a choice, go for a brightness of around 100-120 cd/m2, 6500K or native white point for LCD monitor, and most importantly, an ICC2 Matrix profile rather than an ICC4 or LUT-based profile, as these more recent profiles aren't compatible with many programs yet.

Why is Lightroom changing the colors of my photos?

If Lightroom starts changing the appearance of the newly imported photos automatically, there are a few settings that you might have changed.

Are the photos raw? If so, the changes are likely just a difference in rendering, because raw data is just that—raw—and each raw processor has its own default style. Turn back to the Develop chapter on page 192 for a detailed discussion.

There are a few other possibilities, however, which would also apply to JPEG and other rendered formats:

Develop Preset—You may have selected a Develop preset in the Import dialog. Set the *Develop Settings* pop-up to *None* in the Apply During Import panel and see if the problem recurs on future imports.

Default Settings—You may have changed the Default settings. To check, open a newly imported photo in the Develop module and press the *Reset* button. If the photo doesn't change, hold down the Shift key to change the button to *Reset (Adobe)* and click again.

If the photo now changes, go to *Preferences dialog > Presets tab* and press the *Reset all default Develop settings* button to reset the defaults back to Adobe's own settings.

Existing Edits—Have the photos been edited in Lightroom or ACR previously? If so, they may have Develop settings recorded in the metadata.

For photos that are already imported, select them in Grid view and press the *Reset All* button in the Quick Develop panel to reset them all back to the default settings.

Why doesn't the Library module preview match the Develop module preview?

The Library module uses pre-rendered Adobe RGB JPEGs. At 1:1 view, it's fairly accurate, but the color space is smaller than Develop, so some highly saturated colors may appear slightly desaturated.

The Develop module uses the original data in a large color space, and downsizes the image data on-the-fly. This means that Develop's 1:1 view is the most accurate, but high sharpening and noise reduction values can be wildly inaccurate at Fit or Fill view.

Lightroom says my preview cache is corrupted—how do I fix it?

There's one more problem that can occur with previews—a corrupted preview cache.

The most obvious clue is Lightroom showing an error message telling you that the preview cache is corrupted and then resets the preview cache automatically.

Alternatively you might find that Lightroom displays the wrong preview for some of your photos, some previews or thumbnails disappear when the photo is deselected, or the photo only shows in the Develop module.

If so, you can fix it by manually rebuilding the preview cache:

1. Find your catalog on the hard drive. If you can open Lightroom, go to *Edit menu* (Windows) / *Lightroom menu* (Mac) > *Catalog Settings* > *General tab* and press the Show button to open an Explorer (Windows) / Finder (Mac) window, then quit Lightroom. If you can't open Lightroom, and you don't know where to find your catalog, you'll need to search for *.LRCAT files.

2. Using Explorer (Windows) / Finder (Mac), move or rename the previews folder (*Previews.lrdata) and restart Lightroom.

3. Lightroom can now rebuild the previews from the original files. Select all the photos and go to *Library menu* > *Previews* > *Build Standard-Sized Previews* and leave it to work, perhaps overnight as it takes a long time. If any of the photos are offline (e.g. stored on disconnected external hard drives), these previews will remain blank until you reconnect the drive.

4. Once you're happy they've all rebuilt, you can delete the previous previews folder (*Previews.lrdata) if you haven't already done so. I don't usually recommend deleting the old previews before building new ones, just in case there are any missing original files, and the previews are the only copy you have left. If you're comfortable that you still have all of your original files available, then you can delete the old previews before building the new ones.

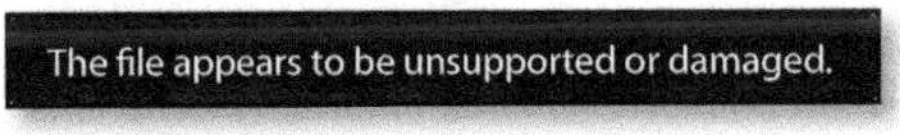

The file appears to be unsupported or damaged.

Figure 19.15 When entering the Develop module, Lightroom may warn that a photo is unsupported or damaged, which usually indicates corruption.

Lightroom appears to be corrupting my photos—how do I stop it?

In the Import chapter error messages starting on page 46, we briefly discussed the problem of images becoming corrupted, especially during import. It can happen to anyone.

Severe file corruption is often picked up at the Import stage, resulting in a *file is unsupported or damaged* error message **(Figure 19.15)**, but less serious corruption might not be discovered until you look at Lightroom's standard size previews.

Initially, Lightroom displays the embedded JPEG preview, which often escapes corruption because it's confined to a small area of the file. Lightroom then reads the whole file to create an accurate preview, at which point the corruption appears. That may lead you to believe that Lightroom's corrupting the files, but it's not.

If a file is corrupted **(Figure 19.16)**, Lightroom's unable turn the leftover data into an accurate image, which results in a distorted view and *There was an error working with the photo* error message in the Loupe view and Develop module.

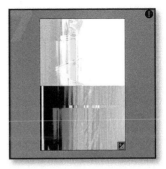

Figure 19.16 A corrupted file may not import at all, may show a low resolution thumbnail with a black border, or may show very visible corruption.

Because most other image browsers only display the uncorrupted embedded JPEG, they often fail to detect the problem. It's therefore important to build standard or 1:1 previews and visually check them for corruption in Lightroom (or another full raw processor) before wiping your memory cards.

But if it's not Lightroom's fault, what causes corruption? Unfortunately the files are usually corrupted before they reach Lightroom, and it's almost always due to hardware problems.

Corrupted files are most frequently caused by a damaged card reader or cable. The good news is the file on the memory card is often uncorrupted, and can be safely imported without corruption by using another card reader.

Other regular suspects include damaged memory cards or problems with the camera initially writing the file, such as the battery dying or the card being removed while writing.

If a photo gets corrupted some time after the original import, your computer likely has a hardware problem. A dying hard drive or damaged connection (e.g. cable) or damaged RAM are frequent causes, but a variety of other hardware issues can also cause problems.

Whatever the cause, you'll need to re-download the file from the memory card or replace it with an uncorrupted backup.

If you don't have an uncorrupted version, Instant JPEG from RAW may be able to extract a readable embedded JPEG preview. You can download it freely from https://www.Lrq.me/instantjpegfromraw

STANDARD TROUBLESHOOTING

If your issue isn't covered by the previous sections, or in the specific topic area of the book, there are some general troubleshooting steps you can try.

As always, make sure you have backups before you try any troubleshooting steps.

1. The Magic Reboot

If you're having odd problems with any computer program, the age-old wisdom "turn it off and turn it on again" still works wonders. First, try restarting the program, and if that doesn't solve it, reboot the computer.

2. Optimize the Catalog

Go to *File menu > Optimize Catalog* and wait for it to tell you it's completed before moving on.

3. Check for Updates

Next, check for updates, as the issue you're running into could be a bug that's been fixed in a later release. Make sure you're running the latest updates, both for Lightroom (by going to *Help menu > Check for Updates*) and also for your operating system. Also update drivers on your machine, particularly the graphics card drivers and any mouse or tablet drivers

4. Turn off the GPU

Buggy graphics card drives can cause no end of trouble. Go to *Preferences > Performance tab* and uncheck *Enable Graphics Processor*. If that helps, you could also check the graphics card manufacturer's website (Windows) / Software Update (Mac) for an updated driver.

5. Reset Preferences

If you're still having problems, resetting Lightroom's Preferences file can solve all sorts of 'weirdness,' so it's a good early step in troubleshooting. See page 453 for detailed instructions.

6. Try a new catalog

If resetting the preferences doesn't help, create a new catalog to rule out minor catalog corruption. To do so:

1. Go to *File menu > New Catalog*.

2. If you can't open Lightroom to access the menu, hold down Ctrl (Windows) / Opt (Mac) while restarting Lightroom, then click the *Create New Catalog* button.

3. Choose a location for the temporary catalog such as the desktop. (Note that this is only a test to check whether the problem is catalog-specific. Don't delete your working catalog or start working in this temporary catalog!)

4. Import some photos into this new catalog to check everything is working as expected.

5. If this works, the problem is likely specific to your catalog. Don't panic, that can usually be fixed! Turn back to the Catalog Corruption section on page 442.

7. Rule out corrupted presets

The next thing to check for is corrupted presets, as they can cause strange problems like module hanging and performance problems. To do so:

Windows

1. Go to *Edit menu > Preferences > Presets tab*.

2. Press the *Show Lightroom Presets Folder* button.

Alternatively, you can navigate directly to C:\Users\[your username]\AppData\ Roaming\Adobe\Lightroom\ Note that this is a hidden folder, so the easiest way to do so is to open the Start menu search box (Windows 7/10) / Search charm (Windows 8) and type *%appdata%\Adobe\Lightroom*

3. Whichever way you choose to find this folder, close Lightroom before going any further.

4. Select the contents of the Lightroom folder, with the exception of the Preferences folder (as we've already ruled out preferences problems).

5. Move these subfolders (e.g. Develop Presets, Print Templates, etc.) to another location, such as the desktop.

6. Restart Lightroom.

Mac

1. Go to *Lightroom menu > Preferences > Presets tab*.

2. Press the *Show Lightroom Presets Folder* button.

Alternatively, you can navigate directly to Macintosh HD / Users / [your username] / Library / Application Support / Adobe / Lightroom / Note that this is a hidden folder, so the easiest way to do so is to open Finder and select the *Go menu*. Hold down the Opt key so *Library* appears in the menu, then click on *Library*. Then navigate through *Application Support > Adobe > Lightroom*.

3. Whichever way you choose to find this folder, close Lightroom before going any further.

4. Select the Lightroom folder and move it to another location, such as the desktop.

5. Reboot your computer (because OS X caches some files), then restart Lightroom.

If the problem isn't solved, you can copy the preset folders back, overwriting the default preset folders that have been automatically created.

If it does solve the problem, copy the presets back a few at a time, to narrow down which specific preset (or group of presets) is causing the problem.

8. Rule out corrupted fonts

Corrupted fonts have also been known to cause problems, particularly in the Print and Book modules. Fonts aren't specific to Lightroom. If you're not familiar with managing your operating system's fonts, Google "uninstall font" and the name of your operating system for instructions on removing fonts.

9. Try a clean user account

Sometimes issues are specific to your computer's user account. Testing a clean user account can rule out a lot of potential problems in one go. If you're not sure how to create a clean user account, here are the official instructions:

Windows - https://www.Lrq.me/winuser (select your Windows version in the pop-up)

Mac - https://www.Lrq.me/macuser

10. Check for hardware and operating system problems

Lightroom taxes your computers hardware more than most of the programs you use, so it often finds hardware and operating system problems that don't show up in other software.

Damaged RAM can also cause some odd problems—Lightroom finds dodgy memory quicker than almost any other program. You can easily check that by running software such as Memtest.

Depending on the issues you're having, check other hardware for issues, for example, if Lightroom's running slowly, check the hard drives, particularly if it's an intermittent problem. They could be dying or just running low on space. If the screen is behaving oddly, check your graphics card, monitor and calibration. If you're having problems importing, check your card reader, USB ports and the destination hard drive.

Also check your boot drive to ensure it has plenty of space available, as a lack of space for operating system temp files can cause all sorts of problems.

DEFAULT FILE & MENU LOCATIONS

If you need to find Lightroom's files at any time, you'll need to know where to look, so here are the most popular Lightroom file locations.

By default, the boot drive is C:\ on Windows and Macintosh HD on Mac. If your operating system is installed on a different drive, you may need to replace the drive letter/name on the file paths that are listed below.

[your username] refers to the name of your user account, for example, mine is called Vic.

The default location of the Lightroom catalog is...

Windows—C: \ Users \ [your username] \ My Pictures \ Lightroom \ Lightroom

Catalog.lrcat

Mac—Macintosh HD / Users / [your username] / Pictures / Lightroom / Lightroom Catalog.lrcat

The default location of the Preferences is...

Windows—C: \ Users \ [your username] \ AppData \ Roaming \ Adobe \ Lightroom \ Preferences \ Lightroom Classic CC 7 Preferences.agprefs

Mac—Macintosh HD / Users / [your username] / Library / Preferences / com. adobe.LightroomClassicCC7.plist

Preference files aren't cross-platform. By default, Preferences are a hidden file on Windows and macOS.

There are also separate startup preferences. These include the last used catalog path, the recent catalog list, which catalog to load on startup and the catalog upgrade history.

Windows—C: \ Users \ [your username] \ AppData \ Roaming \ Adobe \ Lightroom \ Preferences \ Lightroom Classic CC 7 Startup Preferences.agprefs

Mac—Macintosh HD / Users / [your username] / Library / Application Support / Adobe / Lightroom /Lightroom Classic CC 7 Startup Preferences.agprefs

How do I reset Lightroom's Preferences?

There's a simple automated way of resetting preferences—just hold down Alt and Shift (Windows) / Opt and Shift (Mac) while opening Lightroom and it'll ask whether to reset the preferences. The timing is crucial—hold them down while clicking/double-clicking on the app/shortcut. **(Figure 19.17)**

Alternatively, you can reset the preferences manually. Moving or renaming the preferences file, rather than deleting it, means that you can put it back if it doesn't solve the problem, to save you manually recreating your preferences again.

Windows

1. Go to *Edit menu > Preferences > Presets tab.*

2. If *Store presets with this catalog* is unchecked, press the *Show Lightroom Presets Folder* button.

If *Store presets with this catalog* is checked, uncheck it, press the *Show Lightroom Presets Folder* button. Don't forget to check the checkbox again after step 4, otherwise you'll wonder why your presets disappeared.

Alternatively, you can navigate directly to C:\Users\[your username]\AppData\Roaming\Adobe\Lightroom\Preferences

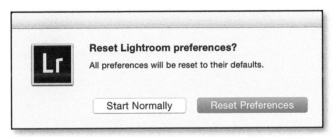

Figure 19.17 *Hold down Alt and Shift (Windows) / Opt and Shift (Mac) while opening Lightroom to reset the preferences.*

Note that this is a hidden folder, so the easiest way to do so is to open the Start menu search box (Windows 7/10) / Search charm (Windows 8) and type *%appdata%\Adobe\Lightroom\Preferences*

3. Whichever way you choose to find the folder, close Lightroom before going any further.

4. Rename, move or delete the Lightroom Classic CC 7 Preferences.agprefs and any earlier versions (but leave the Lightroom Classic CC 7 Startup Preferences there), then restart Lightroom.

Mac

1. Quit Lightroom.

2. Open Finder and select the *Go menu*.

3. Hold down the Opt key so *Library* appears in the menu, then click on *Library*.

4. In the Finder window, open the Preferences folder and scroll down to com.adobe.LightroomClassicCC7.plist

5. Move this file, plus any other Lightroom preference files (e.g. com.adobe.LightroomClassicCC7.LSSharedFileList.plist or older versions), to another folder or delete them.

6. Reboot your computer (because macOS caches some preference files), then restart Lightroom.

7. If your presets are missing, go to *Lightroom menu > Preferences > Presets tab*, check *Store presets with this catalog* and they should reappear.

Some people like to keep screenshots of the Preferences and View Options dialogs, as well as a backup of the preferences file, so they can easily be restored.

What's stored in Preferences?

If you reset your Preferences file, the obvious settings that you lose are those in the Preferences dialog, but it also includes other details such as your View Options settings, last used settings, FTP server details, some plug-in settings, your country, etc.

Your original photos, Develop settings, Develop defaults, collections, presets and other important settings aren't affected by deleting the Preferences file.

The *Store presets with this catalog* setting also reverts to default (unchecked) if you reset the preferences file, but the presets themselves are perfectly safe, and checking the checkbox in Preferences causes the presets to reappear.

There are also separate startup preferences which don't usually need resetting. These include the last used catalog path, the recent catalog list, which catalog to load on startup and the catalog upgrade history.

How do I show hidden files to find my preferences and presets?

On Windows, you can open the Start menu search box (Windows 7/10) / Search charm (Windows 8) and type *%appdata%\Adobe\Lightroom*, and you'll be taken directly to the Lightroom user folder.

On macOS, the user Library folder is hidden by default. If you go to Finder, select the *Go menu*, and hold down the Opt key, you'll see Library appear in the menu, and then you can navigate to the Preferences or Application Support folder. Personally, I drag that Library folder to the sidebar so that it's always easily accessible.

The default location of the Presets is...

Windows—C: \ Users \ [your username] \ AppData \ Roaming \ Adobe \ Lightroom \

Mac—Macintosh HD / Users / [your username] / Library / Application Support / Adobe / Lightroom /

If you've checked the *Store presets with this catalog* checkbox in Preferences, they'll be stored next to your catalog file instead.

To find them easily on either platform, go to *Edit menu* (Windows) / *Lightroom menu* (Mac) > *Preferences* > *Presets tab* and press the *Show Lightroom Presets Folder* button. **(Figure 19.18)**

Each type of preset has its own folder, for example Develop Presets, Filename Templates and Metadata Presets. **(Figure 19.19)**

Presets are cross-platform and are saved in a Lightroom-only format (.lrtemplate). They're just text files with a different extension, so you can open them in any plain text editor.

Your Develop Defaults, Lens Defaults and Custom Point Curves are stored at...

Windows—C: \ Users \ [your username] \ AppData \ Roaming \ Adobe \ CameraRaw \

Mac—Macintosh HD / Users / [your username] / Library / Application Support / Adobe / CameraRaw /

Your Develop default settings, lens defaults and custom point curves are shared with ACR, so they're stored in the shared location, regardless of your *Store presets with this catalog* checkbox setting.

The default location of the Camera Raw Cache is...

Windows—C: \ Users \ [your username] \ AppData \ Local \ Adobe \ CameraRaw \ Cache \

Mac—Macintosh HD / Users / [your username] / Library / Caches / Adobe Camera Raw /

Your custom Camera & Lens Profiles should be installed to the User folders...

Lightroom no longer uses the shared ProgramData (Windows) / Application Support (Mac) folders for Camera or Lens Profiles. Instead, it stores the built-in profiles with its program files.

When you create camera or lens profiles, they must be stored in the user locations listed below. If you previously stored custom profiles in other locations, you'll need to move them to these user folders, otherwise Lightroom won't be able to find them.

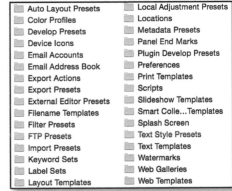

Auto Layout Presets	Local Adjustment Presets
Color Profiles	Locations
Develop Presets	Metadata Presets
Device Icons	Panel End Marks
Email Accounts	Plugin Develop Presets
Email Address Book	Preferences
Export Actions	Print Templates
Export Presets	Scripts
External Editor Presets	Slideshow Templates
Filename Templates	Smart Colle...Templates
Filter Presets	Splash Screen
FTP Presets	Text Style Presets
Import Presets	Text Templates
Keyword Sets	Watermarks
Label Sets	Web Galleries
Layout Templates	Web Templates

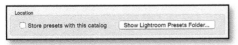

Figure 19.18 *Press the Show Lightroom Presets Folder button in Preferences to easily find the presets.*

Figure 19.19 *Presets are sorted into folders according to their type.*

Windows—C: \ Users \ [your username] \ AppData \ Roaming \ Adobe \ CameraRaw \ CameraProfiles \

Mac—Macintosh HD / Users / [your username] / Library / Application Support / Adobe / CameraRaw / CameraProfiles /

For the lens profiles, substitute the *LensProfiles* folder for the *CameraProfiles* folder in these paths.

The camera and lens profile file extensions are:

.dcpr—camera profile recipe file used for creating/editing a profile in the DNG Profile Editor

.dcp—camera profile

.lcp—lens profile

Preferences & Settings Menu Locations

A few of the menu commands are in different locations on Windows and Mac, depending on the operating system standard. Rather than repeating them every time I refer to Preferences or Catalog Settings, here's a quick reference:

Lightroom Preferences & Catalog Settings are...

Windows—under the *Edit menu*

Mac—under the *Lightroom menu*

Photoshop Preferences are...

Windows—under the *Edit menu*

Mac—under the *Photoshop menu*

TROUBLESHOOTING SHORTCUTS

			Windows	Mac
Reset Preferences			Hold Alt Shift while starting Lightroom	Hold Opt Shift while starting Lightroom

IMPROVING PERFORMANCE

20

The speed of Lightroom— or the lack thereof—is one of the most popular topics among photographers. You may have asked questions such as "why is Lightroom so painfully slow?" and "how do I speed up Lightroom?" or "how do I make Lightroom run faster?"

Browsing the web, you'll find thousands of suggestions on ways to speed Lightroom up. Some of the suggestions work. Others are complete myths. Some suggestions can even make Lightroom slower.

Simply saying, "Lightroom is slow" doesn't help, because different areas of the program benefit from different optimizations. For example, if you're finding it slow in the Develop module, rendering 1:1 previews won't help.

In future, Adobe's main focus is on improving Lightroom's performance, but it's a complex program, and there are many things you can do to help yourself.

To fine-tune performance, you need to understand what Lightroom's doing under the hood, so in this chapter, we're going to take a close look at the different factors that affect Lightroom's performance.

NON-DESTRUCTIVE EDITING

Before we start optimizing Lightroom, let's set some expectations. I frequently hear people say, "But my computer runs fine with everything else," only to then discover that they're only running web browsers and office software, which use minimal resources. Others complain that Photoshop runs fine, but when they try to do the same tasks in Lightroom, it crawls.

Why is Lightroom slower at some tasks than Photoshop?

It's important to understand the nature of Lightroom's non-destructive editing, compared to most other program's pixel-based photo editing. We'll use Photoshop as an example of a pixel editor. (In this context, we're referring to Photoshop itself, as an example of a pixel based editor. Photoshop can also use the Camera Raw plug-in, which works as a non-destructive editor like Lightroom.

Imagine a conversation between you and your computer:

You: *"Computer, increase Exposure to +1.0"*

Photoshop: *"Ok, Exposure +1.0"*

Lightroom: *"Ok, Exposure +1.0"*

You: *"Computer, add Clarity +20"*

Photoshop: *"Ok, Clarity +20"*

Lightroom: *"Ok, Exposure +1.0, Clarity +20"*

Now carry on working for a while, and we'll catch up towards the end of the edit...

You: *"Computer, remove that dust spot"*

Photoshop: *"Ok, dust spot removed"*

Lightroom: *"Ok, Exposure +1.0, Clarity +20, Contrast +24, Temperature 5600, Tint 23, Highlights -40, Shadows +34, Vibrance +13, Tone Curve Strong Contrast, Lens Corrections on, Chromatic Aberration Removal on, Noise Reduction +20, Sharpening Amount +20, Vignette -10, HSL Blue Luminance -23, Upright Auto, Local Adjustment Gradient top to bottom with X settings, Brush mask with long list of coordinates, another brush mask with long list of coordinates, another brush mask with long list of coordinates, first brush spot, second brush spot, third brush spot, fourth brush spot.... ok, that new dust spot removed now too."*

Did you spot the difference? Pixel editors such as Photoshop run a task once, applying the changes to the pixels of the image itself. Each time you make another adjustment, it carries on from the current set of pixels. (That's a generalization as you can use smart objects or adjustment layers, but let's keep things simple for now, as these would also have performance implications.)

Lightroom, on the other hand, is a parametric editor. This means that every time you make an adjustment, it runs a series of text instructions. The more adjustments you make to the image, the more text instructions it has to run each time you make a change. The more complex the instructions, the longer they take to run. (Lightroom silently caches some editing stages to ease this issue, but again, let's keep

things simple.)

What are Lightroom's strengths and weaknesses?

There are pros and cons to both options:

File Size—Lightroom's text instructions are tiny, and since it doesn't touch the original image pixels, you only have to store the text instructions in the catalog and the original image file (plus backups, of course). In Photoshop, the edits are applied to the pixels, so you need to work on a copy of the photo, and if you start saving additional layers, the file size can balloon even further. Winner—Lightroom.

Changing Edits—If you make an edit one day in Lightroom, and change your mind the next day, you can simply move the slider back. No pixels were harmed in the process. In Photoshop, on the other hand, you either have to start all over again from the original, or if the change isn't too huge, you may be able to tweak the edited file, albeit with a lower quality result. (Or if you were really sensible, you may have used layers in Photoshop, at the cost of a larger file.) Winner—Lightroom.

Quality—Photoshop applies adjustments in the order you make them. If you lighten a photo and then darken some areas of it, you can't pull back the detail you've lost in that earlier step (without layers, etc.). Lightroom has the advantage of working on the raw data and silently applies the edits in the optimum order when exporting, with a higher quality result. Winner—Lightroom.

Speed—As we've seen, Lightroom has to constantly re-run text instructions, whereas Photoshop applies them immediately and directly to the pixels. For global edits, that's not too noticeable, but Lightroom can start to drag when using multiple local adjustments and retouching multiple spots. For this reason, pixel editors such as Photoshop and Elements are still better suited to more detailed retouching. On the other hand, when you're doing global edits to a large number of photos, Lightroom is far quicker than opening each of the photos in Photoshop. Winner—for editing lots of photos, Lightroom wins, but for detailed local edits, Photoshop wins.

It's simply a case of understanding their strengths and weaknesses. For editing most of your photos, Lightroom wins hands-down. For building complex local adjustment masks, doing detailed retouching or even removing numerous dust spots from scans, Photoshop is still the better tool for the job.

DEBUNKING MYTHS

I've read much of the information already published online on the topic of Lightroom's performance. Some of the suggestions work. Others are complete myths. Some of the advice (including advice found in my older blog posts and books) is simply outdated. Some suggestions can even make Lightroom slower. These are the main myths to avoid...

Myth #1: GPU—Everyone should turn it off (or on)

I've seen many posts saying that the *Use Graphics Processor* checkbox in *Preferences > Performance* should be turned off. I've seen almost as many saying it should be turned on. The reality is, there isn't a blanket 'best setting' that applies to everyone.

The correct setting for your computer depends on your graphics card, the drive speed, your screen resolution and how you actually use Lightroom. We'll discuss how to select the best setting for you on page 475.

Myth #2: Render 1:1 previews to speed up Develop

Bloggers frequently recommend that you render 1:1 previews in order to speed up loading in the Develop module... however pre-rendered 1:1 previews aren't used AT ALL in the Develop module. There are some good reasons to render 1:1 previews, such as quickly zooming in the Library module, but they won't help in the Develop module. We'll come back to where different types of previews are used on page 460 and page 463.

Myth #3: Make the Camera Raw Cache huge

A long time ago, I recommended enlarging the *Camera Raw Cache* size in *Preferences > Performance* to its maximum saying, "Bigger is better!" Then, in Lightroom 3.6 and later, the cache format was changed and compression applied, meaning the cached files shrunk to a few hundred KB per image, instead of multiple MB, so you could fit a lot more cached images into the same amount of space.

In Lightroom Classic, the rules change again. Now the size of the cached images is linked to the standard preview size set in Catalog Settings, so if you use a high resolution monitor, they may be big.

For most people, it IS worth enlarging the cache from its 5GB default. On the other hand, 200GB is overkill for most people. You'd be better off with a medium sized cache on a fast drive (e.g. SSD) than a much larger cache on a slower drive. We'll look at some rough calculations on page 463.

Myth #4: Use loads of little catalogs

Another frequent "solution" for performance problems is breaking the library up into multiple small catalogs. To be fair, a few things are slightly slower on a big catalog—most notably, opening the catalog and backing it up. But let's just define big catalogs: 1 million photos is a big catalog, 50,000 photos is a small catalog.

These slight delays in opening and backing up are easily offset by the lack of hassle trying to search and maintain multiple catalogs, and the confusion that can result.

We discussed the pros and cons of multiple catalogs on page 428. For the majority of photographers, multiple catalogs create far more problems than they solve. Just optimize the catalog regularly, and keep it on a fast drive.

Myth #5: Delete all of your previews

The final suggestion I frequently see is to empty Lightroom's caches and delete previews regularly. But stop and think about this suggestion for a moment. Lightroom has to display previews, otherwise you're looking at a blank screen. So which is quicker? Loading a small JPEG preview file from the hard drive, or loading a full size raw file and applying complex calculations to it? If you're unsure of the answer, trust me, loading a small JPEG preview is much faster! So why would you want to throw away all of the previews you've already rendered, and force Lightroom to do all these complex calculations again?

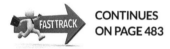

FAST TRACK

CONTINUES ON PAGE 483

PREVIEWS IN THE LIBRARY MODULE

Lightroom is a powerful program, offering far more than just basic raw processing, but it can also tax the most powerful of computer systems. Lightroom uses numerous kinds of previews and caches for different purposes, both in the Library and Develop modules. Having a basic idea of their usage can help you pick the right ones for your needs.

Before Lightroom does anything, it checks to see if the photo is already cached in RAM (random access memory). This is the fastest data to access. This happens automatically so you don't need to do anything to benefit.

If the photo's not already held in RAM, then Lightroom must load a pre-rendered preview, or build one from the original image data. You can see the full decision tree in **Figure 20.1** on page 461. The Library module uses three main kinds of pre-rendered preview—Embedded Previews, Standard Previews and 1:1 Previews.

What are Embedded Previews?

When most cameras write a raw file, they embed a JPEG preview too, although the size varies depending on the manufacturer. During import, you can extract these embedded previews for temporary use in the Library module, so you can start viewing and selecting your photos almost as soon as they've finished importing. We discussed this workflow in more detail on page 83. They don't have any Lightroom adjustments applied, so they look like the camera JPEGs.

What are Standard Rendered Previews?

Standard rendered previews are the most frequently used previews. They're used to display the photo in every module except Develop (where they're shown briefly and then replaced with cached raw data). For speed, Lightroom stores a range of different size AdobeRGB JPEGs as previews, from thumbnails right up to your chosen preview size.

Preview Loading Logic in the Library module

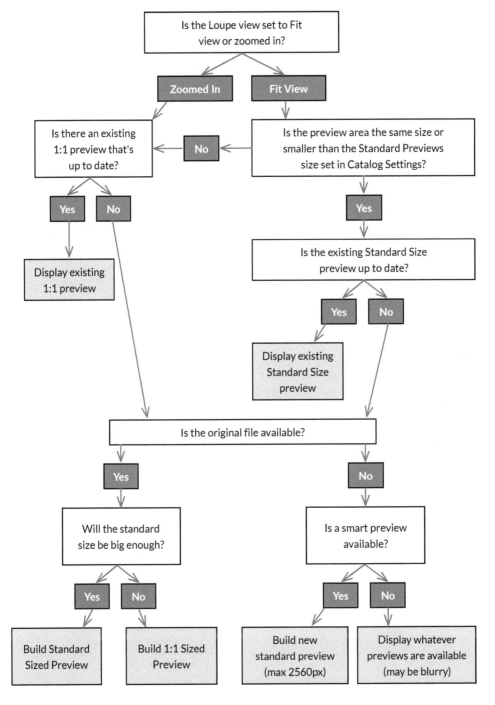

Figure 20.1 *The decision tree Lightroom uses when deciding which preview to load in the Library module.*

The size and quality of the standard-sized previews is set in the Catalog Settings dialog, which we'll come back to on page 469. The default *Auto* setting is ideal for most photographers.

What are 1:1 Rendered Previews?

1:1 rendered previews are full resolution Adobe RGB JPEGs, so they take up more space. If you want to zoom in on your photos in the Library module (e.g. checking focus), building them in advance avoids Lightroom having to build 1:1 previews on the fly, which would slow your browsing experience.

Where are Library module's rendered previews stored?

The previews are stored in a *.lrdata folder (Windows) / package file (Mac) next to your catalog. The standard previews have *.lrprev extensions and the folder/filename ends in Previews.lrdata.

The previews folders/files can grow very large, especially if you're creating 1:1 previews. You can delete any of the previews without permanent damage, but Lightroom will have to rebuild the previews when you next view the photos. If the files are offline, it will just show gray boxes until the files are next online and the previews can be rebuilt, so deleting the *.lrdata files can be a false economy.

If you find your previews are taking up too much space, consider discarding specific 1:1 or smart previews rather than deleting the entire preview cache.

How do I build standard or 1:1 previews?

While embedded previews can only be extracted during import, there are multiple ways of building standard and 1:1 sized previews.

On Demand—The standard sized preview is automatically built when you view a photo in the Library module and 1:1 preview is rendered when you zoom in. The problem with waiting for them to build on demand is you're sat staring at a Loading overlay while Lightroom builds the preview, which slows down your browsing. To avoid this delay, you can build the previews in advance.

On Import—In the File Handling panel of the Import dialog, you can choose to build *Standard* or *1:1 Previews* immediately after import. **(Figure 20.2)**

Menu Command—If you select the photos in the Library module, you can select *Library menu > Previews > Build Standard-Sized Previews* or *Build 1:1 Previews*. This is particularly valuable, as you can leave Lightroom building these previews at a time when you're not using the computer. It can also be used to update existing rendered previews when you've made Develop changes. It automatically skips any previews that are already up to date. **(Figure 20.3)**

If you have no photos selected, or all photos selected, Lightroom builds previews for all the photos in the current view, whether that's a collection, a folder, a filtered view, etc. If you have more than 1 photo selected in Grid mode, it assumes you just want to

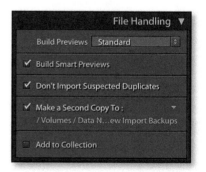

Figure 20.2 *You can build Standard or 1:1 while importing photos.*

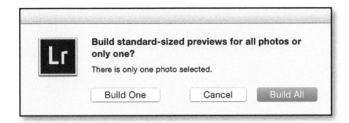

Figure 20.3 *When one photo is selected, Lightroom asks whether to build previews for all the photos or just the selected photo.*

build previews for all of the selected photos. If you have just 1 photo selected, it asks whether you want to build just that one preview, or previews for all photos in the current view.

Automatic Preloading—when you're stepping through photos in the Library module in 1:1 view, Lightroom intelligently creates 1:1 previews for other photos surrounding the selected photo, so when you move on, it loads much quicker.

How do I delete previews?

If you're concerned about the disk space that the 1:1 previews take up, you can discard 1:1 previews on demand by selecting the photos and choosing *Library menu > Previews > Discard 1:1 Previews*.

You can automatically delete 1:1 previews on a regular basis by selecting **Automatically Discard 1:1 Previews** *After One Day / After One Week / After 30 Days* or *Never* in the Catalog Settings dialog.

Lightroom only deletes 1:1 previews that are more than twice the size of your Standard-Sized Previews preference. For example, if your Standard-Sized Previews preference is set to 2048 and your 1:1 preview is 3036, Lightroom will keep the 1:1 preview, whereas if your Standard-Sized Previews preference is set to 1024, the 1:1

preview will be deleted.

The previews are also automatically deleted if you remove or delete a photo from within Lightroom. There's a slight delay in deleting the preview, just in case you press Undo, but they usually disappear at the next relaunch, if not before.

PREVIEWS & CACHES IN THE DEVELOP MODULE

Whereas the Library module displays lower quality rendered previews from the previews cache, the Develop module assumes you need an accurate, rapidly changing view. It first displays the normal preview from Lightroom's main preview cache (if GPU is disabled), then it reads any existing cached data, makes the Basic sliders available for adjustment, and then finishes loading and processing the full resolution data. You can see the full decision process in **Figure 20.4** on page 464. Lightroom mainly uses three main types of data in Develop—a temporary RAM cache, partially processed raw data stored on disk, and the original files.

RAM Cache—Before Lightroom does anything, it checks to see if the photo is already cached in RAM. This is the fastest data to access. When you're working in the Develop module, Lightroom intelligently

Preview Loading Logic in the Develop Module

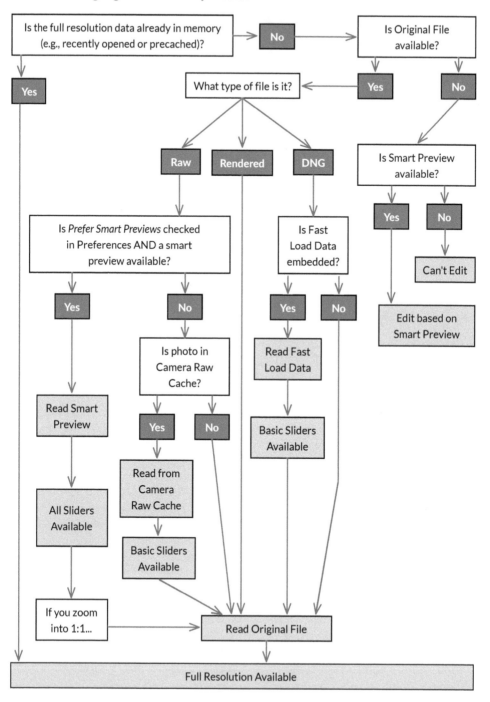

Figure 20.4 *The decision tree Lightroom uses when deciding which preview to load in the Develop module.*

preloads some photos either side of your current photo, so when you move on to the next photo, it loads quickly. This happens automatically so you don't need to do anything to benefit, other than having enough RAM in your computer.

Partially Processed Raw Data—Raw files have to go through some initial processing (such as the demosaic process) before they can be displayed on screen. To save constantly repeating this initial processing, Lightroom caches this low resolution partially processed data in a few different locations. These caches aren't used for rendered files (JPEG/TIFF/PSD) as they don't need this early stage processing.

There are two main caches that hold partially processed raw data: the Camera Raw Cache and Smart Previews. We'll look at each of these caches in more detail shortly.

Originals—Finally, depending on your preference setting, Lightroom may load the original file.

What is the Camera Raw Cache?

The Camera Raw Cache, also known as the ACR Cache, is a folder on your computer that temporarily holds partially processed data (Cache*.dat files) for the most recently accessed raw files, and is used in the Develop module to speed up loading times.

Photos are loaded into the Camera Raw Cache whenever the original raw file is read, for example, when building previews or loading photos into the Develop module. It's a temporary cache, so first in, first out.

Once this data's cached, it's a bit faster doing the initial load in the Develop module and the sliders free up so you can start working, although the Loading overlay may still show

on screen while it does further processing. You'd mainly notice the difference on very large files when you're not working through them consecutively, or when you're moving through them quickly.

The pixel dimensions of the cached image very depending on your selected *Catalog Settings > File Handling tab > Standard Preview Size* setting, essentially making the cached data slightly larger than your screen resolution. This means that the file size also varies, depending on your screen resolution, so if you have a large monitor, you'll need a bigger camera raw cache. We'll come back to figuring out the best size for you on page 468.

What are Smart Previews?

Smart Previews contain the same type of partially processed raw data, and they're always 2560px along the longest edge, regardless of the original file resolution or your screen resolution.

Smart previews can be used as proxy files, in place of the original files, when the original files are offline. They also help with performance when indexing photos for face recognition, when uploading photos to the Lightroom CC cloud, and when editing photos.

They're stored with the catalog, and unlike the Camera Raw Cache, you're in control of building and discarding smart previews. To build smart previews, check the *Build Smart Previews* checkbox in the File Handling panel of the Import dialog, or after import, select the photos in the Library module and go to *Library menu > Previews > Build Smart Previews*. If you decide to delete them later, perhaps because you require the disk space, you'll find *Discard Smart Previews* under the same menu.

If smart previews exist, they're used to speed up loading in the Develop module, and they can also be used to improve interactive performance, simply because there are fewer pixels for Lightroom to compute. We'll come back to the related Preferences checkbox on page 468.

How do I decide whether I'd be better to use the Camera Raw Cache or Smart Previews?

It can all sound very confusing, but as a rule of thumb:

• If you work sequentially through the photos slowly, leave Lightroom to figure it out.

• If you work quickly, mainly in Fit view, and need interactive speed, build smart previews and enable the *Use Smart Previews instead of Originals for Image Editing* checkbox in *Preferences > Performance tab*.

• If you work quickly and often zoom into 1:1 view, keep your originals on fast storage, make your Camera Raw Cache bigger in *Preferences > Performance tab*, and build Standard-Sized Previews if you haven't done so recently, to preload the Camera Raw cache.

How do I solve Develop loading bottlenecks?

As you look through the loading diagram on page 464, you'll note a few potential bottlenecks that you may be able to fix:

RAM—Temporary caches are limited by the amount of RAM available on your system. If you don't have enough RAM, photos are cleared quicker, so you may want to add more RAM to your computer.

Hard drive speed—The speed of the hard

drives containing the catalog, the previews, the smart previews, the Camera Raw Cache and the originals all affect performance. Especially in the case of spinning hard drives, splitting these various caches across multiple hard drives can help, as can upgrading the catalog/previews/cache drive to an SSD.

Computer processing power—Once the data's been read from the disk, it still has to be processed, and this is primarily reliant on the speed of your CPU. That's a more expensive upgrade!

GPU Setting—Enabling the Graphics Processor in Preferences slows down the initial load time, as the data has to be passed from the CPU to GPU, although once it's there, the interactive performance is smoother. Your checkbox setting will depend on your workflow and screen resolution.

PREFERENCES & CATALOG SETTINGS

In addition to selecting the right preview for your workflow, you can optimize your Lightroom Preferences and Catalog Settings for best performance. They're found under the Edit menu (Windows) / Lightroom menu (Mac).

Lightroom Updates

Lightroom is usually updated every 2-4 months, and these updates frequently include performance improvements as well, so it's worth staying up to date. (See page 13.)

Occasionally, an update introduces new bugs that aren't spotted before release. If you're not completely comfortable with this process, you may be safer to wait until the update has been available for a few days, just in case any serious new bugs surface. Keep an eye on my What's New blog posts at https://www.Lrq.me/whatsnew/classic/ for the latest news.

Use Graphics Processor checkbox

In *Preferences > Performance tab*, there's a **Use Graphics Processor** checkbox **(Figure 20.5)**. Extra performance is always a good thing, so you should leave it turned on, right? It's not quite that clear cut. Using the graphics processor or GPU has pros and cons.

1. Your graphics card—you need a card that meets the minimum system requirements (https://www.Lrq.me/classic-sysreq), and even then, some cards are not supported due to driver issues. See https://www.Lrq.me/gpufaq for the list of unsupported cards.

2. Your graphics card driver—there are some horribly buggy drivers out there, which can cause more Lightroom problems than they solve. Check for updated drivers on the manufacturer's website (Windows) / Software Update (Mac).

3. Your screen resolution—you'll see the greatest benefit on high resolution screens (retina, 4K, 5K). If you're using a lower resolution screen, you may find Lightroom faster if you leave GPU disabled.

4. Your usage—Develop is the only module with GPU acceleration, and even then, it's not the whole of Develop (yet).

5. Your workflow—there are compromises, as it takes time for the CPU to pass the data to the GPU, resulting in slower loading times. If loading time takes priority in your workflow, leave it turned off. If interactivity

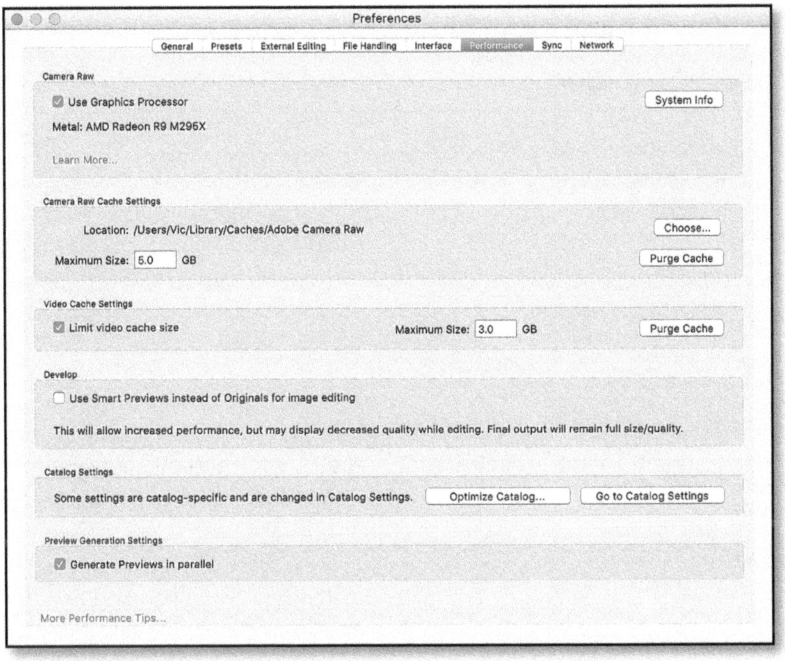

Figure 20.5 *The best Use Graphics Processor checkbox setting depends on your graphics card, driver, screen resolution and Lightroom usage.*

is more important, it may be better turned on.

In short, if you're using a 4K or 5K screen, you probably want it turned on. If you're using a lower resolution screen, try it on and off and see which you prefer.

Camera Raw Cache Settings

By default, the Camera Raw cache is only 5 GB in size, and when new data is added, the oldest data is removed.

You can set the **Maximum Size** of the cache in *Preferences > Performance* tab, up to a maximum of 200 GB. So how big should you make your cache?

The format and size of the individual cache files has changed over the years. In Lightroom Classic, the size varies, based on your standard preview size, which is based on on your screen resolution. Essentially this means you need a larger Camera Raw Cache if you have a high resolution screen. But let's be a little more scientific...

I've done some rough calculations in **Figure 20.6**, to give you an idea of how many photos can be cached in each 5GB of cache space.

Standard Preview Size	Average Size of Cached File	Approx. Number of Photos per 5GB Cache
1024px	0.2 MB	25,000
1440px	0.45 MB	11,100
1680px / 2048px	0.8 MB	6,250
2880px	2.2 MB	2,275

Figure 20.6 *This chart shows average Camera Raw Cache file sizes, to help you figure out the optimal size for your workflow.*

Next, you need to ask yourself roughly how many photos you're likely to be working on at any one time. For example, if I'm going to be working on a 4 weddings over a course of a month, at 1500 photos each, I'm probably going to want space for at least 6000 photos cached at any one time. At 2880px preview size, those previews will average approximately 2.2MB each, so I'll need at least 13.2GB space. (That's 6000 x 2.2 = 13200, then 13200 / 1000 = 13.2)

You can also change the location of this cache, but make sure it's on a fast hard drive or SSD. The Camera Raw cache settings that you change in Lightroom also apply to ACR in Bridge/Photoshop, and can be changed in the ACR Preferences dialog too.

If you start to run low on disk space, or the Develop previews appear to be corrupted, you can purge this cache using the **Purge Cache** button, but it's not something you'd need to do on a regular basis.

Video Cache Settings

Like the Camera Raw cache, the video cache stores recently viewed video data for faster previews. If you regularly work with video, you can enlarge the **Limit Video Cache Size**, so that more of your video footage is cached.

Use Smart Previews Instead of Originals For Image Editing

When it comes to improving Develop performance, Smart Previews are one of Lightroom's best hidden gems. They're much smaller than raw files, so they load much quicker and are a lot less taxing on the computer's processor, so the interactive performance is smoother too. They're not perfectly accurate for adjusting sharpening and noise reduction, however that trade-off is very worthwhile for the smoother performance.

To use the Smart Previews for editing, you need to build the smart previews in advance (page 465), then go to *Preferences > Performance* and check **Use Smart Previews instead of Originals for Image Editing**. When you zoom into 1:1 or export the photos, it's smart enough to automatically switch to the full resolution original, to give the most accurate preview for judging noise reduction and sharpening, although there's a slight delay at this point while it loads the full file.

Optimize the Catalog

Over the course of time, with many imports and deletions, the data in Lightroom's catalog can become fragmented and spread across the whole database, making Lightroom jump around to find the information it needs. The *Preferences > Performnce tab > Optimize Catalog* button "tidies up" and sorts it all back into the right order, bringing it back up to speed.

It's worth running the catalog optimization whenever you've made significant database changes, such as removing or importing a large number of photos, or any time you feel that Lightroom has slowed down. You'll also find it under the File menu, and there's a checkbox in the Back Up Catalog dialog to automatically run the optimization each time you back up your catalog, which saves

you having to remember.

Generate Previews in Parallel

If you have a fast computer, enabling *Preferences > Performance > **Generate Previews in Parallel**** allows multiple previews to be generated concurrently, rather than one at a time. It can, however, have a detrimental effect on interactive performance, so it's best used if you're not going to be using the computer while the previews are building.

Standard Preview Size & Quality

In *Catalog Settings > File Handling tab*, you can set the **Standard Preview Size** and **Preview Quality**. (**Figure 20.7**) (This is a per-catalog setting, so if you use multiple catalogs, you'll need to check each catalog.)

The best size setting depends on your general browsing habits and on your screen resolution. Choosing a size about the width of your screen is a good starting point, and the default *Auto* setting does this automatically. If you always leave the panels open and your hard drive space is very limited, you may prefer a slightly smaller size.

The quality setting is, as with most things, a trade-off. *Low* quality previews take up less

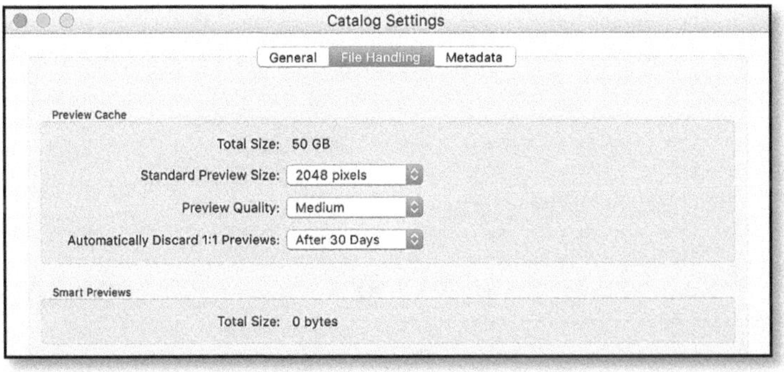

Figure 20.7 *Select your preview size in the Catalog Settings dialog.*

space on disk as they're more compressed, but higher quality previews look better. The default, *Medium*, is a good compromise.

Auto-write XMP checkbox

By default, all of the work you do in Lightroom, such as adding keywords or Develop edits, is stored as text instructions in the Lightroom catalog. If you need to make the metadata available to other programs, such as Bridge or Camera Raw, you need to store it in/with the files using a metadata format called XMP. Some users also use XMP as an additional (but incomplete) backup of edits. (For a full understanding of XMP, see page 345.)

If you frequently edit your photos in other software such as Bridge, writing changes automatically saves you having to remember to do so. However, it can have a notable impact on performance, especially if the photos are stored on a slower drive. To check and change your auto write preference, go to *Catalog Settings > Metadata tab > Automatically Write Changes Into XMP*. **(Figure 20.8)** If you choose to turn auto-write off, you can manually write to XMP at any time by selecting the photos in Grid view and selecting *Metadata menu > Write Metadata to Files*.

View Options Loading Overlay

You don't have to wait for the Loading overlay **(Figure 20.9)** to disappear before starting work on the photo. If you find the overlay distracting, you can turn it off by going to the *View menu > View Options > Loupe tab* and turning off the **Show message when loading or rendering photos** checkbox.

WORKFLOW TWEAKS

Besides optimizing your computer and Lightroom settings, you can also save yourself a lot of frustration by thinking ahead and allowing your computer to do many of its processor-intensive activities at a time when you're not using the computer.

Use embedded previews

Most cameras embed a JPEG preview inside a raw file at the time of capture. To view the photos without having to wait for Lightroom to build its own previews, extract the ready-made previews while importing, by selecting *Import dialog > File Handling panel > Build Previews > Embedded & Sidecar*. They can be replaced later, when you're not using the computer.

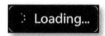

Figure 20.9 *The Loading overlay can be very frustrating when you're in a hurry!*

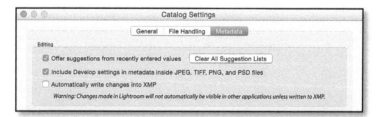

Figure 20.8 *The "Automatically write changes into XMP" setting can have performance implications, so it's worth weighing the pros and cons.*

Build previews overnight

Earlier in the chapter, we learned about the different kinds of previews and caches that can be used to speed up Lightroom. You're going to need rendered previews, but you don't have to sit there waiting for them! Decide which size rendered previews you'll need, then set the standard sized or 1:1 previews building overnight, or at least while you go and make a drink. The same goes for smart previews, if you want to use them to speed up the Develop module. While Lightroom's rendering previews, it's using a lot of the computer's processing power, so you're better off doing something else while it works.

Apply presets before building previews

While we're on the subject of previews, think about Develop settings you apply to all or most of your photos. There's no point building the standard or 1:1 previews and THEN applying a preset, because the previews will need to be updated again. Apply your presets or sync your most-frequently used settings first, and then build your previews to save wasted effort.

Reduce the Window size

The size of your preview area makes a significant difference to the interactive performance, especially in the Develop module. The lower resolution the preview, the fewer pixels Lightroom has to compute, and the quicker it runs. If you don't mind a smaller preview, you can reduce the size of the Lightroom window, enlarge the panels to make the preview area smaller, use Reference View (page 316), or simply select a smaller zoom ratio (e.g. 1:4) in the Navigator panel. **(Figure 20.10)**

Pause background tasks

Lightroom runs a series of background tasks, including Sync, Face Recognition and Reverse Geocoding. These use additional processing power, especially for Sync and Face Recognition, so if you're struggling for speed, it can be useful to pause these tasks while you're working in Lightroom. To do so, click on the Identity Plate in the top left corner and press the *Pause* buttons in the Activity Center. **(Figure 20.11)** Don't forget to start them again when you've finished.

Use optimum slider order

In the Develop module, regardless of the order in which you move the sliders, the end result is always the same (with the exception of spot healing which can be

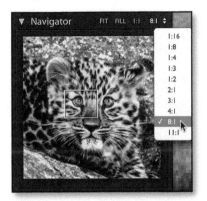

Figure 20.10 *Selecting a smaller zoom ratio means Lightroom has fewer pixels to calculate each time you make an adjustment.*

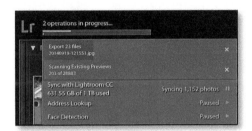

Figure 20.11 *Click on the Identity Plate to view the Activity Center and pause background tasks that are slowing you down.*

affected slightly by lens corrections and also by overlapping spots). There is, however, a slight performance advantage to using the tools in the following order:

1. Tonal Adjustments (e.g. Basic panel, etc.) can be done at any stage, but are often done first

2. Spot Healing

3. Lens Corrections (Profile, Manual Transform sliders, Upright, etc.)

4. Local Corrections (Adjustment Brush, Graduated Filter, Radial Filter)

5. Detail Corrections (Noise Reduction, Sharpening)

If you apply some of these settings (e.g. the lens profile or noise reduction) on import using a preset or default settings, but you're struggling for speed, you can temporarily disable the panel using the panel switch on the left, and then re-enable it when you're finished. **(Figure 20.12)**

Clear history

If the History panel becomes extremely long, particularly with local brush adjustments or spot healing, it can slow down Lightroom's performance. In Lightroom Classic, the history is compressed in the database, to improve performance, but it does still make a difference.

You can clear the History for individual photos by clicking the X button on the panel, or you can clear the History for a large

number of photos by selecting them and navigating to *Develop menu > Clear History*. **(Figure 20.13)**

Clearing the History doesn't remove your current settings. It only clears the list of the slider movements/adjustments you made to get to the current state. Even if you clear the History, your current settings remain, and if you want to change them, you simply move the sliders.

Use a pixel editor for intensive local edits

At the beginning of the chapter, we learned the difference between non-destructive parametric editing (Lightroom) and pixel based editing (Photoshop). Extensive local adjustments, such as detailed adjustment brush masks or large/numerous spot heals,

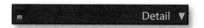

Figure 20.12 You can temporarily turn off adjustments such as Noise Reduction if it's slowing you down.

History		
Temperature	-50	5.3K
Black Clipping	+10	-10
Temperature	-200	5.3K
White Balance: Custom		
Tint	+45	4
Tint	-65	-41
Tint	+20	24
Temperature	-1.8K	5.1K
Temperature	+1.8K	6.9K
Post-Crop Vignette Hig...	+100	100
Post-Crop Vignette Am...	-15	-15
Clarity	-40	10
Contrast	+20	90
Shadows	0	40
Shadows	+20	40
Contrast	+20	70
Exposure	-0.10	0.43
Exposure	+0.40	0.53
Exposure	-0.20	0.13
Shadows	+20	20
Contrast	+20	50
Highlights	-20	-40

Figure 20.13 A large number of History states can slow Lightroom down slightly.

are better suited to Photoshop. While it may be possible to do them in Lightroom, they won't be fast.

Close extra panels

If you're really struggling for speed, you can also help by minimizing the work Lightroom has to do.

This includes closing panels such as the Histogram panel, the Navigator panel, the Develop Detail panel 1:1 preview, the Keywording & Keyword List panels, the Metadata panel and the Filmstrip. Closing the Collections panel and then restarting Lightroom also saves having to count the smart collection contents, which can slow down metadata entry on large catalogs.

When you're moving photos to a new folder, start the move and then switch to an empty folder or collection, such as the Quick Collection, so that Lightroom's not having to constantly redraw the Grid view while it's working. You can also turn off the thumbnail badges in *View menu > View Options*.

Leave exports & merges for when you're not using the computer

Finally, leave large exports for times when you're not using the computer. It's a processor-intensive task that can slow down the fastest of computers, due to the complex calculations involved.

HARDWARE CHOICES

Every single day, I receive emails asking how to choose a new computer for Lightroom. We're not going to go into specific hardware recommendations, because they'd be out of date almost immediately. What we will do is talk about which hardware benefits different Lightroom tasks, so you can make

your own decisions based on your needs and budget.

Adobe publishes minimum system requirements for Lightroom at https://www.Lrq.me/classic-sysreq, but we should be clear... these are MINIMUM system requirements. They allow Lightroom to run... well, it'll walk. If you want to enjoy using Lightroom, you'll definitely want to exceed these minimum requirements. Your hardware requirements depend on how many photos you're editing each week, your budget, the size of the images you're shooting, the amount of time you have available and let's be honest, your tolerance for slow computers.

CPU

There are two primary factors to weigh up when selecting a new CPU: the number of cores on the single CPU (two physical CPU's don't help much) and its clock speed.

Lightroom makes good use of multiple cores for image processing tasks such as building previews, working in the Develop module, and exporting photos, so it's worth selecting a quad-core processor if possible, even though other areas of the program are only lightly threaded.

A high clock speed (measured in GHz) is equally important, as it determines how quickly computations are made, not only for image processing tasks, but also all of the other tasks Lightroom has to perform.

The release date of the processor also affects performance. The clock speed isn't a perfect comparison, because the manufacturers have been working hard on efficiency, so a recent 3.0GHz processor is much faster than a 3.0GHz processor released 10 years ago.

So if you can't trust the clock speed for comparison, how do you figure out which CPU is faster? One easy way to compare is to check other people's Geekbench scores for your chosen processor at http://browser.primatelabs.com/—you're looking for the 64-bit Single and Multi-Core scores.

Need a rule of thumb? If you're looking for a new CPU, a recent generation Intel quad-core desktop processor with a fast clock speed is a great choice. For a high end machine focused primarily on editing, a six-core CPU is also a good choice, although they're a little more expensive and often have a slightly slower clock speed.

Memory (RAM)

The operating system, open programs and their data are held in RAM. The more data you're working with, the more RAM you need. If you don't have enough RAM, some of the data has to be written to the hard drive, which is much slower.

Like most image-editing programs, Lightroom works with large amounts of data, so it needs more RAM than, for example, a word processor. The amount of RAM available affects how many photos can be cached, which can affect image loading time. Some tasks, such as merging panoramas and HDR files, are particularly memory hungry.

Although Adobe lists 4GB of RAM minimum, you don't really want any less than 8GB. 16GB is a much better choice for most users, especially if you're buying a quad-core processor.

If you're running other programs at the same time, perhaps switching to Photoshop to do further editing, you may need additional RAM.

A tip—if you're buying a desktop Mac (not a laptop), it's much cheaper to buy the extra RAM from companies such as OWC (US) or Crucial (International) and install it yourself, rather than paying the Apple premium. Minimal computer knowledge needed!

Hard drives

The speed of the drive that holds the catalog and previews makes a fairly substantial difference, especially in the Library module and also for startup times. This is where an SSD really helps, and therefore it's the first thing I'd put on my shopping list. This is an upgrade that can be beneficial on existing systems, as well as new builds.

Bear in mind that the catalog and its previews—especially if you're building 1:1 and/or smart previews—can grow quite large. For example, my 50k catalog is currently 1.6GB, the previews are 70GB and the smart previews take up another 50GB.

Next, think about where the images will be stored. The access speed primarily affects the loading speed in the Develop module, although Lightroom's smart enough to cache files in advance if you're stepping through images in order. In an ideal world, you'd put the original photos on an incredibly fast drive such as an SSD, but the cost per MB is still quite high. For most users, a 7200rpm internal or fast external drive is adequate for storing photos, but if you need greater speed, a striped RAID is a cost-effective solution.

Also, if your photo storage drive is external, think about connection speed. Even the fastest SSD would be horribly slow in a USB1 external enclosure! If you need to use external drives, look for USB3 or Thunderbolt connections if your computer supports them. The photos can be stored on a NAS (network accessed storage), but the connection speed can be painfully slow, so NAS units are better suited to backups. **(Figure 20.14)**

Don't forget your backup drives. You need a minimum of one backup drive kept onsite, plus some kind of offsite backup, whether that's an additional drive held at a different location or an online backup such as Crashplan (Small Business edition), Carbonite or Backblaze.

As an example configuration, you could choose a good-sized SSD for the operating system and Lightroom catalog/previews, and then a second reasonably fast drive to hold the photos (plus additional backup drives, of course).

While we're thinking about hard drives, remember to leave the operating system and Lightroom space to work. Aim to keep at least 20% free space on your boot and catalog hard drives.

GPU

When deciding on the GPU or graphics card, think about the resolution of the monitor you'll be using. A standard HD screen (1920×1080) is 2 megapixels (MP), a MacBook Retina Pro 15" is 5 MP, a 4K display is 8 MP, and a 5K display is a whopping 15 MP. This means that Lightroom has to calculate and display 4 times as many pixels on a 4K display, compared to a standard HD screen, and nearly 8 times as many on a 5K display. This is why Lightroom slows down on big screens!

Lightroom can use the GPU in place of the CPU to accelerate Develop rendering, especially on high resolution screens/ retina screens. To take advantage of this, you need a mid-range graphics card. The current minimum specifications to take advantage of GPU acceleration are found at https://www.Lrq.me/classic-sysreq. It's also worth checking Adobe's support page

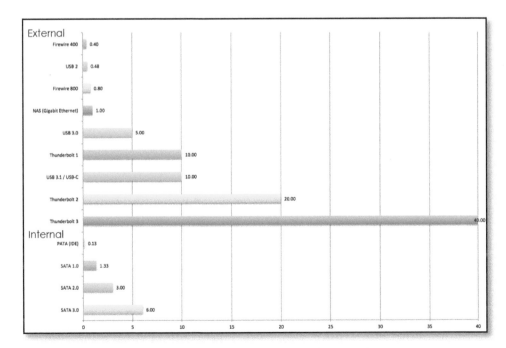

Figure 20.14 *Maximum Transfer Rates (theoretical)*

at https://www.Lrq.me/gpufaq to see which cards are not supported, due to issues with their drivers. Lightroom will still work with an underpowered or unsupported graphics card, but it just can't benefit from the additonal performance acceleration.

On lower resolution screens (e.g. standard HD), there may not be a benefit to utilizing the GPU, and it can actually make Lightroom slower, because it takes time to pass the data from the CPU to the GPU.

If you're using integrated graphics, such as the GPU in many laptops, bear in mind that they share the computer's RAM, so the more RAM, the better. For example, if you're buying a 13" MacBook Pro, which isn't available with a separate graphics card, then it's worth getting 16GB of RAM, as the graphics card will borrow a chunk of it.

It's also important to keep the graphics card driver up to date. To do so, check the graphics card manufacturer's website (Windows) or Software Update (Mac). Check page 477 for instructions.

Monitor & Calibration

Monitor choices are also largely dependent on budget, but IPS screens are generally considered a good choice for photographers. For accurate color, NEC and EIZO are among the best.

4K/5K screens are wonderful for text, but it's a lot more pixels to compute, so bear in mind that the screen resolution will impact performance.

Finally, don't forget you'll need monitor calibration hardware too. This helps to ensure that you're seeing an accurate preview on the screen.

Desktop vs. Laptop

Unless portability is essential, a desktop computer is usually a better choice for Lightroom. There's only a limited amount of space in a laptop, so everything has to be smaller. This means most laptops have slower mobile CPU's, less RAM, and are reliant on slower external hard drives for storage. They're also much more difficult to keep cool due to the lack of space, and when components get hot, they slow down. There are, of course, exceptions: performance laptops are available, but they come at a premium price.

Interaction & Budget

The final thing to remember is that all of these hardware components interact. The fastest CPU in the world won't help if your hard drives can't transfer the data quickly enough. Having 32GB of RAM won't help if your CPU is incredibly slow.

There are also budgetary considerations to weigh up. If you're buying a new machine with a limited budget, $400 for a minor clock speed upgrade on a CPU would be better spent on an SSD, or on 16GB of RAM instead of 8GB, because you'll get a bigger performance boost for the money.

Upgrading Existing Computers

If you're considering upgrading components of your existing computer, take a look at the next section (page 478) and think about what specifically is slow. Slow catalog loading and Library updates may benefit from installing an SSD, but the SSD will have less of an impact in the Develop module. Replacing the GPU will mainly help in the Develop module if you're running a high resolution screen.

Also check Resource Monitor (Windows) /

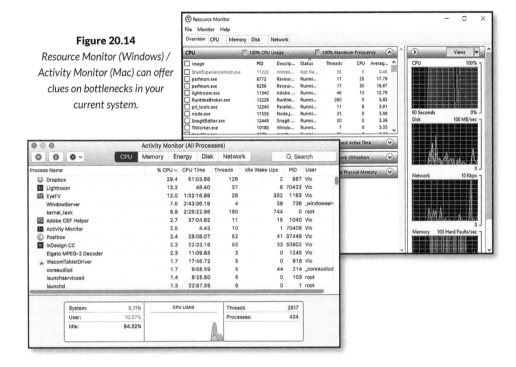

Figure 20.14

Resource Monitor (Windows) / Activity Monitor (Mac) can offer clues on bottlenecks in your current system.

Activity Monitor (Mac) to see where you're hitting your computer's limits. For example, if you're running out of RAM and using virtual memory, then adding additional memory may help. **(Figure 20.14)**

GENERAL SYSTEM MAINTENANCE

Lightroom can't perform well if the operating system is struggling. While not specific to Lightroom, it's worth running regular computer maintenance and optimizing other software running on your computer. This includes operating system and driver updates, keeping hard drives in good condition, and minimizing the number of other programs running in the background.

Operating System Updates

Updates to the Windows or macOS operating systems not only fix bugs and add security fixes, but also improve its performance and compatibility with applications. Windows service packs and other updates are available from the Microsoft Windows Update website and macOS updates are downloaded from the App Store.

Driver Updates

Windows Update includes some drivers, however these are rarely the latest, so you'll need to visit the component manufacturer's website, or for laptops, the laptop manufacturer's website to get the latest drivers. It's important to keep drivers up to date, especially for the graphics card and input devices such as Wacom tablets and other mice, as older or buggy drivers can cause crashes as well as performance issues. For example, see https://www.Lrq.me/gpudriver for instructions on how to update the graphics card driver. Occasionally you may need to roll back one of the drivers, when an updated driver triggers new bugs.

Most macOS driver updates are downloaded from the App Store, but you'll need to check manufacturer's websites for third-party hardware drivers, such as Wacom tablets.

Care of Hard Drives

Both the operating system and Lightroom need room to work, and processes can slow down significantly when they're constrained. Therefore it's important to keep enough space available on your hard drives, especially for the boot drive and the drive containing your catalog.

You can clear space on your hard drive by emptying the Recycle Bin/Trash, deleting files (be careful!) or moving them to another drive. You can also clear out temporary files and caches to help to free up additional space. Windows and macOS both include tools to make this easier.

If you're working with spinning drives on Windows (not SSD's), you also need to defragment/optimize the hard drive from time to time. This moves the data back into contiguous blocks, making it faster to read/write.

macOS automatically defragments small files, so it doesn't require user intervention unless you're working with large numbers of huge files (e.g. 1GB videos).

Other system tasks and software

Other programs running in the background also reduce the resources available to Lightroom. To make these resources available to Lightroom, quit other open applications, including those running in the system tray (Windows) / menubar (Mac), and prevent unnecessary programs running on startup.

Anti-virus/security software running real-time scans also use your computer's resources, so it may be useful to pause the scan while you're working in Lightroom, and exclude specific files such as the catalog and previews.

The same goes for other software that runs automated tasks in the background, such as backup software or cloud sync such as Dropbox. If you're struggling with performance issues, temporarily pausing these tasks can help.

Reboot occasionally

Finally, it's worth rebooting from time to time... yes, even on a Mac!

WHAT'S SLOW?

Throughout this chapter, we've learned the pros and cons of non-destructive editing, how different computer components affect different areas of the program, and the ways you can adjust your Lightroom workflow to get the best performance.

At the beginning of the chapter, we said simply saying "Lightroom is slow" doesn't help, because different areas of the program benefit from different optimizations. In this section, we'll summarize the main places to look for improvement, based on what specifically is slow.

Opening Lightroom

Loading the Lightroom program is primarily dependent on your drive speeds, for both the OS/program files and also for the catalog. If you're finding it slow to load, replacing your spinning drive with an SSD can help, and is a relatively inexpensive upgrade.

Load time is also affected by the size of the catalog, however I wouldn't recommend breaking the catalog up into smaller catalogs to solve this, as this causes more problems than it solves for most people.

Importing Photos

Importing photos is also primarily limited by file transfer rates. This includes the speed of the source—whether that's a camera cable, card reader or hard drive—and the speed of the destination drive(s).

For the source, card readers are usually more reliable than direct camera connections, and faster USB card readers (e.g. USB 3) are available to help improve the import speed.

For the destination, there are potentially two drives in play: the main Destination folder and also the Second Copy location. If these are on external drives, the connection speed (USB2 vs USB3, etc.) is usually the main issue. Many photographers send their second copies to a NAS, which can reduce the speed further.

If you choose to add the photos at their current location, this is a lot quicker than moving/copying the files, however take care that the photos are on a hard drive, not a memory card.

Finally, the additional work you ask Lightroom to do immediately after import can prolong the import time, especially conversion to DNG format or building previews.

Building Previews

The time it takes to build previews is largely dependent on your computer's processing power, but also the drive speed for the catalog and original images.

Improving preview build times frequently requires a newer CPU, so it's not an easy fix. If you're running low on RAM and having to use temp files, this may slow you down further, so it's worth keeping an eye on Resource Monitor (Windows) / Activity Monitor (Mac) to see which computer components are reaching their limits.

The simplest solution for building previews is simply to let them build overnight, or at another time when you don't need the computer. Also, you only need to build the previews you actually use, so if you rarely zoom in the Library module, there's no need to build 1:1 previews.

Viewing In Library

You can speed up viewing in the Library module by building the right size previews in advance. If you need to zoom in, you'll need 1:1 previews. Otherwise, standard sized previews (set to Auto in Catalog Settings) will be plenty. If you've made Develop edits since building the previews, don't forget to rebuild them, otherwise they'll have to update when you select the photo.

Once the previews are built, the drive speed for the catalog/previews is next in line. Putting the catalog/previews on an SSD can make Library browsing smoother.

Applying Metadata

Applying metadata is mainly limited by the speed of the drive containing the catalog, so again, putting the catalog/previews on an SSD makes a notable difference.

It also helps to minimize the amount of work Lightroom has to do, especially closing the Collections, Metadata and Keyword panels if you're not using them.

Don't forget to optimize the catalog

regularly, as this saves Lightroom skipping around the catalog to find the information it needs.

Moving/deleting photos

Moving or deleting photos is also affected by drive speeds—both for the original images as they're moved, and also the catalog as the image records are updated.

Lightroom also has to redraw the grid view as photos disappear, so switching to a different folder or collection (e.g. Quick Collection) can speed the process up slightly.

Finally, rather than trying to delete one photo at a time, consider marking them as rejects and then deleting the rejects when you've finished sorting through the photos.

Loading in Develop

Moving over to the Develop module, let's talk about loading speed. This is primarily dependent on any data that is already cached, then on a mix of processing power (CPU/GPU), screen resolution, drive speeds, and of course, the size and complexity of the image files too.

If you're moving through photos sequentially (and not too quickly!) in the Develop module, Lightroom automatically caches the photos either side in the background to improve loading speed. Once the image data is loaded from the cache (held in RAM), the CPU/GPU is responsible for additional image processing. At this point, buying a computer with a faster CPU/GPU is your main upgrade potential.

If you're not moving sequentially, additional factors come into play. The full resolution image data has to be read from the hard drive, so hard drive speed is a major factor. Once the image data is read from hard drive,

then initial processing has to be applied, which is dependent on the CPU or GPU processing power.

If you're using a standard HD resolution monitor (e.g. 1920×1080), it may be worth leaving the GPU disabled in *Preferences > Performance*, as this increases image loading time without a noticeable benefit, but the smoother interactive performance makes it worth enabling on 4K/5K screens.

The higher the resolution of the image, the more data there is to process, so 50MP images will naturally take longer than 5MP. Some sensors (I'm looking at you, Fuji!) also require more complex calculations.

Whether you're moving sequentially or skipping around, building Smart Previews in advance and checking the *Preferences > Performance > Use Smart Previews for Editing* checkbox is the greatest potential improvement, simply because there's less data to read and process. If you're struggling for loading times in Develop, this is your first place to start.

Editing in Develop

Once the photo is loaded into the Develop module, as long as you have enough RAM, then you're primarily limited by your processing power—the CPU or GPU, depending on your *Use Graphics Processor* checkbox setting.

If you're using a 4K/5K monitor, it's worth enabling the GPU for smoother interactive performance, but on standard resolution monitors or when using an under-powered graphics card, you may be better to leave it disabled and let the CPU do the image processing. Try it both ways and see which you prefer.

The more image data to process, the longer

it takes, so you can reduce the preview size to limit the number of pixels Lightroom has to crunch. You can do this by resizing the Lightroom window, enlarging the panels or selecting a smaller zoom ratio (e.g. 1:4).

We also learned that the slider order can make a slight performance difference. Some tasks are more processor intensive than others, so using a pixel editor such as Photoshop for more complex local adjustments can be a good choice. Temporarily disabling complex calculations such as Lens Corrections can also help with interactive performance.

And finally, like the Develop Loading time, utilizing Smart Previews has the biggest potential gain.

Exporting

Like building previews and working in the Develop module, exporting photos is largely limited by the CPU, where multiple cores can help, and also the speed of the hard drive containing your original photos and the export destination. Alternatively, you could just leave the exports to run when you're not using the computer.

Syncing to Lightroom Cloud

Finally, sync speed is largely dependent on the speed of your internet connection, especially the upload speed, which is often around 1/10 of the download speed.

PERFORMANCE SHORTCUTS

		Windows	Mac
Preferences		Ctrl ,	Cmd ,
Catalog Settings		Ctrl Alt ,	Cmd Opt ,

PERFORMANCE CHECKLIST:

System Maintenance

☐ Install operating system updates

☐ Check for driver updates

☐ Clear hard drive space

☐ Defragment hard drive

☐ Quit OS background tasks

☐ Exclude files from live virus scan

☐ Reboot the computer

Lightroom Settings

☐ Check for Lightroom updates

☐ Optimize the catalog

☐ Set *Enable Graphics Processor* checkbox based on screen resolution

☐ Deselect *Automatically Write Settings into XMP*

Previews & Caches

☐ Build Standard-Sized Previews

☐ Build 1:1 Previews if zooming in

☐ Build Smart Previews and check *Use Smart Previews instead of Originals for Image*

Editing checkbox

☐ Set the Camera Raw Cache size

Workflow

☐ Build previews in advance

☐ Apply presets before building previews

☐ Use a smaller preview area or lower zoom ratio

☐ Pause background tasks

☐ Use the optimum slider order

☐ Clear the History panel

☐ Use a pixel editor for detailed retouching

☐ Close unused panels

☐ Export when you're not using the computer

Upgrade the Computer

☐ SSD (Solid State Drive)

☐ RAM (Memory)

☐ CPU (Processor)

☐ GPU (Graphics Card) especially if 4K/5K monitor

CLOUD SYNC

21

In this increasingly connected world, photography is no longer confined to the desktop. Imagine having easy access to your photos everywhere...

You shoot an event with your DSLR, upload it to the desktop and walk away. Later, you're sat on the train and decide to start sorting through the photos using your tablet. You rate them, organize them into albums/collections and even do some initial edits.

While traveling, you capture a photo with your phone, edit it using Lightroom right there on your phone, and post it to social media.

While you're out, you run into a friend or potential customer, and want to share some photos from your portfolio, so you open Lightroom on your tablet, navigate to the collection and start a slideshow. They want to see more, so you email them a link to view the entire album/collection in their web browser later.

When you return home, the photos taken with your phone have automatically been downloaded to your desktop, complete with

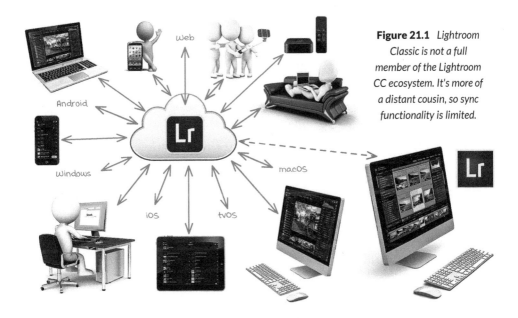

Figure 21.1 *Lightroom Classic is not a full member of the Lightroom CC ecosystem. It's more of a distant cousin, so sync functionality is limited.*

your non-destructive edits and all of the other changes you made while you were out. This is the promise of the new Lightroom CC ecosystem. **(Figure 21.1)**

Lightroom Branding Changes

In October 2017, Adobe announced their plans for the future of Lightroom, and that future has been split into two versions of Lightroom. Why? Because trying to shoehorn cloud functionality into a desktop-focused app just doesn't work very well. Both the cloud and the desktop want to be in charge of the photos, and too many cooks in the kitchen...

The traditional version of Lightroom that we've been using for years has been rebranded as Lightroom Classic, because it continues to use the traditional desktop folder-based organizational system we've used for decades. (Lightroom Classic is the subject of this book, obviously.)

The new Lightroom CC ecosystem, on the other hand, stores all of the photos in the cloud. It has "clients" for Windows, Mac, iOS, Android, Apple TV and most web browsers, all of which access the photos from the cloud. As the Windows and Mac apps are brand new, they have fewer features than Lightroom Classic, although that will change over time. The Lightroom mobile apps that we've used for the last few years, being cloud-focused, have been rebranded to become fully-fledged members of the Lightroom CC ecosystem.

The Limitations of Sync in Lightroom Classic

Lightroom Classic is not a full member of the Lightroom CC cloud ecosystem. It's more like a distant cousin. It has a basic understanding of the sync language, which it's learned over the last few years, but

it'll never become fluent. This means that you can continue to use Lightroom Classic alongside the various Lightroom CC apps, but there are limitations. The gap will grow over the coming months and years, as Lightroom Classic focuses on the desktop workflow and Lightroom CC focuses on cloud sync.

Let's be clear... none of the information in the rest of this chapter is recommended by Adobe, and is therefore used at your own risk. Adobe's recommendation is that you pick either Lightroom Classic or Lightroom CC. But if you've got this far in the book, I think you're smart enough to make your own decision based on all the information that's available.

At this stage, these are the main incompatibilities to be aware of:

Lightroom Classic is a hoarder—When you open Lightroom Classic and enable sync, it downloads anything it finds in the cloud to your local hard drive. Even if you then delete a photo from Lightroom CC, it stays in Lightroom Classic, and if you delete an album in Lightroom CC, the collection just becomes unsynced in Lightroom Classic. Lightroom Classic wants to be in charge of your photos.

Some Features Don't Sync—Lightroom Classic has many features that aren't in Lightroom CC, and other features are available in both apps but work differently. This list is likely to grow further as new features are added to Lightroom CC. **(Figure 21.2)** Right now, most notably:

• Keywords don't sync between Classic and CC.

• Stacks don't sync between Classic and CC.

Task	Sync Up from Classic	Sync Down from CC Cloud
Import		
Add Photos	Originals not uploaded—uploads as a smart preview, and only if mark to sync	Classic downloads all originals from the cloud (as long as you haven't deleted them from CC before they can download)
Add Videos	No	Classic downloads all videos, but sync link is then broken.
Organizing Photos		
Collection / Album Membership	Yes, if collection marked to sync	Yes, if album created in LRCC or marked to sync in Classic
Collection Set / Album Folder Hierarchy	No	No
Collection Custom Sort Order	Yes	Yes
Stack Membership	No	No
Create Copies	Virtual copies upload as smart previews even if originals are already in the cloud	Real copies created in CC become virtual copies in Classic
Delete Photos/Videos	If you delete or unsync, photos are deleted from the cloud	No, just unsynced if already downloaded
Adding / Editing Metadata		
Files Renamed	Yes	N/A
Capture Date Changed	Yes	Yes
Star Ratings	Yes	Yes
Flags	Yes	Yes
Title & Caption	Yes	Yes
Copyright	Yes	Yes
Keywords	Only on first sync, if metadata was written to the files	No
Location (GPS)	Yes, co-ordinates only	Yes, co-ordinates only
Develop Edits		
All Edits	Yes (even if there isn't a user interface for the slider/tool in Lightroom CC)	Yes

Figure 21.2 *Some features exist in both Lightroom CC and Lightroom Classic, but don't sync, or only sync in one direction. This list is likely to grow over time, as new features are added to Lightroom CC. Features that don't exist in Lightroom CC (such as color labels and most metadata fields) are not listed above, but they don't sync either.*

• Location metadata (except GPS coordinates) doesn't sync between Classic and CC.

• Album/Collection hierarchy doesn't sync between Classic and CC.

• Virtual copies created in Classic upload as smart previews only, even if the original's already in the cloud. And real copies created in CC become virtual copies in Classic.

Features Have Different Names—Collections in Lightroom Classic become albums in Lightroom CC, but Album Folders in Lightroom CC don't become Collection Sets. Also, some of the editing features are grouped differently, for example, the White Balance sliders are in the Basic panel in Lightroom Classic but in the Color panel in Lightroom CC. And Lightroom CC doesn't have a user interface for all of Classic's Develop sliders, although it understands them all.

Videos Don't Sync—Videos download to Lightroom Classic, but Classic can't upload videos or metadata changes to the cloud.

Selective Sync—Lightroom Classic only syncs photos you specifically choose to sync. It's easy to miss uploading photos, such as those created by Edit in Photoshop or HDR/Panorama merge. This can be a good thing or a bad thing, depending on whether you want access to all of your photos from other devices or not.

Only Smart Previews Upload—Lightroom Classic only syncs smart previews to the cloud, so even if you remember to sync all of the photos, it can't send the originals to the cloud. However, if you have a slow internet connection, only uploading smart previews may be an advantage, as you'll still be able to view, flag, rate and edit photos on other devices.

Single Catalog—Lightroom Classic only syncs a single catalog, so if you have more than one catalog, you'll need to decide which one you're going to use or merge them into a single catalog using the instructions on page 431.

Sync Bugs—Lightroom Classic's future development is focused on desktop features, so sync bugs in Classic may not be fully investigated or fixed. They're also notoriously difficult to track down.

The Benefits of Sync in Lightroom Classic

Having considered the downsides, there are still some advantages to being able to sync Lightroom Classic with the Lightroom CC ecosystem.

Easy Multi-Computer Use—If you still need the power of Lightroom Classic on your main computer, or you have slow/limited internet access, but you want an easy way to access your photos on other computers or devices, syncing Lightroom Classic on one computer with Lightroom CC on your other devices works pretty well, as long as you're aware of the limitations (and new ones that appear in future). I've detailed this workflow starting on page 406.

Cloud Backup of Originals—If you still need the power of Lightroom Classic on your main computer, but you want your originals in the cloud, it is possible. This is dodgy ground with plenty of potential pitfalls, but the trick is to either:

• Use the Lightroom CC apps to import your photos and upload to the cloud, then let them download into Lightroom Classic. This works reliably, but if your internet connection is slow, you may have to wait a long time before you can start working on the photos in Lightroom Classic.

LIGHTROOM CC - EDIT LIKE A PRO

The Lightroom CC apps for Windows, macOS, iOS, Android, Apple TV and web are simple to use, but there are plenty of hidden features. You could discover many of them on your own, but allow me to save you some time and share some of the insider secrets and power user tips with you. My book on the Lightroom CC ecosystem is called *Adobe Photoshop Lightroom CC—Edit Like a Pro*. It's available from https://www.lightroomqueen.com/shop as well as many online retailers.

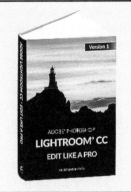

• Add all of your photos to the All Synced Photographs collection in Lightroom Classic's Catalog panel, wait for the smart previews to all upload to the cloud, wait for all of the photos to download to Lightroom CC on the same machine, and then add the same original photos into Lightroom CC. Lightroom CC should be smart enough to recognize that these are originals of existing synced photos, and just upload the originals to the cloud, without duplicating the photos.

Remember, these are not officially recommended or sanctioned workflows, so they won't undergo official testing. However, I know many of my readers like to push technology to the limits, and I'd rather you were aware of the known issues before experimenting by yourself!

SYNCING LIGHTROOM CLASSIC

So, assuming you're going to sync Lightroom Classic with Lightroom CC, let's learn the basics of sync in Lightroom Classic. (I discuss the Lightroom CC side of things in my *Adobe Photoshop Lightroom CC—Edit Like a Pro* book.)

How do I enable sync?

To enable sync, click on the Identity Plate to show the Activity Center, then click **Start**. **(Figure 21.3)**

Sync has three possible states:

Off—The Sync checkboxes are hidden and nothing in the current catalog syncs. To enable it, select *Start* in the Activity Center.

On—The Sync checkboxes show in the Collections panel and Create/Edit Collection dialogs. Lightroom automatically uploads the checked collections of photos and downloads changes made using the Lightroom CC apps.

Paused—The Sync checkboxes show in the collection dialogs, but nothing is transferred to/from the cloud until sync is enabled. To pause or activate sync, click the *Pause* button in the Activity Center.

How do I choose which photos to sync?

Once you've activated Sync, you can

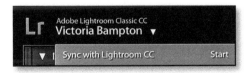

Figure 21.3 *Start syncing a new catalog with the cloud.*

choose which photos to sync to the cloud from Lightroom Classic. Remember, it only uploads lower resolution smart previews, not full resolution originals.

To start syncing photos, drag the photos from Grid view directly to the **All Synced Photographs** collection in the Catalog panel. **(Figure 21.4)**

You can also enable sync for one or more collections of photos. These become albums in the Lightroom CC apps. (If you need a refresher, turn back to the Collections section starting on page 100

for more details on creating and managing collections.)

When you're creating a new collection, check the **Sync with Lightroom CC** checkbox in the New Collection dialog. **(Figure 21.5)**

To sync existing collections, toggle the checkboxes on the left in the Collections panel. **(Figure 21.6)**

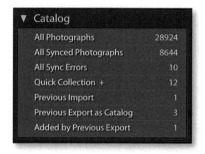

Figure 21.4 *The All Synced Photographs and All Sync Errors collections appear in the Catalog panel.*

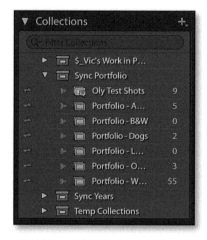

Figure 21.5 *When Sync is enabled, the sync icons appear to the left of the collection names.*

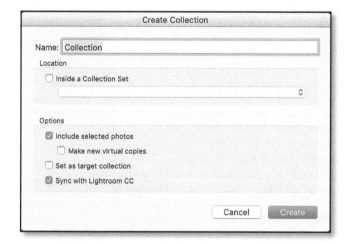

Figure 21.6 *If Sync is enabled, the Sync with Lightroom CC checkbox displays in the Create/Edit Collection dialog.*

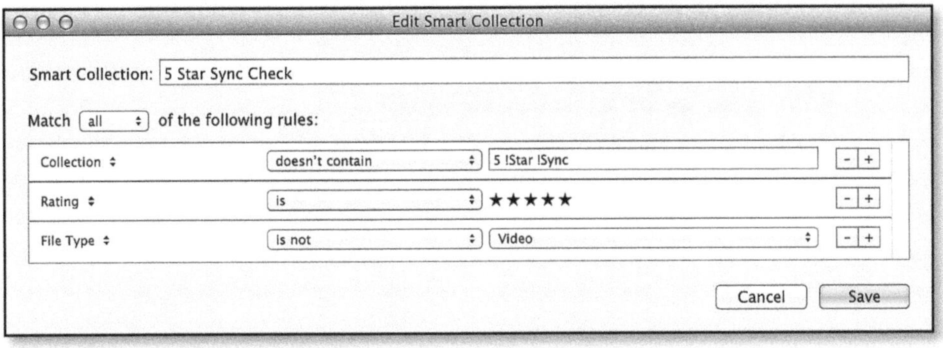

Smart Collection: 5 Star Sync Check

Match [all ⬍] of the following rules:

Collection ⬍	doesn't contain ⬍	5 !Star !Sync	- +
Rating ⬍	is ⬍	★ ★ ★ ★ ★	- +
File Type ⬍	is not ⬍	Video ⬍	- +

[Cancel] [Save]

Figure 21.7 *Although you can't sync smart collections, you can still use them to check you've included the right photos.*

Can I sync smart collections?

Smart Collections would be ideal for ensuring all of the photos shot in the last 60 days, for example, or all of your 5 star photos sync to your iPad. Smart Collections can't be synced for numerous reasons, but there is a workaround. Let's use the 5 star photos as an example.

Create a collection called "5 Star Sync" and mark it to sync to your iPad. Then create a Smart Collection, set to *Rating equals 5 stars* and *File Type is not video* and *Collection doesn't include 5 !Star !Sync.* **(Figure 21.7)**

The Smart Collection checks for any photos that meet the criteria but aren't in your 5 star photos sync collection. If there are ever photos in that Smart Collection, drag them over to the 5 star photos collection to be included in the sync. If everything's synced, the Smart Collection should be set to 0.

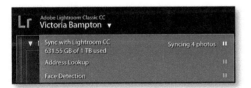

Figure 21.8 *Sync status is displayed in the Activity Center. Click the Pause button to temporarily pause sync.*

How do I check the sync status?

If you click on the Identity Plate, you can access the Activity Center, where it shows a countdown of the photos currently syncing. **(Figure 21.8)** If it can't connect to the Lightroom Sync cloud, it says *Waiting for Connection* instead.

If Lightroom runs into problems syncing, it creates a temporary collection in the Catalog panel called ***All Sync Errors***. In many cases, there's a logical reason for the error, for example, if the original photos are offline and smart previews don't currently exist, Lightroom can't sync these photos. The errors usually clear automatically.

For more detailed feedback, go to *Edit menu (Windows) / Lightroom menu (Mac) > Preferences > Lightroom Sync* and check the ***Sync Activity*** section. This shows the current sync processes and the names of photos that are stuck. **(Figure 21.9)**

If it seems to get stuck, you can also log into your account at https://lightroom.adobe.com and see the current cloud status. This can offer clues on what's stuck, for example, if a thumbnail is grey with a cloud icon, it hasn't finished uploading from Lightroom Classic or from one of the Lightroom CC apps. Float over the thumbnail to show additional

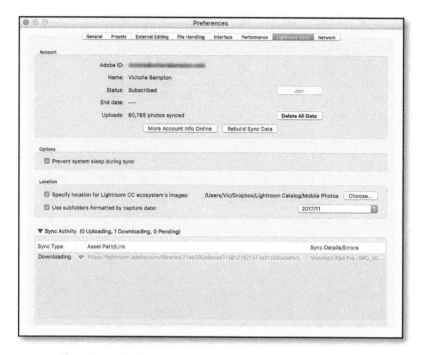

Figure 21.9 *The Pending Sync Activity section shows the current sync activity which is useful for troubleshooting sync errors.*

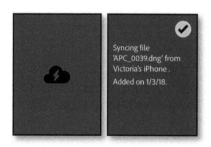

Figure 21.10 *If a photo seems to be stuck syncing, check the web interface to see whether it's safely uploaded to the cloud.*

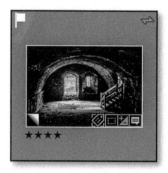

Figure 21.11 *The Sync icon appears in the top right corner of the thumbnail if the photo's included in Sync.*

information, then reopen Lightroom on the device in question and let it finish uploading. If that device is no longer available, click the checkmark then select *Delete* in the menu above to delete the partially uploaded photo from the cloud. **(Figure 21.10)**

Additional icons also appear in the top right

corner of the thumbnails in Grid view. The sync icon simply shows that it's synced to the cloud. Three dots below the sync icon means that something's happening to that photo—it's being synced, the metadata's being read or updated, or previews are being rendered. **(Figure 21.11)**

How do I pause sync?

If you need to pause the sync, perhaps because you need the bandwidth for a higher priority upload, you can pause the sync by clicking the *Pause* button in the Activity Center. When you later click again to turn it back on, Lightroom continues uploading from where it left off.

If you close Lightroom while it's syncing, it automatically continues when you next relaunch Lightroom. It asks for confirmation before it quits, just in case you're unaware that the sync hasn't completed.

Where does Lightroom Classic put the photos I added to Lightroom CC?

When you add photos to one of the Lightroom CC apps (perhaps using your phone), they're uploaded to the Lightroom cloud and then downloaded to your Lightroom Classic catalog. By default, Lightroom puts them in a special folder (Windows) / package file (Mac) on your computer. The full folder path is:

Windows—C:\Users\[your username]\My Pictures\Lightroom\Mobile Downloads. lrdata

Mac—Macintosh HD / Users / [your username] / Pictures / Lightroom / Mobile Downloads.lrdata

This is a fixed location, regardless of where you store your catalog. They show up in the Folders panel as an additional drive. **(Figure 21.12)**

If you select the photos in the Grid view, you can drag and drop them onto a normal folder of your choice. There's more detail on page 118.

Better still, you can change the default location and folder structure for future downloads by going to *Lightroom's Preferences dialog > Lightroom Sync tab.* **(Figure 21.13)**

How do I stop specific photos syncing?

To remove selected photos from the cloud, select them in the *All Synced Photographs* collection and go to *Photo menu > Remove from All Synced Photographs* or press the Delete/Backspace key. This doesn't remove them from the catalog, but does remove them from the cloud and all synced devices.

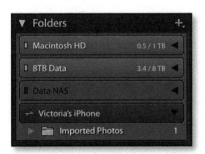

Figure 21.12 *By default, Lightroom CC devices show in the Folders panel as additional drives.*

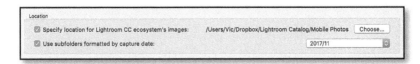

Figure 21.13 *The location and folder structure for mobile/ web uploads can now be selected in Preferences.*

How do I completely disable sync and remove everything from the cloud?

If you need to reset sync and delete everything from the cloud, go to https://lightroom.adobe.com and sign in. Click the Lightroom icon in the top left corner, select Account Info from the menu and then click the **Delete Lightroom Library** button. Your Lightroom Classic catalog remains safely on your desktop, but all of the data is removed from the cloud and the Lightroom CC apps, so double check that everything as safely downloaded to Lightroom Classic before taking this nuclear option. **(Figure 21.14)**

What happens if the same photo changes on the desktop and mobile device while they're offline, creating a conflict?

With many syncing situations, it's possible to end up with conflicts, where the same photo has changed in both locations at the same time, or while they're both offline.

Lightroom resolves these conflicts automatically. If a setting's changed in both Lightroom Classic and a Lightroom CC client while they're both offline, the latest change wins. For example, if you change the flag status on one device, and Develop settings on the other device, both changes will be updated. If you change the flag status on both devices, whichever change was made last is the setting that sticks.

When Lightroom updates the Develop settings from Sync, it adds a *From Lightroom mobile* history state to the History panel.

What happens if I want to sync a different catalog or I need to restore a backup catalog?

You can only have one Lightroom Classic catalog syncing at a time. If you enable sync in a different catalog or an outdated backup catalog, Lightroom asks whether you want to switch to syncing this new catalog.

If you select **Yes, sync this catalog instead**, Lightroom downloads all of the photos from the cloud into the new catalog. It attempts to match up the cloud photos against existing photos, but this only works if the photos are still in their original location, so you may end up with duplicates. **(Figure 21.15)**

While there's nothing to stop you repeatedly switching catalogs, repeatedly wiping data from the cloud and reuploading everything, it takes a lot of time and bandwidth. Sticking to a single catalog is much, much simpler.

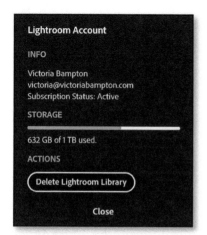

Figure 21.14 *To clear the cloud, log into the Lightroom website.*

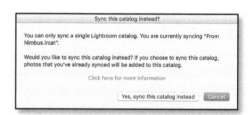

Figure 21.15 *Lightroom can only sync one catalog.*

SHARING WEB GALLERIES

Having your photos in the cloud also means you can share them with others as Lightroom Web Galleries.

How do I share collections as web galleries?

If you right-click on a collection in the Collections panel and choose *Lightroom CC Links*, you can select **Make Collection Public**. This makes the collection accessible to other people, but only if they have the secret link. The link is displayed at the top of the Grid view, or you can select **Copy Public Link** in the same right-click menu to copy it to the clipboard.

When someone visits on the secret link, they can view the photos in Grid or Loupe view and leave Likes and Comments on the photos, but they have much more limited access than your own gallery view.

If you visit https://lightroom.adobe.com, there are additional sharing options for each collection/album, for example, you can allow your viewers to download photos, view additional metadata, or even turn the gallery into a personalized web page including additional text describing the photos. New features are being added all the time.

How do I see my friends comments?

When someone comments on your photos, a little yellow icon appears on the collection in the Collections panel. The quickest way to find the latest comments is to select the *Last Comment Time* sort order from the *Sort By* pop-up on the Toolbar. The thumbnails themselves display a yellow comment badge, which turns gray when you've selected the photo. **(Figure 21.16)**

The comments are displayed in the Comments panel, at the bottom of the right panel group, and if you click in the field at the top, you can reply to the comments too. **(Figure 21.17)**

 ENDS HERE!

Figure 21.16 *The collection icon adds a small speech bubble when there are comments, and it turns orange when the comments are new.*

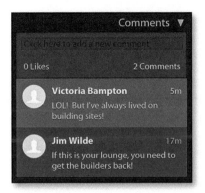

Figure 21.17 *Comments made on the web interface are synced back to the Comments panel on the desktop.*

REGISTER YOUR BOOK FOR ADDITIONAL BENEFITS

With your book purchase, you also get a year's access* to my **Lightroom Classic Premium Members Area**.

The benefits include:

• **Multiple eBook formats** of this book.

• **Updates** as Adobe add new features and other changes to Lightroom Classic, so you always have the latest information.

• **Email Support** from the author, if you can't find the answer in the book. Use the Lightroom Classic CC Premium Email Support form in the Members Area at https://www.lightroomqueen.com/lrclassic-contact

To register your book, I need:

• **Proof of Purchase**, for example, your confirmation email, shipping confirmation, a scan/photograph of the packing slip, or a screenshot of the order confirmation on Amazon's website—I need to be able to read the order number and order/delivery date.

• The **book reference** code: **CL72018LS126**

If you purchased the book direct from https://www.lightroomqueen.com, you'll already be registered, and you'll have received your Members Area login details by email shortly after ordering.

Send me the details using either:

• The book registration form: https://www.lightroomqueen.com/register

• Email: registration@lightroomqueen.com

What happens next?

I'll create your Members Area account and send you the login details. This can take up to 48 hours, as it requires a real human (usually me!) to press the buttons.

You can then log into the Members Area at https://www.lightroomqueen.com/members to access the bonus downloads and email support form.

Members Area access is valid for 365 days (from date of book purchase if new, or from date of publication if purchased used). When your Members Area access expires, you're welcome to extend it at a low cost, so you always have the most up to date information about Lightroom Classic.

INDEX